VISUAL QUICKPRO GUIDE

MACROMEDIA FLASH MX ADVANCED

FOR WINDOWS AND MACINTOSH

Russell Chun

Peachpit Press

Visual QuickPro Guide

Macromedia Flash MX Advanced for Windows and Macintosh

Russell Chun

Peachpit Press
1249 Eighth Street
Berkeley, CA 94710
510/524-2178
800/283-9444
510/524-2221 (fax)

Published by Peachpit Press, a division of Pearson Education.
Find us on the Web at www.peachpit.com.
To report errors, please send a note to errata@peachpit.com.
Published in association with Macromedia Press.

Editor: Rebecca Gulick
Production Coordinator: Lisa Brazieal
Copyeditor: Kathy Simpson
Additional copyediting: Wendy Katz
Technical reviewer: Clint Critchlow, Macromedia Tech Support
Additional technical feedback: Erica Norton and Bentley Wolfe of Macromedia, Inc.
Compositor: Owen Wolfson
Indexer: Emily Glossbrenner
Cover design: The Visual Group
CD-ROM mastering: Victor Gavenda

ISBN 0-201-75846-6

9 8 7 6 5 4 3 2

Printed and bound in the United States of America

Thank you

Many thanks to everyone at Peachpit Press, especially my dedicated editor, Rebecca Gulick, for her support throughout the process and for the polish she put on my words. Thanks also to Lisa Brazieal, Kathy Simpson, Emily Glossbrenner, Owen Wolfson, Victor Gavenda, Marjorie Baer, and Nancy Ruenzel for their tremendous work, and to Gary-Paul Prince and Kim Lombardi for their tireless promotional efforts.

Special thanks to Steve Vargas, my fellow Flash instructor, for cheerfully writing the sections on XML and the CGI GET and POST methods and making sense out of these complex topics.

Thanks to the technical reviewers at Macromedia: Erica Norton and Bentley Wolfe, for their early review; and Clint Critchlow, for his enthusiasm, careful attention, and helpful suggestions.

I'm grateful to the numerous people and friends who lent their time and talents to the video, sound, photos, and illustrations: Eric Stickney, Josh Frost, Ross "Hogg" Viator, Khin Mai Aung, David Harrington, SadSadFun (A. Gass, B. Chulada, F. Parsa, and M. Chulada), Derek Jimenez, and Tim Cramer. Additional images and sound provided courtesy of Benjamin Cummings, Corel Photo, Gary Fisher bikes, Music4Flash.com, RocketClips.com, Kim Steinhaug and SubReal from Flashkit.com, 3DModelz.com, 3DM-MC.com, Help3D.com, and Eden, Jonah, Bennet, David, Alexandra, and Christina Chun and their proud grandpa "Ang-Ang."

TABLE OF CONTENTS

Part III: Navigating Timelines and Communicating 101

Chapter 4: Advanced Buttons and Event Detection 103

Chapter 5: Controlling Multiple Timelines 161

Chapter 6: Managing Outside Communication 191

INTRODUCTION

Macromedia Flash MX is one of the hottest technologies on the Web today. Leading corporate Web sites use its streamlined graphics to communicate their brands; major motion picture studios promote theatrical releases with Flash animations; and online gaming and educational sites provide rich user experiences with Flash interactivity.

As a vector-based animation and authoring application, Flash is ideal for creating high-impact, low-bandwidth Web sites incorporating animation, text, video, and sound. With robust support for complex interactivity and server-side communication, Flash is increasingly the solution for developing Internet applications as well. From designer to programmer, Flash has become the tool of choice for delivering dynamic content across various browsers and platforms.

As the popularity of Flash increases, so does the demand for animators and developers who know how to tap its power. This book is designed to help you meet that challenge. Learn how to build complex animations, integrate sophisticated interfaces and navigation schemes, and dynamically control graphics, video, sound, and text. Experiment with the techniques discussed in this book to create the compelling media that Flash makes possible. It's not an exaggeration to say that Flash is revolutionizing the Web. This book will help you be a part of that revolution. So boot up your computer and get started.

Who Should Use This Book

This book is for the designers, animators, and developers who want to take their Flash skills to the next level. You've mastered the basics of tweening and are ready to move on to more complex tasks involving video, masking, dynamic sound control, or movie-clip collision detection. You may not be a hard-core programmer, but you're ready to learn how ActionScript can control graphics, sounds, and text. You're ready to integrate interactivity with your animations to create arcade-style games, to create complex user-interface elements like pull-down menus, and to learn how Flash communicates with outside applications such as Web browsers. If this description fits you, then this book is right for you.

This book explores the advanced features of Flash MX, so you should already be comfortable with the basic tools and commands for creating simple Flash movies. You should know how to create and modify shapes and text with the drawing tools and be able to create symbols. You should also know how to apply motion and shape tweens, and how to work with frame-by-frame animation. You should know your way around the Flash interface: how to move from the Stage to symbol-editing mode to the Timeline, and how to manipulate layers and frames. You should also be familiar with importing and using bitmaps and sounds, and assigning basic actions to frames and buttons for navigation. Review the tutorials that come with the software, or pick up a copy of *Macromedia Flash MX: Visual QuickStart Guide* by Katherine Ulrich.

Goals of This Book

The aim of this book is to demonstrate the advanced features of Flash MX through a logical approach, emphasizing how techniques are applied. You will learn how techniques build on each other, and how groups of techniques can be combined to solve a particular problem. Each example you work through puts another skill under your belt, so by the end of this book you'll be able to create sophisticated interactive Flash projects.

For example, creating a pull-down menu illustrates how simple elements—invisible buttons, event handlers, button-tracking options, and movie clips—come together to make more complex behaviors. Examples illustrate the practical application of techniques, and additional tips explain how to apply these techniques in other contexts.

How to Use This Book

The concepts in this book build on each other, so the material at the end is more complex than that at the beginning. If you're familiar with some of the material, you can skip around to the subjects that interest you, but you'll find it most useful to learn the techniques in the order in which they appear.

As with other books in the Visual QuickPro Guide series, tasks are presented for you to do as you read about them, so that you can see how a technique is applied. Follow the step-by-step instructions, look at the figures, and try them on your computer. You'll learn more by doing and by taking an active role in experimenting with these exercises.

Tips follow the specific tasks to give you hints on how to use a shortcut, warnings on common mistakes, and suggestions on how the technique can be extended.

Occasionally, you'll see sidebars in gray boxes. Sidebars discuss related matters that are not directly task-oriented. You'll find interesting and useful concepts that can help you understand how Flash works.

What's in This Book

This book is organized into five parts:

- **Part I: Approaching Advanced Animation**
  This part covers advanced techniques for graphics and animation, including strategies for motion tweening, shape tweening, masking, and using digital video and 3D graphics.
- **Part II: Understanding ActionScript**
  This part introduces ActionScript, the scripting language Flash uses to add interactivity to a movie. You'll learn the basic components of the language and how to use the Actions panel to construct meaningful code.
- **Part III: Navigating Timelines and Communicating**
  This part teaches you the ways in which Flash can respond to input from the viewer and how complex navigation schemes can be created with multiple Timelines. You'll also see how Flash communicates with external files and applications such as Web browsers.
- **Part IV: Transforming Graphics and Sound**
  This part demonstrates how to dynamically control the basic elements of any Flash movie—its graphics and sound—through ActionScript.
- **Part V: Working with Information**
  The last part focuses on how to retrieve, store, modify, and test information to create complex Flash environments that can respond to changing conditions.
- **Appendixes**
  Four appendixes give you quick access to the essential ActionScript objects, actions, key code values, and events.

What's on the CD

Accompanying this book is a CD-ROM that contains nearly all the Flash source files for the tasks. You can see how each task was created, study the ActionScript, or use the ActionScript to do further experimentation. You'll also find a trial version of Flash MX as well as a list of Web links to sites devoted to Flash and showcasing the latest Flash examples, with tutorials, articles, and advice.

Additional Resources

Use the Web to your advantage. There is a thriving international community of Flash developers; within it you can share your frustrations, seek help, and show off your latest Flash masterpiece. There are free bulletin boards and mailing lists for all levels of Flash users. Begin your search for Flash resources with the list of Web sites on the accompanying CD and with the Answers panel in the Flash application, which provides links to the Flash developer community on the Web.

What's New in Flash MX

Why "MX"? As its name suggests, Flash MX represents a generational, rather than an incremental, upgrade from Flash 5. Flash MX is now part of a larger family of MX products from Macromedia that can work together to help you develop and deliver rich, dynamic content. You can still use Flash MX by itself, but its potential for server-side integration is greatly expanded by being part of a suite of Web development tools.

Keep in mind that, while the name of the authoring application is Flash MX, the Web browser plug-in that plays Flash MX media is called the Flash 6 Player.

Whether you're a beginner or an advanced user, or a designer or a programmer, a number of new features in Flash MX will appeal to you. The following are just a few that make Flash MX even more powerful, flexible, and easy to use.

Improved Workflow

The user interface has been significantly reorganized to improve your workflow. A single context-sensitive Property Inspector replaces multiple panels, so options for common tasks are consolidated in one place. The remaining panels and windows are fully dockable, enabling you to customize a comfortable workspace. The Timeline supports new features like Layer folders, easier ways to interact with keyframes and tweens, and Distribute to Layers, which can quickly separate graphic elements on the Stage into separate layers on the Timeline.

New Drawing Aids

New features that help you draw include the Distort and Envelope tools to transform your shapes in new and flexible ways, a revamped Color Mixer, and the Snap-to-Pixel command which enables exact placement of objects at a pixel level.

Better Font Handling

Font handling is more sophisticated with the addition of vertical text formats and support for Unicode standards for displaying text in foreign languages. Font substitution during author-time now lets you choose different fonts when your computer doesn't recognize a font in a FLA file.

Rich Media Support

You can now import and display digital video directly within Flash MX with full support for QuickTime, MPEG, AVI, and DV formats. Also, you can dynamically load MP3 sound files and JPG images into Flash during runtime, dramatically increasing flexibility while reducing file sizes.

Expanded Interactivity

The expansion of ActionScript treats buttons and text fields as objects, just like movie clips, so you have even more control over their properties and behavior. A new event model that incorporates a concept known as listeners makes event handling more robust. And of course there is a host of new ActionScript actions, objects, properties, and methods that control elements such as masking, text formatting, and shapes, to name just a few. A new ActionScript panel makes scripting easier with code hinting and an easy-to-access ActionScript reference, and a new Debugger panel adds breakpoints for line-by-line inspection of your movie's interactivity.

Part I: Approaching Advanced Animation

1

Building Complexity

The key to creating complex animations in Flash is building them from simpler parts. Just as the movement of a runner is essentially a collection of rotating limbs, you should think of your Flash project as being a collection of simpler motions. Isolating individual components of a much larger, complicated motion allows you to treat each component with the most appropriate technique, simplifies the tweening, and gives you better control with more refined results.

To animate a head that's turning quickly to face the camera, for example, you would first consider how to simplify the animation into separate motions. Animating the entire sequence at the same time would be difficult, if not impossible, because the many elements making up the head change in different ways as they move. The outline of the head could be a frame-by-frame animation to show the transformation from a profile to a frontal pose. Some of the features of the face could be symbol instances that you squash and stretch in a motion tween to match the turn of the head. And the hair could be a shape tween that lets you show its flow, swing, and slight bounce-back effect when the head stops.

Learning to combine different techniques and break animation into simpler parts not only solves difficult animation problems, but also forces you to use multiple layers and establish symbols of the component parts. By doing so, you set up the animation so that it is easy to manage now and revise later.

This chapter describes approaches to building complex animations through layering, combining, and extending basic Flash capabilities.

Motion-Tweening Strategies

Motion tweening lets you interpolate any of the instance properties of a symbol, such as its location, size, rotation, color, and transparency. Because of its versatility, motion tweening can be applied to a variety of animation problems, making it the foundation of most Flash projects. Because motion tweening deals with instance properties, it's a good idea to think of the technique in terms of instance tweening. Whether or not actual motion across the Stage is involved, changing instances between keyframes requires motion tweening. Thinking of it as instance tweening will help you distinguish when and where to use motion tweening as opposed to shape tweening or frame-by-frame animation.

Creating seamless animated loops

Animated loops are important because they provide a way to continue motion by defining only a few keyframes. You see animated loops in interface elements such as rotating buttons and scrolling menus, as well as in cyclical motions such as a person walking, a butterfly's wings flapping, or a planet revolving. The important point in making seamless loops is making sure that the last and first keyframes are identical (or nearly identical) so that the motion is continuous.

This section shows you how to make two of the most common types of animated loops: scrolling graphics and graphics on closed motion paths. Scrolling graphics are familiar effects in interface elements such as menu options that cycle across the screen. You can also use this technique to create background animations that loop endlessly, such as a field of stars behind a spaceship or passing scenery from a car window.

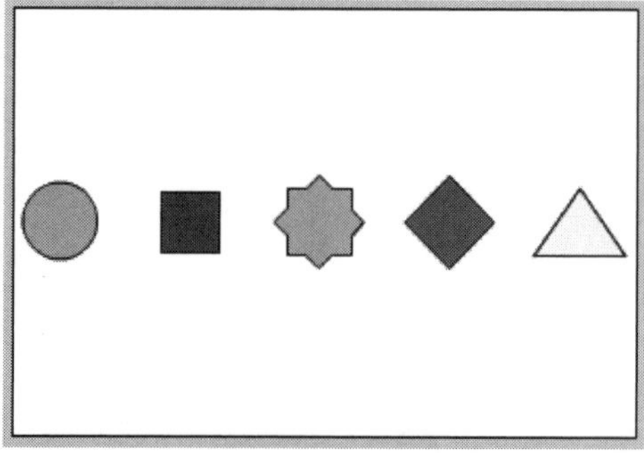

Figure 1.1 Five objects placed across the Stage as they would appear when they begin scrolling across from right to left. The objects could be buttons or simple graphics.

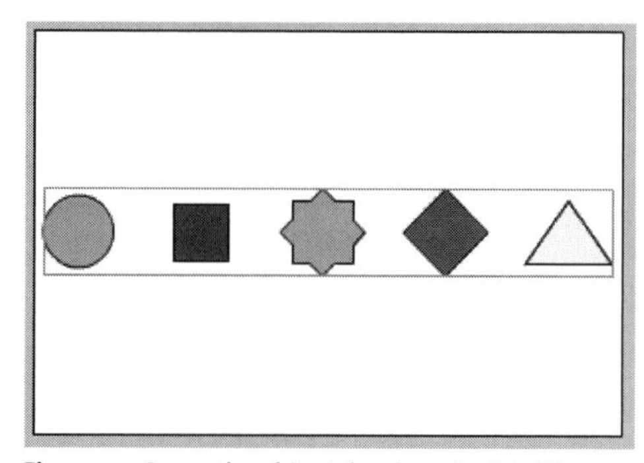

Figure 1.2 Group the objects by choosing Modify > Group.

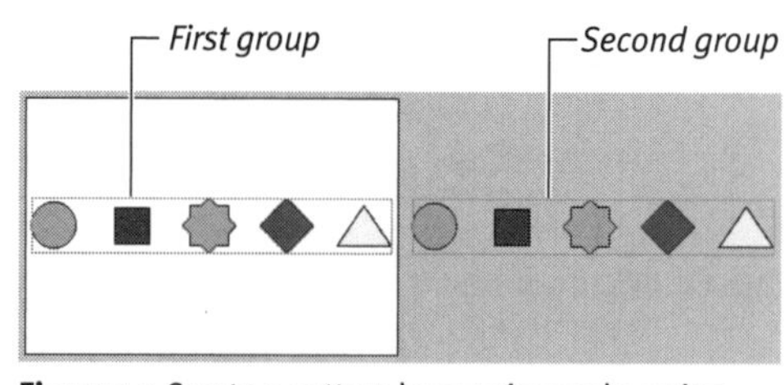

Figure 1.3 Create a pattern by copying and pasting the group.

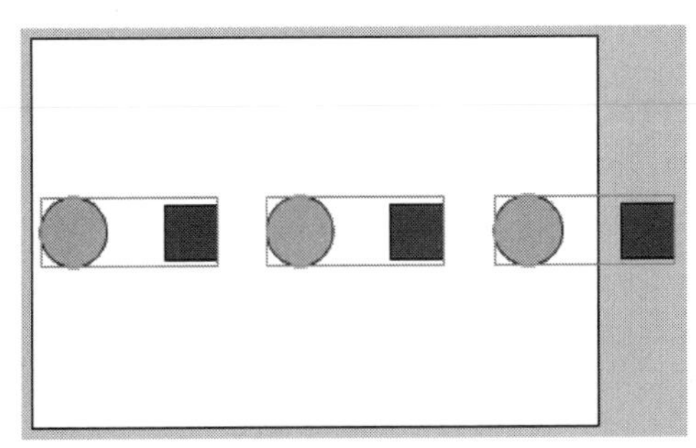
Figure 1.4 This group has only two objects. Repeat the groups to extend well past the Stage.

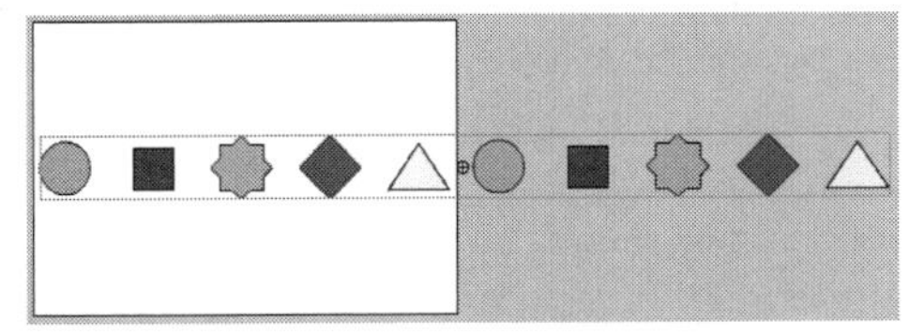
Figure 1.5 Create a graphic symbol of the entire pattern.

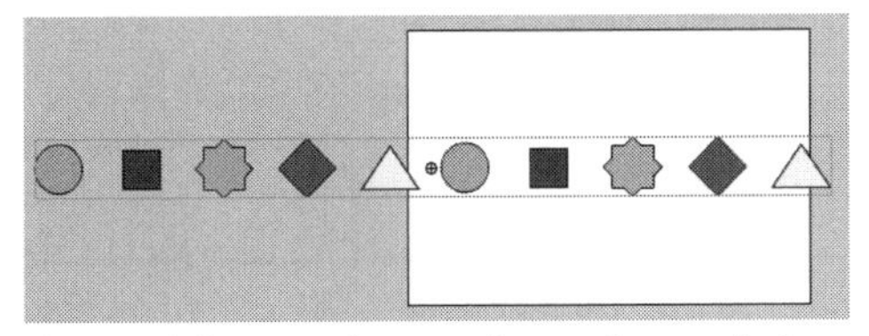
Figure 1.6 The second repeated group is moved where the first group was originally.

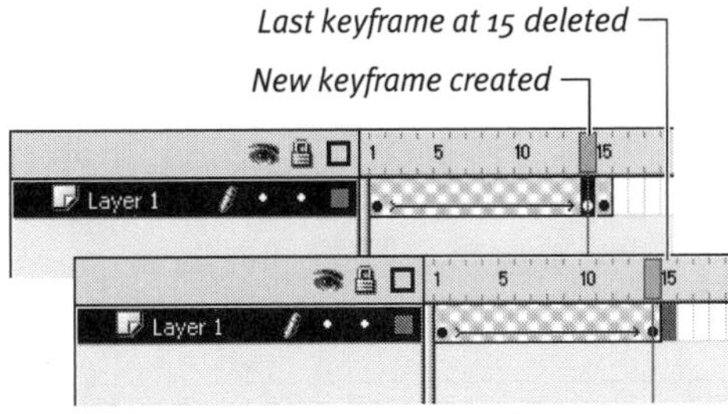

Figure 1.7 Create a new keyframe (top), and delete the last keyframe (bottom).

To create a continuous scrolling graphic:

1. Create the necessary elements that will scroll across the Stage, and place them as they would appear at any given moment (**Figure 1.1**).
2. Select all the elements, and choose Modify > Group (**Figure 1.2**).
3. Copy the group, and paste the copy next to the original group to create a long band of repeating elements.

   If your elements scroll from right to left, for example, place the second group to the right of the first group (**Figure 1.3**).

   Your scrolling elements usually will be larger than the Stage, but if your first group is smaller, you'll need to duplicate it more than once to create a repeating pattern that extends beyond the Stage (**Figure 1.4**).
4. Select all your groups, and convert your selection to a graphic symbol (**Figure 1.5**).

   An instance of the symbol remains on the Stage, allowing you to apply a motion tween.
5. Create a keyframe at a later point in the Timeline.
6. Select the instance in the last keyframe, and move it so that the second repeated group of elements aligns with the first.

   When you move your instance, use its outlines to match its previous position (**Figure 1.6**).
7. Apply a motion tween between the keyframes.
8. Insert a new keyframe just before the last keyframe, and remove the last frame (**Figure 1.7**).

   This technique makes the animation not have to play two identical frames (the first and the last) and creates a smooth loop.

A motion path in a guide layer provides a way to create smooth movement along a path from the beginning point to the end point. If you make the end point of the path match the beginning point, you can create a seamless loop and effectively close the motion path.

To make a closed motion path:

1. Create a graphic symbol, and place an instance of it on the Stage (**Figure 1.8**).
2. Create a guide layer by clicking the Add Motion Guide icon below your layers.

   A new guide layer appears, and your first layer becomes a guided layer (**Figure 1.9**).
3. Draw an empty ellipse in the guide layer.
4. With the Snap to Objects modifier for the Arrow tool turned on, grab your instance by its registration point and place it on the path of the ellipse (**Figure 1.10**).
5. Add frames to both layers, and create a new keyframe in the last frame of the guided layer.

   The first and last keyframes remain the same to create the animated loop (**Figure 1.11**).

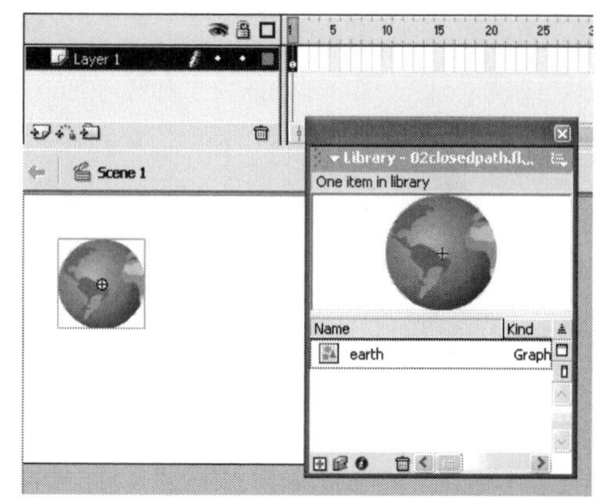

Figure 1.8 An instance of a graphic symbol is placed on the Stage for motion tweening along a path.

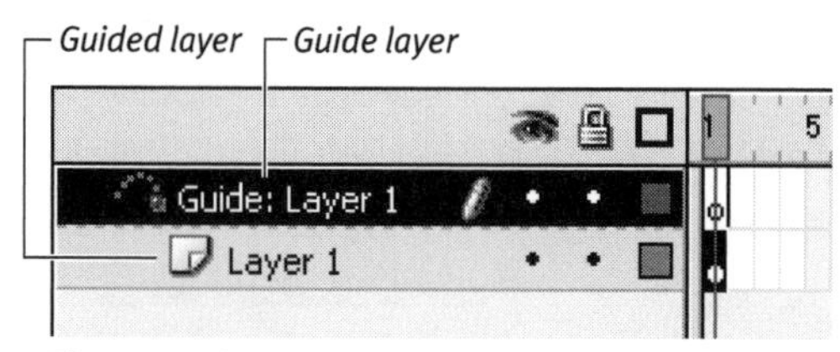

Figure 1.9 The guide layer above Layer 1 will contain the motion path.

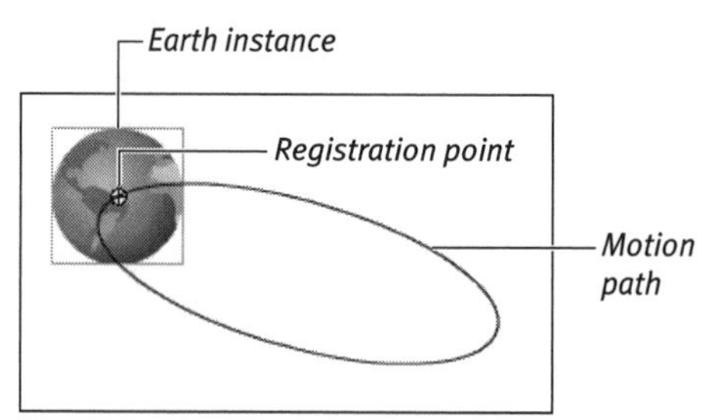

Figure 1.10 The registration point of the earth instance snaps to the motion path.

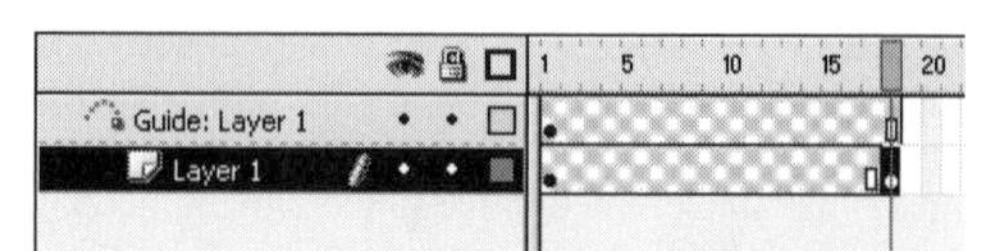

Figure 1.11 The position of the earth at keyframe 1 and at keyframe 18 in Layer 1 are the same.

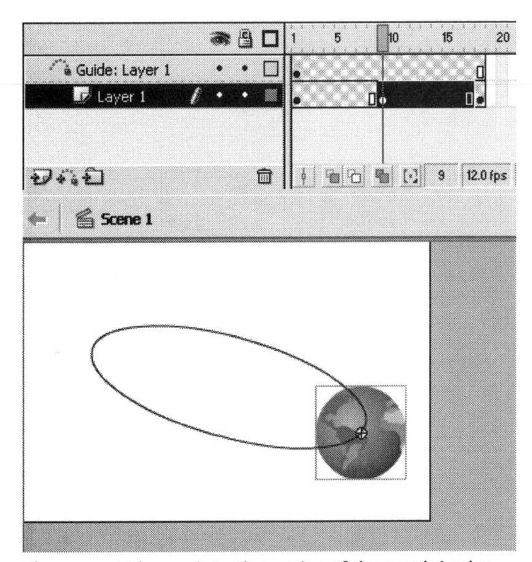

Figure 1.12 The registration point of the earth in the middle keyframe is positioned at the far side of the ellipse.

6. Select the middle frame of the guided layer, and insert a new keyframe, moving your instance in this intermediate keyframe to the opposite side of the ellipse (**Figure 1.12**).
7. Select all the frames between the three keyframes, and in the Property Inspector, choose Motion Tween.

   Your instance now travels along the path of the ellipse, but it returns on the same segment of the ellipse rather than making a complete circuit (**Figure 1.13**).
8. Grab the instance in the last keyframe of the guided layer, and move it slightly closer to the instance in the middle keyframe while maintaining its registration point on the path (**Figure 1.14**).

continues on next page

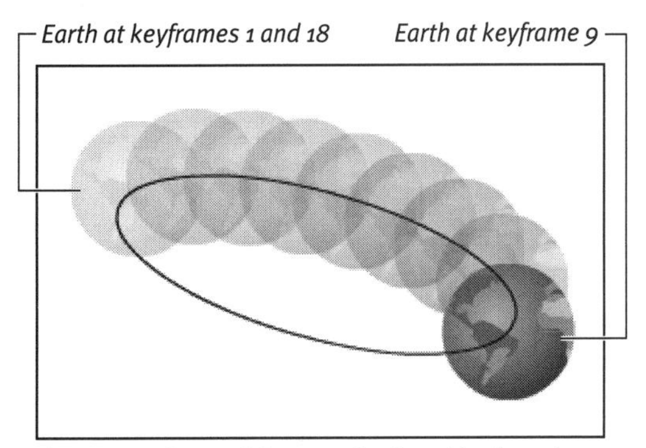

Figure 1.13 The earth bounces back and forth on the same segment of the ellipse.

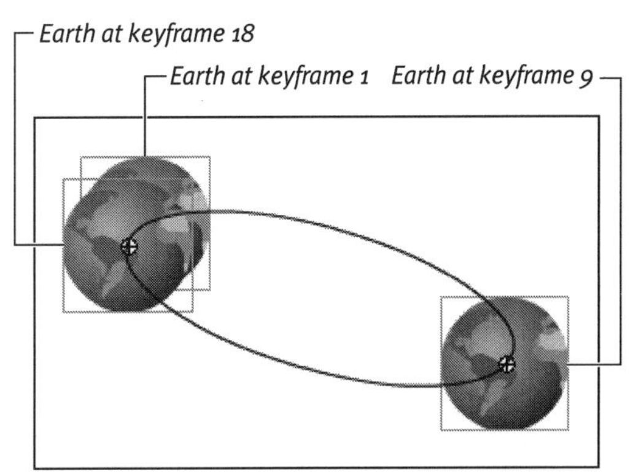

Figure 1.14 The three keyframes of the earth. The first instance is closer to the middle instance on the top path of the ellipse, and the last instance is closer to the middle instance on the bottom path of the ellipse.

Flash tweens two instances by taking the most direct path, so by shortening the distance between the last two keyframes on the bottom segment of the ellipse, you force Flash to use that segment of the ellipse.

Your instance now travels along both sides of the ellipse (**Figure 1.15**).

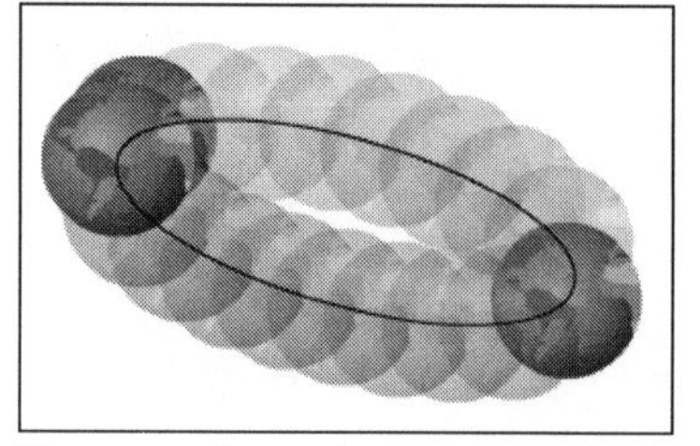

Figure 1.15 The earth moves around the closed path.

✔ Tip

- You can accomplish the same kind of looping effect by deleting a small segment of your path. When you create a gap, you essentially make an open path with beginning and end points for your instance to follow (**Figure 1.16**).

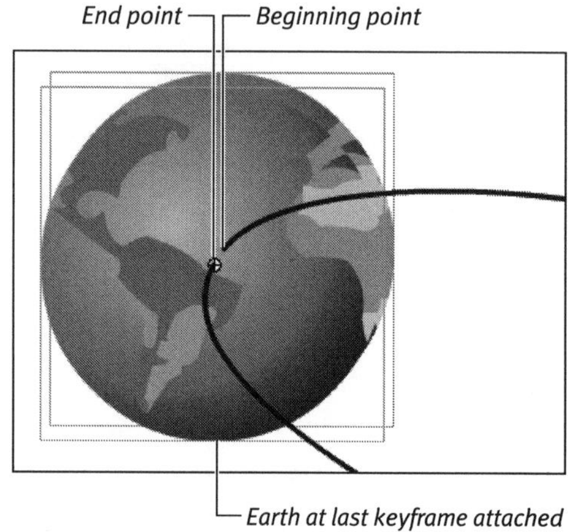

Figure 1.16 A tiny gap provides beginning and end points for your motion path.

Using multiple guided layers

A single guide layer can affect more than one guided layer, letting multiple motion tweens follow the same path. This approach is good for creating complex animations that require many objects traveling in the same direction, such as marching soldiers, blood cells coursing through an artery, rapid gunfire, or a stampeding herd of cattle. Although the individual instances may vary, you maintain control of their general direction with a single guide layer.

Several leaves blowing across the Stage could be animated to follow one guide layer, for example. The guide layer establishes the wind's general direction; the leaves could have slight individual variations by being offset in separate guided layers. Just by changing the path in the guide layer, you make all the leaves change accordingly. Using a single path to guide multiple layers this way is an example of how you build complex animations (in this case, swirling leaves) from very simple parts (one guide layer and one leaf symbol).

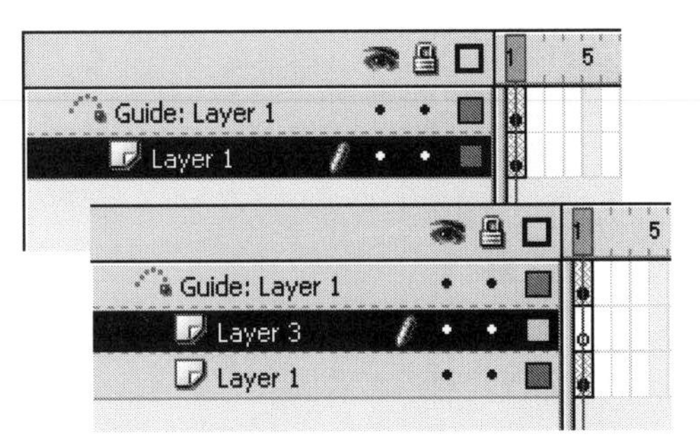

Figure 1.17 Selecting the guided layer (Layer 1 above) and inserting a new layer automatically modifies the new layer as a guided layer (Layer 3).

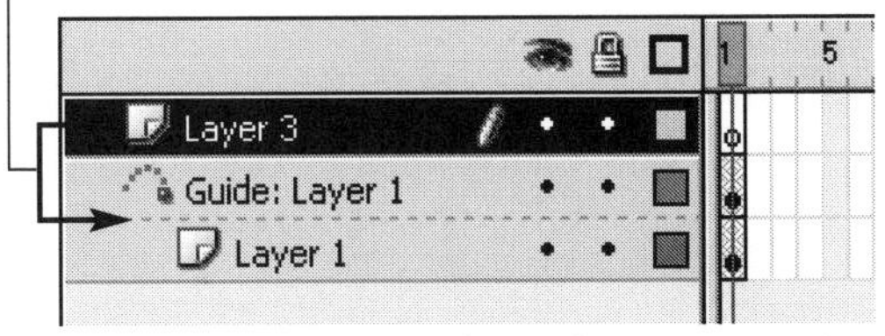

Figure 1.18 A normal layer (Layer 3) can be dragged below the guide layer to become a guided layer.

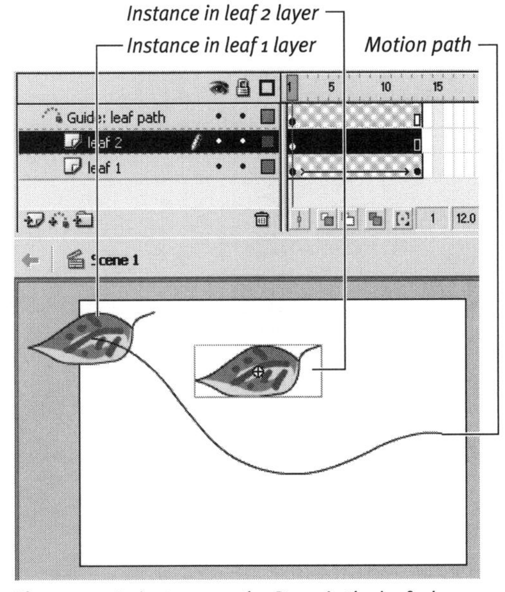

Figure 1.19 An instance on the Stage in the leaf 2 layer.

To assign a second guided layer to a guide layer:

- Select the first guided layer, and click the Insert Layer icon.

  A second guided layer appears above the first (**Figure 1.17**).

  or

- Drag an existing normal layer below the guide layer.

  The normal layer becomes a guided layer (**Figure 1.18**).

To offset a second guided layer:

1. Create the second guided layer as described earlier in this section, and drag in an instance that you want to tween (**Figure 1.19**).
2. Select the instance in the second guided layer, and choose the Free Transform tool in the Toolbox.

   Control handles appears around your instance, along with a white circle in the center marking the current registration point (**Figure 1.20**).

continues on next page

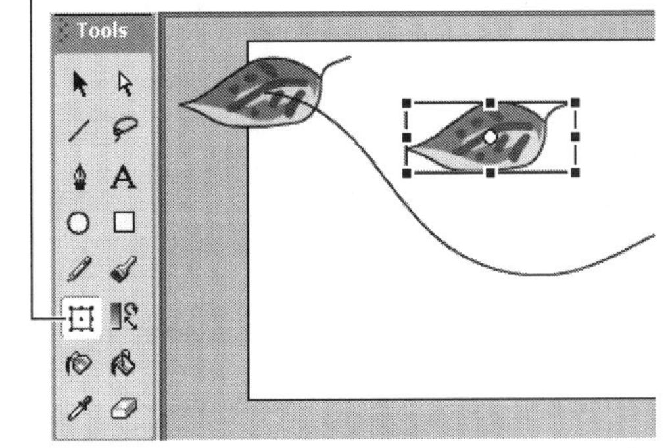

Figure 1.20 Select the instance in the second guided layer, and select the Free Transform tool in the Toolbox.

3. Drag the registration point to a new position.

   An instance's registration point can lie anywhere, even outside the boundaries of the Free Transform tool's control handles.

   The new registration point will be set where you just placed it (**Figure 1.21**).

4. Now select the Arrow tool to exit the Free Transform tool, and make sure that the Snap to Objects modifier is turned on.

5. Grab the instance by its new registration point, and attach it to the beginning of the guide-layer path (**Figure 1.22**).

6. Insert a new keyframe into the last frame.

   The newly created instance in the last keyframe will have the same registration point as the edited instance.

7. Now attach the instance in the last keyframe to the end of the guide-layer path, and apply a motion tween between the two keyframes.

   The motion tween in the second guided layer follows the same path as the first guided layer. The new registration point of the instance in the second guided layer, however, offsets the motion (**Figure 1.23**).

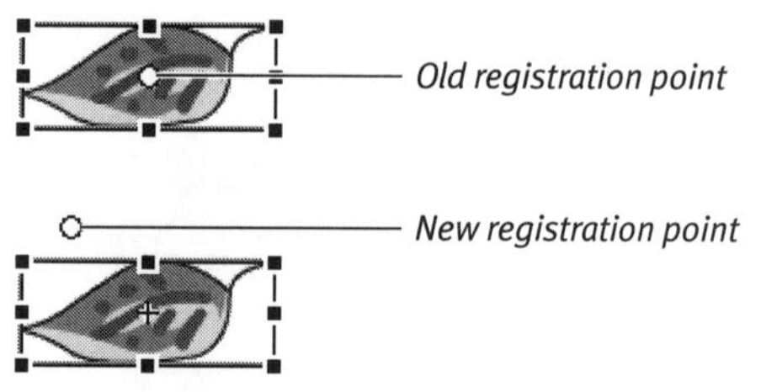

Figure 1.21 Change the registration point of your instance by moving the white circle.

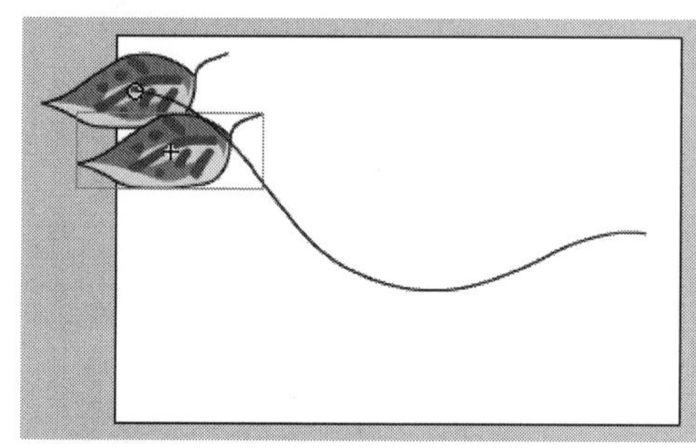

Figure 1.22 The registration point of the leaf, shown selected here, is attached to the path.

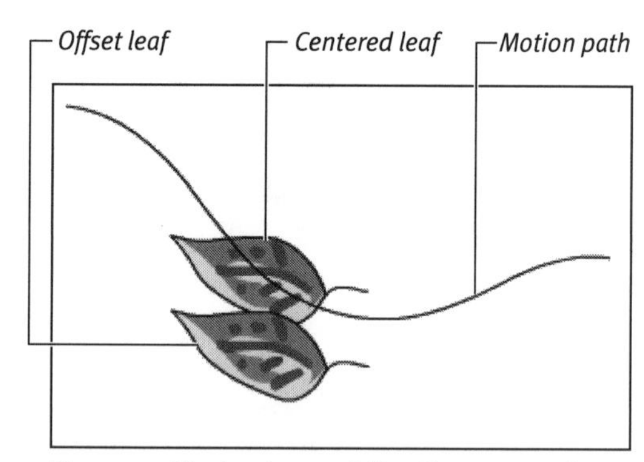

Figure 1.23 The two tweens follow the same motion path. The second leaf is offset because of its moved registration point.

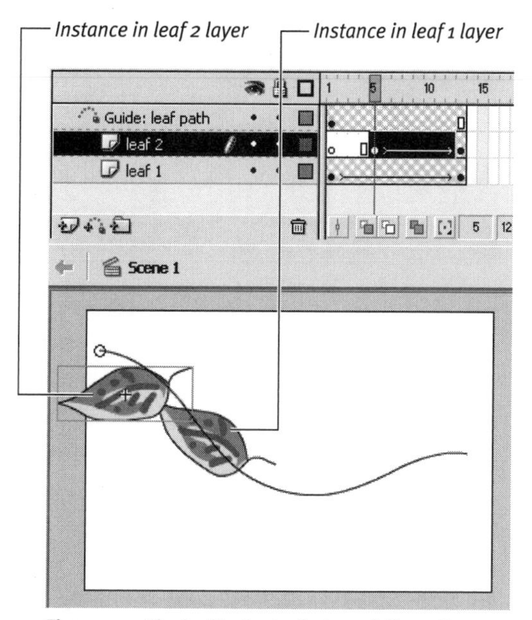

Figure 1.24 The leaf in the leaf 2 layer follows the motion path only after the one in the leaf 1 layer has already started.

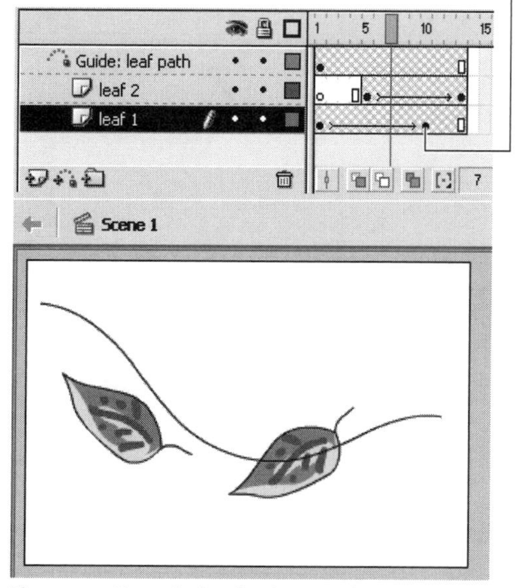

Figure 1.25 Move the last keyframe in the leaf 1 layer closer to the first keyframe.

To vary the timing of a second guided layer:

1. Continuing with the preceding example, drag the first keyframe of the second guided layer to a later point in time.

   The motion tween for that guided layer will begin after the first one starts, but both of the animations will end at the same time (**Figure 1.24**).
2. Drag the last keyframe of the first guided layer to an earlier point in time.

   The motion tweens following the path in the guide layer are staggered relative to each other (**Figure 1.25**).
3. Refine the timing of the motion tweens by moving the first and last keyframes in both guided layers.

✔ Tip

- Create variations in the second guided layer by placing the instances on any point along the path in the guide layer. The instances do not have to lie at the very beginning or end of the path for the motion tween to work.

You can increase complexity by using animated graphic symbol instances along the guide layer's motion path. Animated loops within graphic symbols provide localized motion that still follows the guide layer in the main Timeline.

To add local variations to multiple guided layers:

1. Enter symbol-editing mode for the graphic symbol you use on the motion path.
2. Select the contents of this symbol, and convert it to a graphic symbol.
   You create a graphic symbol within another graphic symbol, which allows you to create a motion tween within your first graphic symbol.
3. Create a looping motion tween (**Figure 1.26**).
   This type of animation ends where it begins.
4. Exit symbol-editing mode, and play the movie to see how the motion tween of the graphic symbol gets incorporated into the motion tween on the main Stage (**Figure 1.27**).

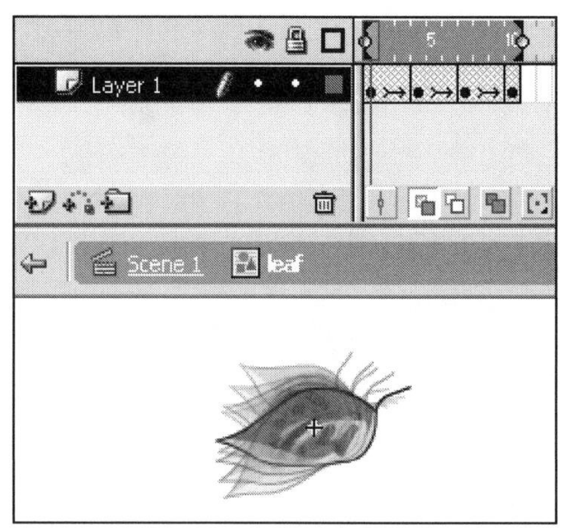

Figure 1.26 An animated graphic symbol of a leaf moving up and down.

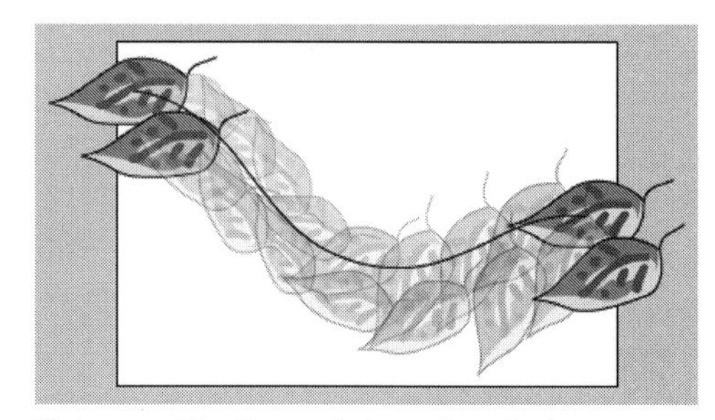

Figure 1.27 Play the movie to see how the leaves follow the motion path while going through their own animation.

✔ Tips

- In the Property Inspector, adjust the play mode option and First parameter to vary how the animated graphic instances play (**Figure 1.28**). By having your loops begin with different frames, you prevent them from being synchronized with one another (**Figure 1.29**).
- Rotating your instances at this point can produce even more complex, interesting, and seemingly random movements. Experiment with rotating your instances as they travel along the motion path.

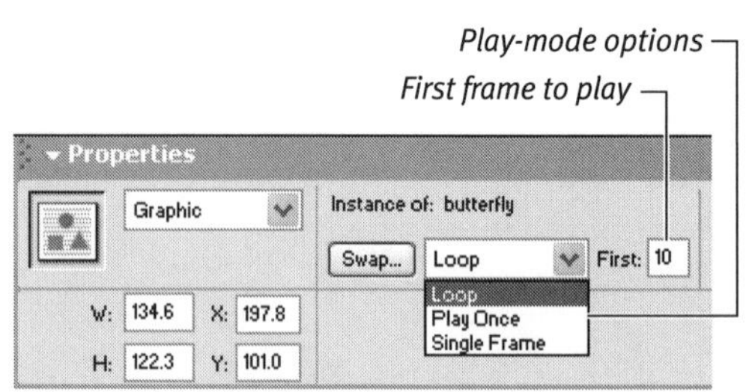

Figure 1.28 The First parameter is set to 10 so that the leaf graphic will loop beginning with frame 10. The other play-mode options in the pull-down menu include Play Once and Single Frame.

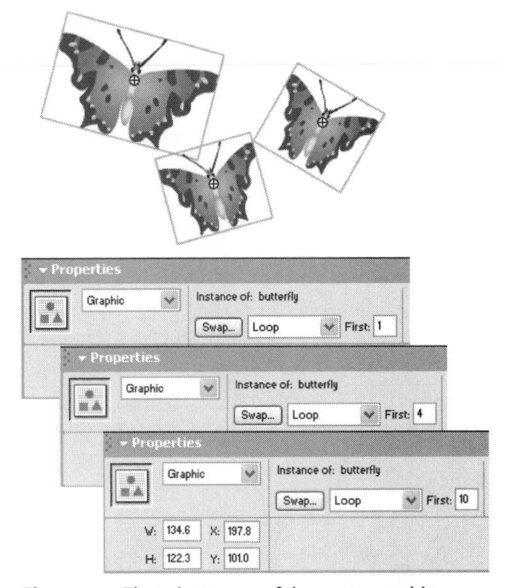

Figure 1.29 Three instances of the same graphic symbol with different first-frame play options. The left butterfly loops beginning with frame 1; its wings will start to close. The middle butterfly loops beginning with frame 4; its wings are already closed and will start to open. The right butterfly loops beginning with frame 10; its wings are opening.

Figure 1.30 Breaking apart a block of static text (top) results in static text of the individual letters (bottom).

Animating titles

Frequently, splash screens on Flash Web sites feature animated titles and other text-related materials that twirl, tumble, and spin until they all come into place as a complete design. Several techniques can help you accomplish these kinds of effects quickly and easily. The Break Apart command, when applied to a block of static text, breaks the text into its component characters while keeping them as live, editable text. This command lets you painlessly create separate text fields for the letters that make up a word or title. Using the new Distribute to Layers command then allows you to isolate each of those characters on its own layer, ready for motion tweening.

When you do start applying motion tweens to your individual letters or words, it's very useful to think and work backward from the final design. Create an end keyframe containing the final positions of all your characters, for example. Then, in the first keyframes, you can change their positions and apply as many transformations as you like, knowing that the final resting spots are secured.

To animate the letters of a title:

1. Select the Text tool, and make sure that Static Text is selected in the Property Inspector.
2. On the Stage, type a title you want to animate.
3. Choose Modify > Break Apart (Cmd-B for Mac, Ctrl-B for Windows).

   Flash replaces the static-text title with individual static-text letters (**Figure 1.30**).

continues on next page

4. Choose Modify > Distribute to Layers (Cmd-Shift-D for Mac, Ctrl-Shift-D for Windows).

   Each selected item on the Stage is placed in its own layer below the existing one. In this case, the newly created layers are named with the individual letters automatically (**Figure 1.31**).

5. Create keyframes at a later point in the Timeline for each layer.

6. In the first keyframe of each layer, rearrange and transform the letters according to your creative urges.

7. Select all the frames in the Timeline, and apply a motion tween.

   Flash automatically converts the static text elements to graphic symbols and stores them in the Library. Your movie animates all these text elements coming together as a complete title (**Figure 1.32**).

✔ Tip

- Make sure that you select all the frames in step 7. If do not include the last keyframe, Flash will leave those text elements as static text while converting the elements in the first keyframe to graphic symbols. In that case, you'll end up with motion tweens with different elements in the first and last keyframes, which could foul up future tweening in those layers.

Figure 1.31 Distribute to Layers separates the selected items in their own layers.

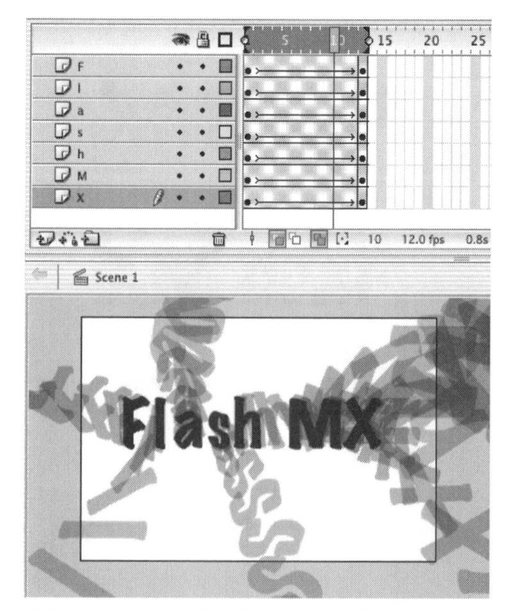

Figure 1.32 These letters tumble and fall into place at the last keyframe.

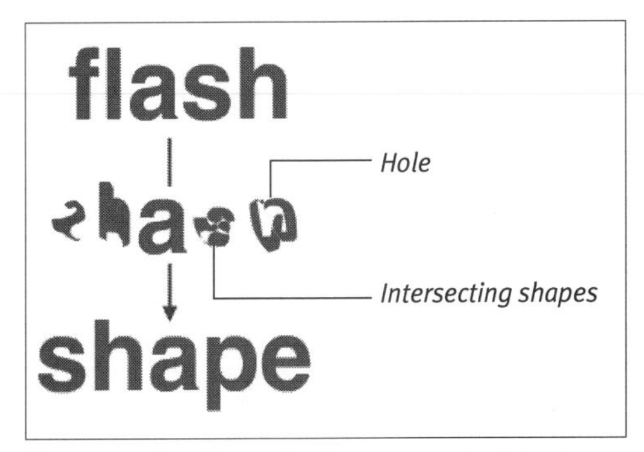

Figure 1.33 An attempt to shape-tween *flash* to *shape* all at once in a single layer. Notice the breakups between the *s* and the *p*, and the hole that appears between the *h* and the *e*.

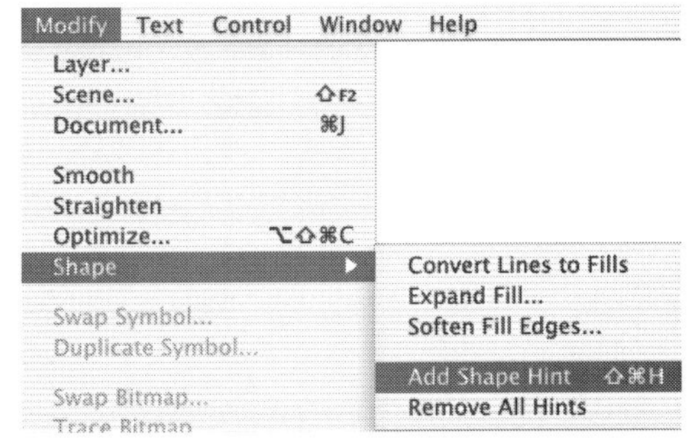

Figure 1.34 Select the first keyframe of the shape tween, and choose Modify > Shape > Add Shape Hint.

Figure 1.35 The first shape hint appears in the center of the Stage in the first keyframe.

Shape-Tweening Strategies

Shape tweening is a technique for interpolating amorphous changes that can't be accomplished with instance transformations such as rotation, scale, and skew. Fill, outline, gradient, and alpha are all shape attributes that can be shape-tweened.

Flash applies a shape tween by using what it considers to be the most efficient, direct route. This method sometimes has unpredictable results, creating overlapping shapes or seemingly random holes that appear and merge (**Figure 1.33**). These undesirable effects usually are the result of keyframes containing shapes that are too complex to tween at the same time.

As is the case with motion tweening, simplifying a complicated shape tween into more basic parts and separating those parts in layers results in a more successful interpolation. Shape hints give you a way to tell Flash what point on the first shape corresponds to what point on the second shape. Sometimes, adding intermediate keyframes will help a complicated tween by providing a transition state and making the tween go through many more-manageable stages.

Using shape hints

Shape hints force Flash to map particular points on the first shape to corresponding points on the second shape. By placing multiple shape hints, you can control more precisely the way your shapes will tween.

To add a shape hint:

1. Select the first keyframe of the shape tween, and choose Modify > Shape > Add Shape Hint (Cmd-Shift-H for Mac, Ctrl-Shift-H for Windows) (**Figure 1.34**).

   A red-circled letter appears in the middle of your shape (**Figure 1.35**).

continues on next page

2. Move the first shape hint to a point on your shape.

   Make sure that the Snap to Objects modifier for the Arrow tool is turned on to snap your selections to vertices and edges.

3. Select the last keyframe of the shape tween, and move the matching circled letter to a corresponding point on the end shape.

   This shape hint turns green, and the first shape hint turns yellow, signifying that both have been moved into place correctly (**Figure 1.36**).

4. Continue adding shape hints, up to a maximum of 26, to refine the shape tween (**Figure 1.37**).

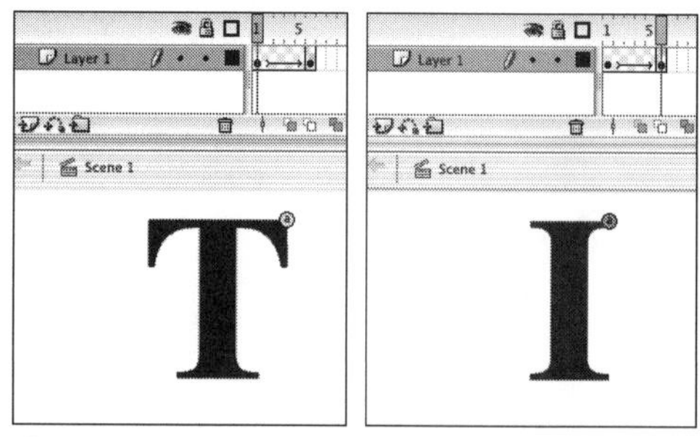

Figure 1.36 The first shape hint in the first keyframe (left) and its matching pair in the last keyframe (right).

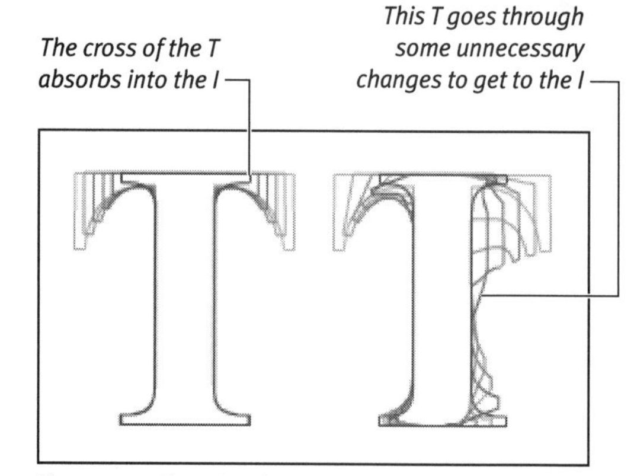

Figure 1.37 Changing from a *T* to an *I* with shape hints (left) and without shape hints (right).

✔ Tips

- Place shape hints in order either clockwise or counterclockwise. Flash will more easily understand a sequential placement than one that jumps around.
- Shape hints need to be placed on an edge or a corner of the shape. If you place a shape hint in the fill or outside the shape, the shape hints will remain red, and Flash will ignore them.
- To view your animation without the shape hints, choose View > Show Shape Hints (Cmd-Option-H for Mac, Ctrl-Alt-H for Windows). Flash deselects the Show Shape Hints option, and the shape hints are hidden.
- If you move your entire shape tween by using Edit Multiple Frames, you will have to reposition all your shape hints. Unfortunately, you cannot move all the shape hints at the same time.

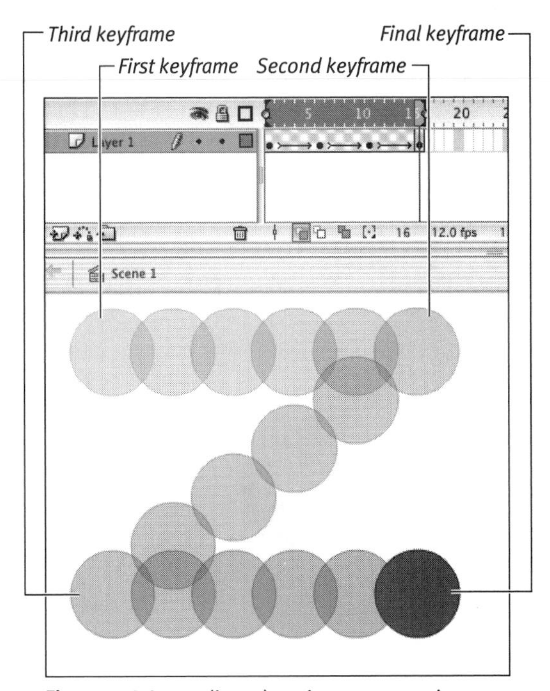

Figure 1.38 A complicated motion tween requires several intermediate keyframes.

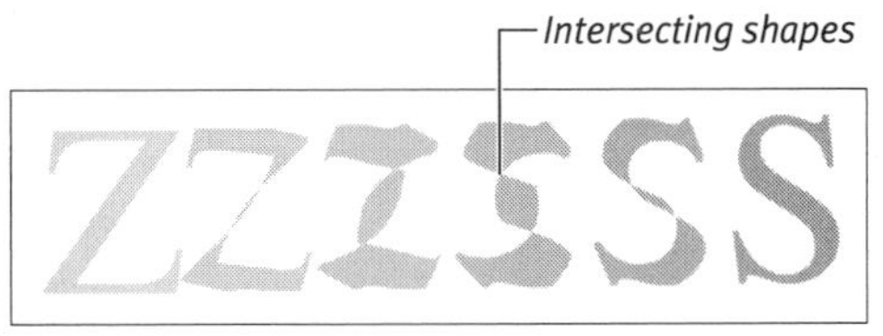

Figure 1.39 Changing a *Z* to an *S* all at once causes the shape to flip and cross over itself.

Figure 1.40 An intermediate shape.

Figure 1.41 The *Z* makes an easy transition to the intermediate shape (middle), from which the *S* can tween smoothly.

To delete a shape hint:

- Drag the shape hint off the Stage.

  The matching shape hint in the other keyframe will be deleted automatically.

To remove all shape hints:

- Choose Modify > Shape > Remove All Hints.

Using intermediate keyframes

Adding intermediate keyframes can help a complicated tween by providing a transition state that creates smaller, more manageable changes. Think about this process in terms of motion tweening. Imagine that you want to create the motion of a ball starting from the top left of the Stage, moving to the top right, then to the bottom left, and finally to the bottom right (**Figure 1.38**). You wouldn't create just two keyframes—one with the ball at the top-left corner of the Stage and one with the ball in the bottom-right corner—and expect Flash to tween the zigzag motion. You would need to establish the intermediate keyframes so that Flash could create the motion in stages. The same is true of shape tweening. You can better handle a dramatic change between two shapes by using intermediate keyframes.

To create an intermediate keyframe:

1. Study how an existing shape tween fails to produce satisfactory results when tweening the letter *Z* to the letter *S* (**Figure 1.39**).
2. Insert a keyframe at an intermediate point within the tween.
3. In the newly created keyframe, edit the shape that provides a kind of stepping stone for the final shape (**Figure 1.40**).

   The shape tween has smaller changes to go through, with smoother results (**Figure 1.41**).

Sometimes, providing an intermediate keyframe isn't enough, and you need shape hints to refine the tween even more. Here are three ways you can add shape hints to a shape tween that uses an intermediate keyframe.

To use shape hints across multiple keyframes:

- Select the intermediate keyframe, and add shape hints as though it were the first keyframe.

  Keep track of which shape hint belongs to which tween by noting their respective colors. Yellow is the shape hint for the beginning keyframe, and green is the shape hint for the end keyframe (**Figure 1.42**).

  or

- Insert a new keyframe adjacent to the second keyframe, and begin adding shape hints.

  A new keyframe allows you to add shape hints without the confusion that overlapping shape hints from the preceding tween may cause (**Figure 1.43**).

  or

- Create a new layer that duplicates the intermediate and last keyframes of the shape tween, and begin adding shape tweens on this new layer.

  By duplicating the intermediate keyframe, you keep shape hints on separate layers, which also prevents the shape hints from overlapping (**Figure 1.44**).

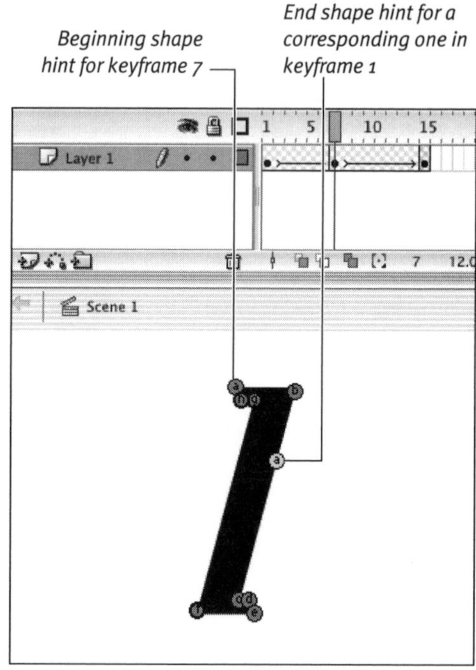

Figure 1.42 This intermediate keyframe contains two sets of shape hints. Some are the ending shape hints for the first tween; others are the beginning shape hints for the second tween.

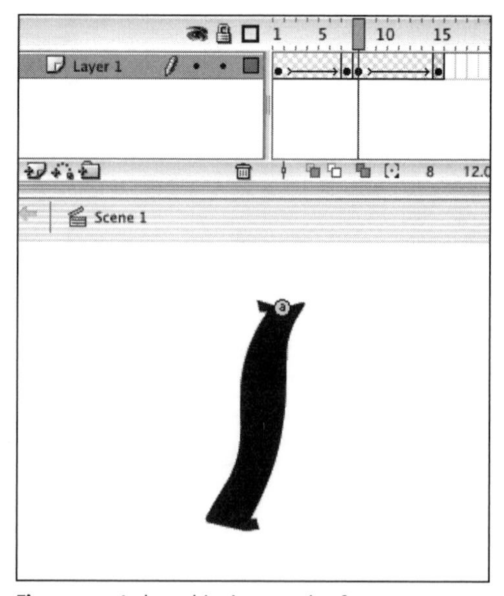

Figure 1.43 A shape hint in a new keyframe.

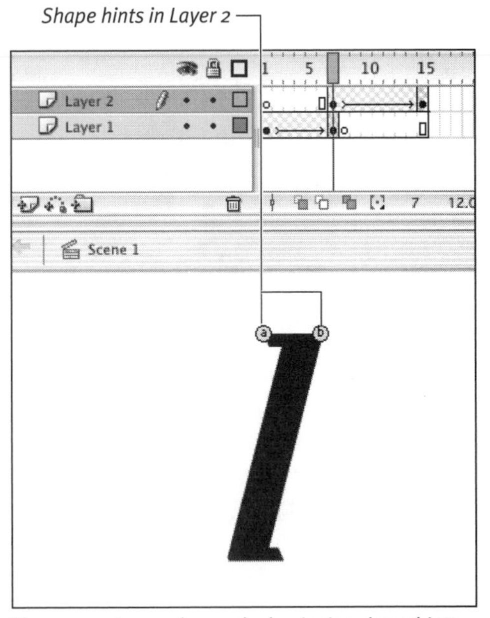

Figure 1.44 Layer 2 keeps the beginning shape hints for the tween from frames 7 to 15 separate from the end shape hints for the tween from frames 1 to 7.

Using layers to simplify shape changes

Shape tweening lets you create very complex shape tweens on a single layer, but doing so can produce unpredictable results. Use layers to separate complex shapes and create multiple but simpler shape tweens.

When a shape tween is applied to change the letter *F* to the letter *D*, for example, the hole in the last shape appears at the edges of the first shape (**Figure 1.45**). Separating the hole in the *D* and treating it as a white shape allows you to control when and how it will appear. Insert a new layer, and create a second tween for the hole. The compound tween gives you better, more refined results (**Figure 1.46**).

Figure 1.45 A hole appears at the outline of the first shape when a shape tween is applied to change an *F* to a *D*.

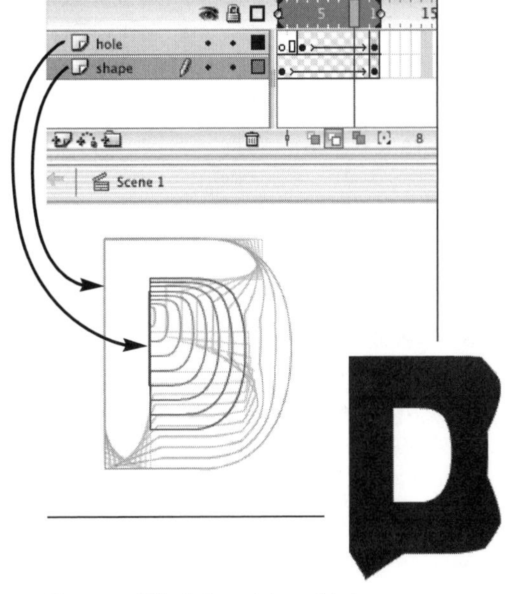

Figure 1.46 The hole and the solid shapes are separated on two layers.

Creating Special Effects

Because Flash's drawing tools are vector-based, you normally wouldn't think of incorporating a special effect, such as a motion blur, which is associated with bitmap applications such as Adobe Photoshop or Macromedia Fireworks. But integrating special effects is possible simply by importing a bitmap that has been altered by a special-effect filter. This technique can give your Flash movie more depth and richness by going beyond the simple flat shapes and gradients of vector drawings.

The following examples demonstrate a motion blur and a blur-to-focus effect. A *motion blur* is a camera artifact produced when something moves too fast for the film to capture; you see a blurry image of where the moving object used to be. Often, these images overlap, creating a streak that trails the fast-moving object. Cameras do create motion blurs automatically and unintentionally, but in Flash, you must put them in yourself.

A *blur* is an effect that occurs when the camera is out of focus. Blurs are particularly effective for transitions; you can animate a blurry image coming into sharp focus.

To create a motion blur:

1. Create the image to which you want to apply a motion blur, and convert it to a graphic symbol (**Figure 1.47**).
2. Copy the graphic, and paste it into a new document in Photoshop.

   The new Photoshop document should be in RGB and at 72-dpi resolution and the same size as your copied Flash graphic.

   The Flash graphic appears in the Photoshop document.
3. Choose Image > Canvas Size.

   The Canvas Size dialog box appears.

Figure 1.47 Create a graphic symbol. This snowboarder will be moving fast enough to cause a motion blur.

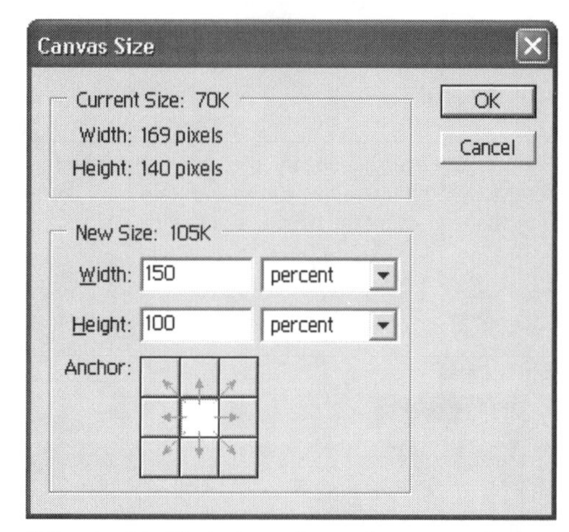

Figure 1.48 In Photoshop, change the canvas size in the direction of the blur. This canvas will get wider on either side by 150%.

Figure 1.49 The image in Photoshop needs room on either side to make room for a horizontal blur.

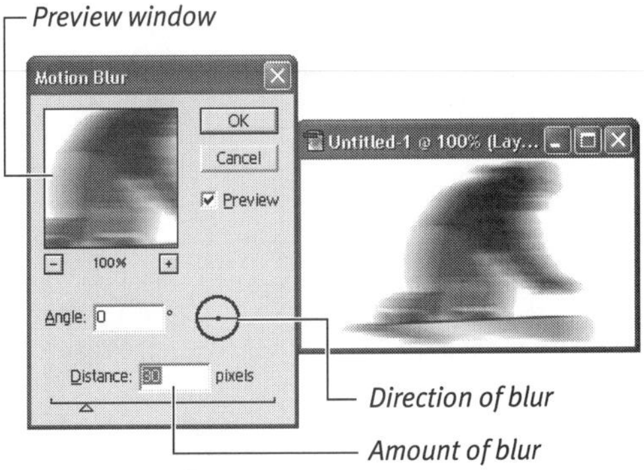

Figure 1.50 The Motion Blur filter in Photoshop provides options for the direction and amount of blur, as well as a preview window of the effect.

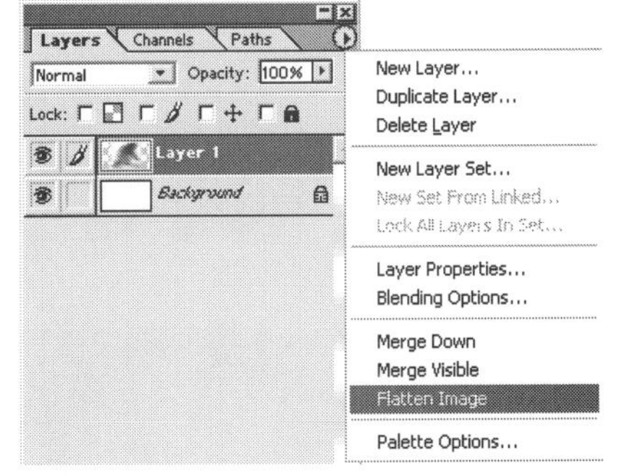

Figure 1.51 In the Layers palette of Photoshop, flatten your image to a single layer.

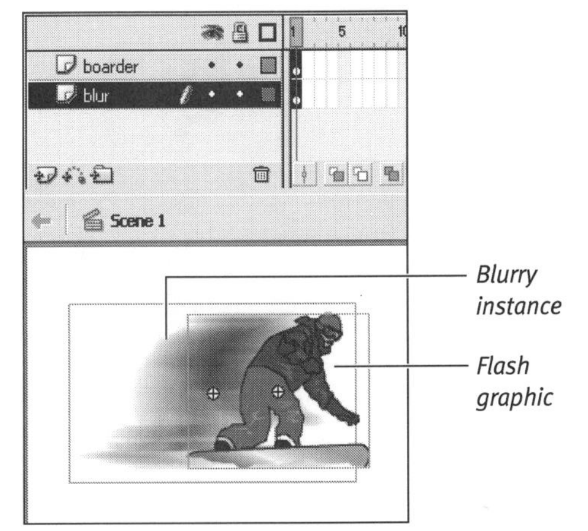

Figure 1.52 The motion blur is positioned behind the image of the snowboarder. Both instances are on separate layers, in preparation for motion tweening.

4. Increase the canvas by about 150 percent in the direction in which you will be applying your motion blur (**Figure 1.48**); then click OK.

   The background of your graphic increases so that you have room for your motion blur (**Figure 1.49**).

5. Choose Filter > Blur > Motion Blur.

   The Motion Blur dialog box appears.

6. Change the angle of the blur to match the direction in which your image will be moving, and set the amount of blur to about one-fifth the overall size of your image (**Figure 1.50**); then click OK.

   The image becomes blurry in one direction only, simulating the speed streaks from a camera.

7. Choose Layer > Flatten Image (**Figure 1.51**).

8. Choose Select > All (Cmd-A for Mac, Ctrl-A for Windows), copy the image, and then paste it back into your Flash file in an empty layer.

   The motion-blurred bitmap image appears on the Stage and in your Library.

9. Convert the blurry bitmap image to a graphic symbol.

10. Move the blurry instance below the original Flash graphic so that the streaks extend in the opposite direction from which the graphic will move (**Figure 1.52**).

11. Create keyframes for both layers later in the Timeline, move both instances across the Stage, and apply a motion tween to both layers.

    The original image and the blurred image move together, but the combined effect isn't quite convincing yet.

continues on next page

12. Adjust the timing of the keyframes so that the blurred image starts a few frames later and the original image finishes a few frames earlier, and add an empty keyframe in the last frame for the blurred image (**Figure 1.53**).

    Having the blurred image lag behind the original graphic makes the streak more of an afterimage and completes the special effect.

Figure 1.53 Play with the timing of the motion tween of the blur so that it appears when the snowboarder is in motion but disappears when he stops.

✔ Tip

- This technique works only if your Stage is a solid color, because the Photoshop filter produces a bitmap that blurs the image to the background.

To create a blur-to-focus effect:

1. As in the preceding example, copy and paste an image from Flash into Photoshop.
2. Adjust the canvas in both width and height to make room for the blur effect.

   For an image that bleeds on all four sides like the example shown here, however, increasing the canvas size isn't necessary.
3. In Photoshop, choose Filter > Blur > Gaussian Blur.

   The Gaussian Blur dialog box appears.
4. Enter a pixel amount that determines the amount of blurring you desire (**Figure 1.54**); then click OK.

   The image blurs.
5. Make sure to flatten the image by choosing Layer > Flatten Image.
6. Select the entire image; then copy and paste it back into Flash in an empty layer.

   This Flash file contains your original, focused image.
7. Convert the blurry imported bitmap to a graphic symbol.

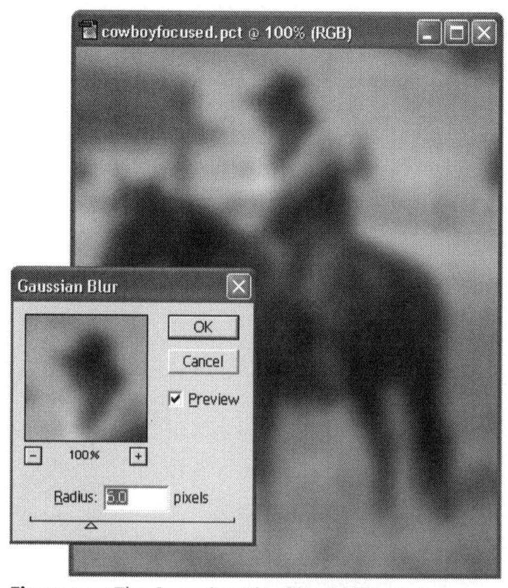

Figure 1.54 The Gaussian Blur filter in Photoshop makes the entire image unfocused.

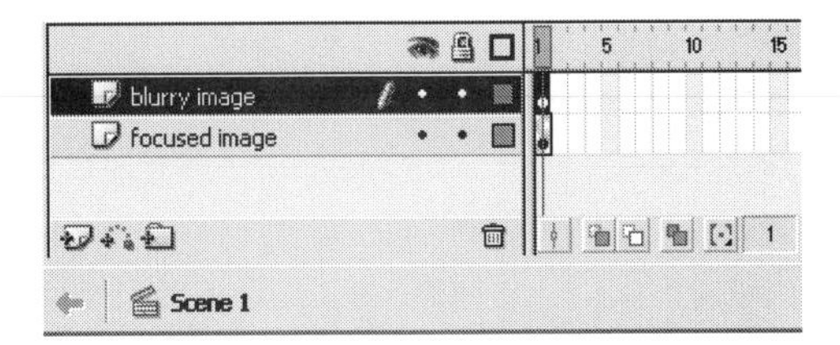

Figure 1.55 Place the blurry instance over the original image. In this figure, the two images are not yet aligned, so you can see their overlapping positions.

8. Align the original, focused image and the blurry image, with the blurry image in the topmost layer (**Figure 1.55**).
9. Later in the Timeline, insert a keyframe into the layer that contains the blurry image, and add a matching number of frames in the layer that contains the focused image.
10. In the last keyframe of the blurry image, change the image's alpha value to 0% (**Figure 1.56**).

    The blurry image in the last keyframe becomes transparent, exposing the focused image in the layer below.
11. Apply a motion tween to the layer that contains the blurry image.

    As the blurry image slowly disappears, it shows the unaltered image, making it seem as though you have one image with a change in focus (**Figure 1.57**).

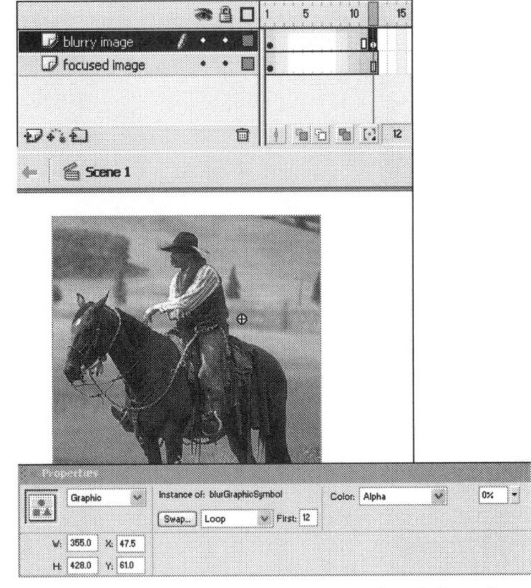

Figure 1.56 In the Property Inspector, the alpha value of the top, blurry image is set to 0%, exposing the original, focused image in the bottom layer.

✔ Tips

- Try increasing the initial size of the blurry image slightly to add a subtle zooming-in effect, which enhances the blur-to-focus transition.
- You can use any Photoshop filter in this manner to create a transition. Experiment with the numerous available filters to suit your movie.

Figure 1.57 The result makes an effective transition.

Animated and Complex Masks

Masking is a simple way to reveal portions of the layer or layers below it selectively. This technique requires making one layer a mask layer and the layers below it the masked layers.

By adding tweening to either or both the mask layer and the masked layers, you can go beyond simple, static peepholes and create masks that move, change shape, and reveal moving images. Use animated masks to achieve such complex effects as moving spotlights, magnifying lenses that enlarge underlying pictures, or "x-ray" types of interactions that show more detail within the mask area. Animated masks are also useful for creating cinematic transitions such as wipes, in which the first scene is covered as a second scene is revealed; and iris effects, in which the first scene collapses in a shrinking circle, leaving a second scene on the screen.

Inserting layers above and below masks can add even more complexity to animated masks. A shape filled with an alpha gradient, for example, can make the hard edges of a mask fade out slowly for a subtle spotlight.

Using movie clips in mask layers opens even more possibilities: multiple masks, masks that move on a motion guide, and even dynamically generated masks that respond to the user. Because dynamic masks rely on ActionScript, however, they'll be covered in detail in Chapter 7.

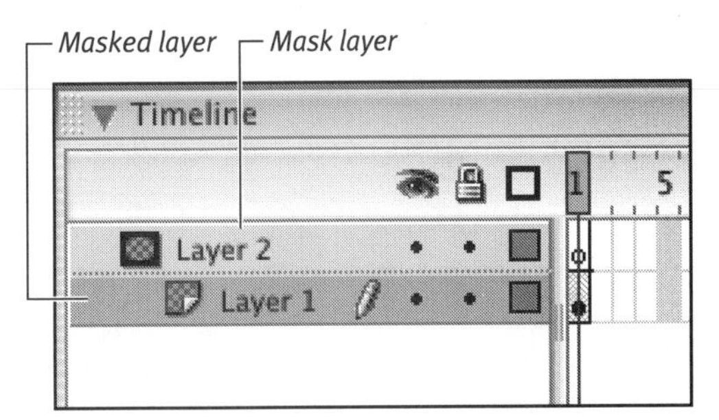

Figure 1.58 Layer 2 is the mask layer, and Layer 1 is the masked layer.

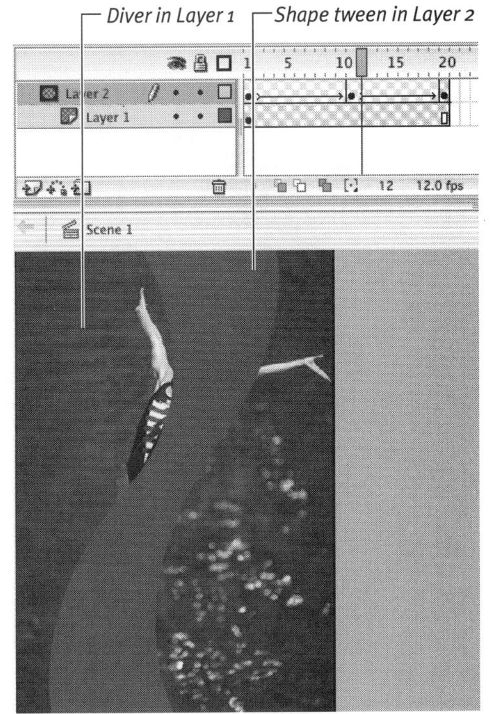

Figure 1.59 A shape tween of a moving vertical swirl is on the mask layer. The diver image is on the masked layer.

To tween the mask layer:

1. In Layer 1, create a background image or import a bitmap.
2. Insert a new layer above the first layer.
3. Select the top layer, and choose Modify > Layer.
4. Select Mask Type.
5. Select the bottom layer, and choose Modify > Layer.
6. Select Masked Type.

   The top layer becomes the mask layer, and the bottom layer becomes the masked layer (**Figure 1.58**).
7. Create a shape tween or a motion tween in the mask layer (the top layer) (**Figure 1.59**).
8. Insert sufficient frames into your masked layer to match the number of frames in the mask-layer tween.
9. Lock both layers to see the effects of your animated mask on the image in the masked layer (**Figure 1.60**).

continues on next page

Figure 1.60 The shape tween uncovers the image of the diver. The portion of the mask that does not reveal the photo is the color of the Stage.

✔ Tips

- Place duplicate images that vary slightly in a normal layer under both the mask and masked layers. This technique makes the animated mask act as a kind of filter that exposes the underlying image. Add a bright image in the masked layer and a dark version of the same image in a normal layer under the masked layer, for example. The mask becomes a spotlight on the image (**Figure 1.61**). Explore other duplicate-image combinations, such as a sharp and a blurry image, a grayscale and a color image, or an offset image (**Figure 1.62**).
- Place a tween of an expanding box in the mask layer that covers the Stage to simulate cinematic wipes between images (**Figure 1.63**).

Figure 1.61 The moving spotlight in the mask layer (spotlight) uncovers the stained-glass image in the masked layer (bitmap). A duplicate darker image resides in the bottom, normal layer (dark bitmap).

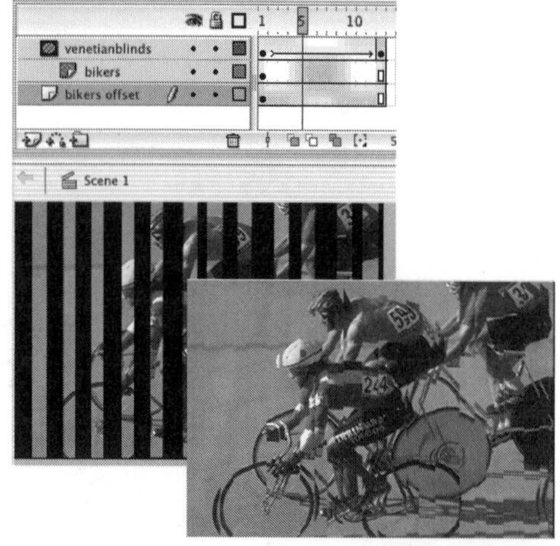

Figure 1.62 The moving vertical shapes in the mask layer (venetian blinds) uncover the image of bicyclists in the masked layer (bikers). A duplicate image in the bottom normal layer (bikers offset) is shifted slightly to create the rippling effect.

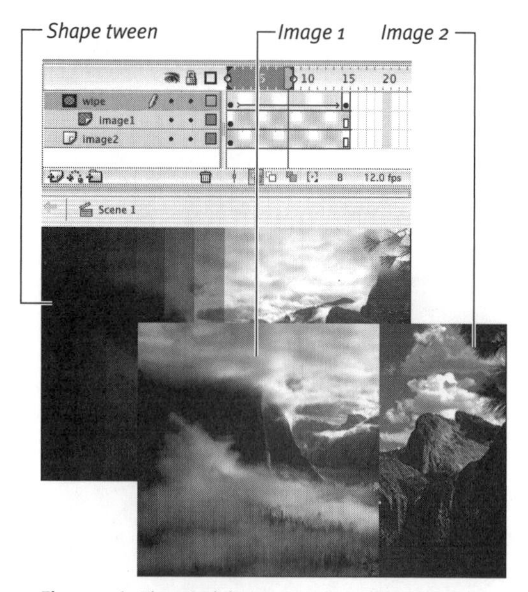

Figure 1.63 The mask layer contains a large shape tween that covers the entire Stage. This technique creates a cinematic wipe between an image in the masked layer (image 1) and an image in the bottom, normal layer (image 2).

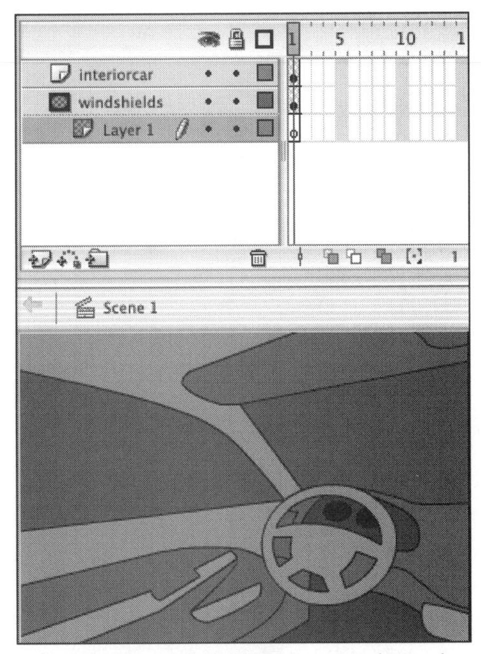

Figure 1.64 The windshield shapes are in the mask layer called windshields. The drawing of the car interior is in a normal layer above the windshields layer.

Figure 1.65 Several motion tweens in masked layers (tree, cow, ground, and sky) move under the windshield shapes in the mask layer.

To tween the masked layer:

1. Beginning with two layers, modify the top to be the mask layer and the bottom to be the masked layer.
2. Draw a filled shape or shapes in the mask layer (**Figure 1.64**).

   This area becomes the area through which you see your animation on the masked layer.
3. Create a shape tween or a motion tween in masked layers that pass under the shapes in the mask layer. You can have as many masked layers as you want under a single mask layer (**Figure 1.65**).
4. Lock both layers to see the effects of your animated masked layers as they show up behind your mask layer (**Figure 1.66**).

continues on next page

Figure 1.66 The images of the tree, cow, ground, and sky move under the mask, creating the illusion of the car's forward motion.

✔ Tip

- This approach is a useful alternative to using shape tweens to animate borders or similar types of objects that grow, shrink, or fill in. Imagine animating a fuse that shortens to reach a bomb (**Figure 1.67**). Create a mask of the fuse, and animate the masked layer to become smaller slowly, making it look like just the fuse is shortening (**Figure 1.68**). Other examples that could benefit from this technique include trees growing, pipes or blood vessels flowing with liquid, and text that appears by filling in with color. Just remember that Flash doesn't recognize strokes in the mask layer, so if you want to create thin lines in the mask layer, use fills only.

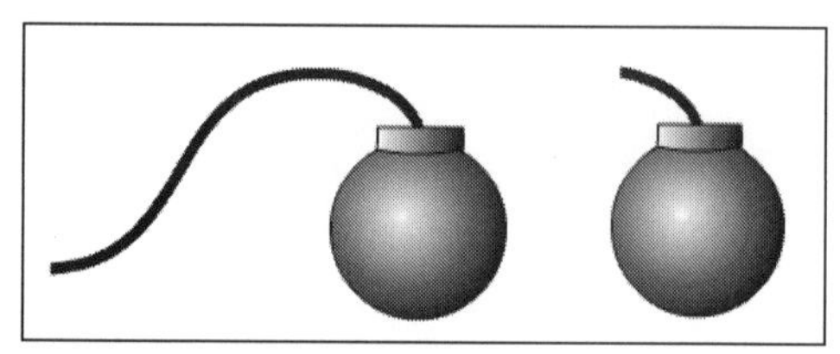

Figure 1.67 The fuse of a bomb shortens.

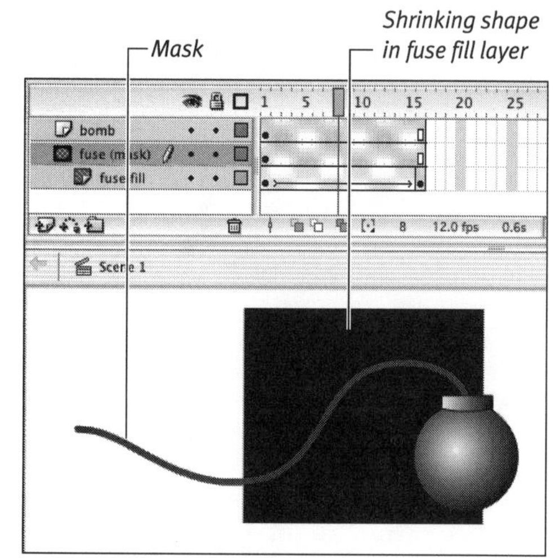

Figure 1.68 The bomb's fuse is a thin shape in the mask layer. The rectangular tween in the masked layer shrinks, making it appear as though the fuse is shortening.

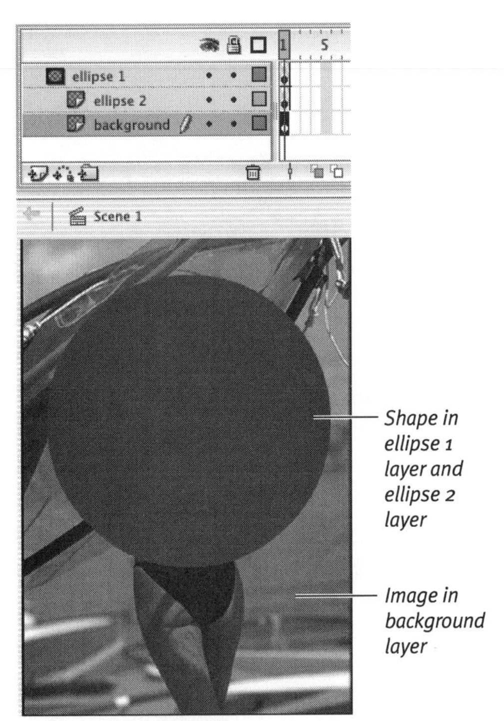

Figure 1.69 The same ellipse appears in both the mask layer (ellipse 1) and the top masked layer (ellipse 2). The image of the windsurfer is in the bottom masked layer (background).

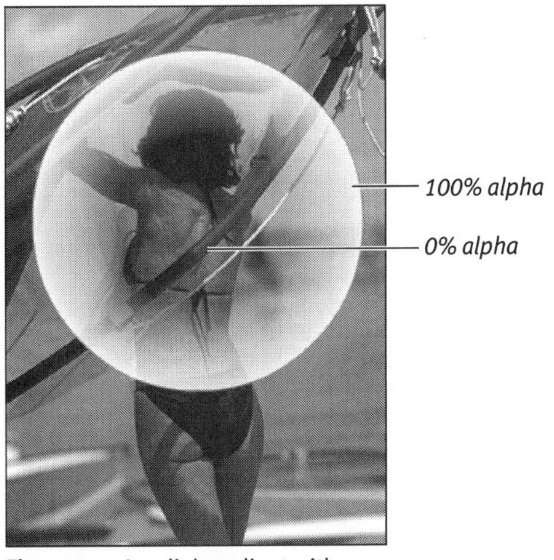

Figure 1.70 A radial gradient with a transparent center in the top masked layer.

In the mask layer, Flash sees all fills as opaque shapes, even if you use a transparent solid or gradient. As a result, all masks have hard edges. To create a softer edge, place a gradient with a transparent center either under or over the mask to hide the edges.

To create a soft-edged mask:

1. Create a mask layer and a masked layer.
2. Place or draw a background image in the masked layer.
3. Draw an ellipse in the mask layer.
4. Copy the ellipse.
5. Insert a new layer between the mask layer and the masked layer.

   Your new layer will become a masked layer.
6. Choose Edit > Paste in Place (Cmd-Shift-V for Mac, Ctrl-Shift-V for Windows).

   A new ellipse appears in the new masked layer, right under the ellipse in the top mask layer (**Figure 1.69**).
7. Fill the pasted ellipse with a radial gradient, defined with a transparent center to an opaque perimeter, in the same color as the Stage (**Figure 1.70**).

continues on next page

8. Lock all three layers to see the effects of the mask (**Figure 1.71**).

   The mask layer lets you see through an elliptical area. The top masked layer hides the edges of the ellipse by creating a gradual fade toward the center. The bottom masked layer holds the contents of your background image (**Figure 1.72**).

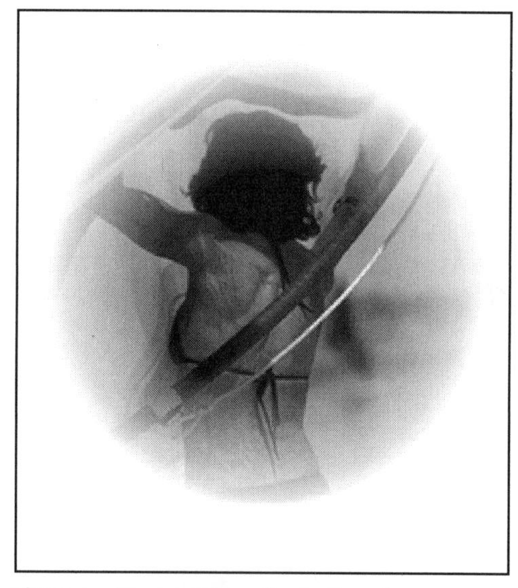

Figure 1.71 The resulting soft-edged mask.

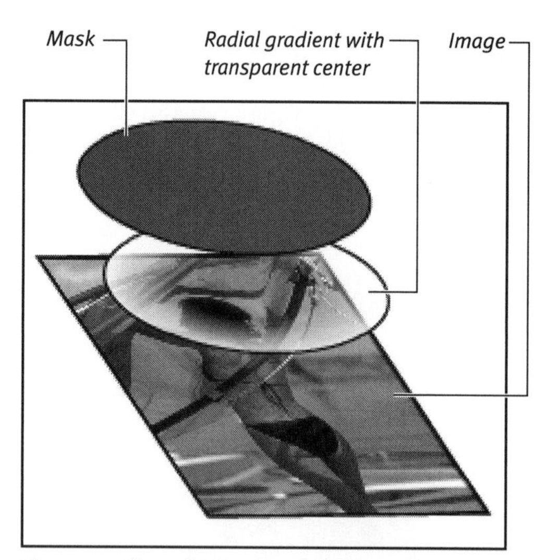

Figure 1.72 The soft-edged mask is the combination of the mask in the top layer (mask layer), a radial gradient in the middle layer (top masked layer), and the background image in the bottom layer (bottom masked layer).

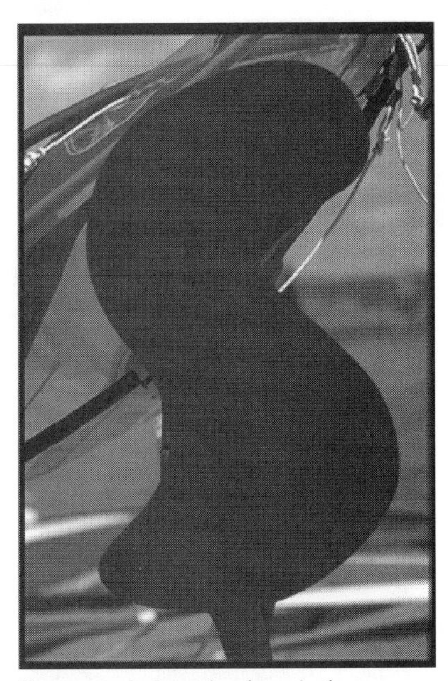

Figure 1.73 An irregular shape in the top masked layer above an image in the bottom masked layer.

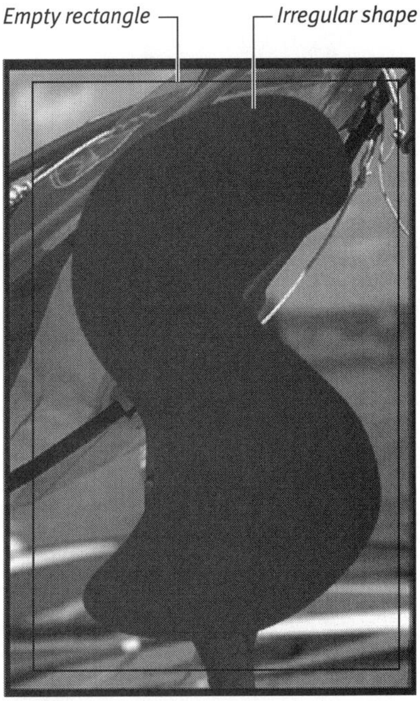

Empty rectangle — *Irregular shape*

Figure 1.74 An empty rectangle drawn around the irregular shape.

Creating soft edges with radial transparent gradients works well with circular masks, but if the shapes of your masks are more complicated, you'll need to resort to customizing the fades of your edges.

To create a soft-edged mask with an irregular shape:

1. Create a mask layer and a masked layer.
2. Place or draw an image in the masked layer.
3. Draw an irregular shape in the mask layer.
4. Copy the shape.
5. Insert a new masked layer between the mask layer and the first masked layer.
6. Choose Edit > Paste in Place.

   Your irregular shape appears in the new masked layer right under the original shape in the top mask layer (**Figure 1.73**).
7. With the Oval or Rectangle tool, draw an outline around your shape (**Figure 1.74**).

continues on next page

8. Fill the area between your shape and the outline with the background color, and delete the fill in the original shape.

   Your complex shape is now the "hole" of a larger shape (**Figure 1.75**).

9. Select the entire shape, and choose Modify > Shape > Soften Fill Edges (**Figure 1.76**).

   The Soften Fill Edges dialog box appears (**Figure 1.77**). The Distance option determines the thickness of the soft edge. The Number of Steps option determines how gradual the transition from opaque to transparent will be. The Direction option determines which way the edge softening will take place.

Figure 1.75 By filling the area between the shape and the rectangle and then deleting the shape, you create a hole.

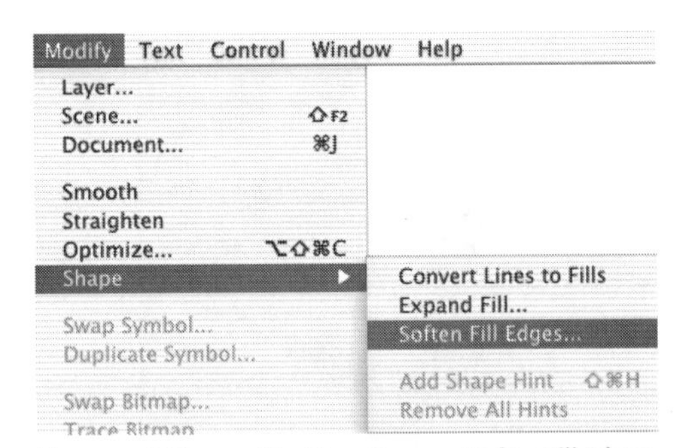

Figure 1.76 Choose Modify > Shape > Soften Fill Edges.

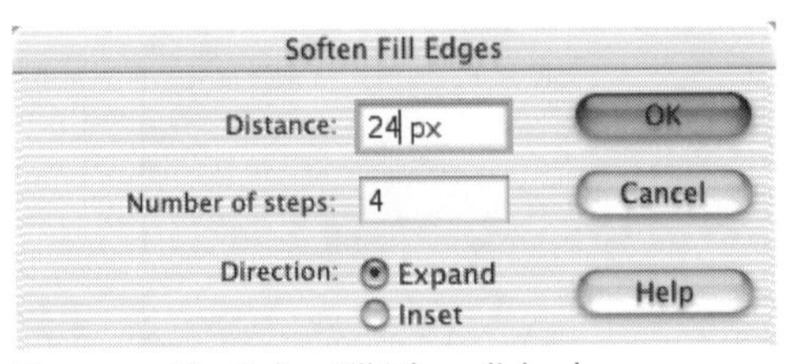

Figure 1.77 The Soften Fill Edges dialog box.

Figure 1.78 The softened edges expand into the "hole," where it is visible through the mask in the top mask layer.

10. Enter the Distance (in pixels) and the Number of Steps, and choose Expand for the Direction.

    All the edges around your shape soften. Because the entire shape expands, the actual hole shrinks (**Figure 1.78**).

11. Lock all three layers to see the effects of the mask (**Figure 1.79**).

Figure 1.79 The soft edges of an irregular mask created with Modify > Shape > Soften Fill Edges.

Although Flash allows multiple masked layers under a single mask layer, you cannot have more than one mask layer affecting any number of masked layers (**Figure 1.80**). To create more than one mask, you must use movie clips. Why would you need to have multiple masks? Imagine creating an animation that has two spotlights moving independently on top of an image (**Figure 1.81**). Because the two moving spotlights are tweened, they have to be on separate layers. The solution is to incorporate the two moving spotlights into a movie clip and place the movie clip on the mask layer.

You will learn much more about the movie clip in chapters 4 and 7. If you'd like, skip ahead to read about movie clips and return when you feel comfortable.

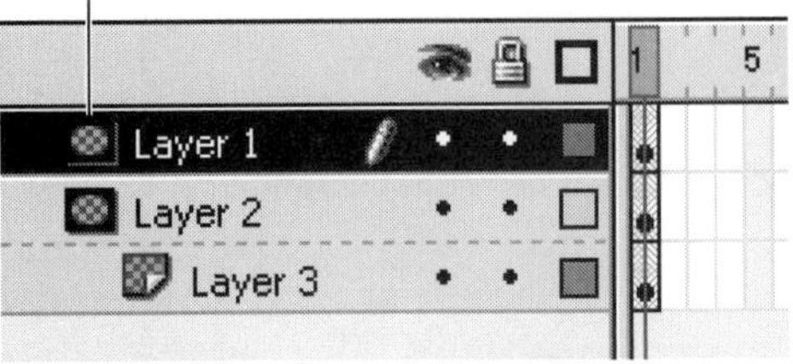

Figure 1.80 Layer 1 and Layer 2 are both defined as mask layers, but only Layer 2 affects Layer 3—the masked layer.

Figure 1.81 Two independent spotlights moving, each uncovering portions of the image.

To create multiple masks:

1. Create a mask layer and a masked layer.
2. Place your image on the masked layer.
3. Choose Insert > New Symbol (Cmd-F8 for Mac, Ctrl-F8 for Windows).

   The Create New Symbol dialog box appears.
4. Enter a descriptive name and choose Movie Clip (**Figure 1.82**); then click OK.

   Flash creates a movie-clip symbol, and you enter symbol-editing mode for that symbol.

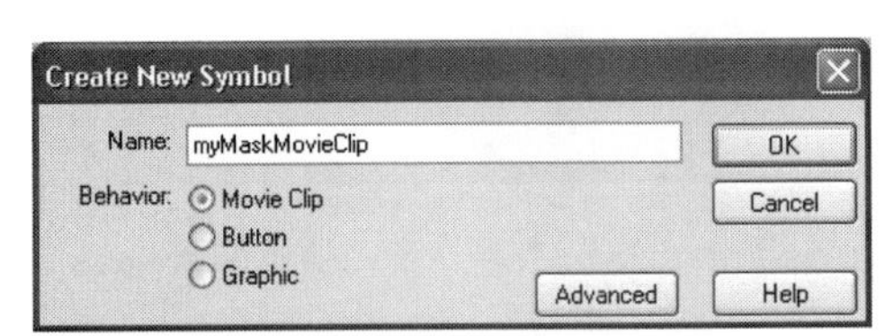

Figure 1.82 Choose Movie Clip to create a new movie-clip symbol.

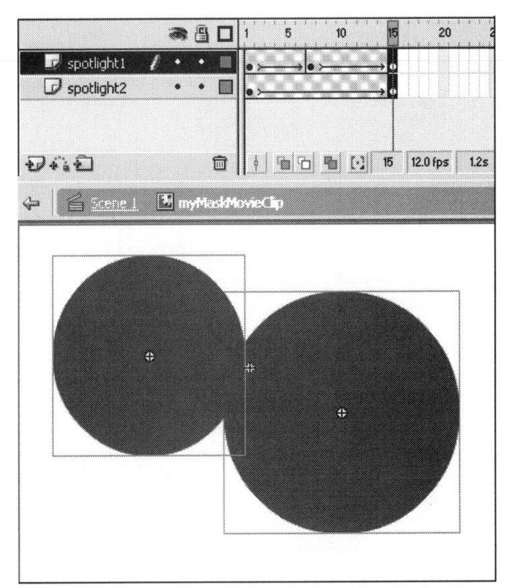

Figure 1.83 The two moving spotlights are motion tweens inside the movie clip called myMaskMovieClip.

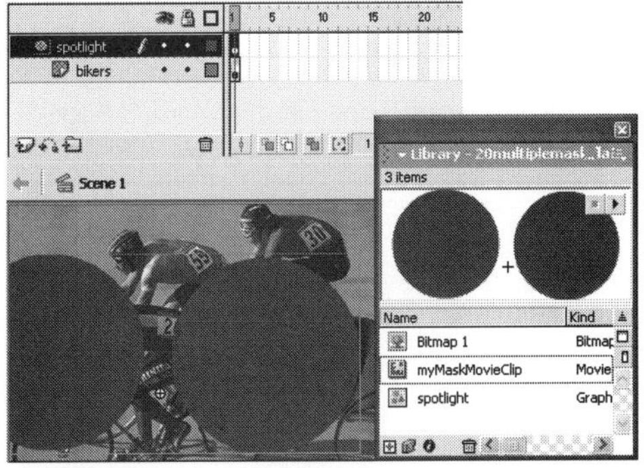

Figure 1.84 An instance of the myMaskMovieClip movie clip is in the top (mask) layer, and the image of the bikers is in the bottom (masked) layer.

5. Create two motion tweens of spotlights moving in different directions on the Timeline of your movie-clip symbol (**Figure 1.83**).

6. Return to the main Stage, and drag an instance of your movie-clip symbol into the mask layer (**Figure 1.84**).

7. Choose Control > Test Movie to see the effects of the movie-clip mask.

   The two motion tweens inside the movie clip both mask the image on the masked layer.

continues on next page

✔ Tips

- To see what your masks are uncovering, use a transparent fill or choose the Outlines option in your Layers Properties (**Figure 1.85**).
- To prevent the animation inside the movie clip from looping constantly, add a keyframe to its last frame and add a `stop` action.

Show as Outlines option

Outline of spotlight 2 layer in a movie clip

Outline of spotlight 1 layer in a movie clip

Figure 1.85 Viewing your masks as outlines lets you see the image underneath; choose the Outlines option in the Layers Properties dialog box, or click the Show as Outlines icon in your layer.

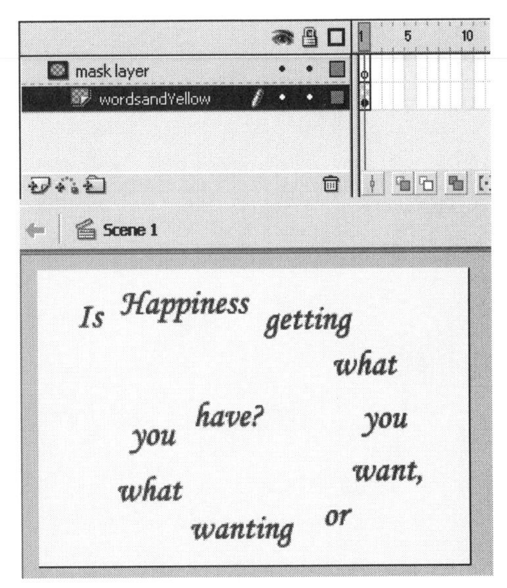

Figure 1.86 The words of this interesting question and a background fill are put on the bottom (masked) layer.

Motion path

Flower graphic instance

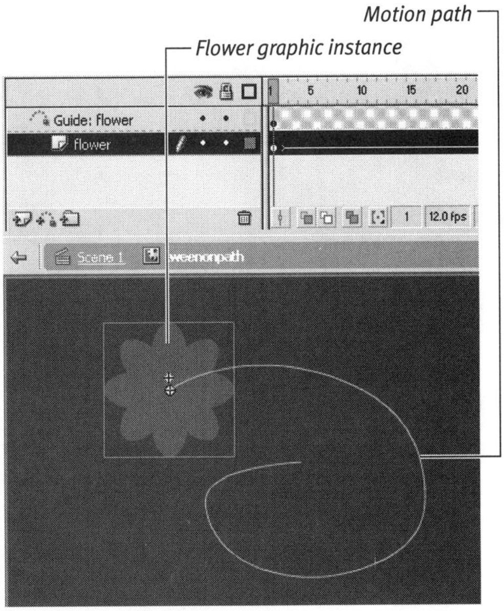

Figure 1.87 Inside a movie clip, the flower graphic instance follows a motion path.

Putting a movie-clip instance inside the mask layer not only makes multiple masks possible, but also provides a way to have a mask follow a motion guide. Build your tween that follows a motion guide inside a movie clip. Place that movie clip in a mask layer on the main Stage, and voilà—you have a mask that follows a path.

To guide a mask on a path:

1. Create a mask layer and a masked layer.
2. Place your image on the masked layer (**Figure 1.86**).
3. Create a new movie-clip symbol.
4. Inside your movie-clip symbol, create a motion tween that follows a motion guide (**Figure 1.87**).

continues on next page

5. Return to the main Stage, and drag an instance of your movie clip into the mask layer (**Figure 1.88**).
6. Edit the motion path to get it exactly the way you want, relative to the other graphics on the Stage, by choosing Edit > Edit in Place or double-clicking the instance (**Figure 1.89**).

   Flash grays out all graphics except for the instance you are editing.
7. Choose Control > Test Movie to see the effect of your movie clip on the mask layer.

   The animation follows its path in the motion guide, and at the same time, it masks the image in the masked layer on the main Stage (**Figure 1.90**).

Figure 1.88 The movie clip containing the moving flower is in the mask layer and positioned over the words.

Figure 1.89 Edit in Place allows you to make changes in your movie-clip symbol and see the graphics on the main Stage at the same time.

Figure 1.90 The moving flower exposes the question as it moves along its motion path.

2

WORKING WITH VIDEO AND 3D

This chapter explores the exciting possibilities of using media created outside Flash in your Flash project. Combining digital video or 3D graphics with Flash lets you develop imagery with all the interactivity of Flash ActionScript but without the limitations of the Flash drawing tools. You can create truly interactive movies, for example, by importing your videos into Flash and then adding buttons and hotspots, sounds, and vector graphics. You can export this combination of video and Flash as either a Flash movie or a QuickTime file. More possibilities of integrating an imported video include using it as a guide for your Flash animation or transforming the video completely by applying Flash's editing tools that turn your video into vector drawings. This kind of effect is used often on Flash Web sites promoting theatrical releases or music videos. Short video clips of band members are imported into Flash as a series of bitmap images, simplified into vectors, and sprinkled throughout other graphics and animation to play along with a soundtrack. The short animated sequences give a live-motion feel, and the vectorized images keep the file size manageable.

Similarly, working with 3D graphics literally adds another dimension to your Flash projects. Although Flash can't actually import and display 3D models, third-party applications let you use models in true 3D space, play with lighting, set camera angles, and export a Flash-compatible vector image. Use 3D objects and animations in Flash as interface elements, buttons, or animated characters and backgrounds.

Integrating Flash and Video

Everybody loves movies. So when you can add video to your Flash Web site, you'll likely create a richer and more compelling experience for your viewers. Several popular formats for digital video include QuickTime, MPEG, AVI, and DV. Fortunately, Flash supports all of them. You can import any of these digital video formats into Flash; add Flash graphics, animation, and interactivity; and in certain cases, even apply motion tweens to your imported video. You can import video into Flash by embedding it or, if you are using the QuickTime format, linking to the video.

Embedding puts the video file inside your Flash project, increasing its file size just like importing a bitmap does. Linking, on the other hand, maintains your video as a separate file outside Flash. Flash keeps track of the video with a path to the filename. If you link a video, however, several restrictions exist. You cannot apply motion tweens to a linked video, and you *must* export your Flash project as QuickTime. (Linked videos will not work in .swf format.) Moreover, the QuickTime format doesn't support the full functionality of Flash ActionScript (see the sidebar "Not All Flash Features Work in QuickTime" later in the chapter). It's safe to say that if you want to create fully functional SWF movies, always embed your videos rather than link them.

You have several ways to acquire digital video. You can shoot your own footage using a digital video camera, or you can shoot with an analog video camera and convert the video using a digitizing board that you install in your computer. Alternatively, you can use copyright-free video clips that have already been digitized and are available on CD-ROM from commercial image stock houses. Any way you go, adding digital video is an exciting way to enrich a Flash Web site.

Figure 2.1 The Import Video dialog box lets you choose to embed the video or link to it.

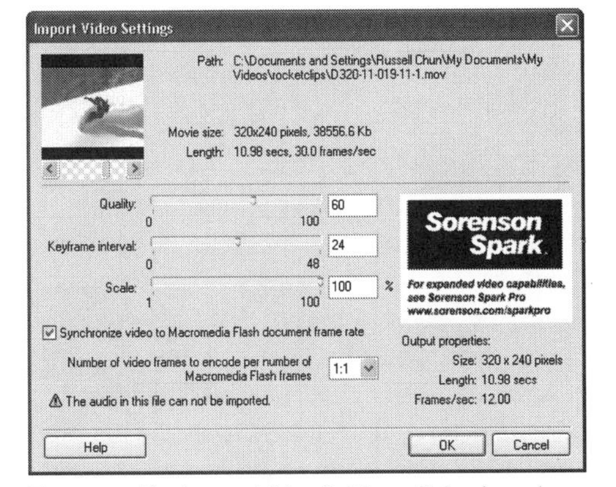

Figure 2.2 The Import Video Settings dialog box gives you control of the way your video will be compressed. Information includes the location and properties of the original file (at top), the compression settings (middle), and the output properties (bottom right).

To embed a digitized video in Flash:

1. From the File menu, choose Import (Command-R for Mac, Ctrl-R for Windows).

   The Import dialog box appears.

2. Select the file you want to import, and click Import (Mac) or Open (Windows).

   The Import Video dialog box appears (**Figure 2.1**), asking whether you want to embed the video or link to it.

3. Choose Embed Video in Macromedia Flash Document, and click OK.

   The Import Video Settings dialog box appears (**Figure 2.2**). Flash uses the Sorenson Spark codec (*co*mpression-*dec*ompression scheme) to import and display video. Choose among these settings to affect the quality, length, and file size of your imported video:

   ▲ **Quality.** Controls the amount of compression that is applied to your video and, hence, the quality of the image. A value of 100 is the best quality but results in a large file, and a value of 0 is the worst quality but produces a small file.

   ▲ **Keyframe Interval.** Determines how frequently complete frames of your video are stored. The frames between keyframes store only the data that changes from the preceding frame. A keyframe interval of 24, for example, stores information on the complete frame every 24 frames of your video. If your video contains action of someone raising his hand between frames 17 and 18, only that portion of the image where his hand is being raised is stored in memory until frame 24, when the full frame is stored. The lower you set the keyframe interval, the more keyframes are stored, and the larger the file will be.

continues on next page

- **Scale.** Controls the size of your video. A setting of 100 percent imports your video at its original size. It's best to keep your video at a maximum of 320 by 240 pixels. Anything larger results in a very large file and poor playback performance.
- **Synchronize Video to Macromedia Flash Document Frame Rate.** Choosing this option matches the frame rate of your video to the frame rate of your Flash movie. This option ensures that a video plays at its intended speed even if the frame rates between it and Flash differ. A video shot at 30 frames per second (fps) and brought into a Flash movie running at 15 fps will play twice as long (and twice as slowly) if you do not synchronize the video. Choose this option for normal use.
- **Number of Video Frames to Encode Per Number of Macromedia Flash Frames.** Controls the mapping of frames between the video timeline and the Flash Timeline. Choosing a ratio in which the first number is smaller than the second number makes the video display less of its frames than Flash. The ratio 1:2, for example, results in one frame of your video playing for every two frames on your Flash Timeline. This setting results in a smaller file (because there are fewer video frames to encode) but a choppier playback. It does *not* affect the duration of your video. Choose 1:1 for normal use.

What Makes a Good Video?

We all know a good video when we see one. But how do you create and prepare digitized videos so they play well and look good within Flash? Knowing a little about the Sorenson Spark compression that is built into Flash will help.

Sorenson compresses video both spatially and temporally. Spatial compression happens within a single frame, much like JPEG compression on an image. Temporal compression happens between frames, so that the only information that is stored is the differences between two frames. Therefore, videos that compress really well are ones that contain localized motion or very little motion (such as a talking head) because the differences between frames are minimal. (In a talking-head video, only the mouth is moving.) For the same reasons, transitions, zooms, and fades do not compress or display well, so stick with quick cuts if possible.

Here are a few other tips for making a good video that are not related to compression:

- Keep the size small (320 by 240 maximum) and the length of the video short. Often, just a few well-placed moments of video is enough to heighten the drama of your Flash movie.
- Maintain reasonable frame rates. Although video may run at about 30 fps, use 12 to 15 fps.
- Shoot in digital. You'll get a cleaner image if your source is digital rather than filming in analog and then converting to digital.

Figure 2.3 Importing a video puts a video symbol in the library and an instance of the movie on the Stage in the active layer.

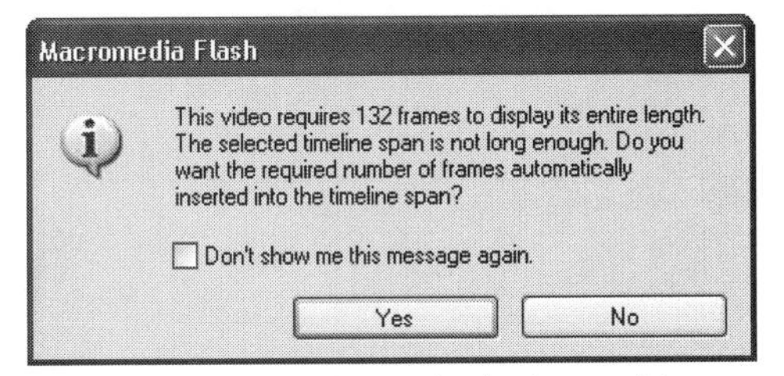

Figure 2.4 Flash will ask you whether it can add enough blank frames to the Timeline automatically to accommodate the length of your imported video.

4. After you have chosen your settings, click OK.

   Flash embeds the video in your document, putting a video symbol in your library and an instance of the video on the Stage in the active layer (**Figure 2.3**). If you do not have enough empty frames to accommodate the entire length of your video, a dialog box appears (**Figure 2.4**). If this happens, click Yes.

✔ Tips

- If you are not satisfied with the result, you can always change the settings by reimporting the video (as described in the following section).
- Macintosh users can import a file quickly by simply dragging the video file from the Desktop to the Stage.
- Flash can't display the soundtrack of imported videos, so if your original video file has sound, you won't hear it within the authoring environment of Flash. When you publish your Flash movie or test it by choosing Control > Test Movie, the sound will be audible again.
- If you have more frames than are needed in a layer containing an embedded video, Flash will display the last frame of the video until the end of the Timeline. To end the Timeline exactly where the video ends, select the excess frames and choose Insert > Remove Frames.

To link a QuickTime video in Flash:

1. Choose File > Import to open the Import dialog box.
2. Select the video file you want to link in Flash.

   The Import Video dialog box appears.
3. Choose Link to External Video File (**Figure 2.5**), and click OK.

   Flash imports a link to the video into your document, putting a video link symbol in your library and an instance of the video on the Stage in the active layer (**Figure 2.6**).

   If you do not have enough empty frames to accommodate the entire length of your video, a dialog box appears, asking to insert frames for the video automatically. If this happens, click Yes.

   Linked videos are visible only when your Flash project is exported as QuickTime (see how to do this later in this section). Be sure to set your publish settings (File > Publish Settings) to Flash Player 4 or earlier before exporting a linked video to QuickTime. QuickTime 5 does not yet support Flash MX media.

✔ Tip

- Unlike embedded videos, if you have more frames than are needed in a layer containing a linked video, Flash displays an empty placeholder that looks like a rectangle with an *X* through it (**Figure 2.7**). To end the Timeline exactly where the video ends, select the excess frames, and choose Insert > Remove Frames.

Figure 2.5 The Import Video dialog box.

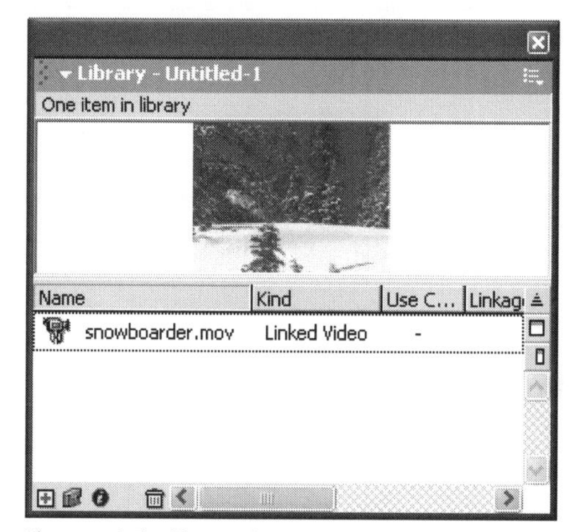

Figure 2.6 The library shows the linked video.

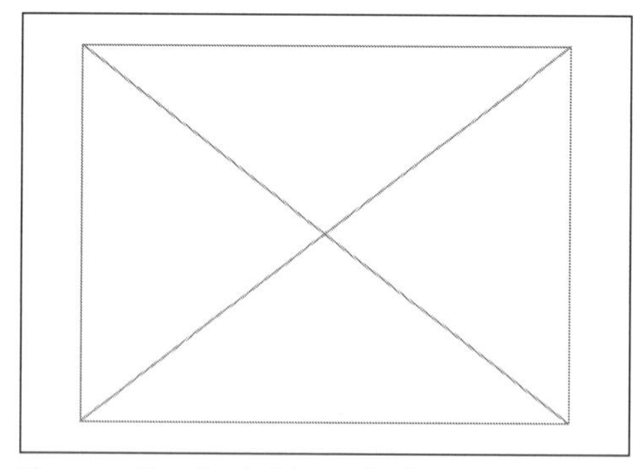

Figure 2.7 The placeholder on the Stage means you're past the end of the linked movie and there are no more frames available to display.

INTEGRATING FLASH AND VIDEO

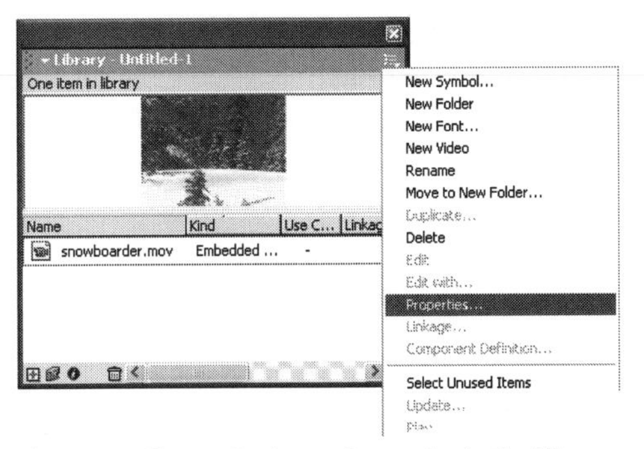

Figure 2.8 Choose Options > Properties in the Library window to get information about the selected symbol.

Figure 2.9 The Embedded Video Properties dialog box shows the name of the symbol and the location of the original video file, as well as the properties of the compressed video (dimensions, time, and size).

Updating and replacing imported videos

When you make changes in your original video file, you'll want those changes to be reflected in your Flash movie as well. Luckily, Flash makes updating your imported videos easy, whether the videos are embedded or linked in Flash. For an embedded video, you can update it or reimport it to modify the compression settings, or you can replace the video with another one. For a linked video, you can update the path to the file if it's been moved or renamed.

If you've linked your video, you can also edit your original video with either QuickTime Player or another external digital video editor. When you do, Flash updates your video symbol in the library automatically. Note that if you use QuickTime Player, you will need QuickTime Pro (the upgrade you buy from Apple) to do any copying, pasting, or resaving of files.

To update an embedded video:

1. Double-click the video icon or the preview window in your library.

   or

   Select the video symbol in the library; then, from the Library window's Options menu, choose Properties (**Figure 2.8**).

   The Embedded Video Properties dialog box appears, showing the symbol name and the original video file's location (**Figure 2.9**).

2. Click Update.

   Flash finds the video file and reimports it, using the original compression settings. Any changes you have made in the video are updated in Flash.

To change the compression settings of an embedded video:

1. Double-click the video icon or the preview window in your library.

   or

   Select the video symbol in the library; then, from the Library window's Options menu, choose Properties.

   The Embedded Video Properties dialog box appears, showing the symbol name and the original video file's location.

2. Click Import.

3. Select the same video file, and click Import (Mac) or Open (Windows).

   The Import Video Settings dialog box appears.

4. Choose new compression settings for your video, and click OK.

   Your video is reimported with the new compression settings.

5. Click OK to exit the Embedded Video Properties dialog box.

   All instances of your video now reflect the changes you made in the compression settings.

To replace an embedded video:

1. Double-click the video icon or the preview window in your library.

   or

   Select the video symbol in the library; then, from the Library window's Options menu, choose Properties.

   The Embedded Video Properties dialog box appears, showing the symbol name and the original video file's location.

2. Click Import.

3. Select the new video file you want to use to replace your old video file, and click Import (Mac) or Open (Windows).

   The Import Video Settings dialog box appears.

4. Choose the compression settings for your new video, and click OK.

   Your replacement video is imported.

5. Click OK to exit the Embedded Video Properties dialog box.

   All instances of your old video symbol now reflect the new video you chose.

To set a new path for your linked video:

1. Double-click the video icon or the preview window in your library.

   or

   Select the video symbol in the library; then, from the Library window's Options menu, choose Properties.

   The Linked Video Properties dialog box appears, showing the symbol name and the original video file's location.

2. Click the Set Path button.

3. Navigate to the new location or renamed video file, select it, and click Open.

   The new path and filename appear in the Linked Video Properties dialog box next to Path.

4. Click OK.

   Flash will now be able to locate the video.

✔ Tip

- The Name field in the Linked Video Properties dialog box is not the name of your original video file, but the name of your symbol in the library. These two names can be different as long as the path to the video file is correct.

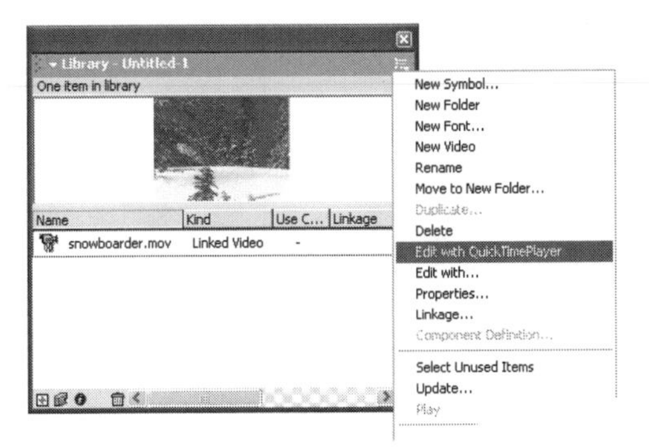

Figure 2.10 In the Library window, choose Options > Edit with QuickTime Player or Edit With to use another application to make changes in your video file.

To edit a linked video:

1. In the library, select the video symbol you want to edit.
2. From the Library window's Options menu, choose Edit with QuickTime Player or Edit With (**Figure 2.10**).

   The external application will launch and open your video file.
3. Edit the video file, and save it.
4. Return to Flash, delete the current instance of the video on the Stage, and drag a new instance from the library to see the changes in your video.

   Flash will use the new video file that you just edited and saved.

Adding Flash elements to your video

After you have imported your video into Flash, you can add Flash elements over the movie, such as titles, labels, and animated special effects. Add graphics next to a talking-head video to mimic a newscast, for example, or use labels to point out important features as they appear in an instructional video on fixing a bicycle.

Put your embedded video inside a graphic symbol, and you can also apply motion tweens to create transitions with the alpha or color effect or create funky rotations, skewing, scaling, and even horizontal or vertical flips.

continues on next page

Add interactivity by integrating buttons or frame actions that control the playback of the video content. Create your own Pause, Stop, Play, Fast Forward, and Rewind buttons to customize the video-playback interface. You can even convert your video to a movie-clip symbol and have at your disposal the methods, properties, and events of the Movie Clip object. Create drag-and-drop video puzzle pieces as a twist on standard puzzles, for example. You will learn much more about the Movie Clip object in later chapters, so be sure to return here after reading about it to see how you can incorporate it into imported videos.

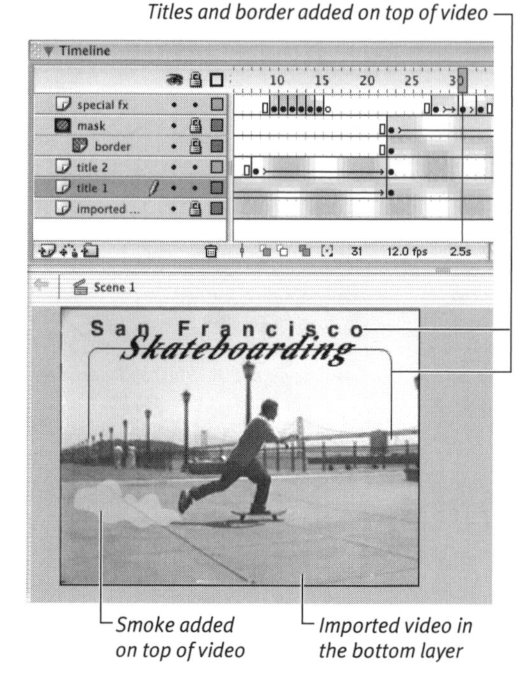

Figure 2.11 Add Flash graphics and animation over your imported video. This example shows two animated titles, a mask that uncovers a border, and the special effect of the shape-tweened smoke behind the skateboarder's foot.

To overlay Flash elements on a video:

1. For this example, set the Stage to the same size as the imported video file (320 by 240 pixels), and position the movie to cover the Stage exactly.
2. Lock the layer that contains the video to prevent it from being moved accidentally.
3. Add separate layers over the video layer to create animated titles, graphics, or special effects.

   Figure 2.11 shows a few animated elements superimposed on the imported video file. Check out the Flash and video files provided on the CD.

To apply a motion tween to an embedded video:

1. Select the video instance on the Stage.
2. Choose Insert > Convert to Symbol (F8).

   The Convert to Symbol dialog box appears.
3. Enter a descriptive name, choose the Graphic option in the Behavior section, and click OK (**Figure 2.12**).

   A warning dialog box appears, asking you whether you want to insert enough frames into the new graphic symbol to accommodate the length of your video.

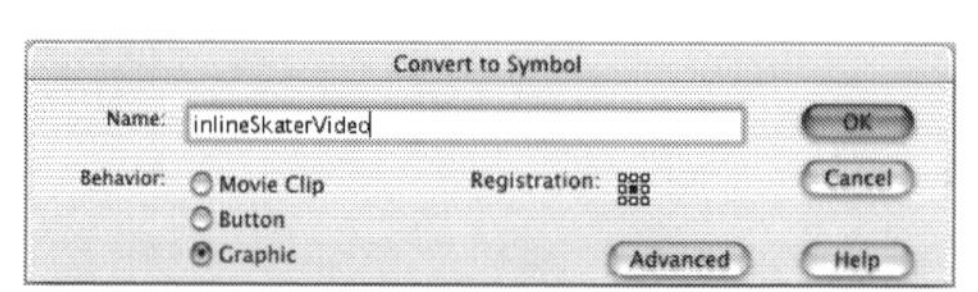

Figure 2.12 Convert your embedded video to a graphic symbol so you can apply motion tweens.

Figure 2.13 This video of an inline skater coming toward the viewer is also given a motion tween that rotates and enlarges it, enhancing the excitement.

Figure 2.14 Add button instances to let your users navigate within the video. These buttons are placed on a separate layer.

4. Click Yes.

   The video on the Stage is now an instance of a graphic symbol to which you can apply motion tweens.

5. Create new keyframes along the Timeline, and modify the instance by changing its color effect, position, scale, rotation, or skew.

6. Apply motion tweens between the keyframes (**Figure 2.13**).

✔ Tips

- You cannot apply tweens to a linked video clip; they will not show up in the final exported QuickTime file.
- You can always add layers and drag out more instances of the graphic symbol containing your video, and your video will play in all the instances. Be aware, however, that new keyframes of the same instance will make your file larger.
- The First parameter in the Property Inspector, which normally establishes which frame of a graphic instance will begin playing, will not affect the playback of the video.

To create interactive controls for a video:

1. Create four buttons: a Play button, a Pause button, a Skip to End button, and a Skip to Beginning button.
2. Place your four button instances in a new layer above the layer containing the imported video file (**Figure 2.14**).
3. Add a third layer, and insert a keyframe at the last frame of the timeline.

continues on next page

4. Label the first keyframe start, and label the last keyframe end (**Figure 2.15**).

5. Assign actions to all four button instances by selecting them individually and then opening the Actions panel.

   ▲ Give the Play button these actions:

   ```
   on (release) {
        play();
   }
   ```

   ▲ Give the Pause button these actions:

   ```
   on (release){
        stop();
   }
   ```

   ▲ Give the Skip to End button these actions:

   ```
   on (release) {
        gotoAndStop("end");
   }
   ```

   ▲ Give the Skip to Beginning button these actions:

   ```
   on (release) {
        gotoAndStop("start");
   }
   ```

   For more information on the Actions panel, see Chapter 3.

6. Test your movie to see how your custom Flash buttons let you navigate to different spots on the Timeline and control the playback of the video (**Figure 2.16**).

Figure 2.15 In another layer, label the start of the Timeline start (top) and the end of the Timeline end (bottom). This method will make assigning frame destinations for your buttons easier.

Figure 2.16 The exported .swf file plays your video while the buttons and actions you've customized control its playback.

Figure 2.17 The Export Movie dialog box.

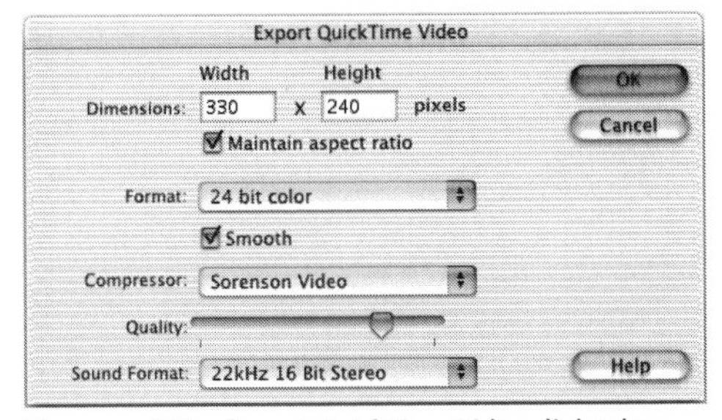

Figure 2.18 The Export QuickTime Video dialog box.

Exporting to QuickTime, QuickTime video, and AVI

Most of the time, you will publish your Flash movie as a .swf file to play with Flash Player in a browser. On some occasions, however, you will need or want to export your Flash movie in alternative formats. The three video formats available for export are QuickTime, QuickTime Video (Mac only), and AVI (Windows only). What are the differences among these file formats, and how do they differ from .swf? To help sort out the confusion, see the sidebar "QuickTime, QuickTime Video, and AVI" in this section.

If you linked a video in Flash, you must export your Flash project as one of these three movie formats for the linked video to display.

If you want to rasterize all your Flash content so that earlier versions of QuickTime Player can display your movie, you will want to export a QuickTime video or an AVI.

To export your Flash movie as a QuickTime video or AVI:

1. Choose File > Export Movie (Ctrl-Alt-Shift-S for Windows, Command-Opt-Shift-S for Mac).

   The Export Movie dialog box appears.

2. Choose a destination folder and name, and choose QuickTime Video or Windows AVI from the Format drop-down menu or Save As Type (**Figure 2.17**).

   The Export dialog box appears. **Figure 2.18** shows the Export dialog box that appears when you choose QuickTime Video.

3. Select your export settings, and click OK.

   Flash exports your Flash movie as a QuickTime video or AVI.

✔ Tip

- If you have animations inside movie clips, only their first frames will display in a QuickTime video or AVI. In the Property Inspector, set their behavior to graphic symbols to play as Loop, and they will play when you export to a QuickTime video or AVI.

To export your Flash movie as a QuickTime file:

1. Choose File > Publish Settings.
2. Select the Flash tab, and change the Version option to Flash Player 4 or earlier.

   Currently, QuickTime 5 does not support Flash MX media. QuickTime 5 supports only Flash 4 functionality.
3. Select the Formats tab, check the box next to QuickTime, and uncheck the others.
4. Select the QuickTime tab, and set the following paramaters for QuickTime (**Figure 2.19**):
   - ▲ **Dimensions.** Allows you to set alternative height and width in pixels.
   - ▲ **Alpha.** Controls how the Flash elements are displayed with the QuickTime movie. Choose Copy to make the Flash Stage opaque. Choose Alpha-Transparent to make the Flash Stage transparent. Choose Auto to make the Flash Stage transparent or opaque, depending on the stacking order of Flash graphics and the QuickTime file.
   - ▲ **Layer.** Controls where you want the Flash track to lie in the exported QuickTime file. Choose Auto for the layering to follow your Flash layers.
   - ▲ **Streaming Sound.** Lets any sounds in Flash be converted to a QuickTime sound track using QuickTime compression settings.
   - ▲ **Controller.** By choosing None, you can create a QuickTime file that doesn't contain the standard QuickTime playback controls. Use this option if you've created custom navigation buttons with Flash (**Figure 2.20**).

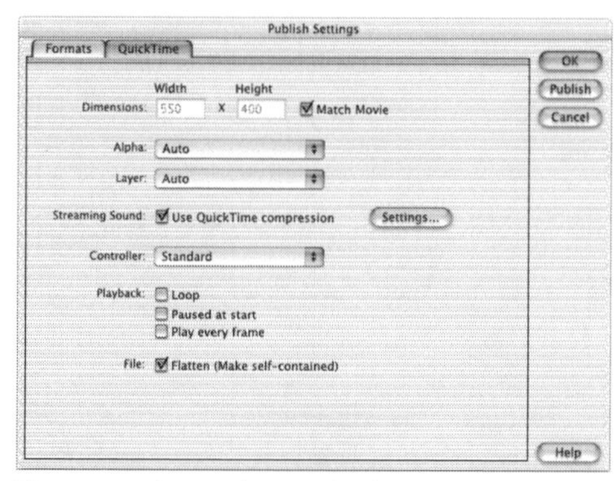

Figure 2.19 The QuickTime tab of the Publish Settings dialog box.

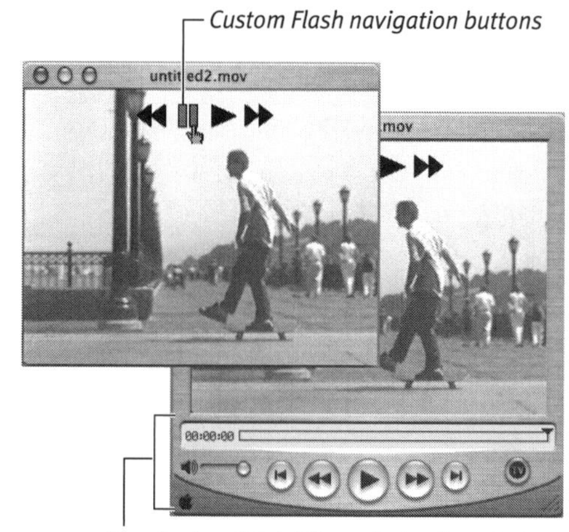

Figure 2.20 Two QuickTime movies, with (bottom) and without (top) the standard playback controls.

- ▲ **Playback.** Choose these options to control how the movie will play. Avoid checking the Play Every Frame checkbox, because it will disable any audio in the QuickTime sound track.
- ▲ **File.** The Flatten (Make Self-Contained) checkbox creates a single file incorporating all externally referenced media, eliminating the need to keep the original imported QuickTime file together with the final exported QuickTime file. The Flatten option also makes the file compatible for both Mac OS and Windows.

5. Click OK or Publish.

   or

   As an alternative to steps 3 through 5, choose Export Movie from the File menu. In the Export Movie dialog box that appears, choose the destination folder, name the destination file, and choose QuickTime from the pull-down menu.

   The Export QuickTime dialog box appears to let you set the same QuickTime parameters that appear in the Publish Settings dialog box.

✔ Tip

- Embedded videos are Flash MX features that are not supported in QuickTime 5; therefore, they will not export as QuickTime.

Not All Flash Features Work in QuickTime

It's very important to understand that QuickTime 5 supports only a subset of current Flash features. The latest QuickTime Player usually is one version behind the Flash Player, so QuickTime 5 supports some Flash 4 features. As a result, many of the more complicated interactive functions and new features in Flash MX movies won't work properly or at all when exported as QuickTime files. Embedded videos, for example, are not supported by QuickTime 5.

You should design your Flash files with these limitations in mind if your intended destination is QuickTime Player. Test early and often, check with Apple for QuickTime updates, and try to stick with basic ActionScripting that controls the playhead of the main Timeline.

QuickTime, QuickTime Video, and AVI

The Export Movie and Publish options give you the choice of QuickTime and either QuickTime Video or AVI, depending on whether you're using a Mac or a Windows computer. These options produce very different formats even though they are all "movie" files.

The QuickTime option allows you to put your Flash content in a separate track of a QuickTime file. The Flash content maintains its functionality and its vector information, so the Flash graphics are still resolution-independent. At the same time, a separate video track plays the bitmap information.

On the Mac, the QuickTime Video option rasterizes your Flash content and puts it on the video track along with the imported QuickTime movie. All interactivity is lost, and buttons become simple graphics that are locked in at a set resolution (**Figure 2.21**). Choose this option if you want to create simple, linear movie files from Flash that don't require the latest version of QuickTime Player.

Figure 2.21 QuickTime (top) separates Flash content on a different track, maintaining Flash's vector information. QuickTime Video and AVI (bottom) combine Flash graphics with the video so that vector information is lost. Recompression of the original imported video file also results in degraded picture quality.

On a Windows computer, you have the option of exporting a movie in AVI format. This format also rasterizes Flash content into a linear movie and disables all interactivity (refer to Figure 2.21).

Table 2.1 will help you decide what kind of export format you need.

Table 2.1

Export Movie Options for Windows

Imported Video	Export Format	Comments
Embedded	SWF	Flash 6 Player required
	AVI	No interactivity
Linked	QuickTime	Limited interactivity
	AVI	No interactivity

Export Movie Options for Mac

Imported Video	Export Format	Comments
Embedded	SWF	Flash 6 Player required
	QuickTime Video	No interactivity
Linked	QuickTime	Limited interactivity
	QuickTime Video	No interactivity

Figure 2.22 A video that is good for rotoscoping contains dramatic or interesting motion with a clear distinction between background and foreground.

Lock the layer containing the video to prevent you from moving it accidentally

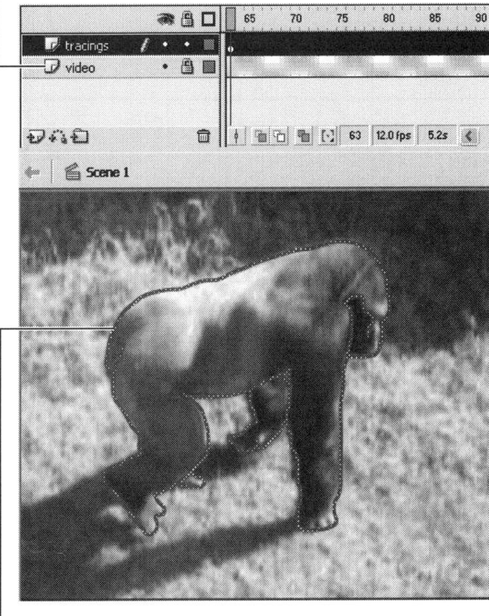

A simple tracing of this gorilla was made with the Pencil tool set on the Smooth modifier

Figure 2.23 Zoom in to the area you want to trace, and use the imported video file as your guide.

Rotoscoping

Rotoscoping is a traditional animator's technique that involves tracing live-motion film to create animation. This process is named after an actual machine, the Rotoscope, which projected live-action film onto an animation board. There, an animator could easily trace the outline of an actor frame by frame to get natural motion that would be too difficult to animate by hand. The old Disney animators often used rotoscoping to do studies, and feature movies and commercials rely on rotoscoping even today.

You can use Flash to import and display digitized videos of actors or moving objects and then do the rotoscoping yourself.

To copy the motion in an imported video:

1. Import a video as described earlier in this chapter (**Figure 2.22**).
2. Lock the layer that contains the video.
3. Add a new layer above the layer that contains your video.
4. Begin tracing the actors or the action in the new layer in keyframe 1 with any of the drawing tools (**Figure 2.23**).

continues on next page

5. Add a blank keyframe by choosing Insert > Blank Keyframe.

   An empty keyframe appears in frame 2.

6. Trace the actors or action in the empty keyframe you just created.

7. Continue the process of adding blank keyframes and tracing until your sequence is complete (**Figure 2.24**).

8. Delete the layer that contains the imported video to see the final rotoscoped animation (**Figure 2.25**).

   In this example, rotoscoping produces a very simple outline of the action, but you can trace any level of detail depending on the desired effect.

Figure 2.24 Rotoscoping this gorilla results in a layer of keyframes with drawings that follow its gait.

Figure 2.25 When you play the finished rotoscoped animation, see how natural the animation appears even if the tracings are very simple.

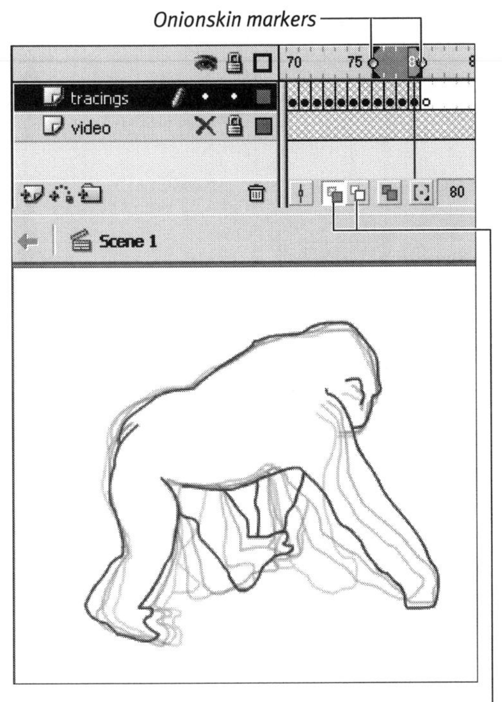

Figure 2.26 Use the Onion Skin buttons below the Timeline to show multiple frames in front of or behind the current frame. Move the onionskin markers to show less or more frames. This onionskin shows three frames behind the current frame 80.

✔ Tips

- To make it easier to see the video below your tracings, you can use the Show Layers As Outlines option in your active layer, or you can use a semitransparent color until you finish the entire sequence.
- Use the Onion Skin buttons (**Figure 2.26**) to help you see your drawings in the previous keyframes.
- Use the comma (,) and period (.) keys to move back or forward on the Timeline in one-frame increments. This technique will help you go back and forth between two frames rapidly to test the differences between your drawings, much like a traditional animator flips between two tracings.

Sometimes, the video you are trying to rotoscope has too many frames, making the motion unnecessarily smooth and the tracing too tedious. You can reduce the number of frames that the video occupies in the Flash Timeline by reimporting your video and changing the video-frames-to-Flash-frames ratio in the Import Video Settings dialog box.

To reduce the number of available frames to trace:

1. In the library, select the video symbol, and choose Properties.

   or

   Double-click the video symbol in the library.

   The Video Properties dialog box appears.
2. Click Import.
3. Select the same video file, and click Import (Mac) or Open (Windows).

   The Import Video Settings dialog box appears.
4. From the Number of Video Frames to Encode Per Number of Macromedia Flash Frames pull-down menu, choose a lower ratio.

   Choosing 1:2, for example, will play one video frame for every two Flash frames, effectively halving the number of tracings. The total length of the video remains the same.
5. Click OK.

Simulating Video

Although Flash can display video directly within Flash Player, there are times when you'll be looking for a more artistic effect than straight video can provide. Converting video to a sequence of bitmap images to create a short frame-by-frame animation is a very effective technique to simulate video and gives you some flexibility to modify the imagery. Although this process can be laborious and relatively low-tech, the rewards are enormous. When you work with bitmap sequences, you can use the Trace Bitmap command to convert them to vector shapes. In the process, you can reduce the number of colors and shapes to create stylized images with posterized effects or delete background shapes to isolate dramatic silhouettes. You can better integrate these short sequences into your Flash movie without being limited by the rectangular boundaries of a direct video. It is also a way to simulate video if you are creating content for Flash Player 5 or earlier.

To create sequential bitmaps from a video:

1. Import a video file, and embed it in your Flash movie.

   You eventually will be importing the same number of bitmap images as you have frames of video, so take care not to import too long a video segment. If possible, reduce the frame rate of your video by using a video-editing application such as Adobe Premiere.
2. Change the dimensions of the Stage to fit the dimensions of your imported video.

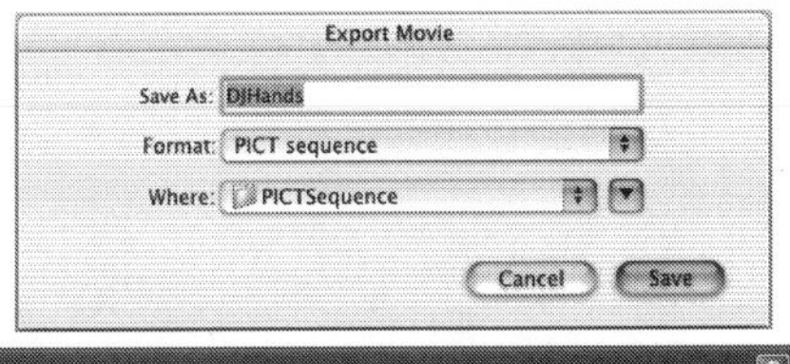

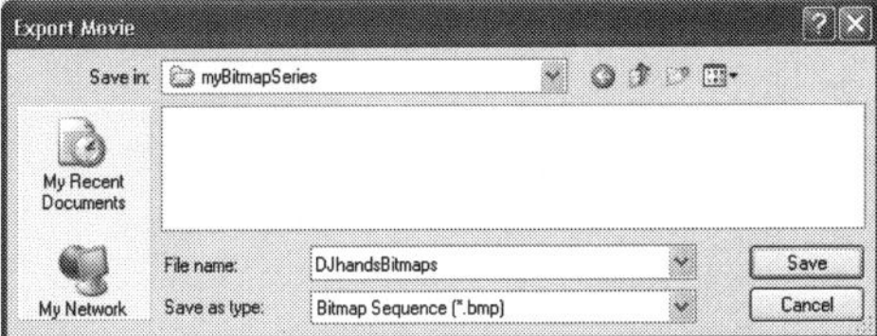

Figure 2.27 The Export Movie dialog box for the Mac (top) and Windows (bottom). The Format and Save As Type pull-down menus give you the choice of export file types. Choose PICT sequence for the Mac or Bitmap Sequence for Windows.

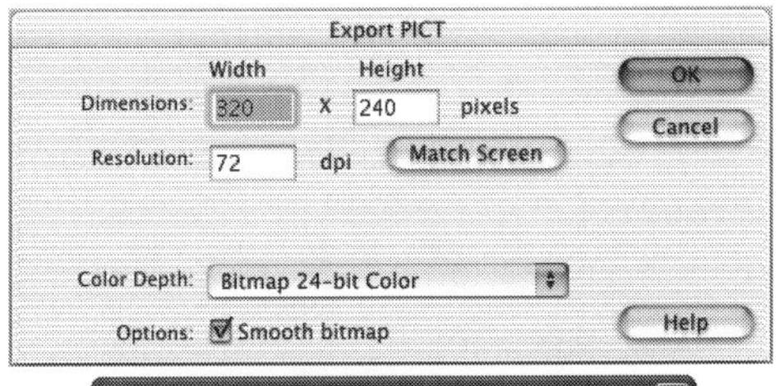

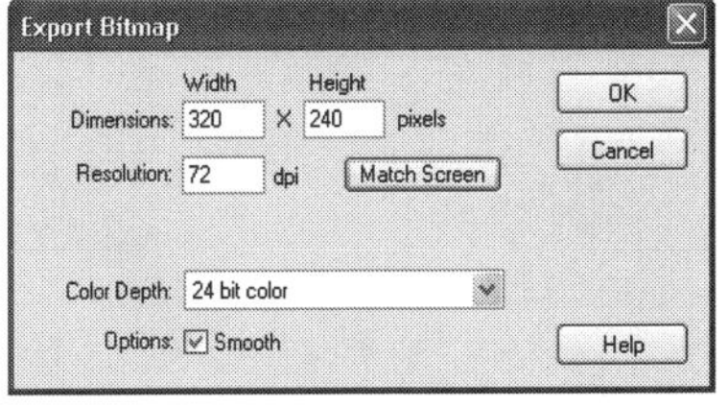

Figure 2.28 The Export PICT dialog box for the Mac (top) and the Export Bitmap dialog box for Windows (bottom).

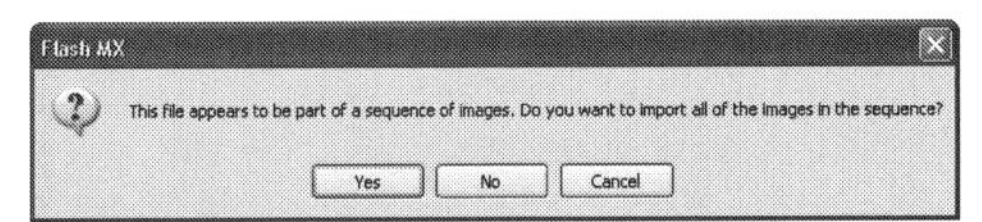

Figure 2.29 The warning dialog box. Click Yes to import the entire sequence.

3. Choose File > Export Movie.

   The Export Movie dialog box appears. This dialog box lets you choose a file format and destination folder.

4. Click New Folder to create a new destination folder.

5. Enter a name for your exported image files.

6. From the Format pull-down menu, choose PICT Sequence (Mac) or Bitmap Sequence (Windows) (**Figure 2.27**).

7. Click Save.

   The Export PICT (Mac) or Export Bitmap (Windows) dialog box appears.

8. Click the Match Screen button to make sure that the width, height, and resolution numbers match your Stage at screen resolution (72 dpi).

9. From the Color Depth pull-down menu, choose the appropriate bitmap level.

   24 bits is the color depth for millions of colors.

10. In the Options section, check the Smooth (Windows) or Smooth Bitmap (Mac) checkbox (**Figure 2.28**).

11. Click OK.

    Flash exports a series of bitmap images and appends a numerical extension to the filenames to keep them in series.

12. Open a new Flash file, and import the first of the images you just created.

    Flash recognizes that this first image is part of a sequence (**Figure 2.29**) and asks you whether you want to import the entire sequence.

continues on next page

13. Click Yes.

Flash places each bitmap in a new keyframe and aligns them all in the active layer (**Figure 2.30**).

✔ **Tip**

- For Mac users, be sure to bump up your memory partition for the Flash application if you plan to import a large PICT sequence. Working with bitmaps can take up a large amount of memory, and imports often fail because of insufficient memory.

To convert the bitmaps to simplified vectors:

1. Select the first keyframe or bitmap on the Stage.
2. Choose Modify > Trace Bitmap.

   The Trace Bitmap dialog box appears (**Figure 2.31**). The parameters in the dialog box determine how accurate the tracing will be to the bitmapped image.
3. Set the following options:
   - ▲ **Color Threshold** (a number between 1 and 200). Controls the tolerance level when Flash is deciding whether neighboring pixels should be considered to be one color or two colors. Flash compares the RGB values of two neighboring regions, and if their difference is less than the color threshold, the color is considered to be the same. The lower the color threshold, the more colors Flash will see and reproduce.
   - ▲ **Minimum Area** (a number between 1 and 1000). Controls how large an area Flash will consider when making the color calculations.

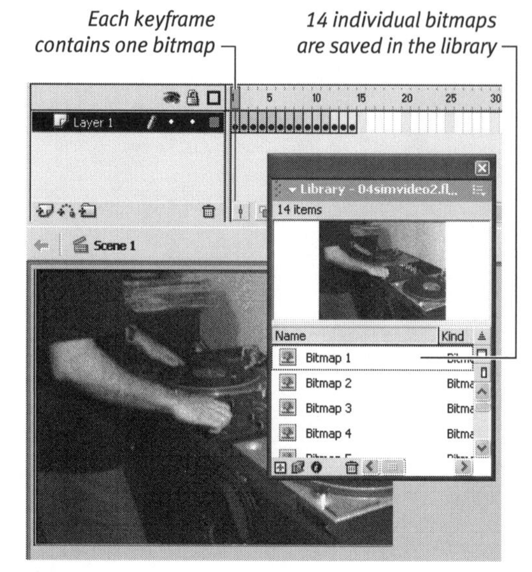

Figure 2.30 After you import a bitmap series, each image is placed in a separate keyframe and also is saved in the library.

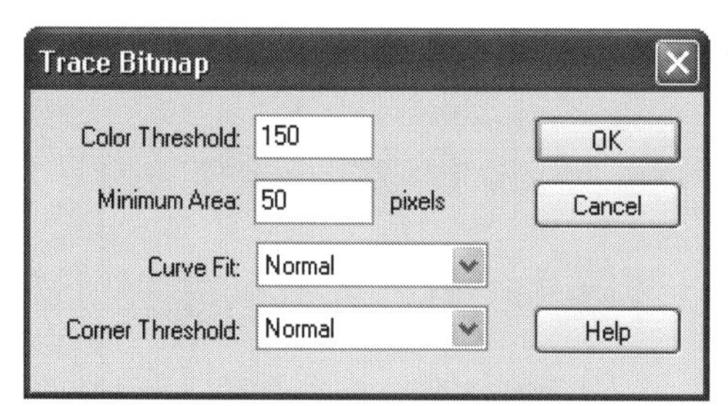

Figure 2.31 The Trace Bitmap dialog box.

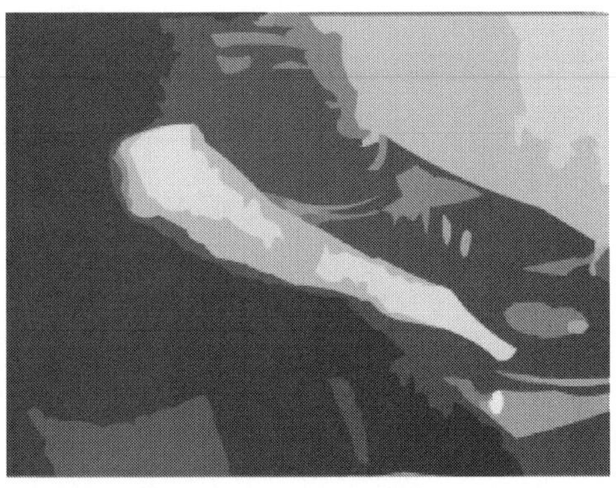

Figure 2.32 This image is the result of a color threshold of 150 and a minimum area of 50.

- ▲ **Curve Fit.** Controls the smoothness of the contours around shapes.
- ▲ **Corner Threshold.** Determines whether Flash will create sharp or smooth corners.

4. After making the first tracing, select the bitmap in the next keyframe and apply Trace Bitmap.

   Continue this process until all the bitmaps in the sequence have been traced (**Figure 2.32**).

5. Add, delete, or change shapes and colors as needed in each keyframe by using the drawing and selection tools in the Toolbar (**Figure 2.33**).

   Look at the finished Flash file on the CD that accompanies this book to see how this short traced video has been modified.

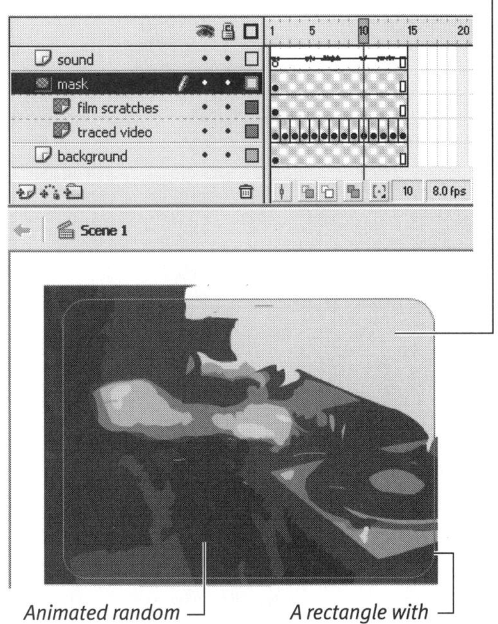

Figure 2.33 Deleting the background in every traced bitmap of the sequence lets you experiment with a more dynamic, animated backdrop. This example masks the traced series, and adds sound and other animated elements.

✔ Tips

- The Trace Bitmap menu command doesn't have a default keyboard shortcut, but you can create one yourself by choosing Edit > Keyboard Shortcuts (Windows) Flash > Keyboard Shortcuts (Mac). When you create a keyboard shortcut for Trace Bitmap, the process of converting a long sequence of bitmaps becomes much easier.
- You should be careful not to select too low a color-threshold value. A traced bitmap that has too many shapes will be a huge drain on performance and often makes the Flash file larger than if you used the bitmap itself.

Although they are vector shapes, sequences of traced bitmaps still can take up a fair amount of space, so it's important to consider ways to maximize their use and get the most bang for your buck.

Copy your keyframes containing the traced animation, and paste them into a graphic symbol or a movie-clip symbol. This technique allows you to treat the keyframes as a single instance, which makes them easier to manipulate.

Following are a few simple strategies you can use to make your one traced animation symbol seem like many different clips (**Figure 2.34**).

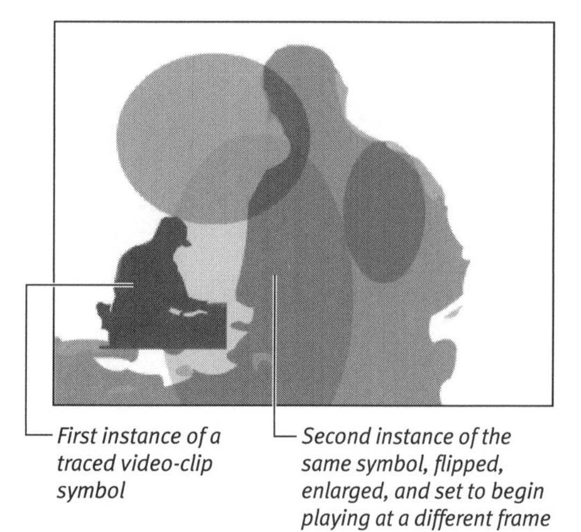

Figure 2.34 A single traced video clip of a DJ spinning some records gets reproduced twice on the Stage. The background instance has been flipped horizontally, enlarged, and made transparent. The foreground instance moves across the Stage and begins looping at a different frame. The circles are extra animated elements.

To use the traced animation:

- Try to keep your simulated video sequences short and small. Most times, you only need a few frames (fewer than 10) to suggest a particular motion if you focus on the most dramatic action of a central character.
- Modify the instances by changing the brightness, tint, or alpha effect. Repetition of graphics with color variations can create Warhol-inspired designs and maintain really small Flash files.
- Transform the instances by flipping them horizontally or vertically, or by changing rotation or scale. An enlarged mirror-image animation can provide a dramatically different backdrop.
- Apply motion tweens to the instances. Create more variety by moving something that's already moving. Tweening instances of an Olympic-diver sequence, for example, can result in many dive varieties.
- Keep some of the instances static in different frames while looping others with different starting frames. In the Property Inspector, choose among three play options (Loop, Play Once, and Single Frame), and designate the First frame to play. Setting these play-mode options will prevent multiple instances on the Stage from being synchronized.

Simulating 3D

Although Flash lacks support for handling true 3D models, you can simulate 3D motion or 3D geometry in several ways. One way is to build a 3D engine with ActionScript, but that topic involves more ActionScripting and much more math. An easier way is to use third-party applications that generate 3D models and can export Flash-compatible images and image sequences. Then the task is a matter of importing those images into Flash. Yet another way of faking 3D is to rely on a little patience and some ingenuity to create shape tweens of 3D geometry that give the illusion of 3D motion.

Third-party applications

You can create 3D images for Flash in two basic ways. The first way is to do all your modeling, rendering, and animation in a powerful 3D application such as 3ds max (formerly known as 3D Studio Max), LightWave 3D, or Maya. Plug-ins such as David Gould's Illustrate!, IdeaWorks3D's Vecta3D, and Electric Rain's Swift 3D then let you output your 3D models and animations as vector images compatible with Flash. These plug-ins are sometimes called cel shaders or cartoon shaders because they render the final images to look like cartoons that were drawn on traditional sheets of acetate, or cels.

The second way to get 3D images to Flash is to use stand-alone tools. Swift 3D, Vecta 3D, and Adobe's Dimensions are available as stand-alone tools that can generate 3D models, animations, and output vector images on their own. Swift 3D will import 3D models and let you build models with primitive objects, text, extrusions, and lathing. Adobe Dimensions doesn't support importing 3D models but has tools for extruding text, revolving objects, and mapping artwork around objects. Vecta3D has functions for importing 3D models and extruding text.

The advantage of using stand-alone tools is that they are simpler to use and much cheaper to buy, but they are meant to create simple rotations or to animate camera moves around a 3D object or scene. For the most part, these products provide all the tools you will need for your Flash work. But if you want to animate a dinosaur and generate a vector sequence of its walk cycle, for example, you must turn to the higher-end packages.

No matter which way you go, the result is vector images or vector image series that you can bring into Flash in individual keyframes (**Figure 2.35**). In this respect, the process is the same as importing sequential bitmaps and tracing them to vectors, except that the conversion to vectors has already been done. Although learning how to use one of these programs is best left for another book, the following example shows how to animate a simple, rotating 3D title quickly by using Swift 3D.

Figure 2.35 3D programs generate vector images and series of vector images that can be imported into Flash. These programs can also render 3D models in a variety of styles. The clown shows the multiple keyframes of his rotation. The clown and the top airplane are rendered in a simple cartoon style. The bottom airplane and car are rendered with gradients.

To animate a 3D title with Flash and Swift 3D:

1. In Swift 3D 2, click the Create Text button in the top menu bar.

   Extruded text appears in the front window (**Figure 2.36**).
2. Select the text.
3. In the left pane, change the text to your own title (**Figure 2.37**).

   The extruded text in the front window changes.
4. Click the Scale button in the top menu.
5. Click your extruded text in the window, and drag it to reduce the text to fit the window.
6. From the Animation palette at the bottom of the screen, select a prescripted animation (a simple spin, for example), and drop it onto your extruded text (**Figure 2.38**).

   Your extruded text now has a 20-frame spin assigned to it. You can test the animation by clicking the Play button below the Timeline.
7. Click the Preview and Export Editor tab.

   This tab allows you to choose the output options for the fill and for the edges, as well as to generate frames to preview.

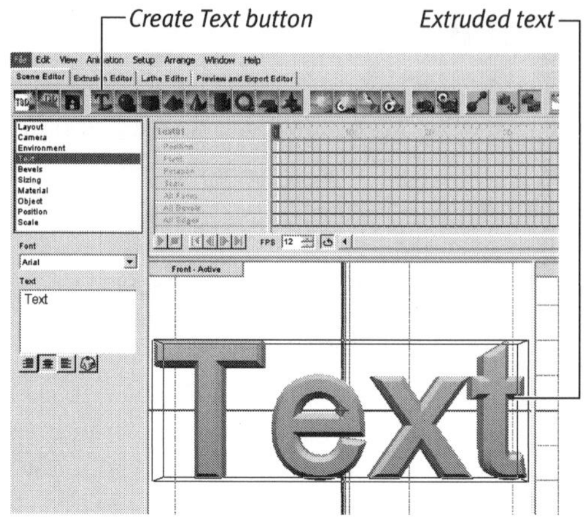

Figure 2.36 In Swift 3D 2,3D objects appear in the front window.

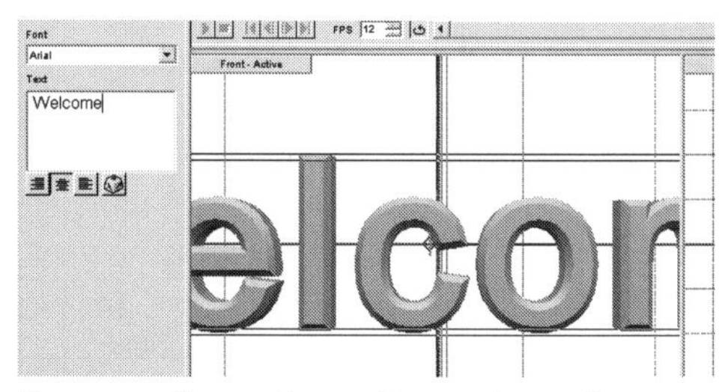

Figure 2.37 Change the word *text* to the word *Welcome*. The extruded text is updated automatically.

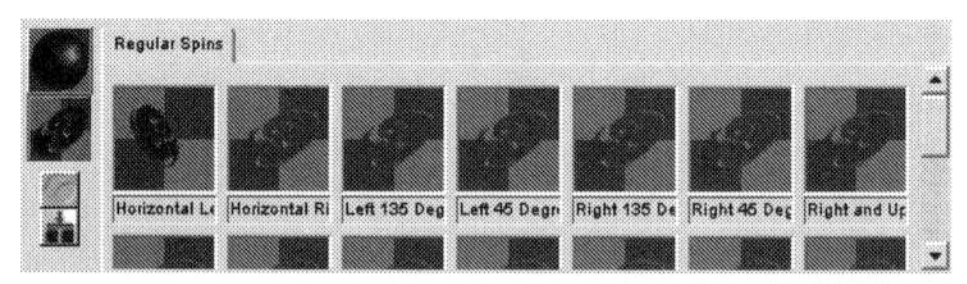

Figure 2.38 The prescripted animations, represented by spinning icons, make it easy to apply common animations to your objects. You can also create your own animations with control of the motion of the camera and the objects.

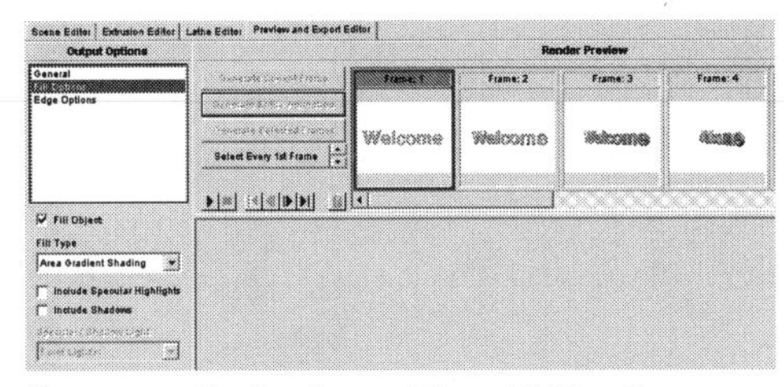

Figure 2.39 The Preview and Export Editor. Choose the output options at the left. Four frames of this animation have been generated.

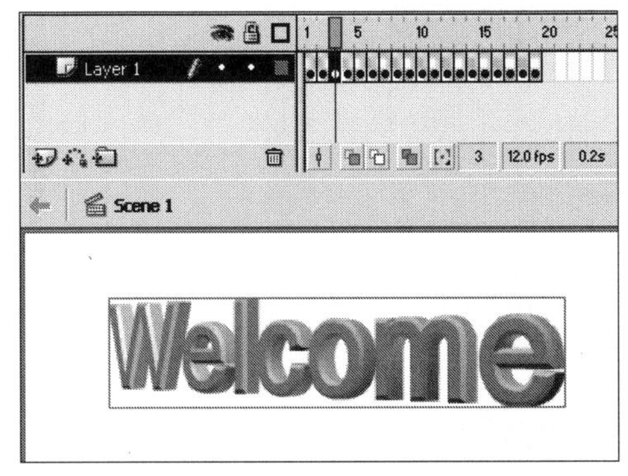

Figure 2.40 The spinning welcome animation is a frame-by-frame animation. Each keyframe contains a group of vector shapes.

8. Choose Area Gradient Shading, and click Generate Entire Animation.

   Swift 3D generates all 20 frames of your rotating text (**Figure 2.39**).

9. Click Export Entire Animation below Export to File, choose a destination folder and filename, and click Save.

   A .swf is generated, containing the frame-by-frame animation of vector images of your rotating text.

10. Open a new file in Flash, choose File > Import, and choose the .swf file you exported from Swift 3D.

    The frame-by-frame animation appears on your Timeline (**Figure 2.40**).

✔ Tip

- Avoid using Swift 3D 2 to render zooms and translations because you can create those effects easily within Flash. Render zooms and translations only if an object's perspective changes dramatically.

When you don't require a complex 3D model and need only a simple object that appears to be moving in 3D space, you can use Flash's existing animation tools (frame-by-frame, motion tween, and shape tween) to create the effect. The result is a much smaller file and quicker download time.

By simplifying an object's motion, you can break its three-dimensionality into flat, individual surfaces and then tween those shapes. A simple rotating cube, for example, consists of rectangles that change shape in a cyclical fashion. The challenge becomes one of defining the keyframes.

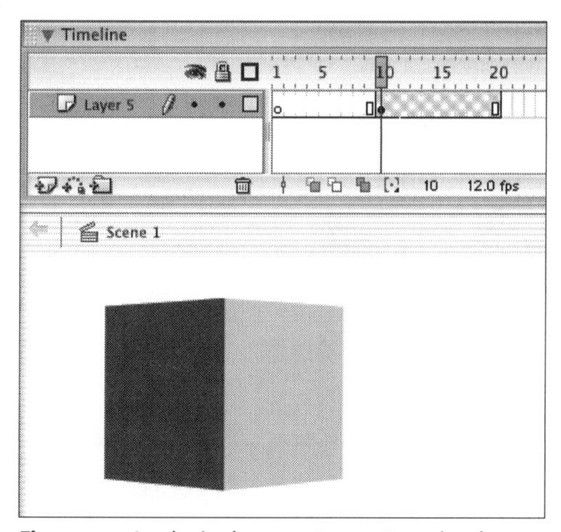

Figure 2.41 A cube is shown as two rectangular shapes.

To simulate a 3D rotation with tweens:

1. Create the cube in Keyframe 10 as two adjacent, filled rectangles with the seam in the center (**Figure 2.41**).

   To keep the perspective correct, use a 3D program to create the initial cube and then import it into Flash.

2. Create a keyframe of the rectangles at Frame 1, with more of the left side showing (**Figure 2.42**).

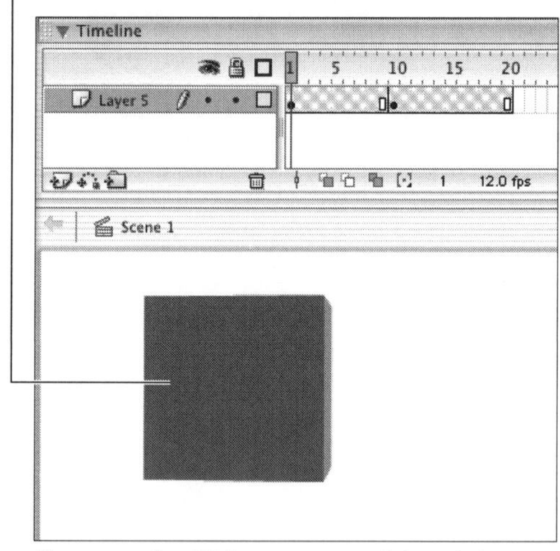

Figure 2.42 Establish one extreme of the cube's rotation in Keyframe 1

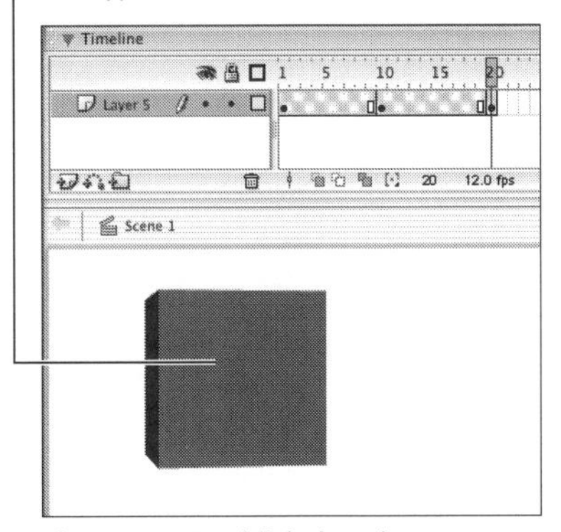

Figure 2.43 Establish the other extreme of the cube's rotation at Keyframe 20.

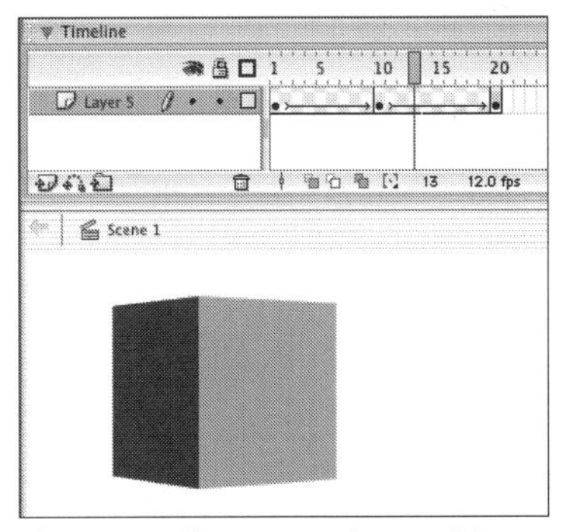

Figure 2.44 Shape tweening provides a smooth transition between the rectangular shapes.

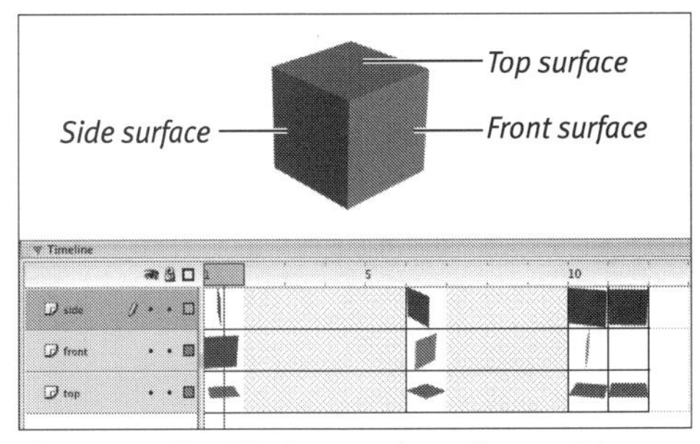

Figure 2.45 The side, front, and top shapes of the cube are separated into three layers for more effective shape tweening. The keyframe at the end lets the shape in the "front" layer disappear.

3. Create a keyframe of the rectangles at Frame 20, with more of the right side showing (**Figure 2.43**).
4. Apply a shape tween between all three keyframes (**Figure 2.44**).

   The filled rectangles change shape, giving the illusion that a cube is rotating in space.

You can use the same approach with even more complicated rotations, as long as you consider how each surface is moving and changing shape independently. For a cube that's tilted so that three surfaces are visible instead of two, you need to separate the three surfaces on different layers and apply three shape tweens (**Figure 2.45**).

Part II: Understanding ActionScript

3 Getting a Handle on ActionScript

ActionScript is Flash's scripting language for adding interactivity to your graphics and movies. You can use ActionScript to create anything from simple navigation within your Flash movie to complex interfaces that react to the location of the viewer's pointer, arcade-style games, and even full-blown e-commerce sites with dynamically updating data. In this chapter, you'll learn how to construct ActionScript to create effective Flash interaction. Think of the process as learning the grammar of a foreign language: First, you must learn how to put nouns and verbs together, and integrate adjectives and prepositions; then you can expand your communication skills and have meaningful conversations by building your vocabulary. This chapter will give you the sound ActionScripting foundation upon which you can build your Flash literacy.

If you are familiar with JavaScript, you'll notice some similarities between it and ActionScript. In fact, ActionScript is based on JavaScript, which is a popular object-oriented programming language for adding interactivity to a Web page. Whereas JavaScript is intended to control the Web browser, ActionScript controls the interactivity within Flash content, so the two scripting languages have slight differences. But the basic syntax of scripts and the handling of objects—reusable pieces of code—remain the same.

Even if you've never used JavaScript, you'll see in this chapter that Flash makes basic scripting easy. You'll learn about the logic of objects and how the Actions panel can automate much of the scripting process while giving you the flexibility to build more sophisticated interaction as your skills improve.

About Objects and Classes

At the heart of ActionScript are objects and classes. *Objects* are data types—such as sound, graphics, text, and numeric values—that you create in Flash and use to control the movie. A date object, for example, retrieves information about the time and the date, and an array object manipulates data stored in a particular order.

All the objects you use and create belong to a larger collective group known as a *class*. Flash provides certain classes for you to use in your movie. These predefined classes are also referred to as objects, but they are named and capitalized. The Color object, for example, is a class from which different color objects are created.

Learning to code in ActionScript centers on understanding the capabilities of these objects and their classes, and using them to interact with one another and with the viewer.

In the real world, we are familiar with objects such as a cow, a tree, and a person (**Figure 3.1**). Flash objects range from visible things, such as a movie clip of a spinning ball, to more abstract concepts, such as the date, pieces of data, or the handling of keyboard inputs. Whether concrete or abstract, however, Flash objects are versatile because after you create them, you can reuse them in different contexts.

Before you can use objects, you need to be able to identify them, and you do so by name just as we do in the real world. Say you have three people in front of you: Adam, Betty, and Zeke. All three are objects that can be distinguished by name. All three belong to the collective group known as humans. You could also say that Adam, Betty, and Zeke are all *instances* of the human class (**Figure 3.2**). In ActionScript, instances and objects are synonymous, and the terms are used interchangeably in this book.

Figure 3.1 Objects in the real world include things like a cow, a tree, and a person.

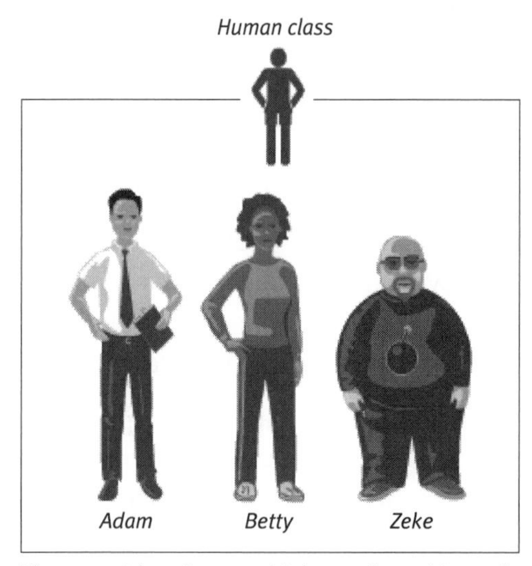

Figure 3.2 Adam, Betty, and Zeke are three objects of the human class. Flash doesn't have such a class, but this analogy is useful for understanding objects.

Figure 3.3 Adam, Betty, and Zeke are human objects with different properties. Properties differentiate objects of the same class.

About Methods and Properties

Each object of a class (Zeke of the humans, for example) differs from the others in its class by more than just its name. Each person differs because of several characteristics that define the individual, such as height, weight, gender, and hair color. In object-oriented scripting, we say that objects and classes have properties. Height, weight, sex, and hair color are all properties of the human class (**Figure 3.3**).

In Flash, each class has a predefined set of properties that let you establish the uniqueness of the object. The Sound class has just two properties: `duration`, which measures the length of a sound, and `position`, which measures the time the sound has been playing. The MovieClip class, on the other hand, has many properties, such as `_height`, `_width`, and `_rotation`, which are measures of the dimensions and orientation of a particular movie-clip object. By defining and changing the properties of objects, you control what each object is like and how each object appears, sounds, or behaves to the user.

Objects also do things. Zeke can run, sleep, or talk. The things that objects can do are known as *methods*. Each class has its own set of methods. The Sound class, for example, has a `setVolume` method that will play its sound louder or softer, and the Date class has a `getDay` method that retrieves the day of the week. When an object does something by using a method, we say that the method is called or that the object calls the method.

Understanding the relationships between objects, classes, properties, and methods is important. Putting objects together so that the methods and properties of one influence the methods and properties of another is what drives Flash interactivity. The key to building your ActionScript vocabulary is learning the properties and methods of different classes.

✔ Tip

- It helps to think of objects as nouns, properties as adjectives, and methods as verbs. Properties describe their objects, whereas methods are the actions that the objects perform.

Writing with Dot Syntax

As in other foreign languages, you must learn the rules of grammar to put words together. *Dot syntax* is the convention that ActionScript uses to put objects, properties, and methods together into statements. You connect objects, properties, and methods with dots (periods) to describe a particular object or process.

```
Zeke.weight = 188
Betty.weight = 135
```

The first statement assigns the value 188 to the weight of Zeke. The second statement assigns the value 135 to the weight of Betty. The dot separates the object name from the property (`weight`) (**Figure 3.4**).

```
Betty.shirt.color = "gray"
```

This statement describes the object Betty that is linked to the object shirt. The object shirt, in turn, has the property `color`, which is assigned the value `"gray"`. Notice that with dot syntax, you use multiple dots to maintain object hierarchy. When you have multiple objects linked in this fashion, it's often easier to read the statement backward. So you could read it as "Gray is the color of the shirt of Betty."

Figure 3.4 The hypothetical `weight` property describes Betty and Zeke. In Flash, the properties of objects can be both read and modified with ActionScript.

Figure 3.5 Dot syntax lets you make objects call methods. Just as the hypothetical method `run()` could make the Adam object begin to jog, the real Flash method `hide()`, when applied to the Mouse object, makes the pointer disappear.

```
Zeke.run ()
```

This statement causes the object Zeke to call the method `run ()`. The parentheses after `run` signify that `run` is a method and not a property. You can think of this construction as noun-dot-verb (**Figure 3.5**). Methods often have *parameters*, or arguments, within the parentheses. These parameters affect how the method is executed.

```
Zeke.run (fast)
Adam.run (slow)
```

Both of these statements will make the Zeke and Adam objects call the `run ()` method, but because each method contains a different parameter, the way the run is performed is different: Zeke runs fast, and Adam runs slowly.

Each method has its own set of parameters that you must learn. Consider the basic Flash action `gotoAndPlay("Scene 1",20)`. `gotoAndPlay` is a method of the MovieClip class. The parenthetical parameters, `("Scene1", 20)`, refer to the scene and the frame number, so the playhead of the object will jump to Scene 1, Frame 20, and begin playing.

✔ Tip

- The dot syntax replaces the slash syntax used in previous versions of Flash. Although you can still use the slash syntax, the dot syntax is recommended because it's more compatible with all the new actions. Use slash syntax only if you are authoring for the Flash 4 Player or earlier.

More on Punctuation

Dot syntax allows you to construct meaningful processes and assignments with objects, properties, and methods. Additional punctuation symbols let you do more with these single statements.

The semicolon

To terminate individual ActionScript statements and start new ones, you use the semicolon. The semicolon functions as a period does in a sentence: It concludes one idea and lets another one begin.

```
stopAllSounds ();
play ();
```

The semicolons separate the statements, so that all the sounds stop first; then the movie begins to play. Each statement is executed in order from the top down, like a set of instructions or a cookbook recipe.

✔ Tip

- Flash will still understand ActionScript statements even if you don't have the semicolons to terminate each one. It is good practice, however, to include them in your scripts.

Curly braces

Curly braces are another kind of punctuation that ActionScript uses frequently. Curly braces group related blocks of ActionScript statements. When you assign actions to a button, for example, those actions appear within curly braces in the `on (release)` statement.

```
on (release) {
   stopAllSounds ();
   play ();
}
```

In this case, both the `stopAllSounds` action and the `play` action are executed when the mouse button is released. Notice how the curly braces are separated on different lines to make the related ActionScript statements easier to read.

Commas

Commas separate the parameters of a method. A method can take many parameters. The `gotoAndPlay ()` method, for example, can take two: a scene name and the frame number. With commas separating the parameters, the ActionScript code looks like this:

```
gotoAndPlay ("Scene 1", 20);
```

Some methods may have three, four, or perhaps even 10 parameters, but as long as you separate the parameters with commas, Flash knows how to handle the code.

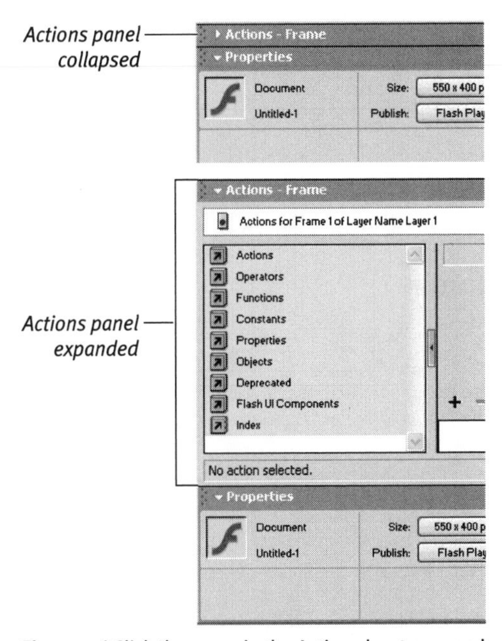

Figure 3.6 Click the arrow in the Actions bar to expand or collapse the Actions panel.

The Actions Panel

The Actions panel is the Flash dialog box that lets you access all the actions that will control your Flash movie. Depending on your level of expertise, you can create, delete, and edit actions in two modes: Normal and Expert. If you're uncomfortable with the ActionScript rules of grammar, the Actions panel can automate some of the scripting process, such as punctuation, generating semicolons and curly braces automatically. The ActionScript panel can also give you real-time code hints as you script and any-time access to the Actions panel reference.

In Flash, the name of the Actions panel appears as either Actions-Frame, Actions-Button, or Actions-Movie Clip, depending on which element you have selected. In any case, the contents of the panel remain the same, so this book always refers to it as the Actions panel.

To open the Actions panel:

- From the Windows menu, choose Actions (F9).

  or

  Click the right-facing triangle in the Actions bar.

  The Actions panel expands, and the triangle points downward (**Figure 3.6**).

  or

  Alt-double-click (Win) or Option-double-click (Mac) an instance on the Stage or a keyframe in the Timeline.

  The Actions panel appears so that you can attach actions to either the keyframe or the instance.

  or

  Right-click (Win) or Ctrl-Click (Mac) on a keyframe or an instance, and choose Actions in the context menu that appears.

  The Actions panel appears so that you can attach actions to either the keyframe or the instance.

To undock the Actions panel:

- Drag the Actions panel by the top-left corner marked by the bumpy area.

  Your pointer will change (hand for Mac, arrows for Windows), indicating that you can undock the Actions panel (**Figure 3.7**).

To redock the Actions panel:

1. Grab the Actions panel by the bumpy area in the left corner, and drag it over the different panels on your desktop.

   Those areas highlight with a bold outline.

2. Drop the Actions panel.

   The Actions panel docks with the highlighted panels (**Figure 3.8**). In Mac OS X, the Actions panel cannot dock with the Property Inspector or the Timeline

✔ Tip

- You can disable docking of all your panels by choosing Edit > Preferences and choosing Disable Panel Docking in the General tab of the Preferences dialog box. (This option is available only on Windows.)

Area to grab to dock or redock Actions panel

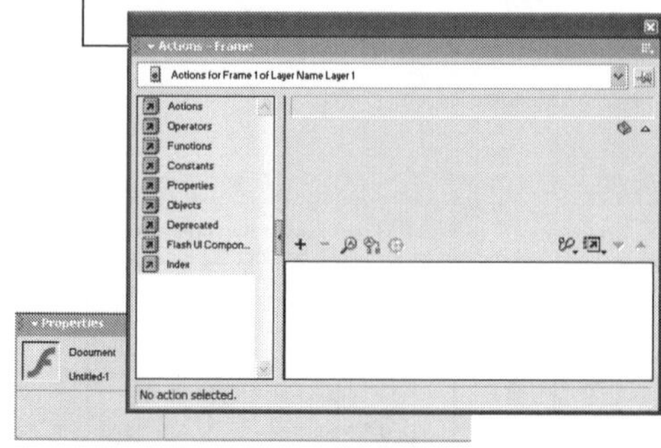

Figure 3.7 The Actions panel can be undocked from the Property inspector (Windows only).

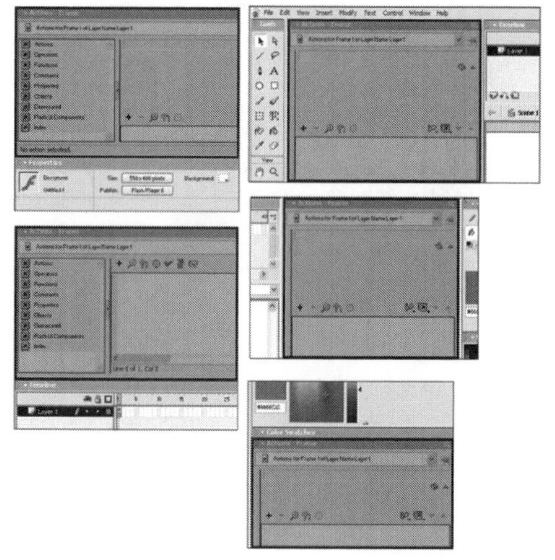

Figure 3.8 You can dock the Actions panel in many places; choose one that suits your own work environment. The Actions panel can be above the Property inspector (top left; the default), above the Timeline (bottom left), to the left or right of the Timeline (right), or among the other panels (bottom).

Normal mode

The Normal mode of the Actions panel features several sections and multiple ways to enter ActionScript statements (**Figure 3.9**). The Actions toolbox on the left side displays all the available commands, organized in logical categories. At the bottom, an index lists all the ActionScript commands in alphabetical order. You choose actions from this categorized list. A brief description of the selected action appears in the top-right section of the Actions panel, and below it, the Parameters pane lets you enter different parameters for that selected action. In the bottom-right section, your completed script appears in the Script pane. At the top of the Actions panel, you can use the pull-down menu to navigate to different scripts within your Flash movie.

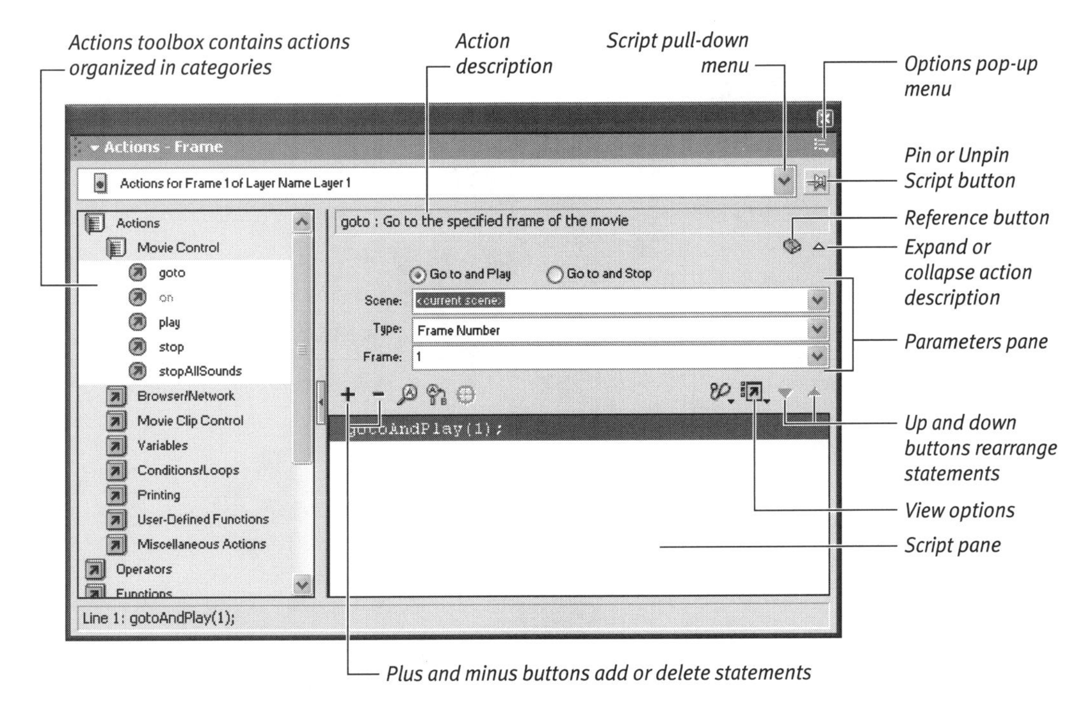

Figure 3.9 The Actions panel in Normal mode.

Expert mode

The Expert mode of the Actions panel is for experienced ActionScript developers who don't need the structured scripting help provided in Normal mode. Expert mode allows you to enter scripts in the Script pane freely, as though you were typing in a text-editing application (**Figure 3.10**).

✔ Tips

- Feel free to switch between Expert and Normal mode. Flash maintains any special formatting you may have used in Expert mode unless you change your script in Normal mode. Then Flash uses its Normal-mode formatting on your script.
- Switching from Expert to Normal can be an easy way to check for errors. Flash won't allow you to switch from Expert to Normal unless your script is free of errors.

To choose Normal or Expert mode:

1. With the Actions panel open, click the Options button in the top-right corner.

   The Options pop-up menu appears (**Figure 3.11**).

2. Choose Normal Mode (Cmd-Shift-N for Mac, Ctrl-Shift-N for Windows) or Expert Mode (Cmd-Shift-E for Mac, Ctrl-Shift-E for Windows).

   or

   Click the View Options button (above and to the right of the Script pane), and choose Normal Mode or Expert Mode from the menu (**Figure 3.12**).

Table 3.1

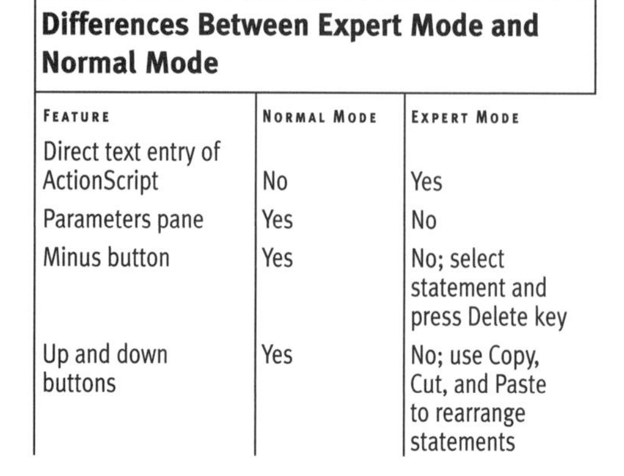

Differences Between Expert Mode and Normal Mode

Feature	Normal Mode	Expert Mode
Direct text entry of ActionScript	No	Yes
Parameters pane	Yes	No
Minus button	Yes	No; select statement and press Delete key
Up and down buttons	Yes	No; use Copy, Cut, and Paste to rearrange statements

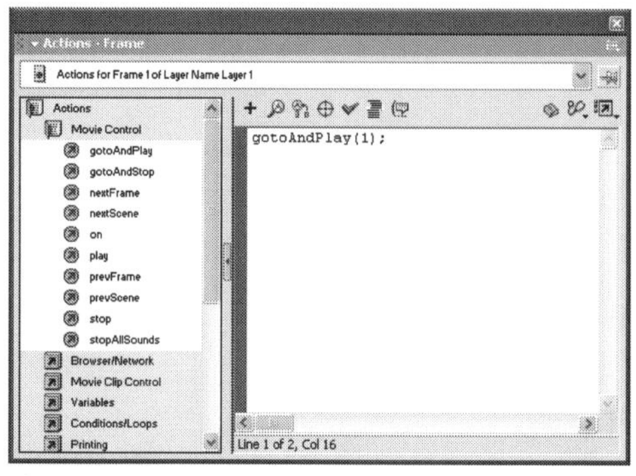

Figure 3.10 The Actions panel in Expert mode.

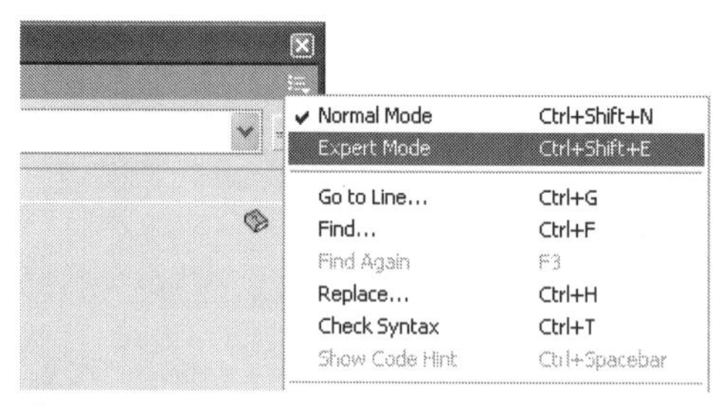

Figure 3.11 The Options menu in the Actions panel gives you the choice of Normal or Expert mode.

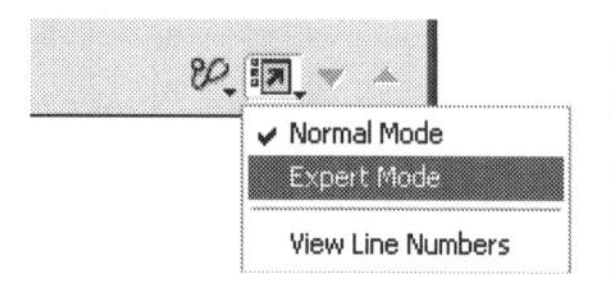

Figure 3.12 Choose Normal Mode or Expert Mode from the View Options menu.

To add an action in Normal mode:

1. Select the instance or frame where you want to assign an action.

   In the Actions toolbox, expand an action category by clicking it.

2. Double-click the desired action.

   The action appears in the Script pane (**Figure 3.13**).

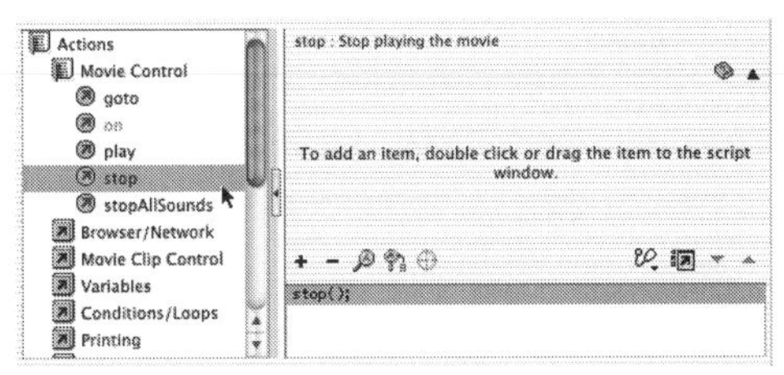

Figure 3.13 Add an action by choosing a statement from the Actions toolbox. Here, the action stop() has been added to the Script pane.

or

1. Select the instance or frame where you want to assign an action.

   In the Actions toolbox, expand an action category by clicking it.

2. Select the action, and drag it into the Script pane (**Figure 3.14**).

   The action appears in the Script pane.

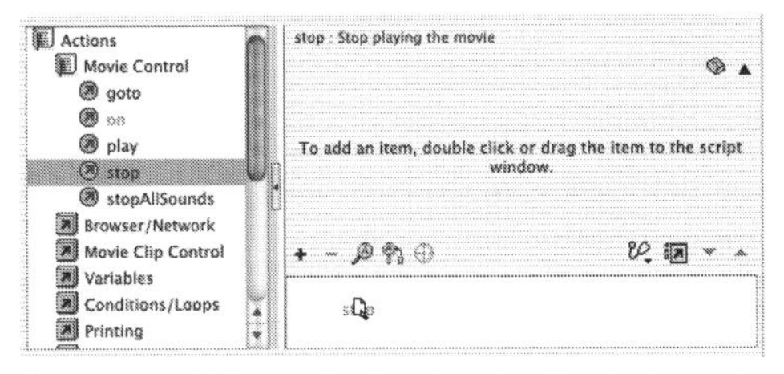

Figure 3.14 Add an action by dragging the statement to the Script pane. The pointer changes temporarily to show you where you can drop the action.

or

1. Select the instance or frame where you want to assign an action.

2. Click the plus button above the Script pane, and choose the action from the pull-down menus (**Figure 3.15**).

   The action appears in the Script pane.

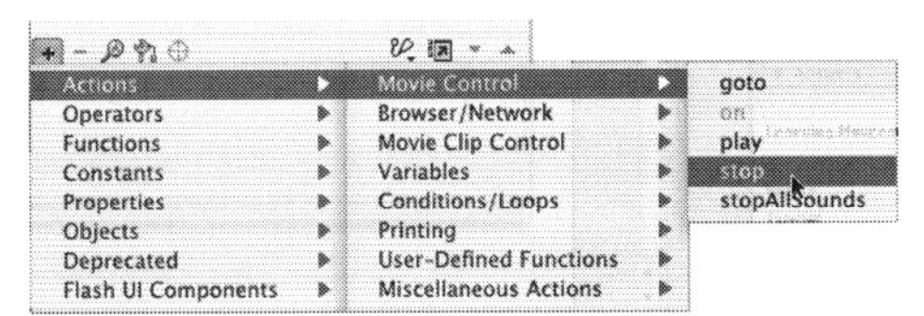

Figure 3.15 Add an action by choosing it from the plus button's pull-down menus.

or

1. Select the instance or frame where you want to assign an action, put your pointer in the Script pane of the Actions panel, and press the Esc key.

2. Type the two-letter code corresponding to the action you want.

   The action appears in the Script pane.

   For a full list of shortcut-key commands for actions, see Appendix C, or choose View Esc Shortcut Keys from the Actions panel's Options menu (**Figure 3.16**) to display them in the Actions toolbox.

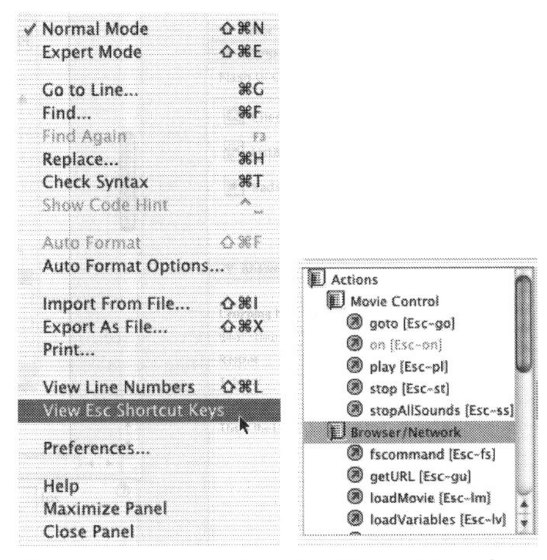

Figure 3.16 Choosing View Esc Shortcut Keys from the Options pull-down menu displays the shortcut keys for every action in the Actions toolbox.

continues on next page

✔ Tip

- While making your selection in the Actions toolbox, you can use the arrow keys, the Page Up and Page Down keys, or the Home and End keys to navigate through the list. Press Enter or the spacebar to open or close categories or to choose an action to put in the Script pane.

To edit actions in Normal mode:

- Select the action, and use the up- and down-arrow buttons to rearrange it in the Script pane.

  or

  Select the action, and drag it to its new location (**Figure 3.17**).

- Select the action, and use the minus button to delete it from the Script pane.

  or

  Select the action, and press the Delete key.

- Select an action in the Script pane, and use the empty text boxes, check-boxes, and pull-down menus of the Parameters pane to change the parameters for the selected action.

  The Script pane shows the action with the parameters in place (**Figure 3.18**).

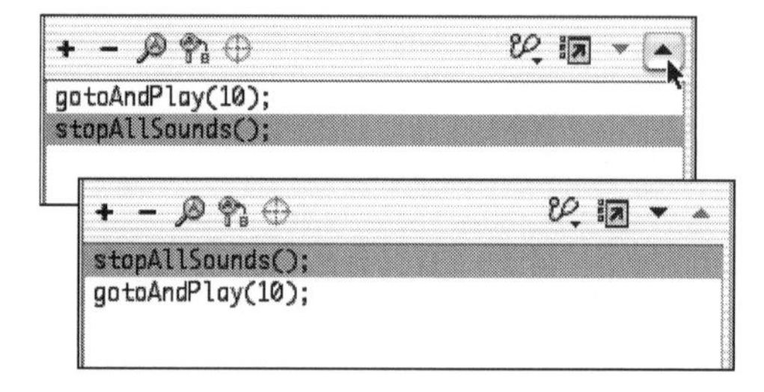

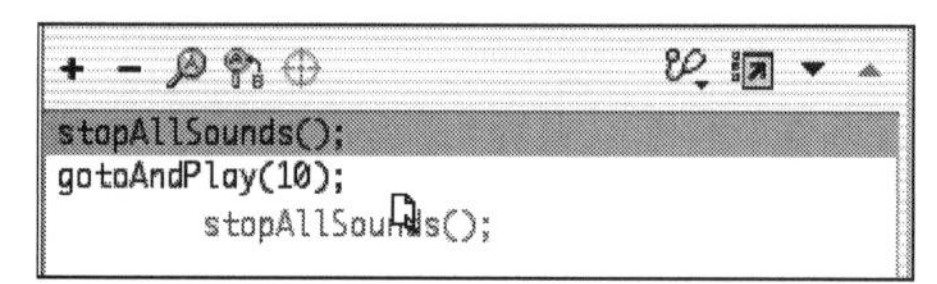

Figure 3.17 Move the stopAllSounds () statement by using the arrow buttons (top) or by dragging it to a new location (bottom). A bold horizontal line shows you where the statement will be when you release the mouse button.

Figure 3.18 The Parameters pane lets you change the parameters of a selected action. The Go To action has two parameter text boxes, a pull-down menu, and radio buttons that affect the way it will work. Entering 10 in the Frame text box and selecting the Go to and Play button change the statement in the Script pane, making the playhead go to Frame 10 and begin playing.

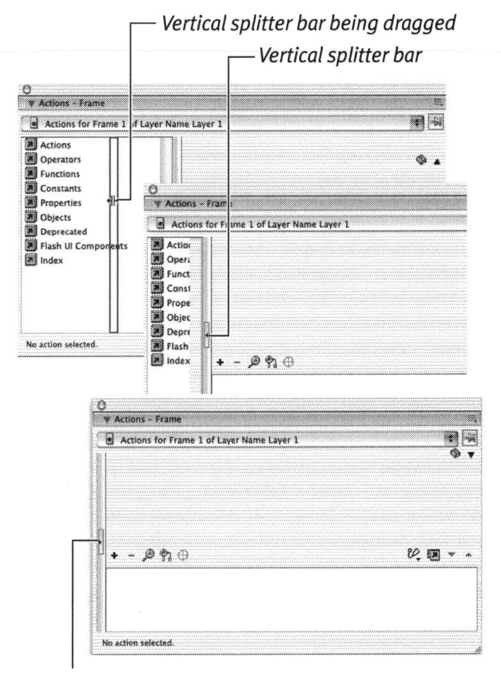

Figure 3.19 Resizing the Actions panel by dragging (top) or clicking the vertical splitter bar. The Actions toolbox can be resized (middle) or completely collapsed (bottom).

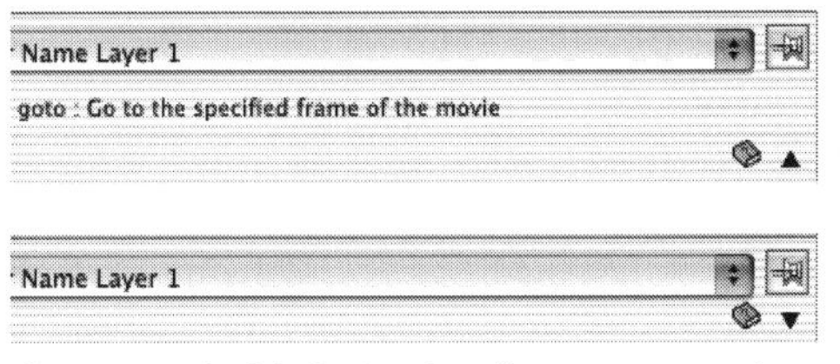

Figure 3.20 The black triangle collapses or expands the description of the action.

✔ Tips

- You can still use familiar editing commands such as Copy, Cut, and Paste to create and rearrange ActionScripts. When you paste a copied script, however, the new script appears after the selection rather than replacing it, as a text-editing application would.
- Use the Shift key to select multiple actions to copy or cut.
- If you copy or delete one line of a larger code block, the entire code block will be copied or deleted.

```
on (release) {
   play();
}
```

  If you select just the first line of this code block and press the Delete key, all three lines will be deleted, because the `on (release)` statement includes the curly braces that span all three lines.

To modify the Actions panel display:

- Drag or double-click the vertical splitter bar, or click the arrow button that divides the Actions toolbox and Script pane, to collapse or expand an area (**Figure 3.19**).
- In Normal mode, click the triangle in the top-right corner of the Actions panel to collapse or expand the action description (**Figure 3.20**).

Actions-panel options

The Actions panel provides many features that can help you write reliable code quickly and easily. Chapter 12 explains many of the debugging tools in detail.

If you're writing ActionScript in Expert mode or entering an expression in a parameters text box in Normal mode, you'll be able to use code hints, which appear as you type. Code hints recognize what kind of action you are typing and offer choices and prompts on how to complete it. Flash makes it easy to be an expert! In Expert mode, you can also customize the format options so that your code looks just the way you want it for ease of reading and understanding.

Regardless of which mode you work in, additional coding help is available in the Actions panel. The Reference button, for example, calls up the Reference panel and sends you directly to the description and usage of any selected action in case you have trouble remembering what a particular action does or how it is used. If you want to keep an ActionScript visible as you select other elements in your Flash movie, you can do so by pinning your script. *Pinning* makes your script "stick" in the Script pane until you unpin it. This technique is very useful if you've forgotten the name of a text box or a movie clip and need to reference it in an ActionScript statement. You can pin your current script and then go look for your text box or movie clip. Your script remains in place, so that you can make the necessary edits.

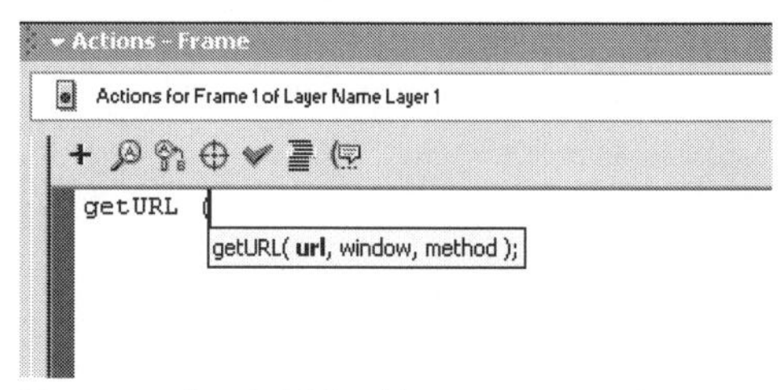

Figure 3.21 A code hint guides you as you enter ActionScript. The first required parameter for this action is the URL.

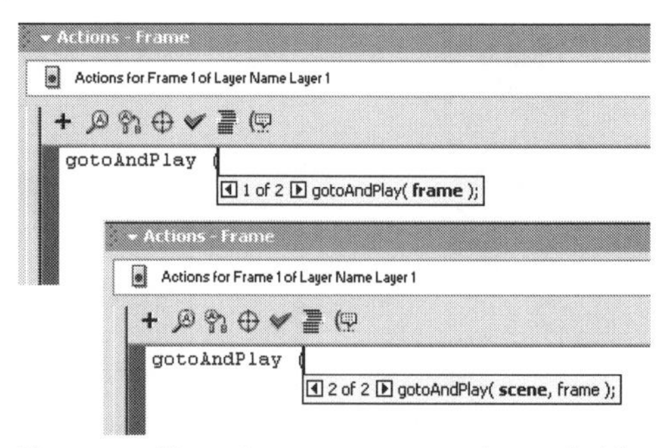

Figure 3.22 The action `gotoAndPlay` can be used with one or two parameters. The code hint shows you both ways.

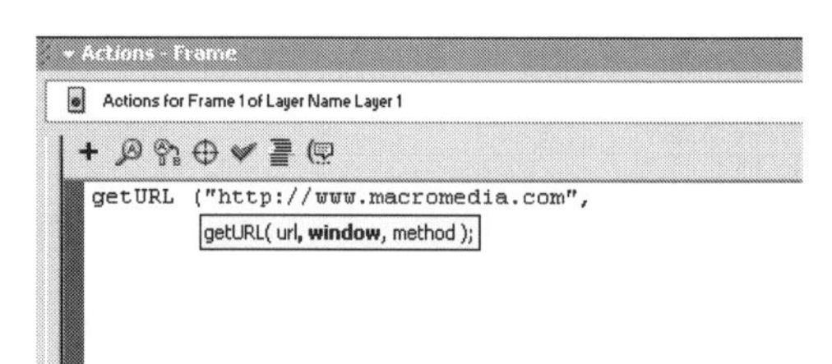

Figure 3.23 After you enter the first parameter, the code hint directs you to the next parameter. The next parameter for this action is the window.

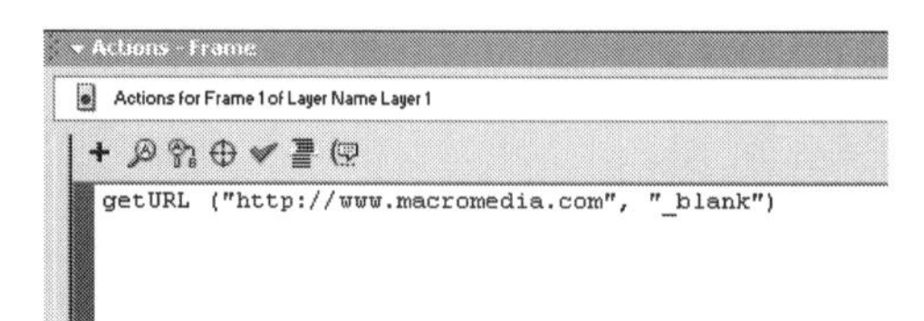

Figure 3.24 When you enter the closing parenthesis, the code hint disappears. The `getURL` action shown here doesn't require the last parameter (the method).

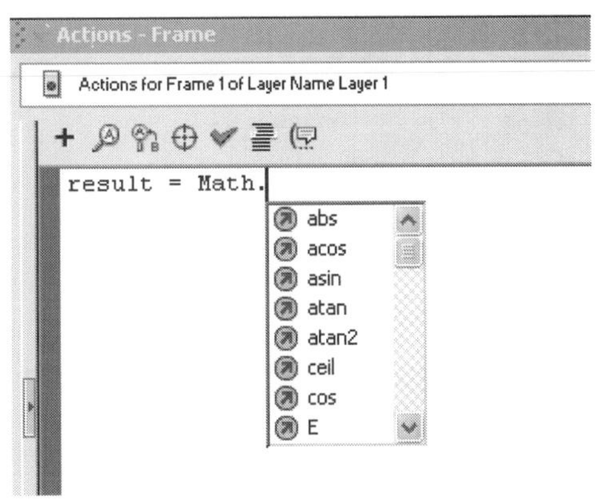

Figure 3.25 The code hint provides a scrolling list of methods and properties for each object. This list contains the methods and properties of the Math object.

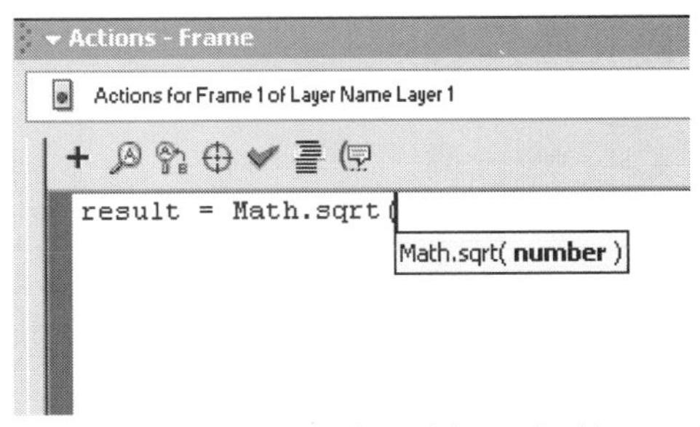

Figure 3.26 The `sqrt()` method of the Math object requires a number for its parameter.

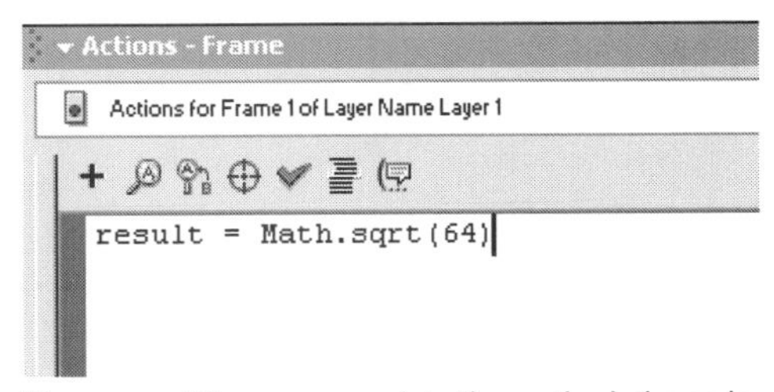

Figure 3.27 When you complete the method, the code hint disappears.

To use code hints in Expert mode:

1. Enter an action in the Script pane by typing the opening parentheses of the action.

   Flash detects the action and anticipates that you will enter its parameters. A code hint appears to guide you (**Figure 3.21**). If an action has different ways of handling parameters, the tool tip shows those options (**Figure 3.22**).

2. Enter the first parameter and then a comma.

   The bold parameter in the code hint advances to highlight the next required parameter (**Figure 3.23**).

3. Continue entering the required parameters, and type a closing parenthesis to finish the action.

   The code hint disappears (**Figure 3.24**).

or

1. Enter an object target path and then a period.

   Flash anticipates that you will enter a method or property of the particular object that appears before the period. A menu-style code hint appears to guide you (**Figure 3.25**).

2. Choose the appropriate method or property from the menu.

   The method or property appears in the Script pane after your dot. Another code hint appears to guide you, providing the parameters of the method (**Figure 3.26**).

3. Enter the parameters of the method, and type a closing parenthesis to finish.

   The code hint disappears (**Figure 3.27**).

✔ Tips

- Dismiss a code hint by pressing the Escape key or clicking a different place in your script.
- Navigate the menu-style code hints by using the arrow keys, the Page Up and Page Down keys, or the Home and End keys. You can also start typing, and the entry that begins with the letter you type will appear in the code hint. Press Enter to choose the selection.
- You can call up code hints manually by pressing Ctrl-spacebar or by clicking the Show Code Hint button above the Script pane when your pointer is in a spot where code hints are appropriate (**Figure 3.28**).
- Change the delay time for code hints to appear or turn off code hints by choosing Preferences from the Actions panel's Options menu. When the Preferences dialog box appears, change your preferences in the ActionScript Editor tab (**Figure 3.29**).

Show Code Hint button

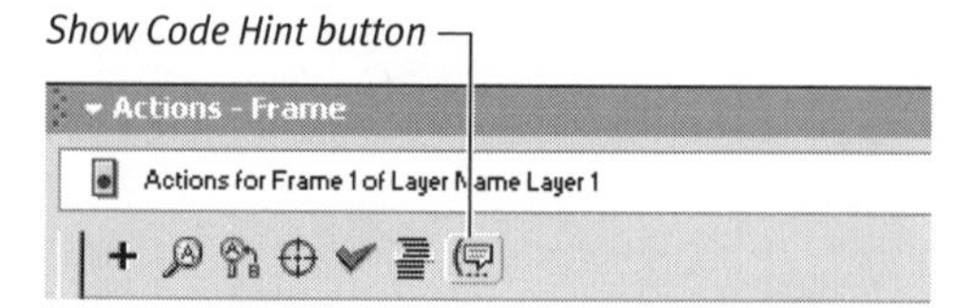

Figure 3.28 The Show Code Hint button is above the Script pane in Expert mode.

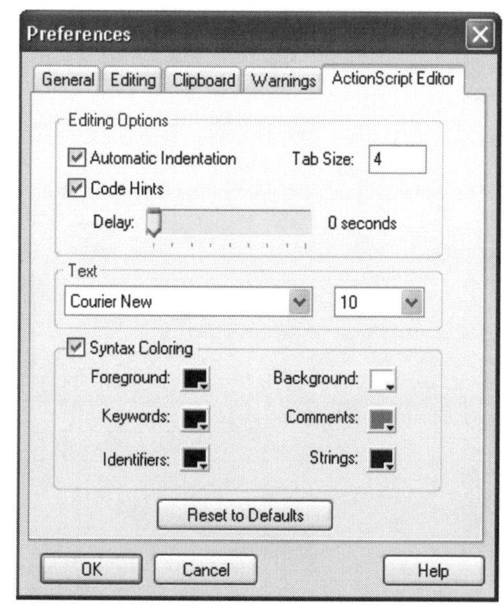

Figure 3.29 In the Preferences dialog box, you can change the time that it takes for code hints to appear.

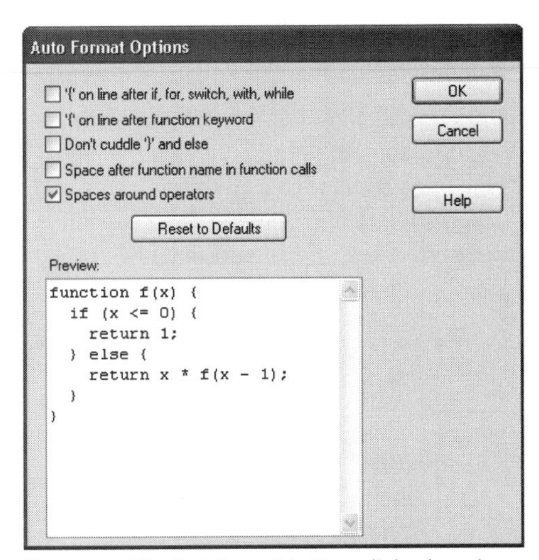

Figure 3.30 The AutoFormat Options dialog box gives you a preview of how a typical block of code would look with the selections you made.

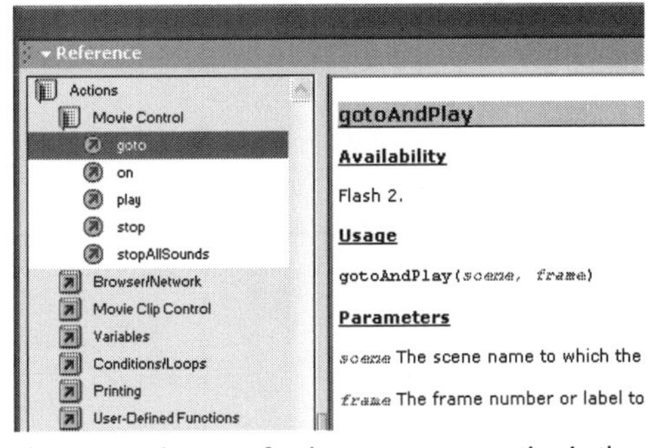

Figure 3.31 The entry for the `gotoAndPlay` action in the Reference panel.

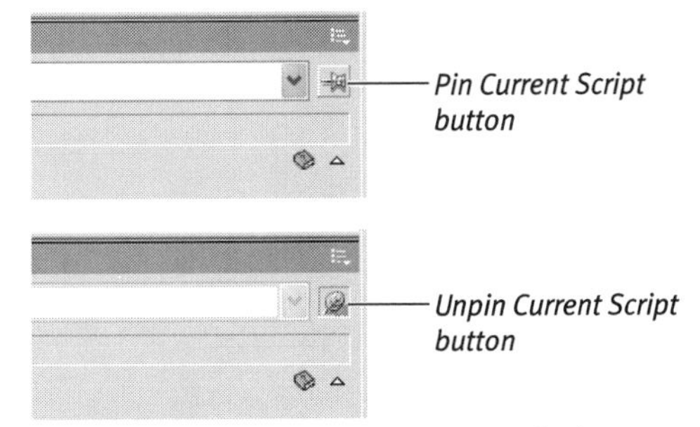

Figure 3.32 The Pin Current Script button (top) toggles to Unpin Current Script (bottom).

To set formatting options in Expert mode:

1. From the Actions panel's Options menu, choose Auto Format Options.

   The Auto Format Options dialog box appears.

2. Set the different formatting options and specify the way a typical block of code should appear (**Figure 3.30**); then click OK.

3. Choose Auto Format from the Actions panel's Options menu (Ctrl-Shift-F for Windows, Cmd-Shift-F for Mac), or click the Auto Format button above the Script pane.

   Flash formats your script in the Script pane according to the preferences you set in the Auto Format Options dialog box.

To look up actions in the Reference panel:

◆ Select an ActionScript term in the Script pane or the Actions toolbox, and click the Reference button above and to the right of the Script pane.

  or

  Right-click (Win) or Ctrl-Click (Mac) an action in the Actions toolbox, and select View Reference from the context menu that appears.

  The Reference panel opens to the selected ActionScript term. The typical entry in the Reference panel contains information about usage and syntax, lists parameters and their availability in various Flash versions, and sample code (**Figure 3.31**).

To pin or unpin a script in the Script pane:

◆ With ActionScript visible in the Script pane, click the Pin Current Script button to the right of the Script pull-down menu (**Figure 3.32**).

  To unpin the script, click the button again.

ActionScript Categories

You've learned that objects, methods, and properties are essential components of ActionScript. But how do they relate to the categories of actions in the Actions toolbox in the Actions panel, and what are the other categories of actions? Flash organizes actions hierarchically in eight categories, plus an index. These categories are Actions, Operators, Functions, Constants, Properties, Objects, Deprecated, and Flash UI Components. Many contain subcategories of actions. Following is a brief description of the categories.

- **Actions** contains the generic commands that control the movie. This category includes actions that manipulate variables (placeholders), expressions (formulas that combine variables), and conditional statements. This category also includes actions that work with movie clips, such as `startDrag(mySpaceship)`. In general, you will be accessing many of the actions in this category to create the interactions between your objects.
- **Operators** contains the symbols that transform variables and expressions or compare one value with another. They include the common mathematical symbols, such as the plus and minus sign, and symbols that modify text elements.
- **Functions** contains actions, such as `getVersion()`, that retrieve specific pieces of information. You can think of functions as being input-output machines that return useful information.
- **Constants** contains keywords that always signify a certain value. You can use constants, such as `true` and `false`, in your expressions.
- **Properties** contains the keywords that refer to descriptions of movie clips that you can modify or evaluate. The property `_rotation` controls the angle of a movie clip, for example.
- **Objects** contains all the objects and their unique methods and properties. An example is `Selection.getFocus()`.
- **Deprecated** contains the actions that are no longer recommended for use because newer actions have replaced them. These actions are collected in this category if you need to create older Flash content.
- **Flash UI Components** contains all the premade interface components provided by Macromedia. Components are specialized movie clips whose contents you can customize. A Component pull-down menu, for example, lets you set the menu's options and its appearance without having to worry about coding its functionality.
- **Index** contains all the ActionScript terms in alphabetical order. If you don't know where to find a term, select it in the Index category and right-click (Windows) or Ctrl-click (Mac). In the context menu that appears, choose View Original, and the correct category opens to show the term.

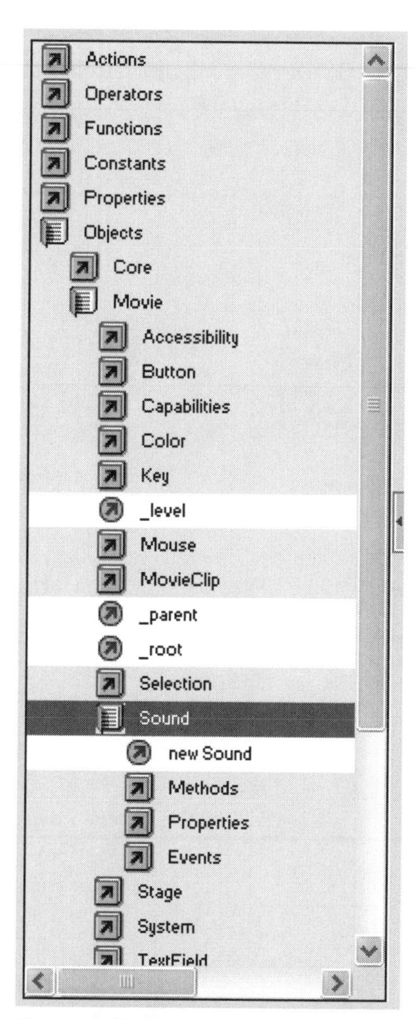

Figure 3.33 Flash's predefined objects control different kinds of information. The Objects category in the Actions toolbox is divided in more categories. Here, you see the Sound object and the contents of its folder.

Using Objects

Now that you know what objects are and how to operate the Actions panel, you can begin to script with objects and call their methods or evaluate and assign new properties.

Flash provides existing classes that it calls objects. The Array object, the Boolean object, the Color object, and all the other objects that Flash provides in the Objects category of the Actions toolbox are really predefined classes. The Array object, for example, should really be called the Array class because you create named individual objects from it. This book refers to the Flash predefined classes as objects with capitalized names, because that's the way they are categorized in the Actions panel's toolbox, but it will continue to use the term *classes* in general discussions for clarity's sake.

These Flash classes have methods and properties that control different elements of your Flash movie, such as graphics, sound, data, time, and mathematical calculations. You can also build your own classes from scratch by combining some of the existing classes and actions with functions (see Chapter 11).

Creating objects

Flash's predefined classes reside in the Objects category in the Actions panel (**Figure 3.33**). Before you can use one of these classes, you must create an instance of the class by giving it a name. The process is similar to creating an instance of, or *instantiating*, a symbol. You need to create an instance of the class to use it in ActionScript, and you do so by naming it. Use the keyword new to assign a unique name to a new instance of the class.

```
Adam = new Human ();
myColor = new Color ();
```

continues on next page

Where do you find the keyword new? In the Objects category of the Actions toolbox, the classes that require you to make new instances include the command new (**Figure 3.34**).

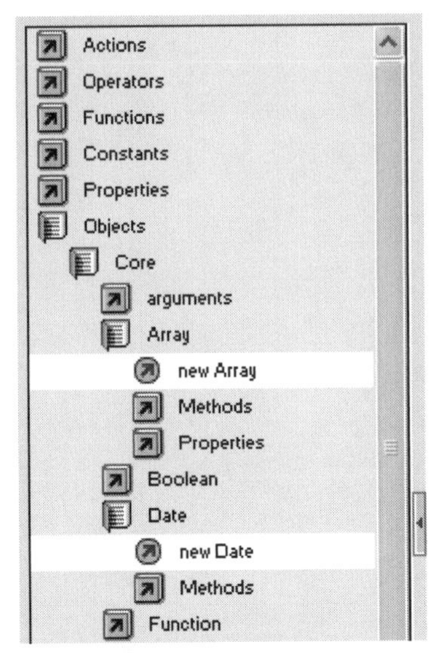

Figure 3.34 In the Array category, the action new `Array` will create a new instance from the Array object. In the Date category, the action new `Date` will create a new instance from the Date object.

The two examples in this section create new objects that you can use and manipulate. The first is a hypothetical statement that makes a new human object called Adam from the Human object. The second is an actual ActionScript statement that makes a new color object called myColor from the Color object. The statement that contains the new operator in front of the class is called a *constructor function*. Constructor functions are specialized functions that create new instances from classes.

The following task demonstrates how to instantiate the Date object. In Normal mode, you can make a new instance of an object in two ways. The first way uses the action `set variable`; the second way uses the action new. The first way is more menu-driven and is slower. The second way requires more typing but is quicker.

To create an object by using set variable:

1. Open the Actions panel in Normal mode.
2. In the Actions toolbox or from the plus button's pull-down menu, choose Actions > Variables > set variable.

   A new statement appears in the Script pane, with empty Variable and Value fields in the Parameters pane (**Figure 3.35**).
3. In the Variable field, enter the name you want to give your object (**Figure 3.36**).

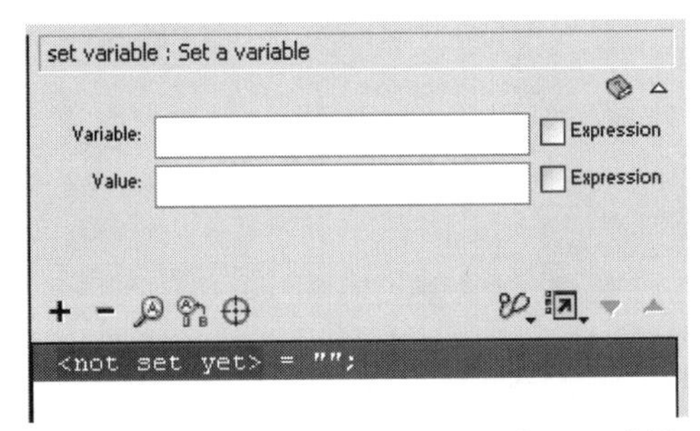

Figure 3.35 The `set variable` action requires a variable and a value.

Figure 3.36 Enter `myDate` as the name of your new Date object.

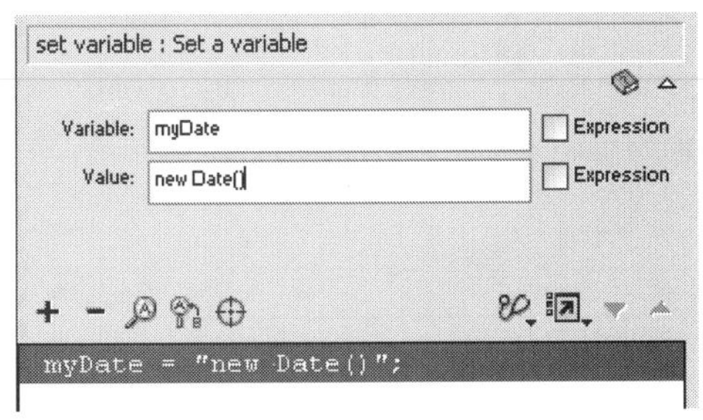

Figure 3.37 The constructor function new Date will make a new instance and assign it to the name in the Variable text box.

Figure 3.38 The new Date() statement is an expression, so check the Expression checkbox.

```
myDate = new Date();
```

Figure 3.39 The finished statement creates an object called myDate from the Date object.

4. Place your pointer in the Value field, and choose Objects > Core > Date > new Date.

   The constructor function new Date appears in the Value field (**Figure 3.37**).

5. Check the Expression checkbox next to the Value field (**Figure 3.38**).

   The quotation marks around the new Date constructor function in the Script pane disappear. This step makes sure that Flash recognizes that the name of your instance evaluates a new Date object and is not assigned to the actual characters in the Value field.

   The Script pane shows the full statement, which assigns the new Date object to the name you entered. Your Date object is instantiated and ready to use (**Figure 3.39**).

To create an object using the keyword new:

1. Open the Actions panel in Normal mode.

2. In the Actions toolbox or from the plus button's pull-down menu, choose Objects > Core > Date > new Date.

   A new statement appears in the Script pane, with new Date() in the Expression field in the Parameters pane (**Figure 3.40**).

continues on next page

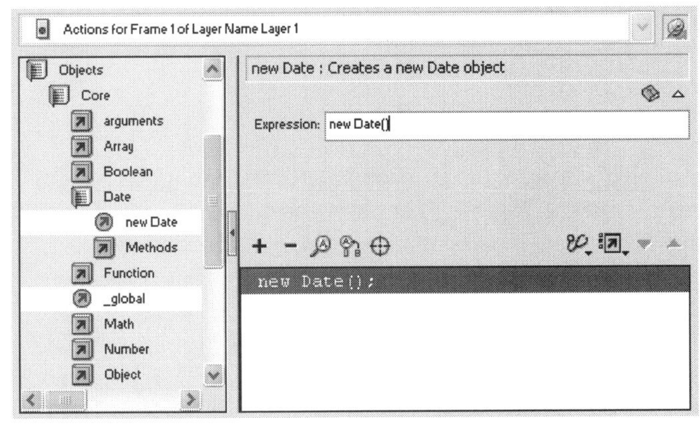

Figure 3.40 Choose new Date in the Actions toolbox.

3. Place your pointer before the `new Date ()` statement, and enter the name you want to call your object, followed by an equal sign (**Figure 3.41**).

   The Script pane shows the full statement, which assigns the new Date object to the name you entered. Your Date object is instantiated and ready to use (**Figure 3.42**).

Figure 3.41 Complete the statement in the Expression text box.

```
myDate = new Date();
```

Figure 3.42 The finished statement in the Script pane.

✔ Tip

- Some of the Flash objects—such as Key, Math, and Mouse—do not need a constructor function to instantiate an object. You can use their methods and properties immediately without having a named object. This practice makes sense because only one unique instance can exist for these special objects. (The Mouse object, for example, can have only one instance because there is only one mouse per computer.) You can tell which of the Flash objects don't require a constructor function by looking in the Objects category in the Actions toolbox. Objects that don't require a constructor function won't list the command `new` among their methods and properties.

About the Expression Box

When you are using the action `set variable`, Expression checkboxes appear for your parameters. Checking the Expression checkbox next to the Value field removes the quotation marks from the actual script, changing a string literal to an expression. A *string literal*, which is always contained within quotation marks, represents the actual collection of characters: numbers, letters, or symbols. An expression, on the other hand, is a formula that may contain variables, or placeholders, that Flash needs to evaluate before knowing what the entire expression represents. The string literal "3+2" is just the three characters 3+2. The expression 3+2, however, is 5. You'll work more with expressions and variables in Part V.

Calling methods

The next step after creating a new object involves calling an object's methods. Recall that you can call a method by using an object's name, followed by a period and then the method with its parameters within parentheses. In the Actions panel in Normal mode, you call a method simply by selecting the method in the particular Objects category (**Figure 3.43**). Depending on the kind of method you choose, the Actions panel displays methods in one of three ways:

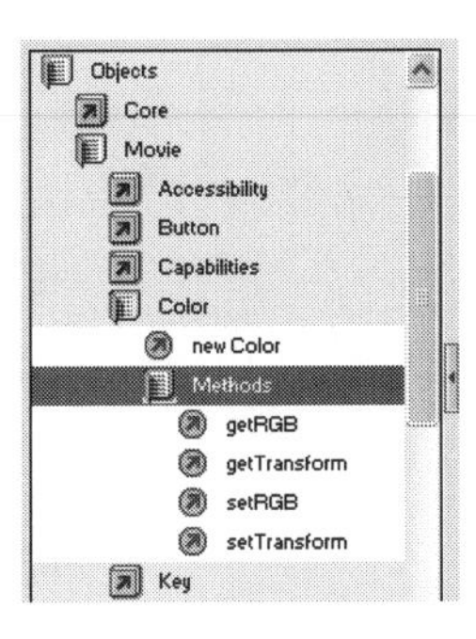

Figure 3.43 Below every object category, a Methods folder lists the methods you can choose to use. The methods of the Color object are shown here.

- The method appears as part of an Expression field in the Parameters pane (**Figure 3.44**). You must provide the object name before the period. Sometimes, you have to create a new line in the Script pane to accommodate this method. Do so by using the `evaluate` action (Actions > Miscellaneous Actions > evaluate) *before* you choose your method.
- The method appears in the Script pane with an empty Object field in the Parameters pane (**Figure 3.45**). You must provide an object name in the Parameters pane.
- The method appears in the Script pane with empty Object and Parameters field in the Parameters pane (**Figure 3.46**). You must provide an object name and the required parameters in the Parameters pane.

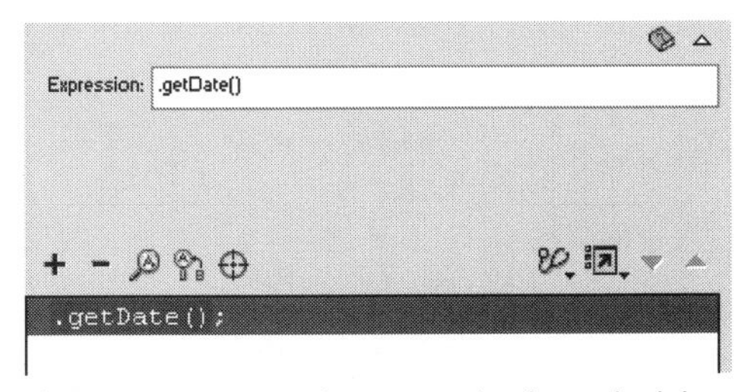

Figure 3.44 `getDate()` is an example of a method that appears in an Expression field.

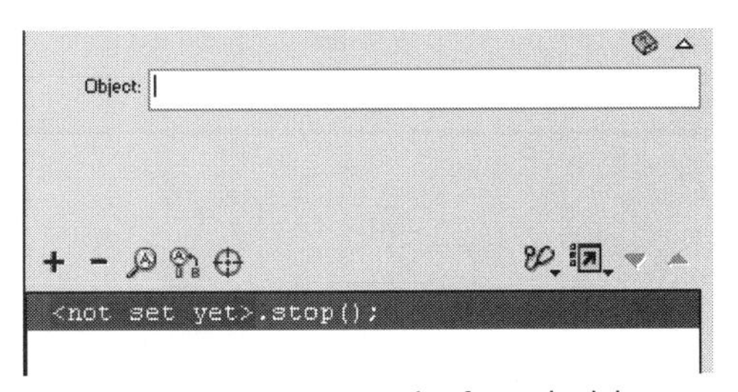

Figure 3.45 `stop()`is an example of a method that requires an object.

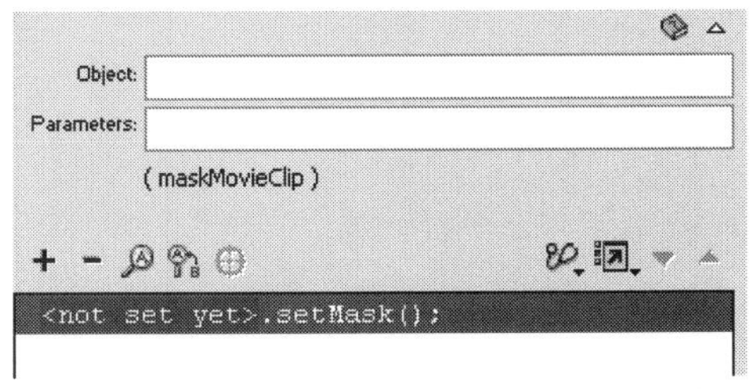

Figure 3.46 `setMask()`is an example of a method that requires an object and parameters.

Ultimately, your final ActionScript in the Script pane will look something like this:

```
myColor.setRGB(0x00CC33)
```

This statement calls the method `setRGB()` to change the color associated with the myColor object. The parameter is the hex number 0x00CC33.

Your ActionScript could also look something like this:

```
currentDate = myDate.getDate ()
```

This statement calls the method `getDate()` from the myDate object and puts the information it retrieves into the variable called `currentDate`.

The following example continues the preceding task and calls a method of the Date object. Later chapters introduce specific objects, provide more information on the Date object, and show you how to use objects' methods to control your Flash movie.

To call a method of an object:

1. Continuing with the preceding task, in the Actions panel, choose Actions > Miscellaneous Actions > evaluate.

   A new statement appears below the first. The semicolon in the Script pane marks the end of the yet-to-be-written statement (**Figure 3.47**).

2. Click inside the Expression field in the Script pane, and choose Object > Core > Date > Methods > getDate.

   A dot and the method appear in the Expression field and in the Script pane. The script is highlighted in red, warning you that the syntax is incorrect and not complete (**Figure 3.48**).

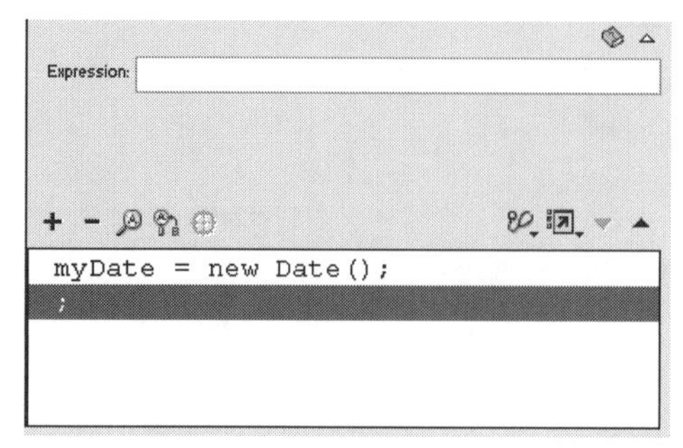

Figure 3.47 The `evaluate` action creates a new line in the Script pane.

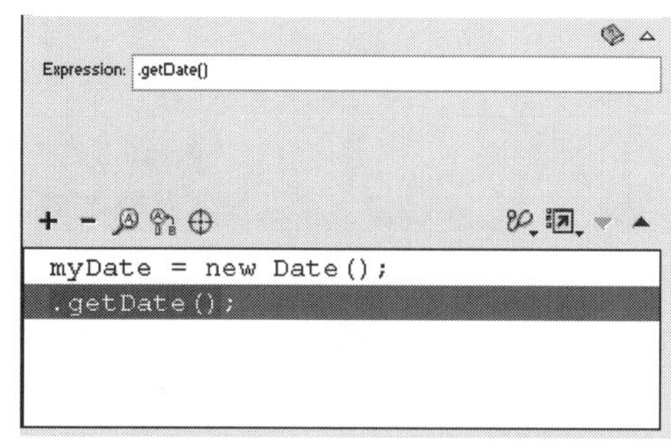

Figure 3.48 A dot and the `getDate()` method appear in the Expression field.

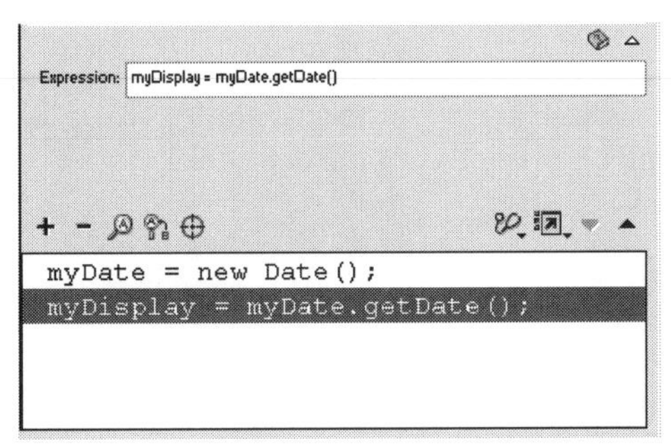

Figure 3.49 Enter the remaining statement to call the method, and put its returned value in a variable called `myDisplay`.

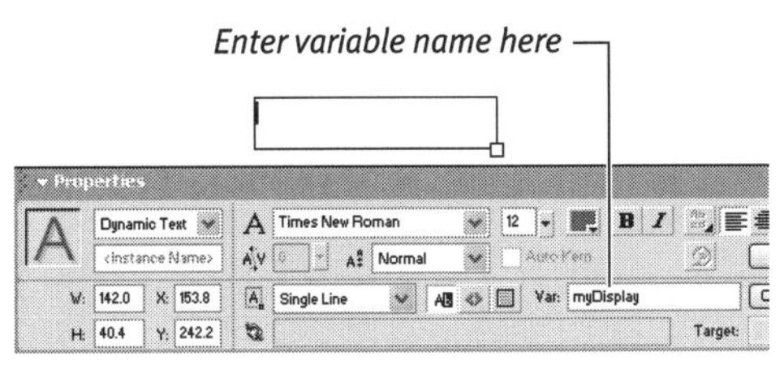

Figure 3.50 The text box at the top is set to Dynamic Text with the variable `myDisplay`. Do not confuse the Instance Name and the Var field in the Property Inspector.

3. Place your pointer before the `.getDate ()` statement; then enter the name of a variable, an equal sign, and the name of the Date object you created in the preceding task (myDate, in this example) (**Figure 3.49**).

   The completed statement appears in the Script pane, and the red highlighting is removed. The statement gets the current date and puts that information in the variable called `mydisplay`. The information that this method gets is called the *returned value*.

4. Select the Text tool, and drag out an empty selection on the Stage.

5. In the Property Inspector, choose Dynamic Text from the pull-down menu, and in the Var text box, enter the name of the variable that holds the current date (**Figure 3.50**).

   The dynamic field on the Stage displays the value of its variable during playback of the movie. You learn more about dynamic text in Chapter 10.

6. Test your movie by choosing Control > Test movie.

   Flash instantiates a Date object and then makes the object call the `getDate()` method. The returned value (the date) is put in the variable called `mydisplay`. You see the value of this variable in the text box on the Stage.

Assigning properties

Just as you have multiple ways to call a method, you have two ways to assign properties in Normal mode of the Actions panel. The first way is to use the `set variable` action (Actions > Variables > set variable). This method gives you a Variable field and a Value field in the Parameters pane. The second way is to use the `evaluate` action (Actions > Miscellaneous Actions > evaluate). This method gives you an Expression field in which you can enter an entire statement, assigning a value to a property or the value of a property to a variable. No matter which way you go, in the end, keep in mind that you want the Script pane to display your object name, followed by a dot and then the property name. If you want to assign a value to a property, that value goes on the right side of an equal sign.

```
myTextField.text = "hello";
```

This statement assigns the word *hello* to the `text` property of the object called myTextField.

If you want to read the value of a property and put it in a variable to use later, your object-dot-property construction goes on the right side of an equal sign.

```
myCurrentText = myTextField.text;
```

This statement puts the value of the `text` property of the object called myTextField in the variable called `myCurrentText`.

When you're working with movie clips, you can use two more actions: `getProperty` and `setProperty`. Chapter 7 explains movie-clip properties.

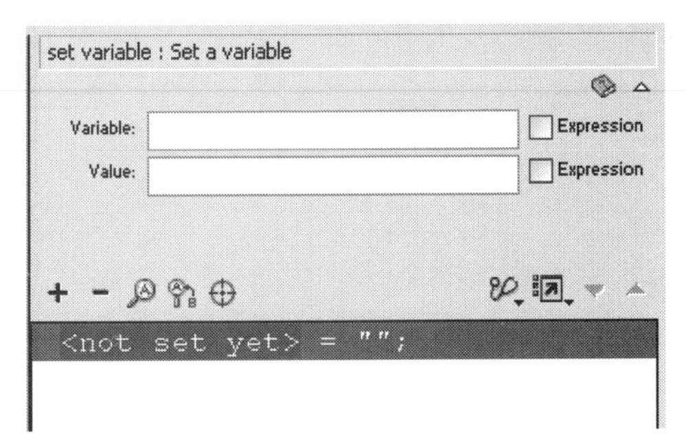

Figure 3.51 Choose the `set variable` action.

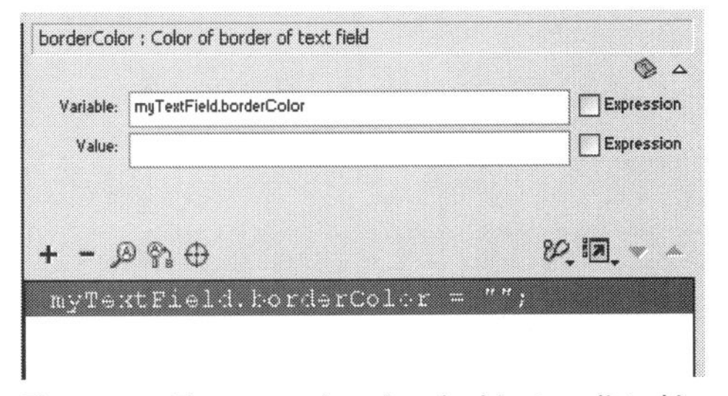

Figure 3.52 The properties of each object are listed in a Properties category. Here, the `borderColor` property of a TextField object is selected.

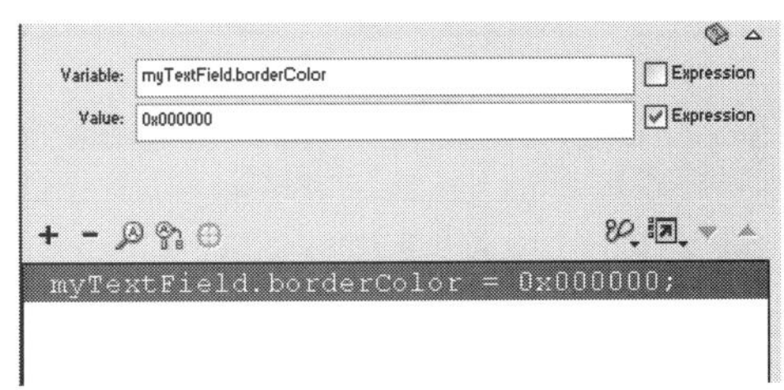

Figure 3.53 The `borderColor` property takes a hex number as its value. The final statement makes the border color of the text box called myTextField black.

To assign a value to a property by using set variable:

1. Choose `set variable` (Actions > Variables > set variable).

   A new line appears in the Script pane, with a Variable field and a Value field in the Parameters pane (**Figure 3.51**).

2. In the Variable field, enter the name of your object.

3. Choose the property in the Actions toolbox.

   Properties are located inside each object's folder in the Object category.

   The property appears after the name of your object, separated from it by a dot (**Figure 3.52**).

4. In the Value field, enter a value.

5. If the value you entered in step 4 is an expression, check the Expression checkbox next to it.

   The completed statement appears in the Script pane (**Figure 3.53**).

To assign a value to a property by using evaluate:

1. Choose `evaluate` (Actions > Miscellaneous Actions > evaluate).

   A new line appears in the Script pane, with an Expression field in the Parameters pane (**Figure 3.54**).

2. In the Expression field, enter the name of your object.

3. Choose a property from the Actions toolbox.

   Properties are located inside each object's folder in the Object category.

   The property appears after the name of your object, separated from it by a dot (**Figure 3.55**).

4. Enter an equal sign, followed by a value.

   The completed statement appears in the Script pane (**Figure 3.56**).

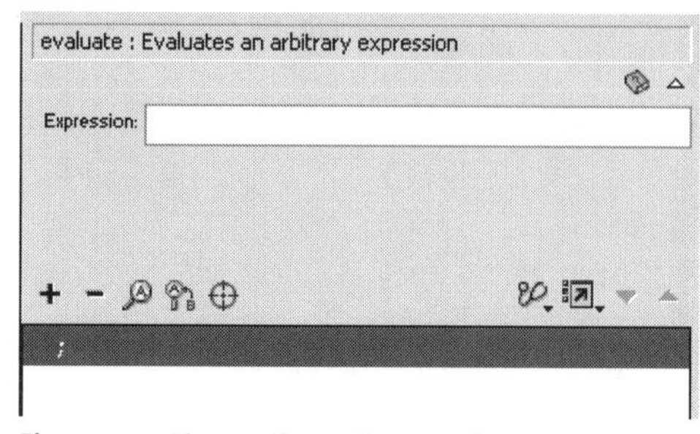

Figure 3.54 Choose the `evaluate` action.

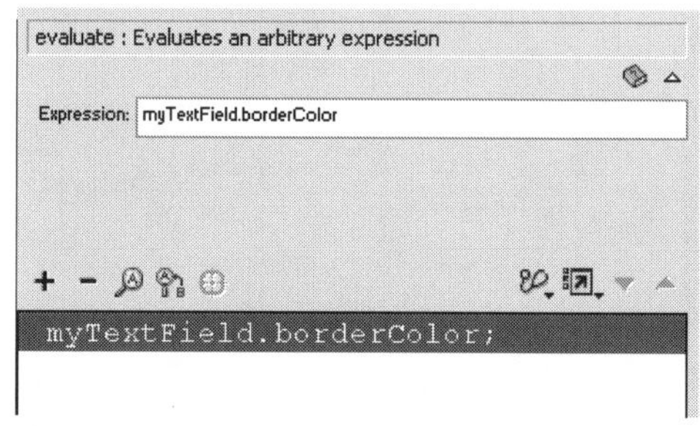

Figure 3.55 Enter the object name, and choose its property.

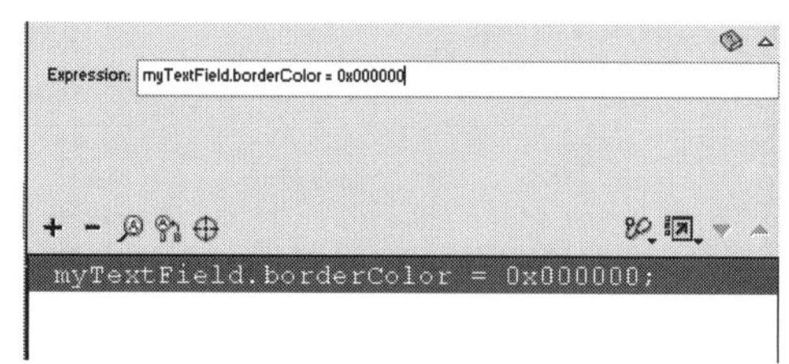

Figure 3.56 The final statement is exactly like the one you created with `set variable`, but it uses a single Expression field rather than Variable and Value fields.

Symbols and Classes

Symbols are not classes. Symbols are not even objects. It's true that movie clips and buttons are both symbols and objects, but these elements are exceptions—and perhaps the source of some confusion. Graphics, sounds, bitmaps, and video clips are all symbols that appear in the Library, but they are not objects or classes because they do not have methods and properties that you can control with ActionScript.

Some parallels exist between classes and symbols. Symbols are reusable assets created in or imported to the Library. With these symbols, you create instances, or copies of the symbols, to use in your movie. Classes, as you have seen, also have instances made from them to be used in your movie.

About Functions

If objects and classes are at the heart of ActionScript, functions must lie in the brain. Functions are the organizers of ActionScript. Functions group related ActionScript statements to perform a specific task. Often, you need to write code to do a certain thing over and over again. Functions eliminate the tedium and the duplication of code by putting it in one place where you can call on it to do its job from anywhere and at any time, as many times as you need.

As you learned earlier in this chapter, the objects Adam, Betty, and Zeke can perform certain tasks, called methods. If these objects were to put on a dinner party, they could organize themselves and do the following:

```
Adam.answerDoor();
Betty.serveDinner();
Zeke.chitChat();
```

But every Friday night when they have a dinner party, you would have to write the same three lines of code—not very efficient if these objects plan to entertain often. Instead, you can write a function that groups the code in one spot.

```
function dinnerParty () {
   Adam.answerDoor();
   Betty.serveDinner();
   Zeke.chitChat();
}
```

Now, every Friday night, you can just invoke the function by name and write the code, `dinnerParty()`. The three statements inside the function's curly braces will be executed. You can add a function in Normal mode by choosing Actions > User-Defined Functions > function (Esc-fn).

You will also be using anonymous functions. As their name suggests, anonymous functions are not named and look something like this:

```
function() {
   Adam.answerDoor();
   Betty.serveDinner();
   Zeke.chitChat();
}
```

Anonymous functions do not work alone and must be assigned to another object.

```
myButton.onPress = function() {
   Adam.answerDoor();
   Betty.serveDinner();
   Zeke.chitChat();
}
```

Now your three friends perform their jobs when the object called myButton is clicked.

You will learn much more about named functions and anonymous functions in the upcoming chapters, after you have a few more actions and concepts under your belt. Anonymous functions are important for handling events (Chapter 4) and for creating your own methods for objects (Chapter 11). Named functions are important for building reusable code (Chapter 11).

Using Comments

After you have built a strong vocabulary of Flash actions and are constructing complex statements in the Actions panel, you should include remarks in your scripts to remind yourself and your collaborators of the goals of the ActionScript. Comments help you keep things straight as you develop intricate interactivity and relationships among objects (**Figure 3.57**).

```
// instantiate the myDate object
myDate = new Date();
//retrieve the date and put it
//in the dynamic textfield variable
//called myDisplay
myDisplay = myDate.getDate();
```

Figure 3.57 Comments interspersed with ActionScript statements help make sense of the code.

To create a comment:

- In the Actions panel, choose Actions > Miscellaneous Actions > comment, and enter your comments in the Comment field of the Parameters pane.

  or

  In Expert mode only, type two slashes (//) in the Actions list, and enter your comments after the slashes.

  Comments appear in a different color from the rest of the script, making them easy to locate.

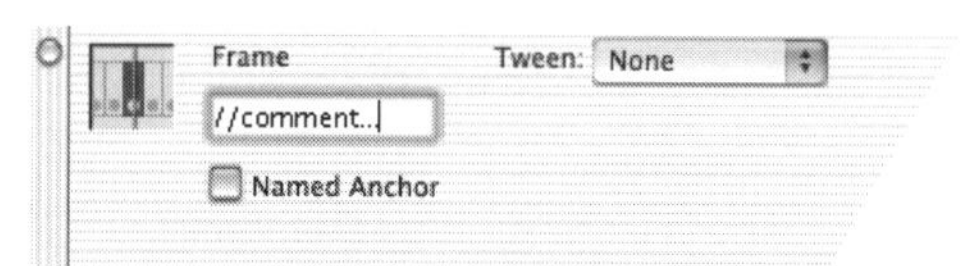

Figure 3.58 In the Property inspector, double slashes indicate a comment in a Frame label.

✔ Tips

- If you have a long comment, break it up with multiple comment statements. That way, you'll have separate lines, and you won't have to scroll the Script pane to see the end of a long remark.
- If you have a long comment spanning multiple lines, you can use a slash and an asterisk (/*) to mark the beginning and end of a comment block. For example:

```
/* This begins the comment.
Even text in between is considered
part of the comment.
/* This is the end of the comment.
```

- Don't worry about creating too many comments. Comments are not compiled with the rest of the script, so they won't bog down performance. Also, because they aren't included in the exported .swf file, they don't increase the final file size.
- The slash convention for creating comments in ActionScript is the same for creating them in keyframes. When you label a frame in the Property Inspector, begin with two slashes (//) to indicate a comment rather than a label (**Figure 3.58**).

Part III: Navigating Timelines and Communicating

Advanced Buttons and Event Detection

4

Creating graphics and animation in Flash is only half the story. You can incorporate interactivity via buttons, the keyboard, and the mouse to give the viewer control of those graphics and animations. Interactivity is essential for basic site navigation and e-commerce interfaces on the Web, as well as for game development, online tutorials, or anything else that requires the viewer to make choices.

What makes a movie interactive? Interactivity is the back-and-forth communication between the user and the movie. In a Flash movie, the user might react to something that's going on by moving the pointer, clicking the mouse button, or pressing a particular key on the keyboard. That reaction may trigger a response from the Flash movie, which in turn prompts the user to do something else. The things that the user does—mouse movements, button clicks, or keyboard presses—are part of things that happen, called *events*. Events form the basis of interactivity. There are many kinds of events; even events that happen without the user knowing about them. You will learn to detect these events and create the responses to events in statements conveniently known as *event handlers*.

This chapter first introduces events, event handlers, and anonymous functions used for event handling. Next, you explore the simplest object that handles events: the Button object. You'll learn how to extend its functionality by creating invisible buttons, tweening button instances, and creating fully animated buttons. You'll tackle the issues involved in creating a more complex button, such as a pull-down menu, which includes different button events, tracking options, and movie clips. You'll also learn about the Key object and the Mouse object, as well as how to create actions that run continuously. Understanding objects and event handling is essential to Flash interactivity, because these elements are the scaffold on which you will hang virtually all your ActionScript.

Events and Event Handlers

Events are things that happen that Flash can recognize and respond to. A button click is an event, as are button rollovers, mouse movements, and key presses on the keyboard. Events can also be things that the user cannot control. The completion of a sound, for example, is also an event. Events can even occur regularly.

With all these events happening, you need a way to detect and respond to them. Event handlers are statements that perform this task. Event handlers perform certain actions as a response to events. You can create an event handler to detect a click of a button, for example. In response, you can make Flash go to another frame in a different scene.

Event handlers are associated with particular Flash objects. Button presses, rollovers, and releases are associated with the Button object. The pressing of a key is associated with the Key object. And the completion of a sound is associated with the Sound object. You will learn about all these events as you learn about the objects themselves. You'll begin with the Button object.

The Button Object

The Button object handles the events involving how the pointer interacts with a button; to a limited extent, it also handles keyboard presses. You can assign event handlers to buttons in one of two ways. First, you can assign an event handler to the button instance that sits on the Stage. When you assign an event handler to the instance, you choose Actions > Movie Control > on in the Actions panel. Flash adds the event handler:

```
on(release){
}
```

The second way to assign an event handler to a button requires that you give your button instance a name in the Property Inspector. Then you assign ActionScript to the main Timeline. Choose Objects > Movie > Button > Events > onRelease. An anonymous function is assigned to your button event:

```
myButton.onRelease=function(){
}
```

In both cases, you then add ActionScript between the curly braces of the event handler. Those actions will be performed whenever the event happens.

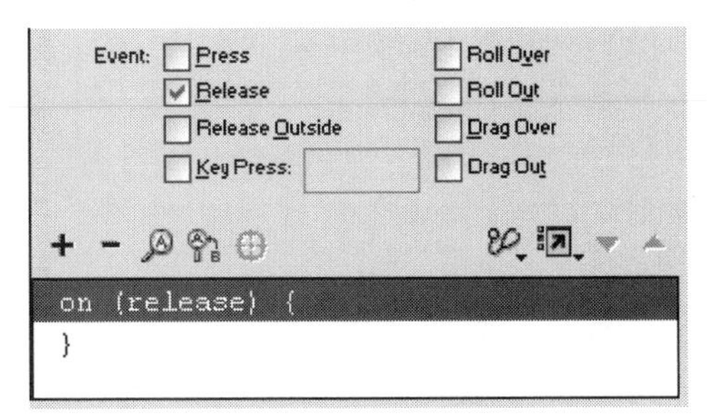

Figure 4.1 Use the on action to assign an event handler to a button instance.

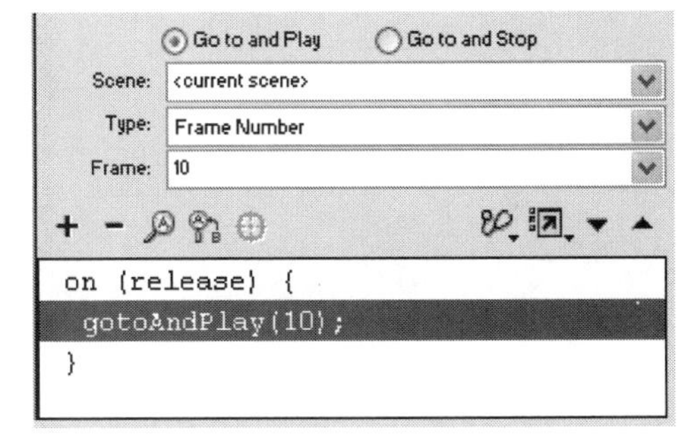

Figure 4.2 When the viewer presses and releases this button, Flash goes to frame 10 and begins playing.

The `release/onRelease` button event is the typical trigger for button interactivity. The event is triggered when the mouse button is released inside the `Hit` state of a button symbol. This setup allows viewers to change their minds and release the mouse button over a safe spot outside the hit area even after they've already clicked a button. Other types of button events make possible a range of interactions. **Table 4.1** lists all the button events.

To assign an event handler to a button instance:

1. Create a button symbol, and place an instance of the button on the Stage.
2. Select the button instance, and open the Actions panel.
3. Choose Actions > Movie Control > on (Esc + on).

   The `on(release)` event handler appears in the Script pane (**Figure 4.1**).
4. Choose another action as the response to the event.

   Additional actions appear between the event handler's curly braces (**Figure 4.2**).

Table 4.1

Button Events

Button Event	Triggered When
on(press)/onPress	When the pointer is over the hit area and the mouse button is pressed.
on(release)/onRelease	When the pointer is over the hit area and the mouse button is pressed and released.
on(releaseOutside)/ onReleaseOutside	When the pointer is over the hit area and the mouse button is pressed and then released outside the hit area.
on(rollOver)/onRollover	When the pointer moves over the hit area.
on(rollOut)/onRollOut	When the pointer moves from the hit area off the hit area.
on(dragOver)/ onDragOver	When the pointer is over the hit area and the mouse button is pressed; then the pointer is moved off the hit area and back over the hit area while the button remains pressed.
on(dragOut)/onDragOut	When the pointer is over the hit area and the mouse button is pressed; then the pointer is moved off the hit area while the button remains pressed.
on(keyPress"WhatKey")	When the key whatKey is pressed.
onSetFocus	When the button receives keyboard focus through the Tab key. (The button is highlighted by a yellow rectangle when the Tab key is used to select a button on the Stage.)
onKillFocus	When the button loses keyboard focus through the Tab key. (The button is highlighted by a yellow rectangle when the Tab key is used to select a button on the Stage.)

To assign an event handler on the Timeline:

1. Create a button symbol, and place an instance of the button on the Stage.
2. Select the button instance, and enter a descriptive name in the Property Inspector (**Figure 4.3**).

   This name is the name of your button object; you will use it to reference the button from ActionScript. This name is *not* the same one that appears in your library.
3. Select the first frame of the main Timeline, and open the Actions panel.
4. Choose Objects > Movie > Button > Events > onRelease.

   An anonymous function appears. The event appears in the Method field of the Parameters pane (**Figure 4.4**).
5. In the Object field, enter the name of your button instance (**Figure 4.5**).

   Your `onRelease` event handler is complete.
6. Choose another action as the response to the event.

   Additional actions appear between the event handler's curly braces (**Figure 4.6**).

✔ Tips

- When naming your button instance in the Property Inspector, keep in mind these simple rules: Do not include spaces, special characters, or punctuation, and do not start your name with a number. These naming rules apply to all objects.
- When you create your event handler on the main Timeline, your button must be present on the Stage at the same time to "receive" its instructions. If you create the event handler in keyframe 1, for example, but your button doesn't appear until keyframe 10, your button will not respond to the event handler.

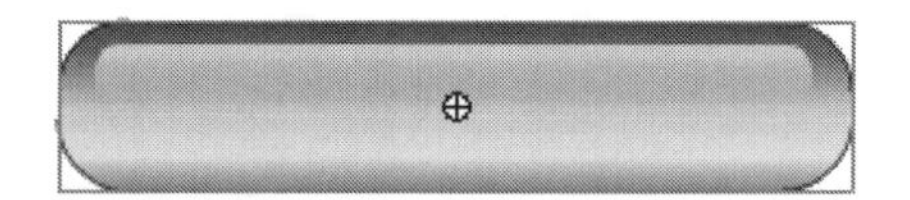

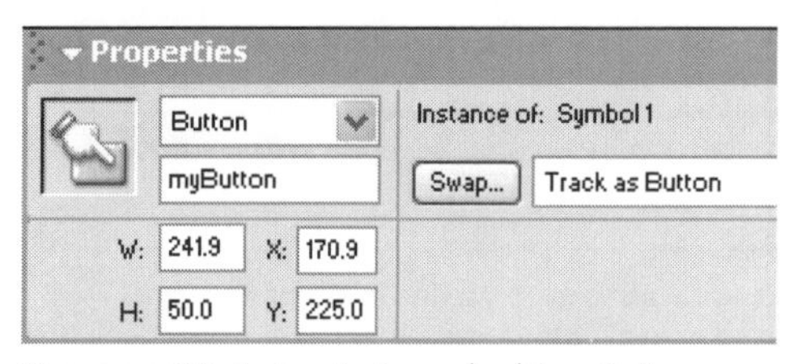

Figure 4.3 This button instance (top) is called myButton in the Property Inspector (bottom).

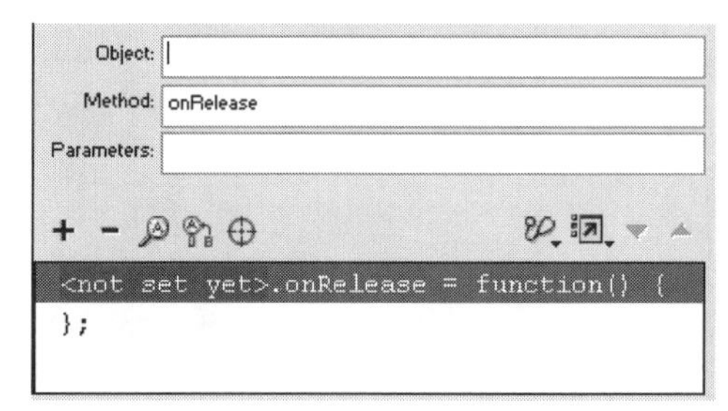

Figure 4.4 This anonymous function has yet to assign the `onRelease` event to a button.

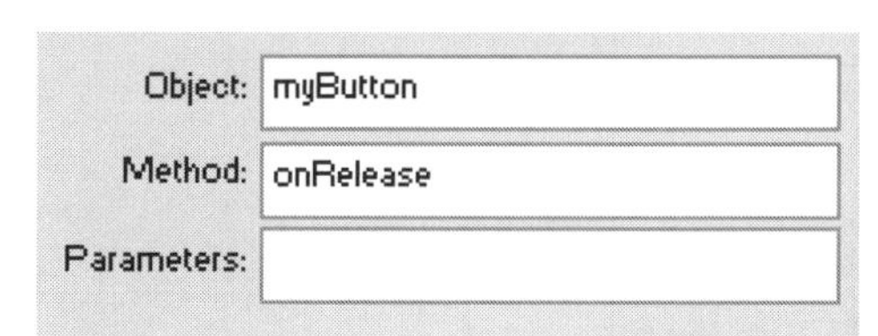

Figure 4.5 The name of your button, myButton, goes in the Object field.

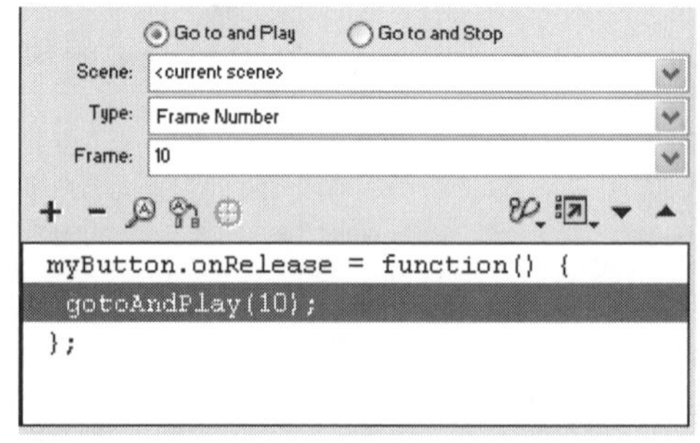

Figure 4.6 When the viewer clicks and releases the button called myButton, Flash goes to frame 10 and begins playing. Compare this script with the one in Figure 4.2.

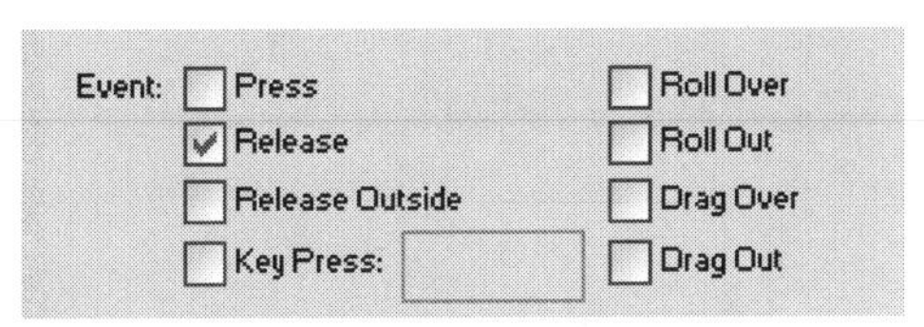

Figure 4.7 The Parameters pane of the on action contains a checkbox list of various events you can assign to the button instance.

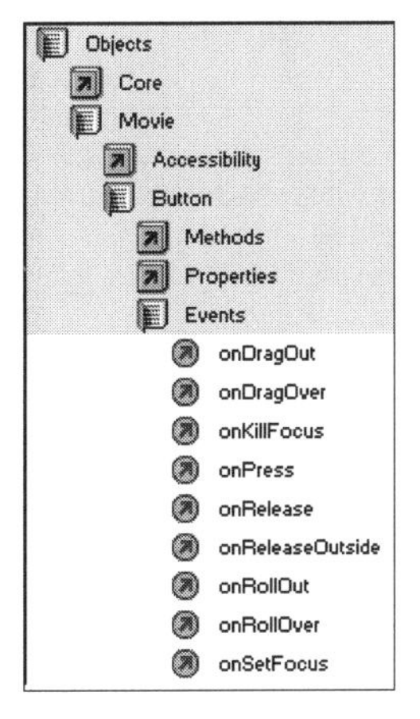

Figure 4.8 The Events category (below the Button category) lists the events you can assign with an anonymous function.

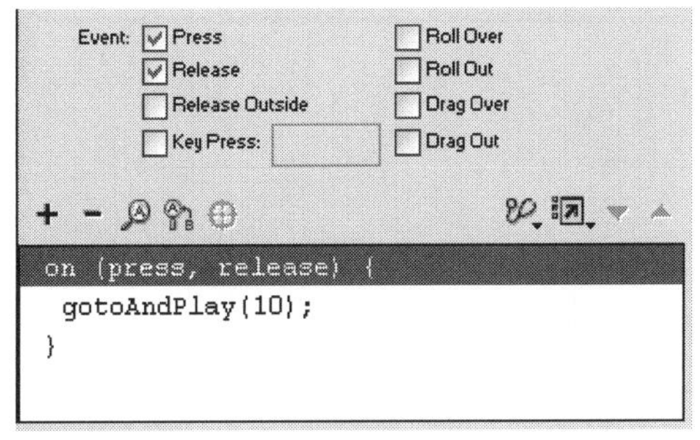

Figure 4.9 If either the `press` or `release` event happens, Flash goes to frame 10 and begins playing.

To select different button events:

1. Choose Actions > Movie Control > on.
2. In the Parameters pane, check additional button events or uncheck unwanted button events (**Figure 4.7**).

   or

   Choose Objects > Movie > Button > Events, and choose a different event from the list of available events (**Figure 4.8**).

✔ Tips

- All the button events except `release` require that you choose Control > Test Movie to see the behavior of the button instance. These other events don't work in the editing environment when you choose Control > Enable Simple Buttons.
- You can assign more than one event for one on action. The action `on (press, release)`, for example, will detect when the mouse button is pressed as well as when the button is released, and will execute any action within its curly braces if either of those two events occurs (**Figure 4.9**).
- If you want to assign more than one event by using an anonymous function, you can create separate function statements or, in Expert mode, write the function in this form:

```
myButton.onPress = myButton.onRelease
= function () {
}
```

continues on next page

- Within one button instance, if you want one event to have a different consequence from another event, you must create separate on action statements or separate anonymous function statements. To have the `rollOver` event make your movie play and the `rollOut` event make your movie stop, your actions would look like this:

```
on(rollOver){
 play();
}
on(rollOut){
 stop();
}
```

- Don't confuse the `rollover/onRollover` button event with the `Over` keyframe of your button symbol. Both involve detecting when the pointer is over the hit area, but the `Over` state describes how your button looks when the mouse is over the hit area, whereas the `rollover/onRollover` event assigns an action when that event actually occurs. So the keyframes of a button symbol define how it looks, and the event handler defines what it does (**Figure 4.10**).

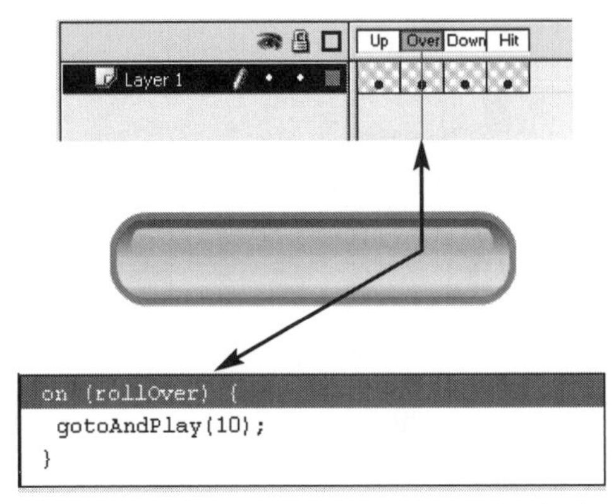

Figure 4.10 The `Over` state of the button symbol (top) defines how the button looks when the pointer is over the `Hit` state. A `rollOver` event handler (bottom) defines what the button does when the pointer is over the `Hit` state.

on(press) or onPress?

With two ways to assign event handlers to buttons, which way do you use? The answer partly depends on the complexity of your Flash project. Although it may be simpler to put event handlers directly on the button instance, in the long run, it's better practice to assign event handlers on the main Timeline. This method keeps all your ActionScript code in one place, rather than scattered among individual buttons on the Stage. As your movie becomes more complex, and you have more buttons to deal with, you'll find it easier to isolate and revise button events. Putting the event handler on the main Timeline also forces you to name your button instances so that you can target and control their properties with ActionScript.

Assigning event handlers directly to button instances, however, offers one distinct advantage: You can copy and paste button instances during author time, and their event handlers will be pasted along with them. In this book, we will use both methods in examples, as you should be comfortable using both `on(press)` and `onPress`.

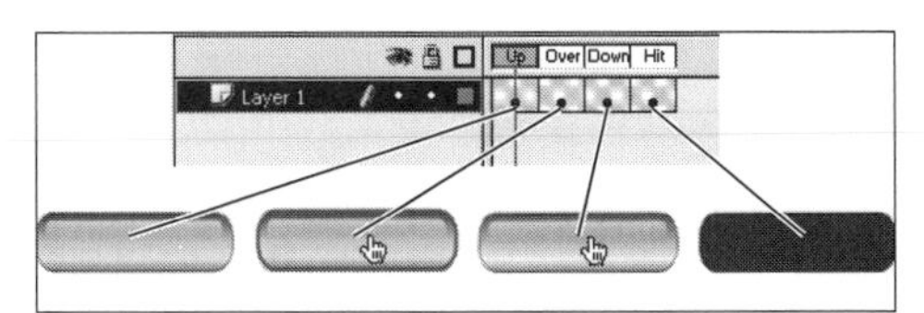

Figure 4.11 The four keyframes of a button symbol.

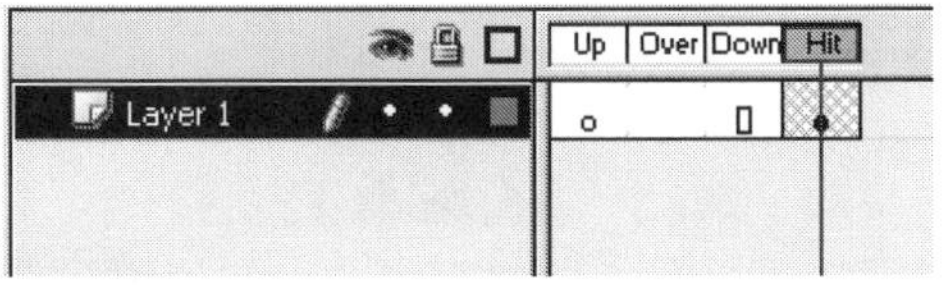

Figure 4.12 An invisible button has only the `Hit` keyframe defined.

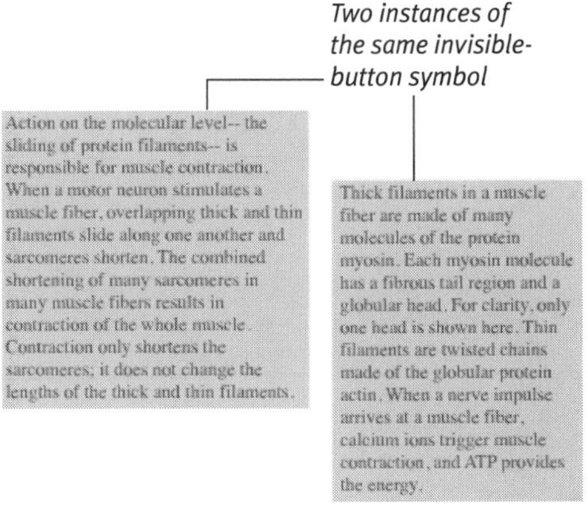

Figure 4.13 Invisible-button instances over text blocks.

Invisible Buttons

Flash lets you define four special keyframes of a button symbol that describe how the button looks and responds to the mouse: the `Up`, `Over`, `Down`, and `Hit` states. The `Up` state shows what the button looks like when the pointer is not over the button. `Over` shows what the button looks like when the pointer is over the button. `Down` shows what the button looks like when the pointer is over the button with the mouse button pressed. And `Hit` defines the actual active, or *hot*, area of the button (**Figure 4.11**).

You can exploit the flexibility of Flash buttons by defining only particular states. If you leave empty keyframes in all states except for the `Hit` state, you create an invisible button (**Figure 4.12**). Invisible buttons are extremely useful for creating multiple generic hotspots to which you can assign actions. By placing invisible button instances on top of graphics, you essentially have the power to make anything on the Stage react to the mouse pointer. If you have several blocks of text that you want the user to read in succession, you can have the user click each paragraph to advance to the next one. Instead of creating separate buttons out of each text block, make just one invisible button, and stretch instances to fit each one. Assign actions to each invisible-button instance that covers the paragraphs (**Figure 4.13**).

When you drag an instance of an invisible button onto the Stage, you actually see the hit area as a transparent blue shape, which allows you to place the button precisely. When you choose Control > Enable Simple Buttons (Ctrl-Alt-B for Windows, Command-Option-B for Mac), the button disappears to show you its playback appearance.

To create an invisible button:

1. From the Insert menu, choose New Symbol.

   The Symbol Properties dialog box appears.

2. Type the symbol name of your button, choose Button as the Behavior, and click OK.

   A new button symbol is created in the library, and you enter symbol-editing mode.

3. Select the `Hit` keyframe.

4. Choose Insert > Keyframe.

   A new keyframe is created in the `Hit` state.

5. With the `Hit` keyframe selected, draw a generic shape that serves as the hotspot for your invisible button (**Figure 4.14**).

6. Return to the main Timeline.

7. Drag an instance of the symbol from the library onto the Stage.

   A transparent blue shape appears on the Stage, indicating the `Hit` state of your invisible button.

8. Move, scale, and rotate the invisible-button instance to cover any graphic.

9. From the Actions panel, assign an action to the button instance.

   When you enable simple buttons, the transparent blue area disappears, but your pointer changes to a hand to indicate the presence of a button.

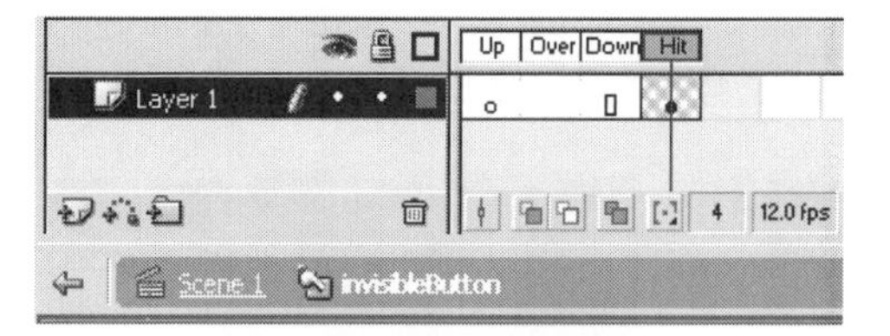

Figure 4.14 An invisible-button symbol. The rectangle in the `Hit` keyframe defines the active area of the button.

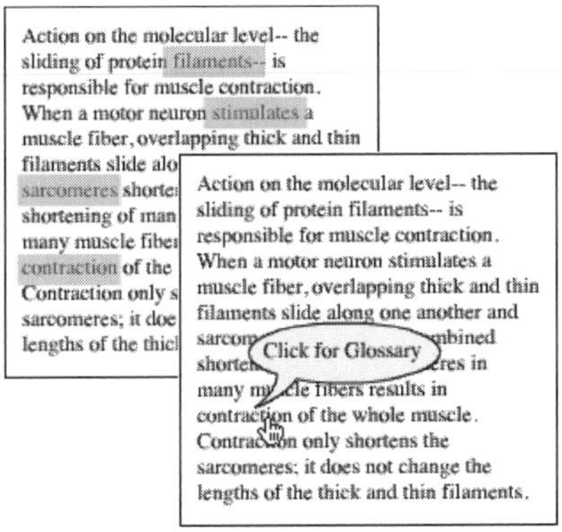

Figure 4.15 The Over state of this invisible button has a balloon with directions to go to a glossary. Multiple instances can cover different words.

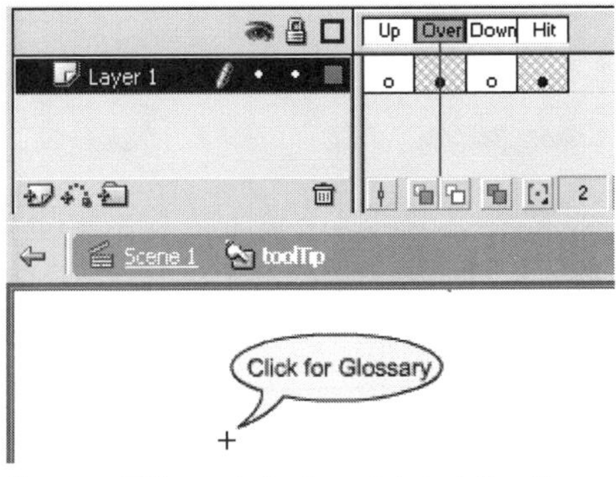

Figure 4.16 When only the Over state is defined in an invisible button, it will appear to pop up when the mouse rolls over the active area.

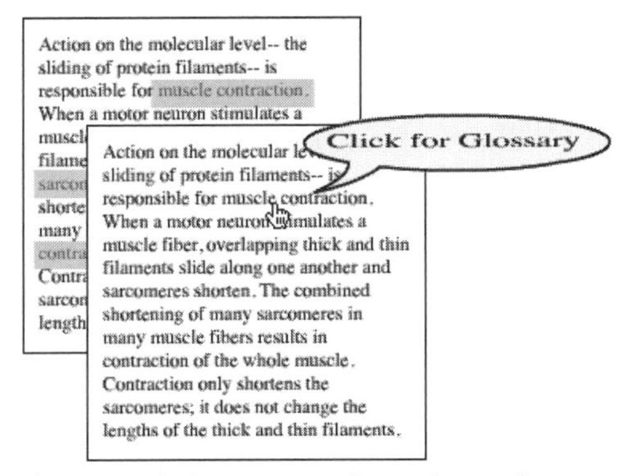

Figure 4.17 The instance over the words *muscle contraction* is stretched, making the Over state of the button stretch as much.

You can also create tool tips or helpful pop-up reminders by using invisible buttons. Create a short message in the Over state of an invisible button, and position these instances wherever the little messages apply (**Figure 4.15**).

To create pop-up tool tips with invisible buttons:

1. Create an invisible button, as described in the preceding task.
2. Select the Over state, and insert a new keyframe.
3. In the Over state, create a graphic that tells users about a particular feature that may be scattered through your Stage or movie (**Figure 4.16**).
4. Return to the main Timeline, and place instances of your invisible button over all the appropriate spots.

✔ Tips

- Be careful about rotating and scaling your instance, because it will affect the button's Over state (**Figure 4.17**).
- Be conscious of the stacking order of invisible buttons and how they are placed in your layers. The topmost button will take precedence over any button underneath it, effectively disabling the action of the bottom button.

Tweening Buttons

You can tween buttons just as you do any other kind of symbol instance and create moving menus and interfaces that still respond to the pointer and carry out actions assigned to them.

To apply a motion tween to a button:

1. From the Insert menu, choose New Symbol, and create a button symbol.
2. Return to the main movie Timeline, and drag an instance of the button symbol onto the Stage.
3. Select the instance, open the Actions panel in Normal mode, and add an action to your button instance (**Figure 4.18**).
4. Create a motion tween as you normally would for a graphic instance.

   Insert new keyframes, move or transform each instance, and then choose Motion Tween in the Property Inspector.
5. On the main Timeline, at the end of your motion tween, add the action `gotoAndPlay(1)`.

   Flash creates an endless loop for your motion-tweened button (**Figure 4.19**).
6. Create a spot on the Timeline where the action assigned to the button instance takes the user.
7. Test your movie.

   Throughout its tween, the button instance is active and responds to your pointer.

✔ Tip

- Tweened button instances use the actions that are assigned to the first keyframe of the motion tween (**Figure 4.20**). Assign an action to the button instance first and then create your motion tween so all subsequent inserted keyframes will contain the same instance with the same actions.

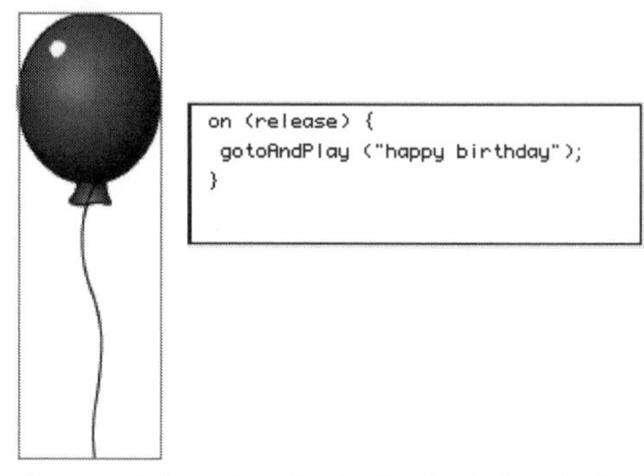

Figure 4.18 The action attached to this balloon button instance makes Flash go to the label called `happy birthday` and begin playing.

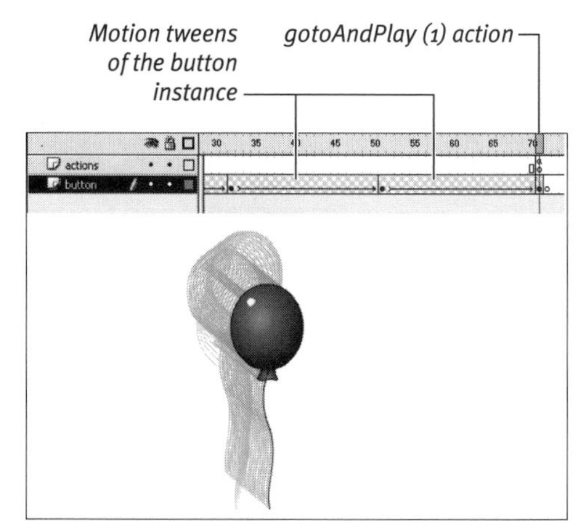

Figure 4.19 This balloon floats up and down in a constant loop.

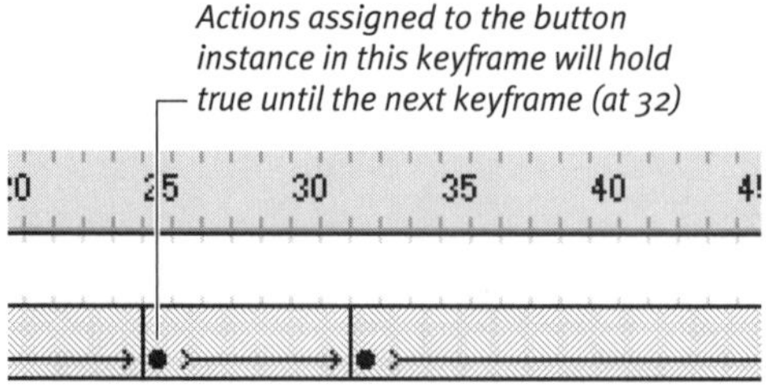

Figure 4.20 Actions assigned to tweened instances. The actions assigned to the first instance of any tween are the ones that are followed.

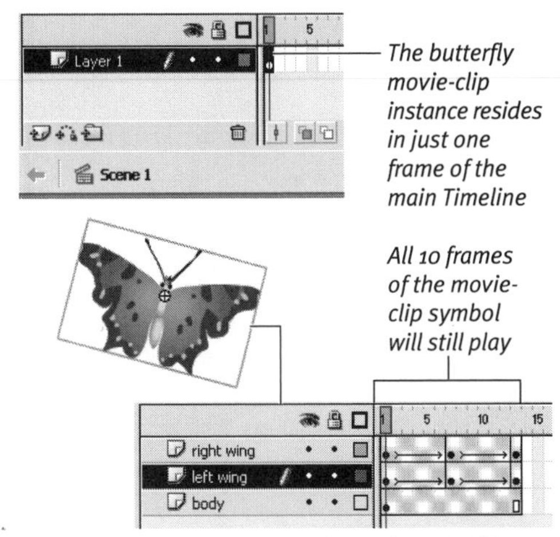

Figure 4.21 Movie clips have independent Timelines.

Comparing a Movie-Clip Instance with a Graphic Instance

How does a movie-clip instance differ from a graphic instance? If you create the same animation in both a movie-clip symbol and a graphic symbol, and then place both instances on the Stage, the differences become clear. The graphic instance shows its animation in the authoring environment, displaying however many frames are available in the main Timeline. If the graphic symbol contains an animation lasting 10 frames, and the instance occupies 4 frames of the main Timeline, you will see only 4 frames of the animation. Movie clips, on the other hand, do not work in the Flash authoring environment. You need to export the movie as a .swf file to see any movie-clip animation or functionality. When you export the movie (you can do so by choosing Control > Test Movie), Flash plays the movie-clip instance continuously, regardless of the number of frames the instance occupies and even when the movie itself has stopped.

Animated Buttons and the Movie-Clip Symbol

Animated buttons display an animation in any of the first three keyframes (`Up`, `Over`, and `Down`) of the button symbol. A button can spin when the pointer rolls over it, for example, because you have an animation of the spinning button in the `Over` state. How do you fit an animation into only one keyframe of the button symbol? The answer: Use a movie clip.

Movie clips are a special kind of symbol that allows you to have animations that run regardless of where they are or how many actual frames the instance occupies. This feature is possible because a movie clip's Timeline runs independently of any other Timeline, including other movie-clip Timelines and the main movie Timeline in which it may reside. This independence means that as long as you establish an instance on the Stage, a movie-clip animation will play all its frames, regardless of where it is. Placing a movie-clip instance in a keyframe of a button symbol makes the movie clip play whenever that particular keyframe is displayed. That is the basis of an animated button.

An animation of a butterfly flapping its wings, for example, may take 10 frames in a movie-clip symbol. Placing an instance of that movie clip on the Stage in a movie that has only one frame will still allow you to see the butterfly flapping its wings (**Figure 4.21**). This functionality is useful for cyclical animations that play no matter what else may be going on in the current Timeline. Blinking eyes, for example, can be a movie clip placed on a character's face. No matter what the character does—whether it's moving or static in the current Timeline—the eyes will blink continuously.

To create a movie clip:

1. From the Insert menu, choose New Symbol.

   The Symbol Properties dialog box appears.

2. Type a descriptive name for your movie-clip symbol, choose Movie Clip as the Behavior, and click OK (**Figure 4.22**).

   You will enter symbol-editing mode.

3. Create the graphics and animation on the movie-clip Timeline (**Figure 4.23**).

4. Return to the main Stage.

   Your movie clip is stored in the library as a symbol, available for you to bring onto the Stage as an instance (**Figure 4.24**).

✔ Tip

- New instances of movie clips begin playing automatically from the first frame, as do instances in different scenes. Imagine that you build a movie-clip animation of a clock whose hand makes a full rotation starting at 12 o'clock. If you place an instance in scene 1 and continue your movie in scene 2, Flash will consider the instance in scene 2 to be new; it will reset the movie-clip animation and begin playing the clock animation at 12 o'clock.

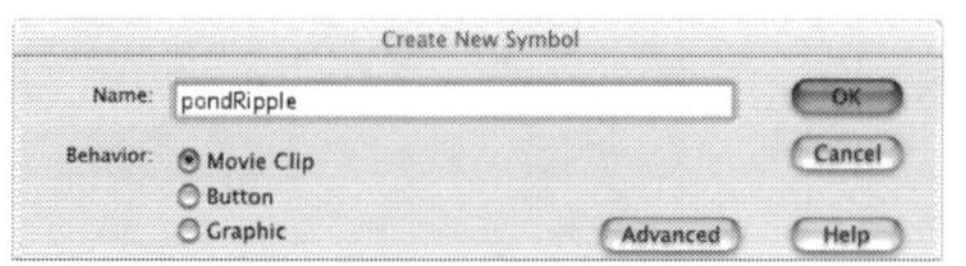

Figure 4.22 Create a new movie-clip symbol by naming it and selecting the behavior.

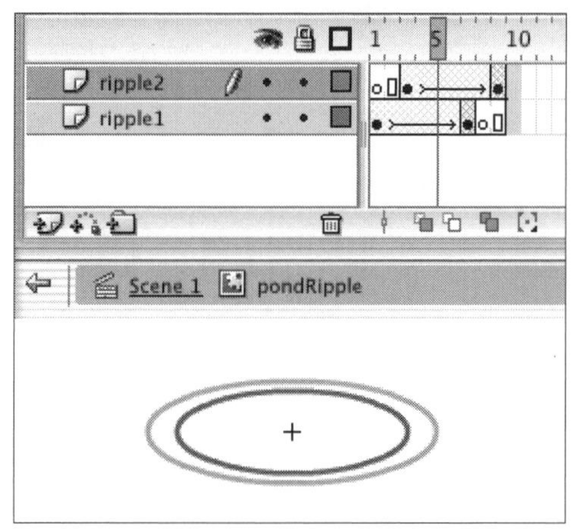

Figure 4.23 The pondRipple movie-clip symbol contains two tweens of an oval getting bigger and gradually fading.

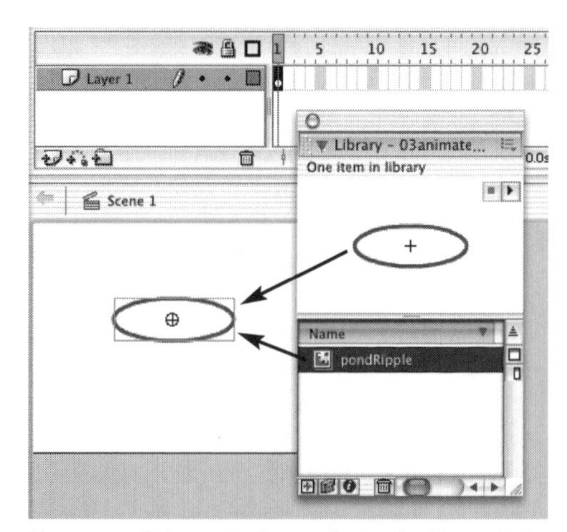

Figure 4.24 Bring an instance of a movie clip symbol onto the Stage by dragging it from the library.

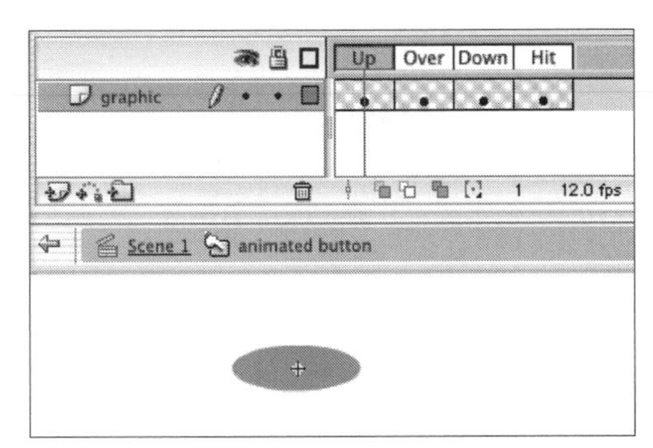

Figure 4.25 A simple button symbol with ovals in all four keyframes.

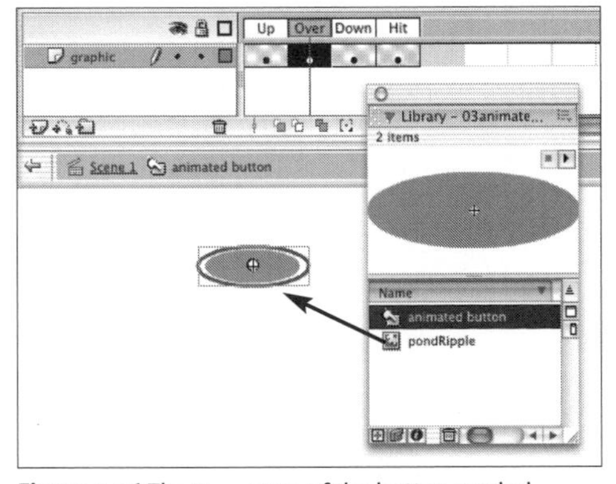

Figure 4.26 The Over state of the button symbol. Place an instance of the pondRipple movie clip in this keyframe to play the pond-ripple animation whenever the pointer moves over the button.

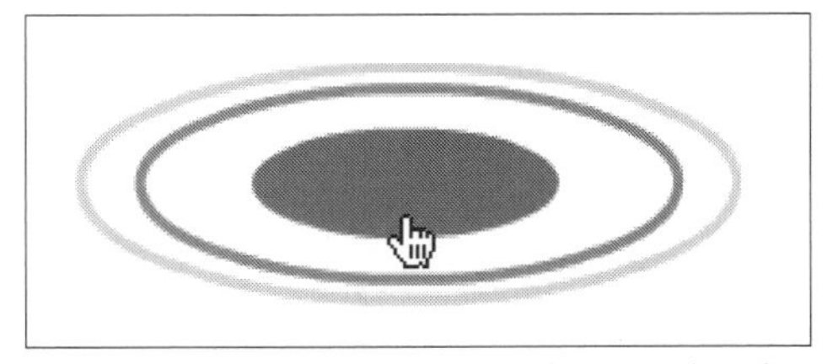

Figure 4.27 The complete animated button. When the pointer passes over the button, the pond-ripple movie clip plays.

To create an animated button:

1. Create a movie-clip symbol that contains an animation, as described in the preceding task.
2. Create a button symbol, and define the four keyframes for the `Up`, `Over`, `Down`, and `Hit` states (**Figure 4.25**).
3. In symbol-editing mode, select the `Up`, `Over`, or `Down` state for your button, depending on when you would like to see the animation.
4. Place an instance of your movie-clip symbol on the Stage inside your button symbol (**Figure 4.26**).
5. Return to the main movie Timeline, and drag an instance of your button to the Stage.
6. From the Control menu, choose Test Movie.

   Your button instance plays the movie-clip animation continuously as your pointer interacts with the button (**Figure 4.27**).

✔ Tip

- Stop the continuous cycling of your movie clip by placing a `stop` action in the last keyframe of your movie-clip symbol. Because movie clips have independent Timelines, they will respond to frame actions. Graphic symbols do not respond to frame actions.

Complex Buttons

You can use a combination of invisible buttons, tweening buttons, animated buttons, and movie clips to create complex buttons such as pull-down menus. The pull-down (or pop-up) menu is a kind of button, common in operating systems and Web interfaces, that is useful for presenting several choices under a single heading. The functionality consists of a single button that expands to show more buttons and collapses when a selection has been made (**Figure 4.28**).

To build your own pull-down menu, the basic strategy is to place buttons inside a movie clip. The buttons control which frames within the movie-clip Timeline to play. Whether the menu is expanded or collapsed is determined within the movie clip. Placing an instance of this movie clip on the Stage allows you to access either the expanded or collapsed state independently of what's happening in your main movie.

Figure 4.28 Typical pull-down menus: the Mac OS File menu (left) and a Web menu from Netscape Navigator (right).

To create a simple pull-down menu:

1. Create a button symbol that will be used for the top menu button, as well as the choices in the expanded list.
2. Fill the `Up`, `Over`, `Down`, and `Hit` keyframes with a filled rectangle (**Figure 4.29**).
3. Create a new movie-clip symbol.
   Enter symbol-editing mode for the movie clip.
4. Insert a new keyframe at a later point in the movie-clip Timeline.
   You now have two keyframes. The first one will contain the collapsed state of your menu, and the second one will contain its expanded state (**Figure 4.30**).

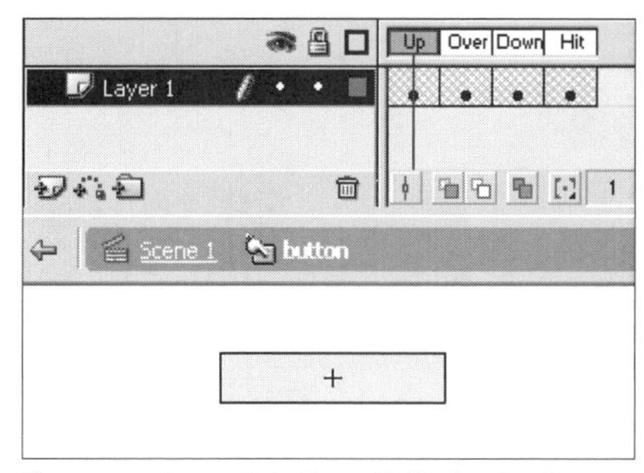

Figure 4.29 A generic button with the four keyframes defined.

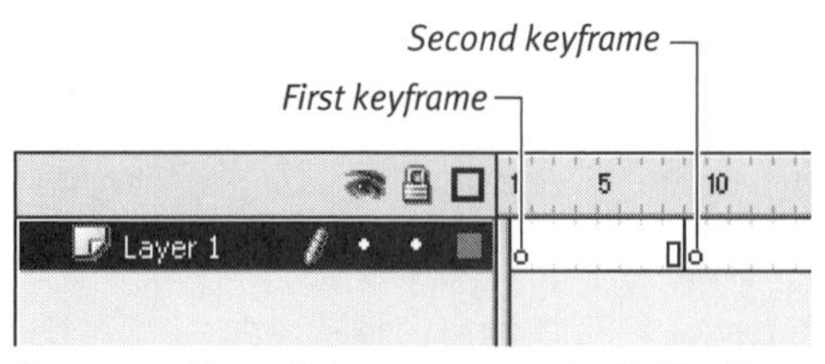

Figure 4.30 The pull-down-menu movie clip Timeline contains two keyframes: one at frame 1, and another at frame 9.

5. Drag one instance of your button symbol into the first keyframe, and add text over the instance to describe the button.

   This is the collapsed state of your menu.

6. Drag several instances of your button symbol into the second keyframe, align them with one another, and add text over these instances to describe the buttons.

   This is the expanded state of your menu (**Figure 4.31**).

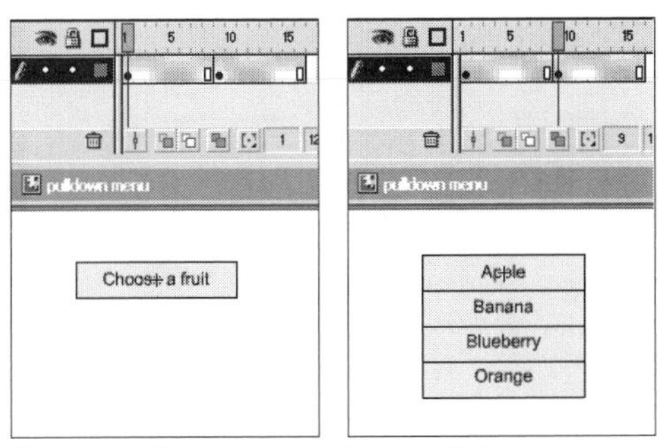

Figure 4.31 The two states of your pull-down menu. The collapsed state is in the first keyframe (left); the expanded state is in the second keyframe (right). The expanded state contains four button instances that represent the menu choices.

7. Add a new layer, and place labels to mark the collapsed and expanded keyframes.

   In the Frame Label field of the Property Inspector, enter `collapsed` for the first keyframe and `expanded` for the second keyframe.

   The labels let you see clearly the collapsed and expanded states of your movie clip, and let you use the `gotoAndStop` action with frame labels instead of frame numbers.

8. Select the instance in the first keyframe.

9. In Normal mode in the Actions panel, choose Actions > Movie Control > goto.

10. From the Type pull-down menu, choose Frame Label.

11. In the Frame field, type `expanded`, and click the Go to and Stop radio button (**Figure 4.32**).

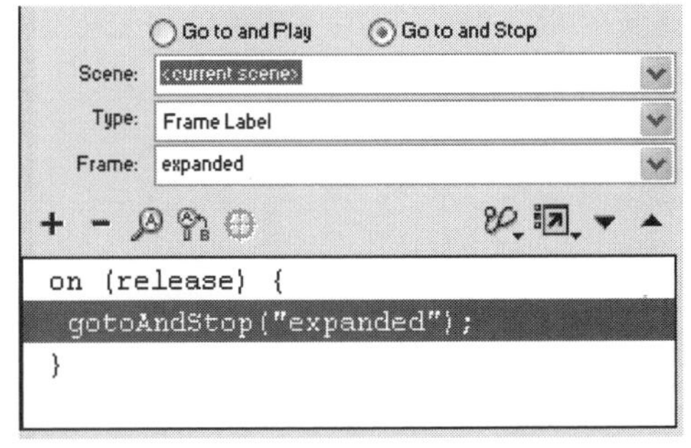

Figure 4.32 This button sends the Flash playhead to the frame labeled expanded and stops there.

12. Select each of the instances in the last keyframe.

13. In the Actions panel, choose Actions > Movie Control > goto.

14. From the Type pull-down menu, choose Frame Label.

15. In the Frame field, type `collapsed`, and click the Go to and Stop radio button (**Figure 4.33**).

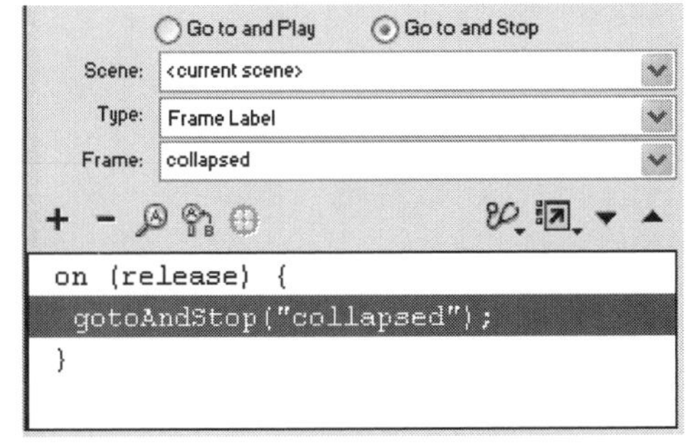

Figure 4.33 This button sends the Flash playhead to the frame labeled collapsed and stops there.

continues on next page

16. Add a third layer, and in the first keyframe, assign the action `stop`.

    Without this `stop` in the first frame of your movie clip, you would see the menu opening and closing repeatedly because of the automatic cycling of movie clips. The `stop` action ensures that the movie clip stays on frame 1 until you click the menu button (**Figure 4.34**).

17. Return to the main movie Timeline, and place an instance of your movie clip on the Stage.

18. From the Control menu, choose Test Movie to see how your pull-down menu works.

    When you click and release the first button, the buttons for your choices appear, because you direct the playhead to go to the expanded keyframe on the movie-clip Timeline. When you click and release one of the buttons in the expanded state, the buttons disappear, returning you to the collapsed keyframe of the movie-clip Timeline. All this happens independently of the main movie Timeline, where the movie-clip instance resides (**Figure 4.35**).

stop action

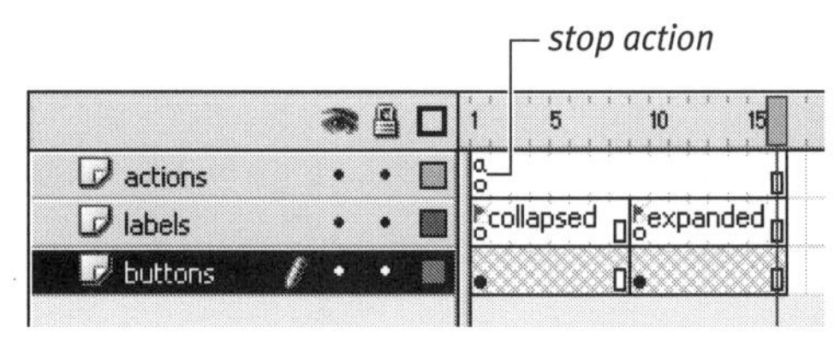

Figure 4.34 The completed movie-clip Timeline for the pull-down menu. A `stop` action is assigned to the first frame in the top layer.

Movie clip in collapsed keyframe

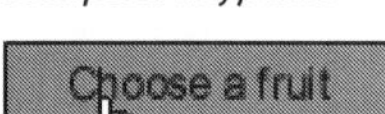

Movie clip in expanded keyframe

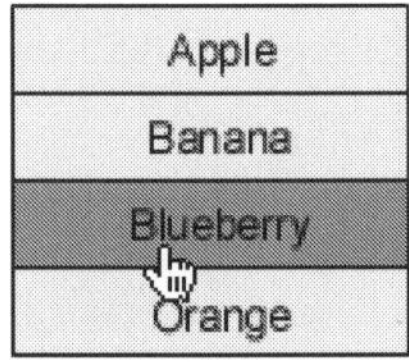

Figure 4.35 The two states of the pull-down menu work independently of the main Timeline.

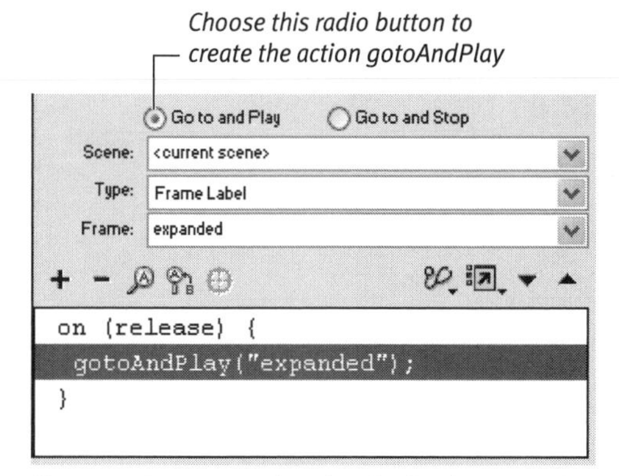

Figure 4.36 Actions assigned to the first button in the collapsed keyframe of the pull-down menu.

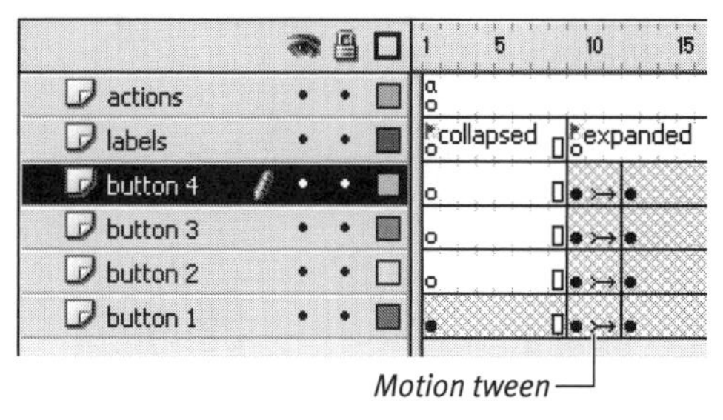

Figure 4.37 The pull-down-menu movie clip. The expanded-menu buttons are separated on different layers so you can motion-tween them.

At this point, you have created a complex button that behaves like a pull-down menu but still does not actually do anything (except modify itself). In Chapter 5, you'll learn how to make Timelines communicate with one another, which enables you to create complex navigation systems.

When you understand the concept behind the simple pull-down menu, you can create more-elaborate ones by adding animation to the transition between the collapsed state and the expanded state. Instead of having the expanded state suddenly pop up, for example, you can create a tween that makes the buttons scroll down gently.

To create an animated pull-down menu:

1. Create a simple pull-down menu, as described in the preceding task.
2. Enter symbol-editing mode for your movie clip.
3. Instead of assigning a `gotoAndStop` action to the button instance in the first keyframe, assign this action:
   ```
   gotoAndPlay("expanded");
   ```
   This action makes the playhead go to the label *expanded* and begin playing (**Figure 4.36**).
4. Create motion tweens for your button instances in the last keyframe (**Figure 4.37**).
5. In the last frame of the movie clip, insert a keyframe, and assign the frame action `stop`.
6. Return to the main movie Timeline, and place an instance of your movie clip on the Stage.
7. From the Control menu, choose Test Movie to see how your pull-down menu works.

   When you click and release the first button, the playhead jumps to the label *expanded* in the movie clip and begins playing, showing the motion tweening of your button choices.

Button-Tracking Options

You can define a button instance in the Property Inspector in one of two ways: Track as Button or Track as Menu Item (**Figure 4.38**). These two tracking options determine whether button instances can receive a button event even after the event has started on a different button instance. The Track as Menu Item option allows this to happen; the Track as Button option does not. The default option, Track as Button, is the typical behavior for buttons; it causes one button event to affect one button instance. More-complex cases, such as pull-down menus, require multiple button instances working together.

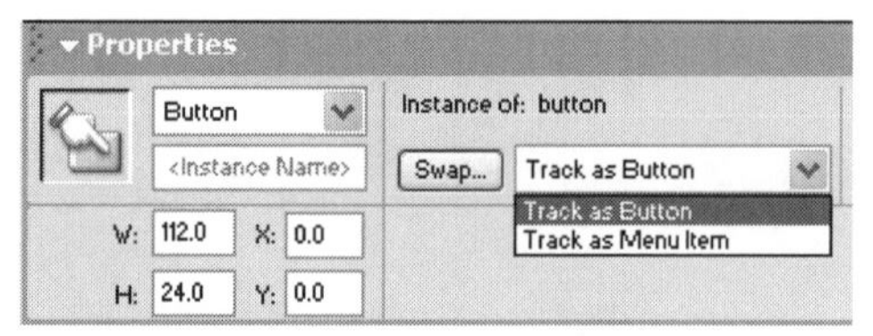

Figure 4.38 The button-tracking options in the Property Inspector.

Imagine that you click and hold down the menu button to see the pop-up choices, drag your mouse to your selection, and then release the mouse button. You need Flash to recognize the `release` event in the expanded menu, even though the `press` event occurred in the collapsed menu for a different button instance (in fact, in a different frame altogether). Choosing Track as Menu Item allows these buttons to receive these events and gives you more flexibility to work with combinations of button events.

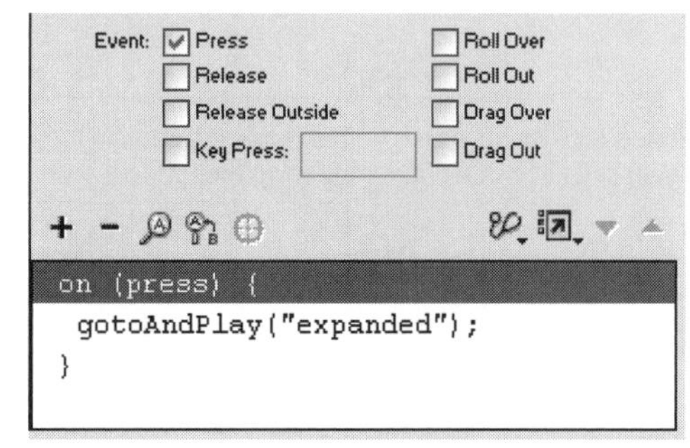

Figure 4.39 The collapsed-menu button is assigned the `press` event.

To set Track as Menu Item with the press event:

1. Create a pull-down menu, as described in the preceding task.
2. Go to symbol-editing mode for the movie clip.
3. Select the button instance in the first keyframe, and change the mouse event to `press` (**Figure 4.39**).

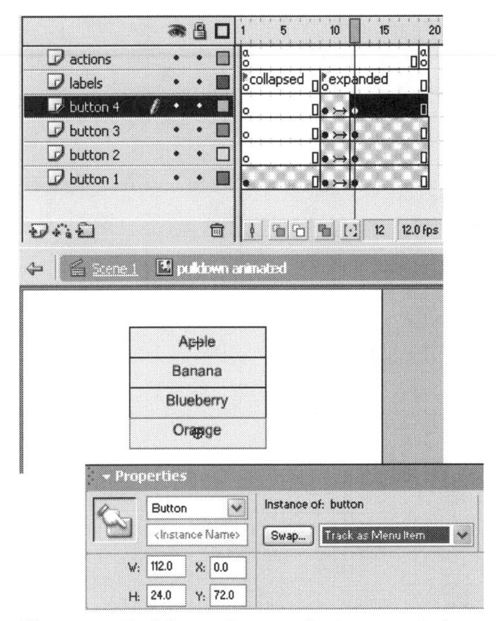

Figure 4.40 Each button instance in the expanded section of the Timeline needs to change to Track as Menu Item, including buttons 1 through 4 in keyframes 9 and 12.

4. Select each button instance in the expanded keyframe.
5. In the Property Inspector, choose Track as Menu Item (**Figure 4.40**).

   The button instances in the expanded menu will now accept a `release` event after the `press` event occurs on a different instance.
6. Return to the main Timeline, and test your movie.

   You now click and hold down the mouse button to keep the menu open.

✔ Tip

- When you set Track as Menu Item for this pull-down menu, the expanded button instances display their Down state as you move your pointer over them. This display occurs because your mouse button is, in fact, pressed, but that event occurred earlier on a different instance.

Refine the pull-down menu with a `dragOver` event so that the menu collapses even if no selection is made. This technique is important to keep pull-down menus expanded only when your viewer is making a choice from the menu.

To set Track as Menu Item with the dragOver event:

1. Continuing with the pull-down menu constructed in the preceding tasks, go to symbol-editing mode for the movie clip.
2. Add a new layer under the existing layers.
3. In the new layer, create an invisible button, and place an instance in a new keyframe corresponding to the expanded keyframe.

   Your invisible-button instance should be slightly larger than the expanded menu (**Figure 4.41**).
4. Select the invisible-button instance.
5. In the Property Inspector, choose the Track as Menu Item option.
6. In the Actions panel, assign these actions:

```
on (dragOver) {
 gotoAndStop ("collapsed");
}
```

7. Return to the main Timeline, and test your movie.

   The invisible-button instance under the expanded menu detects whether the pointer leaves any of the other button instances. If it does, Flash sends the movie clip back to frame 1 and collapses the menu.

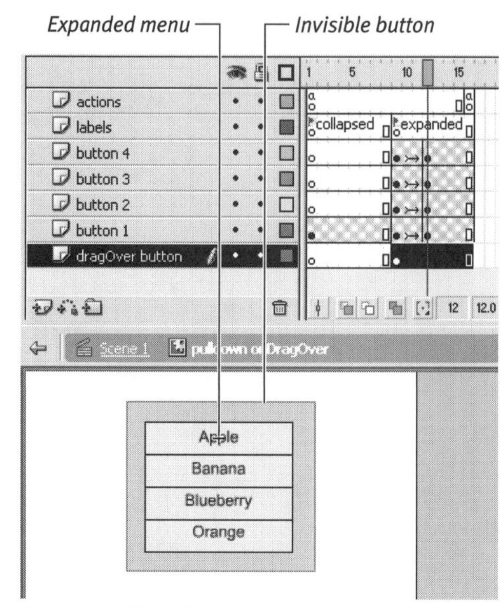

Figure 4.41 When the pointer leaves one of the buttons in the expanded state of the menu, it is dragged over the invisible button that sits in the bottom layer. The `dragOver` event is detected in that button, signaling the playhead to jump to the keyframe labeled `collapsed`.

Button Properties

Because the buttons you create are objects of the Button class, you can control their properties by using dot syntax. Many button properties control the way a button looks (such as its width, height, and rotation), as well as the way a button behaves (such as its button tracking). **Table 4.2** summarizes the properties of the Button object. Many of the properties also control the Movie Clip object (see Chapter 7).

Table 4.2

Button Properties

PROPERTY	VALUE	DESCRIPTION
_alpha	A number from 0 to 100	Specifies the alpha transparency; 0 is transparent, and 100 is opaque.
_visible	True or false	Specifies whether a button can be seen.
_name	A string-literal name	Gets the instance name of the button or sets a new instance name.
_rotation	A number	Specifies the degree of rotation in a clockwise direction from the 12 o'clock position. A value of 45, for example, tips the button to the right.
_width	A number, in pixels	Specifies the horizontal dimension.
_height	A number, in pixels	Specifies the vertical dimension.
_x	A number, in pixels	Specifies the horizontal position of the button's registration point.
_y	A number, in pixels	Specifies the vertical position of the button's registration point.
_xscale	A number	Specifies the percentage of the original button symbol's horizontal dimension.
_yscale	A number	Specifies the percentage of the original button symbol's vertical dimension.
_target	A string	Gets the target path of the button, using slash syntax.
useHandCursor	True or false	Determines whether the pointer changes to a hand icon when hovering over a button.
enabled	True or false	Determines whether the button can receive events.
trackAsMenu	True or false	Determines whether the button will track as a button or track as a menu item.
_focusRect	True or false	Determines whether a yellow rectangle appears around objects as you use the Tab key to select objects.
tabEnabled	True or false	Determines whether the button can receive keyboard focus when you use the Tab key to select objects.
tabIndex	A number	Determines the order of focus when you use the Tab key to select objects. The tab order uses tabIndex in ascending order.

To change a property of a button:

1. Create a button, and drag an instance of it to the Stage.
2. In the Property Inspector, give the button a name.
3. Select the first frame of the main Timeline, and open the Actions panel in Normal mode.
4. Choose Actions > Variables > set variable (Esc + sv).

   A new line appears in the Script pane, with empty Variable and Value fields in the Parameters pane.
5. In the Variable field, enter the name of your button instance.
6. Choose a property by making a choice from the Properties list or by choosing Objects > Movie > Button > Properties.

   If you make a choice from the Properties list, be sure to add a dot to separate the property and the name of your button.

   The Variable field is complete (**Figure 4.42**).
7. In the Value field, enter a value for your property.
8. Check the Expression checkbox for all properties except _name, which takes a string (**Figure 4.43**).

   The completed statement assigns a new value to the property of your button (**Figure 4.44**).

✔ Tip

- You can also choose Actions > Miscellaneous Actions > evaluate to create a dot-syntax expression that assigns a value to a property of a button.

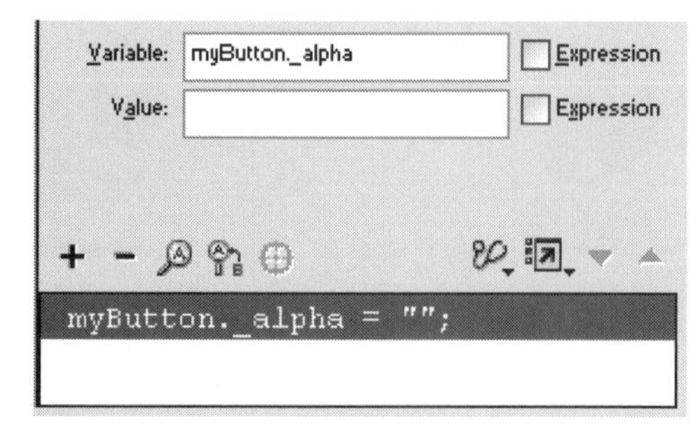

Figure 4.42 The _alpha property of the button called myButton controls its transparency.

Figure 4.43 The value 50 is assigned to the _alpha property of the button called myButton.

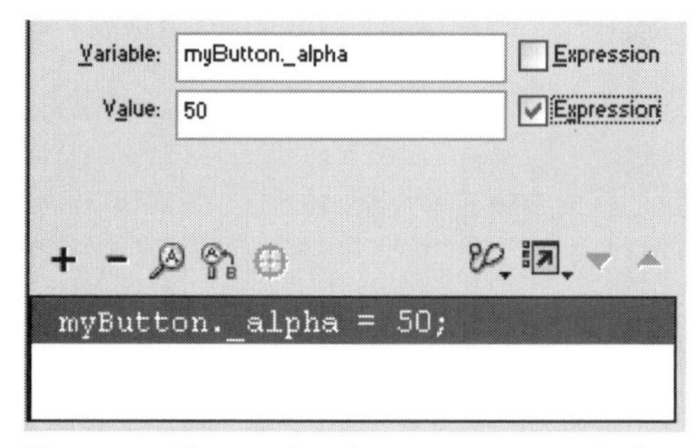

Figure 4.44 The completed statement appears in the Script pane.

BUTTON PROPERTIES

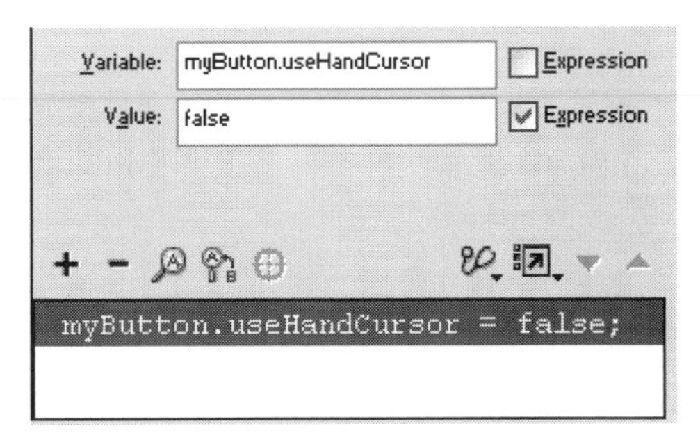

Figure 4.45 The hand pointer is disabled for the button called myButton. Only the arrow pointer will show up.

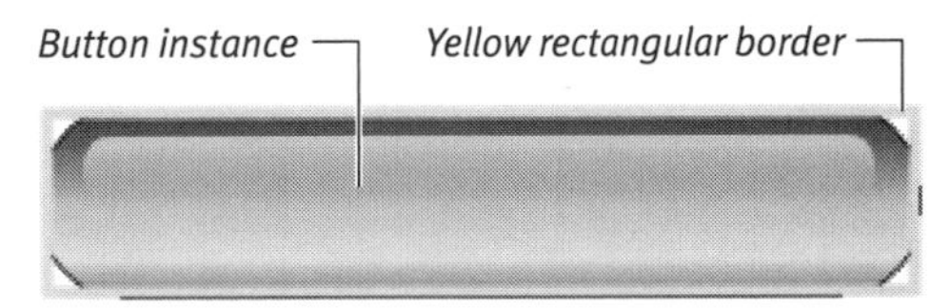

Figure 4.46 When you use the Tab key, buttons show their focus with a yellow rectangular border in their `Over` state.

To disable a button:

- Set the `enabled` property to false.

  If you name your button instance myButton, for example, choose Actions > Variables > set variable or Actions > Miscellaneous Actions > evaluate to create the expression `myButton.enabled = false`.

To disable the hand pointer:

- Set the `useHandCursor` property to `false` (**Figure 4.45**).

  If you name your button instance myButton, for example, choose Actions > Variables > set variable or Actions > Miscellaneous Actions > evaluate to create the expression `myButton.useHandCursor = false`.

Changing button focus with the Tab key

The last several properties listed in Table 4.2–`_focusRect`, `tabEnabled`, and `tabIndex`—deal with controlling the button focus. The *button focus* is a way of selecting a button with the Tab key. When a Flash movie plays within a browser, you can press the Tab key and navigate between buttons, text boxes, and movie clips. The currently focused button displays its `Over` state with a yellow rectangular border (**Figure 4.46**). Pressing the Enter key (or Return key, on the Mac) is equivalent to clicking the focused button. The button property `_focusRect` determines whether the yellow rectangular border is visible. If `_focusRect` is set to `false`, a focused button will display its `Over` state but will not display the yellow rectangular highlight. The property `_tabEnabled`, if set to `false`, will disable a button's capability to receive focus from the Tab key.

continues on next page

The order in which a button, movie clip, or text box receives its focus is determined by its position on the Stage. Objects focus from left to right and then from top to bottom. So if you had a row of buttons at the top of your movie and a column of buttons on the left side below it, the Tab key would focus each of the buttons in the top row first and then focus on each of the buttons in the column (**Figure 4.47**). After the last button is focused, the tab order begins again from the top row.

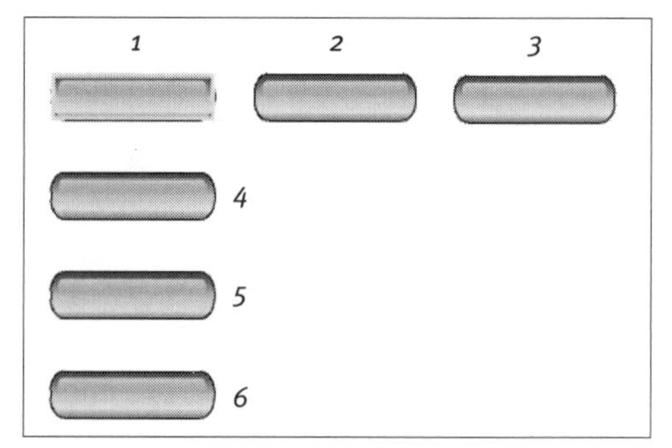

Figure 4.47 The automatic order of button focusing with the Tab key is by position. The numbers show the order in which the buttons will receive focus.

You can set your own tab order with the button property `tabIndex`. Assign a number to the `tabIndex` for each button instance, and Flash will organize the tab order, using the `tabIndex` in ascending order. Take control of the tab order to create more helpful forms, allowing the user to use the Tab and Enter keys to fill out multiple text boxes and click multiple buttons.

To hide the yellow rectangular highlight over focused buttons:

- Set the `_focusRect` property to `false`.

  If you name your button instance myButton, for example, use the expression `myButton._focusRect = false`.

✔ Tip

- You can also hide the yellow rectangular highlight for all your buttons in one statement. Set the `_focusRect` property to `false`, and target the main Timeline by using the keyword `_root`. Use the expression `_root._focusRect = false`.

To disable focusing with the Tab key:

- Set the `tabEnabled` property to `false`.

  If you name your button instance myButton, for example, use the expression `myButton.tabEnabled = false`.

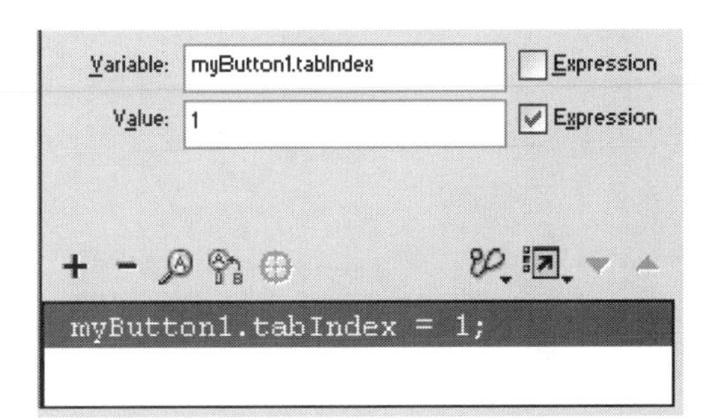

Figure 4.48 The button called myButton1 will receive the first focus with the Tab key.

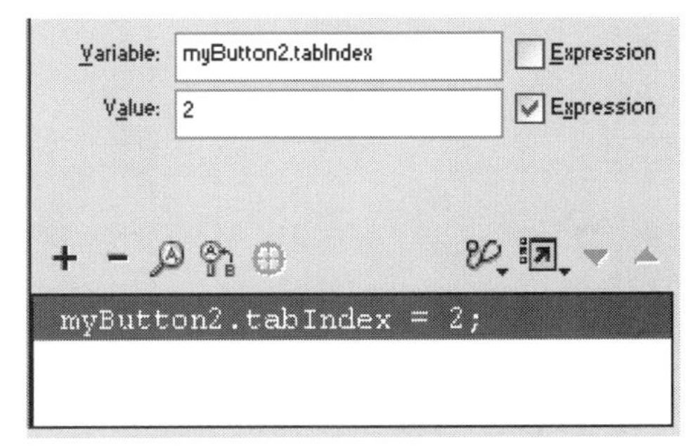

Figure 4.49 The button called myButton2 will receive the second focus with the Tab key.

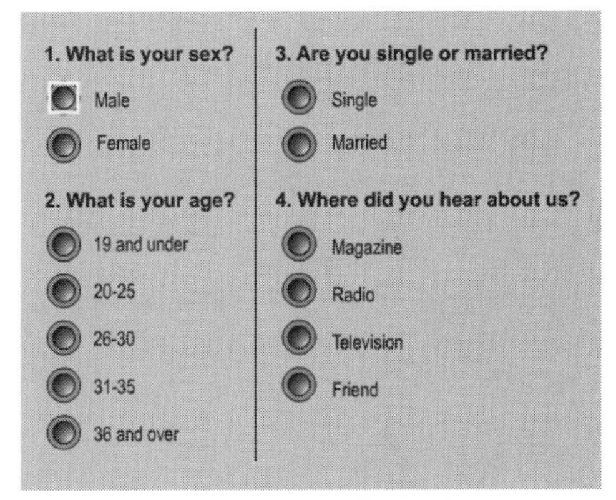

Figure 4.50 Control the order of button focusing to provide easier Tab navigation through forms and questionnaires. This movie focuses buttons in columns to follow the question numbers rather than rely on Flash's automatic ordering.

To change the tab order of button focus:

1. Give each button instance a name in the Property Inspector.
2. Select the first frame of the main Timeline, and open the Actions panel.
3. Choose Actions > Variables > set variable.
4. In the Variable field, enter the name of the button instance you want to receive focus from the Tab key first.
5. Choose Objects > Movie > Button > Properties > tabIndex.
6. In the Value field, type the number 1, and check the Expression checkbox (**Figure 4.48**).

   This button instance will be first in the tab order.
7. Again, choose Actions > Variables > set variable.
8. In the Variable field, type the name of another button instance, and choose the `tabIndex` property.
9. In the Value field, type the number 2, and check the Expression checkbox (**Figure 4.49**).
10. Continue to assign sequential numbers to the `tabIndex` property of your button instances.
11. Choose Publish Preview > Default-(HTML) to view your movie in a browser.

    When you press the Tab key, Flash follows the `tabIndex` in ascending order for button focusing (**Figure 4.50**).

✔ Tip

- Some browsers intercept key presses, so you may have to click the Flash movie in your browser window before you can use the Tab key to focus on buttons.

The Movie Clip As a Button

Movie clips are objects that have their own Timeline in which animations play independently from the main Timeline. This fact lets you put movie clips inside button symbols to create animated buttons, as described earlier in this chapter. But movie clips can also behave like buttons all by themselves. You can assign many of the same event handlers to movie clips that you assign to buttons. Assign an `on(release)` or an `onRelease` event handler to a movie clip, for example, and the event will respond when the viewer clicks the movie-clip instance.

Within the movie-clip Timeline, you can assign the frame labels `_up`, `_over`, and `_down`, and those keyframes will behave like the `Up`, `Over`, and `Down` keyframes of a button symbol (**Figure 4.51**). The `_up` label identifies the state of the movie clip when the pointer is not over the hit area. The `_over` label identifies the state of the movie clip when the pointer is over the hit area. And the `_down` label identifies the state of the movie clip when the pointer is over the hit area and the mouse button is pressed. The hit area of a movie clip is, by default, the shape of the movie clip. You can define a different hit area by assigning another movie clip to the property `hitArea`.

Beware—actions assigned to movie clips behave quite differently from those assigned to buttons. An event handler on a movie clip belongs to that movie clip's Timeline, whereas an event handler on a button belongs to the Timeline on which it is sitting. Consider this simple code:

```
on(release){
   gotoAndStop(10);
}
```

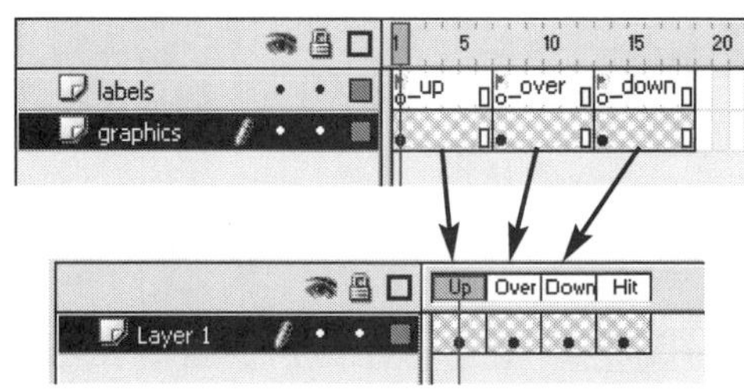

Figure 4.51 The `_up`, `_over`, and `_down` labels of a movie-clip symbol correspond to the `Up`, `Over`, and `Down` keyframes of a button symbol.

Why Have Movie Clips Behave Like Buttons?

Why would you want to use a movie clip as a button? Why not just use a regular button? Movie clips offer you more power and greater flexibility to deal with dynamic situations. Using movie clips as buttons lets you create more complex and sophisticated buttons. Because you can define the hit area of a movie clip yourself, you can shrink, grow, move, and change it dynamically by using ActionScript. You can't do that with buttons. Using movie clips as buttons also makes it easier to combine the methods of movie clips with the events of buttons. The `startDrag()` movie clip method, for example, can be tied to the `on(press)` event handler on a single movie clip.

This doesn't mean that you shouldn't use buttons at all. It does mean you have more options for your creative toolkit.

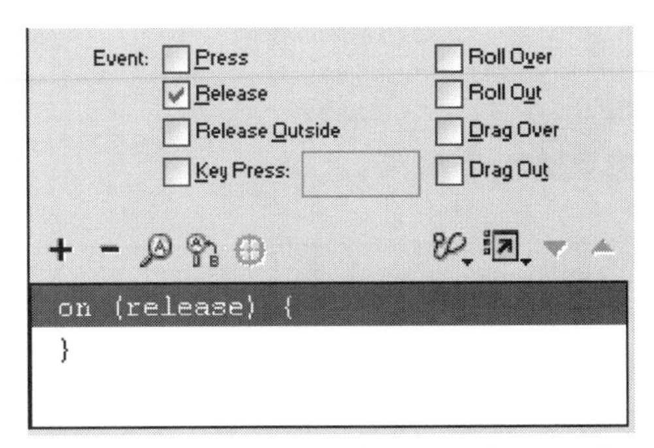

Figure 4.52 The on action can be assigned to a movie clip as well as a button. The Actions panel looks identical for both.

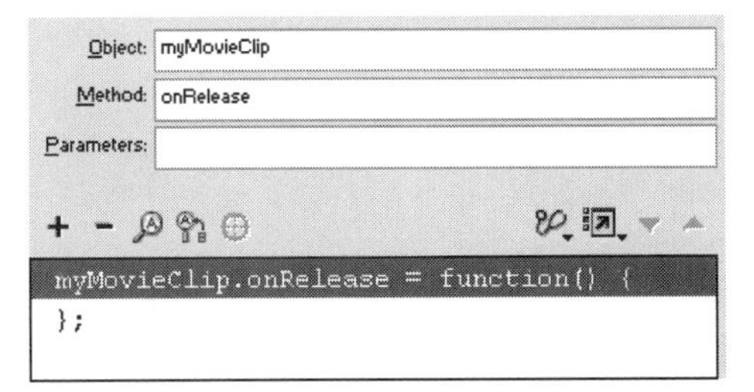

Figure 4.53 The `onRelease` event is assigned to the movie clip called myMovieClip.

When this action is assigned to a movie clip, Flash moves the playhead of the *movie clip's* Timeline to frame 10. When the code is assigned to a regular button, Flash moves the playhead of the *main* Timeline to frame 10. You will learn more about navigating different Timelines in Chapter 5.

To assign a button event handler to a movie clip:

1. Create a movie-clip symbol, and drag an instance of it to the Stage.
2. Select the instance, and open the Actions panel.
3. Choose Actions > Movie Control > on.

   The `on(release)` event handler is assigned to the movie-clip instance.
4. Choose different events in the Parameters pane (**Figure 4.52**).

   or

1. Create a movie-clip symbol, drag an instance of it to the Stage, and give the instance a name in the Property Inspector.
2. Select the first frame of the main Timeline, and open the Actions panel.
3. Choose Objects > Movie > Movie Clip > Events > onRelease.
4. In the Object field, enter the name of your movie-clip instance.

   The `onRelease` event handler is assigned to the movie-clip instance.
5. Choose a different event in the Events category to change the event (**Figure 4.53**).

To define the Up, Over, and Down keyframes of a movie clip:

1. Create a movie-clip symbol, and enter symbol-editing mode for it.
2. Insert a new layer.
3. Choose Insert > Keyframe twice along the Timeline.

   Two more keyframes are created in the movie-clip Timeline (**Figure 4.54**).
4. Select the first keyframe, and type `_up` as its label in the Property Inspector.
5. Select the second keyframe, and type `_over` as its label in the Property Inspector.
6. Select the last keyframe, and type `_down` as its label in the Property Inspector.

   The three keyframes define the `Up`, `Over`, and `Down` states of your movie clip (**Figure 4.55**).
7. In the layer containing your graphics, create keyframes corresponding to the labeled keyframes you just created, and alter your graphics for the `Up`, `Over`, and `Down` states (**Figure 4.56**).
8. Insert another new layer.
9. Select the first frame of the new layer, and open the Actions panel.

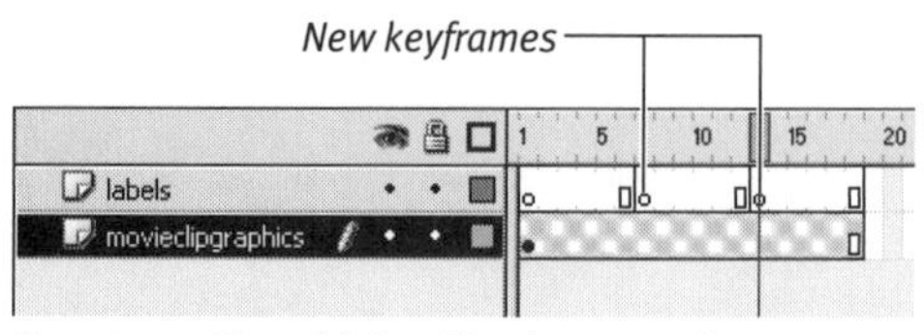

Figure 4.54 Two additional keyframes, at frames 7 and 13, are created in a new layer.

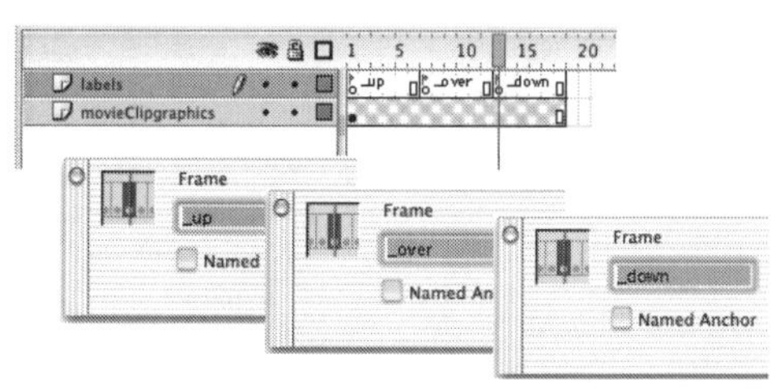

Figure 4.55 Label the three keyframes in the Property Inspector.

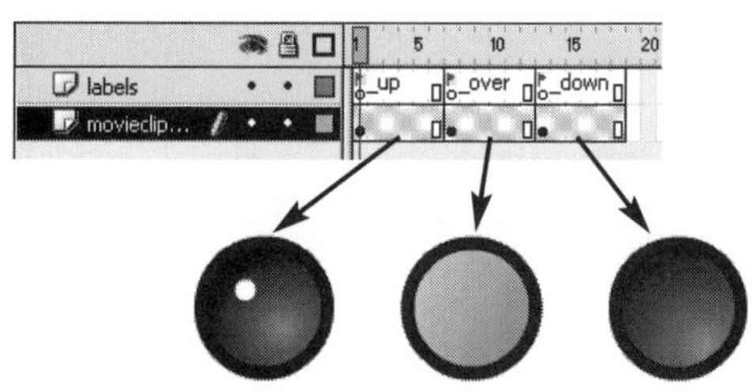

Figure 4.56 The three keyframes contain the `Up`, `Over`, and `Down` states of your movie clip.

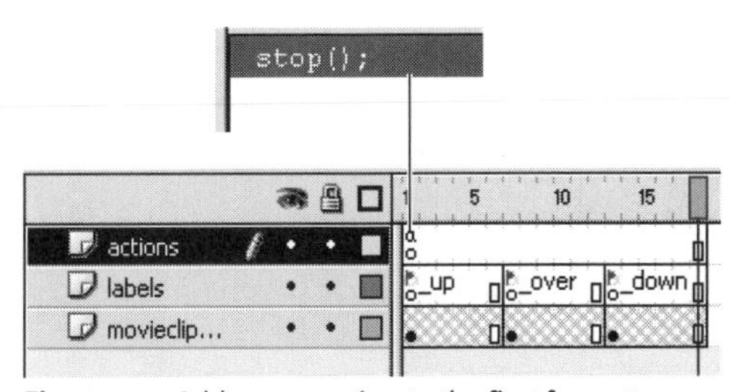

Figure 4.57 Add a `stop` action to the first frame to prevent the movie clip from playing automatically.

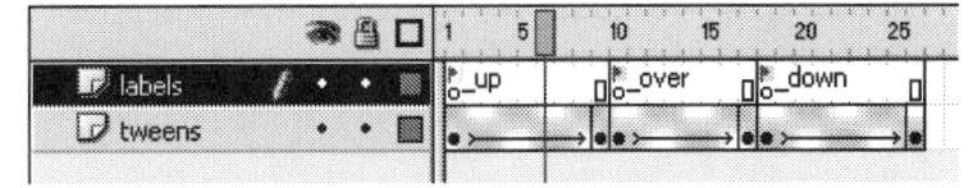

Figure 4.58 Create animations for the `Up`, `Over`, and `Down` states in the `_up`, `_over`, and `_down` keyframes.

10. Choose Actions > Movie Control > stop (Esc + st) (**Figure 4.57**).

    The `stop` action prevents the movie clip from playing automatically.

11. Exit symbol-editing mode.

12. Drag an instance of your movie-clip symbol to the main Stage.

13. Assign a button event handler to your movie-clip instance.

14. Test your movie.

    Flash uses the `_up`, `_over`, and `_down` keyframes for the `Up`, `Over`, and `Down` states of the movie clip. You must have a button event handler assigned to the movie clip to make it behave like a button and recognize the labeled keyframes.

To create an animated button by using a movie clip:

1. Choose Insert > New Symbol.

2. Select Movie Clip, and click OK.

   A new movie-clip symbol is created in your library, and you are put in symbol-editing mode.

3. Insert a new layer, and define the `_up`, `_over`, and `_down` labels for three separate keyframes, as described in the preceding task.

4. In the first layer, create keyframes corresponding to the labeled keyframes you just created.

5. For each keyframe in the first layer, create a motion or shape tween that you want to play for the `Up`, `Over`, and `Down` states of the button (**Figure 4.58**).

6. Insert another new layer, and create keyframes corresponding to the beginning and end of each labeled state.

continues on next page

7. Select each beginning keyframe, and in the Actions panel, choose Actions > Movie Control > play.

   The `play` action will play your tween for the `Up`, `Over`, and `Down` states.

8. Select each ending keyframe, and in the Actions panel, choose Actions > Movie Control > goto.

9. From the Type pull-down menu in the Parameters pane, choose Frame Label.

10. From the Frame pull-down menu, choose the labeled state to which each ending keyframe corresponds.

    For the `Up`, `Over`, and `Down` states, the ending keyframe sends the playhead back to the beginning keyframe, creating a loop for each of your tweens (**Figure 4.59**).

11. Exit symbol-editing mode.

12. Drag an instance of your movie clip to the Stage.

13. Assign a button event handler to your movie-clip instance.

14. Test your movie.

✔ Tip

- You can assign a `stop` action instead of a `goto` action to the end keyframes of the `Up`, `Over`, and `Down` states. Doing so makes the movie clip play the tween only once.

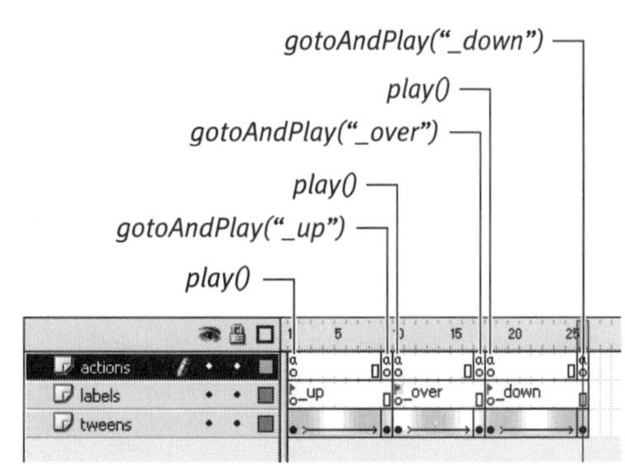

Figure 4.59 The actions in the top layer play and repeat the tweens in each labeled keyframe.

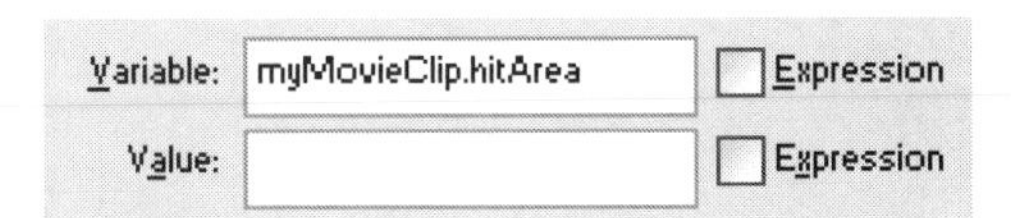

Figure 4.60 The `hitArea` property of a movie clip is the area that responds to the pointer.

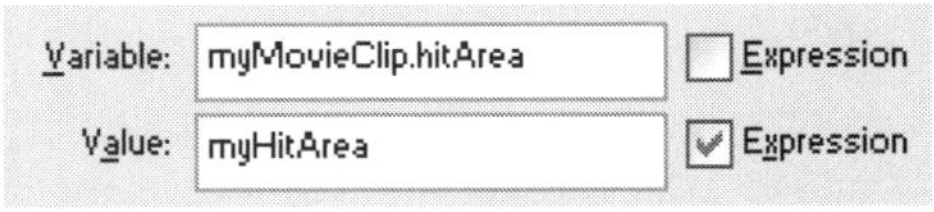

Variable: myMovieClip.hitArea Expression
Value: myHitArea Expression

Figure 4.61 The movie clip called myMovieClip will use the movie clip called myHitArea as its hit area.

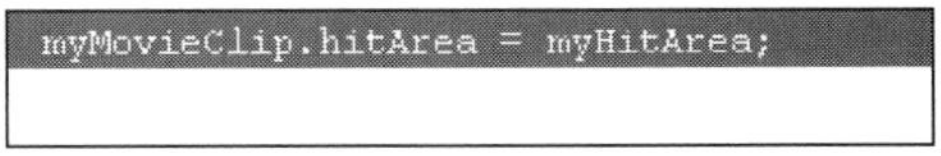

```
myMovieClip.hitArea = myHitArea;
```

Figure 4.62 The completed statement in the Script pane.

To define the hit area of a movie clip:

1. Create a movie-clip symbol, place an instance of it on the Stage, and name it in the Property Inspector.

   This instance is the movie clip to which you will assign a button event handler.

2. Create another movie-clip symbol, place an instance of it on the Stage, and name it in the Property Inspector.

   This instance is the movie clip that will act as the hit area for the first movie clip.

3. Assign a button event handler to the first movie-clip instance.

4. Select the first frame of the main Timeline, and open the Actions panel.

5. Choose Actions > Variables > set variable.

6. In the Variable field, type the name of the first movie-clip instance.

7. Choose Objects > Movie > Movie Clip > Properties > hitArea.

   The `hitArea` property appears in the Variable field after your movie-clip name, separated by a dot (**Figure 4.60**).

8. In the Value field, type the name of the second movie-clip instance, and check the Expression checkbox (**Figure 4.61**).

   The completed expression in the Script pane (**Figure 4.62**) assigns the second movie clip to act as the hit area for the first movie clip, which is behaving like a button.

continues on next page

9. Test your movie.

   The `Up`, `Over`, and `Down` states of your first movie clip respond to the shape of the second movie clip. You can use any movie clip as the hit area for another movie clip, and you can place it anywhere, even inside the movie clip that's acting as a button. As long as you name it, you can target it and assign it to the `hitArea` property of another.

✔ Tip

- The movie clip assigned to the `hitArea` property doesn't need to be visible to work. You can change its alpha transparency in the Property Inspector to be clear, or you can set its `_visible` property to 0. See Chapter 7 for more information on modifying movie-clip properties.

Movie-clip properties that affect button behavior

Like buttons, movie clips have properties that affect its button behavior. **Table 4.3** summarizes these properties. Use these properties as you would for buttons to control whether the movie clip is enabled or whether the hand pointer is visible, or to control the Tab ordering for the focusing of movie clips. Use the `set variable` or the `evaluate` command to assign a value to the property of a movie clip. The following code will disable the hand pointer on a movie clip called myMovieClip that is behaving as a button:

```
myMovieClip.useHandCursor = false
```

Table 4.3

Movie-Clip Properties That Affect Button Behavior

Property	Value	Description
hitArea	Movie clip name	Defines the hit area of a movie clip.
useHandCursor	True or false	Determines whether the pointer changes to a hand icon when hovering over a movie clip.
enabled	True or false	Determines whether the movie clip can receive button events or not.
trackAsMenu	True or false	Determines whether the movie clip will track as a button or track as a menu item.
_focusrect	True or false	Determines whether a yellow rectangle appears around objects as you use the Tab key to select objects.
tabEnabled	True or false	Determines whether the movie clip can receive keyboard focus when you use the Tab key to select objects. Movie clips within a movie clip (its children) may still receive focus even if the parent cannot.
tabIndex	A number	Determines the order of focus when you use the Tab key to select objects. The tabIndex is in ascending order.
tabChilden	True or false	Determines whether movie clips inside movie clips can receive focus when you use the Tab key.
focusEnabled	True or false	Determines whether the movie clip can receive focus even when it is not acting as a button.

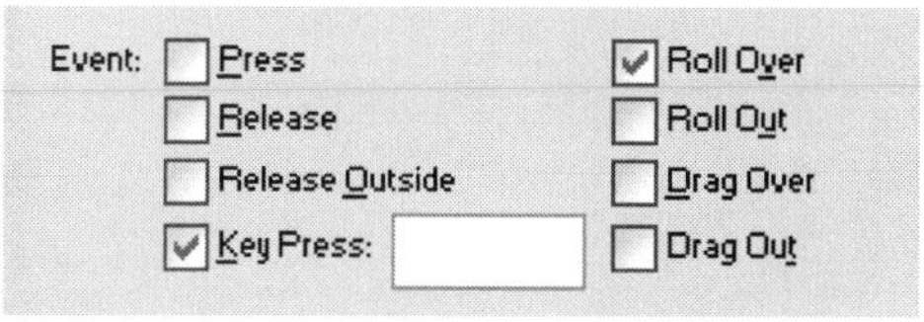

Figure 4.63 The Parameters pane for the on action contains the Key Press checkbox.

Keyboard Detection

The keyboard is just as important an interface device as the mouse, and Flash lets you detect events occurring from single key presses. This arrangement opens the possibility of having navigation based on the keyboard (using the arrow keys or the number keys, for example) or having keyboard shortcuts that duplicate mouse-based navigation schemes. Flash even lets you control live text the viewer types in empty text fields in a movie; these text fields merit a separate discussion in Chapter 10. This section focuses on single or combination keystrokes that trigger things to happen using the `keyPress` event and the Key object.

Key presses using buttons

The `keyPress` event is an option in the Parameters pane of the `on` action (**Figure 4.63**). The `keyPress` event happens when a single key on the keyboard is pressed. To use the `keyPress` event, you need to create a button symbol and place an instance of that button on the Stage. The button instance acts as a container for the event and associated actions, so you should make the button invisible or place the instance just off the Stage so that you can't see it in the final exported .swf file. The `keyPress` event is unusual in that it does not have a parallel event for an anonymous function. You must assign the `keyPress` event to the instance of a button.

To detect a key press with a button:

1. Create an invisible-button symbol, as described earlier in this chapter.
2. Place an instance of the button on or just off the Stage (**Figure 4.64**).
3. Select the instance, and open the Actions panel.
4. Choose Actions > Movie Control > on.

   The `on(release)` event handler appears in the Script pane.
5. In the Parameters pane, uncheck the Release checkbox and check the Key Press checkbox.
6. Choose a specific keyboard character or symbol by typing it in the field next to the Key Press checkbox (**Figure 4.65**).
7. Select an action that will be executed upon detection of the key press (**Figure 4.66**).
8. From the Control menu, choose Test Movie to see how the `keyPress` event responds (**Figure 4.67**).

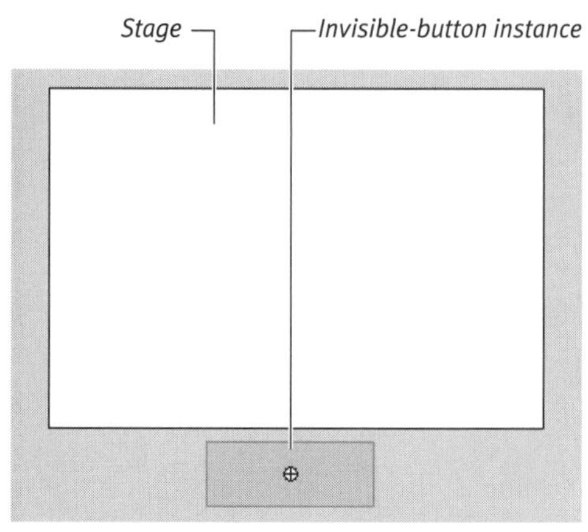

Figure 4.64 Placement of the button instance for a `keyPress` event, just off the Stage.

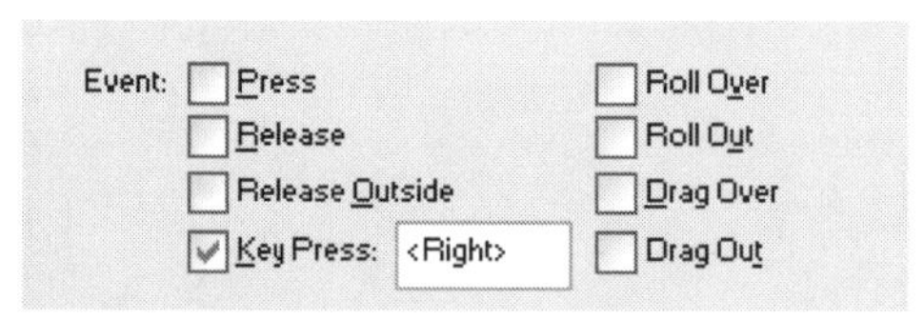

Figure 4.65 The Key Press field lets you enter a single character—in this case, the right arrow.

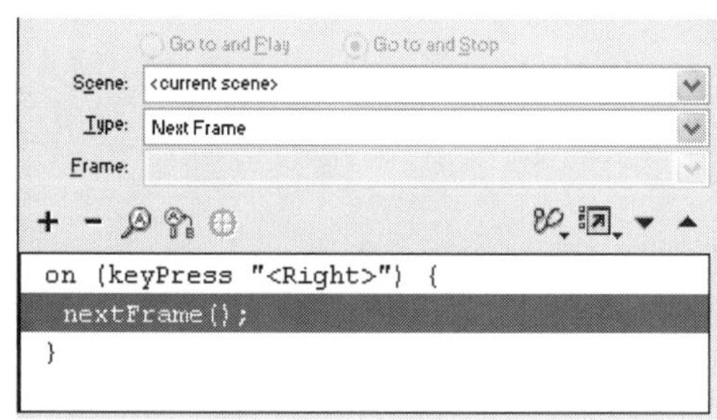

Figure 4.66 The `goto` action is selected, with the type set to Next Frame.

Figure 4.67 This movie has four successive images on the Stage. The `on(keyPress "<right>")` event handler with the response set to `nextFrame` allows you to advance to the next image simply by pressing the right-arrow key.

```
on (keyPress "<Right>") {
  nextFrame();
}
on (keyPress "<Left>") {
}
```

Figure 4.68 A new on action is added after the ending curly brace of the first on action.

```
on (keyPress "<Right>") {
  nextFrame();
}
on (keyPress "<Left>") {
  prevFrame();
}
```

Figure 4.69 Another keyPress event requires two separate on action statements.

To detect multiple key presses with a button:

1. Select the button instance that contains the first `keyPress` event.
2. Open the Actions panel.
3. Add a separate on action (**Figure 4.68**).
4. In the Parameters pane of the second on action, change the event to Key Press, and select another key.
5. Add a different action to be executed upon detection of the second key press (**Figure 4.69**).

   Although multiple keystrokes can be handled with one button instance, each one requires a separate on statement.

To combine a keyPress event with another button event:

1. Create a button symbol that has its Up, Over, Down, and Hit states defined.
2. Place an instance of the button on the Stage.
3. Select the instance, and open the Actions panel.
4. Choose Actions > Movie Control > on.
5. In the Parameters pane for the on action, make sure that the Release checkbox is checked, and also check the Key Press checkbox.
6. Select an action for the event handler.
7. Test your movie (**Figure 4.70**).

   Either clicking the button on the Stage or pressing the key on the keyboard will make your movie perform the action you selected.

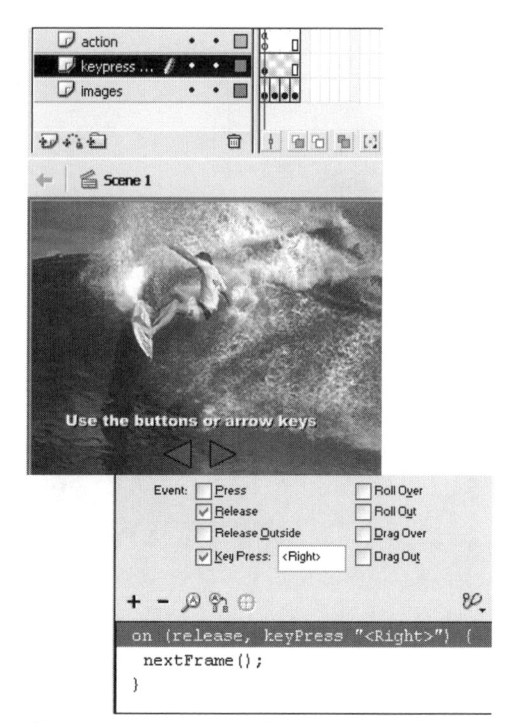

Figure 4.70 The right-arrow button is assigned two events: an on(release) event and an on(keyPress "<right>") event. Either event will advance the movie to the next frame.

✔ Tips

- When your Flash movie plays inside a browser, you must click the movie before any keyPress events can be detected, because the window needs focus.
- The Esc and function keys are not valid keystrokes.
- The keyPress event does not recognize combination keystrokes, such as Option-A and Alt-A. Flash does distinguish between uppercase and lowercase letters, however.

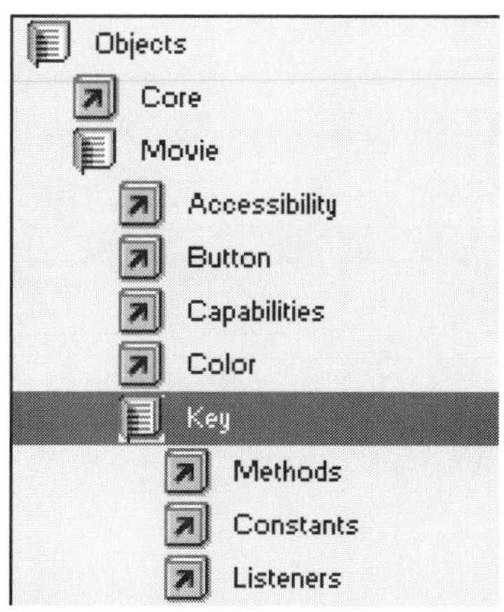

Figure 4.71 The Actions toolbox in the Actions panel contains the actions that handle the Key object.

The Key object

The Key object is an ActionScript class that handles the detection of key presses on the keyboard (**Figure 4.71**). In Chapter 3, you learned that you must instantiate a class before you can use it. The Key object, however, is one of a few objects that don't require a constructor function to create an instance before you can use it. To call one of its methods, you use the object name itself (`Key`).

The Key object has methods that allow you to retrieve the key that was pressed last or to test whether a certain key was pressed. The most common method is `isDown()`, whose parameter is a specific key on the keyboard. This method checks whether that key has been pressed; if so, it returns a value of `true`.

All keys in Flash have a specific number associated with them; this number is known as the *key-code value* (see Appendix B). You use these codes in conjunction with the `isDown()` method to construct a conditional statement that detects the keyboard interaction. `Key.isDown(32)` for example, returns `true` or `false` depending on whether the spacebar (whose key-code value is 32) is pressed.

Fortunately, you don't have to use clumsy numeric key codes all the time. The most common keys are conveniently assigned as properties of the Key object. These properties are constants that you can use in place of the key codes. The statement `Key.isDown(32)`, for example, is the same as `Key.isDown(Key.SPACE)`.

To detect a key press by using the Key object's isDown method:

1. Select the first keyframe in the Timeline, and open the Actions panel in Normal mode.
2. Choose Actions > Conditions/Loops > if.

   The incomplete `if` statement appears in the Script pane, with an empty Condition field in the Parameters pane (**Figure 4.72**).
3. Put your pointer in the empty Condition field in the Parameters pane.
4. Choose Objects > Movie > Key > Methods > isDown.

   The `isDown()` method appears in the Condition field. The key-code parameter is required for this method (**Figure 4.73**).
5. Choose Objects > Movie > Key > Constants > SPACE.

   The property `Key.SPACE` appears as the parameter for the `isDown()` method (**Figure 4.74**).
6. Choose a basic action as the response for this conditional statement (**Figure 4.75**).
7. Insert a new keyframe after the first one, and assign the frame action `gotoAndPlay(1)`.

   This second keyframe loops back to the first so that the conditional statement is checked continuously. This method is the simplest way to have the `if` statement tested (**Figure 4.76**).

We'll explore more-refined ways of dealing with conditionals and action loops later in this chapter. For now, you can use this basic loop to test the `isDown()` method and different Key-object properties.

Figure 4.72 The `if` statement has a condition that it tests. If that condition is true, the actions within the curly braces will be carried out.

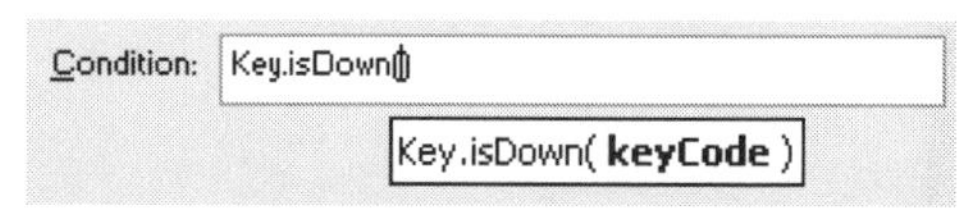

Figure 4.73 The Condition field in the Parameters area of the `if` statement. The method `isDown()` expects a key-code value, as suggested by the code hint.

Condition: Key.isDown(Key.SPACE)

Figure 4.74 The property `key.SPACE` is in place as the key code for the method `isDown()`.

```
if (Key.isDown( Key.SPACE )) {
  gotoAndStop(10);
}
```

Figure 4.75 The Script pane shows the response if the spacebar is pressed.

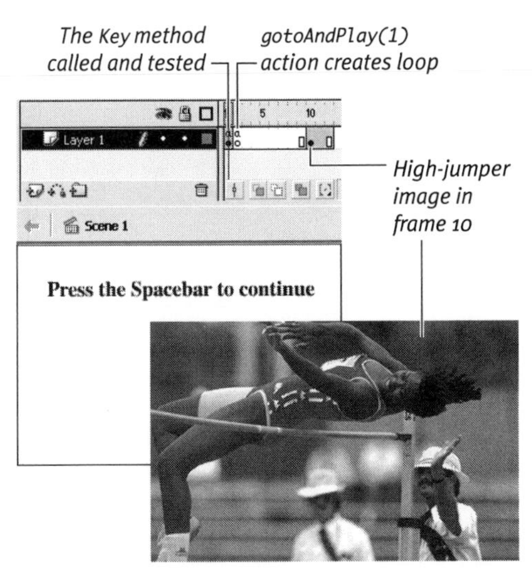

Figure 4.76 This movie loops between frames 1 and 2 until the spacebar is pressed.

Figure 4.77 Add the operator && from the Actions toolbox or simply enter it in the Condition field after the first Key method.

Figure 4.78 The second `isDown()` method follows the first, connected by the && operator.

Condition: Key.isDown(Key.SPACE) && Key.isDown(Key.CONTROL)

Figure 4.79 Both the spacebar and the Ctrl key have to be pressed before this condition can be met.

To create key combinations with the Key object's isDown method:

1. Select the first keyframe from the preceding task, and open the Actions panel in Normal mode.
2. Select the `if` statement.

   The Parameters pane shows the condition, with the Key object's method and property.
3. In the Parameters area, click the Condition field and type a space; choose Operators > Logical Operators > &&; and type another space (**Figure 4.77**).

   The logical operator && joins two statements so that both must be true for the entire statement to be true. You can think of the operator as being the word *and*.
4. In the Condition field after the && operator, choose Objects > Movie > Key > Methods > isDown.

   The `isDown()` method appears in the Condition field after the && operator. Another parameter is required for this method (**Figure 4.78**).
5. Choose Objects > Movie > Key > Constants > CONTROL (**Figure 4.79**).

   The property `key.CONTROL` appears as the parameter for the second `isDown()` method. The conditional will perform the action within its curly braces only if both the spacebar and the Ctrl key are pressed.

Creating listeners for key events

In the preceding section, you had to create a two-frame loop on the main Timeline to test the `isDown()` method. A way to eliminate that loop and detect events of the Key object is to create a listener. A *listener* is an object that you create from the generic Object class. You can create an object called myListener with the statement `myListener = new Object()`. Then you use anonymous functions to assign a key event to your listener. If you want your listener to listen for the `onKeyDown` event and respond by going to frame 10, you create the following function:

```
myListener.onKeyDown = function(){
   gotoAndStop(10);
}
```

When your event is assigned to your listener, you must register your listener with the Key object. Do so by using the `addListener()` method of the Key object, as follows:

```
Key.addListener(myListener)
```

From that point on, whenever the key event occurs, your listener object is notified. The two events that your listener can detect are `onKeyDown` and `onKeyUp`. The `onKeyDown` event happens when a key on the keyboard is pressed. The `onKeyUp` event happens when a key is released.

Listeners are required for the events of the Key, Selection, TextField, and Stage objects. They are available for the Mouse object but not required.

To create a listener for a key event:

1. Select the first frame of the main Timeline, and open the Actions panel.
2. Choose Actions > Variables > set variable.
3. In the Variable field, enter a name for your listener object (**Figure 4.80**).

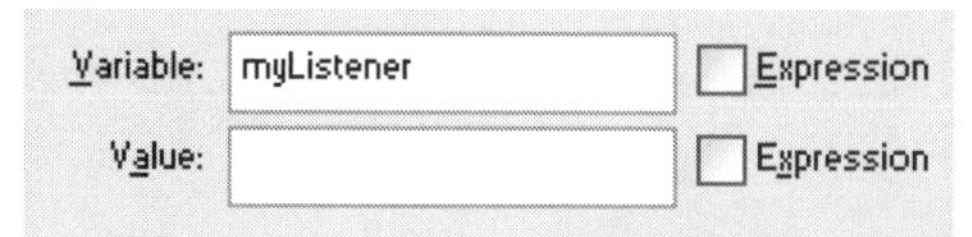

Figure 4.80 The object called myListener will be your listener to detect events of the Key object.

The keyPress Event, the Key Object, and Listeners

Why would you use the Key object and a listener instead of a button with a `keyPress` event? It's really a matter of sophistication versus ease of use and simplicity. Using a listener and the Key object to detect key presses is much more powerful than using a button instance, because you can construct more-complex ActionScript code around the Key object. You can test for key combinations, for example, by requiring two `isDown()` methods to be true before performing certain actions as a response. Using key-code values also opens virtually the entire keyboard. The function keys and the Esc key have key-code values, so they are available to the Key object.

The `keyPress` event is much easier to use, however. If your Flash movie doesn't require much in terms of keyboard interaction, or if you simply want to have a keyboard shortcut accompany a button event, use the `on(keyPress)` action.

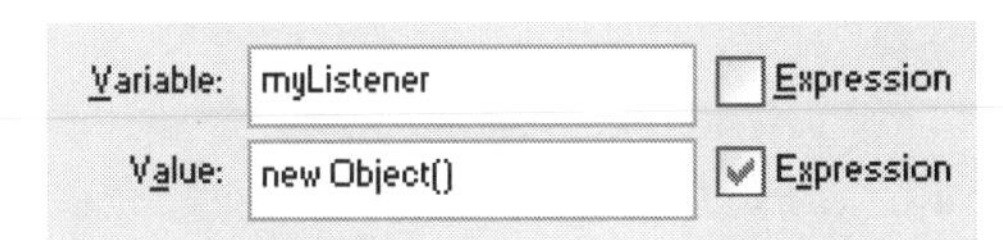

Figure 4.81 The object called myListener is created from the Object class.

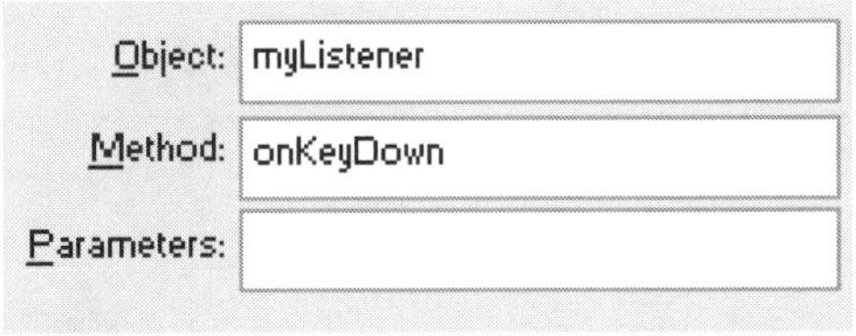

Object: myListener

Method: onKeyDown

Parameters:

Figure 4.82 The onKeyDown event is assigned to your listener.

```
myListener = new Object();
myListener.onKeyDown = function() {
  gotoAndStop(5);
};
```

Figure 4.83 When the listener detects a key being pressed, Flash goes to frame 5 and stops there.

Figure 4.84 The final step in using this listener is registering it to the Key object. The stop action has been added here to keep the movie at frame 1 until the event happens.

4. Put your pointer in the Value field, choose Objects > Core > Object > new Object, and check the Expression checkbox.

   The constructor function `new Object()` appears in the Value field (**Figure 4.81**). Flash instantiates a new generic object, using the name in the Variable field.

5. Choose Objects > Movie > Key > Listeners > onKeyDown.

6. In the Object field, enter the name of your listener that you created in the preceding statement (**Figure 4.82**).

   The onKeyDown event handler for your listener is created.

7. Now choose an action as the response to the onKeyDown event (**Figure 4.83**).

8. Select the closing curly brace of the function.

9. Choose Objects > Movie > Key > Methods > addListener.

10. As the parameter, enter the name of your listener (**Figure 4.84**).

    Your listener is registered and will now listen and respond to the onKeyDown event.

Combine a Key listener with the Key.isDown() method to make Flash respond only to certain key presses. First, your listener detects whether any key is pressed. Then you can use the if statement to test whether a certain key has been pressed.

To listen for a specific key press:

1. Continuing with the preceding task, select the first frame of the Timeline, and open the Actions panel.
2. Delete the gotoAndStop(5) action in the Script pane.
3. Select the onKeyDown event handler in the Script pane.
4. Choose Actions > Conditions/Loops > if.

   The if statement appears within the onKeyDown event handler (**Figure 4.85**).
5. Put your pointer in the Condition field, and choose Objects > Movie > Key > Methods > isDown.

   The isDown() method appears in the Condition field of the if statement.
6. Enter the key code for the specific key you want to detect, or choose a Key property from the category Objects > Movie > Key > Constants (**Figure 4.86**).
7. Add back the gotoAndStop(5) action within the if statement.

   The final script (**Figure 4.87**) creates and registers a listener to detect any key that is pressed with the onKeyDown event. The if statement within the event handler makes sure that there is a response only if a certain key is pressed.

Condition:

```
myListener = new Object();
myListener.onKeyDown = function() {
  if (<not set yet>) {
  }
};
Key.addListener(myListener);
```

Figure 4.85 Add an if statement within the onKeyDown event handler.

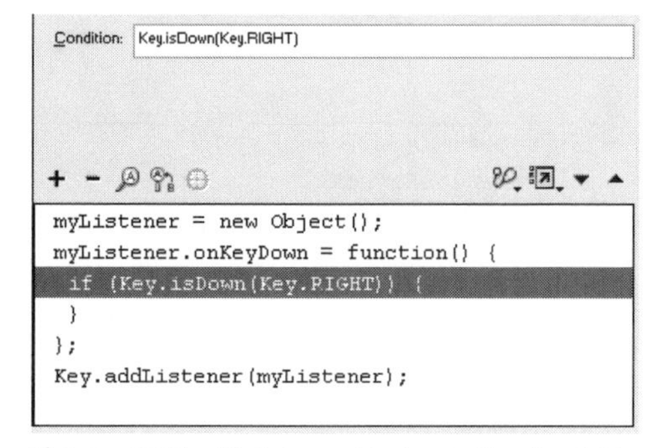

Figure 4.86 The if statement tests whether the right-arrow key is pressed.

```
stop();
myListener = new Object();
myListener.onKeyDown = function() {
  if (Key.isDown(Key.SPACE)) {
    gotoAndStop(5);
  }
};
Key.addListener(myListener);
```

Figure 4.87 The completed script. The stop action has been added at the top to keep the movie at frame 1 until the right-arrow key is pressed.

Mouse Detection

The Mouse object, like the Key object, is one of the few ActionScript classes that do not need to be instantiated before you can use it. Its properties are available immediately, and its methods are called with the object name (`Mouse`). You will learn about its methods and properties in Chapter 7 when you learn more about the movie clip. Here, you'll learn about the mouse events and how to detect them.

You can detect three mouse events: `onMouseMove`, `onMouseDown`, and `onMouseUp`. The `onMouseMove` event happens whenever the user moves the mouse pointer, `onMouseDown` happens when the mouse button is pressed, and `onMouseUp` happens when the mouse button is released. To detect a mouse event, you can assign an anonymous function for it on the main Timeline, like this:

```
_root.onMouseMove = function(){
}
```

(`_root` is an ActionScript word that refers to the main Timeline.)

Another way is to create a listener, just as you do to detect key events. Create a listener from the generic Object class. Assign a mouse-event handler to the listener and then register your listener with the Mouse object, using the method `Mouse.addListener()`.

To detect mouse movement:

1. Select the first frame of the main Timeline, and open the Actions panel.
2. Choose Objects > Movie > Mouse > Listeners > onMouseMove.
3. In the Object field of the Parameters pane, enter `_root` to refer to the main Timeline.

   The `onMouseMove` event handler is assigned to the main Timeline (**Figure 4.88**).
4. Choose an action as a response to this event.

   Whenever the mouse moves, Flash performs the actions listed within the `onMouseMove` event handler (**Figure 4.89**).
5. Choose Actions > Movie Clip Control > updateAfterEvent.

   The `updateAfterEvent` action forces Flash to refresh the display. For certain events, such as `onMouseMove`, `updateAfterEvent` makes certain that the graphics are updated according to the event, not the frame rate.

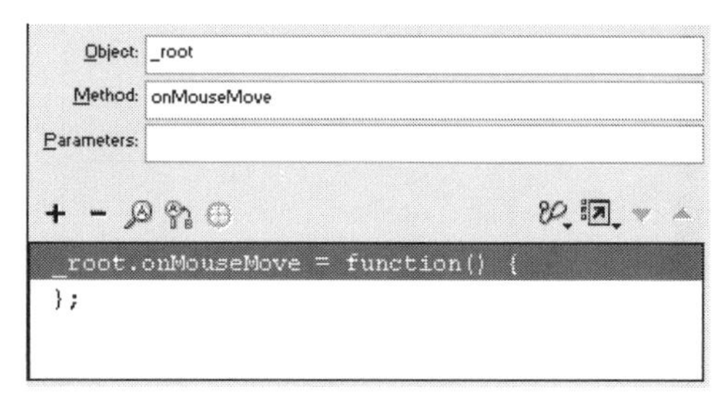

Figure 4.88 An onMouseMove event handler.

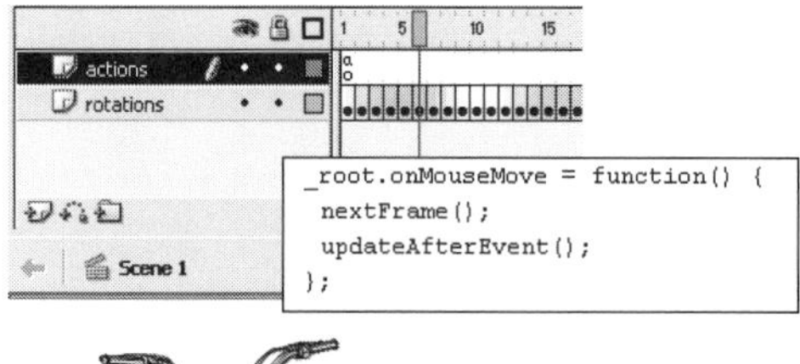

Figure 4.89 This movie contains a frame-by-frame animation of a three-wheeler that rotates. Any time the mouse pointer moves, Flash advances to the next frame.

To create a listener to detect a mouse press:

1. Select the first frame of the main Timeline, and open the Actions panel.
2. Choose Actions > Variables > set variable.
3. In the Variable field, enter a name for your listener object (**Figure 4.90**).

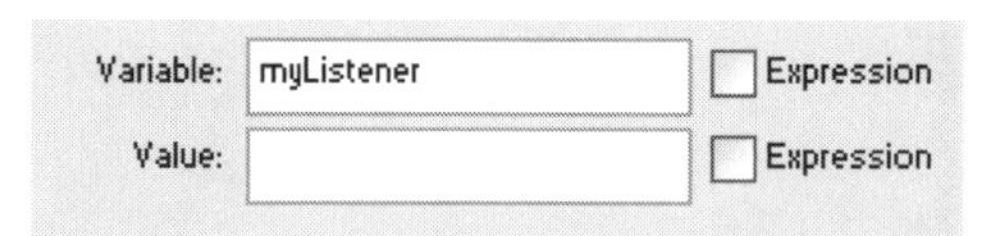

Figure 4.90 The object called myListener will be your listener to detect events of the Mouse object.

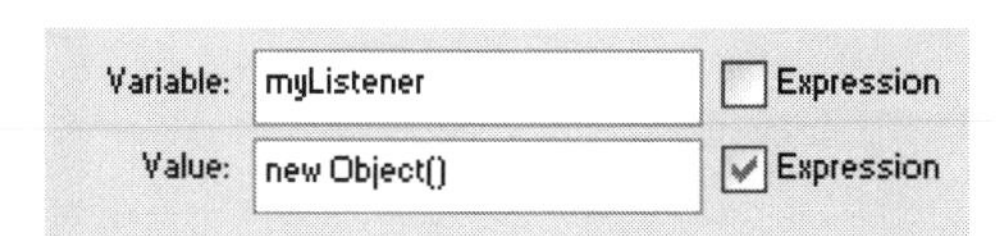

Figure 4.91 The object called myListener is created from the Object class.

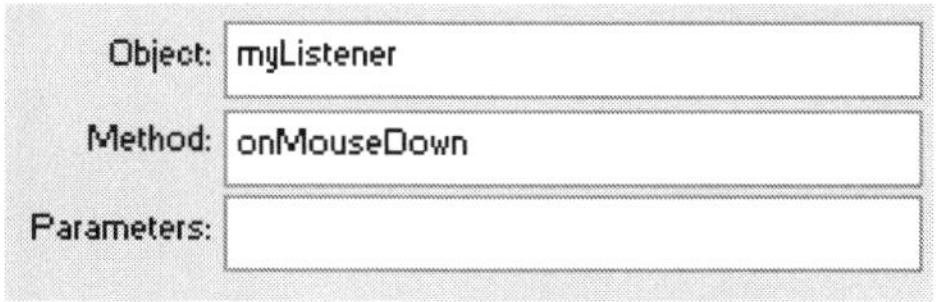

Object: myListener

Method: onMouseDown

Parameters:

Figure 4.92 The onMouseDown event is assigned to your listener.

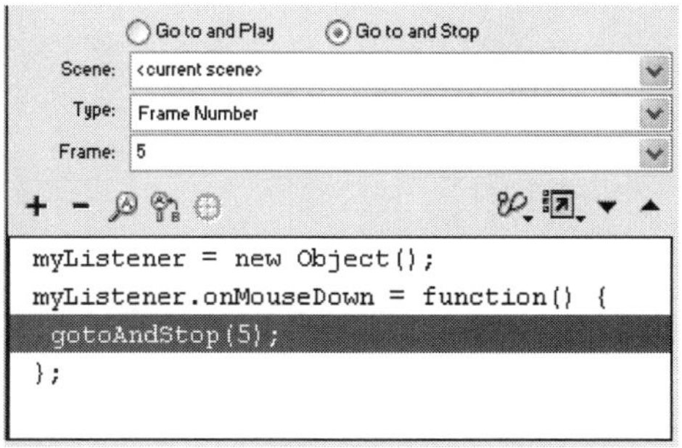

Go to and Play
Go to and Stop

Scene: <current scene>

Type: Frame Number

Frame: 5

```
myListener = new Object();
myListener.onMouseDown = function() {
  gotoAndStop(5);
};
```

Figure 4.93 When the listener detects the mouse button being pressed, Flash goes to frame 5 and stops there.

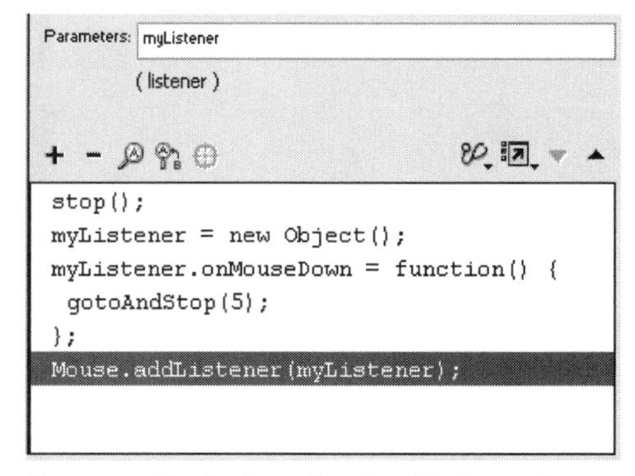

Figure 4.94 The final step in using this listener is registering it to the Mouse object. The stop action has been added here to keep the movie at frame 1 until the event happens.

4. Put your pointer in the Value field, choose Objects > Core > Object > new Object, and check the Expression checkbox.

   The constructor function `new Object()` appears in the Value field (**Figure 4.91**). Flash instantiates a new generic object, using the name in the Variable field.

5. Choose Objects > Movie > Mouse > Listeners > onMouseDown.

6. In the Object field, enter the name of the listener that you created in the preceding statement (**Figure 4.92**).

   The `onMouseDown` event handler for your listener is created.

7. Now choose an action as the response to the `onMouseDown` event (**Figure 4.93**).

8. Select the closing curly brace of the function.

9. Choose Objects > Movie > Mouse > Methods > addListener.

10. For the parameter, enter the name of your listener (**Figure 4.94**).

    Your listener is registered and will now listen and respond to the `onMouseDown` event.

Clip Events

The Movie Clip object, like the Mouse, Key, and Button objects, has its own set of events, which are referred to simply as *clip events*. Many clip events overlap the events of the Key object and the Mouse object; others are unique to the movie clip (**Figure 4.95**). You can assign clip event handlers to the movie-clip instance with the action `onClipEvent` (Actions > Movie Clip Control > onClipEvent (Esc+oc)).

The `onClipEvent` action for movie clips is analogous to the `on` action for buttons: The `onClipEvent` action assigns clip events to movie-clip instances, whereas the `on` action assigns button events to button instances. One notable difference, however, is that actions assigned to an `onClipEvent` pertain to the movie-clip Timeline, not to the main Timeline. You will learn more about navigating different Timelines in Chapter 5.

As you can with buttons, you can assign a clip event handler with anonymous functions on the main Timeline. Give your movie-clip instance a name in the Property Inspector and then assign a function to a clip event, as follows:

```
myMovieClip.onMouseMove = function() {
}
```

myMovieClip is the name of your movie-clip instance, and `onMouseMove` is the clip event.

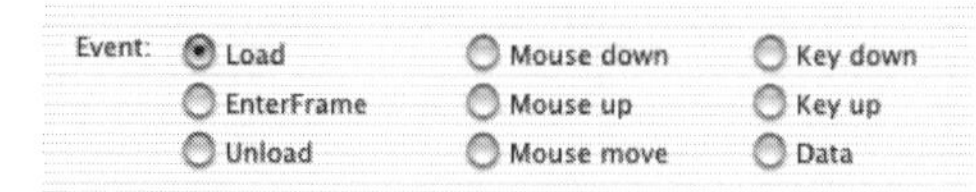

Figure 4.95 The clip events in the Parameters pane of the `onClipEvent` action. Mouse Down, Mouse Up, and Mouse Move are the same events as those for the Mouse object. Key Up and Key Down are the same events as those for the Key object, although they can be used in a slightly different manner.

When you use anonymous functions to assign clip events, sometimes you can specify the main Timeline with the word _root as the name of the movie clip. You can assign the clip event onMouseMove to the main Timeline instead of a movie clip, as follows:

```
_root.onMouseMove = function() {
}
```

Notice that this script is indistinguishable from the event handler for the Mouse object.

The clip events onKeyUp and onKeyDown are handled differently, depending on whether you assign them to a movie-clip instance or on the main Timeline with an anonymous function. When either of these events is assigned with an anonymous function, they must be assigned to a listener and registered to the Key object (see "Creating listeners for key events" earlier in this chapter). If events are assigned to a movie clip with the onClipEvent action, no listener is needed.

For easy reference, **Table 4.4** contains a list of clip events and some information about them.

Table 4.4

Clip Events

Clip Event	Interaction
onClipEvent (mouseDown)/onMouseDown	When the left mouse button is pressed
onClipEvent (mouseUp)/onMouseUp	When the left mouse button is released
onClipEvent (mouseMove)/onMouseMove	When the mouse is moved
onClipEvent (keyDown)/onKeyDown	When any key is pressed
onClipEvent (keyUp)/onKeyUp	When any key is released
onClipEvent (enterFrame)/onEnterFrame	When each frame of the movie clip is updated; triggered at the frame rate of the movie
onClipEvent (load)/onLoad	When the movie clip is instantiated and first appears in the Timeline
onClipEvent (unload)/onUnload	When the first frame after the movie-clip instance is removed from the Timeline
onClipEvent (data)/onData	When either external data or external .swf movies are loaded into the movie clip with the action loadVariables or loadMovie

Clip events are used in many ways. In this example, the keyDown clip event is coupled with a conditional statement that tests which key has been pressed.

To detect a key press with onClipEvent:

1. Create a movie-clip symbol, and drag an instance of it from the library to the Stage.
2. Select the instance, and open the Actions panel.
3. Choose Actions > Movie Clip Control > onClipEvent.
4. In the Parameters pane, choose Key Down (**Figure 4.96**).
5. Choose Actions > Conditions/Loops > if.
6. Put your pointer in the Condition field, and choose Objects > Movie > Key > Methods > getCode.

   The `getCode()` method appears in the Condition field of the `if` statement.
7. After the `getCode()` method, enter two equal signs and the code key for the specific key you want to detect, or choose a Key property from the category Objects > Movie > Key > Constants.

   The `getCode()` method of the Key object retrieves the key code of the last key pressed. Flash checks to see whether that key matches the one you specify after the double equal signs. The double equal signs (==) tell Flash to compare equality (**Figure 4.97**).

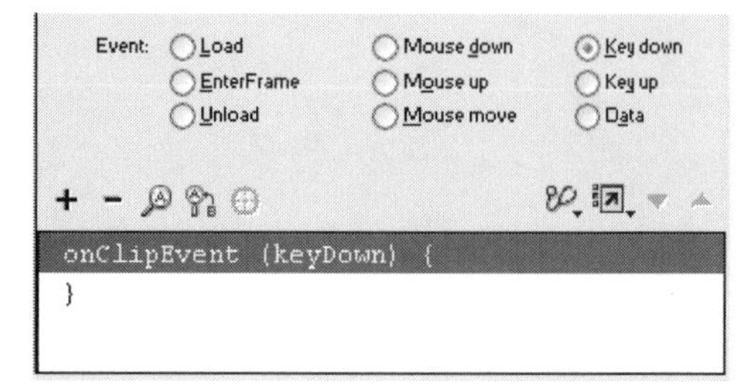

Figure 4.96 The `onClipEvent(keyDown)` clip-event handler.

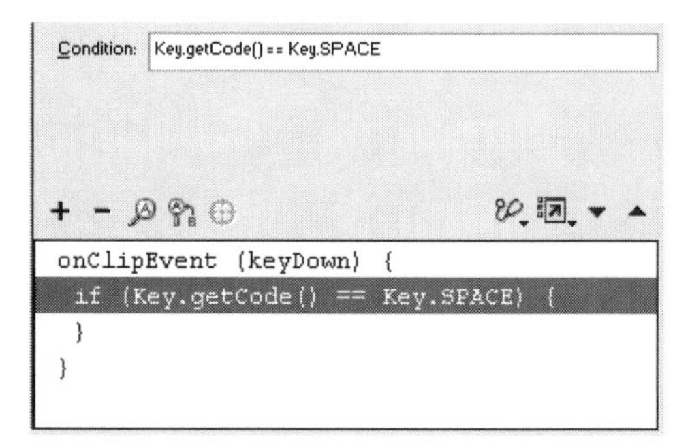

Figure 4.97 When a key is pressed, Flash checks whether it was the spacebar.

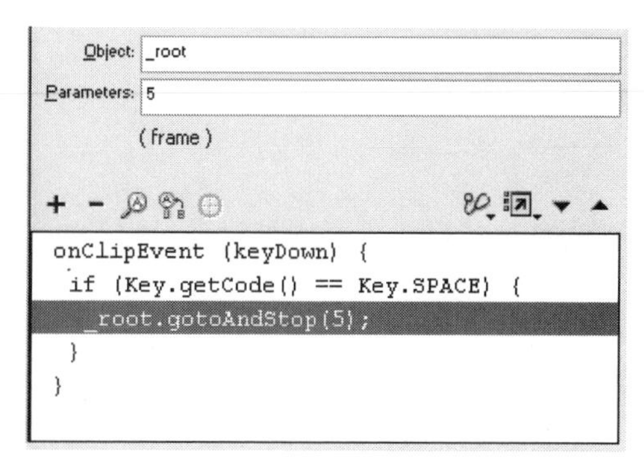

Figure 4.98 Choose the gotoAndStop() method from Objects > Movie > Movie Clip > Methods. You can target the main Timeline with the word _root, so that Flash moves the playhead of the main Timeline to frame 5.

8. Choose an action as the consequence of this `if` statement.

   For this example, choose Objects > Movie > Movie Clip > Methods > gotoAndStop. In the Object field of the Parameters pane, type `_root`, and in the Parameters field, type 5 (**Figure 4.98**).

   Because the `onClipEvent` action assigns code to the movie clip, all its actions pertain to the movie-clip Timeline, not the main Timeline. So you use the word `_root` to make the `gotoAndStop` action target the main Timeline. You'll learn more about targeting different Timelines in Chapter 5.

9. Test your movie.

   The `onClipEvent` action assigned to your movie clip detects when a key is pressed. The `if` statement checks whether the key is the spacebar and makes Flash go to a different frame of the main Timeline.

Creating Continuous Actions with enterFrame

So far, you have learned ways to execute an action in response to events that happen when the user does something. But on many occasions, you'll want to perform an action continuously. An `if` statement, for example, often needs to be performed continuously to check whether conditions in the movie have changed. And often, the command that changes the position of a movie clip needs to be performed continuously to animate it across the Stage.

The clip event `enterFrame` is an event that happens continuously. The clip event happens at the frame rate of the movie, so if the frame rate is set to 12 frames per second, the `enterFrame` event is triggered 12 times per second. Even when the `enterFrame` event is assigned to a movie clip whose Timeline is stopped, the event will continue to happen. This setup is an ideal way to make actions run on automatic pilot; they will run as soon as the `enterFrame` event handler is established and stop only when the movie clip to which the `enterFrame` is attached is removed.

To create continuous actions with enterFrame:

1. Select the first frame of the main Timeline, and open the Actions panel.
2. Choose Objects > Movie > Movie Clip > Events > onEnterFrame.
3. In the Object field, type `_root`.

   The word `_root` refers to the main Timeline (**Figure 4.99**).
4. Choose Actions >Conditions/Loops > if.

   The Condition field appears in the Parameters pane.

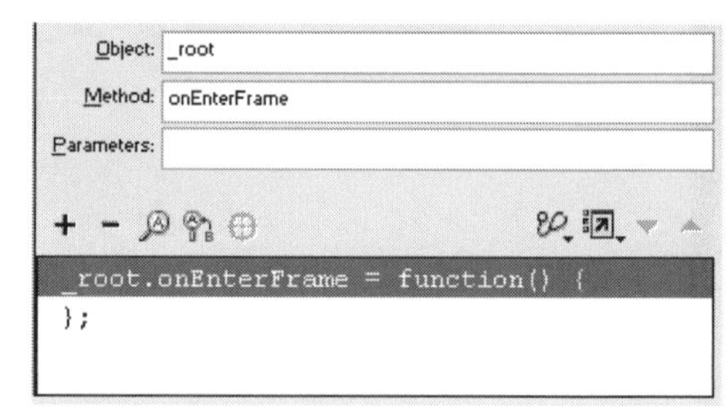

Figure 4.99 The `enterFrame` clip-event handler.

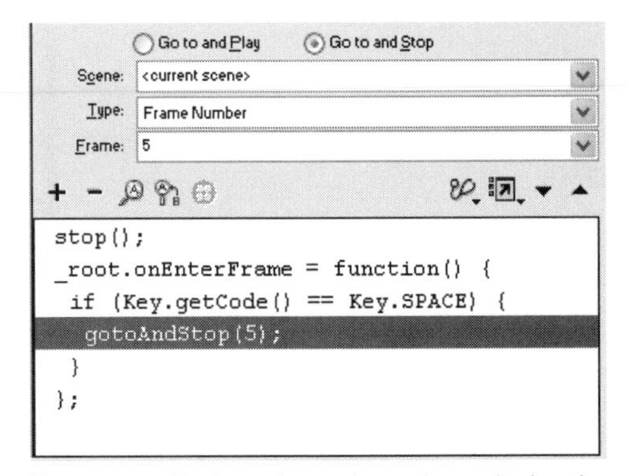

Figure 4.100 Flash continuously monitors whether the last key pressed was the spacebar. If so, it moves the playhead to frame 5 and stops there.

5. In the Condition field, enter this statement:

   `Key.getCode()==Key.SPACE`

   This statement is the same conditional statement that you constructed in the preceding task. In this case, however, Flash does not wait for a `keyDown` event before testing this condition. Here, Flash tests the condition each time a frame in the main Timeline updates. This test happens continuously, even if the Timeline is stopped.

6. Choose an action as the consequence of this `if` statement (**Figure 4.100**).

✔ Tip

- Here's a preview of the kind of dynamic updates you can do with the `enterFrame` clip event by combining it with movie-clip properties. Replace the `if` statement in the preceding task with the expression `ball._xscale += 1`, using the `evaluate` command. Now add a movie-clip instance to the Stage, and name it ball in the Property Inspector. The Script pane should look like this:

```
_root.onEnterFrame = function() {
   ball._xscale += 1;
}
```

  The statement `ball._xscale += 1` adds 1 percent to the horizontal width of your movie clip. Because the action is triggered continuously by the `enterFrame` event, the movie clip keeps growing.

Creating Continuous Actions with setInterval

The enterFrame event, although easy to use and effective for creating most continuous actions, is limited to the frame rate of your Flash movie. If you want to perform an action on a continuous basis but to do so at specific intervals, you should use the action setInterval instead.

You can use the setInterval action in two basic ways. In the first way, you provide two parameters. The first parameter is a function that is invoked on a continuous basis; the second parameter is the interval (in milliseconds) that separates the function invocation. So if you want the function called blinkingLight to be called every 5 seconds, you can write the statement setInterval (blinkingLight, 5000). Then you then must define the blinkingLight function.

The second way to use setInterval is to provide an object, its method, and an interval. Instead of calling a function at a periodic interval, Flash calls the method of the object at a periodic interval. This method can be one that already exists or one that you define yourself. You can call the nextFrame() method on the main Timeline every second with this statement:

```
setInterval (_root, "nextFrame", 1000)
```

Notice that the method name is in quotation marks.

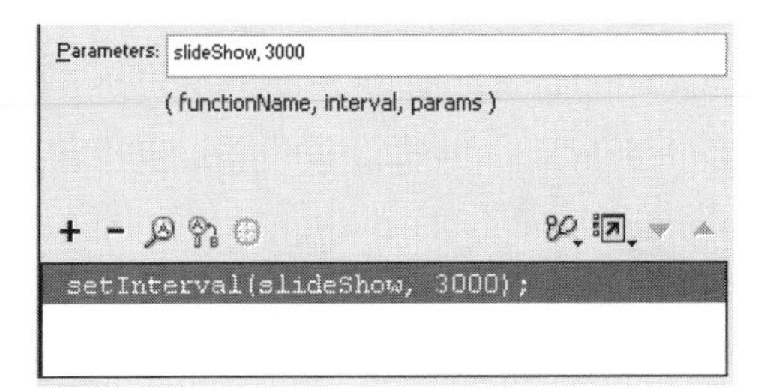

Figure 4.101 The function called `slideshow` will be called every 3 seconds.

Name: slideShow
Parameters:

```
setInterval(slideShow, 3000);
function slideShow() {
}
```

Figure 4.102 Name your function in the Name field of the Parameters pane.

Figure 4.103 This movie contains images from your recent trip to the zoo. The images are in separate keyframes. The `setInterval` action advances to the next image every 3 seconds automatically. The `stop` action has been added to prevent the images from playing until `setInterval` calls the `slideshow` function.

To create continuous actions with setInterval (first way):

1. Select the first frame of the main Timeline, and open the Actions panel.
2. Choose Actions > Miscellaneous Actions > setInterval.
3. In the Parameters field, enter the name of a function, followed by a comma and then an interval (in milliseconds) (**Figure 4.101**).

   The function will be called continuously at the specified interval.
4. Choose Actions > User-Defined Functions > function (Esc + fn).
5. In the Name field of the Parameters pane, enter the name of your function; leave the Parameters field blank (**Figure 4.102**).

   This name is the same one that you used in the `setInterval` action.
6. Choose actions for your function that you want to execute at the periodic interval (**Figure 4.103**).

✔ Tip

- Add the action `updateAfterEvent` (Actions > Movie Clip Control > updateAfterEvent) to your function if you are modifying graphics at a smaller interval than your movie frame rate. This method forces Flash to refresh the display, providing smoother results.

To create continuous actions with setInterval (second way):

1. Select the first frame of the main Timeline, and open the Actions panel.
2. Choose Actions > Miscellaneous Actions > setInterval.
3. In the Parameters field, enter the name of an object, followed by the name of its method in quotation marks, and then an interval (in milliseconds), separating your parameters with commas (**Figure 4.104**).

   The method will be called continuously at the specified interval. This example uses a method of the Movie Clip object, but you can define and use your own method. See Chapter 11 for more information about creating your own methods and objects.

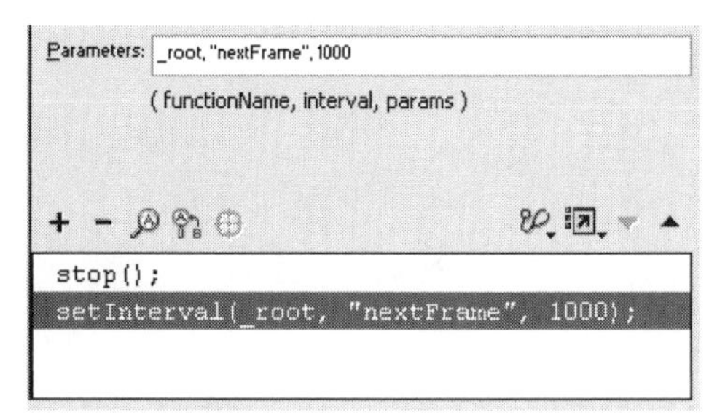

Figure 4.104 This `setInterval` does the same job as in the preceding example, except that it advances every second.

✔ Tips

- In both ways of using the setInterval action, you can pass parameters. In the first way, you can pass parameters to your function; and in the second way, you can pass parameters to your method. If the method you define in setInterval requires parameters, you must provide them at the end of the parameters for setInterval, as in this example:

  ```
  setInterval (myObject, "myMethod",
  1000, parameter1, parameter2)
  ```

  This setInterval will call myObject.myMethod(parameter1, parameter2) every second.

- Although setInterval uses milliseconds to determine when to trigger a function or a method, it must do so during frame transitions set by the movie frame rate. This setup makes the interplay between setInterval and the frame rate a little tricky and makes exact timing less direct than you'd expect. At 10 frames per second, for example, a frame transition occurs every 100 milliseconds. If you define an interval of 200 milliseconds, Flash waits two frames (200 ms) until the interval passes; then it triggers the method or function on frame 3. It waits two more frames (another 200 ms) and then triggers on frame 6. Finally, after two more frames, it triggers on frame 9.

  If you change your movie to play at 20 frames per second, a frame transition occurs every 50 milliseconds. Flash waits four frames (200 ms) and triggers the method or function on frame 5. It waits another four frames and triggers on frame 10. It continues to trigger on every fifth frame—at frame 15 and frame 20. If you compare the two movies, the one at 10 fps gets triggered three times in the first second (frames 3, 6, and 9) whereas the one at 20 fps gets triggered four times in the first second (frames 5, 10, 15, and 20). So even though they both have the same 200-ms interval defined in setInterval, frame rates can have significant effects.

The `setInterval` action continues to call the function or method at regular intervals until the movie ends or until you remove the `setInterval` action with `clearInterval`. The action `clearInterval` requires one parameter, which is the name you give the `setInterval` action. In the preceding examples, you didn't name the `setInterval` action because you had no intention of stopping it. In this next task, you will name your `setInterval` action by using `set variable` or `evaluate`. Then, you can clear it by using the `clearInterval` action.

To clear a setInterval action:

1. Continuing with the preceding example, select the first frame of the main Timeline, and open the Actions panel.
2. Select the `setInterval` action, and delete it.
3. Choose Actions > Variable > set variable.
4. In the Variable field, enter a name to give your `setInterval` action (**Figure 4.105**).
5. In the Value field, create the same `setInterval` action you had before, and check the Expression checkbox (**Figure 4.106**).

   The name in the Variable field identifies the `setInterval` action in the Value field.
6. At a later point in your Flash movie, when you want to stop the `setInterval`, choose Actions > Miscellaneous Actions > clearInterval.
7. In the Parameters field, enter the name identified with the `setInterval` action (**Figure 4.107**).

   When Flash encounters the `clearInterval` action, it removes the `setInterval` and stops the continuous actions.

Figure 4.105 The name of your `setInterval` action goes in the Variable field.

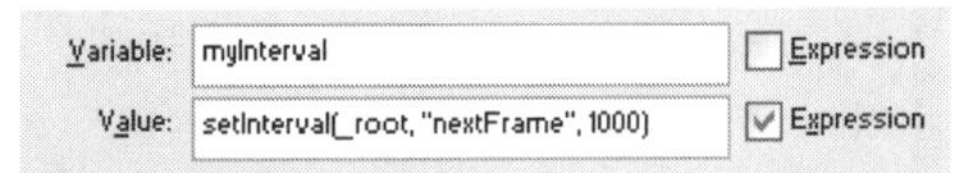

Figure 4.106 The entire `setInterval` action goes in the Value field.

Stop the Slideshow

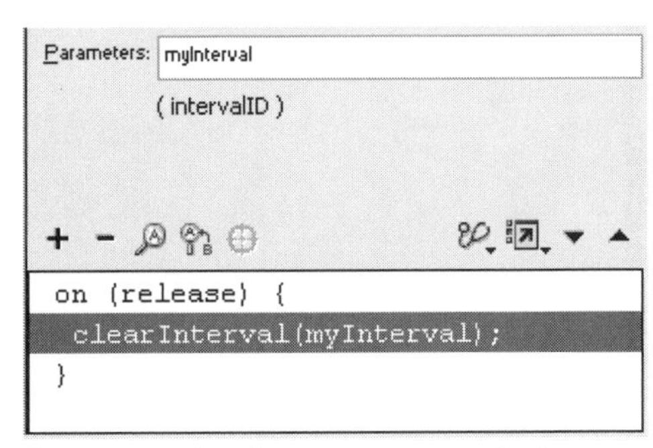

Figure 4.107 When the `clearInterval` action is assigned to a button (top), it will remove the `setInterval` identified as myInterval. The movie will no longer advance to the next frame continuously, and the slide show will stop.

A Summary of Events and Event Handlers

Table 4.5 organizes and compares the many ways you can create event handlers to detect and respond to events.

Table 4.5

A Summary of Events and Event Handlers

Object	Event Handler Assigned on Instance	Event Handler Assigned on Main Timeline	Anonymous Function Assigned to	Listener
Button	on(press)	onPress	button instance	No
	on(release)	onRelease		
	on(releaseOutside)	onReleaseOutside		
	on(rollOver)	onRollover		
	on(rollOut)	onRollOut		
	on(dragOver)	onDragOver		
	on(dragOut)	onDragOut		
	on(keyPress "whatkey")	-		
	-	onSetFocus		
	-	onKillFocus		
Mouse	No	onMouseUp	Listener or _root	Yes*
		onMouseDown		Yes*
		onMouseMove		Yes*
Key	No	onKeyUp	Listener	Yes
		onKeyDown		Yes
Movie Clip (may also receive Button events)	onClipEvent(load)	onLoad	MC/_root	No
	onClipEvent(unload)	onUnload	MC/_root	No
	onClipEvent(data)	onData	MC/_root	No
	onClipEvent(enterFrame)	onEnterFrame	MC/_root	No
	onClipEvent(mouseDown)	onMouseDown	MC/_root/L	Yes*
	onClipEvent(mouseUp)	onMouseUp	MC/_root/L	Yes*
	onClipEvent(mouseMove)	onMouseMove	MC/_root/L	Yes*
	onClipEvent(keyUp)	onKeyUp	Listener	Yes
	onClipEvent(keyDown)	onKeyDown	Listener	Yes

** not required*
MC = movie-clip instance
_root = main Timeline
L = Listener

5 Controlling Multiple Timelines

To create interactivity and direct your users to see, hear, and do exactly what you want, you have to know how to control the Flash playhead on different Timelines. The playhead displays what is on the Stage at any time, plays back any sound, and triggers any actions attached to the Timeline. Jumping from frame to frame on the main movie Timeline is simple enough; you use basic actions you should be familiar with, such as `goto`, `play`, and `stop`. But when you bring movie clips into your movie, you introduce other independent Timelines that can be controlled individually. Your main Timeline can control a movie clip's Timeline; a movie clip's Timeline can, in turn, control the main Timeline; and the Timeline of one movie clip can even control the Timeline of another. Handling this complex interaction and navigation between Timelines is the subject of this chapter.

Navigating Timelines with Movie Clips

The independent Timelines of movie-clip symbols make complicated navigation schemes possible (**Figure 5.1**). While the main Timeline is playing, other Timelines of movie clips can be playing as well, interacting with one another and telling what frames to play or when to stop. It's quite common, in fact, to have enough movie clips on the Stage all talking to one another that the main movie Timeline need be only a single frame for the entire movie to work. Driving all this navigation between Timelines is, of course, ActionScript. The basic actions used to navigate within the main Timeline (`gotoAndStop`, `gotoAndPlay`, `stop`, `play`, `nextFrame`, and `prevFrame`) can also be used to navigate the Timeline of any movie clip. This navigation is possible because you can give a name to every movie-clip instance on the Stage. You name a movie-clip instance in the Property Inspector. When an instance is named, you can identify its particular Timeline and give instructions on where you want to move its playhead.

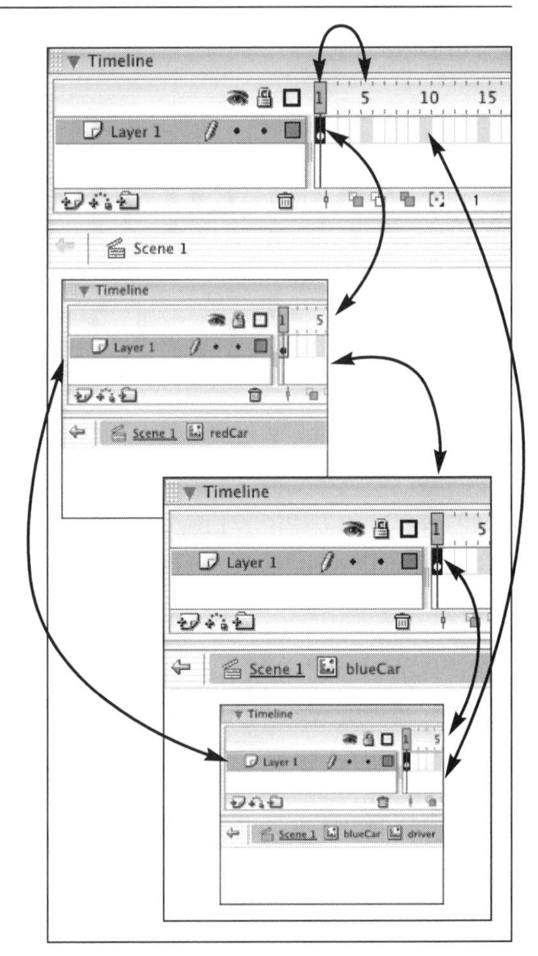

Figure 5.1 A movie can contain many Timelines that interact with one another. This example shows scene 1 as the main Timeline; it contains two movie clips. One of the movie clips contains another movie clip. The arrows show just a few of the possible lines of communication.

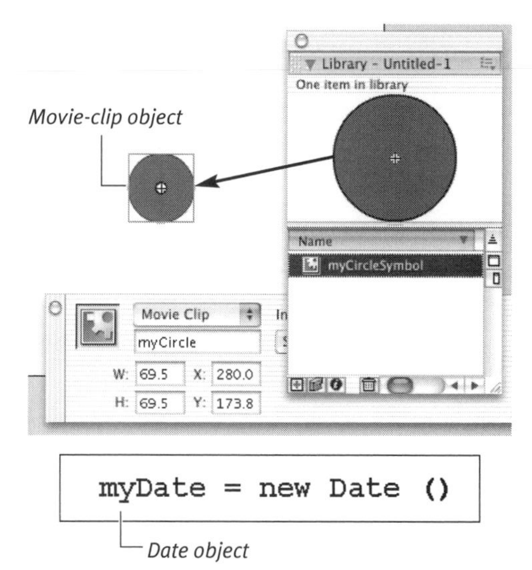

Figure 5.2 Instantiation of a movie-clip symbol (called myCircle) versus instantiation of a Date object (called myDate).

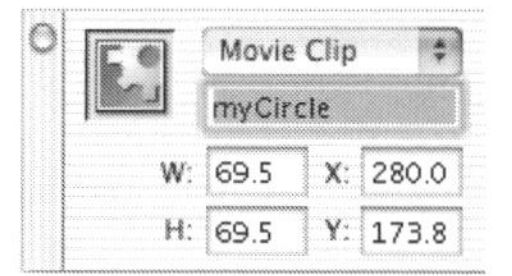

Figure 5.3 The Property Inspector for a selected movie clip. The name of this Movie Clip object is myCircle.

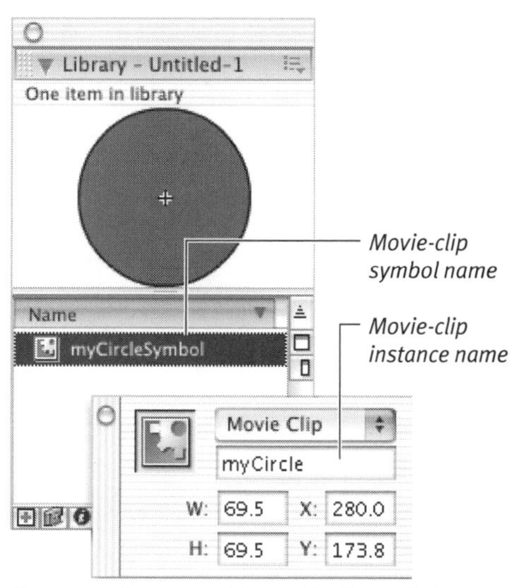

Figure 5.4 The name of the movie-clip symbol appears in the library (myCircleSymbol), and the name of the movie-clip instance appears in the Property Inspector (myCircle).

Naming Instances

Instantiation of a Movie Clip object involves two steps: placing an instance on the Stage and naming that instance in the Property Inspector. You follow the same steps to instantiate a Button object and, as you'll learn in Chapter 10, a TextField object. These two steps accomplish the same task that the constructor function performs for other Flash objects (**Figure 5.2**). The result is the same; a named object is created from a class. You can use that object by calling its methods or evaluating its properties.

To name a movie-clip instance or a button instance:

1. Create a movie-clip symbol or a button symbol.
2. Drag an instance of the symbol from the library to the Stage.
3. Select the instance.
4. In the Property Inspector, below the pull-down menu for the symbol type, enter a unique name for your instance (**Figure 5.3**).

   Now you can use this name to identify your movie-clip instance or your button instance with ActionScript.

✔ Tip

- The name of your symbol (the one that appears in the library) and the name you give it in the Property Inspector are two different identifiers (**Figure 5.4**). The name that appears in the library is a symbol property and basically is just an organizational reminder. The name in the Property Inspector is more important because it is the actual name of the object and will be used in targeting paths. Although the two names can be the same, try to give your symbol a generic name and the instance a specific name to distinguish them.

The Rules of Naming

Although you're free to make up names for your objects, you must adhere to certain simple rules. If you don't, Flash won't recognize your name and will ignore your commands to control the object with ActionScript.

1. Do not use spaces or punctuation (such as slashes, dots, and parentheses), because these characters often have a special meaning to Flash.
2. You can use letters, numbers, and underscore characters, but you must not begin your name with a number.
3. Do not use words that Flash uses for ActionScript. For example, `var` and `new` are reserved for commands and cannot be names.

That's it. Those are the only three rules. Some additional general naming strategies, however, can make your scripts easier to understand, debug, and share.

1. Use a consistent naming practice. A common method is to use multiple names to describe an object and to capitalize the first letter of every word except for the first. The names spinningSquare1, spinningSquare2, and leftPaddle, for example, are intuitive, descriptive, and easy to follow in a script.
2. Consider adding suffixes to your names to describe the object type. Using the standard suffix _mc for movie clips and _btn for buttons readily identifies the object. It also helps the ActionScript panel recognize the object type and will bring up the appropriate code hints. In Expert mode, for example, if you begin typing `leftPaddle_mc` and then a dot, the code hint that appears will display a list of the movie-clip methods and events because it knows that `leftPaddle_mc` is a movie clip.

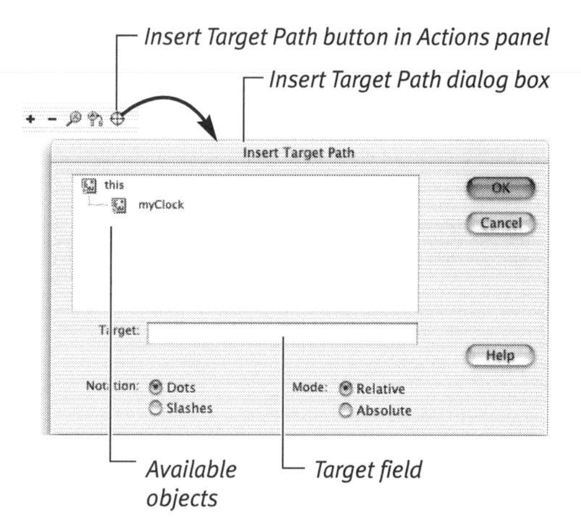

Figure 5.5 The Insert Target Path dialog box allows you to choose a target path by clicking a movie clip, button, or text field within the hierarchy.

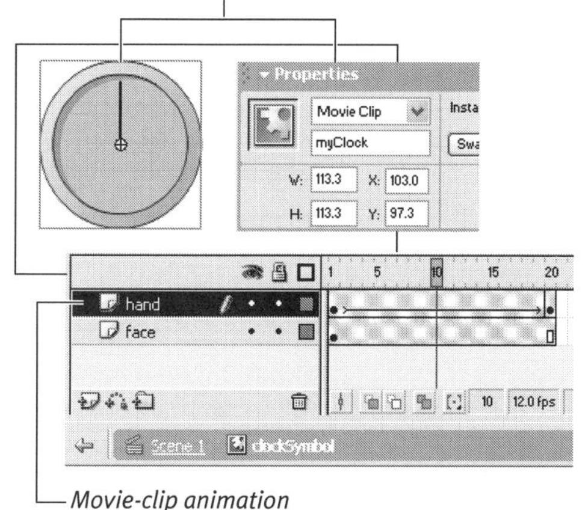

Figure 5.6 The movie-clip instance called myClock is on the main Timeline. The movie clip contains an animation (below) of the hand rotating.

Target Paths

A *target path* is essentially an object name, or a series of object names separated by dots, that tells Flash where to find a particular object. To control movie-clip Timelines, you specify both the target path for a particular movie clip and its method. The target path tells Flash which movie-clip instance to look at, and the method tells Flash what to do with that movie-clip instance. The methods that control the playhead are `gotoAndStop()`, `gotoAndPlay()`, `play()`, `stop()`, `nextFrame()`, and `prevFrame()`. If you name a movie-clip instance myClock, for example, you can write the ActionScript statement `myClock.gotoAndStop(10)`, and the playhead within the movie-clip instance called myClock will move to frame 10 and stop there. `myClock` is the target path, and `gotoAndStop()` is the method.

In the Parameters pane of the Actions panel, the Insert Target Path button opens the Insert Target Path dialog box, which provides a visual way to insert a target path (**Figure 5.5**). All named movie-clip instances, button instances, and text fields are shown in a hierarchical fashion in the display window. You can select individual objects, and the correct target paths appear in the Target field.

To target a movie-clip instance from the main Timeline:

1. Create a movie-clip symbol that contains an animation on its Timeline, and place an instance of it on the Stage.
2. In the Property Inspector, give the instance a name (**Figure 5.6**).
3. Select a keyframe of the main Timeline, and open the Actions panel.

   You will assign an action to the main Timeline that will control the movie-clip instance.

continues on next page

4. Choose Objects > Movie > Movie Clip > Methods > stop.

   The `stop()` method of the movie clip appears in the Script pane (**Figure 5.7**).

5. In the Parameters pane, put your pointer in the Object field and click the Insert Target Path button, located above the Script pane.

   The Insert Target Path dialog box appears.

6. Choose Dots in the Notation section and Relative in the Mode section, and select the movie-clip instance in the display list.

   The target path appears in the Target field (**Figure 5.8**).

7. Click OK.

   The target path appears in the Object field, and the Script pane shows the completed statement (**Figure 5.9**).

8. Test your movie (Control > Test movie).

   Your movie clip normally will play its animation on the main Stage. The action you assign on the main Timeline, however, targets your movie clip and tells the playhead to stop.

✔ Tip

- It's important to choose the methods that control the playhead position (`stop()`, `play()`, `gotoAndStop()`, `gotoAndPlay()`, `nextFrame()`, and `prevFrame()`) from the Objects > Movie > Movie Clip > Methods category, rather than the Actions > Movie Control category. Choosing these methods from the Methods category lets you target different Timelines; choosing the actions from the Movie Control category doesn't.

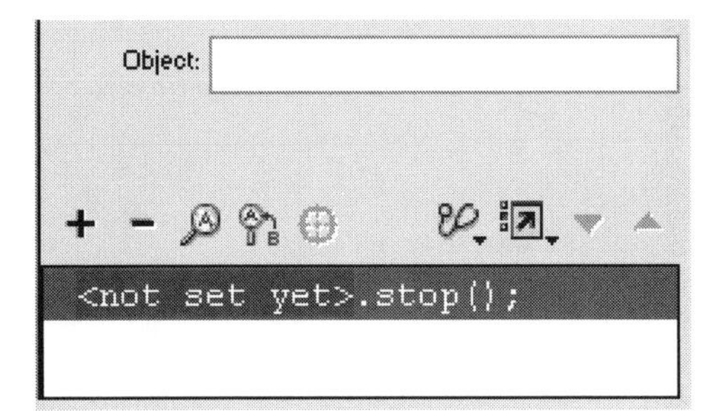

Figure 5.7 The `stop()` method appears in the Script pane.

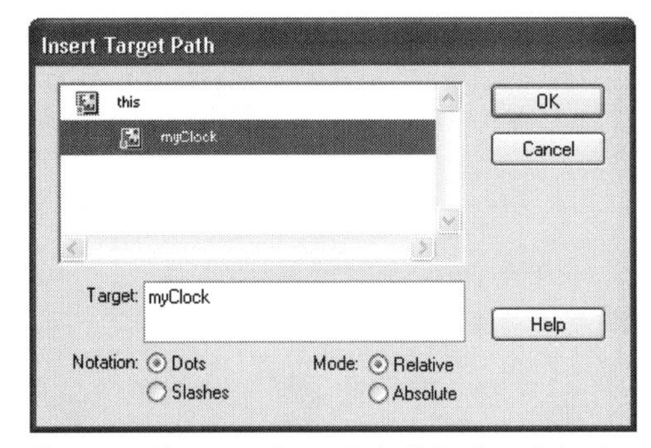

Figure 5.8 The Insert Target Path dialog box. Selecting the movie clip in the display window enters the target path in the Target field.

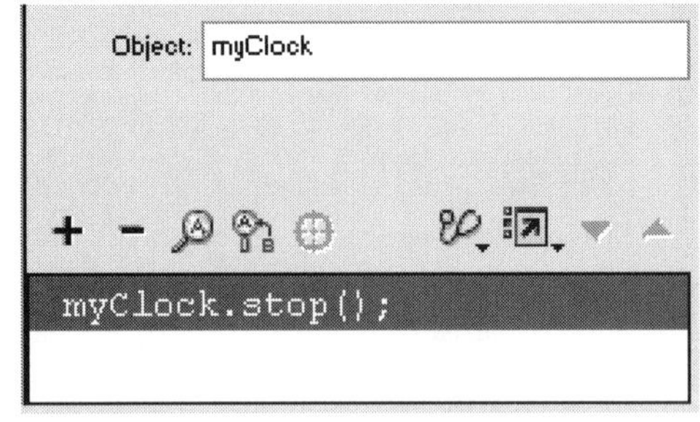

Figure 5.9 The target path is `myClock`, and the method is `stop()`. The playhead of the myClock Timeline stops when this action is triggered.

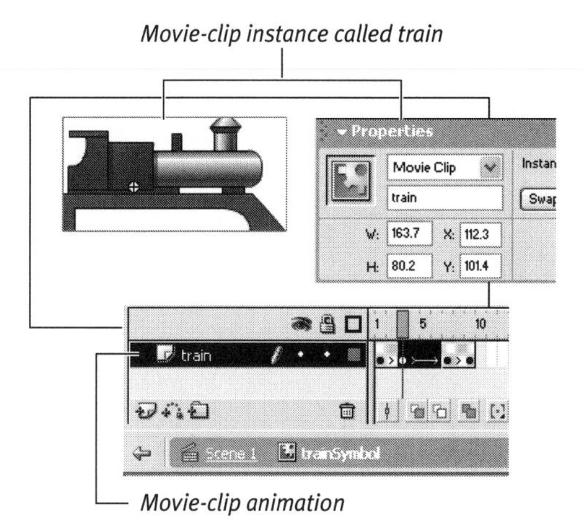

Figure 5.10 The movie-clip instance called train is on the main Timeline. The movie clip contains an animation (below) of the train shaking back and forth.

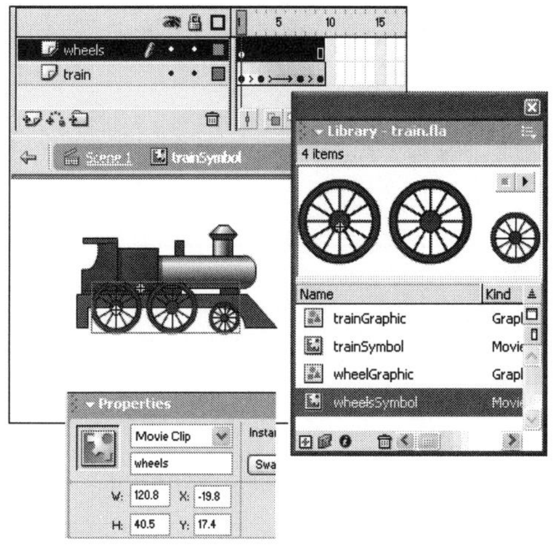

Figure 5.11 Place an instance of a movie clip inside the train movie clip. Name the child movie-clip instance wheels.

You can have a movie clip within another movie clip. The first is the parent, and the second is the child. Any transformation you do to the parent will also affect the child. To control the Timeline of a child movie clip from the main Timeline, use both the parent and the child name in the target path. In the following example, the parent movie clip is a train, and the child movie clip is its wheels.

To target a child of a movie-clip instance from the main Timeline:

1. Create a movie-clip symbol that contains an animation on its Timeline, place an instance on the Stage, and name it in the Property inspector (**Figure 5.10**).
2. Create another movie-clip symbol that contains an animation on its Timeline.
3. Go to symbol-editing mode for the first movie clip, and drag an instance of your second movie clip to the Stage.
4. In the Property Inspector, give the second movie-clip instance a name (**Figure 5.11**).

   You now have a parent movie clip on the main Stage. The parent movie clip contains a child movie clip.
5. Exit symbol-editing mode, and return to the main Stage.
6. Select a keyframe in the main Timeline, and open the Actions panel.
7. Choose Objects > Movie > Movie Clip > Methods > stop.
8. Put your pointer in the Object field and then click the Insert Target Path button.

   The Insert Target Path dialog box opens.
9. Choose Dots in the Notation section and Relative in the Mode section.

continues on next page

10. In the display window, click the triangle (Mac) or the plus sign (Windows) in front of the parent movie clip.

    The hierarchy expands, showing the child movie clip within the parent (**Figure 5.12**).

11. Select the child movie clip as the target path, and click OK.

    The target path, in the form `Parent.Child`, appears in the Object field of the Actions panel.

12. Test your movie.

    The animation of the wheels turning will play within the movie clip of the train, which is bobbing up and down. The action you assign on the main Timeline, however, targets the movie clip of the wheels that is inside the movie clip of the train and tells its playhead to stop. The animation of the train continues (**Figure 5.13**). Despite the parent-child relationship, the Timelines remain independent.

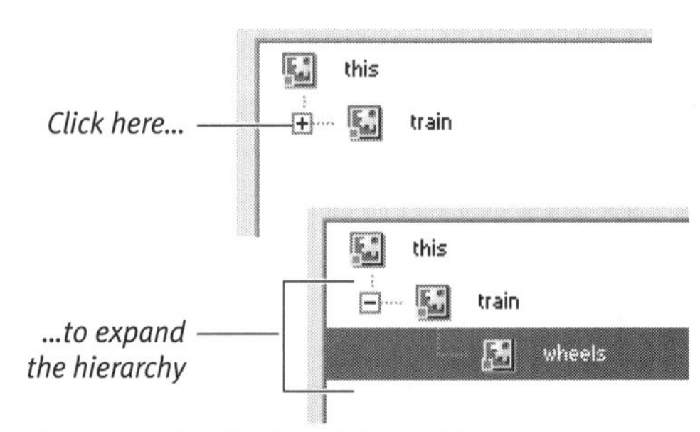

Figure 5.12 The display window of the Insert Target Path dialog box. The hierarchy shows parent-child relationships.

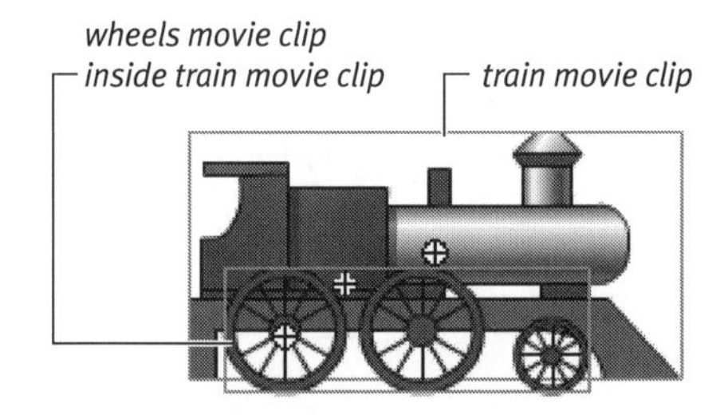

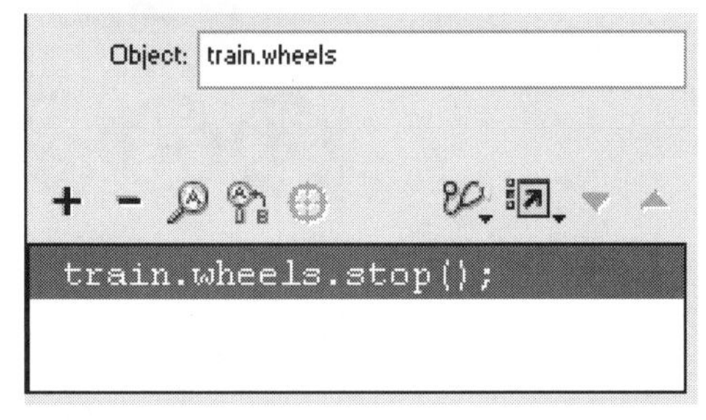

Figure 5.13 The ActionScript statement on the main Timeline tells the wheels movie clip inside the train movie clip to stop.

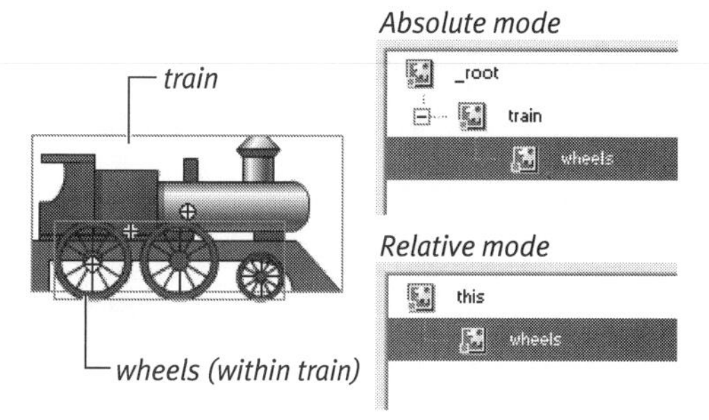

Figure 5.14 Absolute mode versus relative mode of target paths. This example shows the wheels movie clip inside the train movie clip. When you assign actions on the train Timeline, `this` in relative mode refers to train in absolute mode.

Absolute and Relative Paths

Flash gives you two mode options in the Insert Target Path dialog box: relative and absolute. In the preceding example, the method `train.wheels.stop()` originated from the main Timeline. When Flash executes that method, it looks within its own Timeline for the object called train that contains another object called wheels. This is an example of a path that uses relative mode. Everything is relative to where the ActionScript statement resides—in this case, the main Timeline. An alternative way of inserting a target path is to use absolute mode, which has no particular frame of reference. You can think of relative target paths as being directions given from your present location, as in "Go two blocks straight; then turn left." Absolute target paths, on the other hand, are directions that work no matter where you are, as in "Go to 555 University Avenue."

Why would you use one mode instead of the other? If you need to target a Timeline that sits at a higher level than the Timeline you're working in, you can use absolute mode. Imagine that you want to have a movie clip control the main Timeline in which it resides. In relative mode, you see only the Timelines that are inside the current one. In absolute mode, you see all the Timelines no matter where you are. Absolute mode is like having a bird's-eye view of all the movie clips on the Stage at the same time.

Using this and _root

In relative mode, the current Timeline is called `this`. The keyword `this` means *myself*. All other Timelines are relative to the `this` Timeline. In absolute mode, the main movie Timeline is called `_root`. All other Timelines are organized relative to the `_root` Timeline (**Figure 5.14**).

To target the main Timeline from a movie-clip instance:

1. Create a movie-clip symbol that contains an animation on its Timeline, place an instance of it on the Stage, and give the instance a name in the Property Inspector.
2. Go to symbol-editing mode for your movie clip.
3. Select a keyframe on the movie clip's Timeline, and open the Actions panel.

   You will assign ActionScript to the movie clip's Timeline to control the main Timeline (**Figure 5.15**).
4. Choose Objects > Movie > Movie Clip > Methods > gotoAndStop.
5. Put your pointer in the Object field, and click the Insert Target Path button to open the Insert Target Path dialog box.
6. Choose Dots in the Notation section and Absolute in the Mode section (**Figure 5.16**).

   All the movie clips and the main Timeline of the movie appear, not just those inside the current movie-clip Timeline.
7. Select the main Timeline as the target path, and click OK.

   The target path `_root` appears in the Object field (**Figure 5.17**).

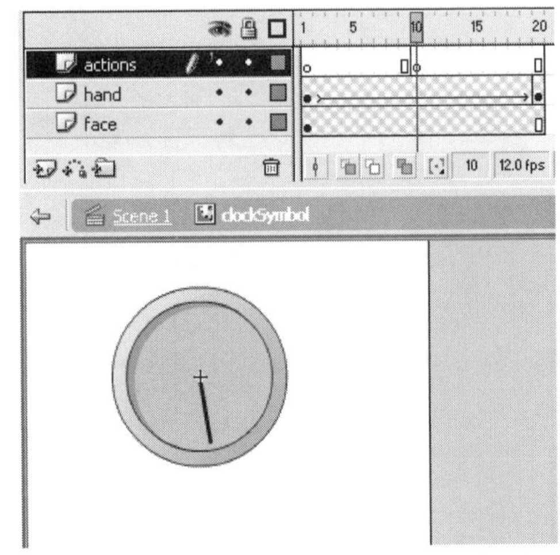

Figure 5.15 This movie clip contains an animation. At keyframe 10, you will assign an action to move the playhead of the main Timeline.

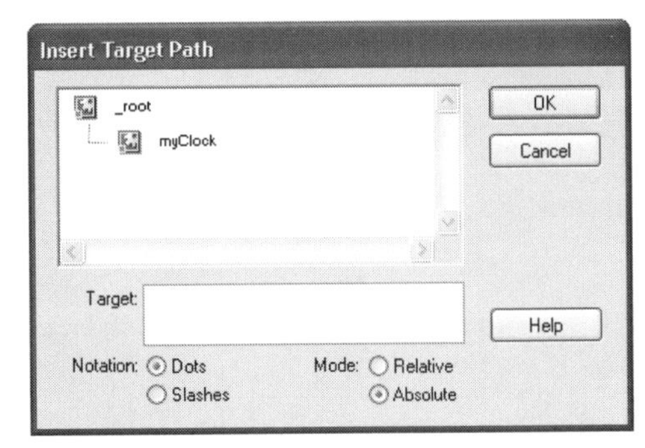

Figure 5.16 Absolute mode, selected in the Insert Target Path dialog box, shows a top-down view of all the Timelines.

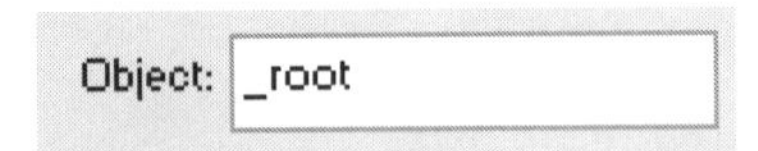

Figure 5.17 The Object field of the `gotoAndStop()` method.

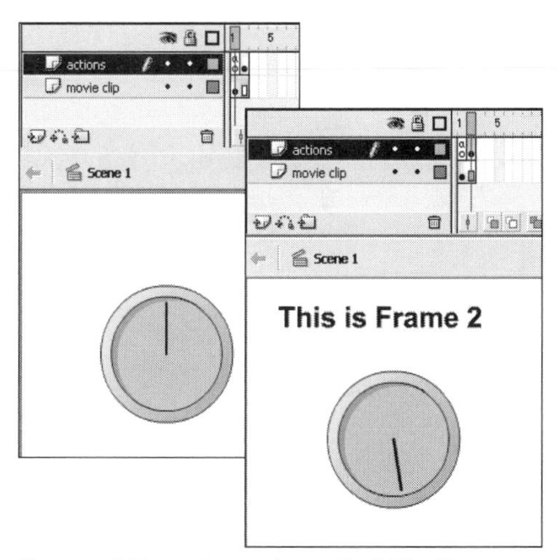

Figure 5.18 The action on the myClock Timeline moves the playhead on the main Timeline to frame 2. There is a `stop` action on the main Timeline at frame 1.

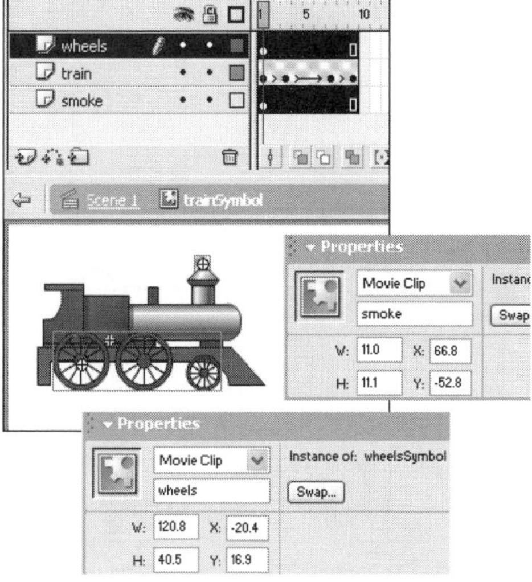

Figure 5.19 The smoke movie clip and the wheels movie clip are dragged into the movie-clip symbol called trainSymbol. The instance of trainSymbol on the Stage is called train (not shown).

8. In the Parameters field, enter a frame number as the main Timeline destination.
9. Test your movie.

   When the ActionScript statement on the movie-clip Timeline is executed, Flash jumps outside that Timeline and looks up to the `_root` Timeline to perform the method there (**Figure 5.18**).

To target a movie-clip instance from another movie-clip instance:

1. Create a movie-clip symbol that contains an animation, place an instance of it on the Stage, and give the instance a name in the Property Inspector.
2. Create two more movie-clip symbols that contain animation.
3. Go to symbol-editing mode for the first movie clip, place instances of the second and third movie clips on the Stage, and give names to both instances in the Property Inspector (**Figure 5.19**).

   You now have a parent movie clip on the main Timeline. The parent movie clip contains two child movie clips.
4. Go to symbol-editing mode for the wheels movie clip.
5. Select a keyframe on the movie clip's Timeline and open the Actions panel.

   You will assign ActionScript on the wheels Timeline to control the smoke Timeline.
6. Choose Objects > Movie > Movie Clip > Methods > stop.

continues on next page

7. Put your pointer in the Object field, and click the Insert Target Path button to open the Insert Target Path dialog box.

8. Choose Dots in the Notation section and Absolute in the Mode section.

9. Select the smoke movie-clip instance, and click OK.

   The target path `_root.train.smoke` appears in the Object field of the Actions panel (**Figure 5.20**).

10. Test your movie.

    When the ActionScript statement on the wheels movie-clip Timeline is executed, Flash starts looking from the `_root` Timeline, drills down through the object called train to the object called smoke, and performs the method on that object (**Figure 5.21**).

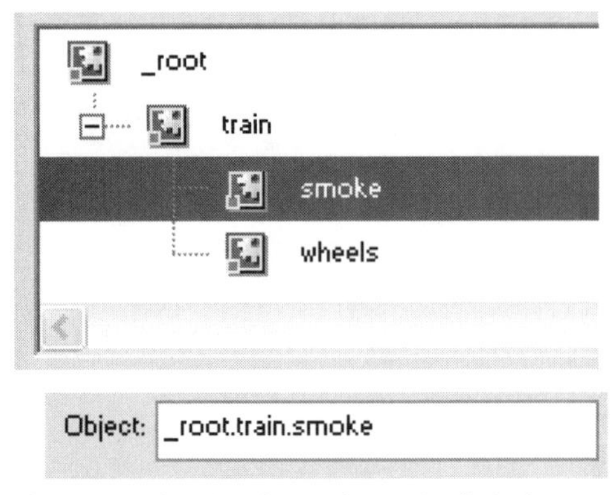

Figure 5.20 Choosing the smoke movie clip in the Insert Target Path dialog box (top) and clicking OK puts the full target path in the Object field of the `stop()` method (bottom).

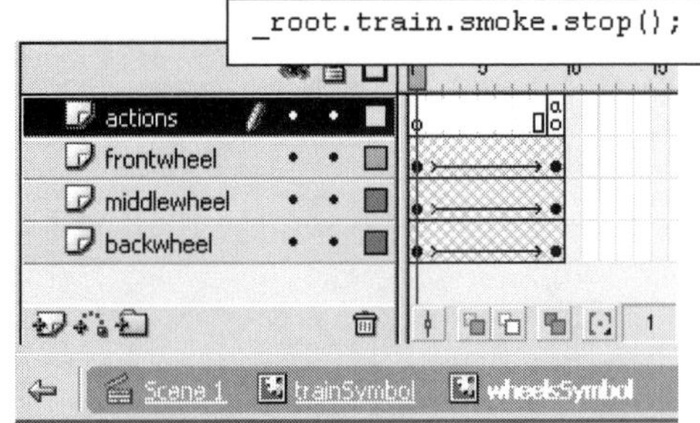

Figure 5.21 The animation in the wheels movie clip plays. When the clip hits frame 9 of its Timeline (bottom), the ActionScript there tells the smoke movie clip to stop playing. The smoke animation has a chance to play only nine frames of itself.

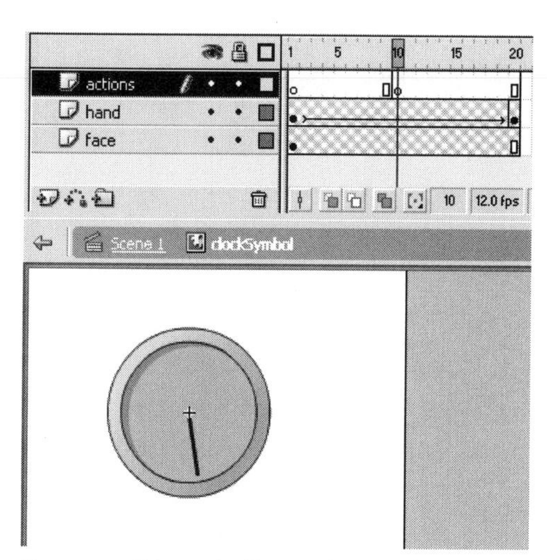

Figure 5.22 This movie clip contains an animation of the hand rotating. The action you'll assign on keyframe 10 will make it stop, so the hand barely makes it to 6 o'clock.

```
this.stop();
```

```
_root.myClock.stop();
```

```
stop();
```

Figure 5.23 Three equivalent statements to target the myClock Timeline from within myClock itself.

To target a movie clip's own Timeline:

1. Create a movie-clip symbol that contains an animation, place an instance of it on the Stage, and give the instance a name in the Property Inspector.
2. Go to symbol-editing mode for your movie clip.
3. Select a keyframe on the movie clip's Timeline, and open the Actions panel.

   You will assign ActionScript to the movie-clip Timeline that controls its own Timeline (**Figure 5.22**).
4. Choose Objects > Movie > Movie Clip > Methods > stop.
5. Click the Insert Target Path button to open the Insert Target Path dialog box.
6. Choose Dots in the Notation section and Relative in the Mode section, and select `this`.

   or

   Click the Insert Target Path button to open the Insert Target Path dialog box; choose absolute mode, and select the absolute target path.

   or

   Choose Actions > Movie Control > stop (**Figure 5.23**).

✔ Tip

- Using `this` or an absolute path to target a movie clip's own Timeline is unnecessary, just as it is unnecessary to use `this` or `_root` when navigating within the main Timeline. It's understood that actions residing in one movie clip pertain, or are *scoped*, to that particular movie clip.

Using _parent in target paths

Although it does not appear in the Insert Target Path dialog box, you can also use the relative term `_parent`. Use `_parent` to target the movie clip at the next-higher level from the current Timeline.

To target the parent of a movie clip:

1. Create a movie-clip symbol that contains an animation, place an instance of it on the Stage, and give the instance a name in the Property Inspector.
2. Create another movie-clip symbol that contains an animation.
3. Go to symbol-editing mode for the first movie clip, place an instance of the second movie clip on the Stage, and give the instance a name in the Property Inspector.

   You now have a parent movie clip on the main Timeline. The parent movie clip contains a child movie clip (**Figure 5.24**).

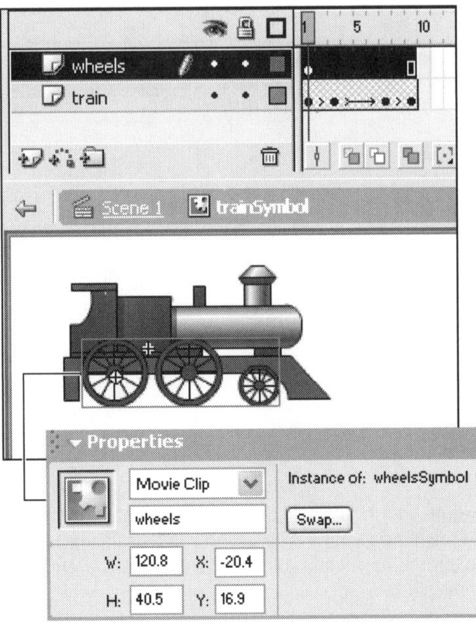

Figure 5.24 Place an instance of a movie clip inside the train movie clip. This child movie clip is called wheels.

Why Relative Paths?

Why use relative paths at all? Absolute paths seem to be a safer construction because they identify an object explicitly no matter where you are.

Relative paths, however, are useful in at least two cases:

- If you create a movie clip that contains actions that affect other movie clips relative to itself, you can move the entire ensemble and still have the target paths work by using relative terms. This method makes it easier to work with complex navigation schemes, because you can copy, paste, and move the pieces without having to rewrite the target paths.

  A direct parallel is managing a Web site and maintaining its links. If you were to create absolute paths to links to your résumé and then move your home page to a different server, you'd have to rewrite your links. The more practical method would be to establish relative links within your home page.

- Relative paths are also useful when you create movie clips dynamically. You will learn how to create movie-clip objects and name them on the fly with ActionScript. In these cases, movie clips are not static, and relative target paths are required to follow them around.

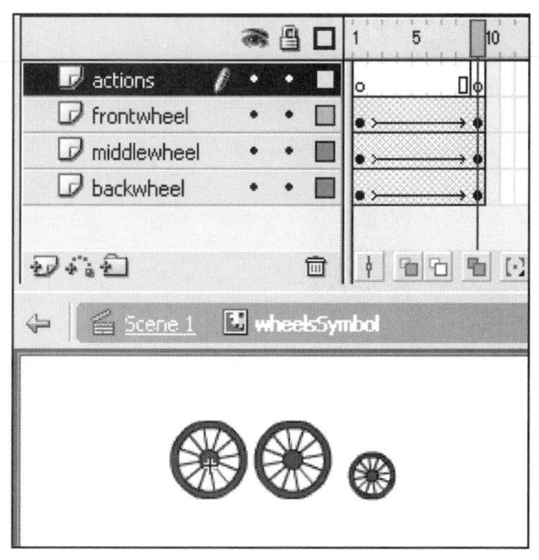

Figure 5.25 The wheels movie clip contains an animation of the wheels rotating.

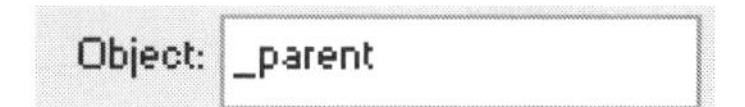

Figure 5.26 The Object field of the `stop()` method.

4. Go to symbol-editing mode for the child movie clip.
5. Select a keyframe on the child movie clip's Timeline, and open the Actions panel.

   You will assign ActionScript to the child movie clip's Timeline to control the parent movie clip's Timeline (**Figure 5.25**).
6. Choose Objects > Movie > Movie Clip > Methods > stop.
7. In the Object field, enter `_parent` (**Figure 5.26**).

continues on next page

8. Test your movie.

   When the ActionScript statement on the wheels movie-clip Timeline is executed, Flash looks up to its parent—the train movie-clip Timeline—and performs the method there (**Figure 5.27**).

   Table 5.1 and **Figure 5.28** summarize the ways you can use absolute and relative paths to target different movie clips.

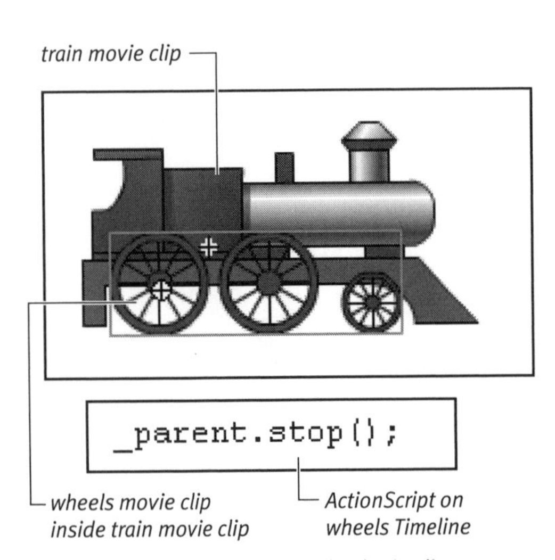

Figure 5.27 The action on the wheels Timeline targets its parent, which is the train Timeline. The action makes the train stop shaking.

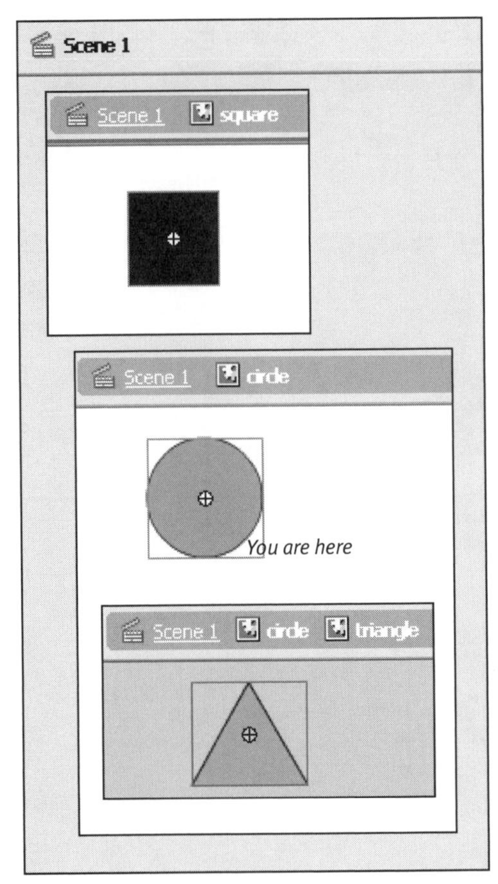

Figure 5.28 A representation of a movie with multiple movie clips. The main Timeline (scene 1) contains the square movie clip and the circle movie clip. The circle movie clip contains the triangle movie clip. These names represent instances. Table 5.1 summarizes the absolute and relative target paths for calls made within the circle movie clip (you are here).

Table 5.1

Absolute versus Relative Target Paths

To target… (from circle)	Absolute Path	Relative Path
Scene 1	_root	_parent
square	_root.square	_parent.square
circle	_root.circle	this
triangle	_root.circle.triangle	triangle

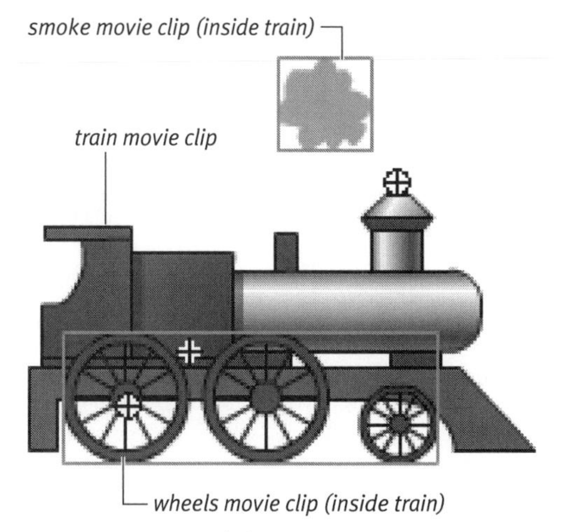

Figure 5.29 Nested `with` statements are an alternative to multiple target paths.

Using the with Action to Target Movie Clips

An alternative way to target movie clips is to use the action `with`. Instead of creating multiple target paths to the same movie clip, you can use the `with` action so that you have to target the movie clip only once. Imagine creating these statements to make the wheels movie clip inside a train movie clip stop and shrink 50 percent:

```
train.wheels.stop();
train.wheels._xscale=50;
train.wheels._yscale=50;
```

You can rewrite those statements with the `with` statement, like this:

```
with(train.wheels){
   stop();
   _xscale=50;
   _yscale=50;
}
```

This `with` action temporarily sets the target path to `train.wheels` so that the method and properties between the curly braces affect that particular target path. When the `with` action ends, any subsequent statements refer to the current Timeline.

The `with` statement can even be nested to affect multiple targets simultaneously (**Figure 5.29**):

```
with(train){
   with(wheels){
      play();
   }
   with(smoke){
      stop();
   }
}
```

continues on next page

These nested with statements accomplish the same thing as the following statements:

```
train.wheels.play();
train.smoke.stop();
```

You should use the with action in Expert mode in the Actions panel. In Normal mode, it is difficult to call methods without providing a target path for the object, so you must use Expert mode to write your methods.

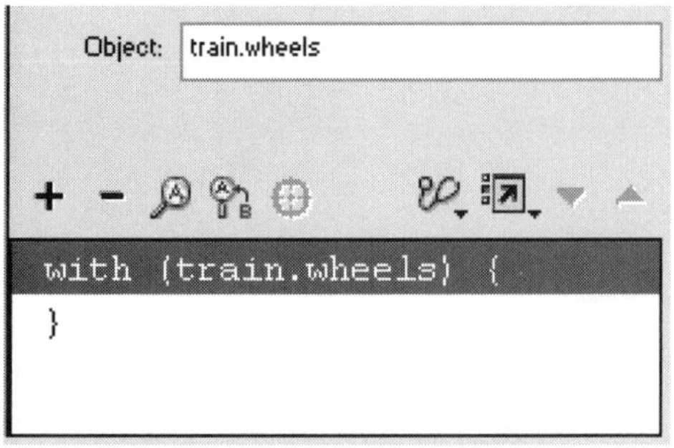

To use the with action:

1. In a keyframe or within an event handler, open the Actions panel.
2. Choose Actions > Variables > with (Esc + wt).

   The Object field appears in the Parameters pane.
3. In the Object field, enter the target path or click the Insert Target Path button (**Figure 5.30**).
4. Between the curly braces of the with action, create your statements for the targeted object (**Figure 5.31**).

Figure 5.30 The with action in the Actions panel. The Object field contains the target path train.wheels.

```
with (train.wheels) {
  stop();
}
```

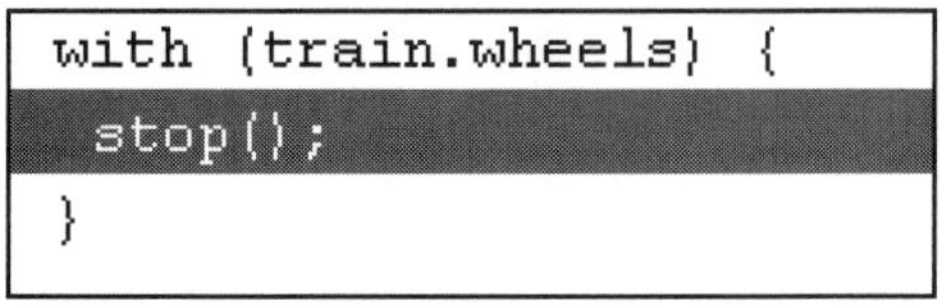

Figure 5.31 The action stop() and any other actions between the inner set of curly braces apply to the target path train.wheels.

```
with (train) {
  with (wheels) {
  }
}
```

Figure 5.32 The action `with(wheels)` is nested within the action `with(train)`.

```
with (train) {
  with (wheels) {
    play();
  }
}
```

Figure 5.33 Selecting the closing curly brace ensures that your next statement will be inserted within the action `with(train)` rather than within the action `with(wheels)`.

```
with (train) {
  with (wheels) {
    play();
  }
  with (smoke) {
    stop();
  }
}
```

Figure 5.34 The complete nested `with` action statements.

To use nested with actions:

1. In a keyframe or within an event handler, open the Actions panel.
2. Choose Actions > Variables > with.
3. In the Object field, enter the first target path.
4. Again, choose Actions > Variables > with.
5. In the Object field, enter the first nested target path (**Figure 5.32**).
6. Create statements for the first nested object.
7. Select the closing curly brace of the first nested `with` statement (**Figure 5.33**).

   If you do not select the closing curly brace before proceeding with the next step, the second nested `with` statement will appear inside the preceding one.
8. Again, choose Actions > Variables > with.
9. In the Object field, enter the second nested target path; then create a statement for this second nested object (**Figure 5.34**).

Slash Notation and tellTarget

So far in constructing your target paths, you've been using dots to separate nested movie-clip objects. Flash also allows you to insert target paths by using slashes. The slash syntax is the notation used by earlier versions of Flash and may provide a more comfortable way of working for some long-time Flash users. The Insert Target Path dialog box gives you the choice of slash or dot notation (**Figure 5.35**).

Slash notation is similar to how computer directories are identified, with slashes separating embedded folders. And as you can in computer directories, you can drill up or down the Timeline hierarchy by using dots. One dot targets the current Timeline; two dots target the next Timeline up. A single slash indicates the root Timeline.

Note how slash notation uses dots to indicate relative paths. You can see how potentially confusing it is to use dot and slash notation together. Fortunately, Flash won't allow mixing the two notations, because it wouldn't understand the statements. If you call the `gotoAndStop()` method of an object, you write it in dot notation as follows:

```
Parent.Child.gotoAndStop(5);
```

In slash notation, however, the statement breaks down. It doesn't make any sense to say:

```
Parent/Child.gotoAndStop(5);
```

Notation: Dots / Slashes   Mode: Relative / Absolute

Figure 5.35 The Notation options are at the bottom of the Insert Target Path dialog box.

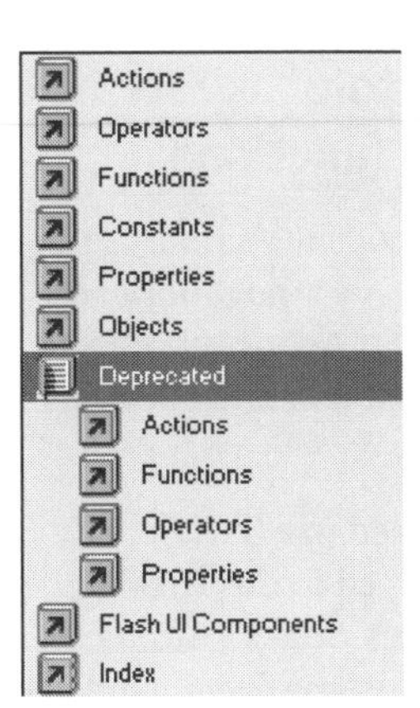

Figure 5.36 Choosing the Deprecated category in the Actions panel displays all the actions that are remnants of earlier versions of Flash and are no longer recommended.

Table 5.2

Dot- and Slash-Notation Equivalents

Dot	Slash
.	/
_root	/
this	.
_parent	..

Slash notation is not compatible with the way Flash adds methods in Normal mode of the Actions panel or with the `with` statement. You should use slash notation only in conjunction with the action `tellTarget`, whose use itself is highly discouraged.

The `tellTarget` action, like slash notation, is a remnant of an earlier version of Flash. It was a very powerful action, but new capabilities for calling methods and evaluating properties of objects via dot syntax make `tellTarget` obsolete. Although you can access `tellTarget` from the Actions panel, it is considered to be a deprecated action. Actions that are *deprecated* are no longer recommended because of their incompatibilities with newer ActionScript statements and syntax. You can view deprecated actions in the Actions panel's Deprecated category (**Figure 5.36**). It's a good idea to be aware of slash notation and `tellTarget`, but you should not use them. To target an object, use the action `with`, or use dot notation.

Table 5.2 shows you the dot and slash notation equivalents.

Scope

You've learned that to direct an ActionScript statement to affect a different Timeline, you need a target path that defines the *scope*. Without a target path, the ActionScript would affect its own Timeline. An ActionScript statement belongs, or is *scoped*, to a particular Timeline or a particular object where it resides. Everything you do in ActionScript has a scope, so you must be aware of it. You could be giving the correct ActionScript instructions, but if it isn't scoped correctly, nothing—or, worse, unexpected—things could happen.

When you assign ActionScript to a frame of the _root Timeline, the statement is scoped to the _root Timeline. When you assign ActionScript to a frame of a movie-clip Timeline, the statement is scoped to that movie-clip Timeline. When you create ActionScript objects by using the constructor function new, that object is scoped to the Timeline where it was created. If you create a Date object (as you did in Chapter 3) on the main Timeline with the statement

```
myDate = new Date();
```

the object myDate is scoped to the _root Timeline. You can target the myDate object with the target path, _root.myDate.

The scope of buttons, movie clips, and functions

Keeping track of the scope of ActionScript assigned to a Timeline is a straightforward matter. When you assign ActionScript to buttons, movie clips, and functions, however, you need to keep a few wrinkles in mind:

- ActionScript assigned to a button with the on action is scoped to the Timeline where the button lies. So if a button is on the main Timeline, the event handler

  ```
  on(release){
     gotoAndStop(10);
  }
  ```

  will send the playhead of the main Timeline to frame 10. The keyword this refers to the main Timeline, so this.gotoAndStop(10) is synonymous with the preceding statement, and this._rotation = 45 will rotate the main Stage, *not* the button.

- ActionScript assigned to a movie clip with the onClipEvent action is scoped to the movie clip's Timeline. So if a movie clip is on the main Timeline, the event handler

  ```
  onClipEvent(mouseDown){
     gotoAndStop(10);
  }
  ```

  will send the playhead of the movie-clip Timeline to frame 10. The keyword this refers to the movie clip, so this.gotoAndStop(10) affects the movie clip's Timeline. The statement this._rotation = 45 will rotate the movie clip.

- ActionScript assigned to a movie clip with the on action (so that it behaves like a button) is scoped to the movie clip's Timeline. So if a movie clip is on the main Timeline, the event handler

```
on(release){
   gotoAndStop(10);
}
```

will send the playhead of the movie-clip Timeline to frame 10. The keyword `this` refers to the movie clip, so `this.gotoAndStop(10)` is synonymous with the preceding statement, and `this._rotation = 45` will rotate the movie clip. Notice how the scope of the on action is different whether it is assigned to a button or to a movie clip.

- ActionScript assigned to a function is scoped to the Timeline on which it was created. So if this event handler is on the main Timeline for a movie clip or a button

```
myInstance.onRelease = function() {
   gotoAndStop(10);
}
```

the playhead on the main Timeline will move to frame 10. The keyword `this` refers to the object of the function, however, so in this example, `this` refers to myInstance. The statement `this._rotation = 45` will rotate myInstance, whether it's a button or a movie clip. The statement `this.gotoAndStop(10)` will move the playhead of myInstance only if it is a movie clip. Buttons do not have Timelines that can be navigated.

Table 5.3 reviews the scope of different event handlers for buttons, movie clips, and functions.

Table 5.3

Scope of Event Handlers

ActionScript Assigned To	Event Handler	Scope
Button	on(event)	Timeline where button instance sits. Keyword this refers to Timeline where button instance sits.
Movie Clip	onClipEvent(event) on(event)	Movie-clip Timeline. Keyword this refers to movie-clip instance.
Function on Timeline	myInstance.onEvent = function()	Timeline where function is created. Keyword this refers to the object of the function (myInstance).

Finding target paths

Sometimes, you'll want to target an object or a movie-clip Timeline, but you don't know the target path. This happens when movie clips are generated dynamically and are given names automatically. If you want the target path of any movie clip, button, or other object, you can use the property `_target` or the function `targetPath`.

The property `_target` returns the absolute target path in slash notation. So if a movie clip called child is inside a movie clip called parent, the `_target` property of child is `/parent/child`.

The function `targetPath` returns the absolute target path in dot notation. It starts the target path with the Level designation. (Chapter 6 covers levels.) `_level0`, for example, refers to the `_root` Timeline in a movie that has no other loaded movies. So if a movie clip called child is inside a movie clip called parent, the `targetPath` function returns `_level0.parent.child`.

In the following examples, you'll use the `trace` command to display the target path in the Output window. This technique is useful for debugging code, but you can also integrate `_target` and `targetPath` into expressions when you need the absolute target path of an object.

Figure 5.37 The `trace` action displays messages in the Output window.

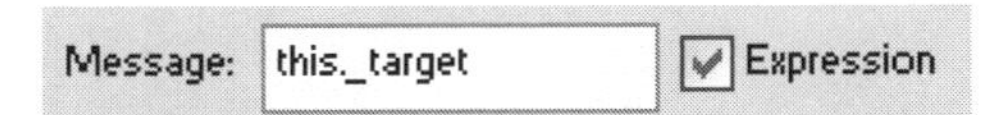

Figure 5.38 This statement in the Message field of the trace action will display the target path in slash notation of the current movie clip (which you see in Figure 5.39).

Figure 5.39 The Output window for the `_target` trace.

To find the target path with _target:

1. Create a movie-clip symbol, place it on the main Stage, and give it a name in the Property Inspector.
2. Create another movie-clip symbol, place it inside the first movie clip, and give it a name in the Property Inspector.

   Now you have a parent movie clip that contains a child movie clip. The parent movie clip sits on the main Timeline.
3. Select the child movie clip inside the parent movie clip, and open the Actions panel.
4. Choose Actions > Movie Control > on.
5. Choose Actions > Miscellaneous Actions > trace (**Figure 5.37**).

   The `trace` command appears within the `on(release)` event handler. The `trace` command displays messages in an Output window when you test a movie for debugging purposes. You will display the target path in the Output window.
6. In the Message field, type `this`, or choose it from the Insert Target Path button.
7. Enter a dot, and then choose Properties > _target.
8. Check the Expression checkbox (**Figure 5.38**).
9. Test your movie.

   When you click the child movie clip, the Output window appears and displays its target path (**Figure 5.39**).

To find the target path with targetPath:

1. Continue with the file you created in the preceding task.
2. Select the child movie clip, and open the Actions panel.
3. Select the `trace` statement in the Script pane.
4. Delete the current contents of the Message field.
5. Choose Functions > targetPath.
6. Between the parentheses of the `targetPath` function, enter the keyword `this`.
7. Make sure that the Expression checkbox remains checked (**Figure 5.40**).
8. Test your movie.

   When you click the child movie clip, the Output window appears and displays its target path (**Figure 5.41**).

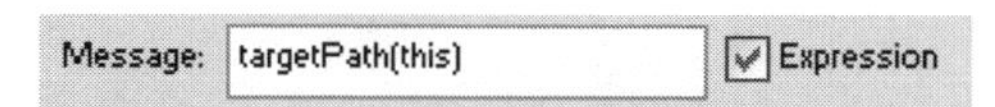

Figure 5.40 This statement in the Message field of the trace action will display the target path in dot notation of the current movie clip (which you see in Figure 5.41).

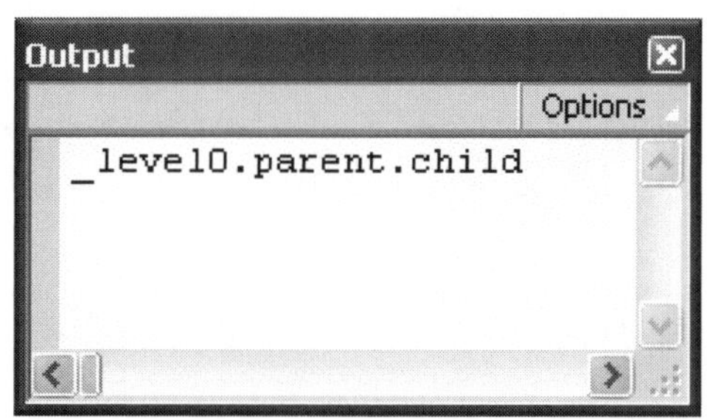

Figure 5.41 The Output window for the `targetPath` trace.

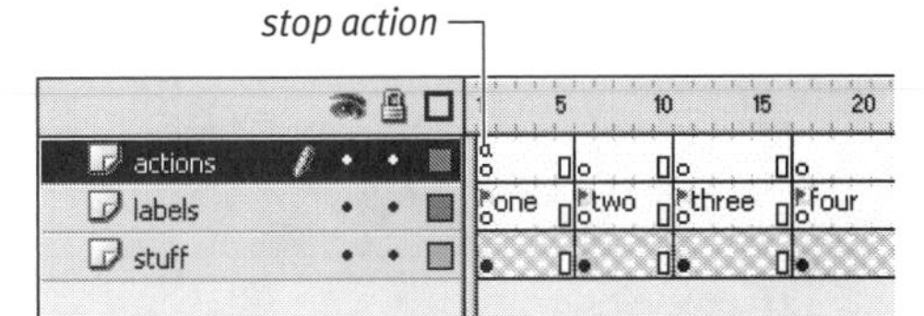

Figure 5.42 The movie clip as a container. This movie clip has a `stop` action in the first keyframe. The other labeled keyframes can contain buttons, graphics, animations, or any other kind of Flash information, which you can access simply by targeting the movie clip and moving its playhead to the appropriate keyframe.

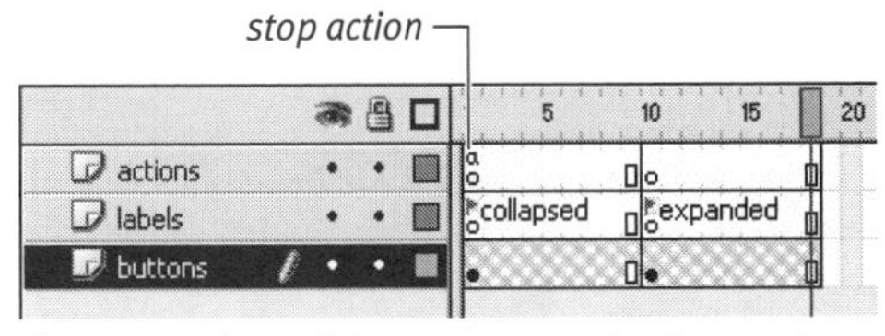

Figure 5.43 The pull-down-menu movie clip contains both collapsed and expanded states.

Movie Clips As Containers

So far in this chapter, you've learned how to name your movie-clip objects, target each one, and navigate within their Timelines from any other Timeline in your movie. But how does the ability to control movie-clip Timelines translate into meaningful interactivity for your Flash project? The key is to think of movie clips as being containers that hold stuff: animation, graphics, sound, and even data. By moving the playhead back and forth or playing certain parts of a particular movie-clip Timeline, you can access that stuff whenever you want, independently of what else is going on (**Figure 5.42**).

A common way to use movie clips, for example, is to have their Timelines contain different states that toggle from one to the other. In Chapter 4, you built pull-down menus that serve exactly that purpose. The pull-down menu is essentially a movie-clip object that toggles between a collapsed state and an expanded state. The buttons inside the movie clip control which of those two states you see, while also providing navigation outside the movie clip's Timeline (**Figure 5.43**).

Another example is using different keyframes of a movie clip to hold different states of a main character in a game. Depending on the circumstances, you can tell the playhead to go to a certain frame of the movie clip to display the character in a sad state, in a happy state, or in a sleepy state.

The following example demonstrates how to create a radio button with a movie clip. Building a radio button is a matter of defining two different keyframes that toggle between an on state and an off state.

To create a radio button:

1. Create a movie-clip symbol.
2. Go to symbol-editing mode for the movie clip, and insert a new keyframe.
3. In the first keyframe, choose Actions > Movie Control > stop.
4. Insert another keyframe, and choose Actions > Movie Control > stop.

   The `stop` actions in both keyframes will prevent this movie clip from playing automatically and stop the playhead on each keyframe.
5. Insert another new layer.
6. Create graphics that correspond to the first keyframe and graphics that correspond to the second keyframe (**Figure 5.44**).
7. Exit symbol-editing mode, and return to the main Stage.
8. Place an instance of your movie clip on the Stage.
9. Select the movie clip, and open the Actions panel.
10. Choose Actions > Movie Control > on.
11. Choose Actions > Movie Control > play.
12. Test your movie.

    When you click the movie clip, the playhead moves to the next keyframe and stops. Each click toggles between two different states, just like a radio button (**Figure 5.45**).

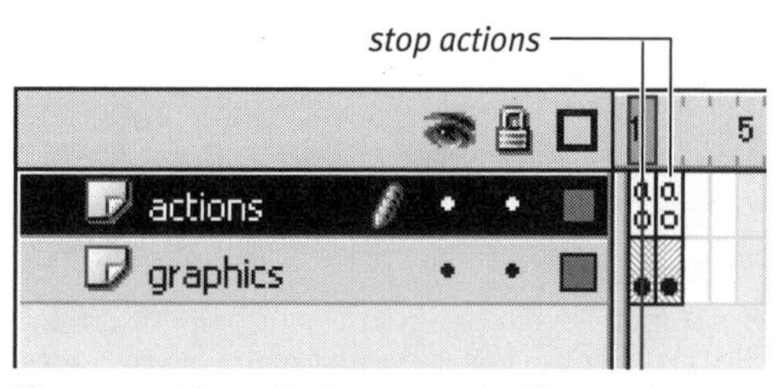

Figure 5.44 The radio-button movie clip contains a `stop` action in both keyframes and two different states that toggle.

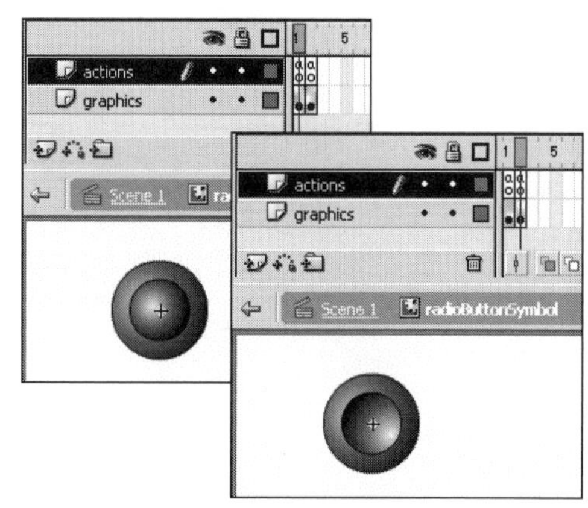

Figure 5.45 The movie clip in the first keyframe (top) sends the playhead to the second keyframe (bottom), and vice versa.

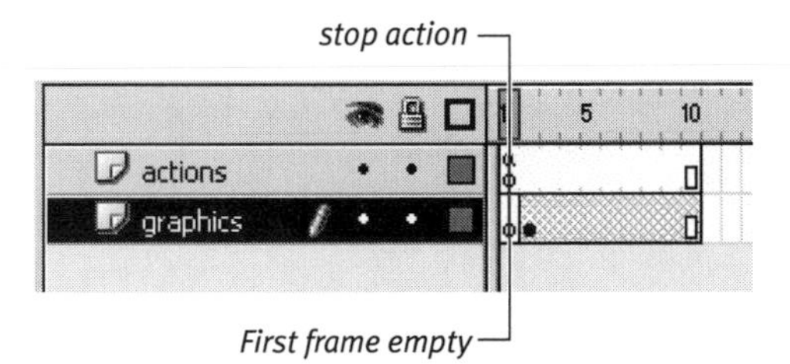

Figure 5.46 A movie clip with an empty first keyframe will be invisible on the Stage. This movie clip has a `stop` action in the top layer and graphics in the bottom layer starting in keyframe 2.

You can do the same thing to a movie clip that you do to a button to make it invisible—that is, leave the first keyframe that is visible to the user blank, so that the instance is invisible on the Stage initially. If the first keyframe of a movie clip is blank and contains a `stop` frame action to keep it there, you can control when to expose the other frames inside that movie-clip Timeline. You could create a movie clip of an explosion, but keep the first keyframe blank. Place this movie clip on a graphic of a submarine, and at the appropriate time, advance to the next frame to reveal the explosion.

Note that you have other ways of using ActionScript to hide or reveal the contents of a movie clip or to place a movie clip on the Stage dynamically; you'll learn about these possibilities in upcoming chapters. But being aware of both the simple (frame-based, as described here) and sophisticated (purely ActionScript-based) approaches will help you tackle a broader range of animation and interactivity challenges.

To create an "invisible" movie clip:

1. Create a movie-clip symbol.
2. Go to symbol-editing mode for the movie clip, and insert a new keyframe into its Timeline.
3. Select the first keyframe, and open the Actions panel.
4. Choose Actions > Movie Control > stop.
5. Leave the first keyframe empty, and begin placing graphics and animations in the second keyframe (**Figure 5.46**).

continues on next page

6. Exit symbol-editing mode, and return to the main Timeline.
7. Drag an instance of the movie clip from the library to the Stage.

   The instance appears on the Stage as an empty circle (**Figure 5.47**). The empty circle represents the registration point of the instance, allowing you to place the instance exactly where you want it.

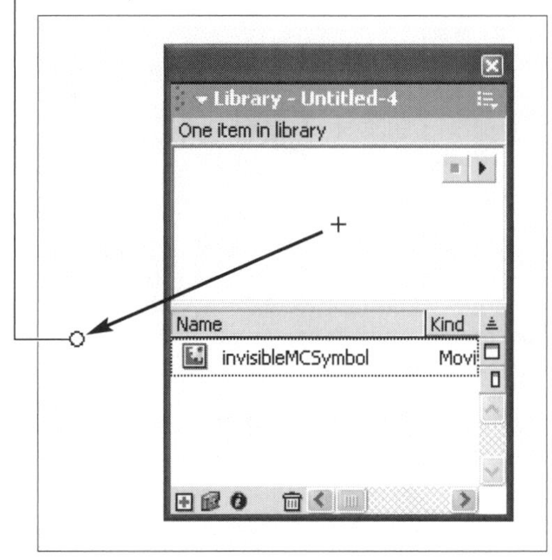

Figure 5.47 An instance of a movie clip with an empty first frame appears as an empty circle.

Managing Outside Communication

6

Flash provides powerful tools to communicate with other applications and external data, scripts, and files to extend its functionality. By using Flash to link to the Web, you can build sites that combine Flash animation and interactivity with non-Flash media supported by the browser. Use Flash to make your browser link to PDF documents, RealMedia files, or even Java applets. Use Flash to send email, communicate with JavaScript, or relay information to and from servers with the CGI GET and POST methods. Flash also supports XML, allowing you to create customized code for data-driven e-commerce solutions. This chapter introduces you to some ways Flash can communicate with HTML, JavaScript, CGI, and XML.

You can also work with multiple Flash movies. Load one or more Flash movies into another Flash movie to create modular projects that are easier to edit and have smaller file sizes. Your main Flash movie might serve simply as an interface that loads your portfolio of Flash animations when the viewer selects them. Learn to communicate from the main Flash movie to its loaded movie or even between two different Flash movies in separate browser windows.

In this chapter, you'll also learn about stand-alone Flash players, called *projectors*, and you'll see how specialized commands affect the way they appear, function, and interact with other programs. Because they don't require a browser to play, projectors are ideal for distributing Flash content on CD-ROM or other portable media.

Finally, you'll learn to communicate with your movie's playback environment. Learn to detect your viewers' system capabilities, Stage size, or Flash Player version so that you can better cater your content to them. Check on the amount of data that has downloaded to users' computers so you can tell them how much longer they have to wait before your movie begins. Keeping track of these external factors will help you provide a friendlier and customized user experience. Along with providing versatile and sophisticated communication options between Flash movies and between the browser and external files, Flash can serve as a key component of dynamic, commercial, and entertainment applications.

Communicating Through the Web Browser

Flash links to the Web browser through the action `getURL` in the Actions panel. This action is very similar to the HTML tag `<A HREF>`, in which the URL of a Web site is specified in the form `http://www.domainname.com/directory`. Use an *absolute URL* (a complete address to a specific file) to link to any Web site, or use a *relative URL* (a path to a file that's described in relation to the current directory) to link to local files contained on your hard drive or a CD-ROM. The `getURL` action also provides ways to target different frames you create within the browser window or in new browser windows. You can create Flash movies that navigate between these frames and windows and control what loads in each one.

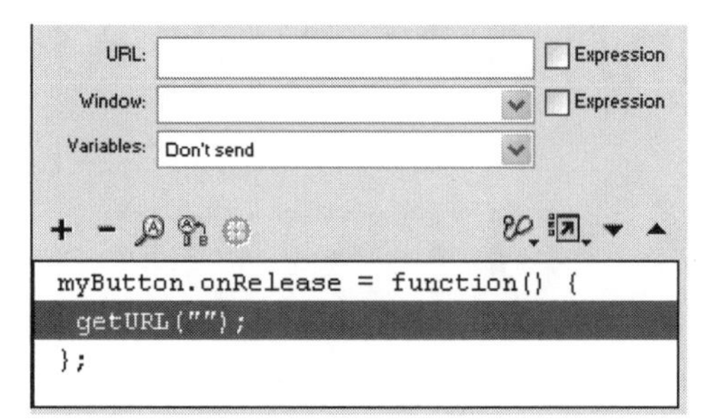

Figure 6.1 The `getURL` action has parameters for a URL, window name, and methods of sending variables to CGI scripts.

Figure 6.2 Enter a URL in the Parameters pane of the `getURL` action.

Linking to the Web

Use the action `getURL` to link to the Web with the standard scheme `http://` followed by the rest of the Web address. Use different schemes to request different protocols, such as `mailto:` for email.

If you test your Flash movie by choosing Control > Test Movie or play it in Flash Player, the action `getURL` automatically launches the default browser and loads the specified Web address in a new window.

To link to a Web site with the getURL action:

1. Create a button symbol, drag an instance from the library to the Stage, and give it a name in the Property Inspector.
2. Select the first frame of the main Timeline, and open the Actions panel.
3. Choose Objects > Movie > Button > Events > onRelease.

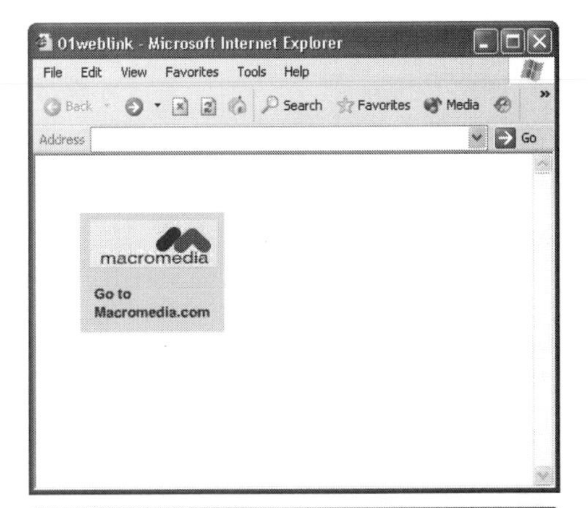

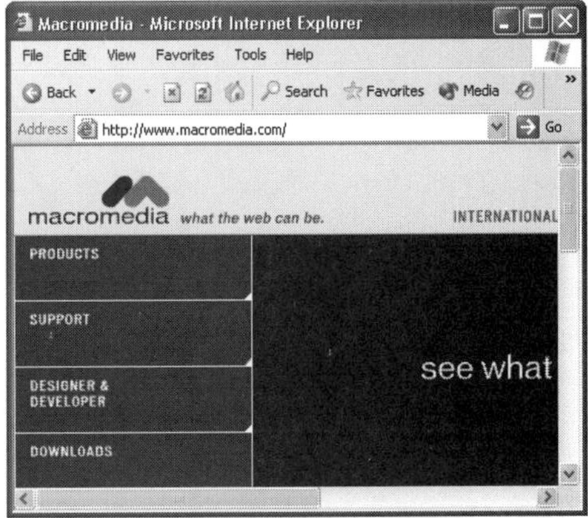

Figure 6.3 The Flash movie (top) links to the Macromedia site in the same browser window (bottom) when the Window field is left blank.

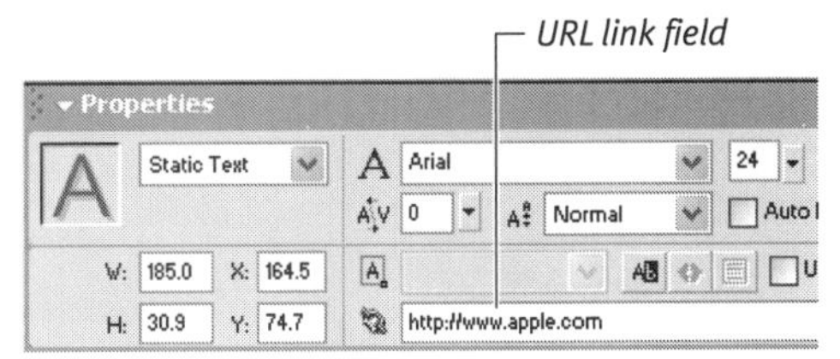

Figure 6.4 A Web address in the link field of the Property Inspector makes the entire static text link to the site.

4. In the Object field, enter the name of your button symbol.

   The `onRelease` event handler for your button is created.

5. Choose Actions > Browser/Network > getURL (Esc + gu).

   The `getURL` action is added to the `onRelease` event handler (**Figure 6.1**).

6. In the URL field, enter the full address of a Web site (**Figure 6.2**).

7. Leave the Expression checkbox unchecked.

8. Export your Flash movie, and play it in either Flash Player or a browser.

   When you click the button you created, the Web site loads in the same window as your Flash movie (**Figure 6.3**). Click the Back button in your browser to return to your Flash movie.

✔ Tips

- You can also link to the Web from a static horizontal text block. Create static text with the text tool, and in the Property Inspector, enter the address of the Web site in the link field (**Figure 6.4**). Your static text will display a dotted underline to show that it is linked to a URL. When your viewers click the text, the Web site will load in the same browser window as your Flash movie.

- In addition to button instances, the `getURL` action can be assigned to a keyframe. If assigned to a keyframe, `getURL` will link to the URL when the playhead enters that particular frame. This method is effective for loading Web links automatically—perhaps after an introductory splash animation or maybe as a way to mimic a series of banner ads that load automatically. You don't give your audience control but essentially pull them along for the ride.

To preaddress an email:

1. Again, create a button symbol, drag an instance from the library to the Stage, and give it a name in the Property Inspector.
2. Select the first frame of the main Timeline, and open the Actions panel.
3. Choose Objects > Movie > Button > Events > onRelease.
4. In the Object field, enter the name of your button symbol.

   The `onRelease` event handler for your button is created.
5. Choose Actions > Browser/Network > getURL.

   The `getURL` action is added to the `onRelease` event handler.
6. In the URL field, enter `mailto:` followed by the email address of the person who should receive the email (**Figure 6.5**).
7. Leave the Expression checkbox unchecked.
8. Export your Flash movie, and play it in either Flash Player or a browser.

   When you click the button you created, an email form appears with the recipient's email address already filled in (**Figure 6.6**). The viewer then types a message and clicks Send. Use `getURL` to preaddress email that viewers can use to contact you about your Web site or to request more information.

✔ Tip

- It's a good idea to spell out the email address of the `getURL mailto:` recipient in your Flash movie (**Figure 6.7**). If a person's browser isn't configured to send email, an error message will appear instead of an email form. By spelling out the address, you allow users to enter it in their email applications themselves.

Figure 6.5 Enter email recipients after `mailto:` in the URL field. Separate additional email addresses with commas.

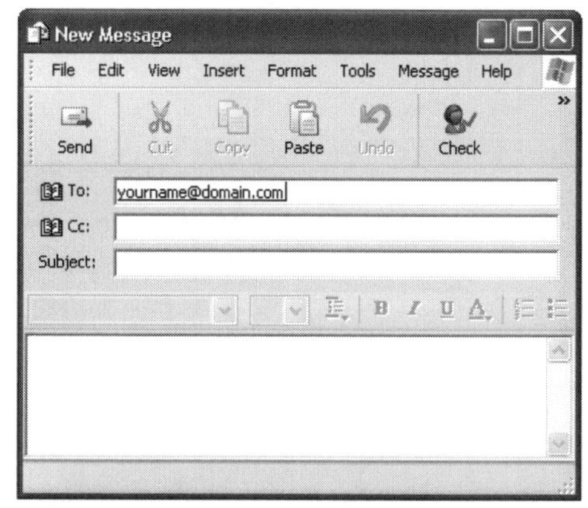

Figure 6.6 A new email message appears in your default mail program.

Contact: yourname@yourdomain.com

Figure 6.7 This email address is also a button that links to the browser via `mailto:`.

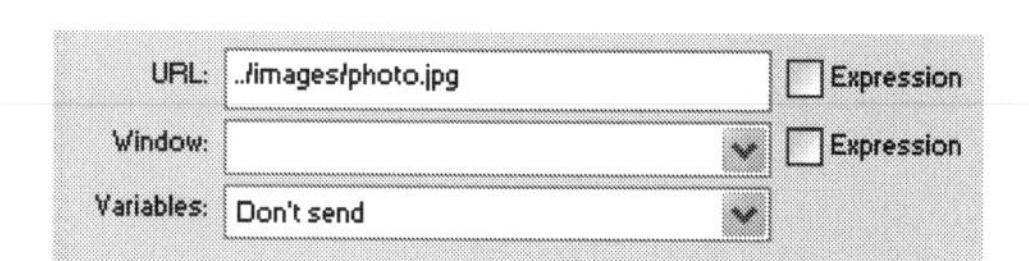

Figure 6.8 This relative URL goes up one directory level and looks for a folder called images, which contains a file called photo.jpg.

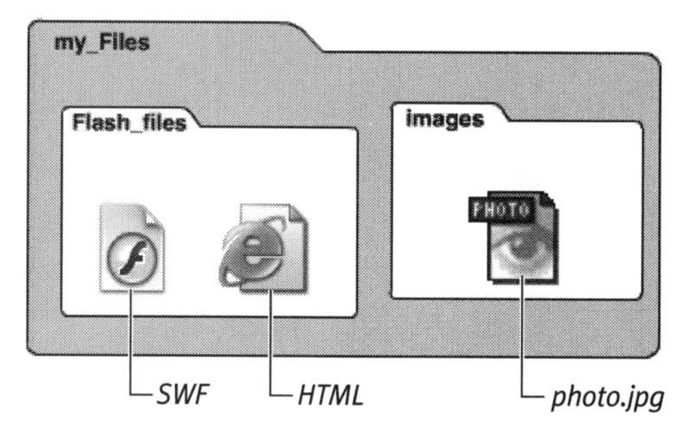

Figure 6.9 Your Flash movie (SWF) and its accompanying HTML file are in a directory that's at the same level as the directory that contains the file `photo.jpg`.

Linking to local files

Use relative paths rather than complete URLs to specify local files instead of files on the Web. This method allows you to distribute your Flash movie on a CD-ROM or floppy disk without requiring an Internet connection. Instead of using the complete URL `http://www.myServer.com/images/photo.jpg`, for example, you can specify just `images/photo.jpg`, and Flash will have to look only inside the images folder to find the file called photo.jpg.

To link to a local file:

1. As before, create a button symbol, drag an instance from the library to the Stage, and give it a name in the Property Inspector.
2. Select the first frame of the main Timeline, and open the Actions panel.
3. Choose Objects > Movie > Button > Events > onRelease.
4. In the Object field, enter the name of your button symbol.

   The `onRelease` event handler for your button is created.
5. Choose Actions > Browser/Network > getURL.

   The `getURL` action is added to the `onRelease` event handler.
6. In the URL field, enter the relative path to the desired file.

   Use a slash (/) to separate directories and two dots (..) to move up one directory (**Figure 6.8**).
7. Leave the Expression checkbox unchecked.
8. Export your Flash movie, and place it and your linked file in the correct folder hierarchy (**Figure 6.9**).

continues on next page

9. Play the movie in either Flash Player or a browser.

   When you click the button you created, Flash looks for the file, using the relative path, and loads it into the same browser window (**Figure 6.10**).

✔ Tip

- Any file type can be targeted in the URL field of the `getURL` action. You can load HTML, JPEG, GIF, QuickTime, and PDF files, and even other Flash movies. Just keep in mind that the viewer's browser must have the required plug-ins to display these different media types.

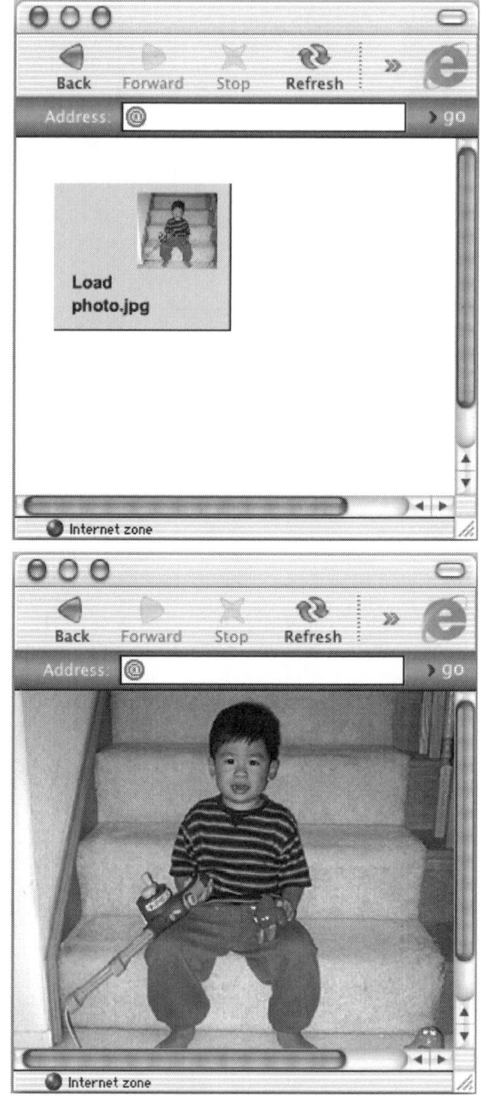

Figure 6.10 The Flash movie (top) links to the local file in the same browser window (bottom).

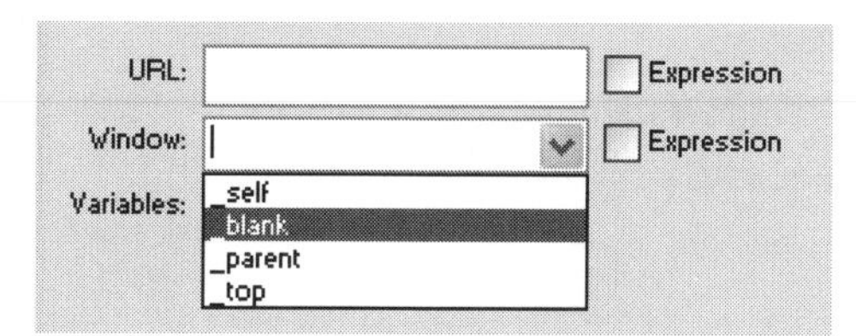

Figure 6.11 The Window field lets you choose reserved keywords from a pull-down menu.

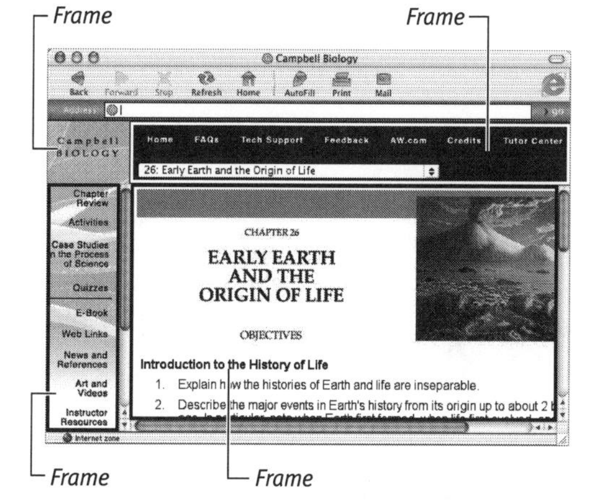

Figure 6.12 A Web site using frames to divide content. The window is divided horizontally into two frames. The bottom and top frames are divided vertically into two more frames. Ad banners, navigation bars, and content usually are separated in this way.

Working with browser framesets and windows

When you play your Flash movie in a browser window, the `getURL` action loads the new Web address in the same window, replacing your Flash movie. To make it load into a new window or a different frame of your window so that your original Flash movie isn't replaced, use the Window options in `getURL` (**Figure 6.11**).

What's the difference between a window and a frame? Browser windows can be divided into separate areas, or *frames*, that contain individual Web pages. The collection of frames is called a *frameset*, and the frameset HTML file defines the frame proportions and the name of each frame (**Figure 6.12**).

The Flash Window parameter can use the name that the frameset HTML file assigns a frame to load a URL directly into that specific frame. This method is very similar to using the HTML `<A HREF>` tag attribute `TARGET`. If you divide a Web page into two frames, for example, you can call the left frame navigator and the right frame contents. Place a Flash movie in the navigator frame with buttons that are assigned the `getURL` action. By entering the frame name contents as the Window parameter of `getURL`, you target the right frame to load the URL.

continues on next page

The Window parameter also provides reserved target names for you to use (**Figure 6.13**). **Table 6.1** summarizes what these names do.

Table 6.1

Window Parameters for getURL

Window Name	Explanation
_self	Specifies the current frame of the current browser window; the default behavior when no Window parameter is specified.
_blank	Specifies a new browser window.
_parent	Specifies the frameset that contains the current frame.
_top	Specifies the top-level frameset in the current browser window.

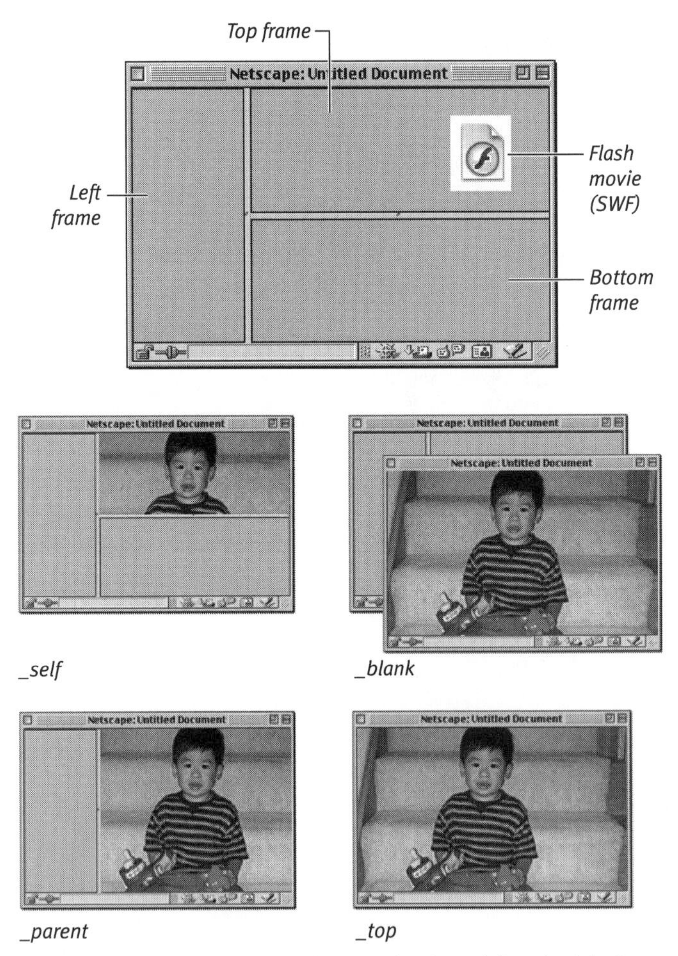

Figure 6.13 At top, a frameset divides a window into a left and a right frame. The right frame contains another frameset that divides itself into top and bottom frames. The Flash movie (SWF) plays in the top frame of the second frameset. The window names specify where the URL loads.

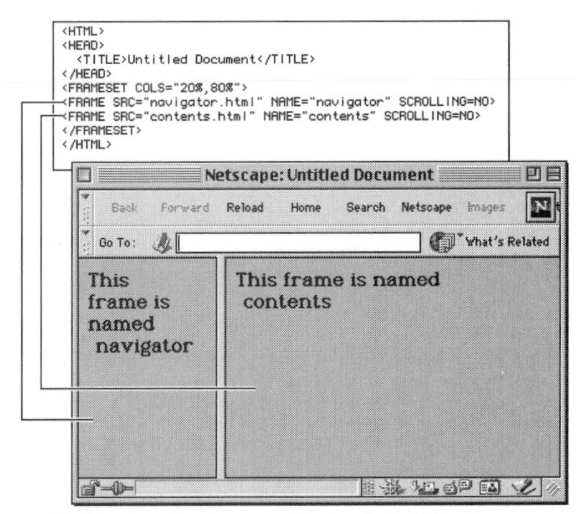

Figure 6.14 The frameset file (top) divides this window into a left column named navigator, which is 20 percent of the browser width, and a right column named contents, which is 80 percent of the browser width (bottom).

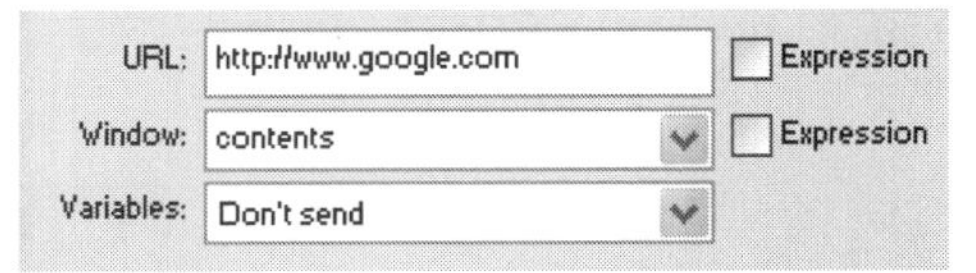

Figure 6.15 The parameters area of the `getURL` action specifies the Google Web site to load in the contents frame.

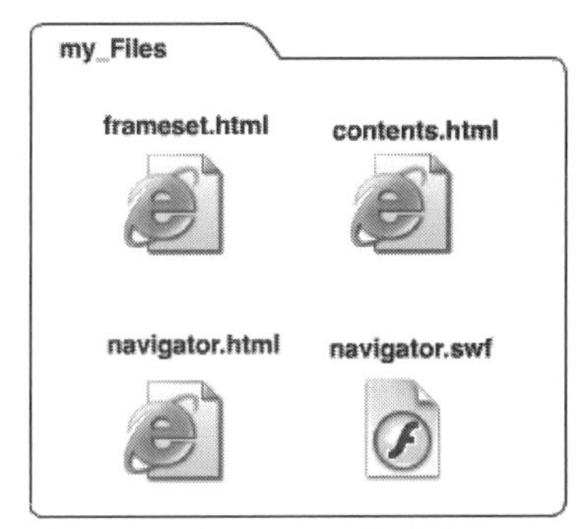

Figure 6.16 The frameset.html file puts the contents.html file in the contents frame and the navigator.html file in the navigator frame. The navigator.html file embeds the Flash movie (navigator.swf).

To open a Web site in a named frame:

1. Create an HTML frameset with two frames and unique names for both.

   Your Flash movie will play in one frame, and the Web-site links will be loaded into the other frame (**Figure 6.14**).

2. Create a button symbol, drag an instance from the library to the Stage as you did in the preceding tasks, and give it a name in the Property Inspector.

3. Select the first frame of the main Timeline, and open the Actions panel.

4. Choose Objects > Movie > Button > Events > onRelease.

5. In the Object field, enter the name of your button symbol.

   The `onRelease` event handler for your button is created.

6. Choose Actions > Browser/Network > getURL.

   The `getURL` action is added to the `onRelease` event handler.

7. In the URL field, enter `http://` and then the address of a Web site.

8. Leave the Expression checkbox unchecked.

9. In the Window field of the Parameters pane, enter the name of the frame established in the HTML frameset (**Figure 6.15**).

10. Publish your Flash movie with its accompanying HTML file.

11. Create another HTML file for the other frame in the frameset.

12. Name both HTML files according to the <FRAME SRC> tags in the frameset document, and place all files within the same folder (**Figure 6.16**).

continues on next page

13. Open the frameset document in a browser.

    Your Flash movie plays in one frame. The button loads a Web site in the other frame (**Figure 6.17**).

To open a Web site in a new window:

1. Create a button symbol, drag an instance from the library to the Stage, and give it a name in the Property Inspector.
2. Select the first frame of the main Timeline, and open the Actions panel.
3. Choose Objects > Movie > Button > Events > onRelease.
4. In the Object field, enter the name of your button symbol.

   The `onRelease` event handler for your button is created.
5. Choose Actions > Browser/Network > getURL.

   The `getURL` action is added to the `onRelease` event handler.
6. In the URL field, enter a Web-site address.
7. Leave the Expression checkbox unchecked.
8. Choose _blank from the Window pull-down menu (**Figure 6.18**); then export your Flash movie and play it in Flash Player or a browser.

   When you click the button you created, a new window appears, and the Web site loads in it.

   or

   In the Window field of the `getURL` action, enter a unique name for your new window (**Figure 6.19**); then export your Flash movie and play it in Flash Player or a browser.

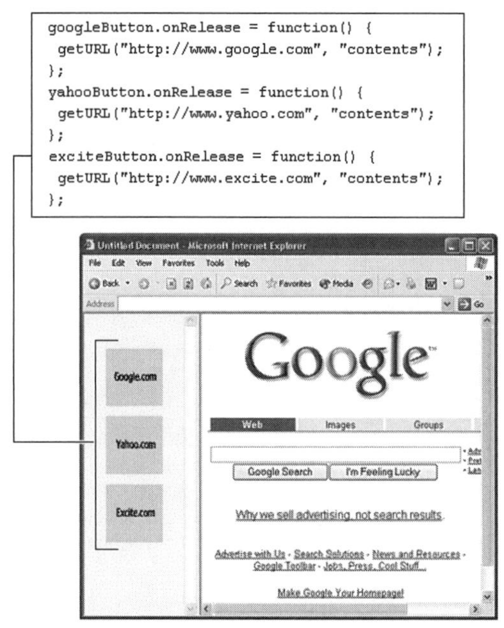

Figure 6.17 The ActionScript for the buttons in the navigator frame is shown. The Google, Yahoo!, and Excite sites load in the other frame, keeping the left frame intact.

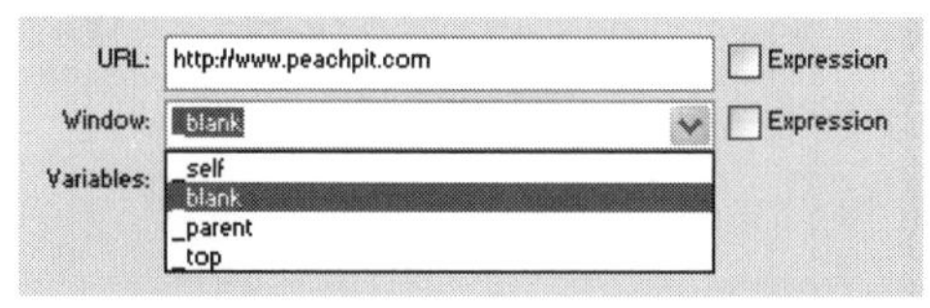

Figure 6.18 When you choose `_blank` from the Window pull-down menu, the Peachpit Web site will load in a new, unnamed window.

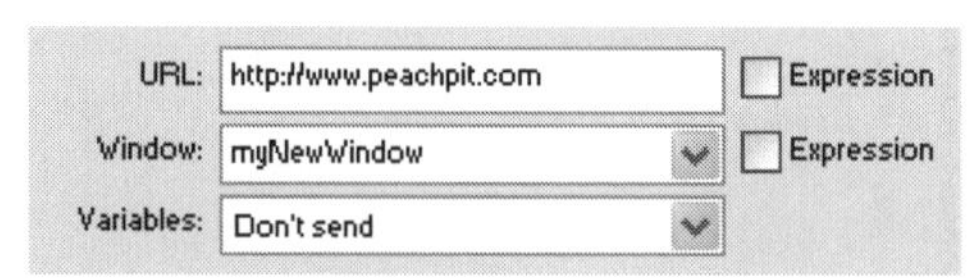

Figure 6.19 The Peachpit Web site will load in a new window called myNewWindow if that name is entered in the Window field.

Figure 6.20 Multiple `getURL` actions with the Window field set to `_blank` (top) and set to a unique name (bottom). This behavior happens on all platforms except Internet Explorer on Windows.

When you click your button, Flash looks for the frame or window with the name that you specified in the Window field of the `getURL` action. Not finding it, Flash creates a new window with that name.

✔ Tips

- There is a crucial difference between opening a new window by using `_blank` and opening a new window by using a name that you enter yourself. If you use `_blank`, each time you click your button to link to a Web site, a new window will be created. If you use a name in the Window field, the first click will open a new window. Subsequent clicks actually find the newly created window you named, so Flash reloads the Web site into that existing window (**Figure 6.20**). Both methods are useful, depending on whether you want your Web links to be in separate windows or to replace each other in the first new window.
- Be careful when you create new browser windows, and keep track of where they are. Sometimes, windows may be hidden behind the active window, loading Web sites that the viewer cannot see.

Using JavaScript to control new window parameters

The Window field in the `getURL` action is useful for directing Web links to new browser windows, but the appearance and location of these new windows are set by the browser's preferences. If you play a Flash movie in a browser that shows the location bar and the toolbar, for example, and you open a new window, the new window will also have a location bar and a toolbar. You can't control these window parameters directly with Flash, but you can control them indirectly with JavaScript.

continues on next page

In the HTML page that holds your Flash movie, you can define JavaScript functions that control the opening and even closing of new browser windows. In your Flash movie, you can call on these JavaScript functions by using the `getURL` action. Instead of entering a Web address in the URL field, you enter `javascript:` followed by the name of the function. Flash finds the JavaScript in the HTML page, and the browser calls the function.

You can use JavaScript to control several window properties. These properties specify the way the window looks, how it works, and where it's located on the screen (**Figure 6.21**). These properties can be defined in the `getURL` action in your Flash movie and passed to the JavaScript function in the HTML page. When you define these window properties, use `yes` (`1`), `no` (`0`), or a number specifying pixel dimensions or coordinates. **Table 6.2** lists the most common window properties that are compatible with both Internet Explorer and Netscape Navigator.

Table 6.2

JavaScript Window Properties

Property	Description
height	Vertical dimension, in pixels.
width	Horizontal dimension, in pixels.
left	X coordinate of left edge.
top	Y coordinate of top edge.
resizable	Resizable area in the bottom-right corner that allows the window to change dimensions (yes/no or 1/0).
scrollbars	The vertical and horizontal scroll bars (yes/no or 1/0).
directories	Also called links, where certain bookmarks are accessible (yes/no or 1/0).
location	Location bar, containing URL area (yes/no or 1/0).
menubar	Menu bar, containing drop-down menus such as File and Edit. Works only in the Windows operating system (yes/no or 1/0).
status	Status bar in the bottom-left corner, containing browser status and security (yes/no or 1/0).
toolbar	Toolbar, containing the back and forward buttons and other navigation aides (yes/no or 1/0)

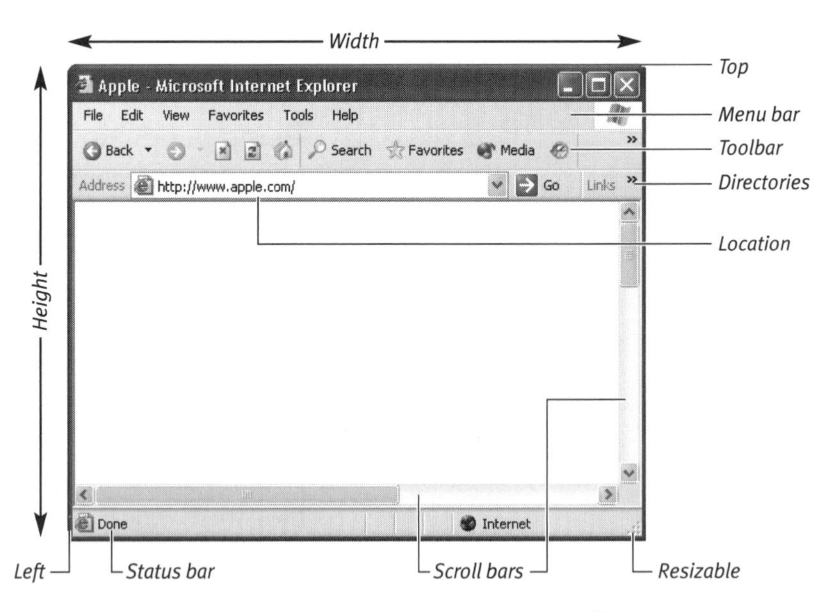

Figure 6.21 You can set the properties of a browser window with JavaScript.

To open a new window with JavaScript:

1. Create a button, name it, and attach the `getURL` action to an `onRelease` event handler as described in the preceding tasks.

   This button will communicate with a JavaScript function in the HTML page.

2. In the URL field, enter the following:

   ```
   javascript:openWindow
   ('http://www.peachpit.com',
   'myNewWindow','toolbar=0,location=0,
   directories=0,status=0,menubar=0,
   scrollbars=0,resizable=0,width=200,
   height=250,left=80,top=180')
   ```

   Because this statement is so long, it may be easier to add the ActionScript in Expert mode. The information that you enter in single quotes between the parentheses are parameters that get passed to the JavaScript function called `openWindow`. You don't have to define all the window properties (**Figure 6.22**).

3. Leave the Expression checkbox unchecked and the Window field blank.

4. Publish your Flash movie with its associated HTML file.

continues on next page

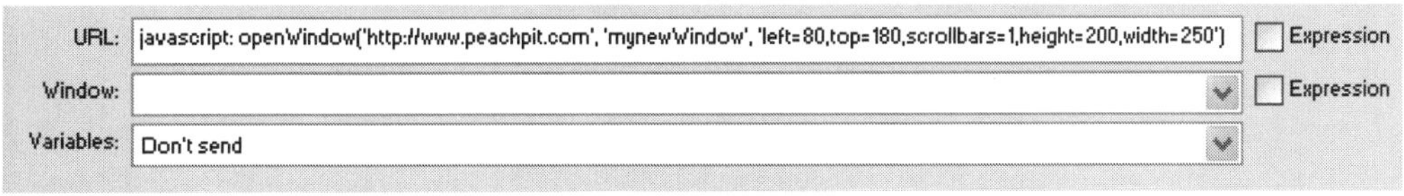

URL: javascript: openWindow('http://www.peachpit.com', 'mynewWindow', 'left=80,top=180,scrollbars=1,height=200,width=250') Expression
Window: Expression
Variables: Don't send

Figure 6.22 The `javascript:` statement calls the `openWindow` function in the HTML page that embeds the Flash movie.

5. Open the HTML page in a text- or HTML-editing application such as BBEdit.

   Now you must define the javaScript function in the HTML page.

6. Add the following script to the head of the HTML page:

```
<SCRIPT LANGUAGE="JavaScript">
function openWindow(URL, windowName,
windowProperties) {
newWindow = window.open(URL,
windowName, windowProperties);
}
</SCRIPT>
```

   This script defines a function called openWindow that has three parameters: URL, windowName, and windowProperties. When this function is called, the object newWindow is created and receives the three parameters from the Flash movie. The HTML page should be similar to **Figure 6.23**.

7. Add the following statement inside the <EMBED> tag after the width and height parameters in the HTML code where your Flash movie (SWF) is referenced:

```
SwLiveConnect=true
```

   This crucial parameter enables Netscape to launch the interface that allows your Flash movie to communicate with JavaScript.

JavaScript

```
<HTML>
<HEAD>
<TITLE>newWindowJS</TITLE>

<SCRIPT LANGUAGE="JavaScript">

<!-- Begin
function openWindow(URL, windowName, windowFeatures) {
newWindow = window.open(URL, windowName, windowFeatures)
}

// End -->
</SCRIPT>

</HEAD>
```

Figure 6.23 JavaScript code in the header of an HTML document. The Flash movie embedded in this HTML document will call on the function openWindow.

9. Save the modified HTML page, and open it in a browser.

   When you click the button that you created, Flash passes the Web address, the window name, and the window properties to the JavaScript function called `openWindow`. Then JavaScript creates a new window with the new properties (**Figure 6.24**).

✔ Tips

- This method of using Flash to talk to JavaScript will not work with older versions of Internet Explorer (version 3 or earlier), or with Internet Explorer 4.5 or earlier for the Macintosh.
- More JavaScript window properties are available, but many of them work in only one of the two most popular browsers. The properties `innerHeight` and `innerWidth`, for example, define the dimensions of the actual window content area, but these properties are unique to Netscape Navigator. You are safe if you stick to the properties listed in Table 6.2.

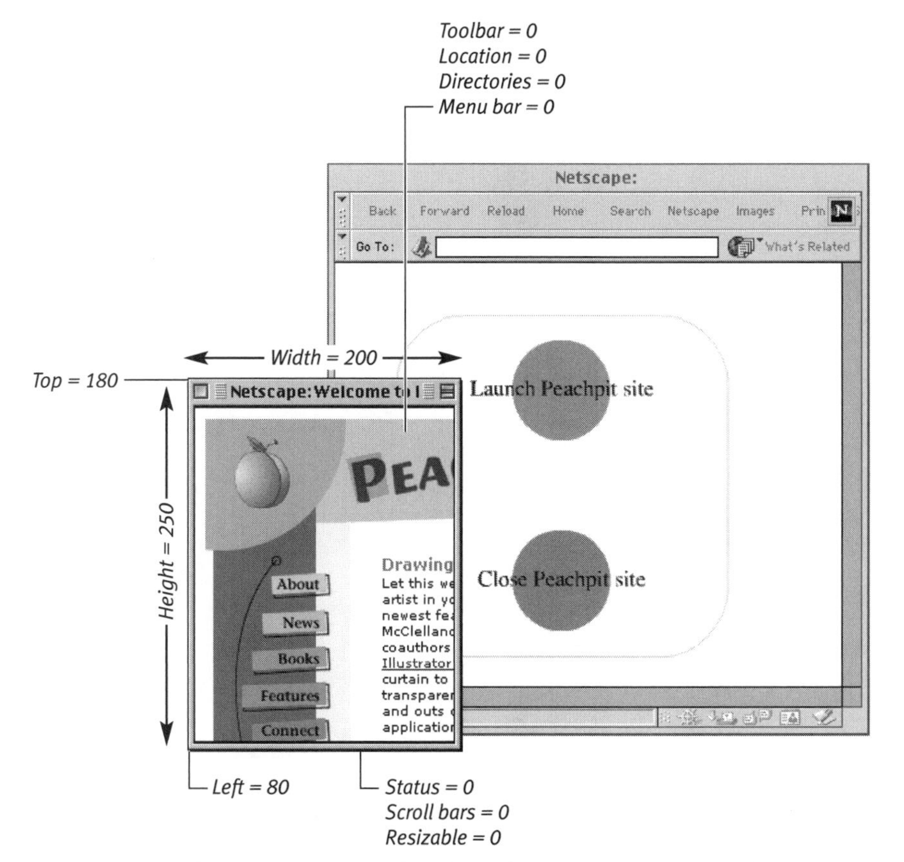

Figure 6.24 A customized window without any features is called *chromeless*. *Chrome* refers to all the interface features of a window.

After you open a window with JavaScript, you can use the same strategy to close it.

To close a window with JavaScript:

1. In your Flash movie, create a second button, and assign the `getURL` action to an `onRelease` event handler.
2. In the URL field, enter the following (**Figure 6.25**):

   `javascript:closeWindow('myNewWindow')`

3. Leave the Expression checkbox unchecked and the Window field blank.
4. Publish your Flash movie and modify its HTML page by adding JavaScript and the `SWLiveConnect` statement as you did in the preceding task.

   Next you must define the function called `closeWindow` in the JavaScript portion of your HTML page.

5. Add the new `closeWindow` function after the `openWindow` function, as follows:

```
function closeWindow(windowName)
{
newWindow.close(windowName)
}
```

   The function `closeWindow` calls the method `close()`. The parameter `windowName` is the name of the window you want to close (**Figure 6.26**).

6. Save your modified HTML page, and open it in a browser.

   When you click the first button, Flash tells JavaScript to create a new window called myNewWindow. When you click the second button, Flash tells JavaScript to close the window called myNewWindow.

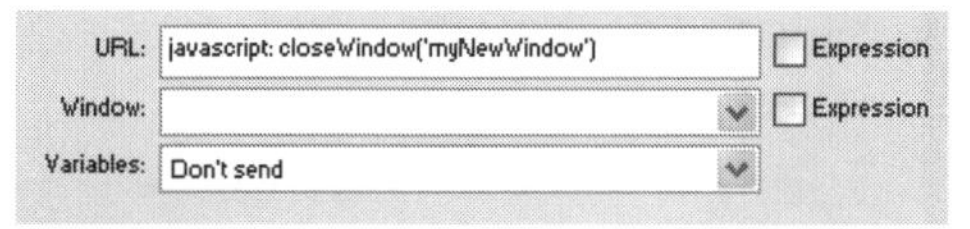

Figure 6.25 The `getURL` action calls the JavaScript `closeWindow` function. The window object called myNewWindow closes.

JavaScript

```
<HTML>
<HEAD>
<TITLE>newWindowJS</TITLE>

<SCRIPT LANGUAGE="JavaScript">

<!-- Begin
function openWindow(URL, windowName, windowFeatures) {
newWindow = window.open(URL, windowName, windowFeatures)
}
function closeWindow(windowName) {
newWindow.close(windowName)
}

// End -->
</SCRIPT>

</HEAD>
```

Figure 6.26 JavaScript code in the header of an HTML document. Both the `openWindow` and `closeWindow` functions are defined here.

Using CGI and the GET and POST methods

The last parameter in the `getURL` action allows you to send information via the `GET` and `POST` methods. These methods send variables that you define in your Flash movie to a server-side application (such as a CGI application) for processing. These methods are most commonly used to send information such as keywords to a search engine or a login name and password to enter a Web site.

The difference between `GET` and `POST` is very simple:

- `GET` appends the variables to the URL in the `getURL` action and is used for very few variables, and for those that contain only a small amount of information. The variables `term=CGI`, `category=All`, and `pref=all` are put at the end of this URL as follows:

  ```
  http://search.domain.com/cgi-bin/
  search?term=CGI&category=All&pref=all
  ```

  You've probably seen this type of long URL after you've requested information from a search engine.

- `POST` sends the variables in the HTTP header of the user's browser. Use `POST` for more security or to send long strings of information in the `getURL` operation. A message board, for example, would do better with a `POST` method.

After the variables are sent to the Web server, they are processed by the CGI scripts in the URL or HTTP headers. These server-side scripts are handled by your Internet service provider or your Webmaster, so you should contact them for more information.

To send information by using GET:

1. Select the text tool, and drag out a text field on the Stage.
2. In the Property Inspector, choose Input Text from the pull-down menu.

   This option lets you use the text field you created to enter information.
3. In the Variable field of the Property Inspector, enter `emailStr` (**Figure 6.27**).

   Whatever you enter in that text field is assigned to the variable `emailStr`.
4. Create a button, place an instance of it on the Stage, and name the button in the Property Inspector.
5. Assign the `getURL` action to the button's `onRelease` event handler.
6. In the URL field of the Parameters pane in the Actions panel, enter the address to the server-side script (such as `http://www.myserver.com/cgi-bin/list.cgi`).
7. From the Window pull-down menu, choose _self.
8. From the Variables pull-down menu, choose Send Using GET (**Figure 6.28**).

   Your Script pane should look as follows:

   ```
   myButton.onRelease = function {
   getURL ( "http://www.myserver.com/
   cgi-bin/list.cgi", "_self", "GET");
   }
   ```

   When a viewer enters an email address in the text field and then clicks the button, the email address is added to the end of the URL and is sent to the CGI script.

   You'll learn more about variables and input text in Part V.

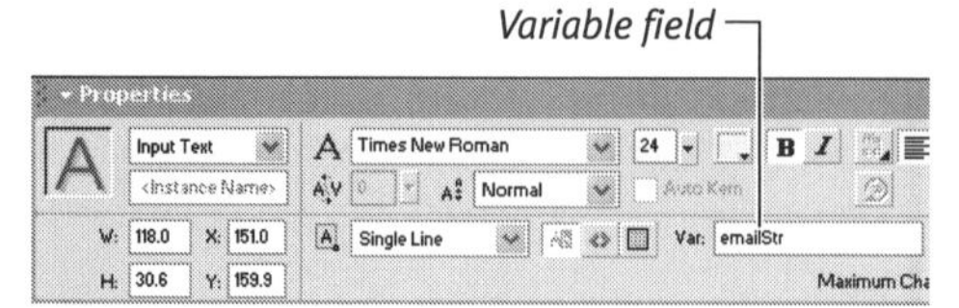

Figure 6.27 Enter `emailStr` in the Variable field of the Property Inspector as your input text.

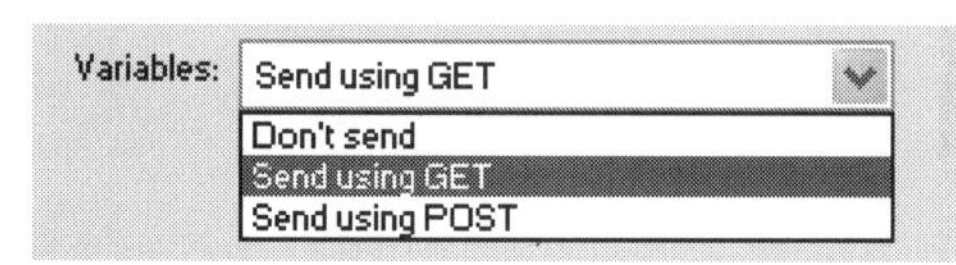

Figure 6.28 You can choose the `GET` or `POST` method from the Variables pull-down menu for the `getURL` action.

Communicating with XML Objects

In addition to HTML and JavaScript, Flash supports XML. Although it's beyond the scope of this book to cover XML in depth, this short discussion will help you understand the exciting possibilities Flash brings to XML.

XML is very different from a traditional markup language such as HTML, which tells the browser how to lay out the content—put this text here, set it to this font, and put it next to this image. Instead, XML allows you to define content according to its meaning and its audience. Content is defined by tags that are easy to read and understand, and not tied to the presentation layer (traditional HTML). A portion of XML could look something like this:

```
<invoice>
<vendorname>Big Tents</vendorname>
<vendorID>MYBDAY021570</vendorID>
<vendorLogo>03SUIRAUQA.GIF</vendorLogo>
<productdescription>
    <name>All-Weather Tent</name>
    <packageDimensions>
        <height>7.25"</height>
<width>7.25"</width>
<depth>48.5"</depth>
<weight>8lbs.</weight>
</packageDimensions>
    <wholesale>$75.43</wholesale>
<retail>$135.99</retail>
</productdescription>
</invoice>
```

In Flash, the XML and XMLSocket objects let you communicate with other applications and style sheets to manage media-rich content that can be unique to each user. Such industries as entertainment, automotive, banking, and e-commerce have recognized the benefits of combining Flash and XML. An example of a real-world application for e-commerce would provide an extensible interface between an online retailer and its partners, vendors, and suppliers in a Flash-enabled extranet. Using Flash as the tool for the interface (buttons, scroll bars, text-input fields, etc.) you could supply a merchant with a drag-and-drop interface for ordering products and placing them in a warehouse. The XML object could enable a vendor to change wholesale and retail prices, while negotiating its product's placement in the retailer's Web site and email campaigns. Done traditionally, all of these different Web-based forms would take enormous amounts of time to create, and still there is the very difficult task of making sure the data matches on both sides. In the code example above, notice how easy it is to find the retail price.

XSL is the style sheet that is applied to XML, and you might need only one or two to supply all the different types of users of your Flash content. The style sheet transforms the interface based on information it has received from the user's client (browser), Web server, or database. A merchant might see some streaming data of what's being purchased and sold daily, and negotiate with a vendor in real time to further increase volume. A partner, on the other hand, may see how well a promotion is progressing with a retailer's customers, and can make the decision to extend the promotion through to the following year. Flash can expose that highly extensible layer between front-end, media-rich content, and middle/back-end negotiating and data. XML won't make your animations tween more smoothly, but it can make it easier to create unique and scalable user experiences. To learn more about Flash's XML and XMLSocket objects, refer to the Flash ActionScript Reference that comes with the software.

Using the browser to navigate Flash content

Most viewers are familiar, if not comfortable, with using their browser's Back and Forward buttons and adding frequently visited sites to their bookmarks (Netscape) or Favorites list (Explorer). So when you have a Flash movie that is conveniently divided into navigable sections, you may want to let the browser handle much of the navigation. Labeling individual keyframes with named anchors provides a way for those keyframes to be accessed with a browser's Back and Forward buttons, or to be saved in the browser's bookmarks or Favorites list.

You create named anchors in the Property Inspector, using the same field you use for labels. A checkbox lets you choose between a normal label or a named anchor. When keyframes are identified as named anchors, your browser adds them to its history list as they are played.

Named anchors come with restrictions: They can be applied only to the main Timeline, and they work only in Windows. (You can still author them on the Mac.) Still, for the right audience (Windows users only), using named anchors is an effective way to take advantage of a browser's navigation and bookmarking features to organize and move through your Flash content.

To create a named anchor:

1. In your Flash movie, add a new layer, and insert keyframes where you want to add anchors.
2. Select the first keyframe.
3. In the Label field of the Property Inspector, enter a name for the anchor.
4. Check the Named Anchor box below the Label field (**Figure 6.29**).

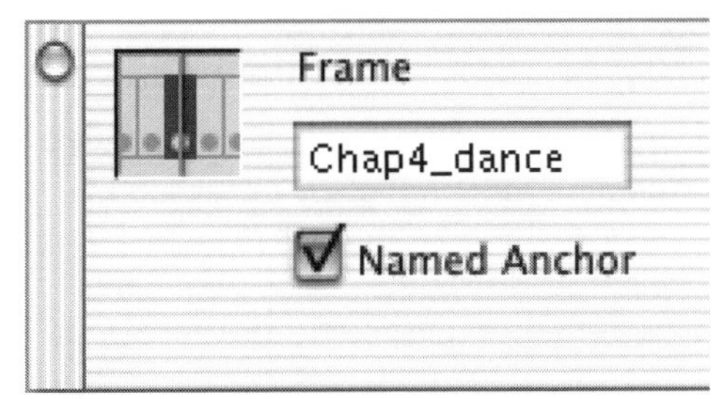

Figure 6.29 The anchor identifies this keyframe as a spot that can be added to Favorites (Explorer) or bookmarks (Netscape) by the browser, and allows the viewer to navigate to the keyframe with the Back and Forward buttons. In Explorer, Chap4_dance will appear in the history list or in the Favorites list. In Netscape, the name of the Flash movie will appear in the history list or in the bookmarks list.

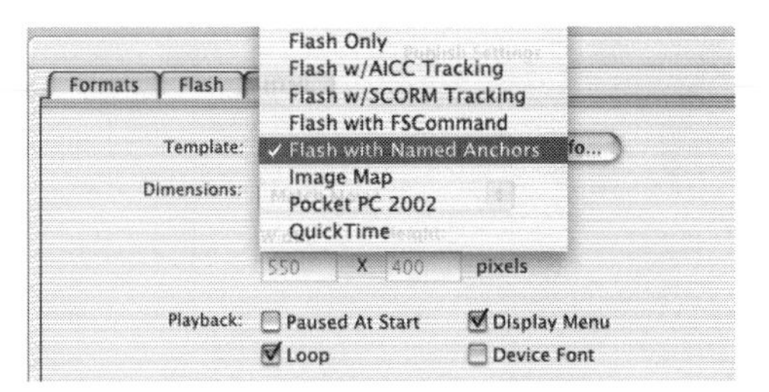

Figure 6.30 The Publish Settings dialog box.

Figure 6.31 The Back button in Explorer lists the named anchors as well as the Web sites you've visited.

5. Enter named anchors for the rest of the keyframes.
6. Choose File > Publish Settings.

   The Publish Settings dialog box appears.
7. Click the HTML tab.
8. From the Template pull-down menu, choose Flash with Named Anchors (**Figure 6.30**).

   This preference adds the necessary code to the HTML page so that both browsers recognize the named anchors in your Flash movie.
9. Publish your movie.
10. Open the HTML page in a browser on a Windows computer.

    After your Flash movie plays through a named anchor, you can use the browser's Back button to navigate to it. Add the anchor to your Favorites or bookmarks list, and you can return directly to that keyframe (**Figure 6.31**).

✔ Tip

- Variables, functions, event handlers, and other information that is initialized in an earlier frame of a movie won't be available to a named anchor if the viewer returns later by using a bookmark or a Favorite. Because a bookmark or Favorite returns the viewer to the middle of your Flash movie, be sure that the anchor locations have no interactivity that depends on ActionScript on earlier frames.

To create automatic named anchors for Scenes:

1. Choose Edit > Preferences (Windows) or Flash > Preferences (Mac).
   The Preferences dialog box appears.
2. Click the General tab.
3. Check the Named Anchor on Scene checkbox (**Figure 6.32**), and click OK.
4. Insert a new scene.
   A named anchor automatically appears in the first frame of the new scene (**Figure 6.33**). Additional scenes will have named anchors added automatically in their first frames. (Scenes made before the preference is set will not have named anchors.) You can change the name of your scene, but their named anchors will not change automatically. You must make that change manually in the Property Inspector.
5. Choose File > Publish Settings. Click the HTML tab and choose Flash with Named Anchors from the Template pull-down menu.
6. Publish your movie.
7. Open the HTML page in a browser.
   When your Flash movie plays through a named anchor in a scene, you can use the browser's Back button to navigate to it. Add the anchor to your browser's Favorites/bookmarks list, and you can return directly to that scene.

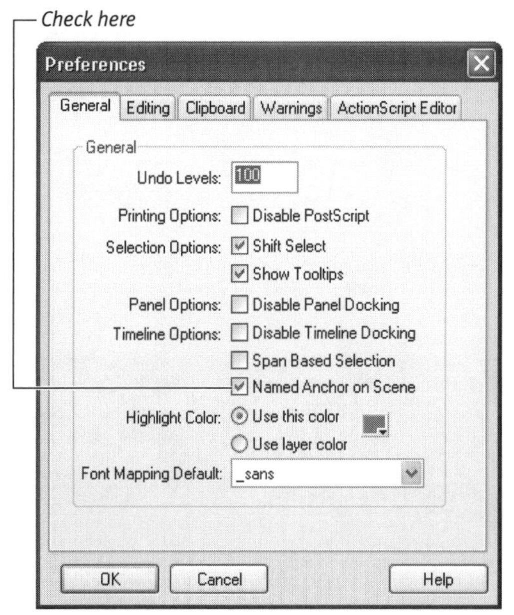

Figure 6.32 Checking Named Anchor on Scene in the Preferences dialog box puts named anchors on additional scenes.

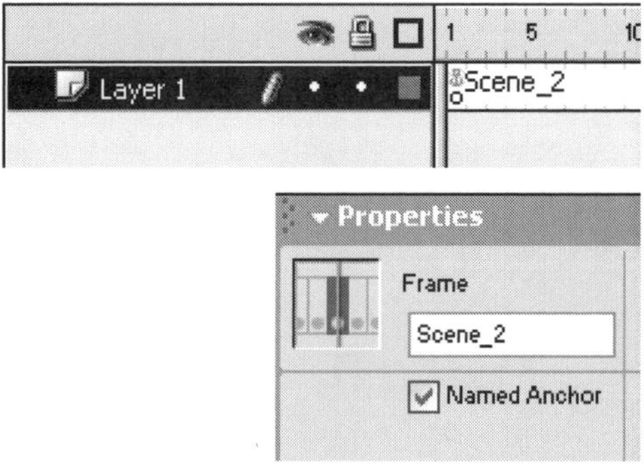

Figure 6.33 Frame 1 of scene 2 is assigned the named anchor Scene_2 automatically.

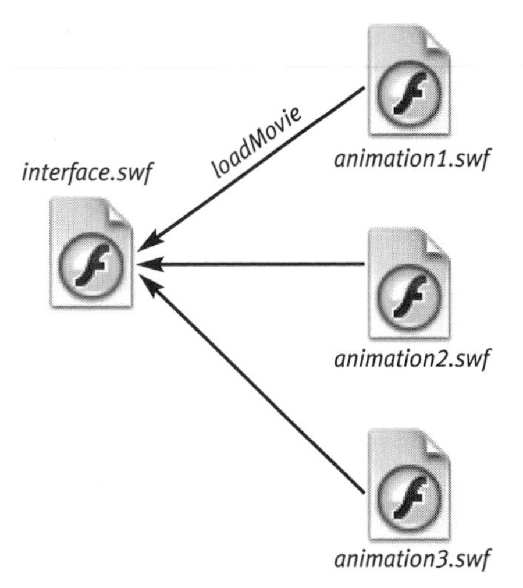

Figure 6.34 A way to keep data-heavy content separate is to maintain external SWF files. Here, the interface.swf movie loads the animation files one by one as they're requested.

Communicating with External Movies

You've learned how a Flash movie can use the action `getURL` to link to any file, including another Flash movie. This action loads the new SWF file into the same browser window, replacing the original movie, or into a new browser window.

Another way to communicate with external Flash movies and combine them with the original Flash movie is to use the actions `loadMovie` and `loadMovieNum`. Both actions allow you to bring in another SWF and integrate it with the current content. The original Flash movie establishes the frame rate, the Stage size, and the background color, but you can layer multiple external SWF files and even navigate within their Timelines. In Chapter 5, you learned to navigate the Timelines of movie clips within a single Flash movie. Now imagine the complexity of navigating multiple Timelines of multiple Flash movies!

One of the benefits of loading external Flash movies is that it allows you to keep your Flash project small and maintain quick download times. If you build a Web site to showcase your Flash animation work, for example, you can keep all your individual animations as separate SWF files. Build the main interface so that your potential clients can load each animation as they request it. That way, your viewers download only the content that's needed, as it's needed. The main interface doesn't become bloated with the inclusion of every one of your Flash animations (**Figure 6.34**).

You can load external SWF files into another Flash movie in two ways. One way is to load a SWF into a level with `loadMovieNum`; the other is to load a SWF into a movie clip with `loadMovie`. Both actions are accessed from the single entry `loadMovie` in the Actions panel, viewed in Normal mode.

Working with levels

Levels hold individual SWF files within a Flash movie. The original Flash movie is always at level 0, and subsequent Flash movies are kept at higher levels. You can have only one movie per level. Higher-level numbers will overlap lower-level numbers, so loaded movies will always appear above your original movie on the screen. To unload a movie, you simply specify the level number; the movie in that level is purged with the action `unloadMovieNum`. Another way to remove a movie in a particular level is to replace it with a new movie. If you load a new movie into a level already occupied by another movie, the old one is replaced.

To load an external movie:

1. Create the external movie you want to load.

   For this example, keep the animation at a relatively small Stage size (**Figure 6.35**).

2. Export your external movie as a SWF file.
3. Open a new Flash document to create the main movie that will load your external movie.
4. Create a button symbol, drag an instance of it from the library to the Stage, and give it a name in the property inspector.
5. Select the first frame of the main Timeline, and create an `onRelease` event handler for your button.
6. Choose Actions > Browser/Network > loadMovie (Esc + lm).

   The `loadMovieNum` action appears within the `onRelease` event handler (**Figure 6.36**).

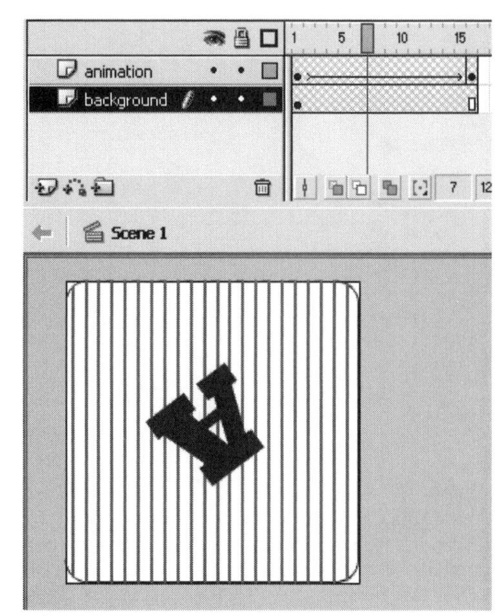

Figure 6.35 An animation of the letter *A* spins on a vertical grid.

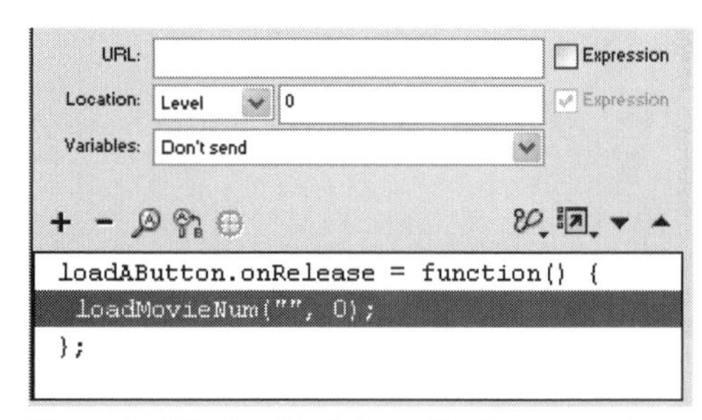

Figure 6.36 The `loadMovieNum` action has parameters for a URL (its target path), for location (its destination), and for variables.

Figure 6.37 This relative URL means that letterA.swf should be in the same directory as the original Flash movie.

Figure 6.38 One level can hold only one Flash movie, but you can many levels.

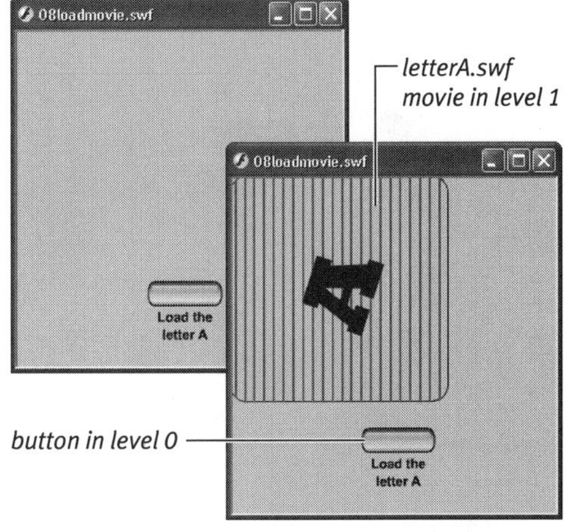

Figure 6.39 The original movie in level 0 (top) and the loaded movie in level 1 (bottom).

7. In the URL field, enter the name of your external SWF file (**Figure 6.37**).

   The URL field specifies the path of the target file. Here, you enter a relative path, so Flash looks within the same directory for the SWF file. You can also change directories by using the slash (/) or double dots (..), or you can enter an absolute path if your SWF file resides on a Web site.

8. Keep the Expression checkbox unchecked.

9. For the Location parameters, keep the pull-down menu set to Level, and enter a number higher than zero (**Figure 6.38**).

10. Publish your movie.

11. Place the SWF file, its HTML file, and the external SWF file in the same directory.

12. Play the main movie in Flash Player or a browser.

    When you click the button, Flash loads the external movie, which sits on top of your original movie and begins playing (**Figure 6.39**).

Characteristics of Loaded Movies

The following is a list of things to keep in mind when working with loaded movies.

- You can have only one movie per level.
- Loaded movies in higher levels will overlap loaded movies in lower levels.
- Loaded movies have transparent Stages. To have an opaque Stage, create a filled rectangle in the bottom layer of your loaded movie (**Figure 6.40**).
- Loaded movies are aligned with the Level 0 movie at their registration points. That means loaded movies are positioned from their top-left corner (x=0, y=0) to the top-left corner of the original movie (x=0, y=0). So loaded movies with smaller Stage sizes will still show objects that are off their Stage (**Figure 6.41**). Create a mask to block objects that may go beyond the Stage and that you don't want your audience to see. Likewise, loaded movies with larger Stage sizes will be cropped at the bottom and right boundaries (**Figure 6.42**).
- Movies loaded into Level 0 replace the original movie, but the Stage size, frame rate, and background color are still set by the original movie. If the loaded movie has a different Stage size from the original, it is centered and scaled to fit.

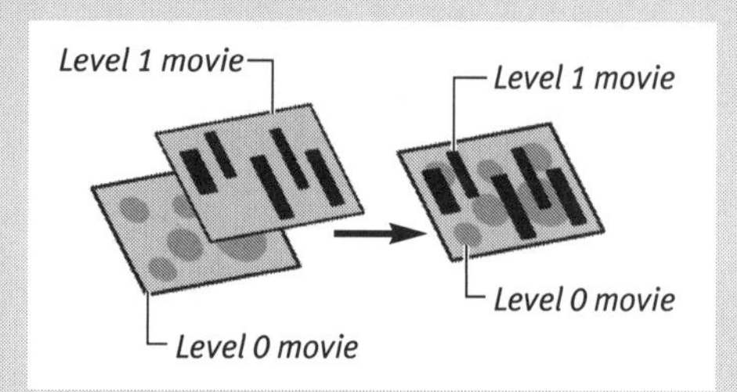

Figure 6.40 The Stage of an external SWF becomes transparent when the SWF is loaded on top of the level 0 movie.

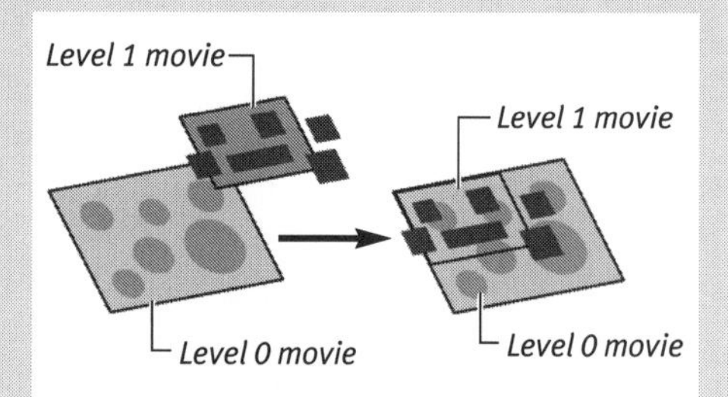

Figure 6.41 Smaller external SWFs are aligned at the top-left corner and display the work area off their Stages. Consider using masks or external SWFs with the same Stage dimensions.

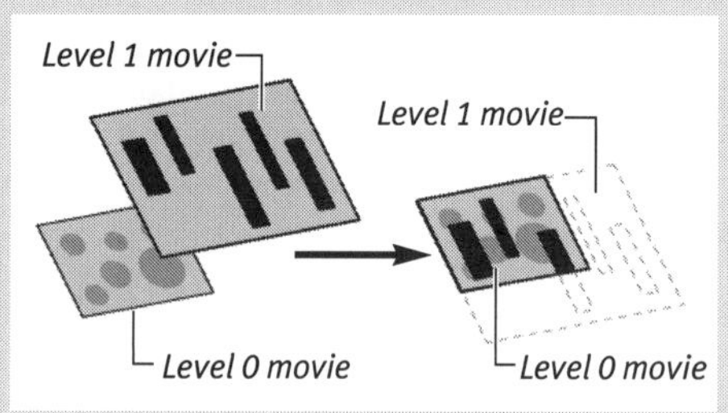

Figure 6.42 Larger external SWFs get cropped when they are loaded on top of the Level 0 movie.

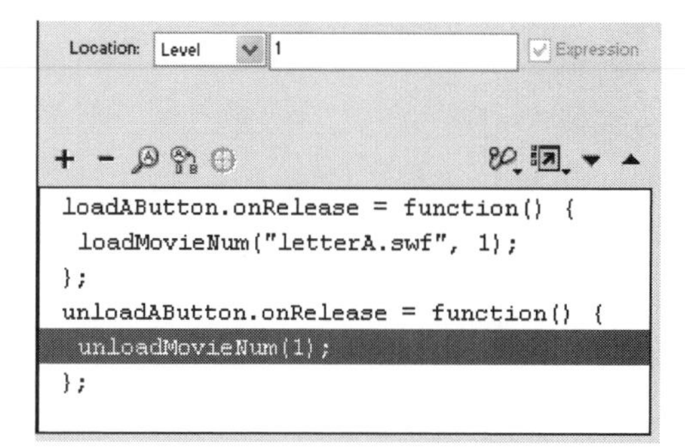

Figure 6.43 The `unloadMovieNum` action has only one parameter for Location. Any movie in level 1 will be removed.

To unload a movie:

1. Using the files from the preceding task, create another instance of the button in the original movie, and give it a name in the Property Inspector.
2. In the first frame of the main Timeline, create an `onRelease` event handler for the second button.
3. Choose Actions > Browser/Network > unloadMovie (Esc + um).

   The `unloadMovieNum` action appears within the `onRelease` event handler.
4. For the Location parameters, choose Level from the pull-down menu, and enter the number that you entered for the `loadMovieNum` action (**Figure 6.43**).
5. Publish your movie, and place it in the same directory as your external SWF file.
6. Play your movie in Flash Player or in a browser.

   The first button loads your external movie in the specified level. The second button unloads that movie from that level.

To replace a loaded movie:

1. Open a new Flash document, and create another small Flash animation to serve as a second external movie.
2. Using the Flash movie that you used as the original in the preceding tasks, add a third instance of your button, and give it a name in the Property Inspector.
3. In the first frame of the main Timeline, create an `onRelease` event handler for the third button.
4. Choose Actions > Browser/Network > loadMovie.

   The `loadMovieNum` action appears below the `onRelease` event handler.
5. In the URL field, enter the name of the second external movie.
6. Leave the Expression checkbox unchecked.
7. For the Location parameters, keep the pull-down menu set to Level, and enter the number that you used for the first `loadMovieNum` action (**Figure 6.44**).
8. Publish your movie, and place both this SWF file and the two external SWF files in the same directory.
9. In Flash Player or a browser, play the original movie that contains the three buttons.

   When you click the first button, Flash loads the first external movie, which sits on top of your original movie. When you click your newly created third button, Flash loads the second external movie in the same level, replacing the first (**Figure 6.45**).

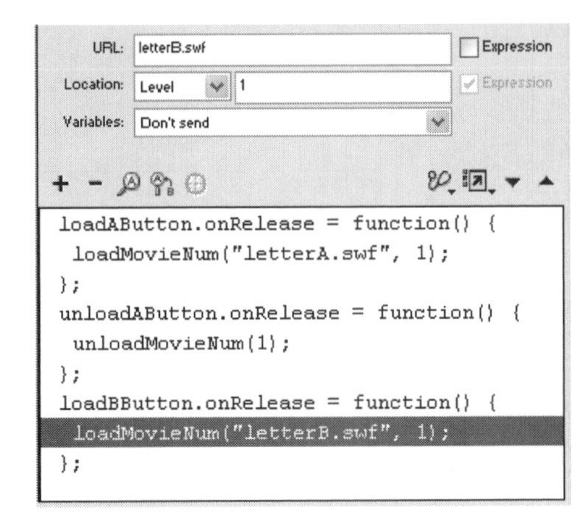

Figure 6.44 The `loadMovieNum` action assigned to the button called loadBButton will load the movie letterB.swf into level 1, replacing anything currently occupying that level.

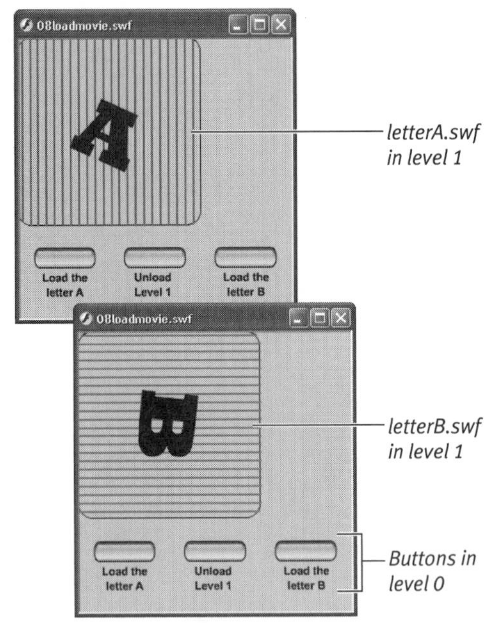

Figure 6.45 Initially, the letterA.swf movie occupies level 1 (top). Loading another movie in the same level replaces letterA.swf.

Loading Movies into movie clips

Loading external movies into levels is somewhat restricting because of the default placement of those movies is at the top-left corner of the original Stage. You can work with that positioning by shifting the elements in your external movie relative to where you know it will appear, or you can change all your external movies so that their Stage sizes correspond to the original Stage size.

A better solution is to load those movies into movie clips instead of levels with the action `loadMovie`. This action places the top-left corner of the loaded movie (x=0, y=0) at the registration point of the targeted movie clip (x=0, y=0) (**Figure 6.46**). Because you can place movie clips anywhere on the Stage, you effectively have a way to place your loaded movie where you want. However, the loaded movie takes over the movie clip; the Timeline of the movie clip is replaced by the Timeline of the loaded movie. However, the movie clip maintains its instance name, and all the scaling, rotation, skewing, color effects, and alpha effects that have been applied to the movie-clip instance are also applied to the loaded movie (**Figure 6.47**).

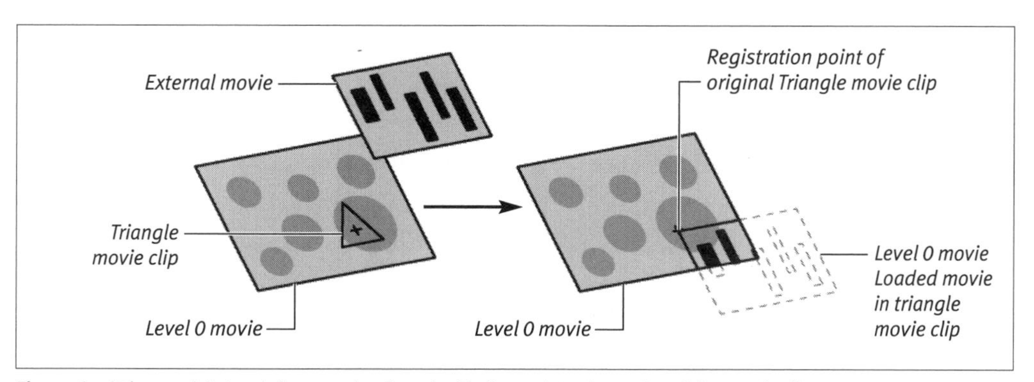

Figure 6.46 The movie's top-left corner is aligned with the registration point of the movie clip.

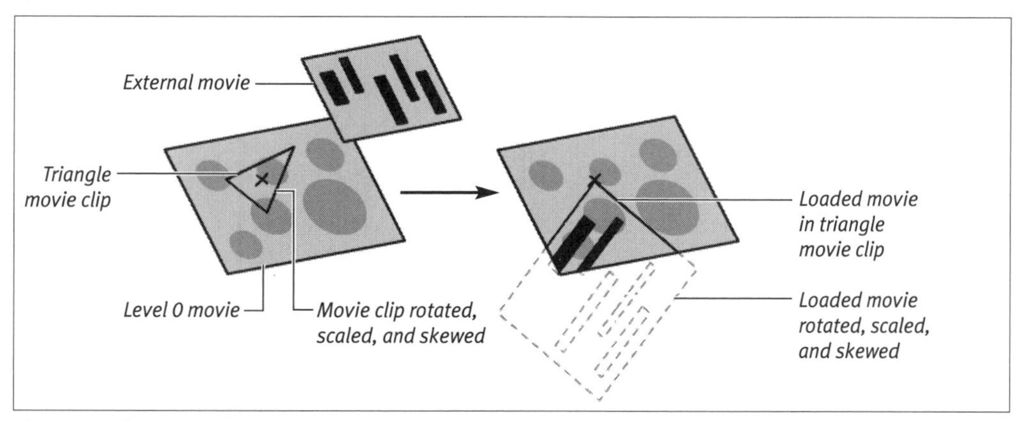

Figure 6.47 The external loaded movie inherits the movie-clip instance's name, position, scaling, skewing, rotation, color effects, and alpha effects.

To load an external movie into a movie clip:

1. Create a movie-clip symbol, and drag an instance of it from the library to the Stage (**Figure 6.48**).
2. Select the instance, and give it a name in the Property Inspector.
3. Create a button symbol, drag an instance of it from the library to the Stage, and give it a name in the Property Inspector.
4. In the first frame of the main Timeline, create an `onRelease` event handler for the button.
5. Choose Actions > Browser/Network > loadMovie.

   The `loadMovieNum` action appears within the `onRelease` event handler.
6. In the URL field, enter the name of an external SWF file.
7. For the Location parameters, choose Target from the pull-down menu, and enter the target path for the movie-clip instance on the Stage. Check the Expression box (**Figure 6.49**).
8. Publish your movie, and place the SWF file, its HTML file, and the external SWF file in the same directory.
9. Play the original movie in Flash Player or a browser.

   When you click the button that you created, Flash loads the external movie into the movie clip. The loaded movie inherits all the characteristics of the movie clip, such as position, scale, rotation, instance name, and color effect, but the Timeline of the movie clip is now the Timeline of the loaded movie (**Figure 6.50**).

Figure 6.48 A movie-clip instance is the future destination for a loaded movie.

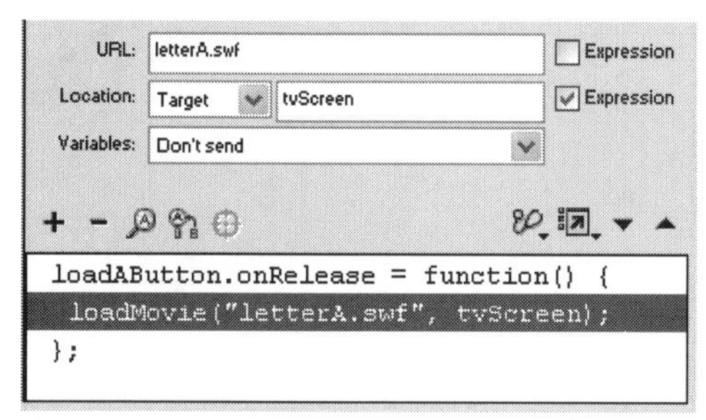

Figure 6.49 When the button called loadAButton is clicked, letterA.swf will load into the movie clip called tvScreen.

✔ Tip

- Make the first keyframe of your movie clip empty so that it acts simply as a container to receive the external movie. Remember that the empty circle that represents the registration point of this movie clip will be the top-left corner of any loaded movie.

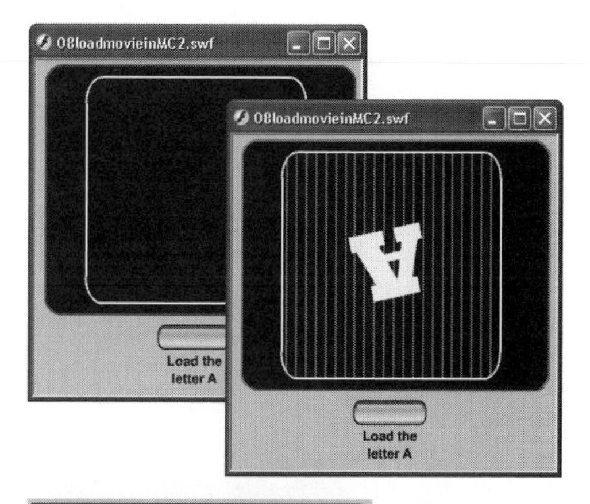

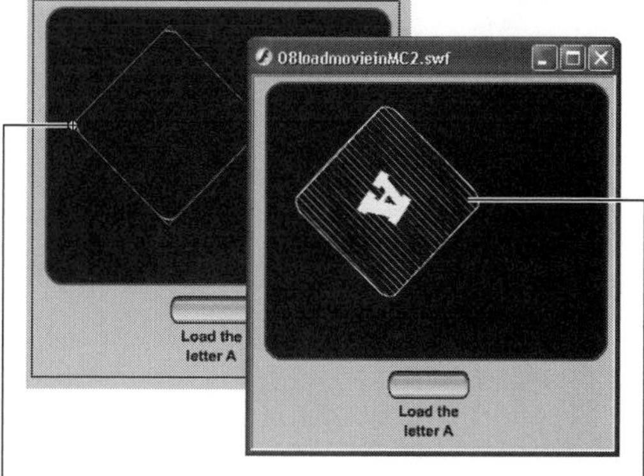

tvScreen movie clip rotated 45 degrees

letterA.swf movie loaded into tvScreen movie clip

Figure 6.50 The letterA.swf movie loads into the tvScreen movie clip (top). When the tvScreen movie clip rotates and shrinks, so does letterA.swf (bottom).

Navigating Timelines of loaded movies

After external movies are loaded into your original movie, you can access their Timelines and control when and where the playback head moves. If you thought that navigation between movie-clip Timelines was complex, just think how intricate navigation can become with multiple movies, each containing its own movie clips!

Flash provides a straightforward way of targeting loaded movies and their Timelines to minimize confusion. Because loaded movies reside on different levels, Flash uses the term `_level1` to refer to the movie in level 1, `_level2` to refer to the movie in level 2, and so on. Movies that are loaded into movie clips simply take on their instance name, so targeting those loaded movies means just targeting movie clips. If loaded movies have movie clips themselves, use dot syntax to drill down the Timeline hierarchy as you do with movie clips on the root Timeline. For example, `_level2.train.wheels` is the target path for the movie clip named wheels inside the movie clip named train that resides in the loaded movie on level 2.

To target a loaded movie:

1. As in the preceding tasks, create an animation to serve as an external Flash movie, and export it as a SWF file.
2. Open a new Flash document.
3. Create a button, drag an instance of it from the library to the Stage, and give it a name in the Property Inspector.
4. In the first frame of the main Timeline, create an `onRelease` event handler for the button.

continues on next page

5. Assign the action `loadMovieNum` to the button event handler, specifying the external SWF file as the URL and a number higher than zero for Location (**Figure 6.51**).

6. Drag another instance of the button onto the Stage, and give it a name in the Property Inspector.

   This button will control the Timeline of the loaded movie.

7. In the first frame of the main Timeline, create an `onRelease` event handler for this second button.

8. Choose Objects > Movie > Movie Clip > Methods > stop.

9. In the Object field, enter `_level` and then the level number (**Figure 6.52**).

   The statement stops the playhead of the movie in the specified level.

10. Publish your movie, and place the SWF and its HTML in the same directory as the external SWF file.

11. Play the movie containing the buttons in Flash Player or a browser.

    The first button loads the external SWF in the specified level. The second button targets that level and stops the playback head.

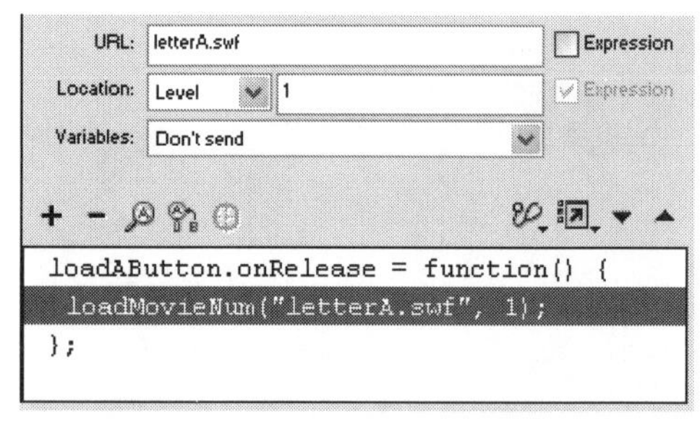

Figure 6.51 The `loadMovieNum` action assigned to the button called loadAButton puts letterA.swf in level 1.

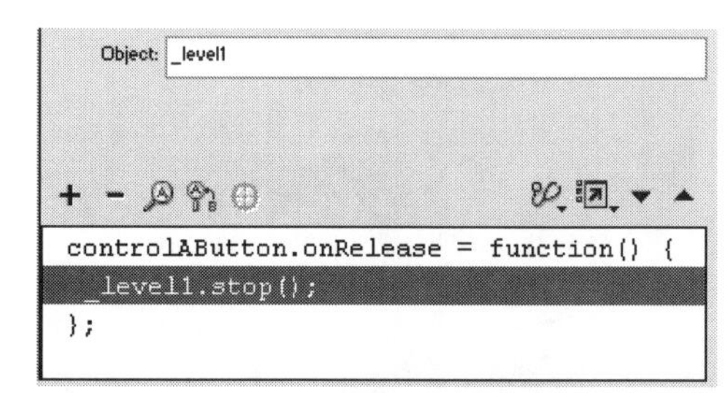

Figure 6.52 The `stop()` method acts on the movie in level 1.

Communicating with External Images

Using the same actions that load external SWF files into your movie dynamically, you can load JPEG images dynamically. Use the action `loadMovie` or `loadMovieNum` to pull images into your movie at run time to reduce the size of your Flash movie and save download time. As is the case with external SWFs, keeping images separate from your Flash movie will make revisions quicker and easier, because you can swap or change the images without messing with the actual Flash file.

Loaded images follow many of the same rules that loaded movies do, and those rules are worth repeating here:

- You can have only one image per level.
- Higher levels overlap lower levels.
- Images loaded into level 0 replace the original movie.
- The top-left corner of an image aligns with the top-left corner of the Stage or the registration point of a movie clip.
- An image loaded into a movie clip inherits its instance name and transformations.

To load an image in a level:

1. Create a button symbol, drag an instance to the Stage, and give it a name in the Property Inspector.

   This button will load a JPEG file into your movie dynamically.

2. Select the first frame of the main Timeline, and open the Actions panel.

3. Create an `onRelease` event handler for your button.

4. Choose Actions > Browser/Network > loadMovie.

   The `loadMovieNum` action appears within the `onRelease` event handler.

5. In the URL field, enter the path to the external JPEG file.

   The URL can be a relative path (such as /images/mypet/dog.jpg), so that Flash looks for the file relative to the current directory, or the URL can be an absolute path (such as http://www.mydomain.com/images/mypet/dog.jpg), so that Flash retrieves the file from any Web site.

6. Keep the Expression checkbox unchecked.

continues on next page

7. For the Location parameters, keep the pull-down menu set to Level, and enter a number higher than zero (**Figure 6.53**).

8. Publish your movie, and place your JPEG image in the correct directory so your Flash movie can find it.

   When you click the button, Flash loads the external JPEG into a higher level. The top-left corner of the JPEG aligns with the top-left corner of the Stage (**Figure 6.54**).

Figure 6.53 The `loadMovie` action can also be used to load JPEG files. Here, myPhoto.JPG is loaded in level 1 when the button is clicked.

Figure 6.54 The buttons on the bottom row load images that are kept external to your Flash movie. The top-left corner of each image aligns with the top-left corner of the Stage.

To load an image in a movie clip:

1. Create a movie-clip symbol, drag an instance of it from the library to the Stage, and give it a name in the Property Inspector.

2. Create a button symbol, drag an instance of it from the library to the Stage, and give it a name in the Property Inspector.

   This button will load a JPEG file into your movie clip dynamically.

3. In the first frame of the main Timeline, create an `onRelease` event handler for the button.

4. Choose Actions > Browser/Network > loadMovie.

   The `loadMovieNum` action appears within the `onRelease` event handler.

5. In the URL field, enter the path to the external JPEG file.

6. For the Location parameters, choose Target from the pull-down menu, and enter the target path for the movie-clip instance on the Stage (**Figure 6.55**).

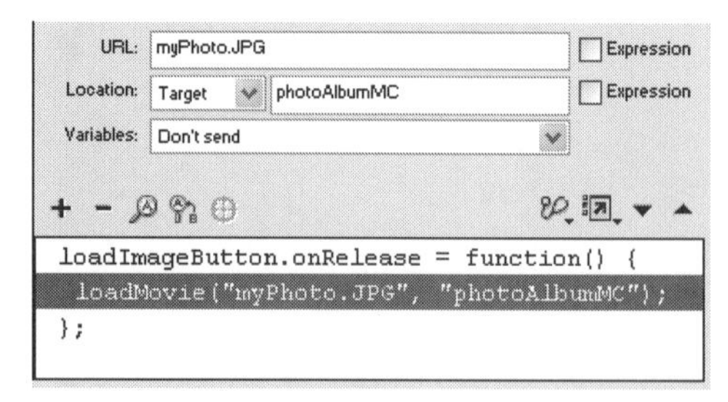

Figure 6.55 The file myPhoto.JPG will be loaded into the movie clip called photoAlbumMC when the button is clicked.

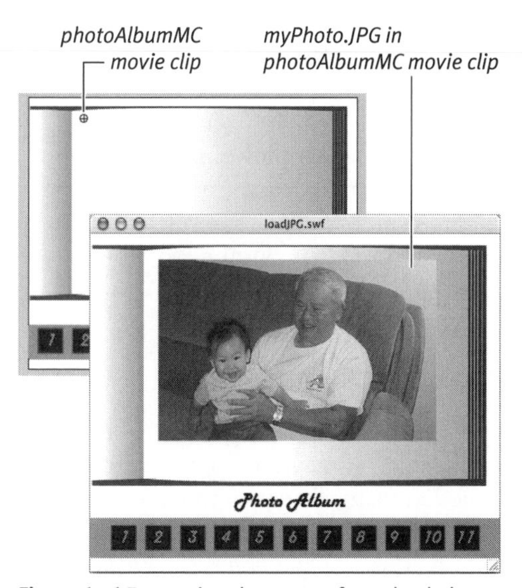

Figure 6.56 For precise placement of your loaded JPEG files, load them into movie clips, which you can position. This movie clip is empty, meaning that it contains no graphics or animation and simply acts as a shell to receive your loaded JPG files.

7. Publish your movie, and place your JPEG image in the correct directory so your Flash movie can find it.

   When you click the button that you created, Flash loads the external JPEG into the movie clip. The top-left corner of the image aligns with the registration point of the movie clip. The image replaces all the movie-clip graphics and inherits all the characteristics of the movie clip, such as position, scale, rotation, instance name, and color effect (**Figure 6.56**).

To remove or replace a loaded image:

- To remove an image, use the action `unloadMovie`, and choose a level or a target to unload the image.
- To replace an image, use the action `loadMovie`, and load another JPEG file into the same level or movie clip. The new JPEG will replace the old one.

✔ Tip

- Flash cannot load progressive JPEG files.

Communicating Between Two Movies

So far, you've learned how a single Flash movie can communicate outside itself—to retrieve a link on the Web, to incorporate another SWF, or to load an image file. But can one Flash movie communicate with another entirely independent Flash movie? The answer is yes, with the help of the LocalConnection object. The LocalConnection object enables communication between two separate Flash movies as long as they are running from the same machine (server). Instructions from one movie can control the appearance, behavior, or interactivity of another. Imagine, for example, creating a frameset that contains a Flash movie in a top frame and a Flash movie in a bottom frame. The movie in the top frame could have buttons or pull-down menus that control the movie in the bottom frame. As another example, you could build a Flash-based laboratory simulation in one browser window and keep a Flash lab notebook in another. Information from the simulation could be sent to the notebook and recorded automatically as the experiment progresses.

Using LocalConnection requires that you create a LocalConnection object in the sender movie as well as the receiver movie. Create the new object in both movies with the `new` constructor function, as follows:

```
myLocalConnection = new LocalConnection()
```

Next, in the sender movie, use the `send()` method to send the name of your message and the name of a function you want the receiver movie to perform:

```
myLocalConnection.send("incomingMessage",
"onReceive")
```

Finally, close the connection:

```
myLocalConnection.close()
```

In the receiver movie, you must define a function that will be performed when that movie receives the message from the sender movie. After the function is established, use the `connect()` method to listen for the name of the message. In the receiver movie, the code would look something like this:

```
myLocalConnection = new LocalConnection()
myLocalConnection.onReceive = function(){
   animation.play();
}
myLocalConnection.connect("incomingMessage")
```

When this receiver movie receives the message called incomingMessage, the movie clip called animation will play.

The LocalConnection object is unlisted in the Actions panel, so you must write the script in Expert mode.

```
myButton.onRelease = function() {
    myLocalConnection = new LocalConnection();
};
```

Figure 6.57 The name of your LocalConnection object is myLocalConnection.

```
myButton.onRelease = function() {
    myLocalConnection = new LocalConnection();
    myLocalConnection.send("incomingMessage", "onReceive");
};
```

Figure 6.58 This `send()` method sends the message identified as incomingMessage and makes the receiver movie perform the function assigned to `onReceive`.

```
myButton.onRelease = function() {
    myLocalConnection = new LocalConnection();
    myLocalConnection.send("incomingMessage", "onReceive");
    myLocalConnection.close();
};
```

Figure 6.59 Close the connection.

To create the sender movie:

1. Create a button symbol, place an instance of it on the Stage, and give it a name in the Property Inspector.
2. In the first frame of the main Timeline, create an `onRelease` event handler for the button.

   This button will tell a movie clip in another Flash movie (the receiver movie) to play.
3. Create a new LocalConnection object by entering the statement, `myLocalConnection = new LocalConnection()` (**Figure 6.57**).
4. Next, call the `send()` method of the `myLocalConnection` object with the two parameters, `"incomingMessage"` and `"onReceive"`. Put quotation marks around both parameters, and separate them with commas (**Figure 6.58**).
5. Call the `close()` method of the `myLocalConnection` object (**Figure 6.59**).

   After sending a connection, you should close it, thereby disconnecting the `LocalConnection`.

To create the receiver movie:

1. In a new file, create a movie clip that contains an animation.

   The movie clip should have a `stop` action in the first frame of its Timeline.

2. Drag an instance of the movie clip to the Stage, and name it in the Property Inspector.

   This movie clip will be the target of a function in this movie. When the incoming message is received, the function will instruct the movie clip to play.

3. Select the first frame of the main Timeline, and open the Actions panel in Expert mode.

4. In the Script pane, enter `myLocalConnection = new LocalConnection()` to instantiate a new `LocalConnection` object.

5. Next, enter `myLocalConnection`, then a dot, and then the name of the incoming message being sent from the sender movie. Enter an equal sign and then function () { }; (**Figure 6.60**).

   You can think of the name of the incoming message like an event. When the message is received, the function is executed. The final form of the function statement, in fact, is identical to an event handler.

6. Within the function statement curly braces, enter the name of your movie clip, a dot, and then the method `play()`.

   This is the receiver movie's response to the incoming message (**Figure 6.61**).

```
myLocalConnection = new LocalConnection();
myLocalConnection.onReceive = function() {
};
```

Figure 6.60 Create the function that responds to the incoming message.

```
myLocalConnection = new LocalConnection();
myLocalConnection.onReceive = function() {
    animation.play();
};
```

Figure 6.61 When this receiver movie gets the message from the sender, it will play its movie clip called animation.

```
myLocalConnection = new LocalConnection();
myLocalConnection.onReceive = function() {
    animation.play();
};
myLocalConnection.connect("incomingMessage");
```

Figure 6.62 The connect() method opens the connection for the message called incomingMessage from the sender movie.

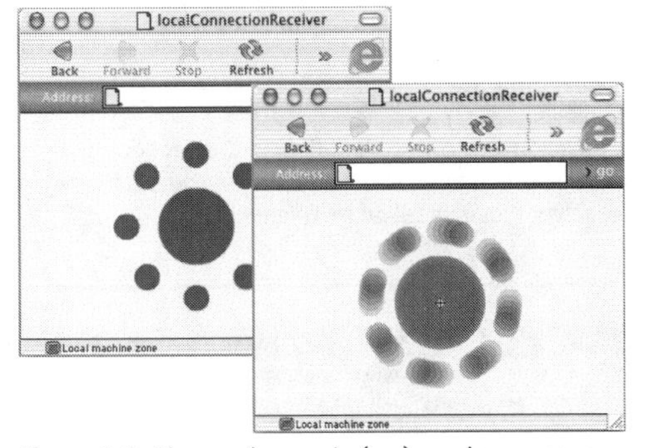

Figure 6.63 The sender movie (top) sends a message when the user clicks the button. The receiver movie in a separate browser window (bottom) responds by playing the animation.

7. On a new line outside the function statement, enter `myLocalConnection`, then a dot, and then the method `connect()`. In between the parentheses of the method, enter the name of the incoming message within quotation marks (**Figure 6.62**).

   The `connect()` method opens the connection for your `LocalConnection` object.

To test communication between the sender and receiver movies:

◆ Publish both movies, and play them in separate browser windows.

  When you click the button in the sender movie, a LocalConnection object is created, and a message is sent. The receiver movie connects to the message and, as instructed by the sender movie, executes the function. As a result, the animation in the receiver movie plays (**Figure 6.63**).

Making a sender movie instruct a receiver movie to perform a function is useful, but it's even more useful to make the sender movie instruct a receiver movie to perform a function with certain parameters. Passing parameters between two independent movies is not only possible, but also allows customized communication. Parameters determine the way the function is performed, much as they determine the way methods are performed. (Learn more about functions and parameters in Chapter 11 and return here to see how they are used with the LocalConnection object.) Sending parameters from the sender movie can make the response in the receiver movie vary according to the interaction in the sender movie.

In this demonstration, you'll create an input text field in the sender movie and a dynamic text field in the receiver movie. You can make the sender movie pass text entered in its input text field to the receiver movie, which displays the text in its dynamic text field.

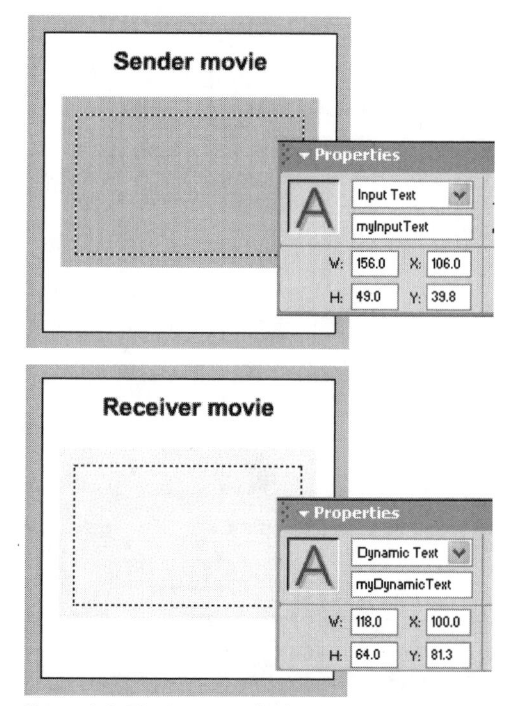

Figure 6.64 The input text field in the sender movie is called myInputText. The dynamic text field in the receiver movie is called myDynamicText.

```
_root.onEnterFrame = function() {
  mySender = new LocalConnection();
  mySender.send("incomingMessage", "onReceive");
  mySender.close();
};
```

Figure 6.65 The `onEnterFrame` event is triggered continuously, so this message is sent to the receiver movie continuously.

To pass parameters from the sender to the receiver movie:

1. Using the sender and receiver movies you created in the preceding tasks, delete the button in the sender movie and the movie clip in the receiver movie.
2. In both movies, select the text tool and create a text field on the Stage.
3. In the Property Inspector, choose input text for the sender movie and dynamic text for the receiver movie, and give them names (**Figure 6.64**).

   The name of a text field, like the names of buttons and movie clips, lets you target the text field and control it.
4. In the sender movie, change the `onRelease` event handler to an `onEnterFrame` event handler scoped to the main Timeline (**Figure 6.65**).

```
_root.onEnterFrame = function() {
  mySender = new LocalConnection();
  mySender.send("incomingMessage", "onReceive", myInputText.text);
  mySender.close();
};
```

Figure 6.66 Flash passes the parameter myInputText.text with its message.

```
myReceiver = new LocalConnection();
myReceiver.onReceive = function(myParameter) {
};
myReceiver.connect("incomingMessage");
```

Figure 6.67 In the receiver movie, the function's parameter is called myParameter.

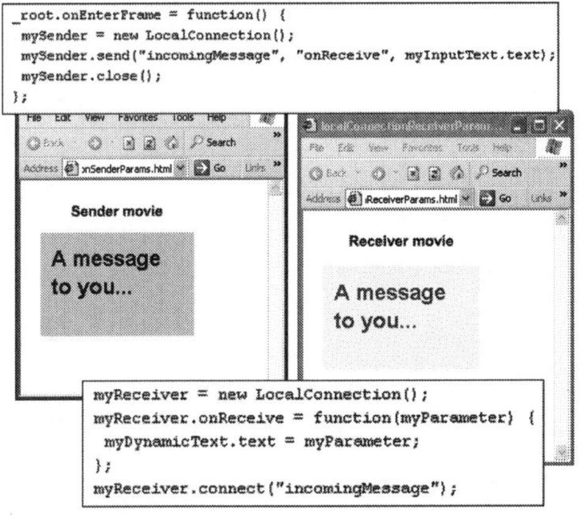

Figure 6.68 The final scripts for the sender movie (top) and receiver movie (bottom). Text in the sender movie's input text field appears in the receiver movie's dynamic text field.

5. Place your cursor after the last parameter in the parentheses of the `send()` method. Add a comma; then enter `myInputText.text` (**Figure 6.66**).

   This parameter and any additional parameters in the `send()` method are sent to the receiver movie. Here, the contents of the text field called `myInputText` are sent as a parameter to the receiver movie.

6. Open the receiver movie, and delete the action within the current function statement.

7. Within the parentheses of the function statement, enter a name to identify the incoming parameter (**Figure 6.67**).

8. In a new line within the function's curly braces, enter the following:

   `myDynamicText.text=myParameter;`

   `myParameter` is the name you entered in step 7, and `myTextField` is the name of the dynamic text field on the Stage.

   The receiver movie receives a single parameter, called `myParameter`, used in the actions within the function. Here, the parameter is assigned to the contents of the dynamic text field called `myDynamicText`.

9. Test your movies by playing them in separate browser windows.

   When you enter text in the sender movie, it is also displayed in the receiver movie because the text is being passed as a parameter (**Figure 6.68**).

Using Projectors and the fscommand Action

Most of the time, you'll play your Flash movie in a browser over the Web. Flash was conceived and developed to deliver content this way. But Flash also provides a way to create *projectors*—self-executable applications that don't require the browser or Flash Player for playback. On either a Windows or Mac system, you can publish projectors for either platform. In Windows, the file extension is .exe, and on the Mac, the word *projector* is appended to the file name. These projector files are larger than the normal exported SWF files, but they contain everything you need to play the content you create, including graphics, animation, sound, and interactivity. Use projectors to deliver your Flash content on transportable media such as floppy disks or CD-ROMs—an ideal scenario for portfolios, presentations, or marketing material.

Playback of Flash content through projectors is different in one respect: Projectors don't use an HTML page that contains tags or instructions to tell it how to be displayed. Will playback be full-screen? Can the window be scalable? You have to give the projector answers to these playback questions rather than rely on an accompanying HTML page. To set or change these kinds of display parameters, use the `fscommand` action, which has just a few simple parameters for projectors, as detailed in **Table 6.3**.

Table 6.3

fscommand Parameters for Projectors

Command	Description and Parameters
fullscreen	Allows playback at full screen and prevents resizing (true/false).
allowscale	Makes the graphics scale when the window is resized (true/false) The scaling mode is always set to showAll.
trapallkeys	Allows the movie, rather than Flash Player, to capture key presses (true/false)
showmenu	Displays the top menu bar. Also shows the control menu when you Control-click (Mac) or right-click (Windows) the movie (true/false).
exec	Opens an executable file (path to file). The target file must be in a folder called fscommand for security reasons.
quit	Quits the projector.

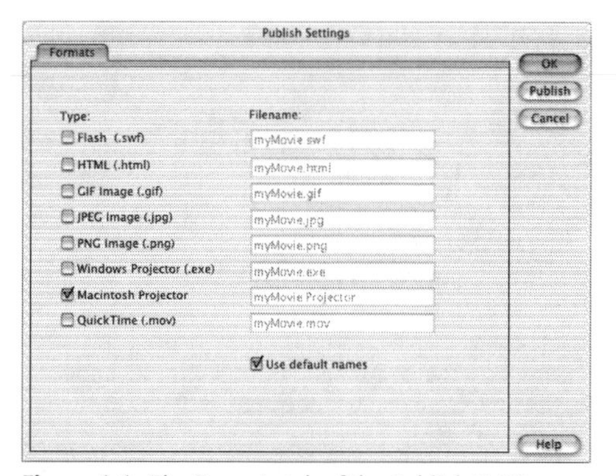

Figure 6.69 The Formats tab of the Publish Settings dialog box. Check the checkboxes to choose the Windows and/or Macintosh projectors.

To publish a projector:

1. Open your Flash file.
2. Choose File > Publish Settings (Opt-Shift-F12 Mac, Shift-Ctrl-F12 Windows).

   The Publish Settings dialog box appears.
3. In the Formats tab, deselect all the checkboxes except the Macintosh Projector and/or Windows Projector checkboxes (**Figure 6.69**).
4. If you want to name your projector something other than the default name, deselect the Use Default Names checkbox, and enter your own file name.
5. Click Publish.

   Your projector file is saved in the same folder as the Flash file.

   or

1. Open your SWF file in Flash Player.
2. Choose File > Create Projector.
3. Choose a file name and destination, and click Save.

   If you choose to create a projector from Flash Player, you can create projectors only for the operating system in which Flash Player is opened.

✔ Tips

- The `getURL` action, when used in a projector, launches your default browser to open any Web link.
- The preferred way to create projectors is through the Publish settings. Flash will not compress the projector if you make it from Flash Player. In larger files you can see a big difference.

To use fscommand to define playback options in a projector:

1. Select the first keyframe of a Flash movie you want to publish as a projector, and open the Actions panel.
2. Choose Actions > Browser/Network > fsCommand (Esc + fs).

   The `fscommand` action appears in the Script pane, with Command and Parameters fields and a pull-down menu specifically for projectors (**Figure 6.70**).
3. From the pull-down menu, choose fullscreen.
4. Check the Expression checkbox next to the Parameters field.

   The Command field contains `fullscreen`, and the Parameter field contains `true` (**Figure 6.71**).
5. Choose `fscommand` again.
6. From the pull-down menu, choose showmenu.

   The Command field contains `showmenu`, and the Parameter field contains `true`.
7. In the Parameter field, change `true` to `false`, and check the Expression checkbox (**Figure 6.72**).
8. Create a button, place an instance of that button on the Stage, and give the instance a name in the Property Inspector.
9. Select the first frame of the main Timeline, and open the Actions panel.
10. Create an `onRelease` event handler for your button.

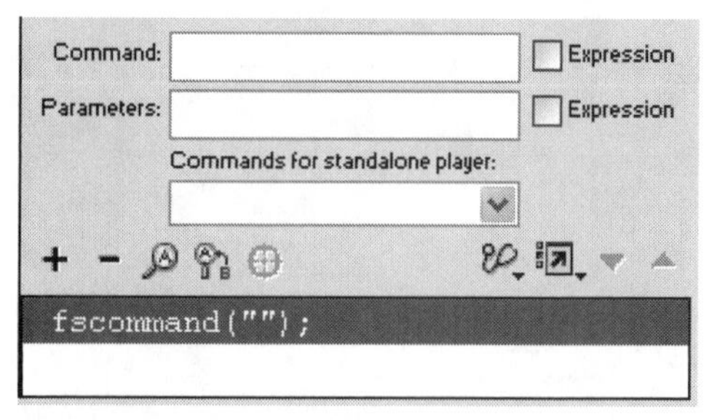

Figure 6.70 `fscommand` options for projectors appear in the pull-down menu at the bottom of the Parameters area.

Figure 6.71 When `fullscreen` is `true`, playback of the projector fills the entire monitor.

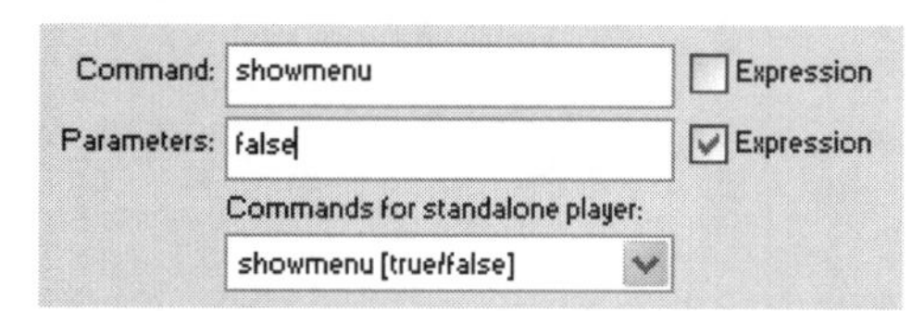

Figure 6.72 When showmenu is false, the menu options (right-click for Windows, Control-click for Mac) are disabled.

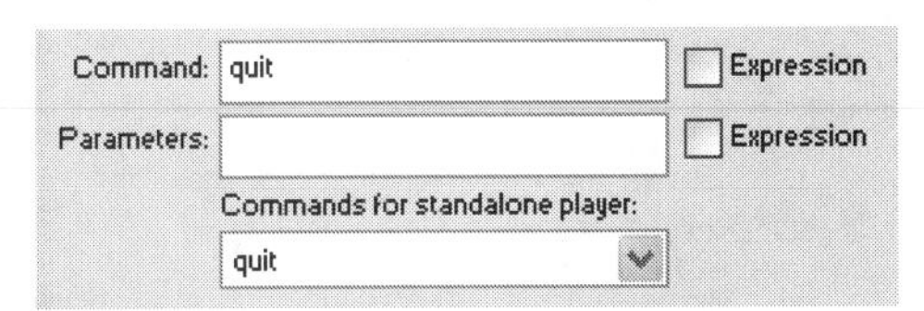

Figure 6.73 The `fscommand quit` assigned to a button closes the projector.

11. Choose Actions > Browser/Network > fscommand.
12. From the Command pull-down menu in the Parameters pane, choose quit (**Figure 6.73**).
13. Publish your movie as a projector.
14. Double-click your projector to play it.

    The Flash projector plays at full screen, effectively preventing the window from being scaled. The menu options are disabled when you right-click (Windows) or Control-click (Mac) the movie. When you click the button, the projector quits.

✔ Tip

- You can also use the Stage properties (discussed later in this chapter) to define some of the ways a projector displays its Flash content. You can define the scale mode for your projector, for example, by setting the `Stage.scaleMode` property. The `fscommand` will always override the Stage properties if a conflict occurs, however.

Communicating with the Printer

Flash can send information directly to a printer to output text and graphics, circumventing the Web browser's print function. Even during playback in Flash Player or as a projector, the print command will function. With the actions `print` and `printAsBitmap`, you can specify a single frame or multiple frames to print, and you can also control which areas of those frames should print. The printable areas do not even have to be visible on the Stage. Graphics and text in any frame in the main Timeline of the movie or any frame of a movie clip's Timeline are available to the printer, making the `print` action more than a simple tool for making hard copies of what is on the computer screen.

Imagine, for example, that you have documents in external SWF files. You easily could load a particular movie into a movie clip or into another level with the action `loadMovie` and then print selected frames from that loaded movie.

In Chapter 10, you'll learn about input text and dynamic text; you can enter information on the keyboard and display text dynamically. You can combine this capability with order forms or receipts, resulting in customized documents that you can send to the printer.

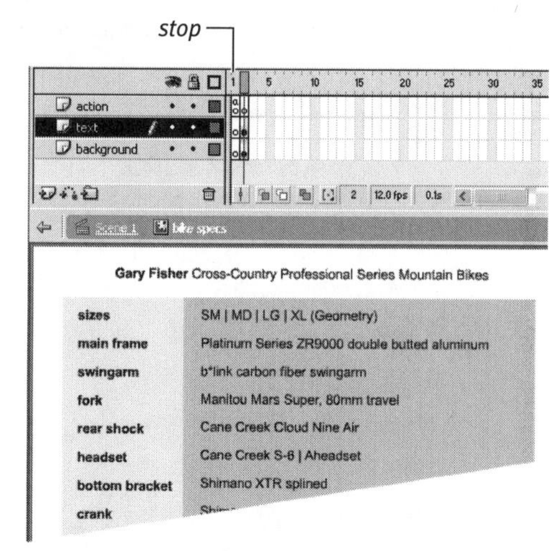

Figure 6.74 This movie clip contains graphics for printing in keyframe 2. In keyframe 1, a `stop` action prevents the clip from playing.

To print a specific frame of a Timeline:

1. Create the graphics you want to be available to the printer in a keyframe.

   It's a good idea to keep them in a movie clip so that they sit in their own Timeline (**Figure 6.74**).

2. Select the keyframe.

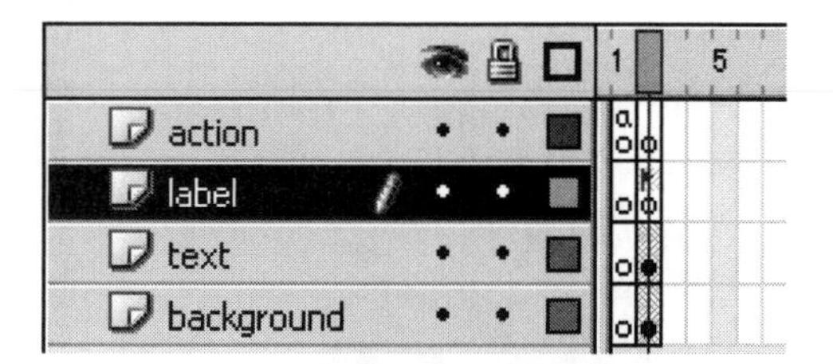

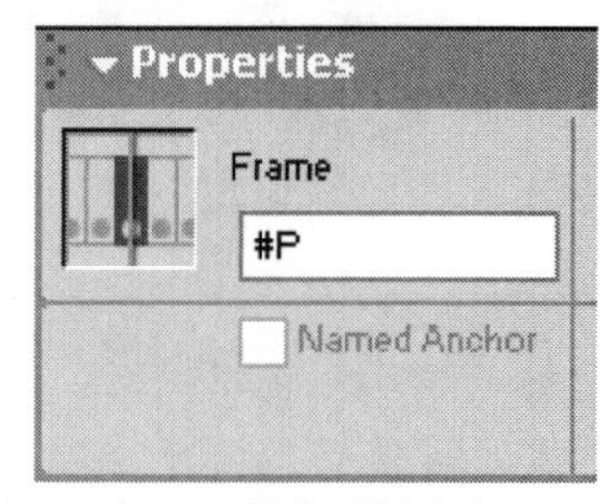

Figure 6.75 In a separate layer, add the #P label to keyframe 2.

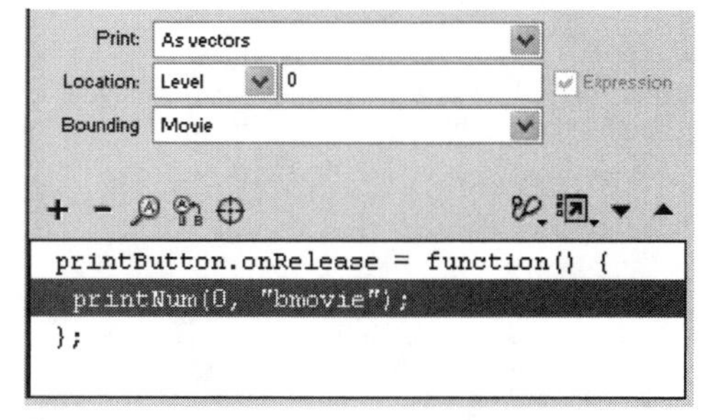

Figure 6.76 The `print` action is assigned to the button called printButton.

Figure 6.77 The movie-clip instance containing the graphics for printing is called bikespecs. This `print` action targets the bikespecs instance.

3. In the Label field of the Property Inspector, enter `#P` (**Figure 6.75**).

   The #P label designates that keyframe to be printed. If you don't add the #P label, all the frames of the movie or targeted movie clip are printed.

4. Return to the main Timeline, drag an instance of your movie clip to the Stage, and give the instance a name in the Property Inspector.

5. Now create a button, drag an instance of this button to the Stage, and name it in the Property Inspector.

6. Select the first frame of the main Timeline, and open the Actions panel.

7. Create an `onRelease` event handler for your button.

8. Choose Actions > Printing > print (Esc + pr).

   The `print` action appears within the `onRelease` event handler (**Figure 6.76**).

9. In the Parameters pane, choose As Vectors from the Print pull-down menu, Target from the Location pull-down menu, and Movie from the Bounding pull-down menu.

10. Enter the target path for your movie-clip instance in the Location field (**Figure 6.77**).

continues on next page

11. Test your movie.

When you click the button that you created, the graphics in the movie clip at keyframe #P are sent to the printer. Your printer dialog box appears. Confirm the print job to begin printing (**Figure 6.78**).

✔ Tips

- Printing a keyframe that contains a movie-clip instance will result in a print of only the first frame of that movie clip. If you want to print frames inside a movie clip, target the movie-clip instance itself.
- To calculate how the area of a graphic translates to the size of the printed piece, multiply the pixel dimensions by the screen resolution, which is 72 ppi (pixels per inch). So an 8.5-by-11-inch sheet of paper is equivalent to a Stage size of 612 pixels (8.5 inches x 72 ppi) by 792 pixels (11 inches x 72 ppi). Then you must take into account the margins for the actual printable area.
- Choose Level from the Location pull-down menu to target a loaded movie in a specific level (**Figure 6.79**). You can specify level 0 to target the main movie. All the frames of that movie will print unless you specify the #P label for certain frames.

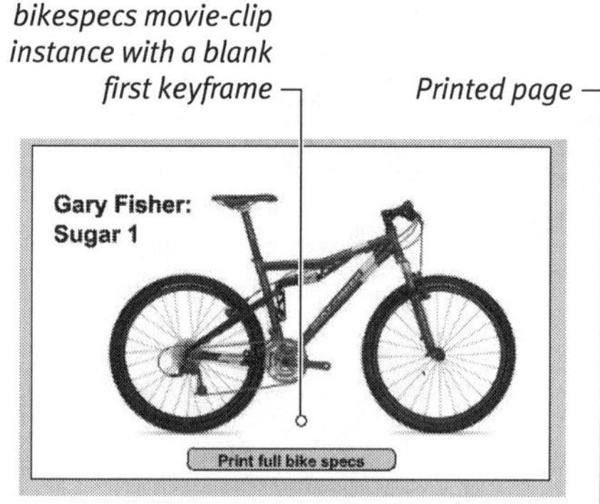

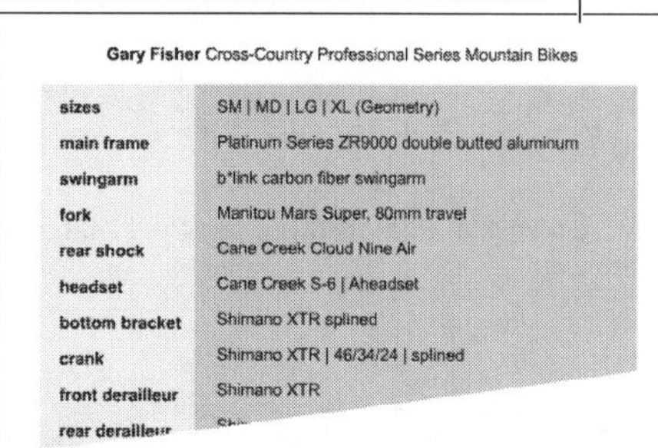

Figure 6.78 The movie-clip instance on the Stage (top) contains the graphics that print (bottom).

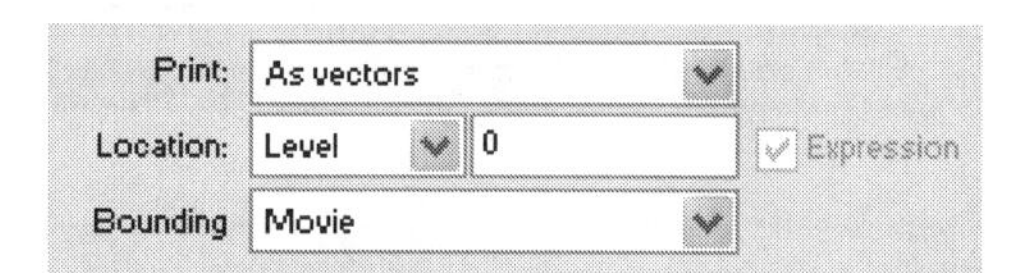

Figure 6.79 The `print` parameters. The movie in Level 0 is targeted to print.

```
on (release) {
 print ("_root.taxforms", "bmovie");
 print ("_root.receipts", "bmovie");
}
```

Figure 6.80 The frames in the taxforms movie clip and in the receipts movie clip will print. Two separate movie clips require two `print` statements.

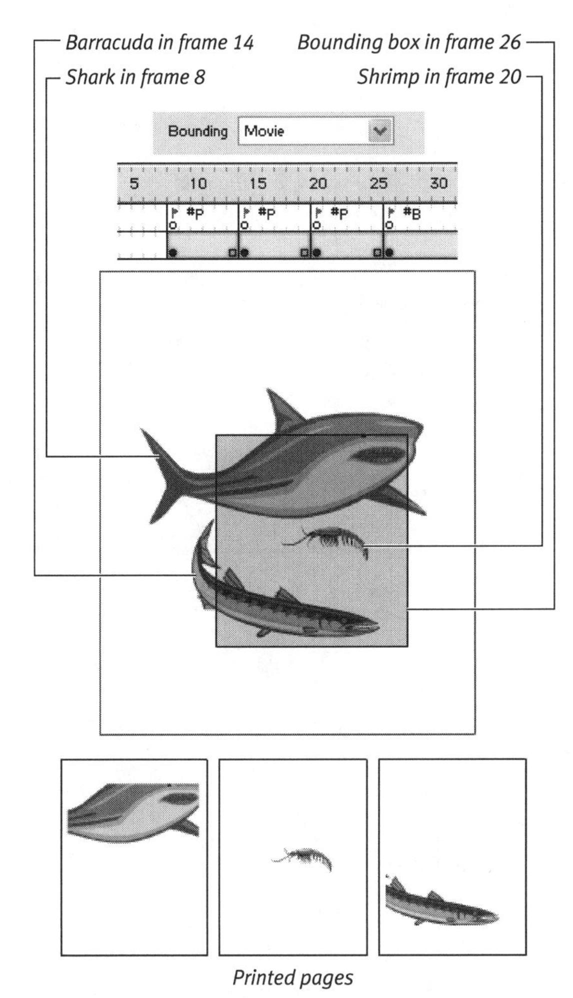

Figure 6.81 The Movie option. Keyframe 26 contains the bounding box that determines the print area for all three images.

To print multiple frames of your movie:

- Mark each keyframe in the target Timeline to print by adding the label #P.
- If you want to print multiple frames that are in separate Timelines, you need to write separate `print` statements in the Actions panel. Multiple print dialog boxes will appear if you choose this method. Flash can print multiple frames, but from only one target path (**Figure 6.80**).

To control the printable area of your movie:

- From the Bounding Box pull-down menu in the Actions panel, choose Movie; then draw a bounding box in a keyframe, and label it #B in the Property Inspector.

  The last parameter in the `print` action changes to `bmovie.` The bounding box you drew defines the print area for all the frames designated with the #P label (**Figure 6.81**).

  or

continues on next page

- From the Bounding Box pull-down menu, choose Frame.

  The last parameter in the `print` action changes to `bframe`. Your graphics in each keyframe labeled #P are scaled to fit the maximum printable area (**Figure 6.82**).

  or

- From the Bounding Box pull-down menu, choose Max.

  The last parameter in the `print` action changes to `bmax`. Flash defines the maximum width and height from all the printable frames and then scales the graphics relative to that printable area (**Figure 6.83**).

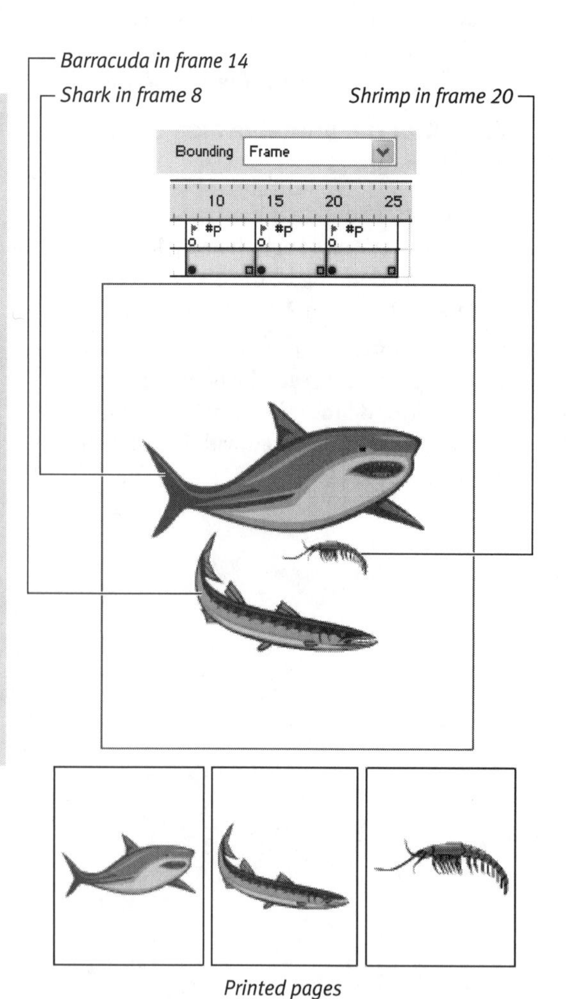

Figure 6.82 The Frame option. No #B labels are necessary. Each image is scaled to fit the printable area. Note that the shrimp prints as big as the shark.

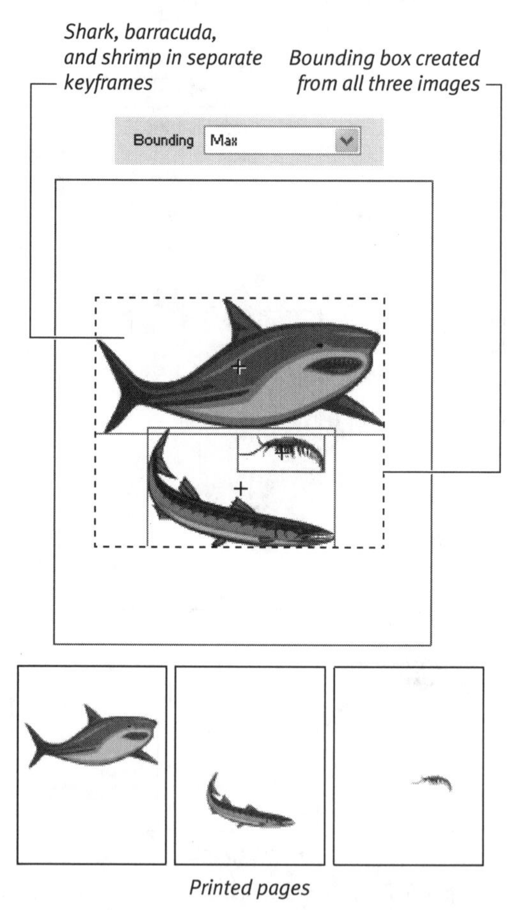

Figure 6.83 The Max option. No #B labels are necessary. A bounding box is created based on the composite sizes and locations of all three images.

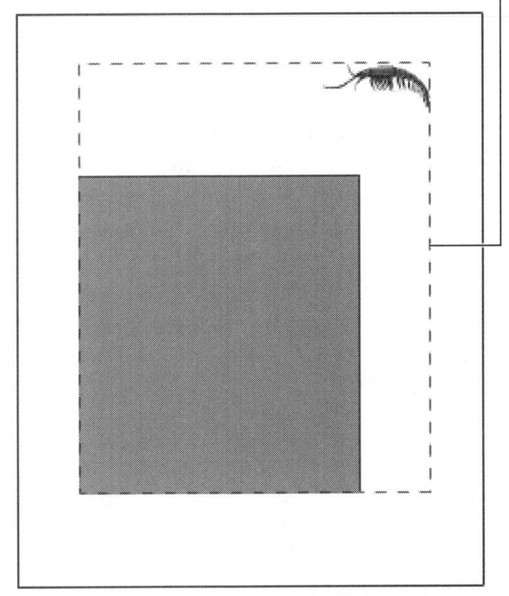

Figure 6.84 These two images in the #B frame force a larger bounding box.

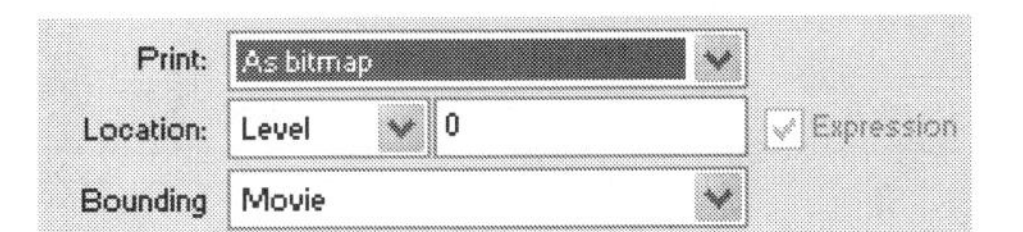

Figure 6.85 The Print As bitmap option is for transparencies and color effects.

✔ Tips

- The bounding box you define in the keyframe labeled #B can be any shape, but Flash will recognize only the minimum rectangle in which that shape would fit. That rectangle defines the printable area.
- It's a good idea to copy and paste your bounding-box shape into a guide layer. That way, you can see how the printable area relates to the graphics that print.
- Make sure that you don't have other shapes or objects in another layer of the same frame that contains the labeled #B keyframe. If you do, your bounding box will be extended, allowing a larger printable area than you intended (**Figure 6.84**).

To print graphics containing transparencies or color effects:

◆ From the Print pull-down menu in the Actions dialog box, choose As Bitmap (**Figure 6.85**).

Graphics that contain alpha or color effects won't print properly unless you choose `printAsBitmap` as the `print` statement. This option, however, results in lower-quality prints than printing as vectors.

Detecting the Movie's Playback Environment

Communicating with a movie's playback environment is important for knowing how your Flash movie will play and be seen by your audience. With that information, you can tailor the movie's display or provide warnings and recommendations to your viewers so they can better enjoy your movie. A viewer might have a lower screen resolution than you require to display the entire Stage of your movie, for example. You could load a different movie that fits, or you could modify the movie's display settings to allow it to be scaled down. Detecting system capabilities and the kind of player hosting the movie is especially important as Flash content becomes more prevalent in devices such as cell phones, PDAs, and television set-top boxes.

Two objects can help you gather information about the playback environment: the System.capabilities object and the Stage object. The System.capabilities object can tell you about screen resolution, the operating system, the color capabilities, and many other useful properties. **Table 6.4** summarizes the System.capabilities properties.

Table 6.4

Properties of the System.capabilities Object

Property	Description
language	Language that Flash Player supports, indicated by a two-letter code (en = English)
os	Operating system
input	Input device type
manufacturer	Manufacturer of Flash Player
serverString	Information to send to a server containing the System.capabilities properties
isDebugger	Debugger capability
version	Flash Player version
hasAudio	Audio capability
hasMP3	MP3 decoder capability
hasAudioEncoder	Audio encoder capability
hasVideoEncoder	Video encoder capability
screenResolutionX	Horizontal size of screen, in pixels
screenResolutionY	Vertical size of screen, in pixels
screenDPI	Screen resolution, in dots per inch
screenColor	Color capability (color, grayscale, or black and white)
pixelAspectRatio	Pixel aspect ratio of the screen
hasAccessibility	Accessibility capability

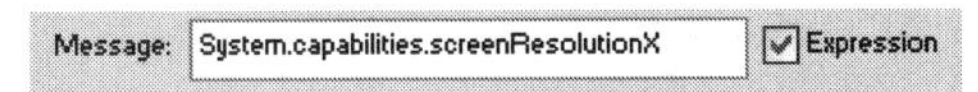

Figure 6.86 The Message field of the `trace` action.

The Stage object can tell you about the display and layout of the movie, detect whether the Stage is resized, and modify the movie's properties in response. **Table 6.5** summarizes the properties of the Stage object.

Both the System.capabilities and the Stage object can be used without a constructor function.

To retrieve the properties of the user's system:

1. Select the first frame in the main Timeline of a new Flash document, and open the Actions panel.
2. Choose Actions > Miscellaneous Actions > trace.

   You will use the `trace` action to display information about your own system in the Output window in test mode.
3. Put your pointer in the Message field, and choose Objects > Movie > System > capabilities.

   The System.capabilities object appears in the Message field.
4. Enter a dot, enter `screenResolutionX`, and check the Expression checkbox (**Figure 6.86**).

   The `trace` action will display the horizontal resolution of your computer screen.

continues on next page

Table 6.5

Properties of the Stage Object

Property	Description
align	Alignment of the Flash content ("T" = top, "B" = bottom, "R" = right, "L" = left, "TR" = top right, "TL" = top left, "BR" = bottom right, "BL" = bottom left, "C" = center)
height	Height of the Stage, in pixels (read-only)
width	Width of the Stage, in pixels (read-only)
scaleMode	Type of scaling display ("showAll", "noBorder", "exactFit", or "noScale")
showMenu	Shows the Control menu when you Control-click (Mac) or right-click (Windows) the movie (true/false)

5. Create another trace action.
6. In the Message field, choose the System.capabilities object, enter a dot, enter `screenResolutionY`, and check the Expression checkbox (**Figure 6.87**).

   The trace will display the vertical resolution of your computer screen.
7. Test your movie.

   In the Output window that appears, the screen resolution of your monitor displays (**Figure 6.88**).

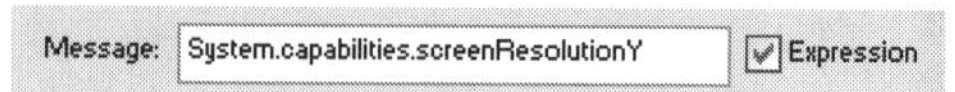

Figure 6.87 The Message field of the second trace action.

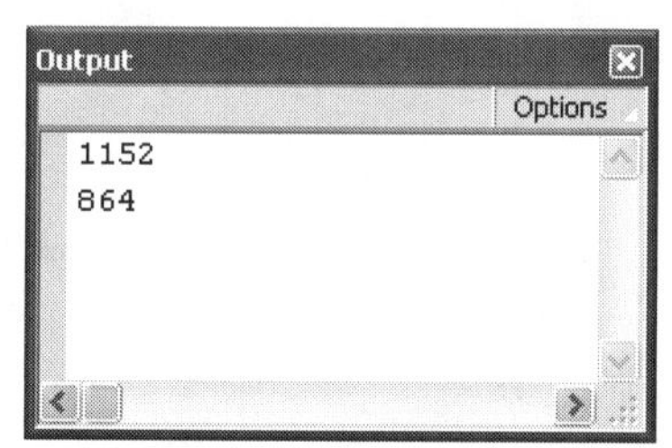

Figure 6.88 The Output window displays trace actions. The monitor for this computer is 1152 x 864 pixels.

✔ Tip

- Instead of `System.capabilities.version`, you can use the global variable `$version`. Both properties report the Flash Player version. The `$version` property is always listed in the Output window when you choose Debug > List Variables in testing mode.

To modify the display mode of the movie:

1. Open an existing Flash movie that contains graphics on the Stage.
2. Select the main Timeline, and open the Actions panel
3. Choose Objects > Movie > Stage > Properties > scaleMode.

   The `Stage.scaleMode` property appears in an Expression field.
4. Place your pointer after `Stage.scaleMode`, and enter an equal sign followed by `"showAll"` (**Figure 6.89**).
5. Choose Objects > Movie > Stage > Properties > align.

   The `Stage.align` property appears in an Expression field.
6. Place your pointer after `Stage.align` and enter an equal sign, followed by `"R"` (**Figure 6.90**).

Figure 6.89 The scaleMode property controls how your Flash movie reacts to resizing. "showAll" displays all the content with no distortions or cropping.

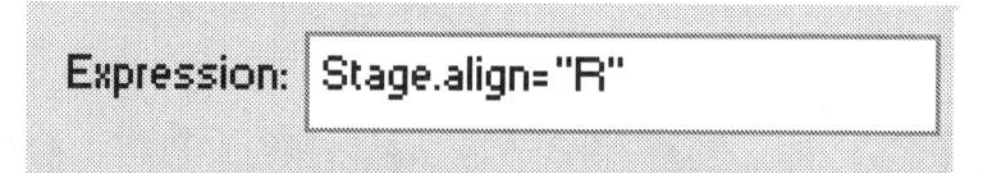

Figure 6.90 The align property controls where your Flash content appears in the window. "R" flushes the movie to the right edge.

"show all"

"noBorder"

"exactFit"

"noScale"

Figure 6.91 The `scaleMode` options. "`showAll`" (top) scales the movie to fit the window without any distortions or cropping to show all the content; this is the default mode. "`noBorder`" (top middle) scales the movie to fit the window without any distortions but will crop content to fill the window. In this mode, none of the background color shows. "`exactFit`" (bottom middle) scales the movie to fill the window on both the horizontal and vertical dimensions. In this mode, none of the background color shows, but the content is distorted. "`noScale`" (bottom) keeps the movie at 100% no matter how big or small the window is. In this mode, the content is cropped if the window is too small, and the background color shows if the window is too big.

7. Test your movie.

   When you resize the test movie window, the graphics on the Stage resize so that one dimension (either height or width) always fills the window. This is the result of the `Stage.scaleMode = "showAll"` statement. The graphics are also aligned to the right side of the window as a result of the `Stage.align = "R"` statement. For a summary of the `scaleMode` property, see **Figure 6.91**.

✔ Tips

- Remember to include the quotation marks for the `align` and `scaleMode` properties, but don't include them for the `height`, `width`, and `showMenu` properties.
- The `width` and `height` properties of the Stage object will report different values depending on how `Stage.scaleMode` is defined. When `Stage.scaleMode = "noScale"`, `Stage.width` and `Stage.height` report the size of the window that contains the Flash movie. This result could be the size of the browser window, the projector, or the window in test movie mode. When `Stage.scaleMode` is set to "`exactFit`", "`showAll`", or "`noBorders`", `Stage.width` and `Stage.height` report the size of the Flash stage when it was created. The default scaling mode for all Flash movies is "`noScale`".
- Avoid using the HTML page to hold your movie if you're going to modify the Stage properties to prevent conflicts with alignments and `scaleMode` settings.

Detection of the resizing of the Stage requires a listener object, just as the Key object does. Create a listener object from the generic Object category, and assign the event `onResize` with an anonymous function. After you register the listener with the Stage object with the method `addListener()`, you can detect and respond to Stage resizings.

To detect when the Stage is resized:

1. Select the first frame of the main Timeline, and open the Actions panel.
2. Choose Actions > Variables > set variable.
3. In the Variable field, enter the name of your listener object.
4. In the Value field, choose Objects > Core > Object > new Object, and check the Expression checkbox (**Figure 6.92**).

   A new object is instantiated for you to use as a listener.
5. Choose Objects > Movie > Stage > Events > onResize.
6. In the Object field, enter the name of your listener object.
7. Leave the Parameters field empty (**Figure 6.93**).

   The `onResize` event handler is completed and assigned to your listener object.

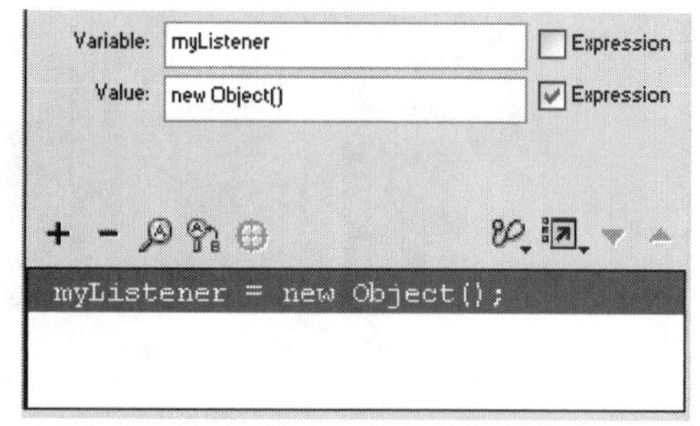

Figure 6.92 Create a new object called myListener.

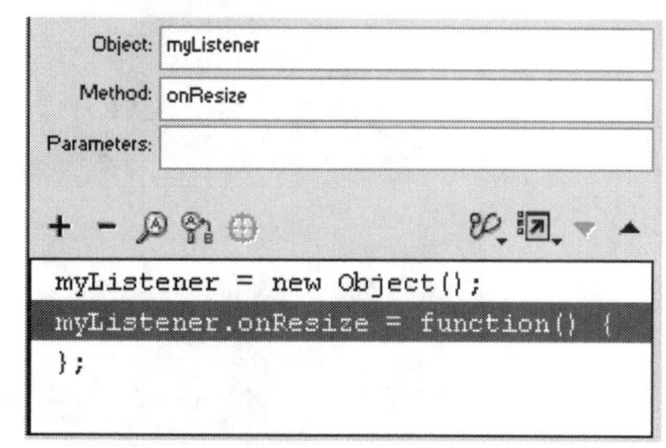

Figure 6.93 The `onResize` event handler.

```
myListener = new Object();
myListener.onResize = function() {
 Stage.align = "C";
 if (Stage.height < 499 || Stage.width < 499) {
  Stage.align = "TL";
  _root._xscale = Math.min(Stage.width, Stage.height)/500*100;
  _root._yscale = Math.min(Stage.width, Stage.height)/500*100;
 }
};
Stage.addListener(myListener);
```

Figure 6.94 The full ActionScript for this example. The Stage for this movie is 500 x 500. If its window is resized smaller, the content is aligned to the top-left corner. The `Math.min()` method decides which dimension (horizontal or vertical) of the window is smaller and scales the movie proportionately according to that size.

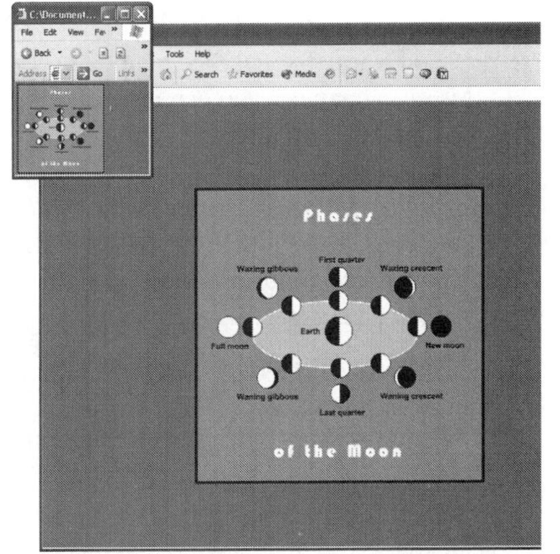

Figure 6.95 Decreasing the size of the window scales the movie so that all its content is still visible (top). Increasing the size of the window scales the movie only to 100%, at which point it maintains its size. This technique would be useful if you want viewers to be able to see your movie on smaller monitors, but you want to prevent other users from enlarging your movie to the point where bitmaps and videos are jagged and lose resolution.

8. Assign actions that will be performed when the `onResize` event occurs (**Figure 6.94**).

   In this example, when the viewer resizes the window, Flash checks whether the size is smaller than the default Stage size. If so, Flash scales the main Stage proportionately according to the smaller of the horizontal and vertical window dimensions. Resizing the window bigger, however, does not make the Flash content scale with the window. The result: You can shrink the window to accommodate smaller monitors and still see the content, but you can't enlarge the Stage more than its normal size.

9. Choose Objects > Movie > Stage > Methods > addListener.

10. In the Parameters field, enter the name of your listener object.

    The listener is registered with the Stage object to listen for the `onResize` event.

11. Test your movie.

12. Resize the movie window.

    Resizing the window triggers the function defining the `onResize` event (**Figure 6.95**).

Detecting Download Progress: Preloaders

All the hard work you put into creating complex interactivity in your movie will be wasted if your viewer has to wait too long to download it over the Web and leaves. You can avoid losing viewers by creating short animations that entertain them while the rest of your movie downloads. These diversions, or *preloaders*, tell your viewer how much of the movie has downloaded and how much longer he or she still has to wait. When enough data has been delivered over the Web to the viewer's computer, you can trigger your movie to start. In effect, you hold back the playhead until you know that all the frames are available to play. Only then do you send the playhead to the starting frame of your movie.

Preloaders must be small, because you want them to load almost immediately, and they should be informative, letting your viewers know what they're waiting for.

Flash provides two ways to monitor the state of the download progress. You can test for the number of frames that have downloaded with the Timeline properties `_framesloaded` and `_totalframes`. Or you can test for the amount of data that has downloaded with the movie-clip methods `getBytesLoaded()` and `getBytesTotal()`. Testing the amount of data is a more accurate gauge of download progress because the frames of your movie most likely contain data that are not evenly spread.

In either approach, the basic concept behind programming the preloader is the same. You tell Flash to compare the amount of frames or data loaded with the total amount of frames or data in the movie. As this ratio changes, you can display the percentage numerically with a dynamic text field or represent the changing ratio graphically as a growing progress bar. Because you often show the progress of the download, these preloaders are known as *progressive preloaders*.

The first frame of the root Timeline contains a `stop` action that prevents the movie from playing. An `onEnterFrame` event handler or a `setInterval` action can test continually whether all the frames or data have been downloaded. If so, Flash can begin playing the movie.

Registration point

Figure 6.96 A rectangular movie clip with its registration point on the far-left edge makes an excellent graphical representation of download progress.

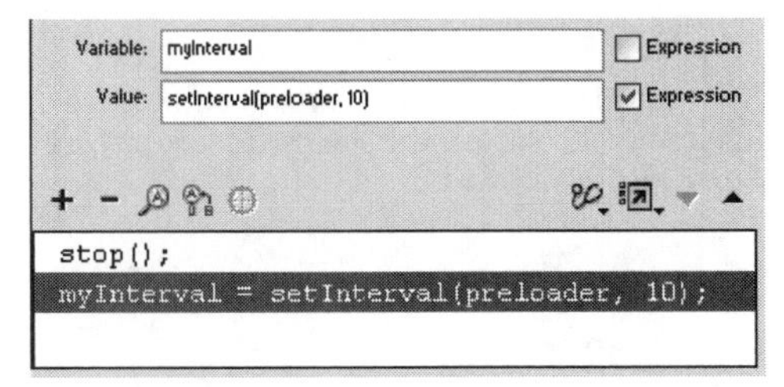

Figure 6.97 Create the `setInterval` action to monitor the download progress continuously.

To create a progressive preloader that detects frames:

1. Create a long rectangular movie-clip symbol.

   Make sure that its registration point is at its far-left edge (**Figure 6.96**).

2. Place an instance of the symbol on the Stage, and give it a name in the Property Inspector.

   Your preloader essentially is a rectangle that grows longer according to the percentage of downloaded frames. You will change the properties of the rectangular movie clip to stretch it dynamically. Because you'll want the bar to grow from left to right, the registration point is placed on the left edge.

3. On the main Stage, draw another rectangle around your movie clip.

   The new rectangle appears below the movie clip. This rectangle will serve as the container that the movie clip will fill as the download progresses.

4. Select the first frame of the main Timeline, and open the Actions panel.

5. Choose Actions > Movie Control > stop.

   The `stop` action prevents your movie from playing until it has downloaded completely.

6. Choose Actions > Variables > set variable.

7. In the Variable field, enter a name to identify a `setInterval` action.

8. In the Value field, choose Actions > Miscellaneous Actions > setInterval.

9. Between the parentheses of the `setInterval` action, enter a name of a function, followed by the interval 10. Click the Expression box (**Figure 6.97**).

   The `setInterval` action calls the function every 10 milliseconds.

   Now you need to create the function.

continues on next page

10. Choose Actions > User-defined Functions > Function.

11. In the Name field, enter the name you gave your function in the `setInterval` action (**Figure 6.98**).

12. Choose Actions > Conditions/Loops > if.

13. In the Condition field, enter the following:

    `_framesloaded>=_totalframes`

    The first part of the statement retrieves the number of frames already downloaded in the main Timeline. The second part retrieves the total number of frames in the main Timeline. The greater than (>) and equals (=) symbols together mean "greater than or equal to."

14. Choose Actions > Movie Control > play.

    If the condition in the `if` statement is `true`, the movie begins to play.

15. Now choose Actions > Miscellaneous Actions > clearInterval.

16. In the Parameters field, enter the name you used to identify your `setInterval` action (**Figure 6.99**).

    After all the frames have downloaded and the movie plays, you no longer need the `setInterval` action. The `clearInterval` action removes it.

17. Select the closing brace of the `if` statement.

18. Choose Actions > Miscellaneous Actions > evaluate.

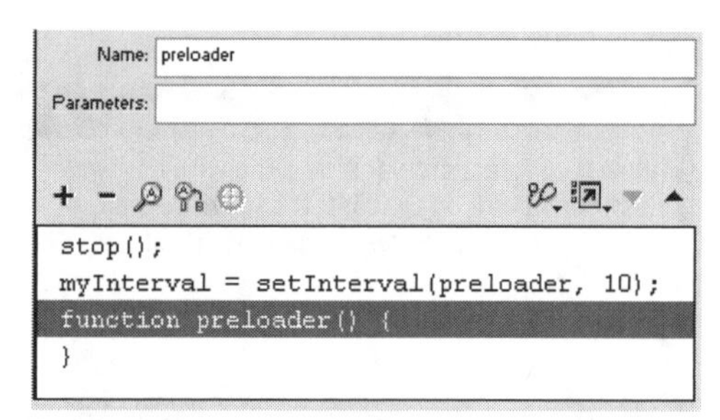

Figure 6.98 The function called preloader is called at regular intervals by the `setInterval` action. The function will contain the actions to test and display the download progress.

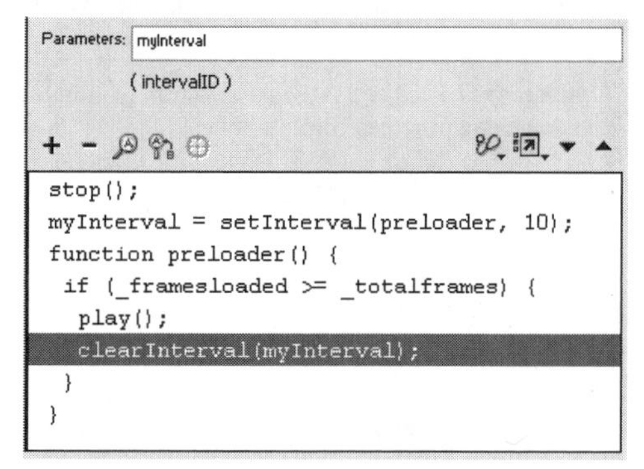

Figure 6.99 When the number of frames downloaded equals the total number of frames, the actions between the curly braces of the `if` statement are executed. Flash will begin playing the main Timeline and will remove the `setInterval` action.

Expression: progressBar._xscale = (_framesloaded/_totalframes)*100

```
stop();
myInterval = setInterval(preloader, 10);
function preloader() {
 if (_framesloaded >= _totalframes) {
  play();
  clearInterval(myInterval);
 }
 progressBar._xscale = (_framesloaded/_totalframes)*100;
}
```

Figure 6.100 The horizontal dimension of the movie clip called progressBar changes according to the percentage of downloaded frames.

Movie begins from this point forward

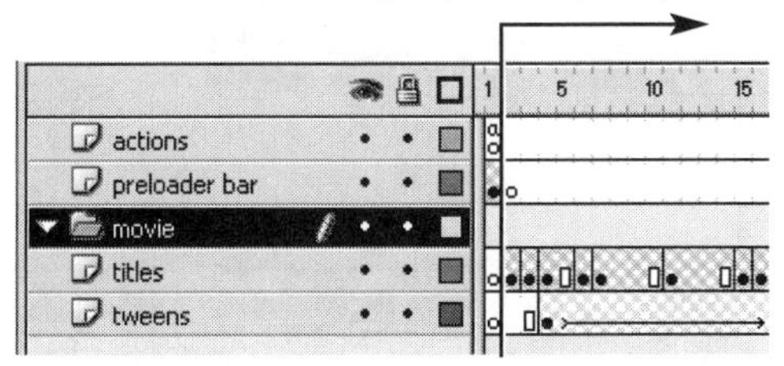

Figure 6.101 The "real" movie begins at keyframe 2, after the rectangular movie clip is removed.

19. In the Expression field, enter the following:

`progressBar._xscale = (_framesloaded/_totalframes)*100;`

This statement dynamically changes the width of your rectangular movie clip. The statement may look complicated, but it's simple when you break it down. The statement, `_framesloaded/_totalframes`, gives the proportion of downloaded frames. This fraction is multiplied by 100, which results in a percentage. The percentage is used to modify the horizontal dimension of your rectangular movie clip, called progressBar (**Figure 6.100**).

20. In the main Timeline, insert a new keyframe, and delete the progressBar movie clip and the background rectangle.

21. Begin creating your animation from keyframe 2 (**Figure 6.101**).

continues on next page

22. Test your movie with the Bandwidth Profiler and with Show Streaming on.

The Bandwidth Profiler is an information window above your movie in Test Movie mode; it displays the number of frames and the amount of data in each frame as vertical bars. If the vertical bars extend over the bottom of the red horizontal line, there is too much data to be downloaded at the bandwidth setting without causing a stutter during playback. The Show Streaming option simulates actual download performance (**Figure 6.102**). The green bar at the top shows the download progress. The triangle marks the current location of the playhead. The playhead remains in frame 1 until the green progress bar reaches the end of the Timeline. Only then does the playhead begin moving.

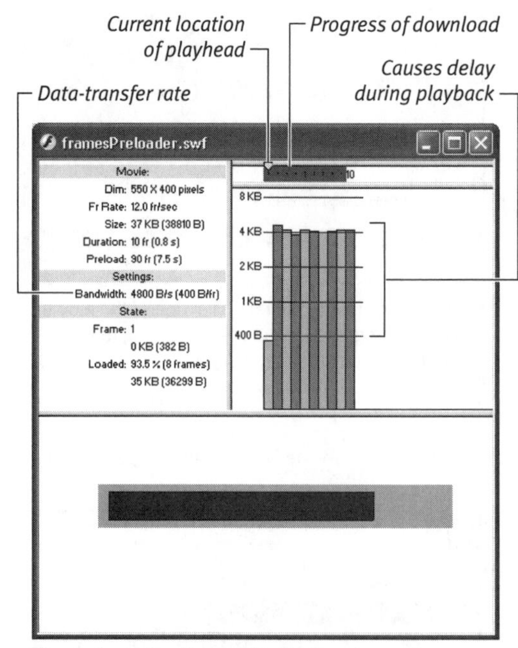

Figure 6.102 The Bandwidth Profiler shows the individual frames that cause pauses during playback because the amount of data exceeds the data-transfer rate. The alternating light and dark bars represent different frames. Notice how the progress of the download (about 8 out of 10 frames have loaded completely) affects the proportion of the movie clip (about 80%).

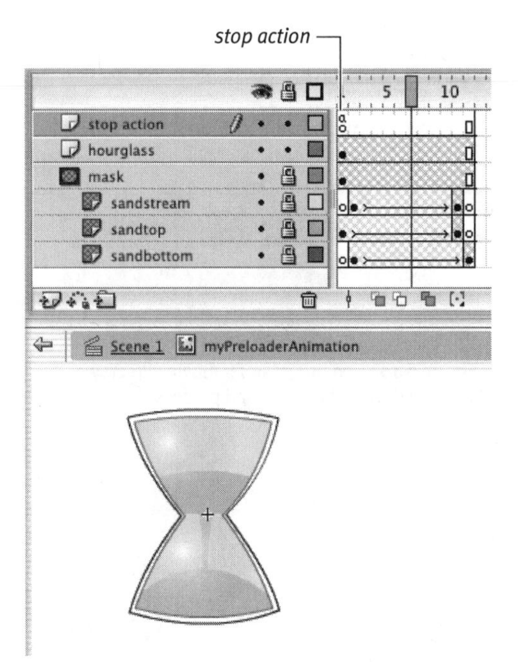

Figure 6.103 This 12-frame movie clip contains an animation of an hourglass whose sand falls from the top bulb to the bottom bulb. A `stop` action is in the first frame to prevent the clip from playing automatically. You can tell a movie clip like this one to play a frame corresponding to the percentage of the download progress. When the download starts, the sand is still in the top bulb at frame 1. When the download ends, the sand would be in the bottom bulb at frame 12.

✔ Tips

- You won't see your preloader working unless you build an animation with many frames containing fairly large graphics that require lengthy download times. If your animation is small, you'll see your preloader whiz by, because all the data will download quickly and begin playing almost immediately.
- Explore other graphical treatments of the download progress. Stretching the length of a movie clip is just one way to animate the download process. With subtle changes to your ActionScript, you can apply a variety of animated effects to your preloader. You can create an animation in a movie clip and make Flash display successive frames of that animation based on the download percentage. In the Expression field of the `evaluate` action, enter this statement:

  ```
  myMovieClip.gotoAndStop(Math.round
  (_framesloaded/_totalframes*
  (myMovieClip._totalframes))
  ```

  This statement calculates the download progress not as a percentage, as you did earlier, but as a proportion of the total number of frames in the movie clip called myMovieClip. The `Math.round()` method is applied to the result to round it to a whole number, and Flash goes to that frame (**Figure 6.103**).

To create a progressive preloader that detects data:

1. Using the file you created in the preceding task, select the first frame of the main Timeline, and open the Actions panel.
2. Select the `if` statement.
3. Replace the contents of the Condition field with this statement:

   `getBytesLoaded()>=getBytesTotal()`

   Flash checks whether the number of bytes (data) that have been loaded is greater than or equal to the total number of bytes in the main Timeline. You can find the `getBytesLoaded()` and `getBytesTotal()` methods by choosing Objects > Movie > Movie Clip > Methods.
4. Select the last statement in the function, and replace it with this statement:

   `progressBar._xscale=getBytesLoaded()/getBytesTotal()*100;`

   The horizontal dimension of the movie clip called progressBar now stretches based on the percentage of bytes loaded (**Figure 6.104**).
5. Test your movie with the Bandwidth Profiler and with Show Streaming on.

   Notice how the progress bar stretches more smoothly here than in the preceding task because of its finer division into bytes rather than frames.

```
stop();
myInterval = setInterval(preloader, 10);
function preloader() {
 if (getBytesLoaded()>=getBytesTotal()) {
  play();
  clearInterval(myInterval);
 }
 progressBar._xscale = (getBytesLoaded()/getBytesTotal())*100;
}
```

Figure 6.104 The progressBar movie clip grows steadily during the download process.

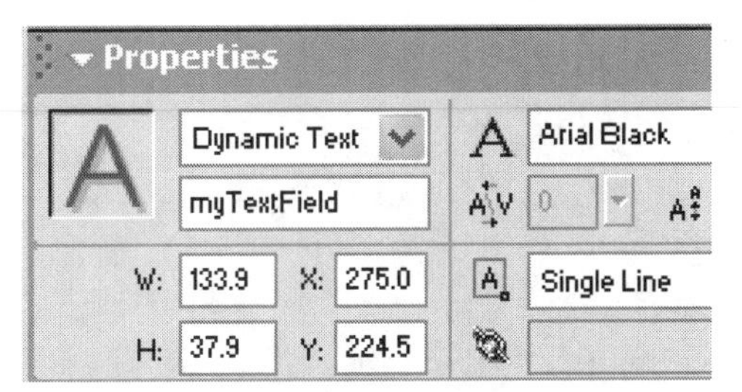

Figure 6.105 This dynamic text field is called myTextField.

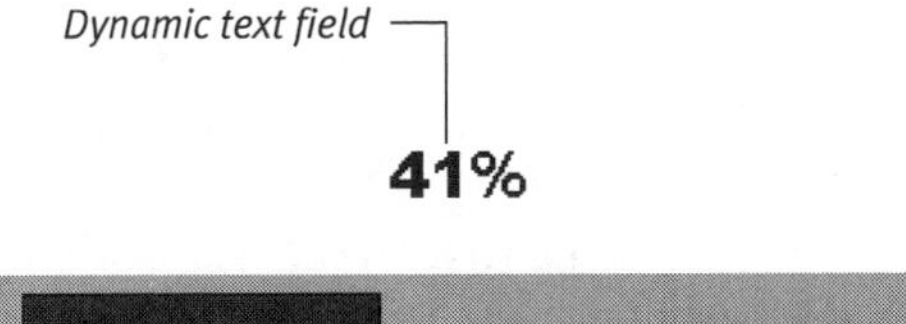

Figure 6.106 The dynamic text field displays the percentage of the download progress along with the graphical representation.

Often, a preloader has an accompanying display of the percentage of download progress. This display is accomplished by a dynamic text field placed on the Stage. You will learn more about dynamic text in Chapter 10, but you can follow these steps now to add a simple numeric display.

To add a numeric display to the progressive preloader:

1. Continuing with the file from the preceding task, select the text tool, and drag out a text field on the Stage.
2. In the Property Inspector, give the text field a name (**Figure 6.105**).

   The name of the text field, like the names of buttons and movie clips, lets you target the text field and control it.
3. Select the first frame of the main Timeline, and open the Actions panel.
4. Select the last line in the function statement.
5. Choose Actions > Miscellaneous Actions > evaluate.

   A new line appears in the Script pane.
6. In the Expression field, enter:

   ```
   myTextField.text = Math.round
   (getBytesLoaded()/getBytesTotal()
   *100)+"%"
   ```

   The percentage of download progress is rounded to a whole number by the `Math.round()` method. The percent (%) character is appended to the end, and the result is assigned to the `text` property of your text box, displaying it on the Stage (**Figure 6.106**).

The Bandwidth Profiler

The Bandwidth Profiler is a handy option to see how data is distributed throughout your Flash movie and how quickly (or slowly) it will download over the Web. In Test Movie mode, choose View > Bandwidth Profiler (Command-B for Mac, Ctrl-B for Windows) to see this information.

The left side of the Bandwidth Profiler shows movie information, such as Stage dimensions, frame rate, file size, total duration, and preload time in frames and seconds. It also shows the Bandwidth setting, which simulates actual download performance at a specified rate. You can change that rate in the Debug menu and choose the rate for a modem that your viewer is likely to have. Flash gives you options for 28.8 and 56KB modems, for example.

The bar graph on the right side of the Bandwidth Profiler shows the amount of data in each frame of your movie. You can view the graph as a streaming graph (choose View > Streaming Graph) or as a frame-by-frame graph (choose View > Frame by Frame Graph). The streaming graph indicates how the movie downloads over the Web by showing you how data streams from each frame, whereas the frame-by-frame graph simply indicates the amount of data in each frame. In Streaming Graph mode, you can tell which frames will cause hangups during playback by noting which bar exceeds the given Bandwidth setting.

To watch the actual download performance of your movie, choose View > Show Streaming. Flash simulates playback over the Web at the given Bandwidth setting. A green horizontal bar at the top of the window indicates which frames have been downloaded, and the triangular playhead marks the current frame that plays.

Part IV: Transforming Graphics and Sound

7 Controlling the Movie Clip

The movie clip is a powerful object. Its power comes from the myriad of properties, methods, and events that are available to it. Essentially, Flash lets you control the way movie clips look and behave. Movie-clip properties such as position, scale, rotation, transparency, color, and even instance name can all be changed with ActionScript. As a result, you can create arcade-style interactivity, with characters changing in response to viewer input or conditions. Imagine a game of Tetris created entirely in Flash. Each geometric shape could be a movie clip, and the viewer would control its rotation and position with the keyboard. A game of Asteroids could feature an alien ship that moves in response to the viewer's position. This kind of animation isn't based on tweens you create while authoring the Flash movie. Rather, this is dynamic animation that is essentially "created" during playback.

Flash also gives you powerful methods to control a movie clip's behavior. Make movie clips draggable so that viewers can actually pick up puzzle pieces and put them in their correct places, or develop a more immersive online shopping experience in which viewers can grab merchandise and drop it into their shopping carts. You'll learn how to detect where draggable movie clips are dropped on the Stage, as well as control collisions and overlaps with other movie clips. You'll learn how to generate movie clips dynamically, so that new instances appear on the Stage during playback. You can use movie clips to create moving masks and even to create drawings—lines, curves, fills, and gradients.

Learning to control movie-clip properties, methods, and events is your first step in understanding how to animate entirely with ActionScript.

Dragging the Movie Clip

Drag-and-drop behaviors give the viewer one of the most direct interactions with the Flash movie. Nothing is more satisfying than grabbing a graphic on the screen, moving it around, and dropping it somewhere else. It's a natural way of interacting with objects, and it's easy to give your viewers this experience. Creating a drag-and-drop behavior in Flash involves just two basic steps: creating the movie clip and then assigning ActionScript to an event handler that triggers the drag action.

The usual behavior for drag-and-drop interactivity is for the dragging to begin when the viewer presses the mouse button over the movie clip. Then, when the mouse button is released, the dragging stops. Hence, the action to start dragging is tied to an `on (press)` or an `onPress` event handler, and the action to stop dragging is tied to an `on (release)` or an `onRelease` event handler. If you use `on (press)`, you assign ActionScript directly to the movie-clip instance. If you use `onPress`, you assign ActionScript to the root Timeline. Both ways are valid. As you learned in Chapter 4, although it may initially be simpler to assign scripts to the instance, in the long run, as you develop more complicated code, it is better practice to put all your code in one place on the main Timeline.

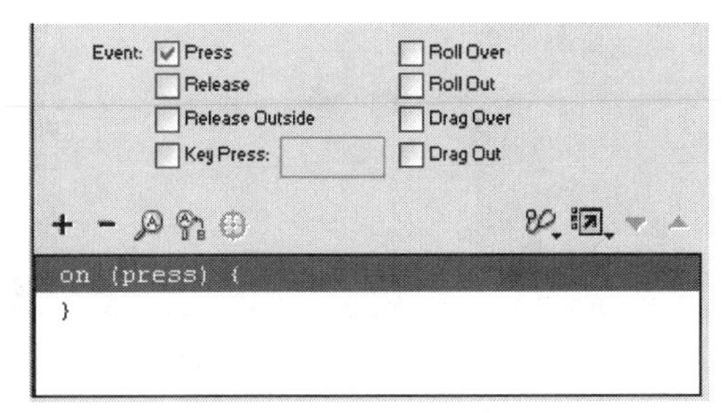

Figure 7.1 Select the Press event for the on handler assigned to the movie clip.

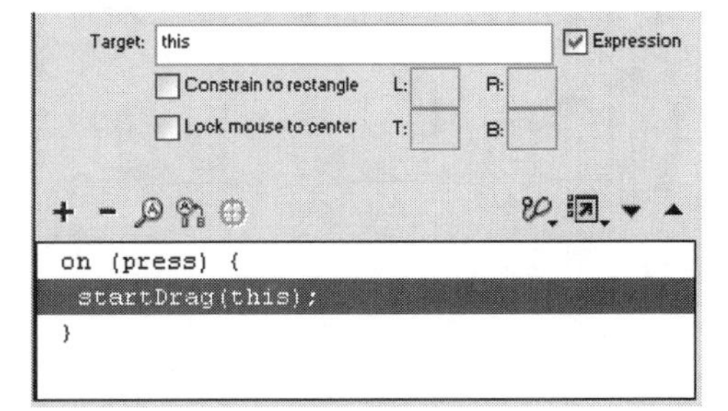

Figure 7.2 The target `this` makes the `startDrag` action affect the current movie clip.

To start dragging a movie clip by using the on (press) event handler:

1. Create a movie-clip symbol, and place an instance of it on the Stage.
2. Select the movie-clip instance, and open the Actions panel.
3. Choose Actions > Movie Control > on (Esc+on).

   The `on (release)` statement appears in the script window.
4. In the Parameters pane, uncheck the box next to Release, and check the box next to Press (**Figure 7.1**).

   The `on (release)` statement changes to `on (press)`.
5. Choose Actions > Movie Clip Control > startDrag (Esc+dr).

   The `startDrag` action appears under the `on (press)` event handler.
6. In the Parameters pane, in the Target field, enter `this`, and check the Expression box (**Figure 7.2**).

   The keyword `this` refers to the current movie clip. Checking the Expression box removes the quotation marks around `this` in the Script pane so that Flash recognizes the word as the keyword rather than a string literal.
7. Test your movie.

   When you press your mouse button over the movie clip, you can drag it around.

To start dragging a movie clip by using the onPress event handler:

1. Create a movie-clip symbol, place an instance of it on the Stage, and name it in the Property Inspector (**Figure 7.3**).
2. Select the first frame of the root Timeline, and open the Actions panel.
3. Choose Objects > Movie > Movie Clip > Events > onPress.

   The `onPress` event handler appears in the Script pane, with empty fields for Object and Parameters.
4. In the Object field in the Parameters pane, enter the name of your movie clip; leave the Parameters field empty (**Figure 7.4**).

   The completed statement creates an `onPress` event handler for your movie clip.
5. Choose Actions > Movie Clip Control > startDrag (Esc+dr).

   The `startDrag` action appears between the function curly braces.
6. In the Parameters pane, in the Target field, enter `this`, and check the Expression box (**Figure 7.5**).

   The keyword `this` refers to the current movie clip.
7. Test your movie.

   When you press your mouse button over the movie clip, you can drag it around.

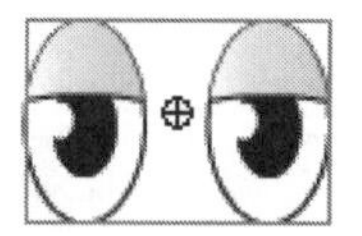

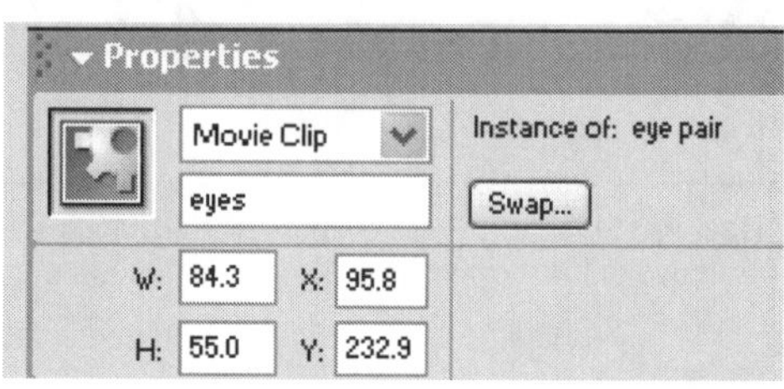

Figure 7.3 The movie-clip instance of these cartoon eyes is given the name eyes in the Property Inspector.

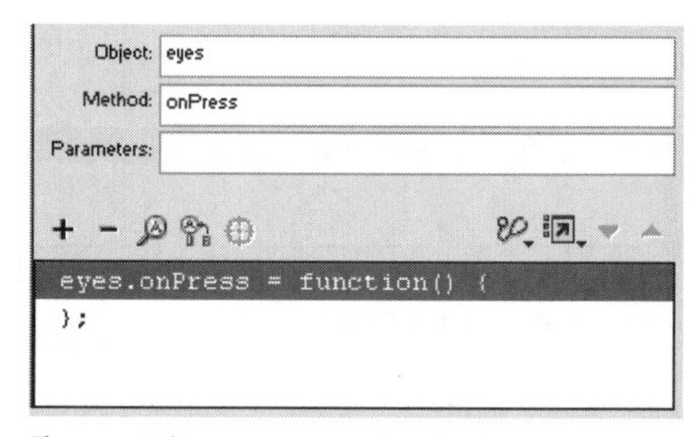

Figure 7.4 The `onPress` event handler is created with an anonymous function.

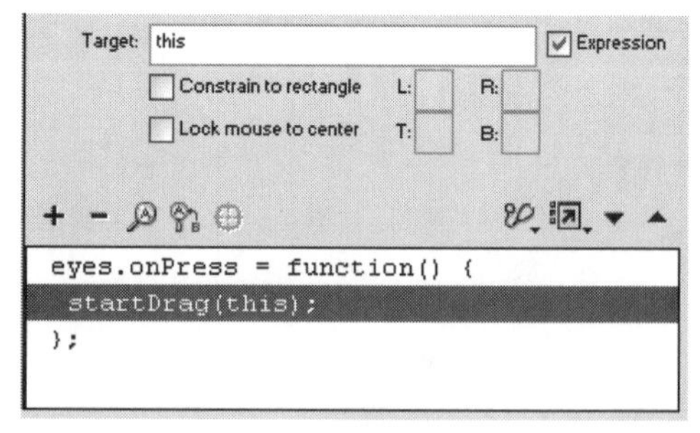

Figure 7.5 The target `this` makes the `startDrag` action affect the movie clip called eyes. Compare this figure with Figure 7.2.

```
on (press) {
 startDrag(this);
}
on (release) {
 stopDrag();
}
```

```
eyes.onPress = function() {
 startDrag(this);
};
eyes.onRelease = function() {
 stopDrag();
};
```

Figure 7.6 Each of the three facial features are movie clips that can be dragged to the potato face and dropped into position. The ActionScript can be assigned to the movie-clip instance (top) or on the root Timeline (bottom).

To stop dragging a movie clip:

1. Using the file you created in the preceding task, select the closing curly brace in the Script pane.
2. If you are continuing with assigning actions to the movie instance, choose Actions > Movie Clip Control > on.

   The `on (release)` statement appears.

   or

   If you are continuing with assigning actions to the main Timeline, choose Choose Objects > Movie > Movie Clip > Events > onRelease. In the Object field, enter the name of your movie clip.

   The `onRelease` event handler is completed for your movie clip.
3. Choose Actions > Movie Clip Control > stopDrag (Esc+sd).

   The `stopDrag` statement appears, with no parameters.
4. Test your movie.

   When you press your mouse button over the movie clip, you can drag it. When you release your mouse button, the dragging stops (**Figure 7.6**).

✔ Tip

- Only one movie clip can be dragged at any one time. For this reason, the `stopDrag` action doesn't need any parameters; it will stop the drag action on whichever movie clip is currently draggable.

In many cases, you may want the movie clip to snap to the center of the user's pointer as it is being dragged, rather than wherever the user happens to click.

To center the draggable movie clip:

1. Select the `startDrag` action in the Script pane.
2. In the Parameters pane, check the box next to Lock Mouse to Center (**Figure 7.7**).

   After you press the mouse button over the movie clip to begin dragging, the registration point of your movie clip snaps to the mouse pointer.

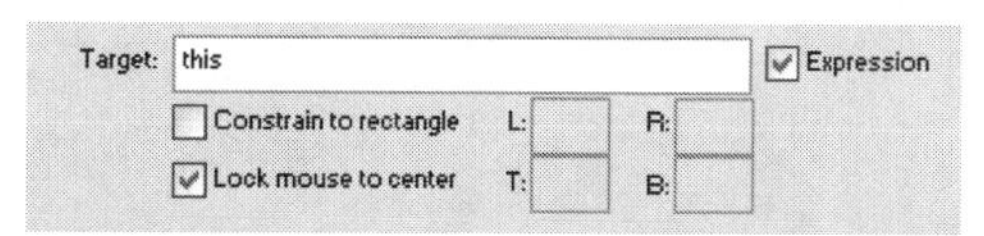

Figure 7.7 The Lock Mouse to Center option forces the viewer to drag the movie clip by its registration point.

✔ Tip

- If you select the Lock Mouse to Center option, make sure that the hit area of your movie clip covers its registration point. (By default, the hit area of your movie clip is the graphics it contains.) If it doesn't , after the movie clip snaps to your mouse pointer, your pointer will no longer be over any hit area, and Flash won't be able to detect when to stop the drag action.

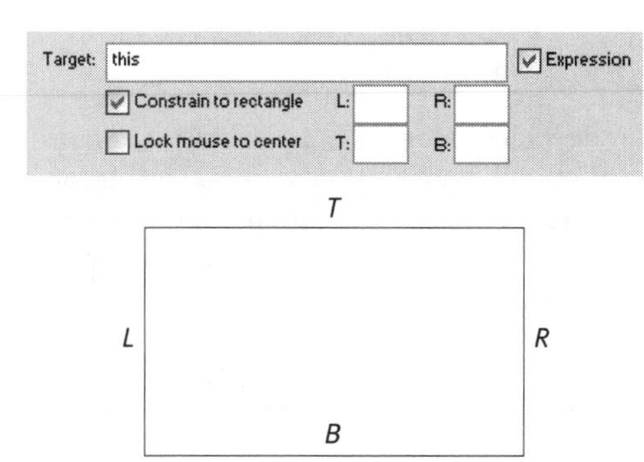

Figure 7.8 The Constrain to Rectangle option has settings for the left (L), right (R), top (T), and bottom (B) boundaries.

You may also want to limit the area where viewers can drag movie clips.

To constrain the draggable movie clip:

1. Select the `startDrag` action in the Script pane.
2. In the Parameters pane, check the box next to Constrain to Rectangle, and enter pixel coordinates for each of the four fields representing the maximum and minimum limits for the registration point of your draggable movie clip (**Figure 7.8**).
   - *L:* the leftmost margin (minimum *x* position) where the registration point of the movie clip can go.
   - *R:* the rightmost margin (maximum *x* position) where the registration point of the movie clip can go.
   - *T:* the topmost margin (minimum *y* position) where the registration point of the movie clip can go.
   - *B:* the bottommost margin (maximum *y* position) where the registration point of the movie clip can go.

   The pixel coordinates are relative to the Timeline in which the movie clip resides. If the draggable movie clip sits on the root Timeline, the pixel coordinates correspond to the Stage, so L=0, T=0 refers to the top-left corner. If the draggable movie clip is within another movie clip, L=0, T=0 refers to the registration point of the parent movie clip.

✔ Tip

- You can use the Constrain to Rectangle parameters to force a dragging motion along a horizontal or a vertical track, as in a scroll bar. Set the L and R fields to the same number to restrict the motion to up and down, or set the T and the B fields to the same number to restrict the motion to left and right.

Actions versus Methods

You may have noticed that despite our emphasis on the "object-dot-method" construction of calling an object's method, we did not follow that syntax in the previous examples. The reason is that certain methods, such as `startDrag` and `stopDrag`, can be used as either a method or an action. In fact, you'll see that these methods are listed in both the Actions > Movie Clip Control category and in the Objects > Movie > Movie Clip > Methods category.

What's the difference? In general, when you make a choice from the Actions category, as we have done here, Flash guides you through the parameters and writes the script in the correct form based on the choices you make in the Parameters pane. When you make a choice from the Methods category, Flash gives you less guidance and assumes that you know what kind of values are required for each parameter. Compare the Actions panel for `startDrag` as either an action or a method (**Figure 7.9**).

Several other action/method duplicates exist. But don't think that you have to learn the same ActionScript twice. Although the scripts may look slightly different, their effect, usage, and parameters are the same.

Be aware, however, that the one exception is the action `goto` (Actions > Movie Control > goto). The action `goto` lets you move the playhead only in the current Timeline. You must choose the method `gotoAndStop()` or `gotoAndPlay()` to move the playhead in different Timelines.

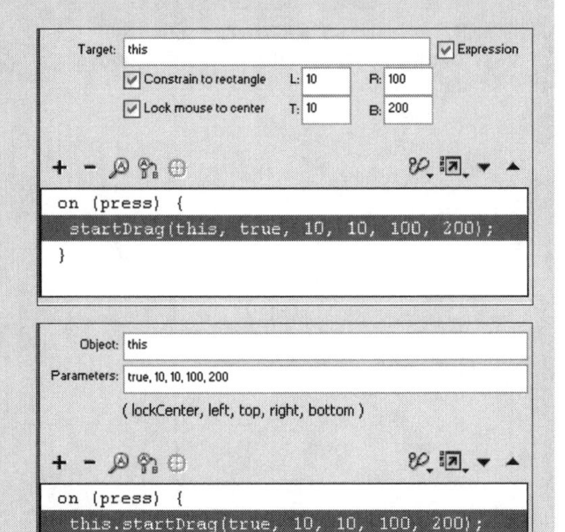

Figure 7.9 The Actions panels for `startDrag` as an action (top) and as a method (bottom) differ in the way that the parameters are input.

Setting the Movie-Clip Properties

Many movie-clip properties—size, transparency, position, rotation, and quality—define how the movie looks. By using the action `setProperty` or by using dot syntax, you can target any movie clip and change any of those characteristics during playback. **Table 7.1** summarizes properties that are available from the action `setProperty`. A few of these properties affect the entire movie, not just a single movie clip.

Table 7.1

Properties Available Through setProperty

Property	Value	Description
`_alpha` (Alpha)	A number from 0 to 100	Specifies the alpha transparency, where 0 is totally transparent and 100 is opaque.
`_visible` (Visibility)	true or false	Specifies whether a movie clip can be seen.
`_name` (Name)	A string-literal name	Specifies a new instance name of the movie clip.
`_rotation` (Rotation)	A number	Specifies the degree of rotation in a clockwise direction from the 12 o'clock position. A value of 45, for example, tips the movie clip to the right.
`_width` (Width)	A number in pixels	Specifies the horizontal dimension.
`_height` (Height)	A number in pixels	Specifies the vertical dimension.
_x (X Position)	A number in pixels	Specifies the horizontal position of the movie clip's registration point.
_y (Y Position)	A number in pixels	Specifies the vertical position of the movie clip's registration point.
_xscale (X Scale)	A number	Specifies the percentage of the original movie-clip symbol's horizontal dimension.
_yscale (Y Scale)	A number	Specifies the percentage of the original movie-clip symbol's vertical dimension.
`_focusrect` (Show focus rectangle)	true or false	Determines whether a yellow rectangle appears around objects as you use the Tab key to select objects.
`_highquality` (High quality)	A number 0, 1, or 2	Specifies the level of antialiasing for playback of the movie. 2 = best: antialiasing and bitmap smoothing. 1 = high: antialiasing and bitmap smoothing if there is no animation. 0 = low: no antialiasing. This property is a global property that affects the entire movie, rather than a single movie clip. This property is also considered to be deprecated.
`_quality` (Quality)	LOW, MEDIUM, HIGH, or BEST	Specifies the level of antialiasing for playback of the movie. BEST = antialiasing and bitmap smoothing. HIGH = antialiasing and bitmap smoothing if there is no animation. MEDIUM = lower-quality antialiasing. LOW = no antialiasing. This property is a global property that affects the entire movie, rather than a single movie clip.
`_soundbuftime` (Sound buffer time)	A number	Specifies the number of seconds before the movie begins to stream sound. The default value is 5. This property is a global property that affects the entire movie, rather than a single movie clip.

✔ Tips

- There is a difference between an Alpha of 0 and a Visibility of false, although the result may look the same. When Visibility is false, the movie clip literally cannot be seen. Mouse events in the movie clip and buttons within that movie clip aren't responsive because they are invisible. When Alpha is 0, on the other hand, mouse events and buttons within the movie clip still function.
- The *x* and *y* coordinate space for the root Timeline is different from movie-clip Timelines. In the root Timeline, the *x* axis begins at the left edge and increases to the right; the *y* axis begins at the top edge and increases to the bottom. Thus, x = 0, y = 0 corresponds to the top-left corner of the Stage. For movie clips, the coordinates x = 0, y = 0 correspond to the registration point (the crosshair). The value of *x* increases to the right of the registration point and decreases into negative values to the left of the registration point. The value of *y* increases to the bottom and decreases into negative values to the top (**Figure 7.10**).
- The X Scale and Y Scale properties control the percentage of the original movie-clip symbol, which is different from what may be on the Stage. If, for example, you place an instance of a movie clip on the Stage and shrink it 50 percent, and then you apply an X Scale of 100 and a Y Scale of 100 during playback, your movie clip will double in size.

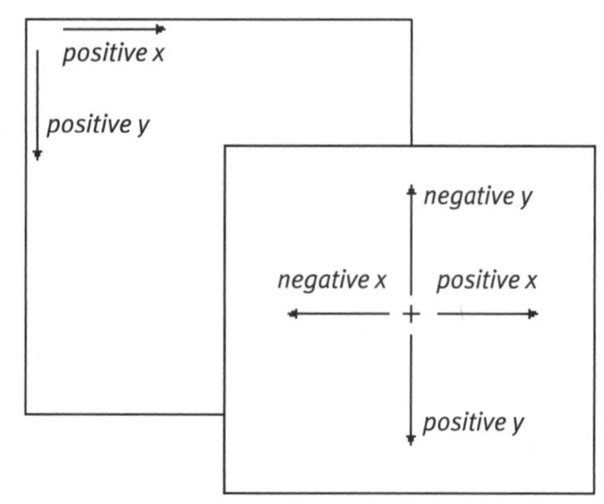

Figure 7.10 The x, y coordinates for the root Timeline (top) are centered at the top-left corner of the Stage. The x, y coordinates for movie clips (bottom) are centered at the registration point.

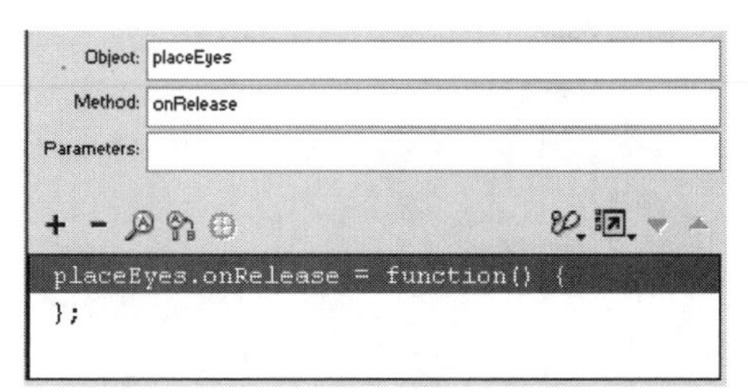

Figure 7.11 The `onRelease` event handler for the placeEyes button is completed. In this example, this button will modify the *x* and *y* positions of a movie clip.

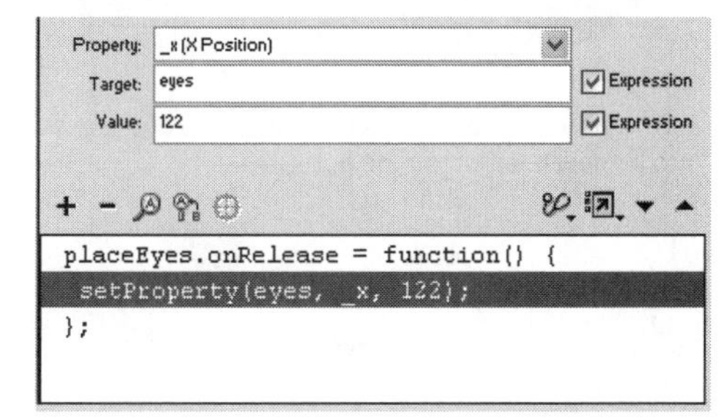

Figure 7.12 The x position of the movie clip eyes on the root Timeline is set to 122.

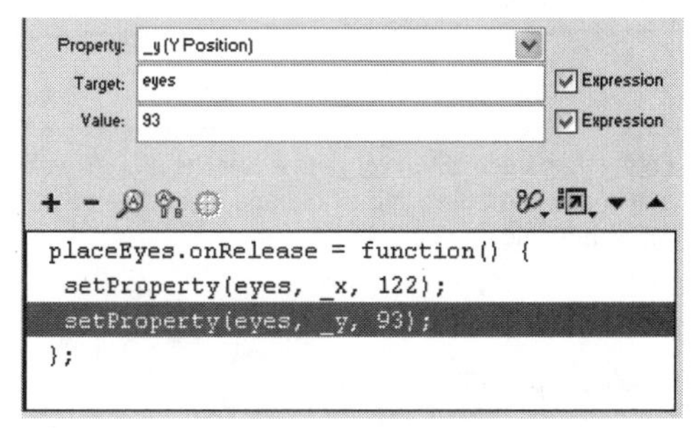

Figure 7.13 The y position of the movie clip eyes on the root Timeline is set to 93.

To change the position of a movie clip:

1. Create a movie-clip symbol, place an instance of it on the Stage, and name it in the Property Inspector.
2. Create a button symbol, place an instance of it on the Stage, and name it in the Property Inspector
3. Select the first frame of the root Timeline, and open the Actions panel.
4. Choose Objects > Movie > Button > Events > onRelease.
5. In the Object field, enter the name of your button (**Figure 7.11**).
6. Choose Actions > Movie Clip Control > setProperty (Esc+sp).

   The `setProperty` statement appears within the `onRelease` event handler.
7. From the Property pull-down menu in the Parameters pane, choose _x (X Position).
8. In the Target field, enter the target path of your movie clip, or use the Insert Target Path button at the bottom of the Parameters pane, and check the Expression box.
9. In the Value field, enter a number for the *x* position, and check the Expression box. (**Figure 7.12**).
10. Again, choose Actions > Movie Clip Control > setProperty.

    A second `setProperty` statement appears below the first.
11. For Property, select _y (Y Position); for Target, enter the target path; for Value, enter a number for the *y* position; and check the Expression box (**Figure 7.13**).

continues on next page

12. Test your movie.

    When you click the button that you created, your movie clip jumps to the new position defined by your two `setProperty` actions (**Figure 7.14**).

An alternative way of setting movie-clip properties is to use dot syntax in this form: `target._property=value`. Use the `set variable` or the `evaluate` action as described in the following task to assign a value to the property of a particular movie clip.

To set movie-clip properties in dot syntax:

1. In the Actions panel, choose Actions > Variables > set variable (Esc+sv).
2. In the Variable field, enter the target path to the movie clip whose property you want to modify.

   Enter a dot, followed by the property you want to affect.
3. In the Value field, enter the required value, and check the Expression box if it is a number or an expression (**Figure 7.15**).

or

1. In the Actions panel, choose Actions > Miscellaneous Actions > evaluate (Esc+ev).
2. In the Expression field, enter the target path to the movie clip, a dot, and then the property you want to affect.
3. Enter the equal sign and then the value you want to assign to the property (**Figure 7.16**).

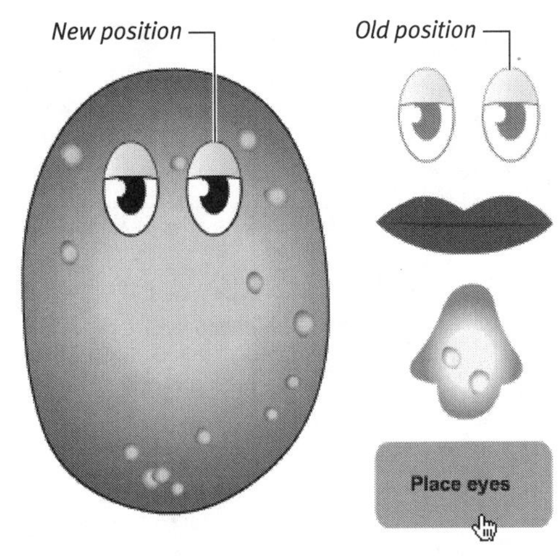

Figure 7.14 The button sets the movie clip of the eyes into its new position on the potato.

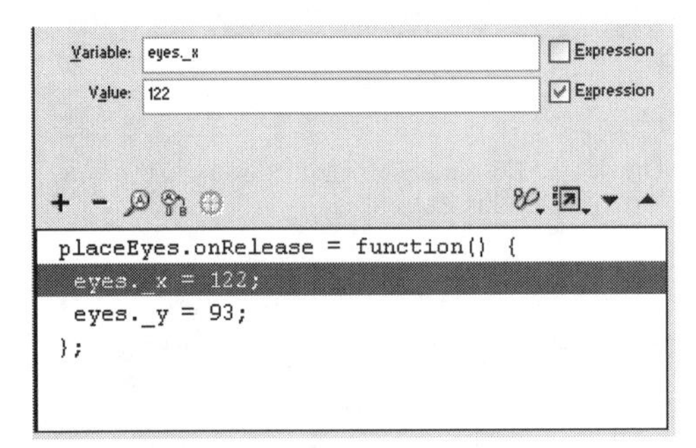

Figure 7.15 Use `set variable` to enter the property of a movie clip in the Variable field and its new value in the Value field.

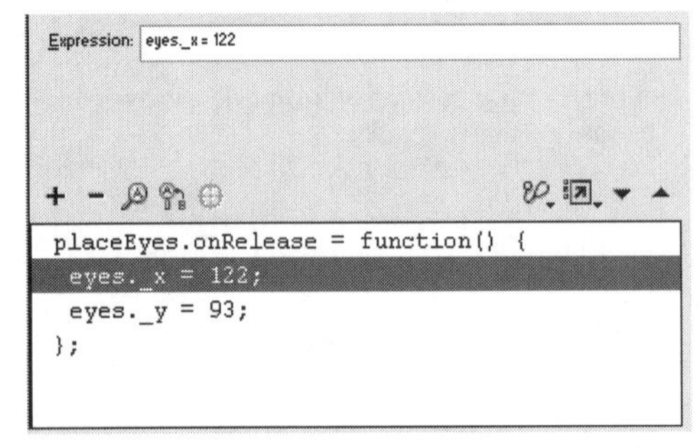

Figure 7.16 Use `evaluate` to assign the property of a movie clip to its new value all in one parameter field.

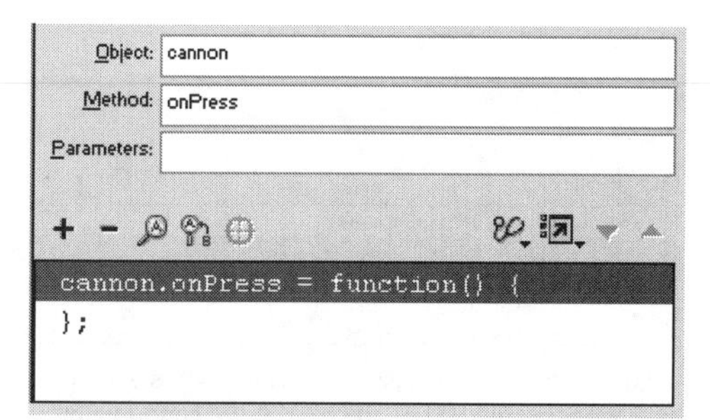

Figure 7.17 The onPress event handler for the cannon movie clip is completed.

Getting the Movie-Clip Properties

Very often, you will want to change a movie clip's property relative to its current value. You may want to rotate a cannon 10 degrees each time your viewer clicks a button, for example. How do you find out the current value of a movie clip's property? You can get a property in two ways. The first way is to use the function `getProperty`. The second way is far simpler because it only requires that you write the target path and property in dot syntax. So if you want to change a movie clip's property based on its current value, you can write the expression

```
cannon._rotation = cannon._rotation + 10
```

This expression will add 10 degrees to the current angle of the movie clip called cannon.

To get a property by using getProperty:

1. Create a movie clip, place an instance on the Stage, and name it in the Property Inspector.

   In this example, you will get the rotation property of this movie clip and add 10 degrees each time you click it.

2. Select the first frame of the root Timeline, and open the Actions panel.

3. Choose Objects > Movie > Movie Clip > Events > onPress.

4. In the Object field, enter the target path to your movie clip (**Figure 7.17**).

5. Choose Actions > Miscellaneous Actions > evaluate.

6. In the Expression field, enter: `this._rotation =`

continues on next page

7. Now choose Functions > getProperty.

   The `getProperty` function appears in the Expression field.

8. Between the `getProperty` parentheses, enter the target path of the movie clip whose property you want to get, followed by the property; separate the parameters with a comma (**Figure 7.18**).

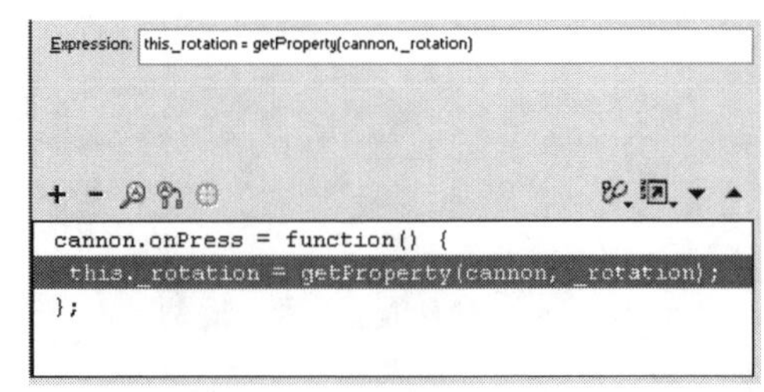

Figure 7.18 The `getProperty` function in this example retrieves the `_rotation` property of the cannon movie clip. This expression is not yet finished.

9. Enter + `10` to complete the expression (**Figure 7.19**).

   Each time the movie clip is clicked, Flash gets the value of its `rotation` property and adds 10 to it.

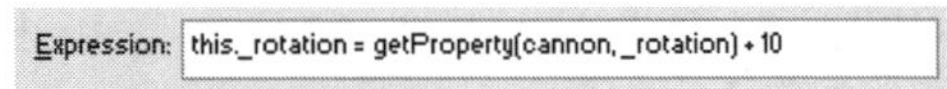

Figure 7.19 The completed expression adds 10 to the current rotation of the cannon movie clip.

To get a property by using dot syntax:

1. Continue with the example in the preceding task.

2. Select the first frame of the root Timeline, and open the Actions panel.

3. Select the statement within the `onPress` event handler, and change it as follows:

   `this._rotation = this._rotation + 10`

   Each time the movie clip is clicked, Flash gets the value of its `rotation` property and adds 10 to it (**Figure 7.20**).

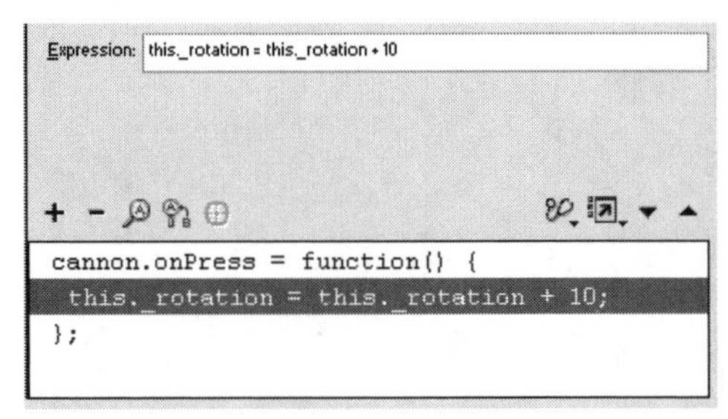

Figure 7.20 Use this dot-syntax expression to change a property relative to its current value.

✔ Tip

- You can use shortcuts to add and subtract values by using combinations of the arithmetic operators. You learn about these combinations in Chapter 9.

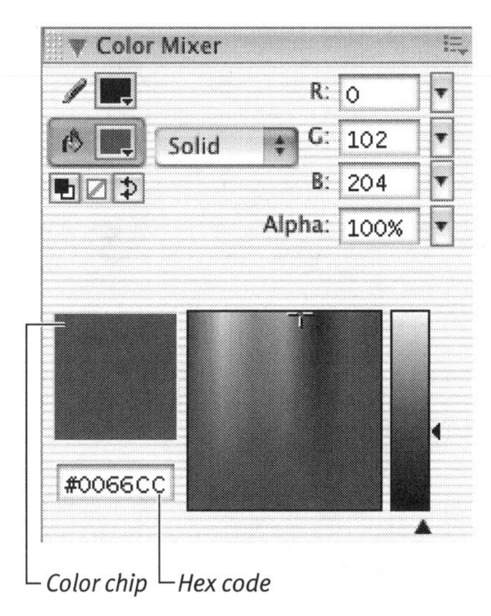

Figure 7.21 The Mixer panel has a display window to show the selected RGB color in hexadecimal code.

Modifying the Movie-Clip Color

One conspicuous omission from the list of movie-clip properties that `setProperty` controls is color. But you can use the Color object—a predefined class—to change the color of movie clips.

The first step in modifying a movie clip's color is instantiating a new color object with a constructor function such as this:

```
nameofColorObject = new
Color(movieClipInstance)
```

In this function, `nameofColorObject` is the name of your new color object, and `movieClipInstance` is the target path of the movie clip you want to control.

Next, you can use your new color object to set the RGB values of the movie clip by using the method `setRGB()`. To define your new color, use the hexadecimal equivalents of each color component (red, green, and blue) in the form of 0xRRGGBB. You may have seen this six-digit code in HTML to specify the background color of a Web page. You can find these values for a color in the Color Mixer panel. Choose a color in the color spectrum, and the hexadecimal value for that color appears in the display to the left (**Figure 7.21**).

To set the color of a movie clip:

1. Create a movie-clip symbol whose color you want to modify, place an instance of it on the Stage, and name it in the Property Inspector.
2. Create a button symbol, place an instance of it on the Stage, and name it in the Property Inspector.

   You will use this button to call the `setRGB()` method of your new color object.
3. Select the first frame of the root Timeline, and open the Actions panel.
4. Choose Actions > Variables > set variable.
5. In the Variable field, enter the name for your new color object.
6. Place your pointer in the Value field, and choose Objects > Movie > Color > new Color.

   The expression `new Color()` appears. The `new Color()` constructor requires a target path to a movie clip as its parameter.
7. Enter your movie-clip name as the parameter, or use the Insert Target Path button below the Parameters pane (**Figure 7.22**). Check the Expression box.

   The completed statement instantiates a new color object and is ready to be used.
8. Choose Objects > Movie > Button > Events > onRelease.
9. Enter the name of your button in the Object field (**Figure 7.23**).

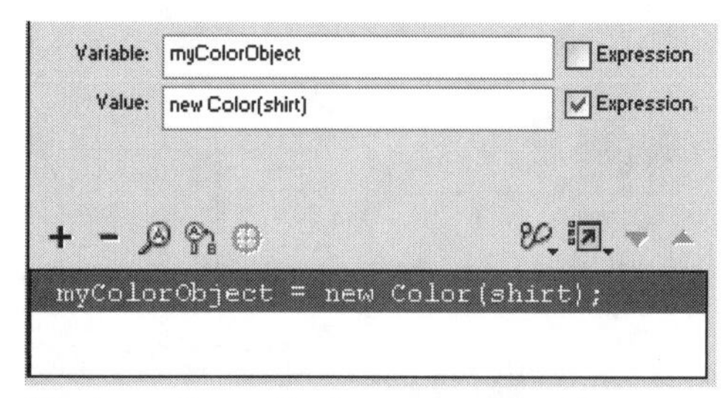

Figure 7.22 The `new Color` constructor function creates a new color object. The new color object is called `myColorObject` and is associated with the movie clip called shirt.

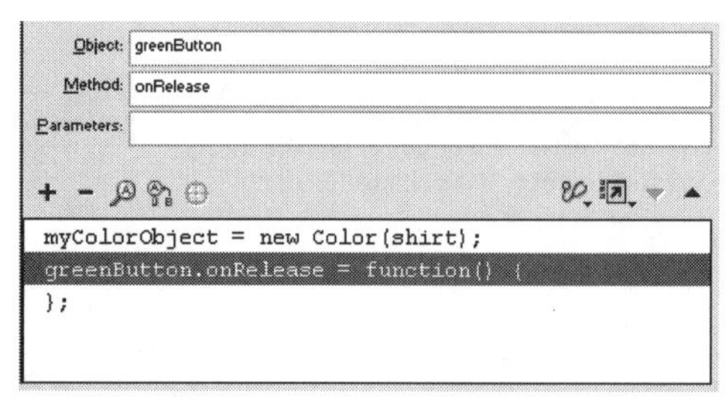

Figure 7.23 The `onRelease` event handler is completed for the greenButton button.

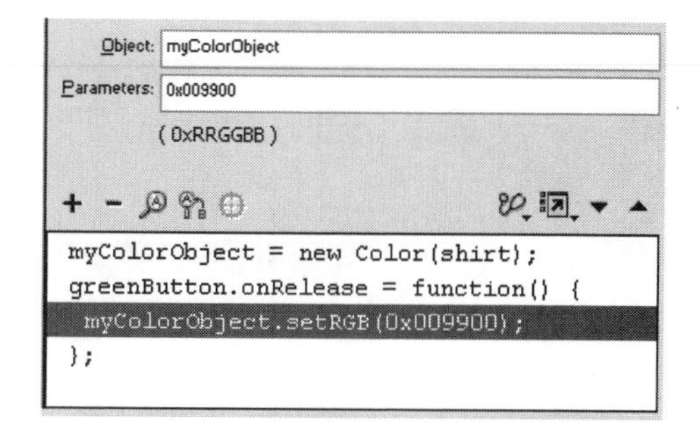

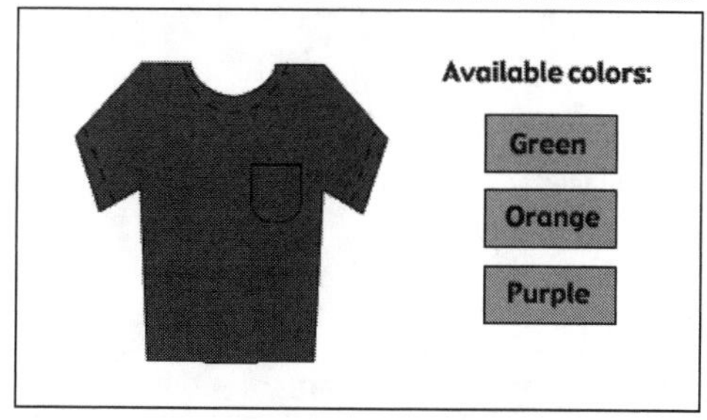

Figure 7.24 The `setRGB` method takes the parameter oxRRGGBB, which is the hex code for a color. Use `setRGB` with different hex codes to change the color of this movie clip, shirt.

10. Choose Objects > Movie > Color > Methods > setRGB.

The `setRGB()` method appears within your button event handler, with an Object field and a Parameters field in the Parameters pane.

11. In the Object field, enter the target path to your color object.

12. In the Parameters field, enter `0x`, followed by the six-digit hexadecimal code for the new color (**Figure 7.24**).

13. Test your movie.

In the first frame, a color object is instantiated. When you click your button, that color object calls its `setRGB()` method. The movie clip associated with the color object is assigned a new RGB value.

Using the color-transform object

The method `setRGB()` lets you change only a movie clip's color. To change its brightness or its transparency, you must use the method `setTransform()`. This method allows you to define both the percentages and the offset values for each of the RGB components, as well as the alpha transparency. These parameters are the same as the ones in the Advanced Effect dialog box. This dialog box appears when you apply an advanced color effect to an instance (**Figure 7.25**).

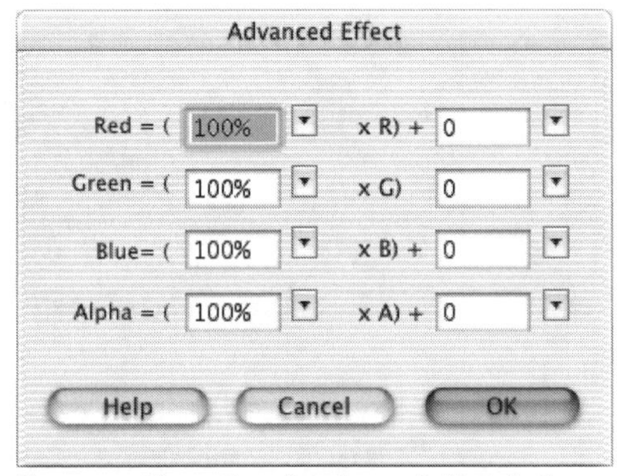

Figure 7.25 The options for advanced effects in the Property Inspector control the RGB and alpha percentages and the offset values for any instance.

To use the `setTransform()` method for your color object, you must first create another object that essentially holds the color-transformation information, which is in the parameters ra, rb, ga, gb, ba, bb, aa, and ab (**Table 7.2**). The color-transform object is created via the generic class called Object. After you define the color-transform object, you use it in the `setTransform()` method of your color object. This process may be a little confusing, but the basic idea is this: Where you normally would see numbers or strings as parameters for a method—the number 5 in the method `gotoAndStop(5)`, for example—you now use an object such as `setTransform(myColorTransformObject)`.

The baseline `setTransform()` parameters (the values that maintain the movie clip's color) are as follows:

```
ra=100    ba=100
rb=0      bb=0
ga=100    aa=100
gb=0      ab=0
```

Table 7.2

setTransform Parameters

Parameter	Value
ra	Percentage (–100 to 100) of red component
rb	Offset (–255 to 255) of red component
ga	Percentage (–100 to 100) of green component
gb	Offset (–255 to 255) of green component
ba	Percentage (–100 to 100) of blue component
bb	Offset (–255 to 255) of blue component
aa	Percentage (–100 to 100) of alpha transparency
ab	Offset (–255 to 255) of alpha transparency

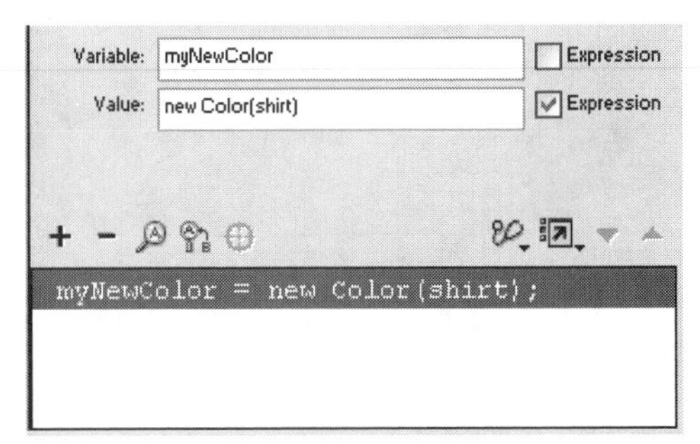

Figure 7.26 A new color object called myNewColor is created for the shirt movie clip.

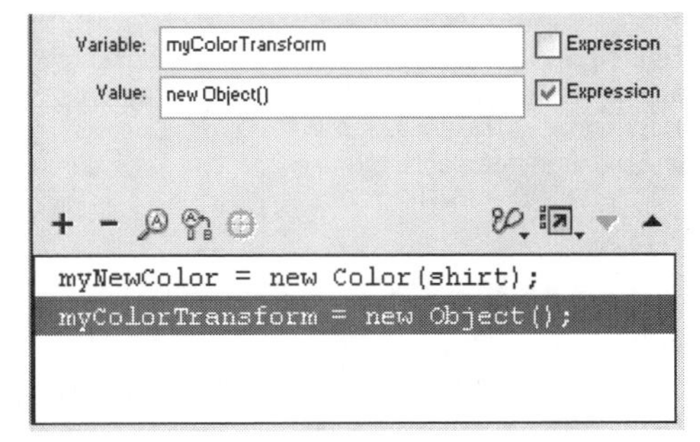

Figure 7.27 Create a new generic object called myColorTransform with the constructor function `new Object`. This object will hold the RGB and alpha information.

To transform the color and alpha of a movie clip:

1. Create a movie-clip symbol whose color or transparency you want to modify, place an instance of it on the Stage, and name it in the Property Inspector.
2. Create a button symbol, place an instance of it on the Stage, and name it in the Property Inspector.

   You will use this button to call the `setTransform()` method of your color object.
3. Select the first frame of the root Timeline, and open the Actions panel.
4. Instantiate a new color object as described in "To set the color of a movie clip" earlier in this chapter (**Figure 7.26**).
5. Choose Actions > Variable > set variable.
6. In the Variable field, enter the name for a color-transform object.
7. Place your pointer in the Value field, and choose Objects > Core > Object > new Object. Check the Expression box.

   The `new Object()` constructor function appears in the Value field. Your new color-transform object is instantiated (**Figure 7.27**). This object is a generic object that has no premade properties or methods.
8. Choose Actions > Variables > set variable.
9. In the Variable field, enter the name of your color-transform object, a dot, and then one of the set transform parameters.

continues on next page

10. In the Value field, enter a number. Check the Expression box.
11. Repeat steps 8 to 10 for all eight parameters (**Figure 7.28**).

    The parameters for the color transformation are defined in the properties of your color-transform object.
12. Choose Objects > Movie > Button > Events > onRelease.
13. In the Object field, enter the name of your button.
14. Choose Object > Movie > Color > Methods > setTransform.
15. In the Object field, enter the name of your color object.
16. In the Parameters field, enter the name of your color-transform object (**Figure 7.29**).

    The full script should look like the one in **Figure 7.30**.
17. Test your movie.

    First, a color object and a color-transform object are instantiated. When you click the button that you created, the color object calls the `setTransform()` method, which uses the color-transform object as its parameter. The movie clip associated with the color object changes color and transparency.

✔ Tip

- Instead of creating eight separate statements to define the parameters of your color-transform object, you can write just one statement that lists them all. You can use this syntax:

  ```
  myColorTransform = { ra: '100', rb:
  '150', ga: '75', gb: '200', ba: '20',
  bb: '188', aa: '50', ab: '255'}
  ```

  The parameters are separated from their values by colons, and the parameter/value pairs are separated by commas.

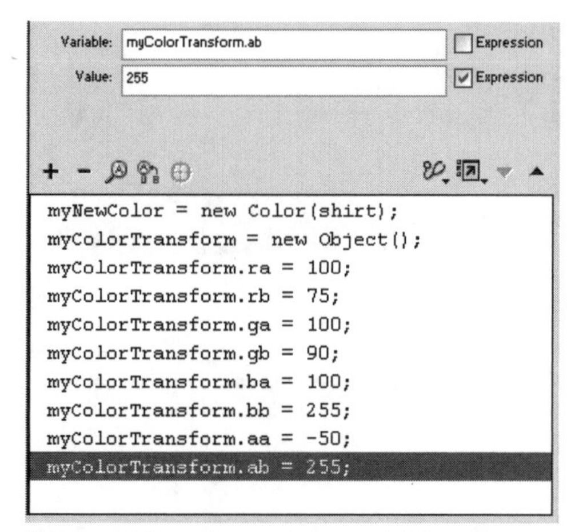

Figure 7.28 The red, green, blue, and alpha percentage and offset values are set with a series of set variable statements. ra, rb, etc. are properties of the myColorTransform object.

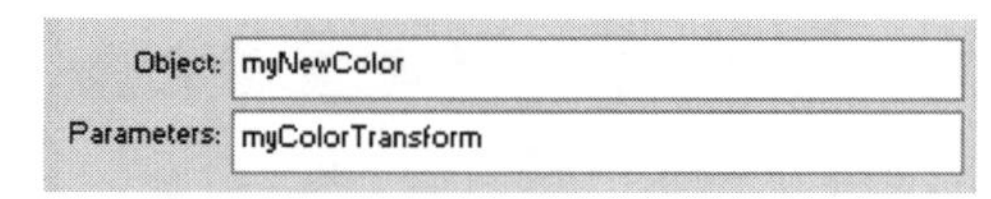

Figure 7.29 The Parameters pane of the `setTransform()` method. The `setTransform()` method requires, as its parameter, an object that holds the color-transformation information. That object, in this example, is called myColorTransform.

```
// instantiate a new color object
myNewColor = new Color(shirt);
// instantiate a new color transform object
myColorTransform = new Object();
// set the properties of the
// color transform object
myColorTransform.ra = 100;
myColorTransform.rb = 75;
myColorTransform.ga = 100;
myColorTransform.gb = 90;
myColorTransform.ba = 100;
myColorTransform.bb = 255;
myColorTransform.aa = -50;
myColorTransform.ab = 255;
transformButton.onRelease = function() {
 // call the setTransform method using the
 // color transform object as the parameter
 myNewColor.setTransform(myColorTransform);
};
```

Figure 7.30 The full ActionScript changes the color and alpha of the movie clip shirt with a button click.

To change the brightness of a movie clip:

- Increase the offset parameters for the red, green, and blue components equally, but leave the other parameters unchanged.

  If your color-transform object is called myColorTransform, for example, set its properties as follows:

```
myColorTransform.ra=100
myColorTransform.rb=125
myColorTransform.ga=100
myColorTransform.gb=125
myColorTransform.ba=100
myColorTransform.bb=125
myColorTransform.aa=100
myColorTransform.ab=0
```

  A color object using these parameters would increase the brightness of a movie clip to about 50 percent . Or you could set the offset parameters of red, green, and blue to their maximum (255), as follows:

```
myColorTransform.ra=100
myColorTransform.rb=255
myColorTransform.ga=100
myColorTransform.gb=255
myColorTransform.ba=100
myColorTransform.bb=255
myColorTransform.aa=100
myColorTransform.ab=0
```

  A color object using these parameters would increase the brightness of a movie clip to 100 percent, so that it would turn white.

To change the darkness of a movie clip:

- Decrease the offset parameters for the red, green, and blue components equally, but leave the other parameters unchanged.

  To darken a movie clip about 50 percent, for example, set the color-transform properties as follows:

```
myColorTransform.ra=100
myColorTransform.rb=-125
myColorTransform.ga=100
myColorTransform.gb=-125
myColorTransform.ba=100
myColorTransform.bb=-125
myColorTransform.aa=100
myColorTransform.ab=0
```

To change the transparency of a movie clip:

- Decrease either the offset or the percentage parameter for the alpha component, and leave the other parameters unchanged.

  Decrease aa to –100 or decrease ab to –255 for total transparency.

Swapping Overlapping Movie Clips

When you have multiple draggable movie clips, you'll notice that the objects maintain their stacking order even while they're being dragged, which can seem a little odd. You would expect that the one you pick up would come to the top. You can make it do so by using the `swapDepths()` method to swap the stacking order of movie clips dynamically. `swapDepths()` can switch the stacking order of movie clips either by swapping two named movie clips or by swapping a named movie clip with whatever movie clip is in a designated depth level. The *depth level* is a number that refers to a movie clip's stacking order. Higher depth-level numbers will overlap lower ones, much like levels of loaded movies.

The amazing thing about `swapDepths()` is that it even works across layers, so a movie clip in the bottom layer can swap with a movie clip in the topmost layer.

Knowing where a movie clip lies in the stacking order can also be quite useful. The method `getDepth()`, which returns the depth level of any movie clip, is the logical counterpart to the `swapDepths()` method.

To swap a movie clip with another movie clip:

1. Create two draggable movie clips on the Stage, as outlined earlier in this chapter.

   Your script should look similar to **Figure 7.31**.

2. In the Script pane, select the first `startDrag` statement, and choose Objects > Movie > Movie Clip > Methods > swapDepths.

3. In the Object field, enter `this`.

```
puzzle1.onPress = function() {
 startDrag(this);
};
puzzle1.onRelease = function() {
 stopDrag();
};
puzzle2.onPress = function() {
 startDrag(this);
};
puzzle2.onRelease = function() {
 stopDrag();
};
```

Figure 7.31 The ActionScript to make the movie clips called puzzle1 and puzzle2 draggable.

Figure 7.32 The Parameters pane for the swapDepths() method. The current movie clip and the movie clip puzzle2 swap in the stacking order.

```
puzzle1.onPress = function() {
  startDrag(this);
  this.swapDepths(puzzle2);
};
puzzle1.onRelease = function() {
  stopDrag();
};
puzzle2.onPress = function() {
  startDrag(this);
  this.swapDepths(puzzle1);
};
puzzle2.onRelease = function() {
  stopDrag();
};
```

Figure 7.33 Each swapDepths() method is associated with a `startDrag` action. When you click puzzle1, it swaps with puzzle2. When you click puzzle2, it swaps with puzzle1.

4. In the Parameters field, enter the target path of the second movie clip (**Figure 7.32**).

   Whenever you click the first draggable movie clip, it will swap its stacking order with that of the other movie clip.

5. Select the second `startDrag` statement, and add a similar `swapDepths` statement below it.

6. In the Parameters field for this `swapDepths` statement, choose the target path of the first movie clip.

   The completed scripts should look like the one in **Figure 7.33**.

7. Test your movie.

   When you drag the first movie clip, it will swap its stacking order with that of the second movie clip, and vice versa.

To swap the depth level of a movie clip:

1. Continue with the same file you created in the preceding task.
2. Select the first `swapDepths` statement.
3. Replace the target path in the Parameters field with a number specifying the depth level (**Figure 7.34**).
4. Select the second `swapDepths` statement, and replace its Parameters field with the same depth-level number.
5. Test your movie.

   The first movie clip you drag is put into the specified depth level. The second movie clip you drag is swapped with whatever is currently in that depth level (**Figure 7.35**).

✔ Tip

- The difference between using a target path and using a depth number as the `swapDepths()` parameter depends on your needs. Use a target path simply to swap the two named movie clips, so that a movie clip that is overlapping the other movie clip will be sent behind it. To keep a draggable movie clip above all other movie clips, use depth level to send it to the top of the stacking order.

```
Object: this
Parameters: 2
         ( target )

puzzle1.onPress = function() {
 startDrag(this);
 this.swapDepths(2);
};
puzzle1.onRelease = function() {
 stopDrag();
};
puzzle2.onPress = function() {
 startDrag(this);
 this.swapDepths(2);
};
puzzle2.onRelease = function() {
 stopDrag();
};
```

Figure 7.34 The current movie clip swaps with the one in depth level 2.

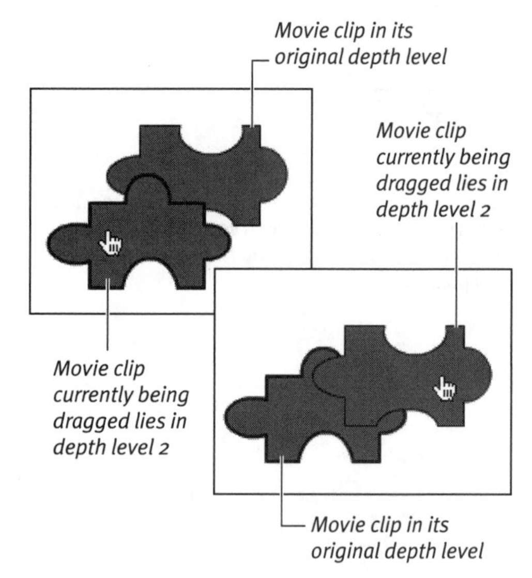

Figure 7.35 Swapping depth levels is ideal for dealing with multiple draggable movie clips, such as these puzzle pieces.

Figure 7.36 This `trace` command displays the depth level of the movie clip puzzle1.

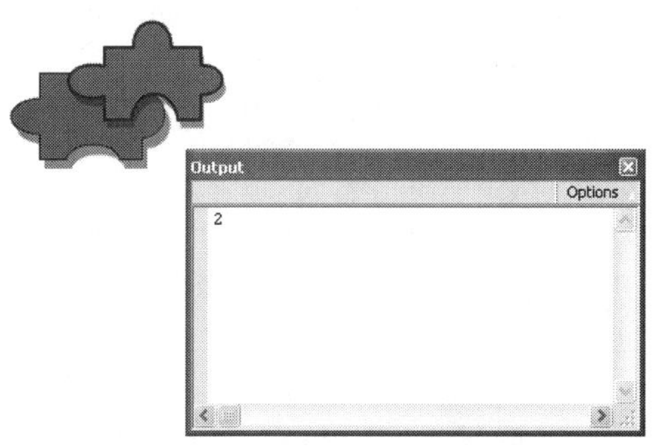

Figure 7.37 The `trace` command shows in the Output window that the currently dragged movie clip is in depth level 2. The Output window appears only when you test your Flash movie. It does not appear in your final .swf file.

To determine the depth level of a movie clip:

1. Continue with the same file you created in the preceding task.
2. Select the first `swapDepths` statement, and choose Actions > Miscellaneous Actions > trace.

   The `trace` command will display information in the Output window when you test your movie. You will add the `swapDepths()` method to the `trace` command to see the depth level of your movie clip.
3. Place your pointer in the message field, and choose Objects > Movie > Movie Clip > Methods > getDepth.
4. Place your pointer before the dot and the `getDepth()` method in the Message field, enter the target path to the first draggable movie clip, and check the Expression box (**Figure 7.36**).
5. Select the second `swapDepths` statement, and add another `trace` command with a `getDepth()` method for the second draggable movie clip.
6. Test your movie.

   When you drag the first movie clip, the Output window appears and displays the movie clip's depth level. When you drag the second movie clip, its depth level displays in the Output window (**Figure 7.37**).

✔ Tip

- The method `getDepth()` is also a method of the Button object and the TextField object, so you can use it in the same way to determine the stacking order of those objects.

Detecting Dropped Movie Clips

Now that you can make a movie clip that can be dragged around the Stage, you'll want to know where the user drops it. If the movie clips are puzzle pieces, for example, you need to know whether or not those pieces are dragged and dropped on the correct spots. One of the simplest ways to detect the dropped movie clip's location is to use the movie-clip property `_droptarget`. This property retrieves the absolute target path of another movie clip where the draggable movie clip was dropped. The second movie clip essentially is the destination for the draggable movie clip. Use a conditional statement to compare whether the `_droptarget` of the draggable movie clip is the same as the target path of the destination movie clip. Perform any actions based on whether the condition is true or false.

A common practice with drag-and-drop movie clips is to create snap-to and bounce-back behaviors. When the user drops a movie clip very near a correct location, you can detect that situation with `_droptarget` and then adjust, or *snap*, the movie clip to a more exact position by using the `setProperty` action, which sets its X and Y Positions. When the user drops a movie clip in an inappropriate location, you can detect that situation with `_droptarget` and then send, or *bounce*, it back to its original position by using the `setProperty` action.

A word of caution here: The `_droptarget` property returns the absolute target path in slash syntax. This property originated in Flash 4, which supported only the slash syntax. So to test whether the `_droptarget` property matches the target path of a destination movie clip, you construct a conditional statement that looks like the following:

```
draggableMovieClip._droptarget ==
"/destinationMovieClip"
```

Alternatively, you can use the `eval` function (Functions > eval) to resolve the `_droptarget` slash syntax to dot syntax. Using `eval` would look something like this:

```
eval(draggableMovieClip._droptarget) ==
_root.destinationMovieClip
```

```
Condition: this._droptarget == "/destination"

drag.onPress = function() {
 startDrag(this, true);
};
drag.onRelease = function() {
 stopDrag();
 if (this._droptarget == "/destination") {
 }
};
```

Figure 7.38 This condition tests whether the current movie clip has been dropped on the movie clip called destination. The slash (/) refers to the root Timeline.

```
drag.onPress = function() {
 // begin dragging this movie clip
 startDrag(this, true);
};
drag.onRelease = function() {
 // stop dragging this movie clip
 stopDrag();
 // check to see if this movie clip
 // is dropped on the destination movie clip
 if (this._droptarget == "/destination") {
  // if it's true, then make it invisible
  setProperty(this, _visible, false);
 }
};
```

Figure 7.39 If the draggable movie clip is dropped on the movie clip called destination, its visibility is set to false.

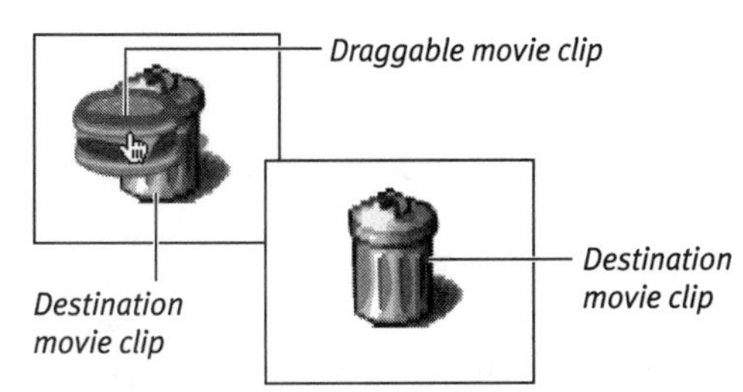

Figure 7.40 This hamburger disappears when it is dropped on the trash can.

To detect a dropped movie clip:

1. Create a draggable movie clip, place an instance of it on the Stage, and name it in the Property Inspector.
2. Create a movie clip, place an instance of it on the Stage, and name it in the Property Inspector. Then assign actions on the main Timeline to make it draggable.

   This movie clip is the destination for the draggable movie clip.
3. Select the first frame of the root Timeline, and open the Actions panel.
4. Select the `stopDrag` action, and choose Actions > Conditions/Loops > if (Esc+if).

   The `if` statement appears below the `stopDrag` statement.
5. In the Condition field, enter `this`, followed by a dot.
6. Choose Properties > _droptarget.
7. Enter two equal signs.

   A pair of equal signs tests whether one value is the same as another. A single equal sign is used to assign one value to a variable.
8. Enter the target path of the destination movie clip within quotation marks, using slash syntax.

   The final conditional statement is constructed (**Figure 7.38**).
9. Choose an action to be performed when this condition is met.

   The final script should look like **Figure 7.39**.
10. Test your movie (**Figure 7.40**).

    When you drop the draggable movie clip, Flash checks whether its `_droptarget` property matches the target path of the second movie clip. If so, the `_visibility` property of the draggable movie clip is set to true, and the clip disappears.

To create a bounce-back effect:

1. Continue with the same file you created in the preceding task.
2. Select the last action within the `if` statement, and choose Actions > Conditions/Loops > else (Esc+el).

   The `else` statement appears. It gives you the opportunity to choose an alternative consequence if the condition in the `if` statement returns false (**Figure 7.41**).

```
drag.onPress = function() {
  startDrag(this, true);
};
drag.onRelease = function() {
  stopDrag();
  if (this._droptarget == "/destination") {
    setProperty(this, _visible, false);
  } else {
  }
};
```

Figure 7.41 The `else` action provides an alternative to the `if` condition.

3. Choose Actions > Movie Clip Control > setProperty.
4. Choose X Position from the Property pull-down menu, enter `this` in the Target field, enter the original *x* coordinate in the Value field, and check both Expression boxes (**Figure 7.42**).

   This `setProperty` statement changes the *x* position of the draggable movie clip when it's not dropped over the destination movie clip.

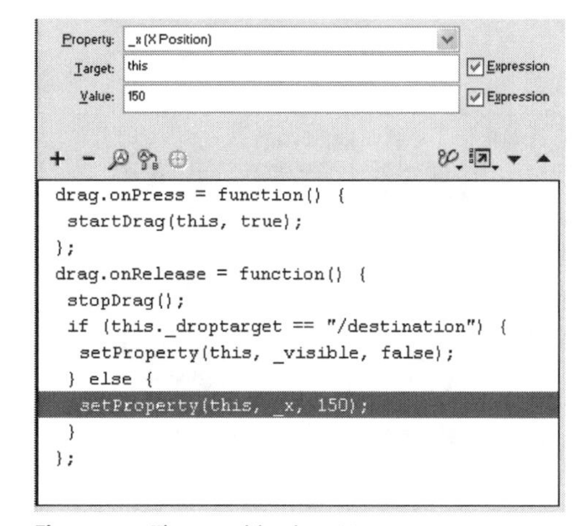

Figure 7.42 The *x* position is set to 150.

5. Choose Actions > Movie Clip Control > setProperty.
6. Choose Y Position from the Property pull-down menu, enter `this` in the Target field, enter the original *y* coordinate in the Value field, and check both Expression boxes.

   This `setProperty` statement changes the *y* position of the draggable movie clip when it's not dropped over the destination movie clip. The complete script looks like **Figure 7.43**.

7. Test your movie.

   When the draggable movie clip isn't dropped over the destination movie clip, Flash sets the *x* and *y* coordinates so that the movie clip bounces back to its original position.

✔ Tip

- Flash determines the dropped movie clip's location at its registration point. If the registration point of the dropped movie clip does not land in the graphic area of the destination movie clip, it will not be detected even if other parts overlap.

```
drag.onPress = function() {
 // begin dragging this movie clip
 startDrag(this, true);
};
drag.onRelease = function() {
 // stop dragging this movie clip
 stopDrag();
 // check to see if this movie clip
 // is dropped on the destination movie clip
 if (this._droptarget == "/destination") {
  // if it's true, then make it invisible
  setProperty(this, _visible, false);
 } else {
  // if it's false, send it back
  // to its previous location
  setProperty(this, _x, 150);
  setProperty(this, _y, 100);
 }
};
```

Figure 7.43 The actions for a bounce-back effect are assigned to the `else` condition.

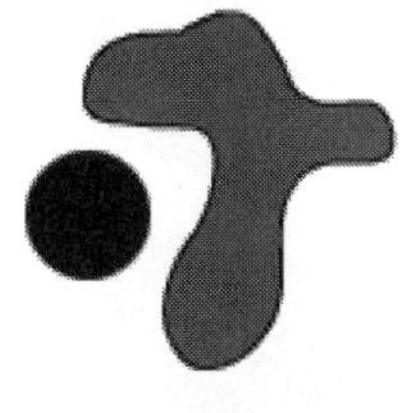

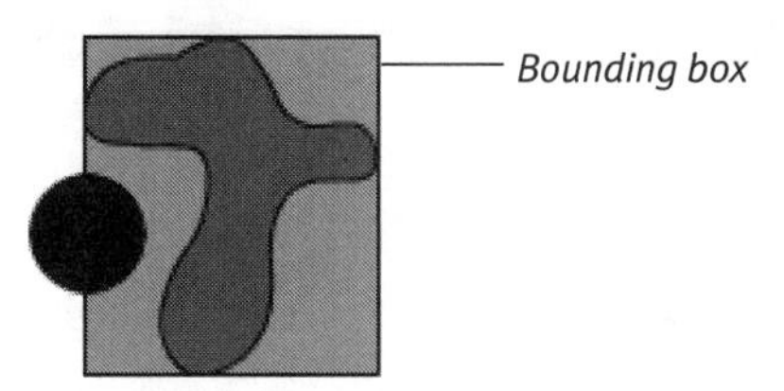

Figure 7.44 When the `shapeflag` parameter is true (top), the two objects won't intersect; only the shapes are considered. When the `shapeflag` parameter is false (bottom), the two objects will intersect; the bounding box is considered.

Detecting Movie-Clip Collisions

Another condition you can test for is whether a movie clip intersects another movie clip. The game of Pong, for example, simply detects collisions between the ball, the paddles, and the wall, all of which are movie clips. Detecting movie-clip collisions can be useful on sophisticated e-commerce sites as well. Suppose that you develop an online-shopping site that lets your customers drag merchandise into a shopping cart. You can detect when the object intersects with the shopping cart and provide interaction such as highlighting the shopping cart or displaying the product price before the user drops the object.

Collision detection uses the movie-clip method `hitTest()`. You can use `hitTest()` in two ways. One way is to check whether the bounding boxes of any two movie clips intersect. The *bounding box* of a movie clip is the minimum rectangular area that contains the graphics. This method is ideal for graphics colliding with other graphics, such as a ball with a paddle, a ship with an asteroid, or a book with a shopping cart. In this case, you enter the target path of the movie clip as the parameter—for example, `hitTest(_root.target)`.

The second way is to check whether a certain *x-y* coordinate intersects with a graphic. This method is point-specific, which makes it ideal for checking whether only the registration point of a graphic or the mouse pointer intersects with a movie clip. In this case, the `hitTest()` parameters are an *x* value, a *y* value, and the `shapeflag` parameter, as in `hitTest(x, y, shapeflag)`. The `shapeflag` parameter is true or false. This parameter determines whether the bounding box of a movie clip is considered (`false`) or just the shape of the graphics is considered (`true`) (**Figure 7.44**).

To detect an intersection between two movie clips:

1. Create a movie clip, place an instance of it on the Stage, and name it in the Property Inspector.
2. Create another movie clip, place an instance of it on the Stage, and name it in the Property Inspector. Then assign actions on the main Timeline to make it draggable.
3. Select the first frame of the root Timeline, and open the Actions panel.
4. Select the last line in the Script pane, and choose Objects > Movie > Movie Clip > Events > onEnterFrame.
5. In the Parameters pane, enter `_root` in the Object field.

   The `onEnterFrame` event handler for the root Timeline is established. This event occurs at the frame rate of the movie, which makes it ideal for checking the `hitTest` condition continuously (**Figure 7.45**).
6. Choose Actions > Conditions/Loops > if.
7. In the Condition field, enter the name of the draggable movie clip.
8. Choose Objects > Movie > Movie Clip > Methods > hitTest.
9. Within the parentheses of the `hitTest` statement, enter the path of the stationary movie clip.
10. Enter two equal signs, followed by the word `true` (**Figure 7.46**).

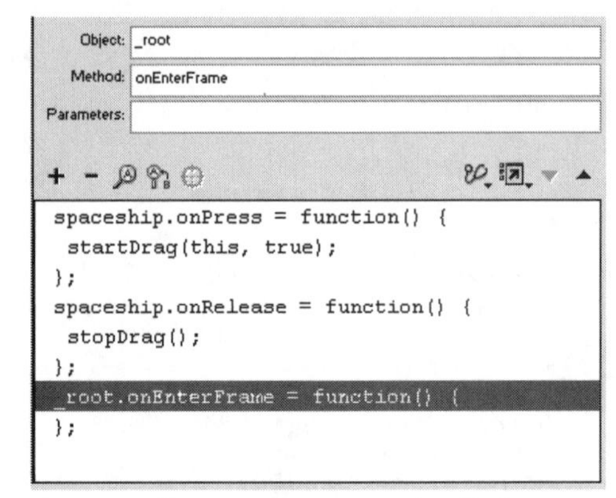

Figure 7.45 The `onEnterFrame` event handler is an ideal handler for checking a condition continuously.

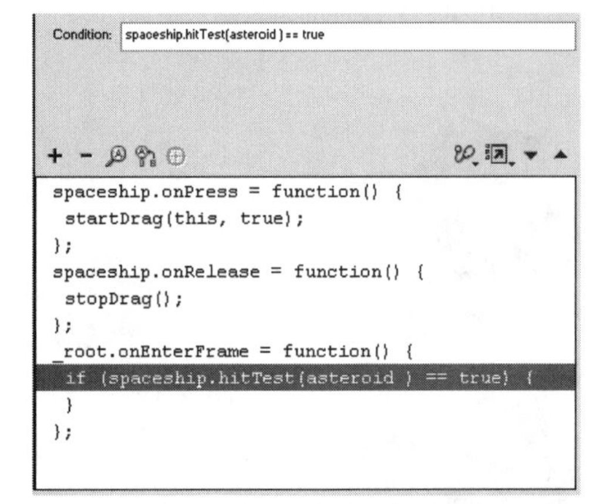

Figure 7.46 This condition checks whether the spaceship movie clip intersects the asteroid movie clip.

```
spaceship.onPress = function() {
 startDrag(this, true);
};
spaceship.onRelease = function() {
 stopDrag();
};
_root.onEnterFrame = function() {
 if (spaceship.hitTest(asteroid ) == true) {
  spaceship.nextFrame();
 }
};
```

Figure 7.47 The consequence of an intersection is the `nextFrame` action.

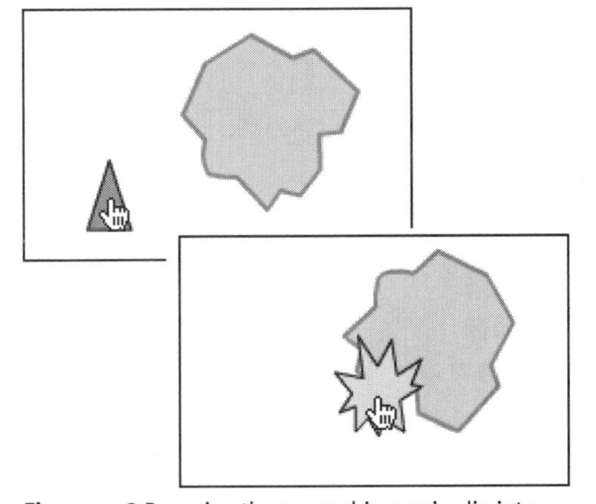

Figure 7.48 Dragging the spaceship movie clip into the bounding box of the asteroid movie clip advances the spaceship movie clip to the next frame, which displays an explosion.

11. Choose an action to be performed when this condition is met.

    The final script should look like **Figure 7.47**.

12. Test your movie (**Figure 7.48**).

✔ Tips

- For true/false conditions (known as *Booleans*) like the one in this task, you can simply state the condition and leave out the last part, `== true`. Flash automatically returns a true or a false when you call the `hitTest()` method, and the `if` statement automatically tests whether the condition is true. You'll learn more about conditional statements in Part V.
- It doesn't really matter whether you test the moving movie clip to the target or the target to the moving movie clip. The following two statements detect the same kind of collision:

  ```
  spaceship.hitTest(asteroid)
  asteroid.hitTest(spaceship)
  ```
- If the target of the `hitTest()` method is a movie clip that contains moving graphics, the bounding box of that movie clip will be the bounding box of the last keyframe in the animation.

To detect an intersection between a point and a movie clip:

1. Continue with the same file you created in the preceding task.
2. Select the first frame of the root Timeline, and open the Actions panel.
3. Select the `if` statement.
4. In the Condition field, change the expression so it reads as follows:
   `asteroid.hitTest(spaceship._x, spaceship._y, true)`
   The `hitTest()` method now checks whether the *x* and *y* positions of the draggable movie clip called spaceship intersect with the shape of the movie clip called asteroid (**Figure 7.49**).
5. Test your movie.

```
spaceship.onPress = function() {
 startDrag(this, true);
};
spaceship.onRelease = function() {
 stopDrag();
};
_root.onEnterFrame = function() {
 if (asteroid.hitTest(spaceship._x, spaceship._y, true) == true) {
  spaceship.nextFrame();
 }
};
```

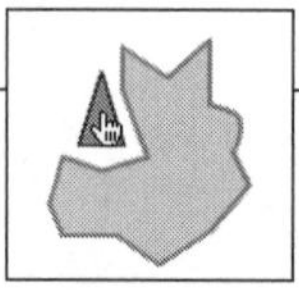

Figure 7.49 The ActionScript (above) tests whether the registration point of the spaceship movie clip intersects with any shape in the asteroid movie clip. Notice that the spaceship is safe from collision, because its registration point is still within the crevice and clear of the asteroid.

✔ Tip

- The properties `_xmouse` and `_ymouse` are values of the current *x* and *y* positions of the pointer on the screen. You can use these properties in the parameters of the `hitTest()` method to check whether the pointer intersects a movie clip. This expression returns true if the pointer intersects the movie clip called asteroid:
  `asteroid.hitTest(_xmouse, _ymouse, true)`

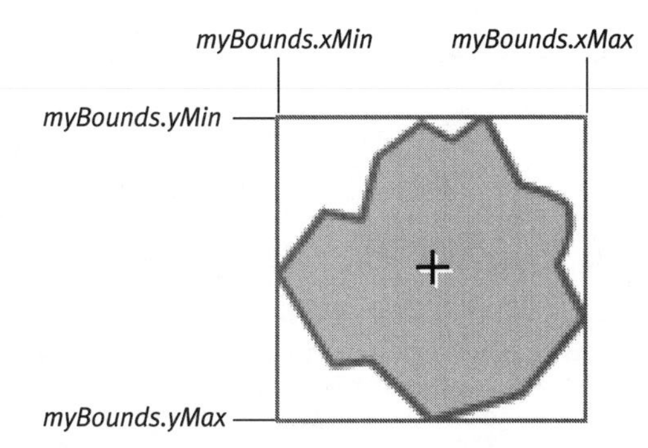

Figure 7.50 The xMin, xMax, yMin, and yMax properties of a boundary object refer to the edges of a movie clip whose boundaries have been retrieved.

Getting the Boundaries of Movie Clips

Often, when you are changing the dimensions and location of a movie clip dynamically, you'll need to know its boundaries to keep limitations on those changes. You could create a map that your viewer can move around or zoom in on for more details by setting the `_x`, `_y`, `_xscale`, and `_yscale` properties of the map. But you would also want to know where the edges of the map are so that you can make sure they are never exposed. The method you need to use is `getBounds()`. This method gets the minimum and maximum dimensions of the bounding box of a movie clip and puts the information in a generic object containing the properties `xMin`, `xMax`, `yMin`, and `yMax`. If you call your bounding-box object myBounds, the value of the movie clip's left edge would be `myBounds.xMin`, the right edge would be `myBounds.xMax`, the top edge would be `myBounds.yMin`, and the bottom edge would be `myBounds.yMax` (**Figure 7.50**).

To get the boundaries of a movie clip:

1. Create a movie-clip symbol, place an instance of it on the Stage, and give it a name in the Property Inspector.

   This clip will be the movie clip whose boundaries you will determine.

2. Select the first frame on the root Timeline, and open the Actions panel.

3. Choose Objects > Movies > MovieClip > Methods > getBounds.

4. Put your pointer in front of the dot and the `getBounds()` method, and enter a name for an object that will hold the boundary information, followed by an equal sign.

continues on next page

5. On the right side of the equal sign but before the dot, enter the target path to the movie clip whose boundary box you want to retrieve (**Figure 7.51**).

   The results of the `getBounds()` method will be assigned to the name of your object. The method, however, still needs a parameter for its `targetCoordinateSpace`.

6. Between the parentheses of the `getBounds()` method, enter a target path to the Timeline whose *x-y* coordinate space you want to serve as the reference for the boundary information (**Figure 7.52**).

   Flash gets the boundaries of the movie clip on the Stage. The boundaries are made relative to the root Timeline. All this information is put in an object whose properties contain the minimum and maximum *x* and *y* values.

7. Test your movie.

   Choose Debug > List Variables to verify the boundaries of the movie clip (**Figure 7.53**). Use the object properties `xMin`, `yMin`, `xMax`, and `yMax` as constraints on other interactivity. Use the boundary properties to constrain a draggable movie clip, for example (**Figure 7.54**).

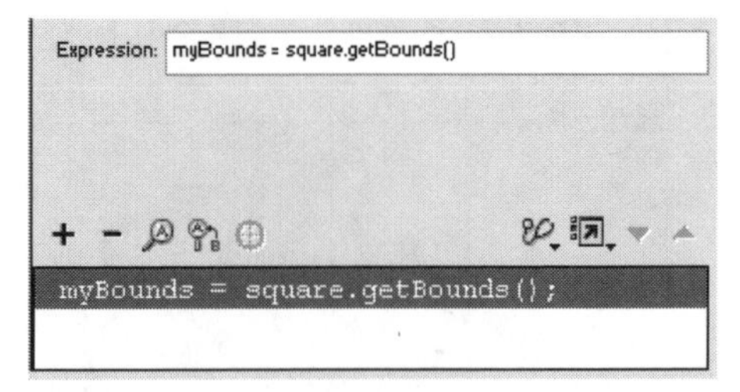

Figure 7.51 myBounds is the name of the boundary object, and square is the name of the movie clip, whose boundaries you are interested in finding.

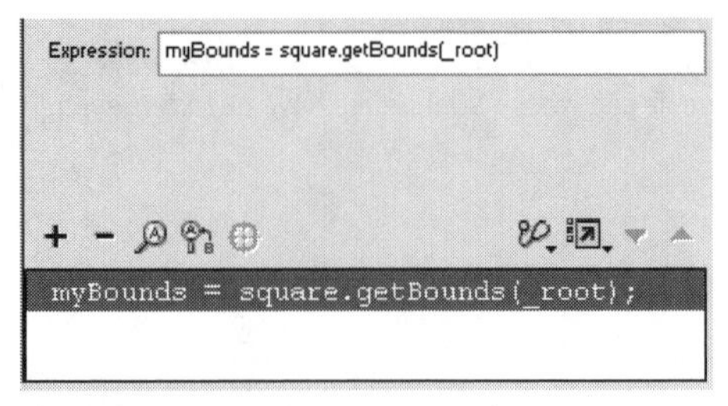

Figure 7.52 `getBounds()` retrieves the minimum x (xMin), minimum y (yMin), maximum x (xMax), and maximum y (xMax) values of the movie clip called square relative to the `_root` coordinates, and stores that information in your boundary object called myBounds.

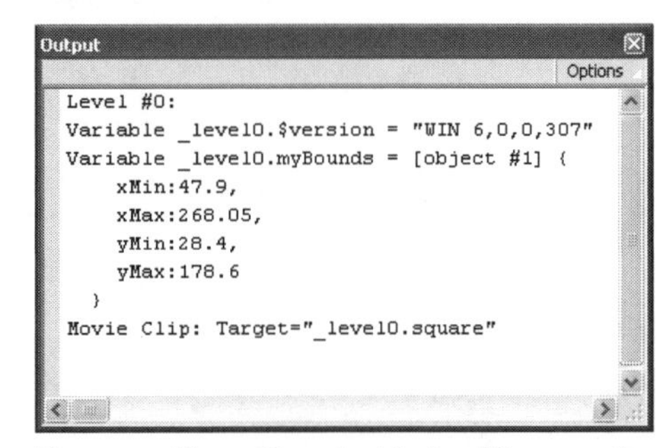

Figure 7.53 The myBounds object and its properties are listed in the Output window when you choose List Variables in test mode.

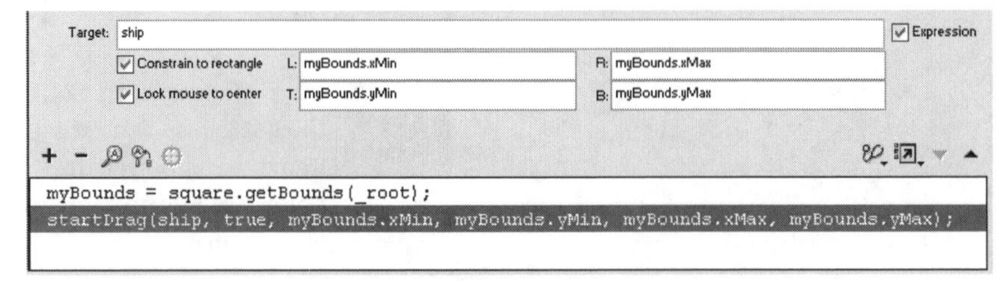

Figure 7.54 Using the boundary information in the L, T, R, and B fields of a `startDrag` action will constrain a draggable movie clip to the edges of the square movie clip.

Generating Movie Clips Dynamically

Creating movie clips on the fly—that is, during playback—opens a whole new world of exciting interactive possibilities. Imagine a game of Asteroids, in which enemy spaceships appear as the game progresses. You can store those enemy spaceships as movie-clip symbols in your library and create instances on the Stage with ActionScript as you need them. Or, if you want an infinite supply of a certain draggable item (such as merchandise) to be pulled off the shelf of an online store, you can make duplicates of the movie clip each time the viewer drags it away from its original spot. Or create after-images of a movie clip's motion, much like onionskinning, by duplicating a movie clip and making it lag as it moves across the screen. All the while, you maintain the power to modify properties, control the position of the playhead in those Timelines, and use the clips like any other movie clips.

Flash has many methods that enable dynamically generated movie clips. Among them are `duplicateMovieClip()`, `attachMovie()`, and `createEmptyMovieClip()`.

Duplicating movie clips

When you use the method `duplicateMovieClip()`, an exact replica of an instance on the Stage is created in the same position as the original. Duplicate movie-clip instances are given their own unique names, as well as a specific depth level for each instance. This depth level determines stacking order, just as it does with the movie-clip method `swapDepths()`.

It's common practice to duplicate movie clips by using looping functions that append successive numbers to the instance name and assign depth levels automatically. You can duplicate a movie clip named asteroid in this manner, producing asteroid1 in depth level 1, asteroid2 in depth level 2, asteroid3 in depth level 3, and so on. Check out Chapter 9 to learn about the looping actions that complement the duplication of movie clips.

To duplicate a movie-clip instance:

1. Create a movie-clip symbol, place an instance on the Stage, and name it in the Property Inspector.
2. Create a button symbol, place an instance of it on the Stage, and name it in the Property Inspector.
3. Select the first frame of the root Timeline, and open the Actions panel.

continues on next page

4. Choose Objects > Movie > Button > Events > onRelease.

5. Enter the name of your button in the Object field (**Figure 7.55**).

6. Choose Actions > Movie Clip Control > duplicateMovieClip (Esc+dm).

   The `duplicateMovieClip` action appears within the `onRelease` event handler in the Script pane.

7. In the Target field, enter the target path for the movie clip, and check the Expression box.

8. In the New Name field, enter the name for the new duplicate movie clip, and leave the Expression box unchecked.

9. In the Depth field, enter a number to specify the stacking order for your duplicate movie clip (**Figure 7.56**).

   At this point, when you play your movie, the actions assigned to your button duplicate the nerd movie clip, but the new instance appears right above the original, so you can't see whether anything happened. To see the duplicate, you need to move or change it in some way to make it stand out from the original.

10. Choose Actions > MovieClip Control > setProperty.

11. From the Property pull-down menu, choose X Position.

12. In the Target field, enter the target path of the duplicate movie clip, and check the Expression box.

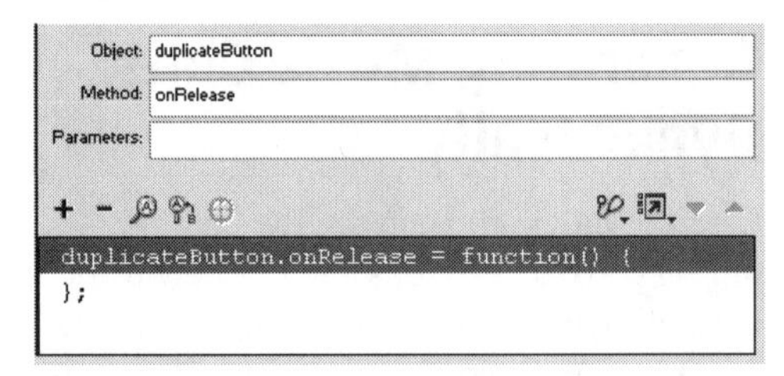

Figure 7.55 The `onRelease` event handler for the button called duplicateButton is created.

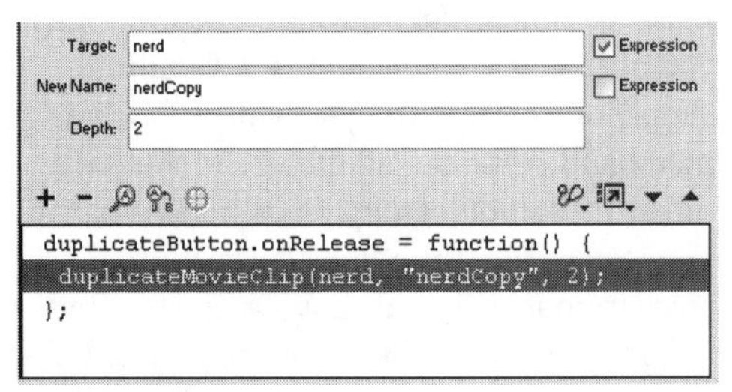

Figure 7.56 The duplicate movie clip called nerdCopy is made in depth level 2 from the movie clip called nerd.

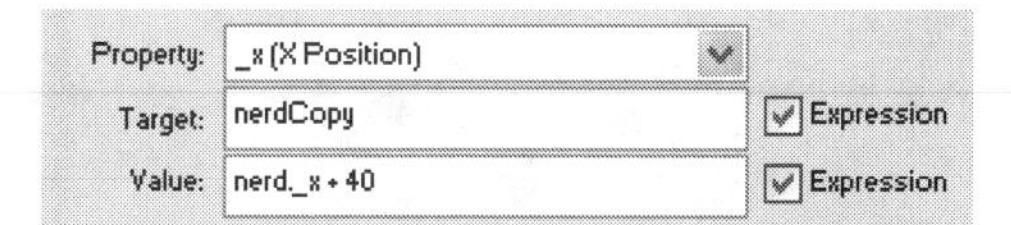

Figure 7.57 The Parameters pane for the `setProperty` action. The nerdCopy movie clip is shifted 40 pixels to the right of the nerd movie clip.

```
duplicateButton.onRelease = function() {
 duplicateMovieClip(nerd, "nerdCopy", 2);
 setProperty(nerdCopy, _x, nerd._x + 40);
 setProperty(nerdCopy, _xscale, 75);
 setProperty(nerdCopy, _yscale, 110);
};
```

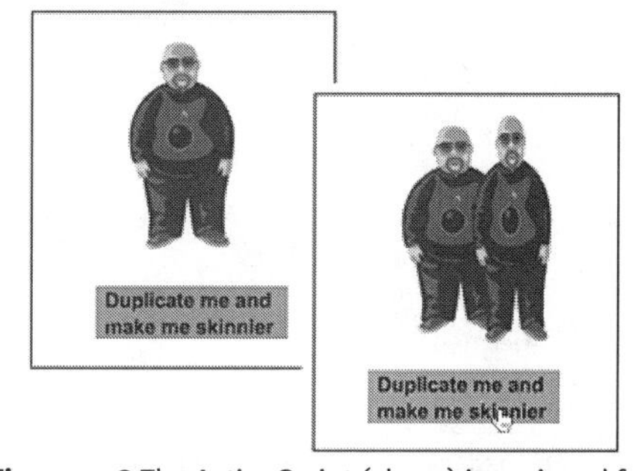

Figure 7.58 The ActionScript (above) is assigned for the button instance at the bottom of the Stage. When the original movie clip (left) is duplicated, the copy can be targeted and controlled just like any other (right). This movie-clip copy, called nerdCopy, has its *x* position, *x* scale, and *y* scale properties modified.

13. In the Value field, enter an expression that adds 40 to the *x* position of the original movie clip (**Figure 7.57**), and check the Expression box.

14. Add more `setProperty` statements to transform the duplicate movie clip (**Figure 7.58**).

15. Test the movie.

✔ Tips

- You can have only one movie-clip instance per depth level. If you duplicate another instance in a level that's already occupied, that instance replaces the first one.
- Duplicate movie clips inherit the properties of the original instance. If the original instance has an alpha transparency of 50 percent, for example, the duplicate movie-clip instance will also have an alpha transparency of 50 percent. Duplicate instances will always start in frame 1, however, even if the original movie-clip instance is in a different frame when it is duplicated.
- Duplicate movie clips also take on any ActionScript that may be assigned to the original instance. If the original instance contains ActionScript that makes it a draggable movie clip, for example, the duplicate will also be draggable.
- The depth level corresponds to the same depth level in the movie-clip method `swapDepths()`. Use `swapDepths()` to change the stacking order of duplicated movie clips.

Attaching movie clips

The technique of duplicating movie clips is useful for existing movie clips, but what if you need to place a *new* movie clip on the Stage from the library dynamically? In this situation, you would turn to the `attachMovie()` method. This method lets you create new instances of movie clips from the library and attach them to existing movie-clip instances already on the Stage or to the root Timeline. The attached movie clip doesn't replace the original, but actually becomes part of the movie-clip object in a parent–child relationship. If the original instance on Stage is called `parentInstance`, the target path for the attached movie clip would be something like
`_root.parentInstance.attachedInstance`

If a movie clip attaches to the root Timeline, the target path is simply:
`_root.attachedInstance`

To attach a movie clip from the library:

1. Create a movie-clip symbol, place an instance of it from the library on the Stage, and give it a name in the Property Inspector.

   This instance will be the original, parent instance to which you'll attach another movie clip.

2. Create another movie-clip symbol, and select it in the library.

3. From the Library Options pull-down menu, choose Linkage (**Figure 7.59**).

   The Linkage Properties dialog box appears.

4. In the Linkage section, select Export for ActionScript and leave Export in first frame checked; in the Identifier field, enter a unique name for your movie clip; then click OK (**Figure 7.60**).

   This identifier allows you to call on this movie clip by this name from ActionScript and attach it to an instance on the Stage.

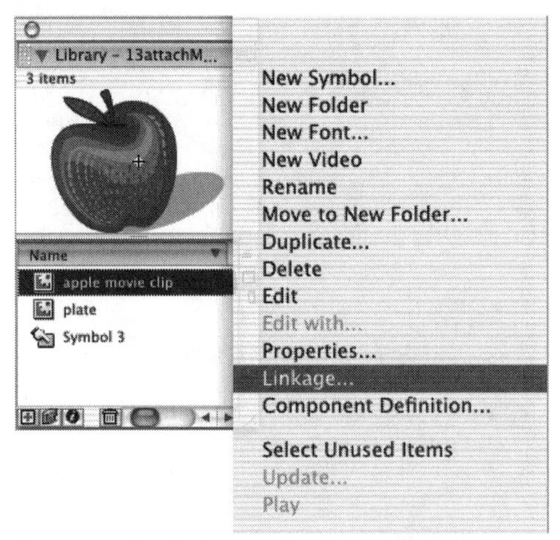

Figure 7.59 The Linkage option in the Library window.

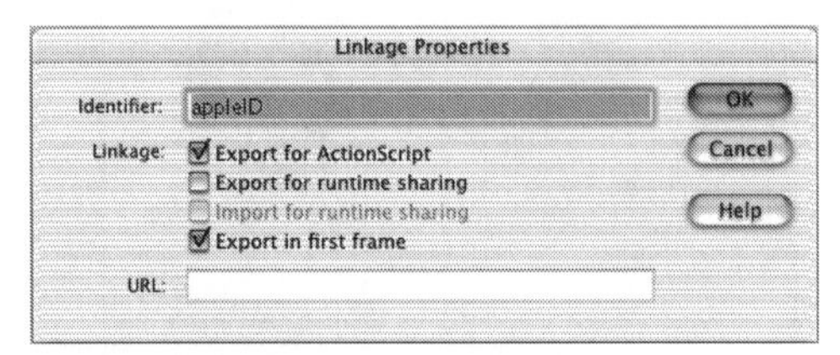

Figure 7.60 The Linkage Properties dialog box.

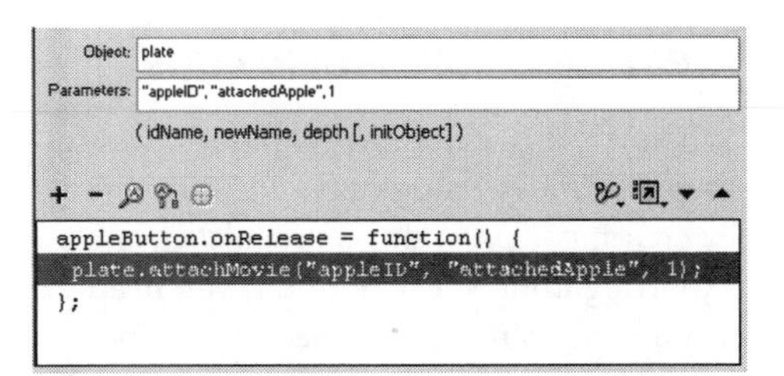

Figure 7.61 The attachMovie() method requires the parameters idName, newName, and depth. This attachMovie() method attaches the movie clip identified as appleID to the instance plate in depth level 1 and names the attached instance attachedApple.

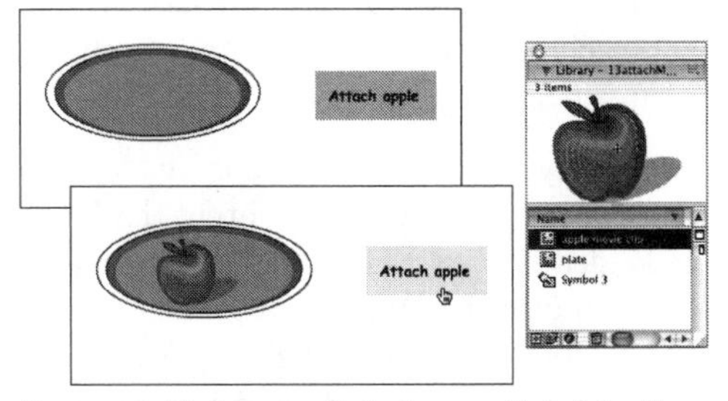

Figure 7.62 The movie-clip instance called plate sits on the Stage (top). The actions assigned for the button attach an instance of the apple movie clip from the library (right) to the plate instance (bottom).

5. Create a button, drag an instance of it to the Stage, and name it in the Property Inspector.
6. Select the first frame of the root Timeline, and open the Actions panel.
7. Create an `onRelease` event handler for your button.
8. Choose Objects > Movie > Movie Clip > Methods > attachMovie.
9. In the Object field, enter the target path of the movie-clip instance on the Stage.

   This instance is the one to which you will attach the new instance.
10. In the Parameters field, enter the identifier of the movie clip in the Library window, a name for the attached instance, and a depth level, separating your parameters with commas (**Figure 7.61**).

    The identifier and new name must be in quotation marks.
11. Test your movie.

    When you click the button that you created, the movie clip identified in the library attaches to the instance on Stage and overlaps it. The registration point of the attached movie clip lines up with the registration point of the parent instance (**Figure 7.62**).

You need to keep several names straight when you use the `attachMovie()` method. In this example, the name of the movie clip symbol in the library is apple movie clip. The name of the identifier is appleID. The name of the attached instance is attachedApple.

continues on next page

✔ Tips

- You can always attach movie clips to the root Timeline by entering `_root` in the Object field in the Parameters pane of the `attachMovie()` method. The registration point of the attached instance will be aligned with the top-left corner (x=0, y=0) of the Stage.
- An attached movie clip takes on the properties of the movie-clip instance to which it attaches. If the original movie clip instance is rotated 45 degrees, the attached movie clip will also be rotated 45 degrees.
- You can attach multiple movie clips to the same parent instance as long as you specify different depth levels. Each depth level can hold only one movie clip.
- You can also attach movie clips to a recently attached movie clip itself. The target path for the first attached movie clip becomes `_root.parentInstance.attachedInstance1`. The target path for another attached movie clip becomes `_root.parentInstance.attachedInstance1.attachedInstance2`, and so on.
- You cannot attach a movie clip to another movie clip that has an external .swf file loaded into it (see Chapter 6 for the `loadMovie` action).

Creating empty movie clips

When you attach a movie clip, you need to prepare a movie-clip symbol in your library by creating it, assigning an identifier, and exporting it for ActionScript. If you need just an empty movie clip—a movie clip without graphics, animations, or attached scripts—you can use the method `createEmptyMovieClip()`. This method is similar to `attach movie clip` in that it attaches a movie clip dynamically to another movie clip already on the Stage. But instead of attaching a movie clip symbol from the library, you attach an empty movie clip. You give each newly created empty movie clip a unique name and depth level.

Use empty movie clips as "shells" in preparation for additional content that may be loaded into your Flash movie. Create an empty movie clip on the root Timeline and modify its *x* and *y* properties to position it anywhere on the Stage. Now you can use `loadMovie()` to load external .swf files into your empty movie clip.

Empty movie clips are also important for movie-clip drawing methods. You'll learn to draw lines, curves, fills, and gradients just by using ActionScript. An empty movie clip provides the anchor for all these drawing methods.

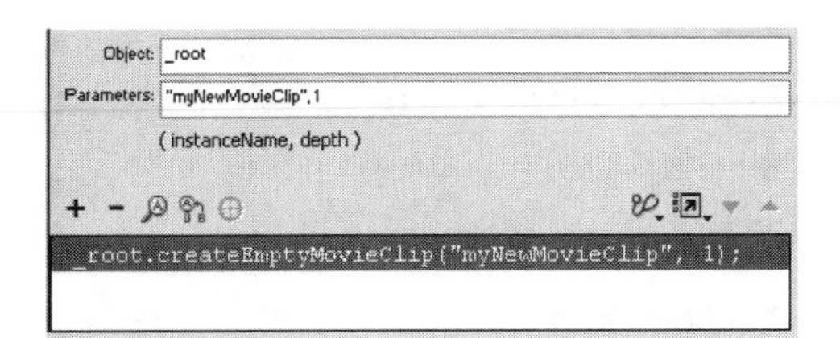

Figure 7.63 The empty movie clip called myNewMovieClip is created on the root Timeline in depth level 1.

To create an empty movie clip on the root Timeline:

1. Select the first frame of the root Timeline, and open the Actions panel.
2. Choose Objects > Movie > Movie Clip > Methods > createEmptyMovieClip.
3. In the Object field, enter `_root`.

   An empty movie clip will be attached and scoped to the root Timeline.
4. In the Parameters field, enter a unique name for your empty movie clip, as well as a unique depth level.

   Separate your parameters with commas, and make sure that your name is in quotation marks (**Figure 7.63**).

   A movie clip with the name you've chosen is created on the root Timeline at the specified depth level.

Removing Movie Clips Dynamically

Just as you can generate movie clips dynamically, you can remove them dynamically. You can delete movie-clip instances that have been duplicated or attached, delete empty movie clips, and even delete movie-clip instances that were put on the Stage at author time. **Table 7.3** lists the different ways to remove movie clips.

To remove a duplicated, attached, or empty movie clip by using removeMovieClip:

1. Choose Actions > Movie Clip Control > removeMovieClip (Esc+rm).
2. In the Target field of the Parameters pane, enter the target path of the movie clip. Check the Expression box (**Figure 7.64**).

To remove a duplicated, attached, or empty movie clip by using unloadMovie:

1. Choose Actions > Browser/Network > unloadMovie (Esc+um).
2. From the Location pull-down menu in the Actions panel, select Target.
3. Enter the target path of the movie clip. Check the Expression box (**Figure 7.65**).

To remove a movie clip placed on the Stage at author time by using unloadMovie:

1. Choose Actions > Browser/Network > unloadMovie (Esc+um).
2. From the Location pull-down menu in the Actions panel, choose Target.
3. Enter the target path of the movie clip. Check the Expression box.

Table 7.3

Removing Movie Clips

Movie Clips Created By	Remove With
duplicateMovieClip	removeMovieClip, unloadMovie
attachMovie	removeMovieClip, unloadMovie
createEmptyMovieClip	removeMovieClip, unloadMovie
manual placement on Stage during author time	unloadMovie

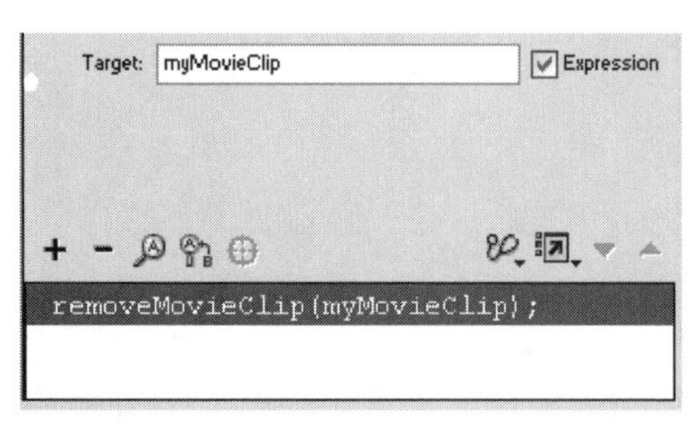

Figure 7.64 The myMovieClip movie clip is removed from the Stage. Use `removeMovieClip` to remove dynamically generated movie clips.

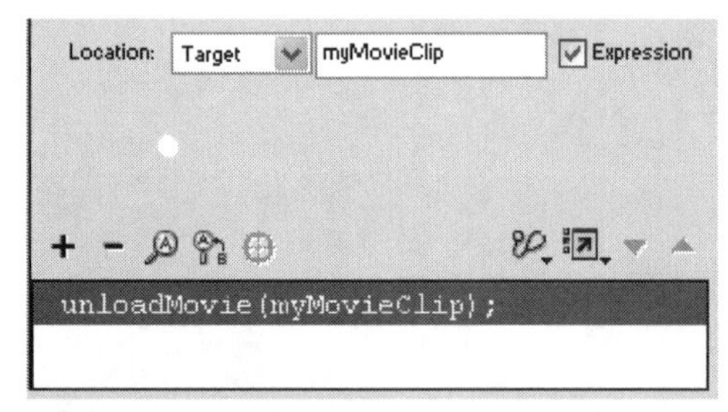

Figure 7.65 `UnloadMovie`, which usually removes external SWF files, can be used to remove dynamically generated movie clips as well as movie clips placed on the Stage during author time.

Creating Shapes Dynamically

A special category of the movie clip is reserved for creating lines, curves, fills, and gradients. These methods are the drawing methods of the movie clip. With these methods, you can create your own shapes with control of color, transparency, stroke width, and even the kind and placement of gradient fills. You could use the drawing methods to create your own simple paint and coloring application, or you could draw bar graphs, pie charts, or connect data points to visualize numerical data that your viewer inputs.

To use the drawing methods, you must start with a movie clip. The movie clip acts as the point of reference for all your drawing coordinates. So if your movie clip is anchored at the top-left corner of the Stage (at x=0, y=0), all the drawing coordinates are relative to that registration point. The movie clip also acts as though it were a pen tip, anchoring the start of a line or curve and keeping track of its end point as you tell it to draw. The movie clip doesn't actually move, however. Think of the movie clip as being a virtual pen tip.

Although you can use any movie clip to begin drawing, the most common way is to use the method `createEmptyMovieClip()` to create an empty movie clip on the root Timeline. The new movie clip is positioned at the top-left corner of the Stage automatically, so its drawing coordinates are identical to the Stage coordinates.

Creating lines and curves

Three methods draw lines and curves: the `moveTo()`, `lineTo()`, and `curveTo()` methods. The `moveTo()` method sets the beginning point of your line or curve. The `lineTo()` and `curveTo()` methods set the end point and, in the case of curves, determines its curvature.

The `lineStyle()` method changes the characteristics of your stroke, such as its point size, color, and transparency. The `clear()` method erases the drawings made with your movie clip.

To create lines:

1. Select the first frame of the root Timeline, and open the Actions panel.
2. Choose Objects > Movie > Movie Clip > Methods > createEmptyMovieClip.

continues on next page

3. In the Object field, enter `_root`.

4. In the Parameters field, enter a name for this movie clip and a depth level, making sure that your instance name is in quotation marks (**Figure 7.66**).

   An empty movie clip is created on the root Timeline and positioned at the top-left corner of the Stage.

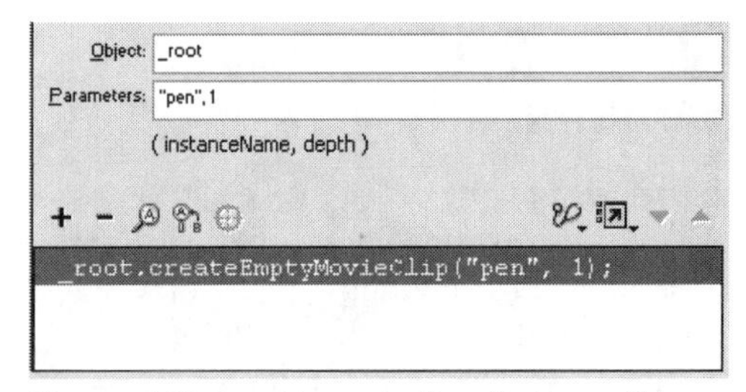

Figure 7.66 The empty movie clip called pen will be the coordinate space for the drawing and will act as a virtual pen.

5. Choose Objects > Movie > Movie Clip > Drawing Methods > lineStyle.

6. In the Object field, enter the target path to your empty movie clip.

7. In the Parameters field, enter the thickness of the line, the RGB color in hex code, and its transparency, separating your parameters with commas (**Figure 7.67**).

   The thickness is a number between 0 and 255. 0 is hairline thickness, and 255 is the maximum point thickness.

   The RGB parameter is the hex code referring to the color of the line. You can find the hex code for any color in the Color Mixer panel below the color swatch. Red, for example, is 0xFF0000.

   The transparency is a number between 0 and 100 for the line's alpha value. 0 is completely transparent, and 100 is completely opaque.

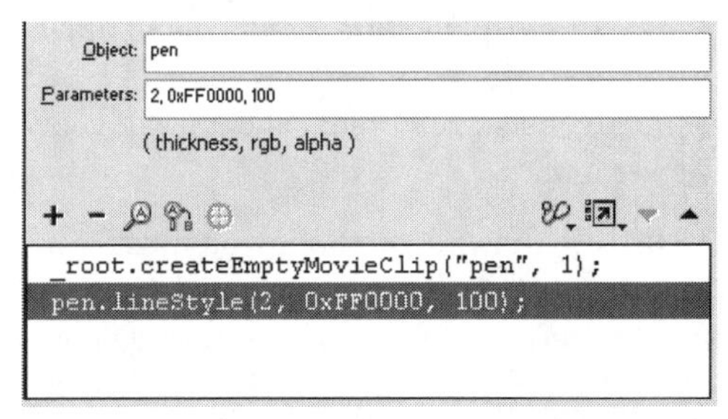

Figure 7.67 Define the line style (stroke thickness, color, and transparency) before you begin drawing.

8. Choose Objects > Movie > Movie Clip > Drawing Methods > moveTo.

9. In the Object field, enter the target path to your movie clip.

10. In the Parameters field, enter the *x* and *y* coordinates where you want your line to start, separating your parameters with commas (**Figure 7.68**).

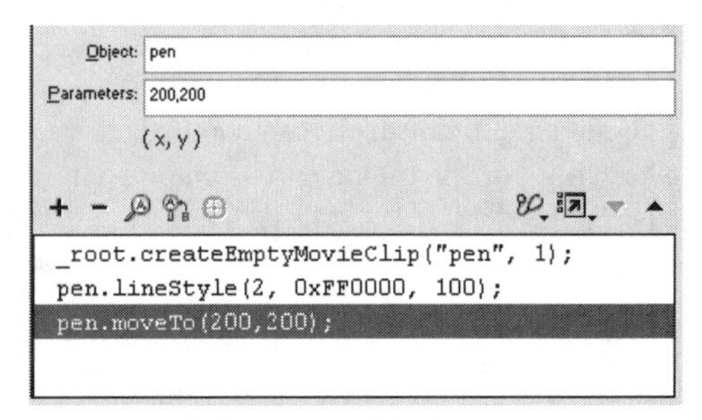

Figure 7.68 The beginning of this line is at x=200, y=200.

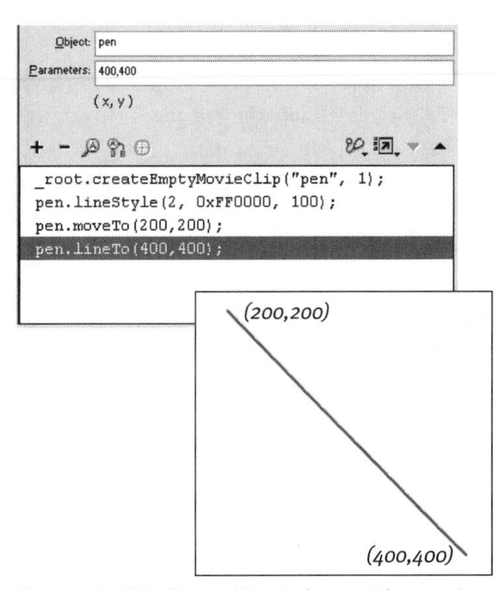

Figure 7.69 This diagonal line is drawn with a 2-point red stroke. The virtual pen tip is now positioned at x=400, y=400 and ready for a new `lineTo()` method.

11. Choose Objects > Movie > Movie Clip > Drawing Methods > lineTo.
12. In the Object field, enter the target path to your movie clip.
13. In the Parameters field, enter the *x* and *y* coordinates of the end point of your line, separating your parameters with commas (**Figure 7.69**).

    The end point of your line segment automatically becomes the beginning point for the next, so you don't need to use the `moveTo()` method to move the coordinates.
14. Continue adding more `lineTo()` methods to continue drawing more line segments.

✔ Tips

- You can change the line style at any time, so that multiple line segments can have different thicknesses, colors, or transparencies. Add a `lineStyle()` method before the `lineTo()` method whose line you want to modify.
- After you finish your drawing, you can modify its properties by modifying the properties of the empty movie clip. Or you can affect the behavior of your drawing by calling a method of the empty movie clip. The drawing still "belongs" to the empty movie clip, so whatever you do to it will affect the drawing. You can duplicate your drawing, for example, by using the `duplicateMovieClip` action on the empty movie clip.
- Instead of creating an empty movie clip to control the drawing methods, you could use the root Timeline to control the drawing methods. But you won't have as much control of the root Timeline as you would an empty movie clip.

To create curves:

1. Create an empty movie clip on the root Timeline as described in the preceding task.
2. Choose Objects > Movie > Movie Clip > Drawing Methods > lineStyle.
3. Define the style of your curve as described in the preceding task.
4. Choose Objects > Movie > Movie Clip > Drawing Methods > moveTo.
5. Move the starting point of your curve as described in the preceding task.
6. Choose Objects > Movie > Movie Clip > Drawing Methods > curveTo.
7. In the Object field, enter the target path to your empty movie clip.
8. In the Parameters field, enter *x* and *y* coordinates for the control point and *x* and *y* coordinates for the end of the curve (**Figure 7.70**).

   The *control point* is a point that determines the amount of curvature. If you were to extend a straight line from the control point to the end point of the curve, you would see that it functions much like the handle of a curve (**Figure 7.71**). Check out the sample file in this section on the accompanying CD-ROM to see how the control point affects your curve in real time.

✔ Tip

- When editing in Expert mode, you can reduce the repetition of the target path by using a `with` statement to change the scope temporarily . For example:

```
_root.createEmptyMovieClip("pen", 1);
with (pen) {
   lineStyle(5, 0xff0000, 100);
   moveTo(200, 100);
   curveTo(300, 100, 300, 200);
   curveTo(300, 300, 200, 300);
   curveTo(100, 300, 100, 200);
   curveTo(100, 100, 200, 100);
}
```

  is the same as

```
_root.createEmptyMovieClip("pen", 1);
pen.lineStyle(5, 0xff0000, 100);
pen.moveTo(200, 100);
pen.curveTo(300, 100, 300, 200);
pen.curveTo(300, 300, 200, 300);
pen.curveTo(100, 300, 100, 200);
pen.curveTo(100, 100, 200, 100);
```

Object: pen
Parameters: 300,100,400,200
(controlX, controlY, anchorX, anchorY)

```
_root.createEmptyMovieClip("pen", 1);
pen.lineStyle(2, 0xFF0000, 100);
pen.moveTo(200,200);
pen.curveTo(300,100,400,200);
```

Figure 7.70 The curveTo() method requires *x* and *y* coordinates for its control point and for its end point. This curve starts at (200,200) and ends at (400,200), with the control point at (300,100) (see Figure 7.71).

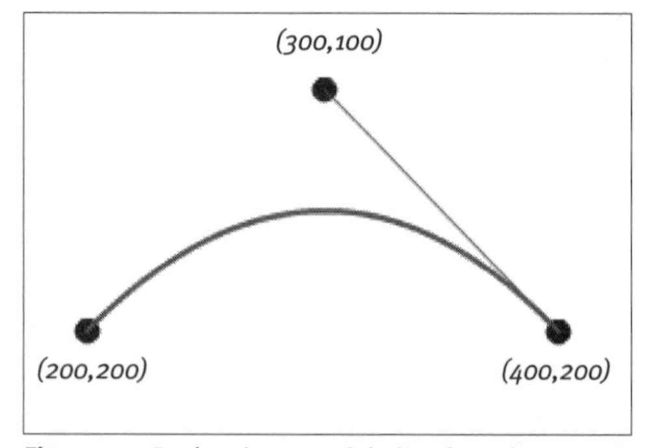

Figure 7.71 By drawing a straight line from the control point to the end point, you can visualize the curve's Bézier handle. The dots have been added to show the two anchor points and the control point.

Quadratic Bézier Curves

If you were to try to draw a circle with the curveTo() method using four segments, you might be surprised by the results. The following script does not produce a perfect circle, as you might expect (**Figure 7.72**):

```
_root.createEmptyMovieClip("pen", 1);
with (pen) {
   lineStyle(5, 0xff0000, 100);
   moveTo(200, 100);
   curveTo(300, 100, 300, 200);
   curveTo(300, 300, 200, 300);
   curveTo(100, 300, 100, 200);
   curveTo(100, 100, 200, 100);
}
```

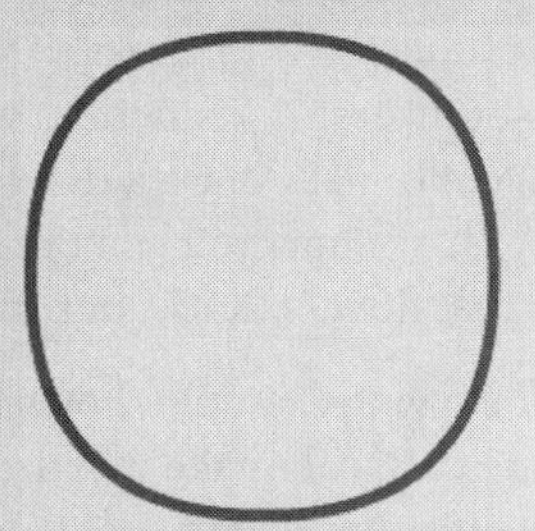

Figure 7.72 An imperfect circle drawn with four curveTo() statements.

The curveTo() method uses what are called quadratic Bézier curves—the same kind that it uses for the Oval tool in the Tools panel. Four segments don't produce a perfect circle, because Flash needs eight (**Figure 7.73**). So how do you determine their anchor points and control points? The answer involves a fair bit of math and trigonometry (which you will explore in Chapter 11), but the code to produce a perfect circle in eight segments is presented here. Essentially, the start and end points of each curve lie on a circle of a certain radius (r). The *x* coordinate is r*cos(theta), and the *y* coordinate is r*sin(theta). *Theta* is the angle that one segment covers. So for eight segments, theta is 45 degrees. The control points lie exactly between the start and end anchor points at a distance of r/cos(0.5*theta).

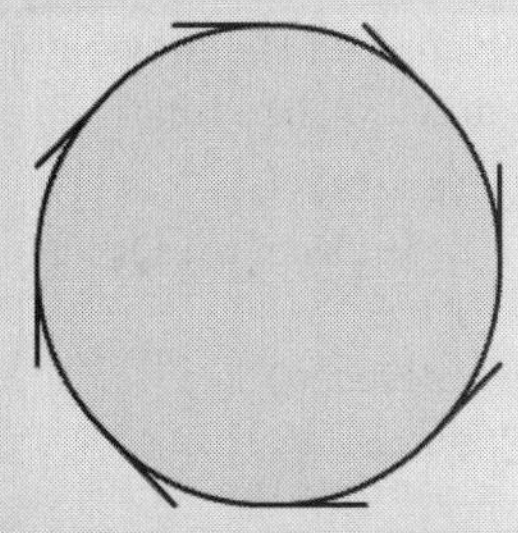

Figure 7.73 A perfect circle drawn with eight curveTo() statements. Line segments from the control points to the end points have been added to show the eight curves.

```
function radians(degrees) {
   return (Math.PI/180)*degrees;
}
theta = 45;
r = 100;
d = r/Math.cos(radians(0.5*theta));
this.lineStyle(1, 0x000000, 100);
this.moveTo(r, 0);
for (k=(theta/2); k<361; k=k+theta) {
   xControl = d*Math.cos(radians(k));
   yControl = d*Math.sin(radians(k));
   xAnchor = r*Math.cos(radians(k+(theta/2)));
   yAnchor = r*Math.sin(radians(k+(theta/2)));
   this.curveTo(xControl, yControl, xAnchor, yAnchor);
}
```

The clear() method erases the drawings made with the movie-clip drawing methods. In conjunction with an onEnterFrame event or a setInterval() function, you can make Flash continually erase a drawing and redraw itself. This is how you can create curves and lines that are not static, but change.

The following example shows the dynamic updates you can make in a drawing by moving their vertices with draggable movie clips.

Figure 7.74 The onEnterFrame event handler is created for the root Timeline.

To use clear to update a drawing dynamically:

1. Create four small draggable movie clips with the code assigned to their instances.

   The code on the movie-clip instances should look like this:

   ```
   on (press) {
      startDrag(this);
   }
   on (release) {
      stopDrag();
   }
   ```

2. Give each draggable movie clip a unique name in the Property Inspector.
3. Select the first frame of the root Timeline, and open the Actions panel.
4. Create an empty movie clip on the root Timeline as described in the previous tasks.
5. Choose Objects > Movie > Movie Clip > Events > onEnterFrame.
6. In the Object field, enter _root (**Figure 7.74**).

   The onEnterFrame event handler is created. This event happens at the frame rate of the movie, providing a way to perform actions continuously.

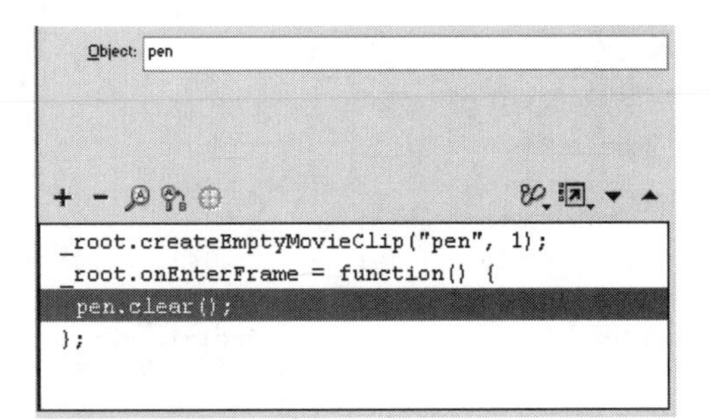

Figure 7.75 All drawings created with the pen movie clip are cleared continuously.

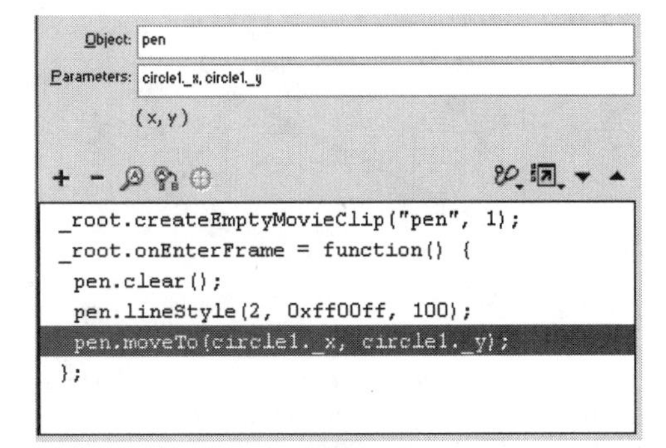

Figure 7.76 The first line segment will begin where the registration point of circle1 lies.

7. Choose Object > Movie > Movie Clip > Drawing Methods > clear.
8. In the Object field, enter the target path to your empty movie clip (**Figure 7.75**).

   The `clear()` method erases the previous drawings made with your empty movie clip.
9. Choose Objects > Movie > Movie Clip > Drawing Methods > lineStyle.
10. In the Object field, enter the target path to the empty movie clip.
11. In the Parameters field, enter the thickness, hex code for its color, and its alpha value.
12. Choose Objects > Movie > Movie Clip > Drawing Methods > moveTo.
13. In the Object field, enter the target path to the empty movie clip.
14. In the Parameters field, enter the _x property and the _y property for one of your draggable movie clips (**Figure 7.76**).
15. Choose Objects > Movie > Movie Clip > Drawing Methods > lineTo.
16. In the Object field, enter the target path to the empty movie clip.
17. In the Parameters field, enter the _x property and the _y property for the second draggable movie clip.

continues on next page

18. Continue adding `lineTo()` methods whose *x* and *y* coordinates correspond to the *x* and *y* properties of the draggable movie clips.

    The final script should look like **Figure 7.77**.

19. Test your movie.

    Flash continuously erases the line segments with the `clear()` method and redraws them according to where the draggable movie clips lie. You can drag the movie clips around the Stage to change the shape dynamically (**Figure 7.78**).

✔ Tip

- In this example, you could use `onMouseMove` instead of `onEnterFrame`, because the only time the drawing needs to be updated is when the viewer is dragging one of the movie clips. If you do use `onMouseMove`, add the `updateAfterEvent()` statement (Actions > Movie Clip Control > updateAfterEvent) to force Flash to refresh the screen whenever the mouse pointer moves.

```
_root.createEmptyMovieClip("pen", 1);
_root.onEnterFrame = function() {
  pen.clear();
  pen.lineStyle(2, 0xff00ff, 100);
  pen.moveTo(circle1._x, circle1._y);
  pen.lineTo(circle2._x, circle2._y);
  pen.lineTo(circle3._x, circle3._y);
  pen.lineTo(circle4._x, circle4._y);
};
```

Figure 7.77 The line segments are drawn to where the draggable movie clips circle2, circle3, and circle4 are located.

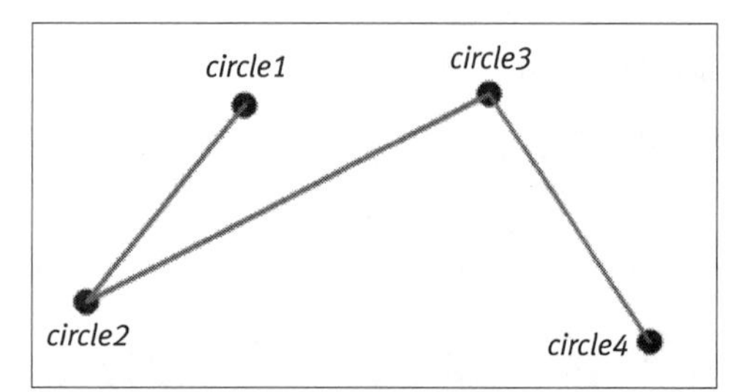

Figure 7.78 The three line segments between the four draggable movie-clip circles are redrawn continuously, creating a moveable, Tinker Toys-like shape that moves where you position the vertices.

Creating fills and gradients

You can fill shapes with solid colors, transparent colors, or radial or linear gradients by using the methods `beginFill()`, `beginGradientFill()`, and `endFill()`. You start the beginning of your shape to be filled by calling either the `beginFill()` or the `beginGradientFill()` method, and mark the end of the shape with `endFill()`. If your path is not closed (the end points do not match the beginning points), Flash automatically closes it when the `endFill()` method is applied.

Applying solid or transparent fills with `beginFill()` is fairly straightforward; you specify a hex code for the color and a value between 0 and 100 for the transparency. Gradients are more complex. You control five parameters: gradient type, colors, alphas, ratios, and matrix type.

- **Gradient type** is either the string `"radial"` or `"linear"`. You must include the quotation marks. Radial parameters begin from the inside to the outside. Linear parameters begin from the left to the right.
- **Colors** is a special object called an array object. An array holds information in an ordered way. You must create an array object and put the hex codes for the gradient colors into the array in the order in which you want them to appear. If you want blue on the left side of a linear gradient and red on the other, for example, you create an array like this:

```
colors = new Array(0x0000FF,0xFF0000)
```

continues on next page

- **Alphas** is also an array object that contains the alpha values (0 through 100) corresponding to the colors in the order in which you want them to appear. If you want your blue on one side to be 50 percent transparent, you create an array like this:

  ```
  alphas = new Array (50,100)
  ```

- **Ratios** is an array object that contains values (0 through 255) corresponding to the colors that determine how they will mix. The ratio value defines the width where the color is at 100 percent. An array like `ratios = new Array(0, 127)` means that the blue is 100 percent at the left side and the red is 100 percent starting at the middle (**Figure 7.79**).

- **Matrix type** is a generic object whose properties you define. These properties determine the orientation of your gradient. You can use matrix type in two ways: box and matrix. The box way lets you set the orientation of the gradient with *x* and *y* coordinates, width and height properties (in pixels), and an angle property (in radians) (**Figure 7.80**). The matrix way uses a 3-by-3 matrix. Because matrices involve a high-level math background, we'll restrict the discussion of the matrix type to the box way.

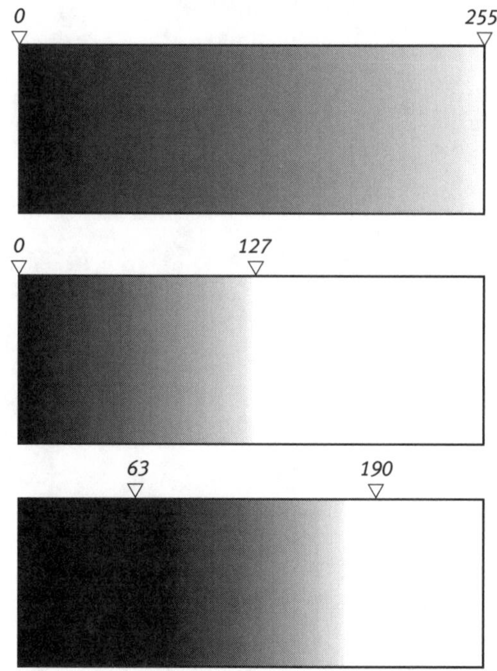

Figure 7.79 Ratios determine the mixing of colors for your gradient. The entire width of your gradient (or radius, for a radial gradient) is represented on a range from 0 through 255. Ratio values of (0,255) represent the typical gradient where each color is at the far sides (top). Ratio values of (0,127) create a tighter mixing in the first half of the gradient (middle). Ratio values of (63,190) would create a tighter mixing in the middle of the gradient (bottom).

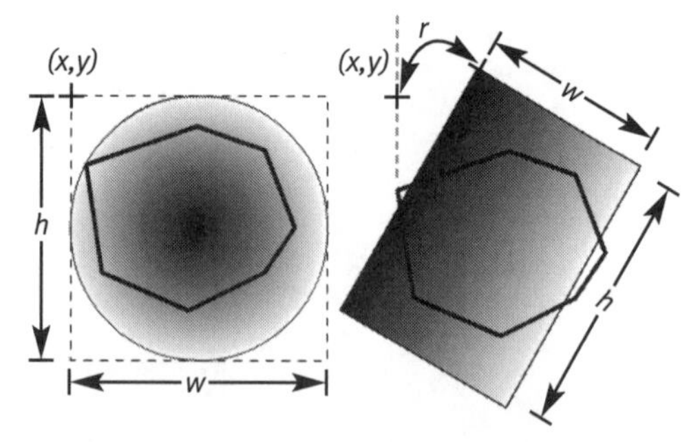

Figure 7.80 Parameters for the box matrix type. A radial gradient (left) and a linear gradient (right) are shown superimposed on a shape it would fill. *x* and *y* are the coordinates for the top-left corner of the gradient. *w* and *h* are its width and height. *r* is the clockwise angle that it makes from the vertical.

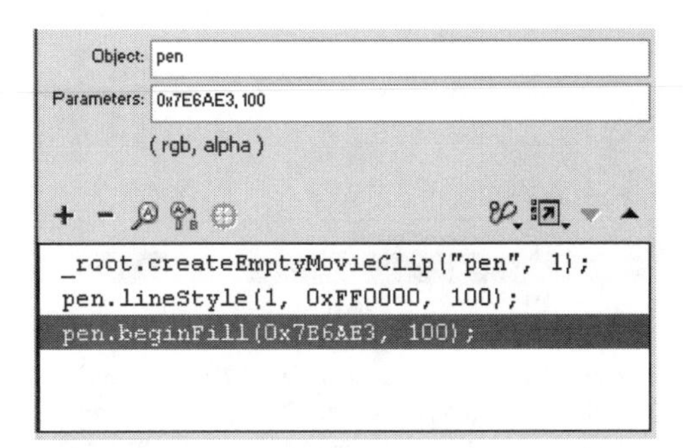

Figure 7.81 This fill is light blue at 100 percent opacity.

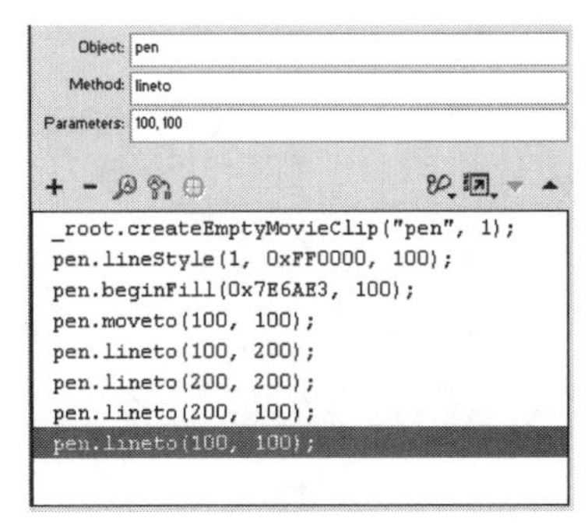

Figure 7.82 The end point of the last `lineTo()` method (100,100) matches the beginning point (100,100), creating a closed shape that can be filled.

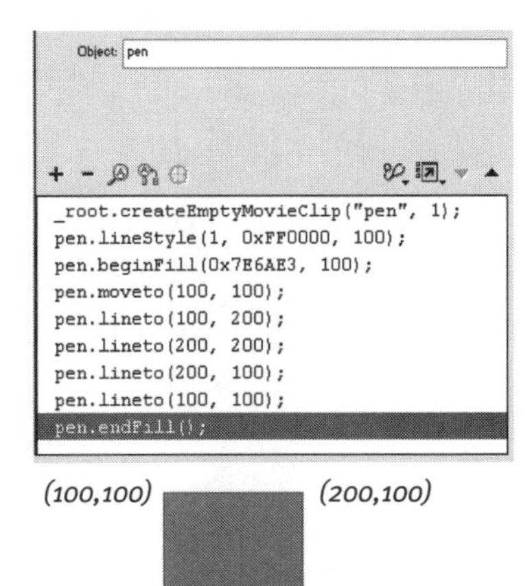

Figure 7.83 A blue box appears as a result of this code. The box was drawn counterclockwise from its top-left corner, but the order of line segments is irrelevant.

To fill a shape with a solid color:

1. Create an empty movie clip on the root Timeline.
2. Choose Objects > Movie > Movie Clip > Drawing Methods > lineStyle, and define the style of your line.
3. Choose Objects > Movie > Movie Clip > Drawing Methods > beginFill.
4. In the Object field, enter the target path of the empty movie clip.
5. In the Parameters field, enter the hex code for a color and a value for the alpha, separating your parameters with commas (**Figure 7.81**).
6. Choose Objects > Movie > Movie Clip > Drawing Methods > moveTo, and move the starting point of your line.
7. Use the `lineTo()` or `curveTo()` method to draw a closed shape (**Figure 7.82**).
8. When the end points match the beginning points of your shape, choose Objects > Movie > Movie Clip > Drawing Methods > endFill.

   No parameters are required for the `endFill()` method. Flash fills the closed shape with the specified color (**Figure 7.83**).

To fill a shape with a gradient:

1. Create an empty movie clip on the root Timeline.
2. Choose Actions > Variables > set variable.
3. In the Variable field, enter a name for your color array.
4. Put your pointer in the Value field, choose Objects > Core > Array > new Array.

   The constructor function creates a new array object.
5. Between the parentheses of the `new Array()` statement, enter the colors of your gradient in hex code, separating your hex codes with commas, and check the Expression box (**Figure 7.84**).

   By adding parameters to the `new Array()` statement, you instantiate a new array object and populate the array at the same time. The first color refers to the left side of a linear gradient or the center of a radial gradient.
6. Again, choose Actions > Variables > set variable.
7. In the Variable field, enter a name for your alpha array.
8. In the Value field, choose Objects > Core > Array > new Array.
9. Between the parentheses of this `new Array()` statement, enter the alpha values that correspond to each color, and check the Expression box (**Figure 7.85**).
10. For a third time, choose Actions > Variables > set variable.
11. In the Variable field, enter a name for your ratios array.
12. In the Value field, choose Objects > Core > Array > new Array.

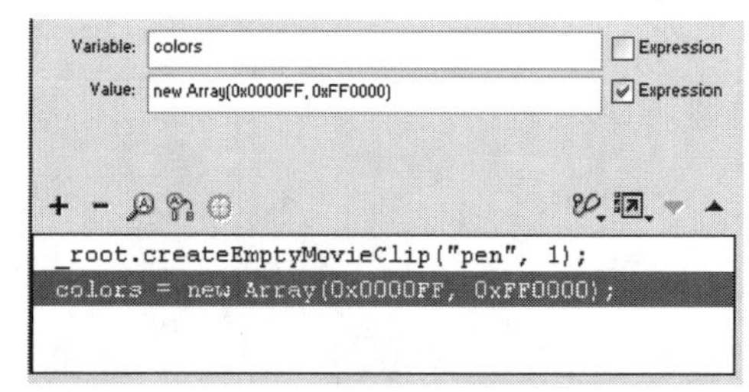

Figure 7.84 The colors array is created with blue on one side and red on the other. If this gradient is going to be a linear gradient, blue (0x0000FF) will be on the left. If it is going to be a radial gradient, blue will be in the center.

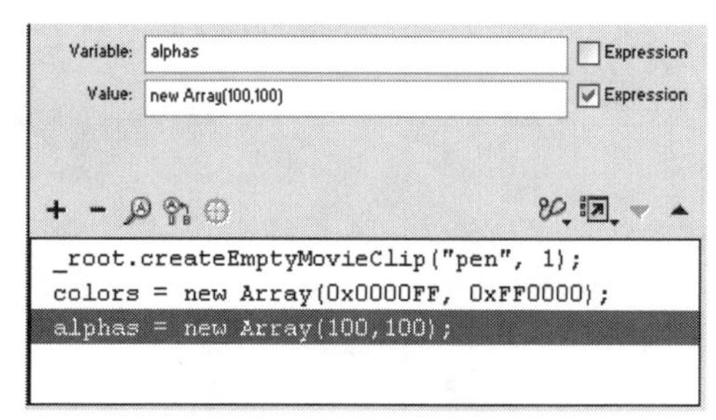

Figure 7.85 The alphas array is created with 100 percent opacity for both the blue and the red.

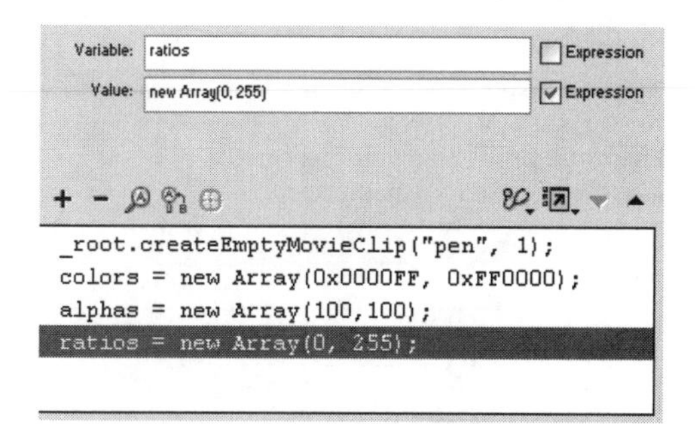

Figure 7.86 The ratios array is created with blue on the far left side (or the center, in the case of a radial gradient), and with red on the far right side (or the edge of a radial gradient).

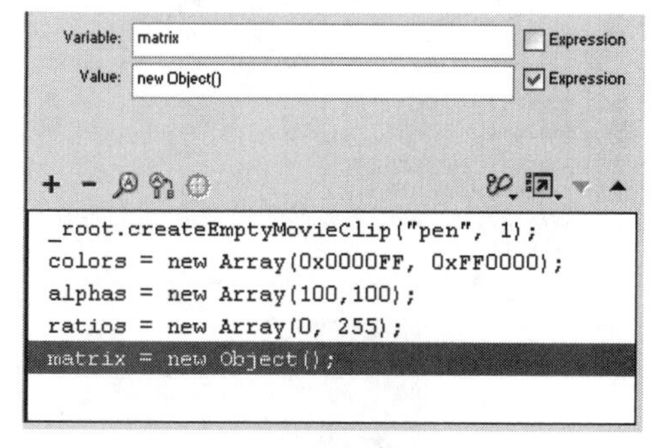

Figure 7.87 The matrix generic object is created.

```
_root.createEmptyMovieClip("pen", 1);
colors = new Array(0x0000FF, 0xFF0000);
alphas = new Array(100,100);
ratios = new Array(0, 255);
matrix = new Object();
matrix.matrixType = "box";
matrix.x = 100;
matrix.y = 100;
matrix.w = 100;
matrix.h = 100;
matrix.r = 0;
```

Figure 7.88 The *x, y* coordinates, width and height, and angle of the gradient are defined as properties of the matrix object.

13. Between the parentheses of this new `Array()` statement, enter the ratio values that correspond to each color, and check the Expression box (**Figure 7.86**).
14. For a fourth time, choose Actions > Variables > set variable.
15. In the Variable field, enter a name for your matrix object.
16. In the Value field, choose Objects > Core > Object > new Object.
17. Check the Expression box.

    Unlike the previous `set variable` statements, which create arrays, your matrix object is created from the generic Object category (**Figure 7.87**).
18. In a series of statements, define the properties of your matrix object.

    Using the `evaluate` statement (Actions > Miscellaneous Actions > evaluate), enter the name of your matrix object, a dot, and then its property. Next, enter an equal sign and a value. Remember that the `matrixType` property is assigned the word `"box"` (in quotation marks).

    The Script pane should look similar to **Figure 7.88**.
19. Choose Objects > Movie > Movie Clip > Drawing Methods > lineStyle, and define the style of your line.
20. Choose Objects > Movie > Movie Clip > Drawing Methods > beginGradientFill.
21. In the Object field, enter the target path to the empty movie clip.

continues on next page

22. In the Parameters field, enter the string "linear" or "radial" to choose your gradient type; then enter the name of your color array, alphas array, ratios array, and your matrix object.

    Separate the parameters with commas (**Figure 7.89**).

    All the information about your gradient that you defined in your arrays and matrix object is fed into the parameters of the `beginGradientFill()` method.

23. Choose Objects > Movie > Movie Clip > Drawing Methods > moveTo, and enter starting coordinates for your shape.

24. Create a series of lines or curves with `lineTo()` or `curveTo()` to create a closed path.

25. Choose Objects > Movie > Movie Clip > Drawing Methods > endFill.

    Flash fills your shape with the gradient (**Figure 7.90**).

✔ Tips

- The color array that you create for the `beginGradientFill()` method is not the same as an object you create from the Color object. The Color object controls a movie clip's color. The color array is used as a parameter in the `beginGradientFill()` method.
- The *r* property of the matrix-type object takes radians, not degrees. To convert degrees to radians, you must multiply by the number pi and then divide by 180. Using the Math object for pi (Math.PI), you can use the formula `radians = degrees*(Math.PI/180)`
- The *r* property of the matrix-type object affects only linear gradients and has no effect on radial gradients.

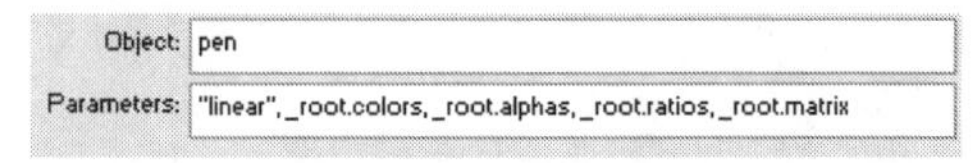

Figure 7.89 The Parameters pane of the `beginGradientFill()` method.

```
_root.createEmptyMovieClip("pen", 1);
colors = new Array(0x0000FF, 0xFF0000);
alphas = new Array(100,100);
ratios = new Array(0, 255);
matrix = new Object();
matrix.matrixType = "box";
matrix.x = 100;
matrix.y = 100;
matrix.w = 100;
matrix.h = 100;
matrix.r = 0;
pen.lineStyle(5, 0xFF0000, 100);
pen.beginGradientFill("linear", _root.colors,
      _root.alphas, _root.ratios, _root.matrix);
pen.moveto(100, 100);
pen.lineto(100, 200);
pen.lineto(200, 200);
pen.lineto(200, 100);
pen.lineto(100, 100);
pen.endFill();
```

Figure 7.90 The complete ActionScript code creates a box with a linear gradient from blue to red.

Figure 7.91 Combining draggable movie clips (the vertices), drawing methods (the lines connecting the vertices), and dynamic masking (uncovering the image "behind" the wrapping paper).

Figure 7.92 A movie clip containing a bitmap cityscape will be the masked movie clip.

Using Dynamic Masks

You can turn any movie clip into a mask and specify the movie clip to be masked with the method `setMask()`. To use the method, you define the movie clip you want to be masked as the target path before the method and then define the movie clip you want to act as a mask as its parameter: `masked.setMask(mask)`. Because you can control all the properties of movie clips, you can make your mask move or grow and shrink in response to viewer interaction. You can even combine the `setMask()` method with the movie-clip drawing methods to create masks that change shape (**Figure 7.91**).

One of the limitations of the `setMask()` method is that button events applied to the movie clip mask do not work. The events `onPress`, `onRelease`, `onReleaseOutside`, `onRollover`, `onRollout`, `onDragOver`, and `onDragOut` fail because they conflict with the masked movie clip beneath them. You have ways around this limitation, however. One way is to create an invisible button inside the mask movie clip. Make the movie clip into a mask, and assign button events to the invisible button. The other way is to create a movie clip within a movie clip. Use the `setMask()` method on the inner movie clip, and assign button events to the outer movie clip. Make sure that the outer movie clip contains graphics it can recognize as a hit area. Use one of these workarounds to assign `startDrag()` and `stopDrag()` methods to button events so that you can create draggable masks.

To set a movie clip as a mask:

1. Create a movie clip, place an instance on the Stage, and name it in the Property Inspector (**Figure 7.92**).

   This movie clip will be masked.

continues on next page

2. Create another movie clip, place an instance on the Stage, and name it in the Property Inspector (**Figure 7.93**).

   This movie clip will act as a mask.

3. Select the first frame of the root Timeline, and open the Actions panel.

4. Choose Objects > Movie > Movie Clip > Methods > setMask.

5. In the Object field of the Parameters pane, enter the target path to the movie clip you want to be masked.

6. In the Parameters field, enter the name of the target path to the movie clip you want to use as a mask (**Figure 7.94**).

7. Test your movie.

   The opaque shapes of the mask movie clip reveal the masked movie clip (**Figure 7.95**).

✔ Tips

- You can specify the root Timeline as the movie clip to be masked, and all the graphics on the main Timeline (including movie clips on the Stage) will be masked. To do so, enter `_root` in the Object field of the Parameters pane.
- Holes in the opaque shapes of your mask movie clip are not recognized and do not affect the mask (**Figure 7.96**).
- To undo a `setMask()` method, use the `null` keyword for its parameter as follows: `masked.setMask(null)`.

Figure 7.93 A movie clip of vertical shapes will be the mask movie clip.

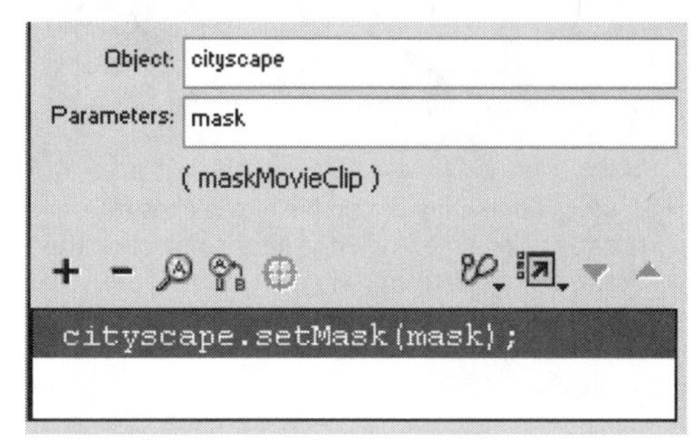

Figure 7.94 The mask movie clip will mask the cityscape movie clip.

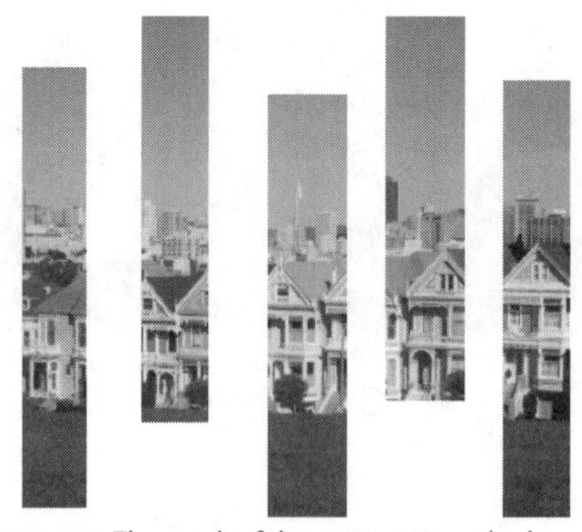

Figure 7.95 The result of the `setMask()` method.

Figure 7.96 If this shape were to be used in a movie clip for the `setMask()` method, Flash would recognize only a square for the mask.

Figure 7.97 You'll create a draggable mask to uncover this movie clip to make the viewer look for the monkey in the bush.

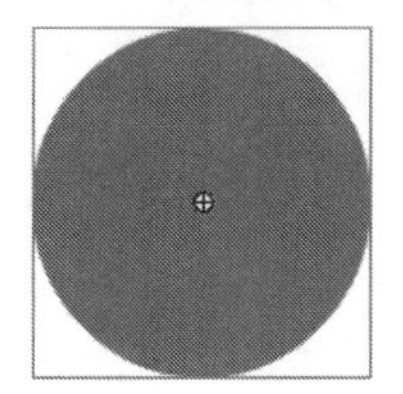

Figure 7.98 A simple circle will be the mask.

To create a draggable mask:

1. Create a movie clip, put an instance of it on the Stage, and name it in the Property Inspector.

   This movie clip will be masked (**Figure 7.97**).

2. Create another movie clip, put an instance of it on the Stage, and name it in the Property Inspector.

   This movie clip will act as a mask (**Figure 7.98**).

3. Double-click the circular movie clip to edit the symbol, create an invisible button inside this movie-clip symbol, and name the button in the Property Inspector.

   The invisible button inside your movie clip will be assigned the `startDrag` and `stopDrag` actions (**Figure 7.99**).

4. Exit symbol-editing mode, select the first frame of the root Timeline, and open the Actions panel.

continues on next page

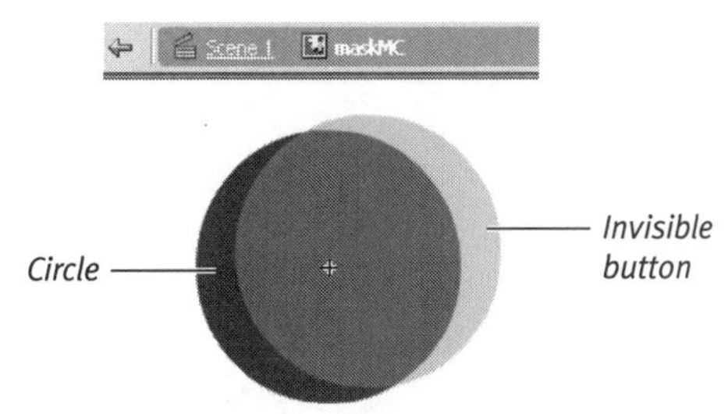

Figure 7.99 Inside the circular movie clip, called maskMC, place an invisible button. Here, the invisible button is offset so that you can see it. Superimpose the invisible button on the circle.

5. Choose Objects > Movie > Movie Clip > Methods > setMask.
6. In the Object field, enter the target path of the movie clip to be masked.
7. In the Parameters field, enter the target path of the mask movie clip (**Figure 7.100**).
8. Choose Objects > Movie > Button > Events > onPress.
9. In the Object field, enter the target path to your invisible button (**Figure 7.101**).
10. Choose Actions > Movie Clip Control > startDrag.
11. In the Target field, enter the target path of your mask movie clip, and check the Expression box (**Figure 7.102**).
12. Select the closing brace of the `onPress` event handler, and choose Objects > Movie > Button > Events > onRelease.
13. In the Object field, enter the target path to your invisible button.
14. Choose Actions > Movie Clip Control > stopDrag.
15. Test your movie.

    The movie clip acts as a mask, and the invisible button inside it provides a way to drag and drop the mask (**Figure 7.103**).

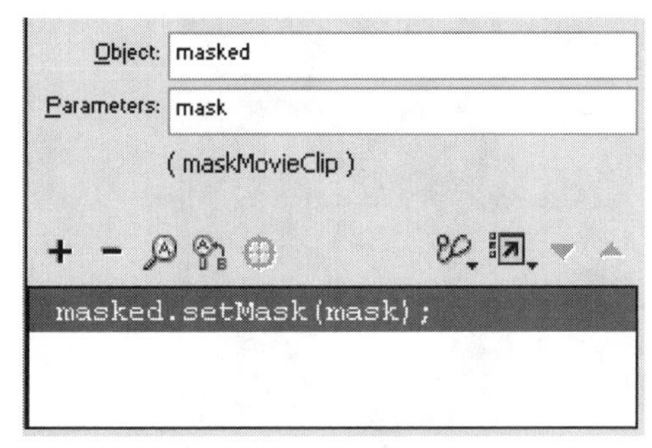

Figure 7.100 Create the mask of the circle over the masked image (the monkey in the bush).

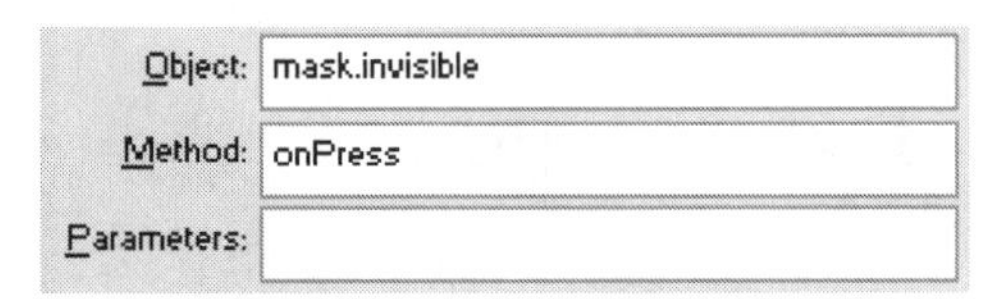

Figure 7.101 The `onPress` event handler is created for the invisible button called invisible inside the movie clip called mask.

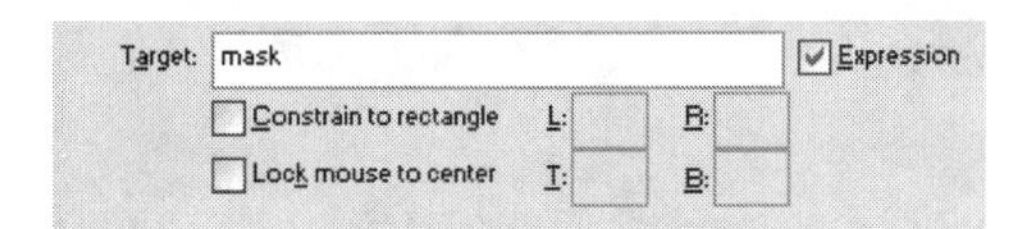

Figure 7.102 The Parameters pane for the `startDrag` action.

```
masked.setMask(mask);
mask.invisible.onPress = function() {
  startDrag(mask);
};
mask.invisible.onRelease = function() {
  stopDrag();
};
```

Figure 7.103 The final ActionScript code (top) assigns interactivity to both the movie clip and the invisible button inside the movie clip.

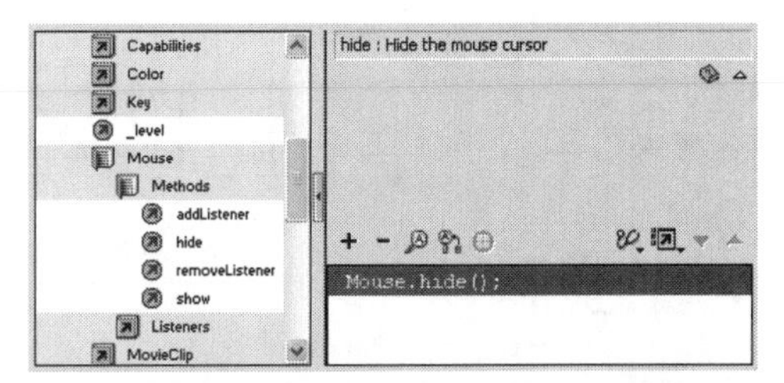

Figure 7.104 The `hide()` method of the Mouse object doesn't require previous instantiation.

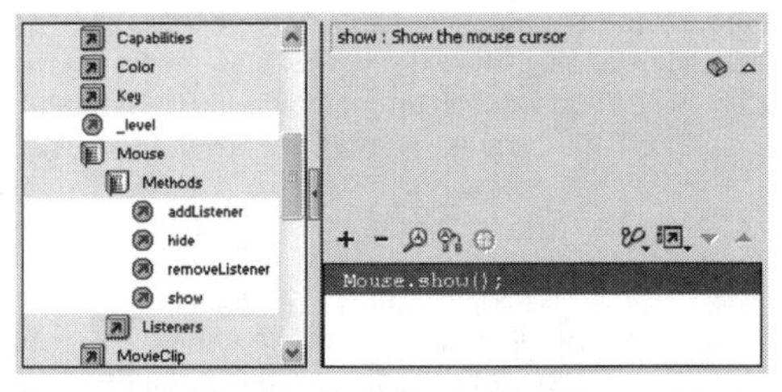

Figure 7.105 The `show()` method of the Mouse object makes a hidden mouse visible again.

Customizing Your Pointer

When you understand how to control the movie clip, you can build your own custom pointer. Think about all the different pointers you use in Flash. As you choose different tools in the Tools palette—the Paint Bucket, the Eyedropper, the Pencil—your pointer changes to help you understand and apply those tools. Similarly, you can tailor the pointer's form to match its function.

Customizing the pointer involves first hiding the default mouse pointer. Then you must match the location of your new graphic to the location of the hidden (but still functional) mouse pointer. To do this, you set the `X Position` and `Y Position` properties of a movie clip to the *x* and *y* positions of the mouse pointer. The *x* and *y* positions of the mouse pointer are defined by the properties `_xmouse` and `_ymouse`.

To hide the mouse pointer:

1. Select the first frame, and open the Actions panel.
2. Choose Objects > Movie > Mouse > Methods > hide (**Figure 7.104**).

   When you test your movie, the mouse pointer becomes invisible.

To show the mouse pointer:

- From the Actions panel, choose Objects > Movie > Mouse > Methods > show (**Figure 7.105**).

To create your own mouse pointer:

1. Create a movie-clip symbol, place an instance of it on the Stage, and name it in the Property Inspector.

   This movie clip will become your pointer.

2. Select the first frame of the root Timeline, and open the Actions panel.

3. Choose Objects > Movie > Mouse > Methods > hide.

   The `Mouse.hide()` method appears. When this movie begins, the mouse pointer disappears.

4. Choose Objects > Movie > Movie Clip > Events > onMouseMove.

5. In the Object field, enter `_root`.

   The on`MouseMove` event handler is completed.

6. Choose Actions > Movie Clip Control > setProperty.

7. From the Property pull-down menu, choose X Position.

8. In the Target field, enter the name of your movie clip.

9. In the Value field, enter `_xmouse`.

10. Check both Expression boxes.

11. Again, choose Actions > Movie Clip Control > setProperty.

12. From the Property pull-down menu, choose Y Position.

13. In the Target field, enter the name of your movie clip.

14. In the Value field, enter `_ymouse`.

15. Check both Expression boxes (**Figure 7.106**).

16. Test your movie (**Figure 7.107**).

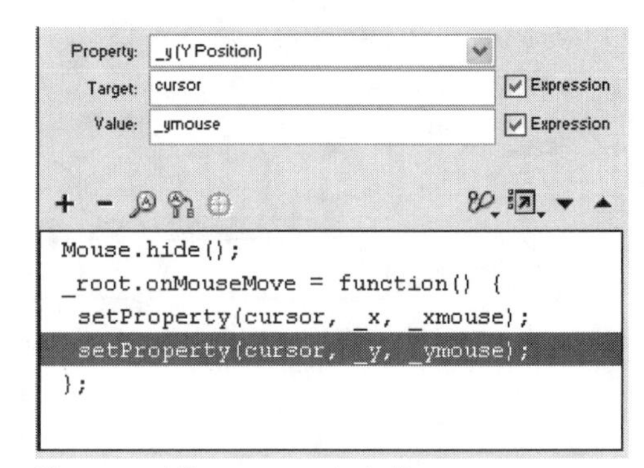

Figure 7.106 The mouse pointer disappears as soon as this movie begins. The `setProperty` statements set the *x* and *y* positions of the current movie clip to the *x* and *y* positions of the mouse pointer whenever it moves.

Figure 7.107 This magnifying glass is a movie clip that matches the *x* and *y* positions of the pointer. Create helpful pointers like this one with an appearance that matches function.

```
Mouse.hide();
_root.onMouseMove = function() {
  setProperty(cursor, _x, _xmouse);
  setProperty(cursor, _y, _ymouse);
  updateAfterEvent();
};
```

Figure 7.108 Add the `updateAfterEvent` function to force Flash to refresh the display and create smoother motion.

Use the function `updateAfterEvent()` to force Flash to redraw the screen independent of the movie's frame rate. This function eliminates the flicker associated with graphics moving around the screen faster than Flash can update the display and is especially important when you use a custom pointer. The action `updateAfterEvent` can be used only with the events `mouseMove`, `mouseDown`, `mouseUp`, `keyDown`, and `keyUp` or as part of a function passed from `setInterval()`.

To update the graphics on-screen:

1. Continue with the file you created in the preceding task.
2. Select the last `setProperty` statement within the `onMouseMove` event handler.
3. Choose Actions > Movie Clip Control > updateAfterEvent (**Figure 7.108**).

   The `updateAfterEvent` function appears in the Script pane. Flash updates the graphics on the screen each time the pointer moves, creating smoother motions.

✔ Tip

- Explore using multiple movie clips that track the location of your pointer. A vertical line that follows `_xmouse` and a horizontal line that follows `_ymouse` create a moving crosshair.

Beginning to Animate with ActionScript

The actions and methods discussed so far in this chapter—scripts that let you control and test virtually all aspects of the movie clip (appearance, position, draggability, collisions, depth level, duplication and creation, drawing capability, and masking capability)—are the basic tools for animating entirely with ActionScript. Whereas motion tweens and shape tweens are created before playback, ActionScript animation is generated during playback, so it can respond to and change according to your viewer's actions. You can use the mouse properties `_xmouse` and `_ymouse` as parameters in movie-clip methods or to control movie-clip properties so that the location of your viewer's pointer determines the behavior and appearance of graphics on-screen.

The following examples show how to use the mouse properties `_xmouse` and `_ymouse` to create responsive animations. The first example is a simple game of tag. You create a movie clip that follows your pointer, and if the movie clip catches up to you, you lose the game. The second example combines `_xmouse` and `_ymouse` with the movie-clip drawing methods so you can draw with the pointer. The third example is a scrolling menu that moves according to where the pointer is located.

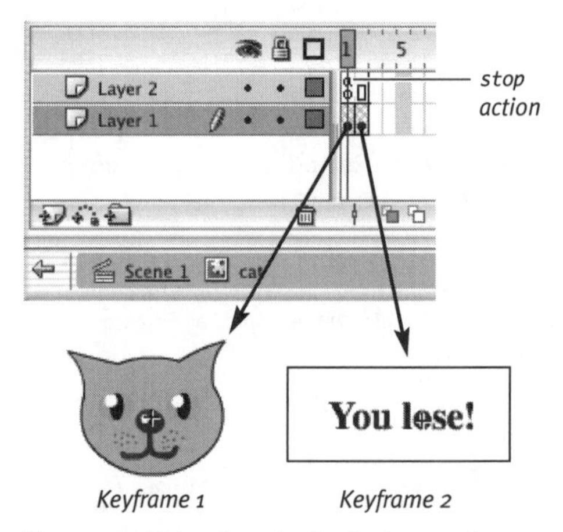

Figure 7.109 This cat movie clip displays a cat graphic in keyframe 1 when it chases your pointer and a different graphic in keyframe 2 when you lose the game.

To create a mouse-tracking game:

1. Create a movie-clip symbol with two keyframes.

   The first keyframe contains a graphic and a `stop` action, and the second keyframe contains a "You lose!" message (**Figure 7.109**).

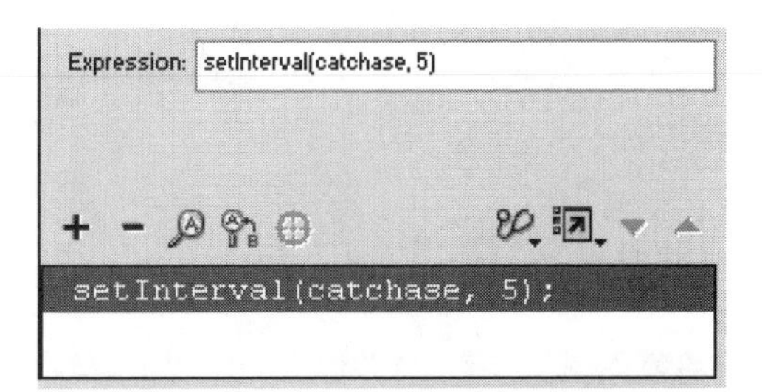

Figure 7.110 The action `setInterval`, like the event handler `onEnterFrame`, is a good way to execute ActionScript statements continuously.

Name: catchase

Parameters:

```
setInterval(catchase, 5);
function catchase() {
}
```

Figure 7.111 The function called `catchase` will be called every 5 milliseconds.

2. Place an instance of the movie clip on the Stage, and name it in the Property Inspector.

   In this example, the clip is called cat.

3. Select the first frame of the root Timeline, and open the Actions panel.

4. Choose Actions > Miscellaneous Actions > setInterval.

5. In the Parameters field, enter the name of a function, followed by a comma and then 5 (**Figure 7.110**).

   The function you specify in the `setInterval` statement will be called every 5 milliseconds.

6. Choose Actions > User-Defined Functions > function.

7. In the Name field, enter the name of your function; leave the Parameters field blank (**Figure 7.111**).

8. Choose Actions > Variables > set variable.

9. In the Variable field, enter the target path of the movie clip, followed by a dot and then the `X Position` property.

   The statement should look like the following:

   ```
   cat._x
   ```

10. In the Value field, enter the following:

    ```
    cat._x + (_xmouse - cat._x)/100
    ```

continues on next page

11. Check the Expression box next to the Value field.

    This statement starts with the *x* position of the cat movie clip and adds the difference between the mouse position and the cat position. If the mouse is to the right of the cat, the statement adds a positive value. If the mouse is to the left of the cat, the statement adds a negative value. In either case, the cat gets closer to the mouse. The division by 100 makes sure that the cat doesn't jump on the mouse immediately. The increment is small (one-hundredth of the distance), so the cat lags behind the position of the mouse.

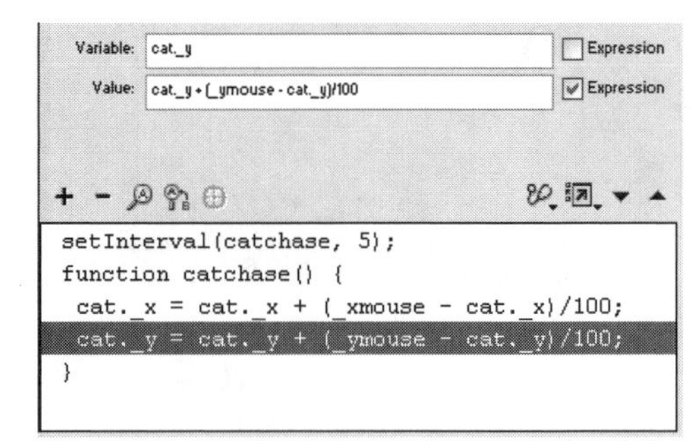

Figure 7.112 The *x* and *y* positions of the cat movie-clip instance change according to the position of the pointer.

12. Choose Actions > Variables > set variable.
13. In the Variable and Value fields, enter the same information for the *y* coordinate (**Figure 7.112**).
14. Choose Actions > Conditions/Loops > if.
15. In the Condition field, enter the following:

    `cat.hitTest(_xmouse,_ymouse, true)`

    This statement uses the `hitTest()` method to test whether the *x* and *y* positions of the mouse intersect the cat movie clip. The `shapeflag` argument is set to `true` so that only the graphics of the cat movie clip are considered, rather than the entire bounding box (**Figure 7.113**).

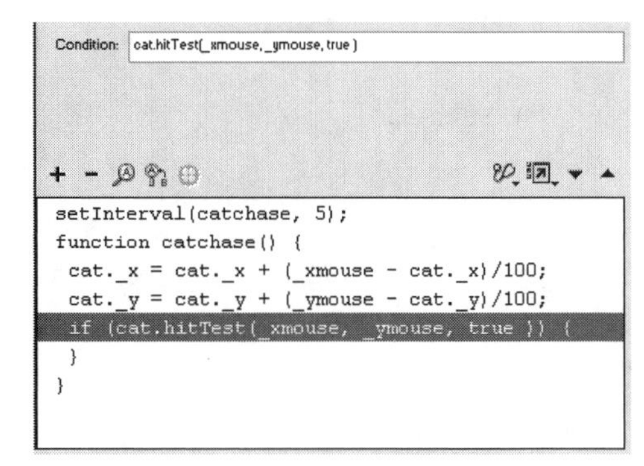

Figure 7.113 The condition checks whether the pointer intersects the cat movie-clip instance.

16. Choose Object > Movie > Movie Clip > Methods > nextFrame.
17. In the Object field, enter the target path for the cat movie clip.

    When the `hitTest()` returns `true`, the cat movie clip goes to the next frame, displaying the "You lose!" message (**Figure 7.114**).

Object: cat

```
setInterval(catchase, 5);
function catchase() {
  cat._x = cat._x + (_xmouse - cat._x)/100;
  cat._y = cat._y + (_ymouse - cat._y)/100;
  if (cat.hitTest(_xmouse, _ymouse, true)) {
    cat.nextFrame();
  }
}
```

Figure 7.114 The cat movie clip advances to the next frame in its Timeline.

18. Chose Actions > Movie Clip Control > setProperty.

Property: _name (Name)
Target: cat ☑ Expression
Value: youLoseMessage ☐ Expression

```
setInterval(catchase, 5);
function catchase() {
 cat._x = cat._x + (_xmouse - cat._x)/100;
 cat._y = cat._y + (_ymouse - cat._y)/100;
 if (cat.hitTest(_xmouse, _ymouse, true )) {
  cat.nextFrame();
  setProperty(cat, _name, "youLoseMessage");
 }
}
```

Figure 7.115 These parameters for `setProperty` change the instance name of the cat movie clip to youLoseMessage.

```
setInterval(catchase, 5);
// call the catchase function every 5 ms
function catchase() {
 // set x, y for cat closer to x, y of mouse
 cat._x = cat._x + (_xmouse - cat._x)/100;
 cat._y = cat._y + (_ymouse - cat._y)/100;
 // test if x,y of mouse intersects cat
 if (cat.hitTest(_xmouse, _ymouse, true )) {
  // if it does, display a you lose message
  cat.nextFrame();
  // and change the name of the cat instance so
  // it no longer follows the mouse
  setProperty(cat, _name, "youLoseMessage");
 }
 // refresh screen
 updateAfterEvent();
}
```

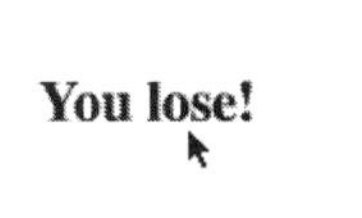

Figure 7.116 The ActionScript assigned to the `catchase` function (top) provides all the interactivity for the mouse-chasing game. The cat movie clip chases the pointer (left) and displays a message that was hidden on frame 2 of its Timeline when it intersects with the pointer (right).

19. From the Property pull-down menu, choose Name.

20. In the Target field, enter the target path of the cat movie clip, and check the Expression box.

21. In the Value field, enter a new name (**Figure 7.115**).

The instance name of the cat movie clip changes, preventing the first set of action statements from moving the cat movie clip around any more.

22. Select the closing brace of the `if` statement, and choose Actions > Movie Clip Control > updateAfterEvent.

23. Test your movie (**Figure 7.116**).

To draw with the pointer:

1. Select the first frame of the root Timeline, and open the Actions panel.
2. Choose Objects > Movie > Movie Clip > Events > onMouseMove.
3. In the Object field, enter `_root` (**Figure 7.117**).
4. Choose Objects > Movie > Movie Clip > Drawing Methods > lineStyle.
5. In the Object field, enter `_root`.
6. In the Parameters field, enter a thickness, a hex-code value, and an alpha value (**Figure 7.118**).
7. Choose Objects > Movie > Movie Clip > Drawing Methods > lineTo.
8. In the Object field, enter `_root`.
9. In the Parameters field, enter `_xmouse`, a comma, and `_ymouse` (**Figure 7.119**).

   Whenever the pointer moves, Flash draws a line segment from the previous position to the current position of the pointer.
10. Choose Actions > Movie Clip Control > updateAfterEvent.
11. Test your movie (**Figure 7.120**).

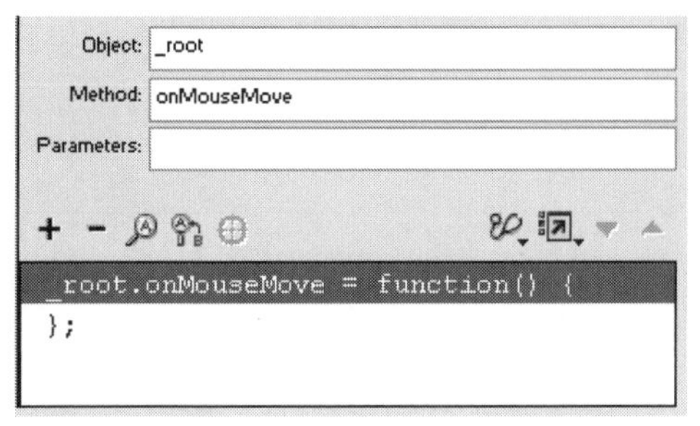

Figure 7.117 The onMouseMove event handler is created for the root Timeline.

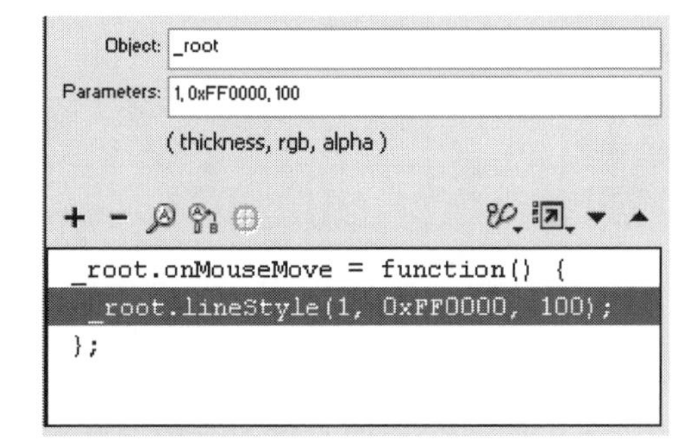

Figure 7.118 This line style is defined as a 1-point red line.

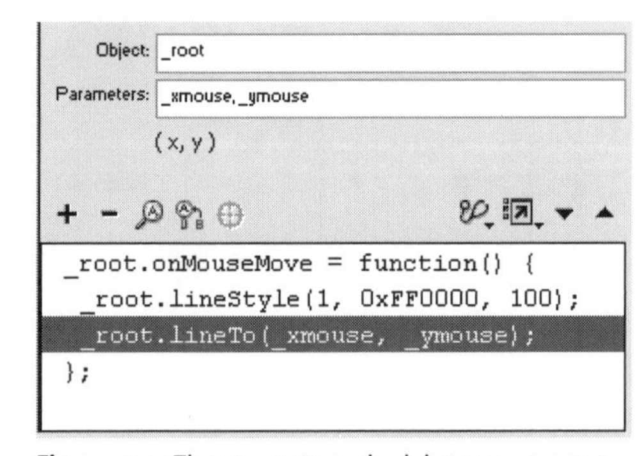

Figure 7.119 The `lineTo()` method draws a segment to the *x*, *y* position of the mouse pointer.

```
_root.onMouseMove = function() {
 _root.lineStyle(1, 0xFF0000, 100);
 _root.lineTo(_xmouse, _ymouse);
 updateAfterEvent();
};
```

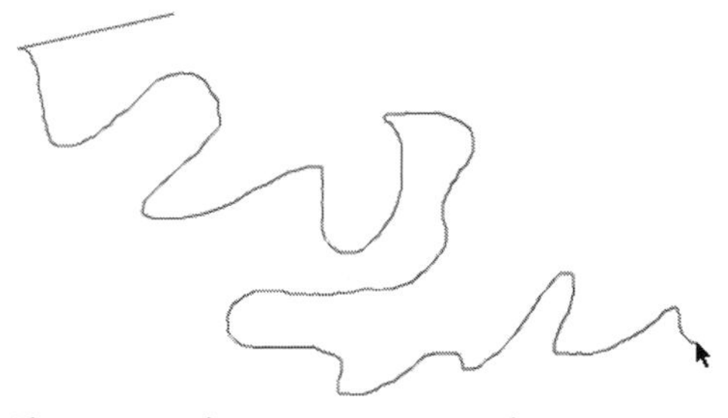

Figure 7.120 Whenever your mouse pointer moves, a new line segment is drawn, creating a simple drawing program.

Figure 7.121 A movie clip with a long row of buttons extends off the Stage. To provide access to the buttons, the movie clip will scroll to the right or to the left, depending on where the mouse pointer is located.

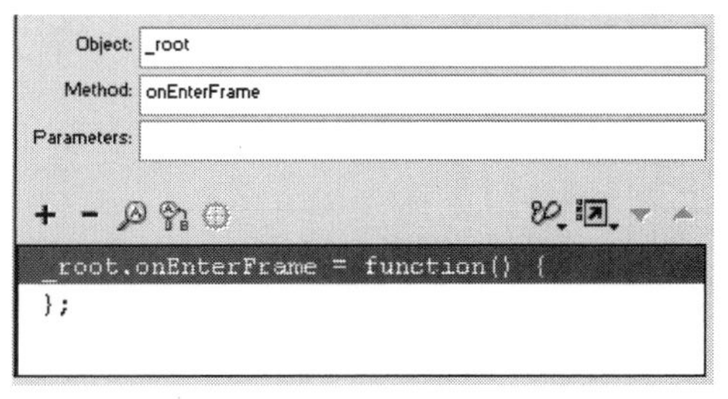

Figure 7.122 The `onEnterFrame` event handler is created on the root Timeline.

To create a scrolling menu that responds to the mouse pointer:

1. Create a movie clip that contains a long row of buttons or graphics (**Figure 7.121**), put it on the Stage, and name it in the Property Inspector.
2. Select the first frame of the root Timeline, and open the Actions panel.
3. Choose Objects > Movie > Movie Clip > Events > onEnterFrame.
4. In the Object field, enter `_root` (**Figure 7.122**).
5. Choose Actions > Variables > set variable.
6. In the Variable field, enter the name of your movie clip, followed by a dot and then `_x` for its *x* property.
7. In the Value field, enter the name of your movie clip, followed by a dot and `_x`; then add this expression:

   `(.5 * Stage.width - _xmouse)/10`

continues on next page

8. Check the Expression box (**Figure 7.123**).

   When you subtract the horizontal position of the mouse pointer from half of the Stage width, you get a number that is positive if the pointer is on the left or negative if the pointer is on the right. Use this value to move the *x* position of your movie clip. The division by 10 makes the increments smaller and, hence, the movement of the movie clip slower.

9. Test your movie.

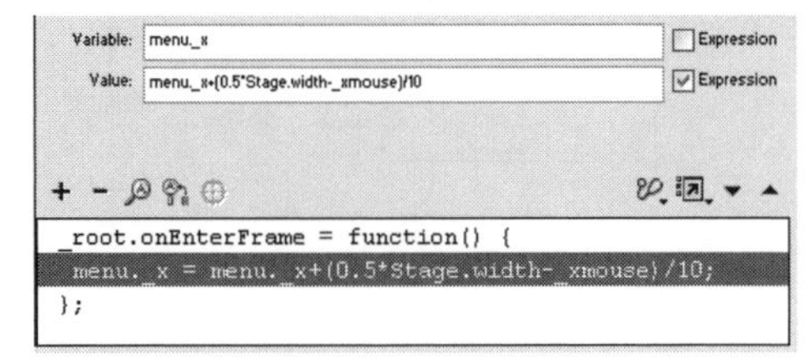

Figure 7.123 The horizontal position of the mouse pointer is used to calculate the new position of the movie clip called menu.

✔ Tip

- The next step for this scrolling menu would be to script boundaries so that the movie clip can't scroll off the screen. You'll learn about creating `if` statements in Chapter 9.

8 Controlling Sound

Incorporating sound into your Flash movie can enhance the animation and interactivity and add excitement to even the simplest project by engaging more of the user's senses. You can play background music to establish the mood of your movie, use narration to accompany a story, or give audible feedback to interactions such as button clicks and drag-and-drop actions. Flash supports several audio formats for import, including WAV, AIF, and MP3, which enables you to work with a broad spectrum of sounds. Flash also gives you many options for sound export, from speech-quality compression to high-quality MP3 compression, to help keep your Flash file size to a minimum.

This chapter explores the Sound object—the Flash class that lets you control sound with ActionScript. You should already be familiar with basic sound handling in Flash, such as importing sounds and assigning them to keyframes with the Event, Start, Stop, and Stream Sync options. If you are unsure about some of these techniques, review the tutorials and the Help files that accompany Flash for additional information. Moving forward, you'll learn how to use the Sound object to play sounds from the library dynamically without having to assign them to keyframes. You'll also learn to load sounds that reside outside your movie, enabling efficient management of your Flash and sound content. Using ActionScript, you can start, stop, and adjust the sound volume or its stereo effect, giving you control based on user interactions or movie conditions. You'll learn to use the Sound object's properties and events to time your sounds with animations or with other sounds.

All these methods, properties, and events of the Sound object give you the flexibility and power to integrate sounds into your movies creatively. You can create a slider bar that lets your viewers change the volume, for example, or add sounds to an arcade game that are customized to the game play. Develop dynamic slide shows synchronized to music or narration, or even make your own jukebox to play MP3 tunes.

Using the Sound Object

Attaching a sound file to a keyframe in the Timeline is an easy way to incorporate sounds into your movie. Two common ways to integrate sound on the Timeline are to use the Event Sync option to play a clicking sound in the down state of a button symbol and to use the Stream Sync option to synchronize dialogue with an animation. But if you need to control when a sound plays, change its volume and playback through the left and right speakers dynamically, or retrieve information about the number of seconds it has been playing, turn to the Sound object.

The Sound object is a Flash-defined class whose methods control its playback behavior and whose properties can help you control its timing. You need to instantiate the Sound object by using a constructor function to give it a name, just as you did with the Color object in Chapter 7. When the Sound object is named, you'll be able to use it to play and modify sound files that you associate with it.

To create a global Sound object:

1. Select the first frame of the main Timeline, and open the Actions panel.
2. Choose Actions > Variables > set variable (Esc + sv).
3. In the Variable field, enter the name of your new Sound object (**Figure 8.1**).
4. Click the Value field, choose Objects > Movie > Sound > new Sound, and check the Expression checkbox.

   The `new Sound()` constructor function appears in the Value field (**Figure 8.2**). The constructor takes an optional parameter that specifies a movie clip. This movie clip contains the sounds that would be controlled by the Sound object. By not specifying a movie clip, you create a Sound object that controls all the sounds in the Timeline (**Figure 8.3**).

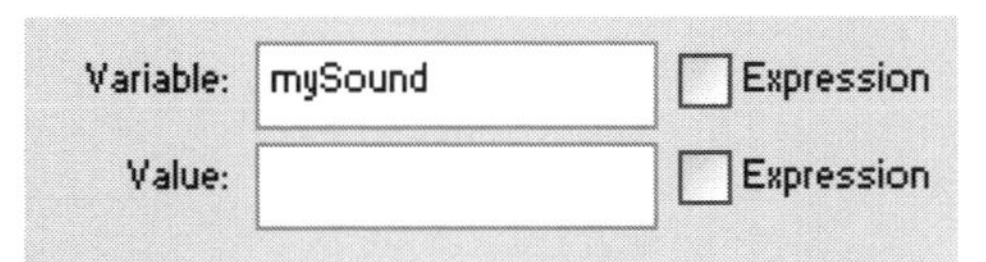

Figure 8.1 Enter `mySound` as the name of your Sound object, and leave the Expression checkbox unchecked.

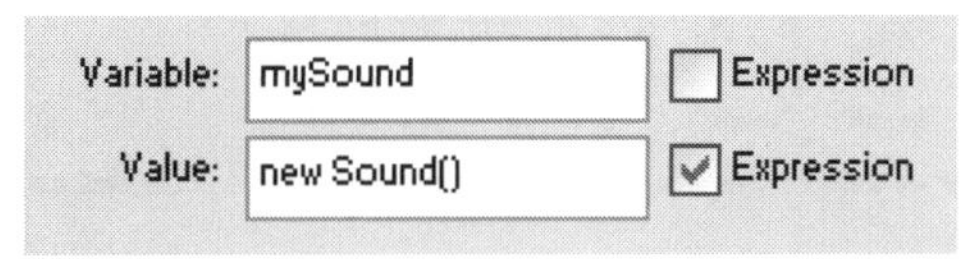

Figure 8.2 The `new Sound()` constructor function in the Value field instantiates a new Sound object.

```
mySound = new Sound();
```

Figure 8.3 The completed statement in the Script pane creates the Sound object called mySound.

Figure 8.4 Choose the Linkage option from the library for each sound you want to attach.

Attaching Sounds

After your new Sound object is instantiated, you must associate a sound with it. You can load an external MP3 file into your Sound object (which is covered later in this chapter), or you can attach a sound from the library. When you have multiple imported sounds in your library, you have to convey to the Sound object which one to play and control. You identify sounds in the library by using the Linkage option, just as you did in Chapter 7 when you attached a movie clip from the library to a movie-clip instance on the Stage. In addition to identifying your sound, the Linkage option exports it with the SWF file so that it will be available when called by the Sound object. When the sound is identified with the Linkage option, you attach it to the Sound object by using the method `attachSound()`.

To attach a sound to the Sound object:

1. Continuing with the file you created in the preceding task, import a sound file by choosing File > Import (Command-R for Mac, Ctrl-R for Windows).

   Your selected sound file appears in the library. You may import these sound formats: AIF (Mac), WAV (Windows), and MP3 (Mac and Win). More formats may be available if QuickTime is installed on your system.

2. Select the sound symbol in your library.

3. From the Options menu, choose Linkage (**Figure 8.4**).

   The Linkage Properties dialog box appears.

4. In the Linkage section, check the Export for ActionScript checkbox. Leave Export in first frame checked.

continues on next page

5. In the Identifier field, enter a name to identify your sound (**Figure 8.5**).
6. Click OK.

   Flash exports the selected sound in the SWF file with the unique identifier so that it is available to play when called by the Sound object.
7. Select the first frame of the main Timeline, and open the Actions panel.
8. Select the new Sound() statement in the Script pane.

   By selecting the new Sound() statement, you make sure that your next ActionScript statement appears below it.
9. Choose Objects > Movie > Sound > Methods > attachSound.
10. In the Object field, enter the name of your Sound object.
11. In the Parameters field, enter the identifier of your sound file within quotation marks (**Figure 8.6**).

    Your sound file is attached to the Sound object.

    It's very important that you specify the sound-file identifier within quotation marks. They tell Flash that the word is the literal name of the identifier and not an expression that it must evaluate to determine the name of the identifier.

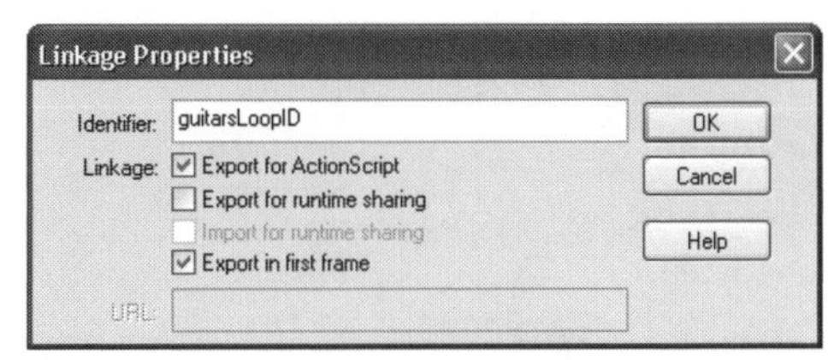

Figure 8.5 This sound is called guitarsLoopID and will be included in the exported SWF file.

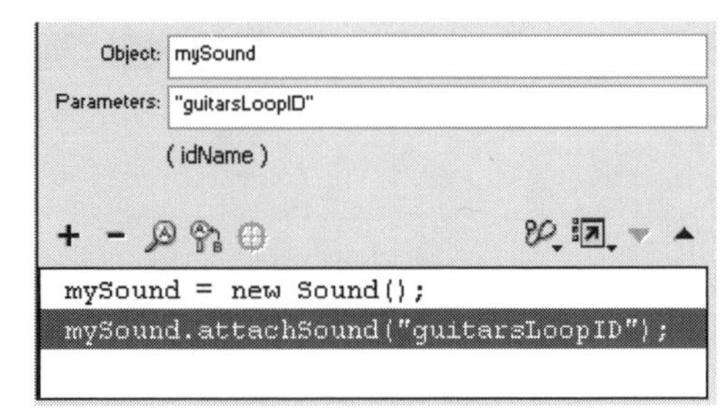

Figure 8.6 The attachSound() method attaches a sound from the library ("guitarsLoopID") to the Sound object (mySound).

Playing Sounds

After you have created a new Sound object and attached a sound to it from the library, you can play that sound. Use the `start()` method to play a sound from your Sound object. The `start()` method takes two parameters: `secondOffset` and `loops`.

The `secondOffset` parameter is a number that determines how many seconds into the sound it should begin playing. You can set the sound to start from the beginning or at some later point. If you have a 20-second sound attached to your Sound object, for example, a `secondOffset` setting of 10 makes the sound play from the middle. It doesn't delay the sound for 10 seconds, but begins immediately at the 10-second mark.

The `loops` parameter is a number that determines how many times the sound will play. A `loops` setting of 2 plays the entire sound two times with no delay in between.

If no parameters are defined for the `start()` method, Flash plays the sound from the beginning and plays one loop.

To play a sound:

1. Continuing with the file you used in the preceding task, create a button symbol, place an instance of it on the Stage, and give it a name in the Property Inspector.
2. Select the first frame of the main Timeline, and open the Actions panel.
3. Assign an `onRelease` event handler to your button.
4. Choose Objects > Movie > Sound > Methods > start.
5. In the Object field, enter the name of your Sound object.

continues on next page

6. In the Parameters field, enter `0`, followed by a comma and then 5 (**Figure 8.7**).

   The `secondOffset` parameter is set to 0, and the `loops` parameter is set to 5.

7. Test your movie.

   When your viewer clicks the button, the sound plays from the beginning and loops five times.

✔ Tips

- Unfortunately, you have no way of telling the `start()` method to loop a sound indefinitely. Simply set the `loops` parameter to a ridiculously high number, such as 99999.
- The `start()` method plays the attached sound whenever it's called, even when the sound is already playing. This situation can produce multiple, overlapping sounds. In the preceding task, for example, when the viewer clicks the button multiple times, the sounds play over one another. To prevent overlaps of this type, insert a `stop()` method (as outlined in the following task) right before the `start()` method. This technique ensures that a sound always stops before it plays again.
- The `start()` method always plays the latest sound attached to the Sound object. This means you can attach more sounds from the Library to the same Sound object, and the `start()` method will play the most current sound. You could create three buttons and assign the following script:

```
mySound = new Sound ();
firstButton.onRelease = function() {
   mySound.attachSound("Hawaiian");
}
secondButton.onRelease = function() {
   mySound.attachSound("Jazz");
}
startButton.onRelease = function() {
   mySound.start(0,1)
}
```

  When you click firstButton and then startButton, you'll hear the Hawaiian sound. When you click secondButton and then startButton, you'll hear the Jazz sound. If you begin playing the Jazz sound before the Hawaiian sound finishes, you'll hear overlapping sounds.

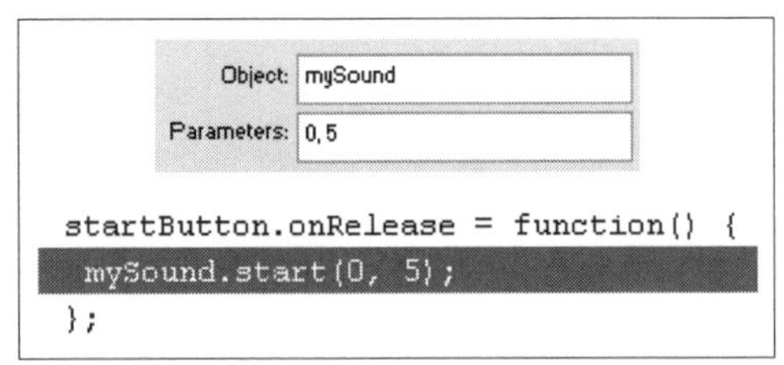

Figure 8.7 A portion of the Script pane shows just the `onRelease` handler for the button called startButton. This `start()` method plays the sound that is attached to mySound 5 times.

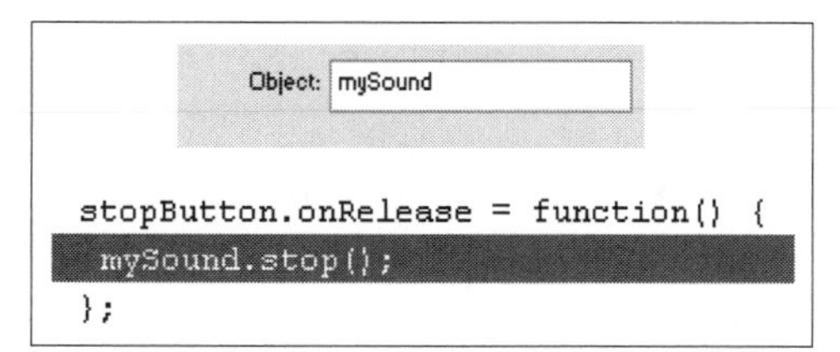

Figure 8.8 A portion of the Script pane shows just the `onRelease` handler for the button called stopButton. This `stop()` method stops playing any sounds attached to the mySound Sound object. The `stop()` method has no parameters.

To stop a sound:

1. Continuing with the file you used in the preceding task, place another instance of the button symbol on the Stage, and give it a name in the Property Inspector.
2. Select the first frame of the main Timeline, and open the Actions panel.
3. Assign an `onRelease` event handler to your new button instance.
4. Choose Objects > Movie > Sound > Methods > stop.
5. In the Object field, enter the name of your Sound object (**Figure 8.8**).
6. Test your movie.

   When your viewer clicks this button, any sound attached to the Sound object that is playing stops.

You can have all sounds stop indiscriminately by using the action `stopAllSounds`.

To stop all sounds:

- Choose Actions > Movie Control > stopAllSounds (Esc + ss).

  When this action is performed, Flash stops all sounds, whether they are attached to a Sound object or playing from the Timeline.

Modifying Sounds

When you use the Sound object, Flash gives you full control of its volume and its output through either the left or right speaker, known as *pan control*. With this level of sound control, you can let your users set the volume to their own preferences, and you can create more-realistic environments. In a car game, for example, you can vary the volume of cars as they approach or pass you. Playing with the pan controls, you can embellish the classic Pong game by making the sounds of the ball hitting the paddles and the walls play from the appropriate sides.

The two methods for modifying sounds are `setVolume()` and `setPan()`. The method `setVolume()` takes a number between 0 and 100 as its parameter, representing the percentage of full volume. So 100 represents the maximum volume, and 0 is silence. The method `setPan()` takes a number between –100 and 100. The setting –100 plays the sound completely through the left speaker, 100 plays the sound completely through the right speaker, and 0 plays the sound through both speakers equally.

To set the volume of a sound:

1. Continuing with the file you used in the preceding task, place another instance of the button symbol on the Stage, and give it a name in the Property Inspector.
2. Select the first frame of the main Timeline, and open the Actions panel.
3. Assign an `onRelease` event handler to your button.
4. Choose Objects > Movie > Sound > Methods > setVolume.
5. In the Object field, enter the name of your Sound object.
6. In the Parameters field, enter a number between 0 and 100 (**Figure 8.9**).
7. Test your movie.

   First, play your sound. When you click this button, the volume changes according to the volume parameter.

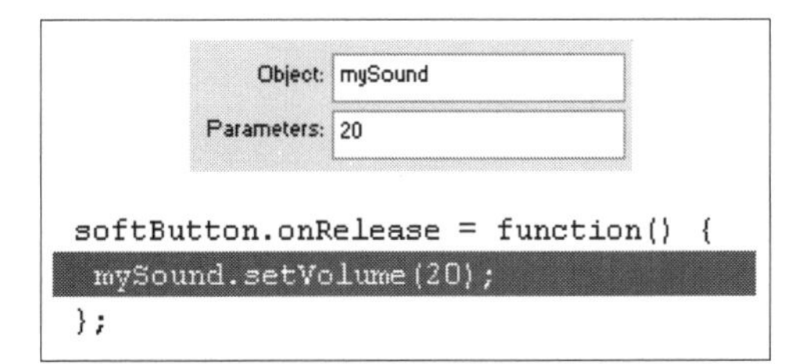

Figure 8.9 A portion of the Script pane shows just the `onRelease` handler for the button called softButton. This `setVolume()` method reduces the volume for the mySound Sound object to 20 percent. (The default value is 100 percent.)

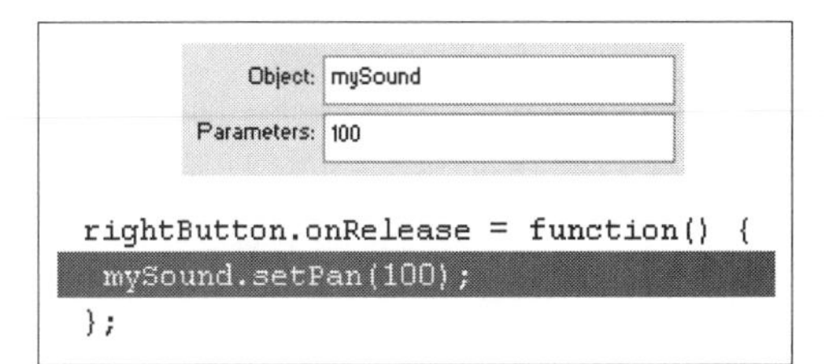

Figure 8.10 A portion of the Script pane shows just the onRelease handler for the button called rightButton. This setPan() method for the mySound Sound object makes all its sound play out of the right speaker.

To set the right and left balance of a sound:

1. Continuing with the file you used in the preceding task, place another instance of the button symbol on the Stage, and give it a name in the Property Inspector.
2. Select the first frame of the main Timeline, and open the Actions panel.
3. Assign an `onRelease` event handler to your button.
4. Choose Objects > Movie > Sound > Methods > setPan.
5. In the Object field, enter the name of your Sound object.
6. In the Parameters field, enter a number between –100 and 100 (**Figure 8.10**).

   This single number controls the balance between the left and right speakers.
7. Test your movie.

   First, play your sound. When you click this button, the left–right balance changes according to the pan parameter.

Modifying Independent Sounds

When you instantiate your Sound object and do not specify a movie clip for its parameter, such as `mySound = new Sound ()`, the `setVolume()` and `setPan()` methods will have a global effect, controlling all the sounds in the root Timeline. Even if you create two separate Sound objects like the following,

```
mySound1 = new Sound ();
mySound2 = new Sound ();
```

you cannot use the `setPan()` method to play mySound1 through the left speaker and mySound2 through the right speaker.

To modify sounds independently, you must create your Sound objects with parameters that target specific movie clips. Thereafter, Sound objects will be applied to different movie clips, and you can use the `setVolume()` and `setPan()` methods to control the two sounds separately.

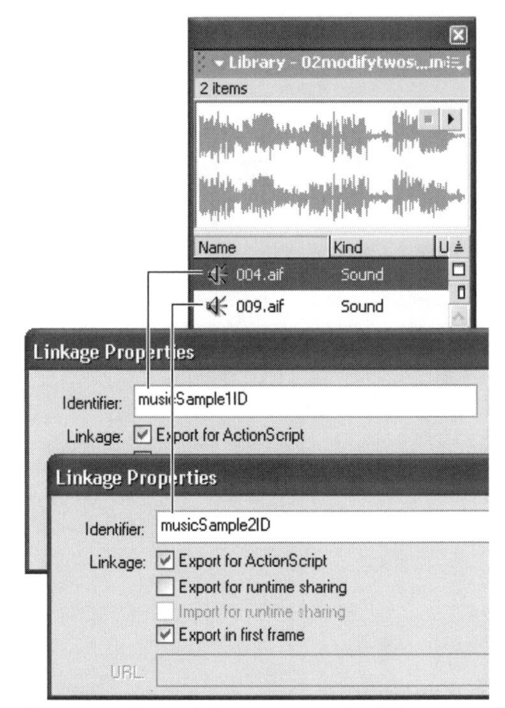

Figure 8.11 Give each imported sound a different identifier in the Linkage Properties dialog box.

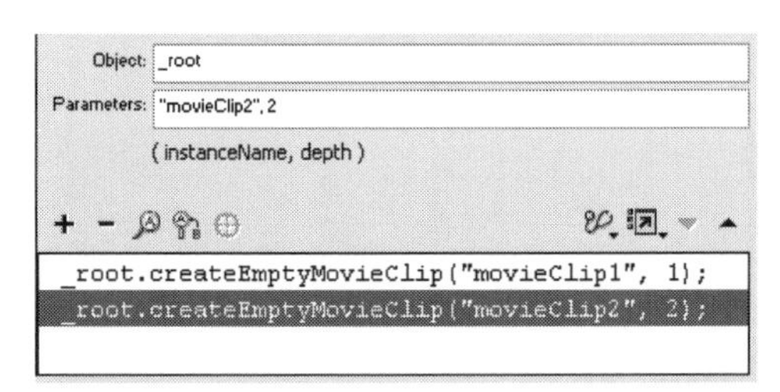

Figure 8.12 Create two empty movie-clip instances on the main Timeline to act as targets for the new Sound objects. The two movie-clip instances here are called movieClip1 and movieClip2.

To modify two sounds independently:

1. Import two sound files into Flash.
2. From the Options menu in the Library window, choose Linkage.

   The Linkage Properties dialog box opens.
3. Check the Export for ActionScript box, and give both sounds unique identifiers (**Figure 8.11**).
4. Select the first frame of the main Timeline, and open the Actions panel.
5. Using the method `createEmptyMovieClip()` (Objects > Movie > Movie Clip > Methods > createEmptyMovieClip), create two movie-clip instances on the root Timeline, using unique names in different depth levels (**Figure 8.12**).

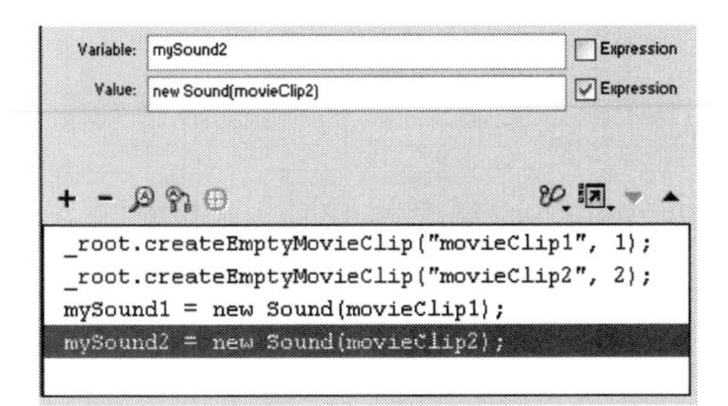

Figure 8.13 The mySound1 Sound object is created; it targets movieClip1. The mySound2 Sound object is created; it targets movieClip2.

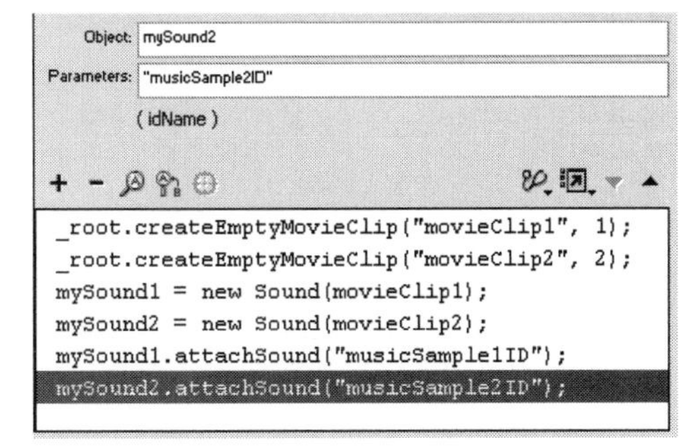

Figure 8.14 Attach the two sounds from the library to the two Sound objects.

```
start1Button.onRelease = function() {
  mySound1.start(0, 1);
};
```

Figure 8.15 A portion of the Script pane shows just the `onRelease` handler for the button called start1Button. This `start()` method plays the mySound1 object. Notice that although mySound1 targets movieClip1, movieClip1 need not be referenced at all in the target paths of mySound1's methods. The methods `attachSound()` and `start()` refer to the Sound object, not to the targeted movie-clip instance.

Flash creates two movie clips dynamically. You will use these movie clips as targets for your Sound objects. (See Chapter 7 for more information about the `createEmptyMovieClip()` method.)

6. Choose the `set variable` action to instantiate two new Sound objects, as you did earlier in this chapter.
7. Between the parentheses of each constructor function, enter the names of the empty movie clips (**Figure 8.13**).

   Now each Sound object is associated with its own movie clip (its own independent Timeline).
8. Use the `attachSound()` method to attach the two sounds from the library to each of your Sound objects (**Figure 8.14**).
9. Create a button symbol, place an instance of it on the Stage, and name it in the Property Inspector.
10. Select the first frame of the main Timeline, and open the Actions panel.
11. Assign an `onRelease` event handler to the button.
12. Assign the `start()` method for the first Sound object (**Figure 8.15**).

continues on next page

13. Repeat steps 9 through 12 to create a button that starts to play the second Sound object (**Figure 8.16**).

14. Place two more instances of button symbols on the Stage, and name them in the Property Inspector.

15. For the first button instance, assign the `setPan()` method to the first Sound object with a pan parameter of –100 (**Figure 8.17**).

    This button plays the first Sound object in the left speaker.

16. For the second button instance, assign the `setPan()` method to the second Sound object with a pan parameter of 100 (**Figure 8.18**).

    This button plays the second Sound object in the right speaker.

17. Test your movie.

    When this movie starts, two empty movie clips are created. Then two Sound objects are created, targeting the newly created movie clips. Finally, a different sound is attached to each Sound object. This technique enables you to control the left-right balance of each sound separately with the buttons called leftButton and rightButton.

```
start2Button.onRelease = function() {
  mySound2.start(0, 1);
};
```

Figure 8.16 A portion of the Script pane shows just the `onRelease` handler for the button called start2Button. This `start()` method plays the mySound2 object.

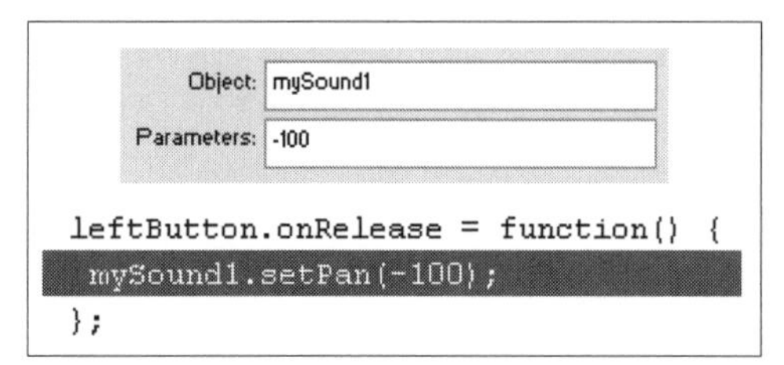

Figure 8.17 A portion of the Script pane shows just the `onRelease` handler for the button called leftButton. The `setPan()` method for mySound1 plays it in the left speaker.

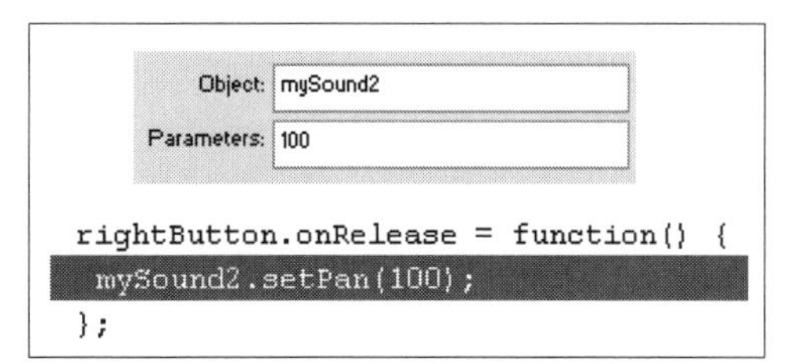

Figure 8.18 A portion of the Script pane shows just the `onRelease` handler for the button called rightButton. The `setPan()` method for mySound2 plays it in the right speaker.

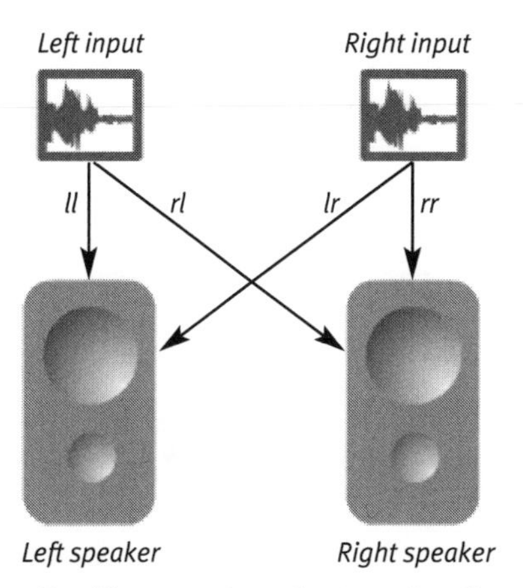

Figure 8.19 The parameters of `setTransform()` determine distribution of sounds between the left and right speakers. The first letter refers to the output speaker; the second letter refers to the input sound.

Transforming Sounds

For advanced users who want more precise control of how a sound is playing through the left and right speakers, Flash provides the method `setTransform()`. This method allows you to set percentages that determine how much of the right or left channel plays through the right and left speakers. Using this method, your sound can switch speakers from left to right dynamically or switch from stereo to mono.

The `setTransform()` method of the Sound object is very similar to the `setTransform()` method of the Color object discussed in Chapter 7. As with the Color object, using `setTransform()` with the Sound object requires that you create a generic object to hold the information specifying the distribution of left and right sounds. The properties of the sound-transformation object are `ll`, `lr`, `rr`, and `rl` (**Figure 8.19**). **Table 8.1** summarizes the functions of these properties.

Table 8.1

setTransform Parameters for the Sound Object

Parameter	Value
ll	Percentage value specifying how much of the left input plays in the left speaker.
lr	Percentage value specifying how much of the right input plays in the left speaker.
rr	Percentage value specifying how much of the right input plays in the right speaker.
rl	Percentage value specifying how much of the left input plays in the right speaker.

To switch the left and right speakers:

1. Import a sound file into Flash.
2. From the Options menu in the Library window, choose Linkage.

   The Linkage Properties dialog box opens.
3. Check the Export for ActionScript box, and give the sound an identifier (**Figure 8.20**).
4. Create a button symbol, place an instance of it on the Stage, and give it a name in the Property Inspector.
5. Select the first frame of the main Timeline, and open the Actions panel.
6. Choose the `set variable` action to instantiate a new Sound object, as you did earlier in this chapter (**Figure 8.21**).

   Don't specify a target movie clip for the parameter.
7. Attach the sound to this Sound object with the method `attachSound()`.
8. Assign an `onRelease` event handler to your button.
9. Choose the `start()` method for your Sound object (**Figure 8.22**).

   This button plays your sound.
10. Place another instance of the button symbol on the Stage, and give it a name in the Property Inspector.
11. In the Actions panel, assign an `onRelease` event handler to the second button.
12. Choose Actions > Variables > set variable.
13. In the Variable field, enter a name for your transformation object.
14. Click inside the Value field, and choose Objects > Core > Object > new Object.

Figure 8.20 This sound is identified in the library as conversationID.

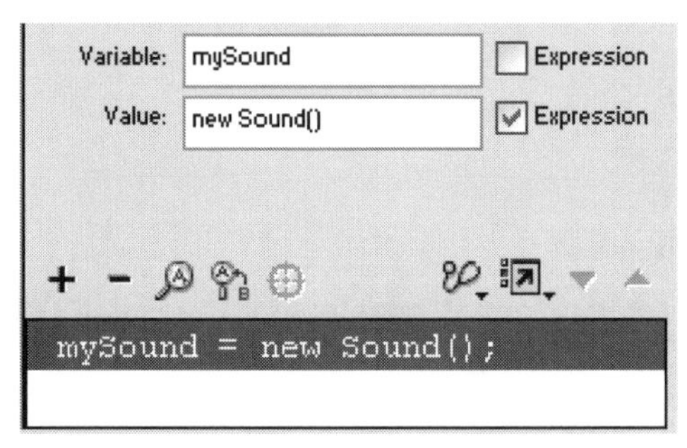

Figure 8.21 The mySound Sound object is created.

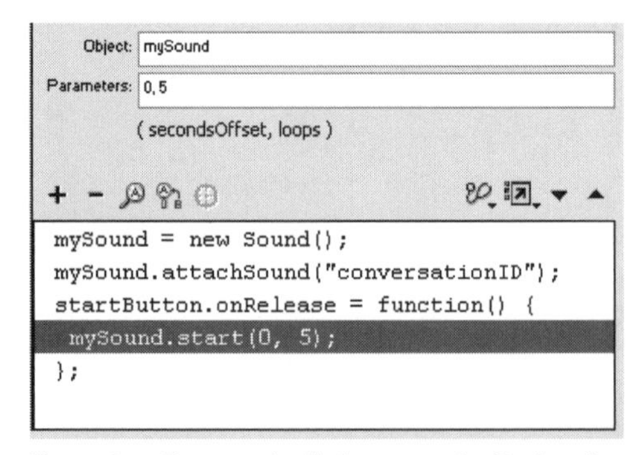

Figure 8.22 The sound called conversationID plays five times when the button called startButton is clicked.

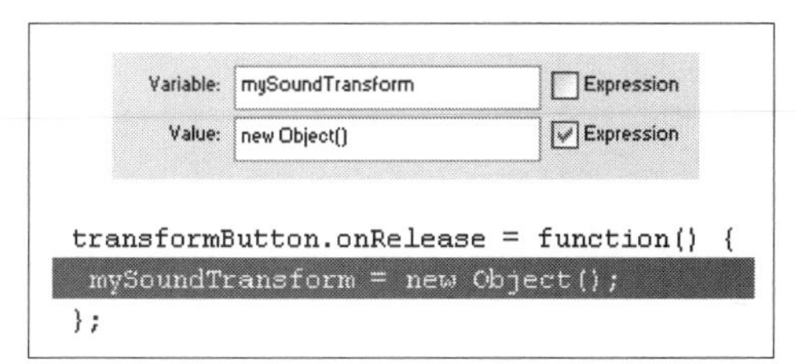

Figure 8.23 A portion of the Script pane shows just the `onRelease` handler for the button called transformButton. The mySoundTransform object is created from the generic Object class.

```
Variable: mySoundTransform.rr     [ ] Expression
Value:    0                       [✓] Expression

transformButton.onRelease = function() {
 mySoundTransform = new Object();
 mySoundTransform.ll = 0;
 mySoundTransform.lr = 100;
 mySoundTransform.rl = 100;
 mySoundTransform.rr = 0;
};
```

Figure 8.24 A portion of the Script pane shows just the `onRelease` handler for the button called transformButton. The four parameters of the `setTransform()` method are defined as properties of the mySoundTransform object.

```
Object:     mySound
Parameters: mySoundTransform
            ( sxform )

transformButton.onRelease = function() {
 mySoundTransform = new Object();
 mySoundTransform.ll = 0;
 mySoundTransform.lr = 100;
 mySoundTransform.rl = 100;
 mySoundTransform.rr = 0;
 mySound.setTransform(mySoundTransform);
};
```

Figure 8.25 A portion of the Script pane shows just the `onRelease` handler for the button called transformButton. The `setTransform()` method uses the object called mySoundTransform as its parameter. The four properties of the mySoundTransform object supply the method the information required to distribute the sounds to the left and right speakers.

15. Check the Expression checkbox next to the Value field (**Figure 8.23**).

    Your new sound-transformation object is instantiated.

16. Choose Actions > Variables > set variable.

17. In the Variable field of the Actions panel, enter the name of your sound-transformation object, followed by a dot and then one of the parameters. In the Value field, enter a percentage, and check the Expression checkbox. Do this for all four parameters (**Figure 8.24**).

    The properties of your sound-transformation object are defined. These properties will be used as the parameters of the `setTransform()` method.

18. Choose Objects > Movie > Sound > Methods > setTransform.

19. In the Object field, enter the name of your Sound object.

20. In the Parameters field, enter the name of your sound-transformation object (**Figure 8.25**).

    The hint below the Parameters field displays *sxform*. This hint stands for *sound transform* and is a reminder that the method requires a sound-transformation object.

21. Test your movie.

    When you click the second button, Flash creates a generic object whose properties (`mySoundTransform.ll`, `mySoundTransform.lr`, and so on) hold the sound-transformation information. Then this information is passed to the Sound object by the `setTransform()` method. The distribution of sound in the left and right speakers changes.

Creating Dynamic Sound Controls

One of the most effective uses of the Sound object and its methods is to create dynamic controls that allow the user to set the desired volume level or speaker balance. A common strategy is to create a draggable movie clip that acts as a sliding controller. By correlating the position of the draggable movie clip with the volume parameter of the `setVolume()` method, you can make the volume change dynamically as the viewer moves the movie clip.

For a vertical slider bar that controls volume, you can create two elements: the actual handle or slider and the track or groove that it runs along (**Figure 8.26**). First, you create a movie clip called groove. To make things easy, make the groove movie clip 100 pixels high with its center point at the bottom of the rectangle. Making the groove 100 pixels high will make it simpler to correlate the position of the slider on the groove with the `setVolume()` parameter. To create the draggable slider, create a movie clip called slider and assign the `startDrag()` action with constraints on the motion relative to the groove movie clip.

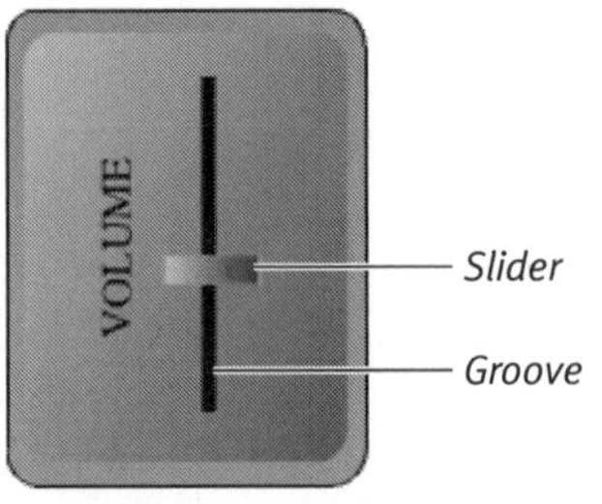

Figure 8.26 The components of a volume control are the slider that moves up and down and the groove.

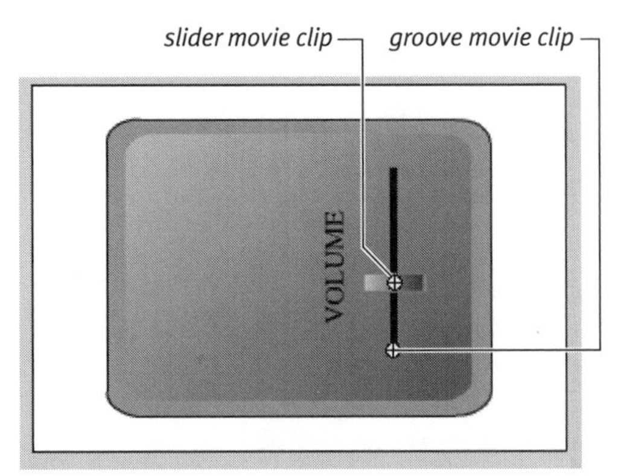

Figure 8.27 The movie-clip instance called groove will limit the motion of the draggable movie clip called slider. Notice that the registration point of the groove movie clip lies at its bottom edge.

To constrain a slider over a groove for a volume-control interface:

1. Create a movie clip of a tall rectangle that is 100 pixels high and whose registration point lies at the bottom edge.
2. Place an instance of the clip on the Stage, and name it groove in the Property Inspector.
3. Create another movie clip of a slider.
4. Place the clip on the groove movie clip, and name it slider in the Property Inspector (**Figure 8.27**).

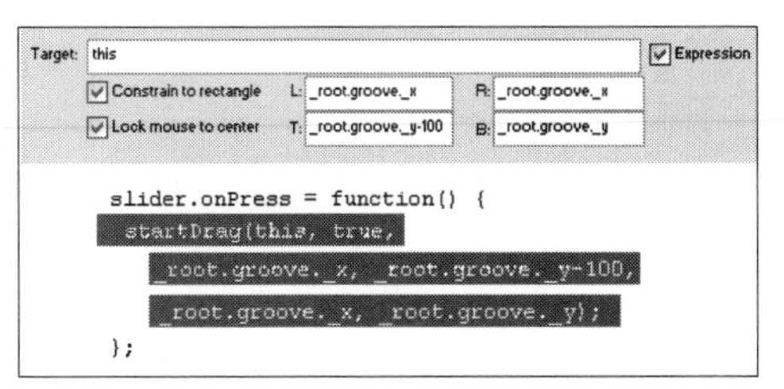

Figure 8.28 A portion of the Script pane shows just the onPress handler for the slider movie clip. The startDrag() action has been broken into three lines to fit the page only. The Constrain to Rectangle parameters constrain the slider movie clip from the center point to 100 pixels above the center point of the groove movie clip.

```
slider.onPress = function() {
 startDrag(this, true,
    _root.groove._x, _root.groove._y-100,
    _root.groove._x, _root.groove._y);
};
slider.onRelease = function() {
 stopDrag();
};
```

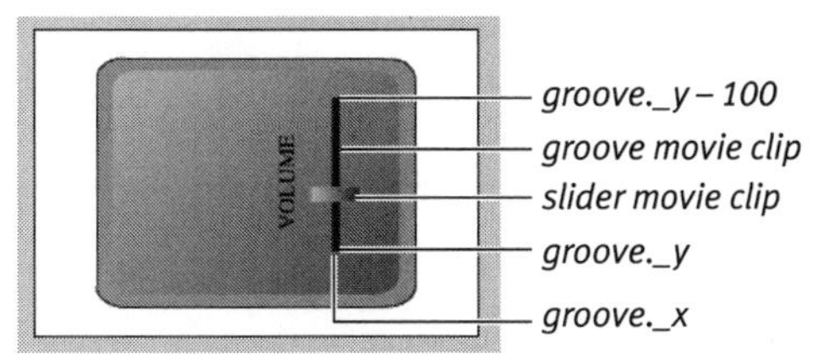

Figure 8.29 The full script. The startDrag() action has been broken into three lines to fit the page only. The slider movie clip can be dragged along the groove movie clip.

5. Select the first frame of the main Timeline, and open the Actions panel.
6. Assign an `onPress` event handler to the slider movie clip.
7. Choose Actions > Movie Clip Control > startDrag.
8. In the Target field, enter `this`, and check the Expression checkbox.
9. Check the Lock Mouse to Center and Constrain to Rectangle checkboxes.
10. Enter the following parameters:
    - In the L field, enter `_root.groove._x`.
    - In the R field, enter `_root.groove._x`.
    - In the T field, enter `_root.groove._y-100`.
    - In the B field, enter `_root.groove._y`.

    The actions assigned to the slider movie clip constrain the left and right sides to the center of the groove movie clip. The top is constrained to 100 pixels above the lower edge of the groove movie clip, and the bottom is constrained to the lower edge of the groove movie clip (**Figure 8.28**).
11. Assign an `onRelease` event handler to the slider movie clip.
12. Choose Actions > Movie Clip Control > stopDrag.
13. Test your movie (**Figure 8.29**).

The GlobaltoLocal movie-clip method

The second part of creating a dynamic sound control for volume is correlating the *y* position of the slider bar with the parameter for the `setVolume()` method. You want the top of the groove to correspond to a volume of 100 and the bottom of the groove to correspond to a volume of 0 (**Figure 8.30**).

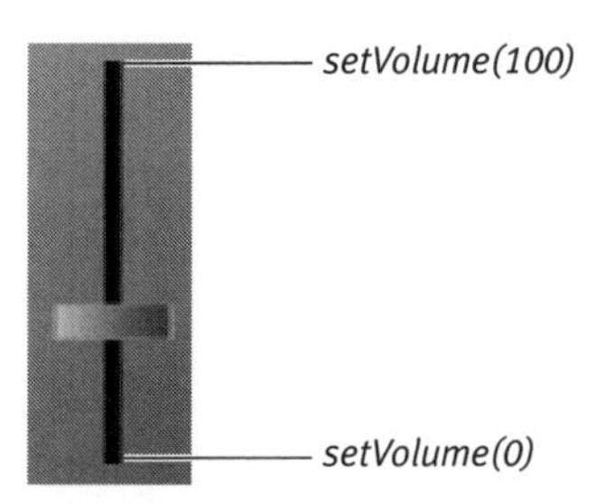

Figure 8.30 The `setVolume()` parameters need to correspond with the position of the slider movie clip on top of the groove movie clip.

But how do you get the *y* coordinates of the moving slider to match up with a number from 0 to 100? One way is to use the movie-clip method `globaltoLocal()`, which can convert the coordinates of the slider bar to coordinates that are relative to the groove movie clip. Because the groove movie clip is 100 pixels high and the slider bar is constrained to the groove movie clip's height, the groove movie clip's local coordinates provide a convenient correlation with the volume settings (**Figure 8.31**).

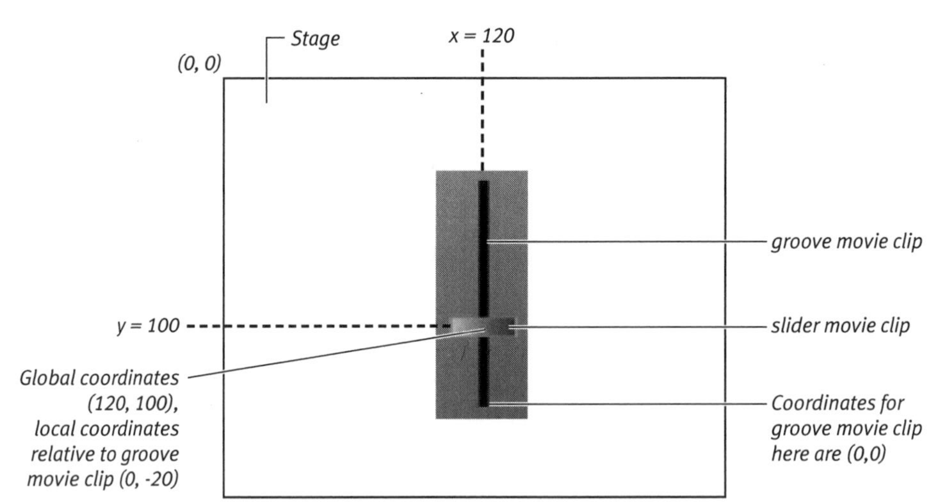

Figure 8.31 The global coordinates of the slider movie clip are determined by the root Timeline's Stage. The local coordinates are relative to the groove movie clip.

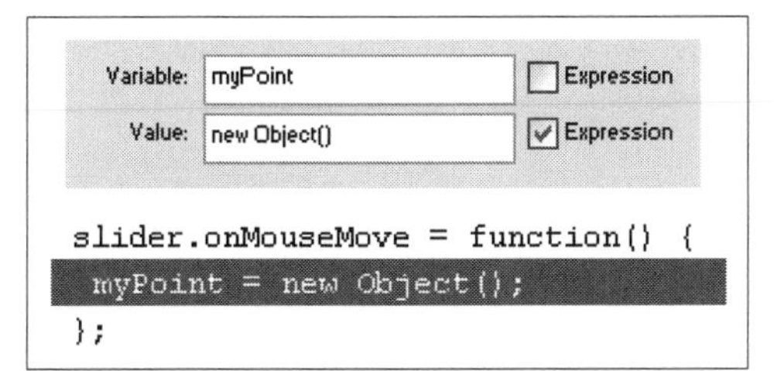

Figure 8.32 A portion of the Script pane shows just the onMouseMove handler for the slider movie clip. The myPoint object is created from the generic Object class.

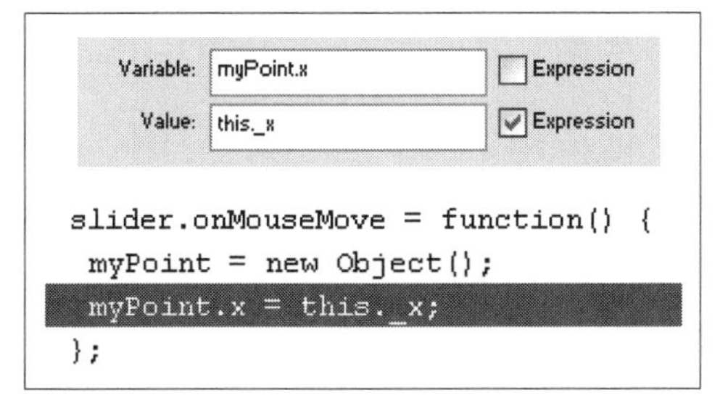

Figure 8.33 A portion of the Script pane shows just the onMouseMove handler for the slider movie clip. The current x position of the slider movie clip is assigned to `myPoint.x`.

To transform global coordinates to local coordinates:

1. Continuing with the file you used in the preceding task, select the first frame of the main Timeline, and open the Actions panel.
2. Choose Objects > Movie > Movie Clip > Events > onMouseMove.
3. In the Object field, enter the name of your slider movie clip.

   The slider moves whenever the pointer moves, so the onMouseMove event provides a good way to trigger a volume change based on the slider position.
4. Choose Actions > Variables > set variable.
5. In the Variable field, enter a name for the object that will hold the *x* and *y* information to be transformed from global to local coordinates.

   This object is your point object.
6. With the pointer in the Value field, choose Objects > Core > Object > new Object, and check the Expression checkbox (**Figure 8.32**).
7. Again, choose Actions > Variables > set variable.
8. In the Variable field, enter the name of your point object, followed by a dot and then the property x.
9. In the Value field, enter `this._x`, and check the Expression checkbox (**Figure 8.33**).

   This step sets the x property of your point object to the *x* position of the draggable movie clip.

continues on next page

10. Again, choose Actions > Variables > set variable.
11. In the Variable field, enter the name of your point object, followed by a dot and then the property y.
12. In the Value field, enter `this._y`, and check the Expression checkbox.

    This step sets the y property of your point object to the *y* position of the draggable movie clip.
13. Now choose Objects > Movie > Movie Clip > Methods > globalToLocal.
14. In the Object field, enter the target path of the movie clip whose coordinate system you want to use.
15. In the Parameters field, enter the name of your point object (**Figure 8.34**).

    Flash transforms the coordinates of your point object (relative to the root Timeline) to the coordinates of the targeted movie clip (relative to the groove movie clip's Timeline).

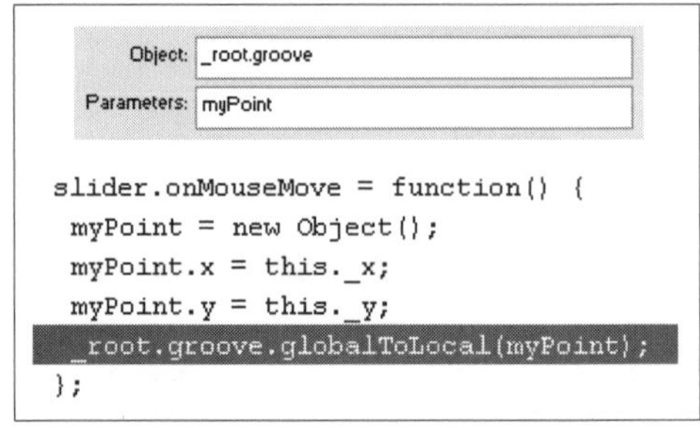

Figure 8.34 A portion of the Script pane shows just the `onMouseMove` handler for the slider movie clip. The global coordinates of `myPoint` (`myPoint.x` and `myPoint.y`) change to the local coordinates of the groove movie clip.

To link the slider position to the volume setting:

1. Continuing with the file you used in the preceding task, import a sound file into Flash.
2. From the Options menu in the Library window, choose Linkage.

   The Linkage Properties dialog box opens.
3. Check the Export for ActionScript box, and give the sound an identifier.
4. Create a button symbol, place an instance of it on the Stage, and give it a name in the Property Inspector.
5. Select the first frame of the main Timeline, and open the Actions panel.

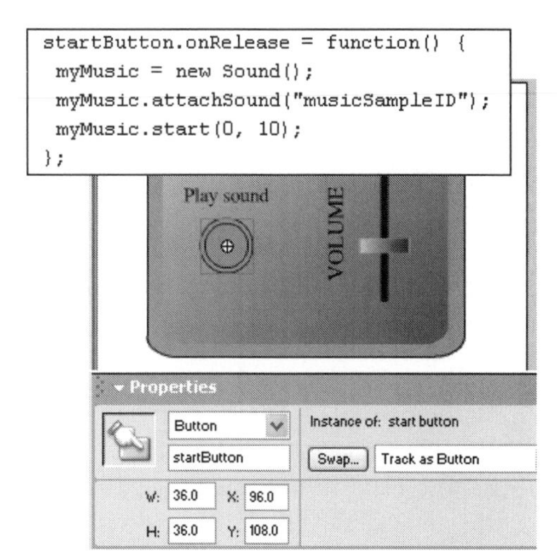

Figure 8.35 The event handler of the startButton creates a Sound object, attaches a sound from the library, and plays it.

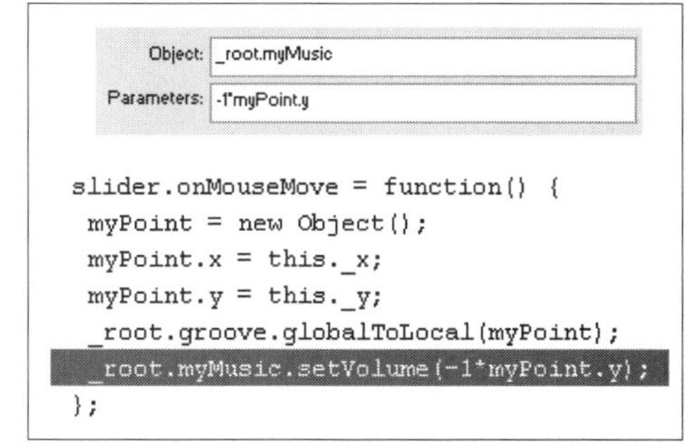

Figure 8.36 A portion of the Script pane shows just the `onMouseMove` handler for the slider movie clip. The groove movie-clip symbol is 100 pixels tall, with its center point at the bottom edge. Hence, the local coordinates of the groove movie clip range from –100 to 0. To change this range, multiply by (–1). The result is a range from 100 at the top to 0 at the bottom that can feed into the `setVolume()` parameter.

6. Assign an `onRelease` event handler to your button and actions as you did in the preceding tasks to create a new Sound object.
7. Attach the sound from the library to the Sound object; then assign the method that starts the sound (**Figure 8.35**).
8. Select the last statement within the `onMouseMove` event handler, and choose Objects > Movie > Sound > Methods > setVolume.
9. In the Object field, enter the target path for your Sound object.
10. In the Parameters field, enter `-1*myPoint.y`.

    The *y* position of your slider moves between –100 to 0. By multiplying the point object by –1, you convert the range of values from 100 to 0 (**Figure 8.36**).
11. Choose Actions > Movie Clip Control > updateAfterEvent.
12. Test your movie.

    When you drag the slider up or down in the groove, you change the sound volume dynamically.

Loading External Sounds

Each time you use the Linkage Properties dialog box to identify a sound in the library and mark it for export, that sound is added to your SWF file, increasing its size. Sounds take up an enormous amount of space, even with MP3 compression, so you have to be judicious with your inclusion of sounds. One way to manage sounds so that your file stays small is to keep sounds as separate files outside your Flash movie. Use the method `loadSound()` to bring MP3 sounds into Flash and associate them with a Sound object only when you need them. (MP3 is the only allowable format.) This method also allows you to change the sound file easily without having to edit your Flash movie. You can maintain several background-music tracks that users can choose among, for example. To turn the music on, you use the method `loadSound()`. To choose a different track, you call the method again and load a different sound file.

The method `loadSound()` requires two parameters. The first parameter is the path to the MP3 file. The second parameter determines whether you want the sound to be a streaming or an event sound. Enter `true` for streaming or `false` for not streaming (event). Streaming sounds will begin to play as soon as enough data downloads. For this reason, streaming sounds do not need the `start()` method. Event sounds, however, must download in their entirety and do require the `start()` method to begin playing.

To load and play an external sound:

1. Instantiate a Sound object with the constructor function `new Sound()`.
2. Choose Objects > Movie > Sound > Methods > loadSound.
3. In the Object field, enter the name of your Sound object.
4. In the Parameters field, enter the path to your MP3 file.

   If the file resides in the same directory as your Flash movie, you can enter just the name of the file. Put the path or file name in quotation marks. Enter a comma; then enter `true` for a streaming sound (**Figure 8.37**).
5. Test your movie.

   As soon as your movie begins, it creates a Sound object, then loads an MP3 file into it, and plays.

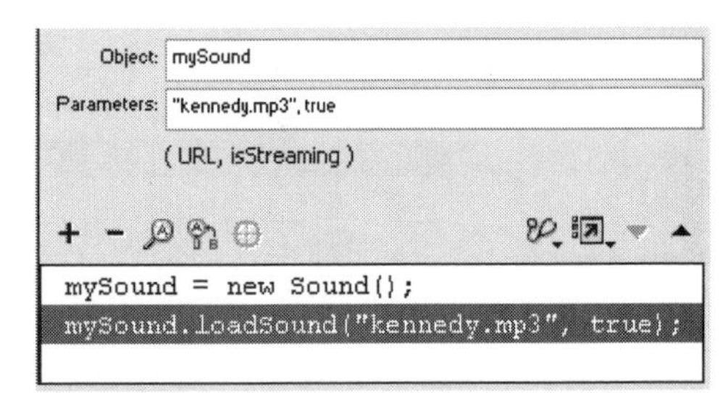

Figure 8.37 The `loadSound()` method streams the MP3 file called kennedy.mp3 that resides in the same directory as the Flash movie. The sound plays as soon as enough data has downloaded.

To stop a loaded sound:

- Use the `stop()` method.

  The loaded sound associated with your Sound object will stop playing.

✔ Tip

- After you stop a loaded sound, you have two ways to make it play again, depending on whether your sound is a streaming or an event sound. If your sound is a streaming sound, you must reload it with `loadSound()` to begin playing again. If your sound is an event sound, you must use the `start()` method.

Event or Streaming: Sound-Sync Options

Sounds behave differently depending on their sync options. The method `loadSound()` requires that a sound have a Stream or an Event sync option. (Two additional sync options, Start and Stop, are available only to sounds that are assigned to a keyframe.) Understanding the differences between the two sync options will help you decide when to use one or the other.

- Streaming sounds begin playing before they have downloaded completely. You can have only one stream per Sound object, so overlapping sounds are not possible (unless you instantiate more Sound objects). Streaming sounds are ideal for long passages of music or narration. To stop a streaming sound, call the `stop()` method; to start a streaming sound, call the `loadSound()` method again.
- Event sounds must be downloaded completely before they can play. Event sounds play when you call the `start()` method. If you call the `start()` method again before the first sound has finished, another instance begins, creating overlapping sounds. To stop an event sound, call the `stop()` method. Event sounds are appropriate for short sounds and sound effects for user-interface elements such as button rollovers and mouse clicks.

Reading Sound Properties

The Sound object provides two properties that you can use to find out more about the lengths of sounds. `position` is a property that measures the number of milliseconds that a sound has been playing. `duration` is a property that measures the total number of milliseconds of the sound. Both properties are read-only.

Use `position` and `duration` to time your animations to your sounds. In the following task, you modify an image according to the length of time a sound has been playing. As the sound plays, the image slowly reveals itself. When the sound ends, the image is revealed completely.

To use the position and duration properties:

1. Continuing with the file you used in the preceding task, import an image, convert it to a movie clip, place the movie-clip instance on the Stage, and name it in the Property Inspector.

   You will modify the scale and the alpha of this movie clip according to the length of time that your sound plays.

2. Select the first frame of the main Timeline, and open the Actions panel.

3. Choose Objects > Movie > Movie Clip > Events > onEnterFrame.

4. In the Object field, enter `_root`.

   The `onEnterFrame` event handler is created (**Figure 8.38**).

5. Choose Actions > Variables > set variable.

6. In the Variable field, enter the name of your movie clip, followed by a dot and then `_alpha`.

7. In the Value field, enter the following:

   `(mySound.position/mySound.duration)*100`

Table 8.2

Sound Properties	
Property	**Description**
position	length of time a sound has been playing (in milliseconds)
duration	total length of a sound (in milliseconds)

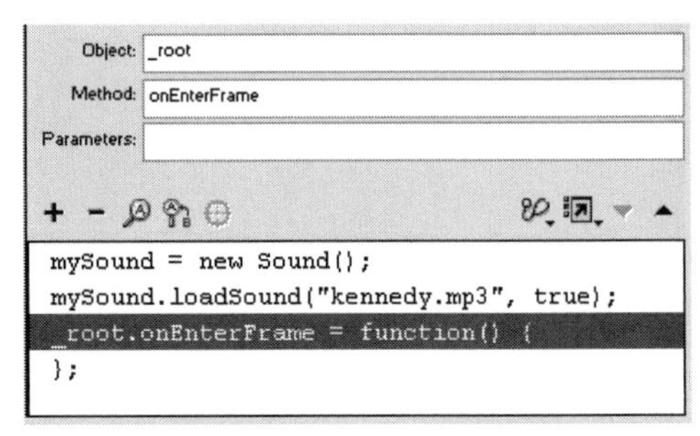

Figure 8.38 Assign the `onEnterFrame` event handler to the root Timeline.

Figure 8.39 The position and duration properties of the mySound object modify the _alpha property of the movie clip called image. As the value of position reaches duration, the image increases opacity.

```
mySound = new Sound();
mySound.loadSound("kennedy.mp3", true);
_root.onEnterFrame = function() {
  image._alpha = (mySound.position/mySound.duration)*100;
  image._xscale = 50+((mySound.position/mySound.duration)*50);
  image._yscale = 50+((mySound.position/mySound.duration)*50);
};
```

Figure 8.40 The full script (above). As the sound progresses, the image slowly appears (middle). When the sound is complete (position equals duration), the image is opaque and full-size. (Photo courtesy of the U.S. Senate)

Check the Expression box.

mySound is the name of your Sound object. mySound.position is the number of milliseconds that the sound has been playing. mySound.duration is the total duration of the sound, in milliseconds. So when you carry out the division and multiply by 100, you get the percentage of the progress of the sound (**Figure 8.39**).

The complete statement increases the alpha value of the movie clip as the sound plays so that the movie clip begins completely transparent and ends completely opaque when the sound stops.

8. Create two more statements that use the duration and position properties of the Sound object to modify the _xscale and _yscale properties of the movie clip.

The statements should look like the following:

```
image._xscale = 50+((mySound.position/
mySound.duration)*50);
image._yscale = 50+((mySound.position/
mySound.duration)*50);
```

The movie clip called image slowly increases from 50 percent of its size to 100 percent of its size.

9. Test your movie.

As you hear the words spoken by Senator Ted Kennedy at his brother's funeral, an image of Robert Kennedy slowly appears. The duration and position properties of the Sound object enable you to synchronize the sound to the transparency and size of the image (**Figure 8.40**).

✔ Tip

- The position property behaves a little differently when you use loadSound() set to streaming. When you load several streaming sounds, the Sound object does not recognize the start of each new sound, so the position property does not reset. In this case, the position measures the cumulative length of time that your sounds have played.

Detecting Sound Events

You can detect when a sound loads with the event onLoad or detect when a sound ends with onSoundComplete. Assign an anonymous function to the event to build the event handler. For example, consider the following script:

```
mySound.onSoundComplete = function(){
    gotoAndStop(10);
}
```

In this script, when the sound assigned to mySound is complete, Flash goes to frame 10.

The onSoundComplete event lets you control and integrate your sounds in several powerful ways. Imagine creating a jukebox that randomly plays selections from a bank of songs. When one song finishes, Flash knows to load a new song. Or you could build a business presentation in which the slides are timed to the end of the narration. In the following example, the completion of the sound triggers a graphic to appear on the Stage, providing a visual cue for the end of the sound.

To detect the completion of a sound:

1. Continuing with the file you used in the preceding task, select the first frame of the main Timeline, and open the Actions panel.
2. Choose Objects > Movie > Sound > Events > onSoundComplete.
3. In the Object field, enter the name of your Sound object (**Figure 8.41**).

   Your onSoundComplete event handler detects when the sound associated with the Sound object ends. When that happens, the function is triggered.

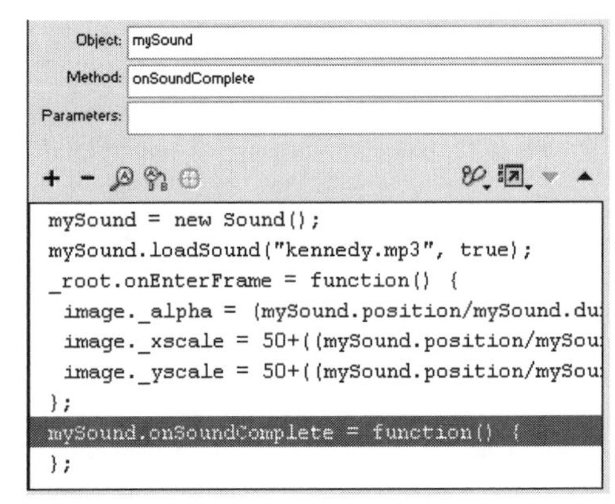

Figure 8.41 Create the onSoundComplete event handler for your Sound object called mySound.

Figure 8.42 The statement within the onSoundComplete event handler (above) attaches a movie clip from the library to the image movie clip.

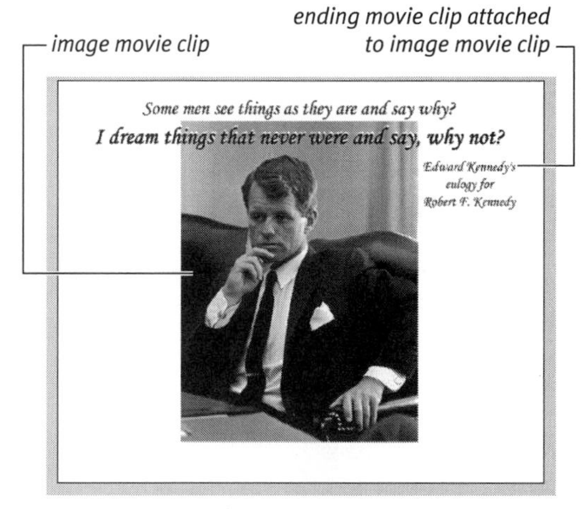

Figure 8.43 When the onSoundComplete event is triggered, a movie clip containing a quote from the sound attaches to the image movie clip. The registration point of the attached movie clip was modified so that when it appears, it is positioned correctly. (Photo courtesy of the U.S. Senate)

4. Within the event handler, add actions to be performed when the sound ends (**Figure 8.42**).

5. Test your movie (**Figure 8.43**).

✔ Tip

- If a sound is looping, the onSoundComplete event is triggered when all the loops have finished.

Working with Information

9 Controlling Information Flow

As your Flash movie displays graphics and animation and plays sounds, a lot can be happening behind the scenes, unapparent to the viewer. Your Flash document may be tracking many bits of information, such as the number of lives a player has left in a game, a user's login name and password, or the items a customer has placed in a shopping cart. Getting and storing this information requires *variables*, which are containers for information. Variables are essential in any Flash movie that involves complex interactivity, because they let you create scenarios based on information that changes. You can modify variables and use them in *expressions*—formulas that can combine variables with other variables and values—and then test the information against certain conditions to determine how the Flash movie will unfold. This testing is done in *conditional statements*, which control the flow of information. Conditional statements are the decision-makers of your Flash movie; they evaluate information that comes in and then tell Flash what to do based on that information. You would use conditional statements to make a ball bounce back if it collides with a wall, for example, or increase the speed of the ball if the game time exceeds one minute.

This chapter is about managing information by using variables, expressions, and conditional statements. You've dealt with all three in limited ways in earlier chapters, but here, you'll learn how to work with them in more detail. Understanding how to get, modify, and evaluate information lets you truly direct your Flash movie and change the graphics, animation, and sound in dynamic fashion.

Initializing Information

Variables hold information. You can create, change the contents of, and discard variables at any time. The first time you put information into a variable is called *initialization*. Initializing a variable in Normal mode of the Actions panel involves the `set variable` action, which assigns a value to a variable. You can also write out a statement that initializes a variable without using the `set variable` action as long as you have a variable name on the left side of an equal sign and a value on the right side. This point is crucial, because a=b is *not* the same as b=a.

You've initialized variables before; you just didn't call it that. When you create new objects by using `set variable`, as in the statement `myColor= new Color (myMovieClip)`, you initialize the variable `myColor`. In this case, the variable contains the Color object, but a variable can hold any kind of information, such as a number, letters, a true or false value, or even a reference to another variable. The different kinds of information that variables can contain are known as *data types*.

Variables and data types

Examples of typical types of variables are a user's score (number data type), an Internet address (string data type), a Sound object (object data type), and the on/off state of a radio button (Boolean data type). You can easily change the data type that a variable holds. A variable that was initialized with a number data type can be changed later in the movie to hold a string data type with a new `set variable` action. It's good practice to keep the data type of variables constant, however, so that when you manipulate them, you don't get unexpected results (trying to multiply a string by a string, for example). **Table 9.1** lists the data types that variables can hold.

Variable names should describe the information that they hold. The variable names `playerScore` and `spaceshipVelocity`, for example, are appropriate and will cause fewer headaches than something like `xyz` or `myVariable`. Use the same rules to name variables as you would to name movie clips, buttons, and other objects: Do not use special characters or spaces, and always begin your variable with a letter. The common practice is to use multiple words strung together to describe a variable, with every word capitalized except the first.

Table 9.1

Variable Data Types

Data Type	Description	Example
Number	A numeric value.	myScore = 24
String	A sequence of characters, numbers, or symbols. A string is always contained within quotation marks.	yourEmail = "johndoe@domain.com"
Boolean	A value of either true or false. The words are not enclosed in quotation marks. Alternatively, you can use 1 for true and 0 for false.	radioButton = true
Object	The name of an object that you create from a constructor function.	myColor = new Color(myMovie)
Null	A value representing no data.	A variable that hasn't yet been assigned a value or no longer contains a value.
Undefined	A value representing a variable that hasn't yet been assigned a value.	An empty input text field.

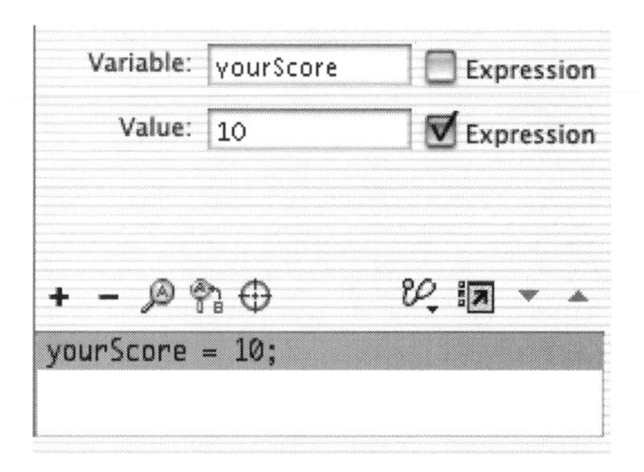

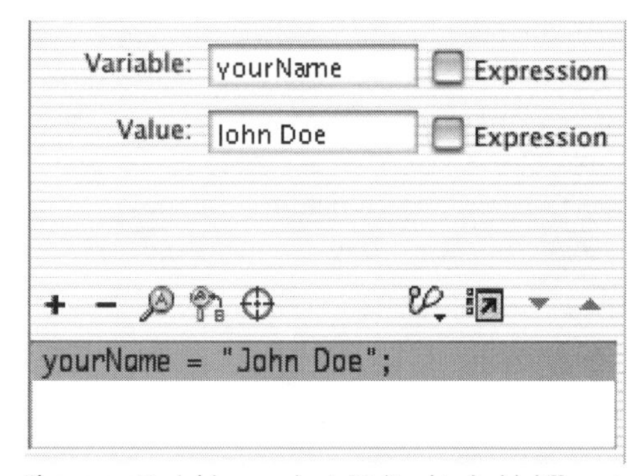

Figure 9.1 Variables can be initialized to hold different kinds of information. The Value Expression checkbox needs to be checked for a number (top). The Value Expression checkbox doesn't need to be checked for a string (bottom).

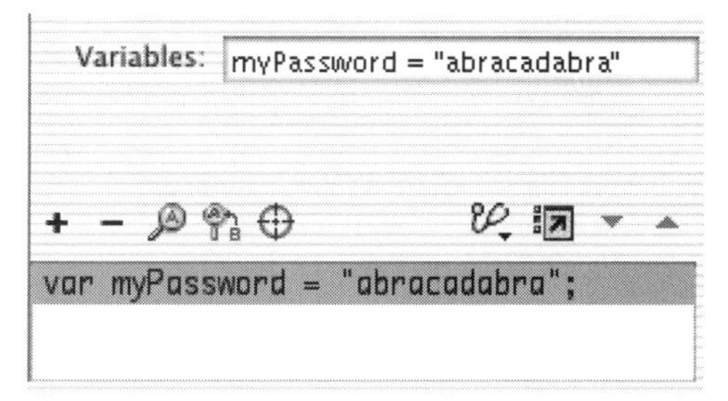

Figure 9.2 The keyword var identifies the word myPassword as a variable.

To initialize a variable:

1. Select the first frame of the root Timeline, and open the Actions panel.
2. Choose Actions >Variables > set variable (Esc + sv).
3. In the Variable field of the Actions panel, enter the name of your variable, and leave the Expression checkbox unchecked.
4. In the Value field, enter the information that the variable holds (a number, a new object, a string, or a Boolean value), leaving the Expression checkbox unchecked for a string data type (**Figure 9.1**).

✔ Tips

- You can also use the var action to initialize a variable. Choose Actions > Variables > var. In the Variable field, enter the name of your variable, an equal sign, and then a value (**Figure 9.2**). The var keyword signifies that the name that follows is a variable, which may make scripts easier to read. In addition, when you use var within a function, the variable is defined only for that function and expires at the end of the function call.
- You cannot use certain words for variable names because they are reserved for special functions or for use as keywords in ActionScript. You will just confuse Flash by trying to use them as variables. These words are `break`, `else`, `instanceof`, `typeof`, `case`, `for`, `new`, `var`, `continue`, `function`, `return`, `void`, `default`, `if`, `switch`, `while`, `delete`, `in`, `this`, and `with`.
- It's good practice to initialize your variables in the first frame of your Timeline. That way, you keep them all in the same place and can edit their initial values easily.

continues on next page

- When you assign a property to a variable, or assign a reference to another variable to a variable, Flash determines the value and puts it in your variable at that moment. If the property or the referenced variable subsequently changes, the value of your variable will not change unless you reassign it. For example:

  `xPosition = _xmouse`

  When you initialize the variable called `xPosition` in the first frame of your movie, it holds the *x* coordinate of the pointer. As you move the pointer around the screen, the property `_xmouse` changes, but the variable `xPosition` does not. The variable `xPosition` still holds the original *x* coordinate from when it was initialized. To have a variable updated continually, you must put it within an event handler that is triggered continuously (such as `onEnterFrame`) or within a function call of a `setInterval` action.

If you no longer need a variable, it's a good idea to delete it so you can free memory. To remove a variable, use the `delete` action.

To delete a variable:

1. In the Actions panel, choose Actions > Variables > delete.
2. In the Variable field, enter the name of the variable you want to remove.

   When this statement is executed, the variable is deleted.

Strings vs. expressions

When you use the action `set variable` to put information into a variable, you have the option of checking an Expression checkbox in the Parameters pane for the Variable and Value fields (**Figure 9.3**). Checking the Expression checkbox next to the Value field removes the quotation marks around the entry and makes it an expression rather than a string. An *expression* is a statement that may include variables, properties, and objects that must be resolved (figured out) before Flash can determine its value. Think of an expression as being an algebraic formula, like $a^2 + b^2$. The value of the expression has to be calculated before it can be assigned to the variable name (**Figure 9.4**).

Figure 9.3 The Variable and Value fields in the Parameters pane of `set variable` both have Expression options.

```
myVolume = myLength*myWidth;
dogYears = 7*Age;
downloadProgress = _root._framesloaded/_root._totalframes;
```

Figure 9.4 Some examples of expressions. The variable names are on the left side of the equal signs, and the expressions are on the right.

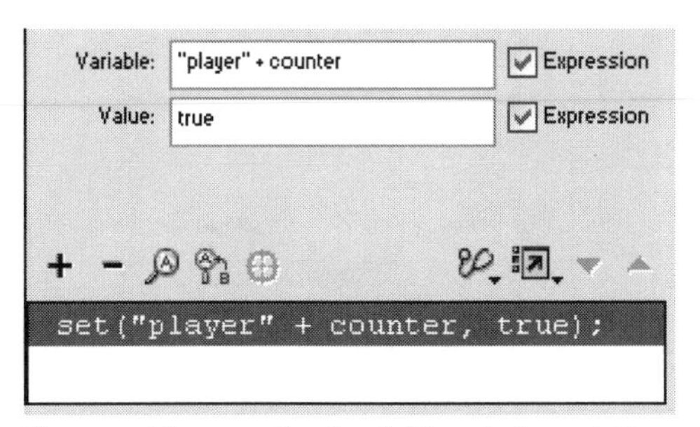

Figure 9.5 The `set` action (available only through the `set variable` action) lets you use an expression for a variable name.

A *string*, on the other hand, is a statement that Flash uses as is and considers simply to be a collection of characters. The string $a^2 + b^2$ is literally a sequence of seven characters (counting the spaces around the plus sign). When you initialize a variable with a string data type, you must leave the Expression checkbox unchecked. For all other data types, you must check the Expression checkbox.

Checking the Expression checkbox next to the Variable field changes the entire statement in the Actions list to the form `set (variable, value)`. This syntax lets you enter an expression for the variable. You could have variable names `player1`, `player2`, and `player3` created dynamically by using the expression `"player" + counter`, in which `counter` itself is a variable that contains a number (**Figure 9.5**). This method is a way of referencing variable names dynamically and is discussed later in this chapter.

✔ Tip

- If quotation marks always surround a string, how do you include quotation marks in the actual string? You use the backslash (\) character before including a quotation mark. This technique is called *escaping* a character. The string “`The line \"Call me Shane\" is from a 1953 movie Western"` produces the following result: The line “Call me Shane” is from a 1953 movie Western. **Table 9.2** lists a few common escape sequences for special characters.

Table 9.2

Common Escape Sequences

Sequence	Character
\b	Backspace
\r	Return
\t	Tab
\"	Quotation mark
\'	Single quotation mark
\\	Backslash

Using Variables and Expressions

Use variables and expressions as placeholders for parameters within your ActionScript. In virtually every action or method that requires you to enter a parameter, you can place a variable or an expression instead of a fixed value. The basic action `gotoAndStop`, for example, gives you the option to enter an expression instead of a frame number in the Frame field. This expression might be a variable called `myCard` that holds a number between 1 and 52. Frames 1 through 52 in the Timeline could contain graphics of the 52 playing cards, so changing the variable `myCard` in the `gotoAndStop` action would make Flash display different cards.

In the action `getURL`, the URL field can be an expression rather than a static Internet address. The expression might be a string concatenated with a variable such as `"http://"+yourWebSite`. Changing the variable called `yourWebSite` makes Flash load different URLs with the `getURL` action. Values for the properties of objects and target paths for objects can be replaced with expressions in the `setProperty` action (**Figure 9.6**).

Another way to use a variable is as a simple counter. Rather than taking the place of a parameter, a counter variable keeps track of the number of a certain kind of occurrence for later retrieval and testing. A player's score can be stored in a variable so that Flash knows when the player reaches enough points to win the game. Or a variable could keep track of a certain state. You can set the variable `myShield=true` if a character's force field is turned on, for example, and change the variable to `myShield=false` if the force field is turned off.

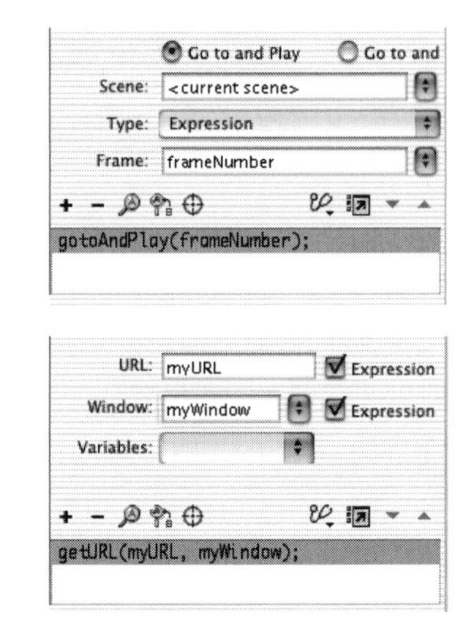

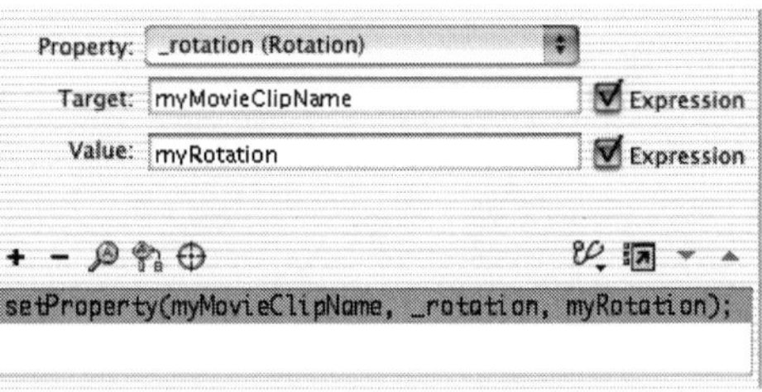

Figure 9.6 Examples of using variables and expressions in parameters fields of actions: the variable `frameNumber` in `gotoAndPlay` (top), the variables `myURL` and `myWindow` in `getURL` (middle), and the variables `myMovieClipName` and `myRotation` in `setProperty` (bottom).

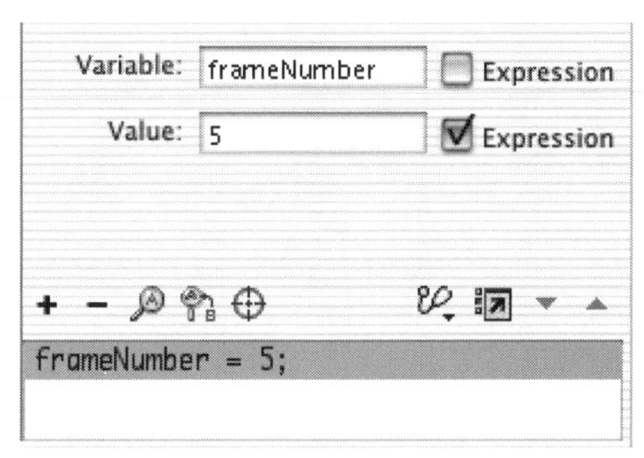

Figure 9.7 The variable `frameNumber` is initialized to 5.

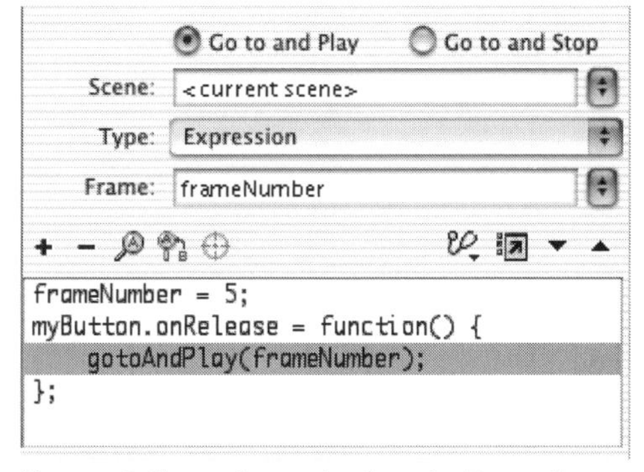

Figure 9.8 Choose Expression from the Type pull-down menu so you can put the variable `frameNumber` in the Frame field.

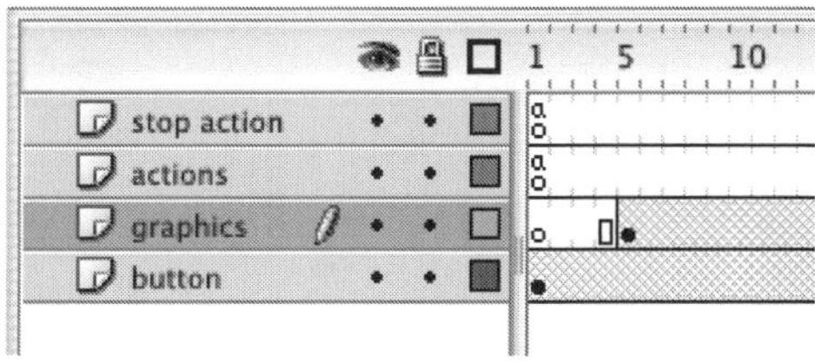

Figure 9.9 When the user clicks the button in the bottom layer, Flash goes to the value of `frameNumber`, which is 5.

To use a variable in a parameter field:

1. In the first keyframe of the root Timeline, choose Actions > Variables > set variable.
2. In the Variable field of the Actions panel, enter the name of your variable.
3. In the Value field, enter a number, and check the Expression checkbox (**Figure 9.7**).
4. Create a button symbol, drag an instance of it to the Stage, and give it a name in the Property Inspector.
5. Select the first frame of the root Timeline again, and open the Actions panel.
6. Assign an `onRelease` event handler to your button.
7. Choose Actions > Movie Control > goto.
8. In the Parameters pane, from the Type pull-down menu, choose Expression.
9. In the Frame field, enter the name of the variable you initialized in the root Timeline (**Figure 9.8**).
10. Provide additional frames so that the playhead has somewhere to go.
11. Test your movie (**Figure 9.9**).

    Your variable contains a number. When Flash performs the `gotoAndPlay` action, it uses the information contained in your variable as the frame to go to. If you change the value of your variable, Flash will go to a different frame.

✔ Tip

- If you want Flash to go to a frame label instead of a frame number, you must define a string data type for your variable. Assign the string `"Conclusion"` to the variable `myFrameLabel`, for example. By using `myFrameLabel` as the parameter in the `gotoAndPlay` action, you can have Flash go to the frame labeled Conclusion.

The scope of variables

When you initialize variables, they belong to the Timeline where you create them. This is known as the *scope* of a variable. Variables have their own scope, just as you learned in Chapter 4 that functions and event handlers have a scope. If you initialize a variable on the root Timeline, the variable is scoped to the root Timeline. If you initialize a variable inside a clip event handler, the variable is scoped to that movie clip.

Think of a variable's scope as being its home. Variables live on certain Timelines, and if you want to use the information inside a variable, first you must find it with a target path. This process is analogous to targeting movie clips and other objects. To access either a movie clip or a variable, you identify it with a target path. When you construct a target path for a variable, you can use the absolute term `_root` or the relative terms `this` and `_parent`.

In the following task, you will build a pull-down menu that loads a Web site, using the `getURL` action. The URL for the action is stored in a variable that is initialized and scoped to the main Timeline. Because the `getURL` action resides in a movie clip, the variable and the action that uses the variable have different scopes. Use a target path to identify the variable on the main Timeline from the movie clip's Timeline.

To target a variable with a different scope:

1. Create a movie clip of a pull-down menu, as demonstrated in Chapter 4.
2. Drag an instance of the movie clip from the library to the Stage (**Figure 9.10**), and give the instance a name in the Property Inspector.

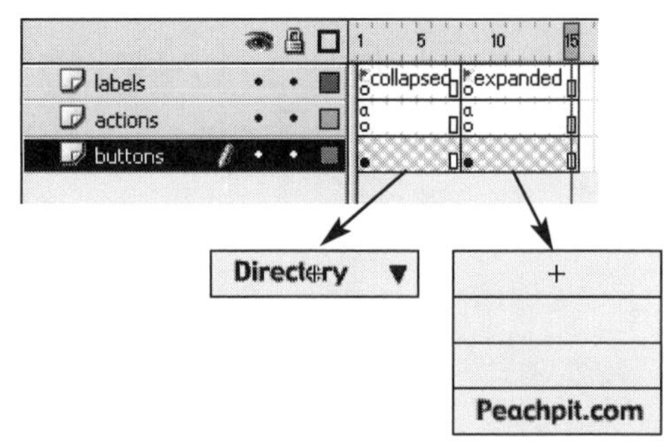

Figure 9.10 A movie clip of a pull-down menu has two states—collapsed and expanded—that toggle back and forth.

Figure 9.11 Initialize `myURL` by assigning the Peachpit Press Web site to it.

myURL scoped to root Timeline

initializeVariable

pulldownmenu

Scene 1

Peachpit.com

getURL action assigned to button inside movie clip targets _root.myURL

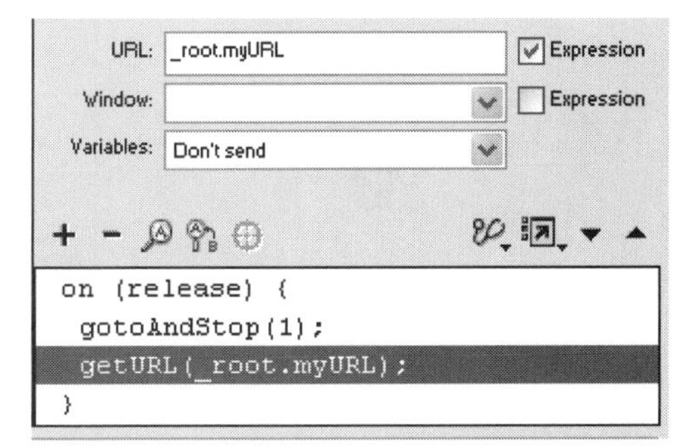

Figure 9.12 For the last button of the pull-down menu, assign `_root.myURL` to the URL field. Because this action is inside the movie clip of the pull-down menu, `_root` is necessary to target the variable `myURL` in the root Timeline.

3. Select the first frame of the root Timeline, and open the Actions panel.
4. Choose Actions > Variable > set variable.
5. In the Variable field, enter a name.
6. In the Value field, enter an Internet address.
7. Leave both Expression checkboxes unchecked (**Figure 9.11**).

   This variable is initialized in the root Timeline and holds a string data type.
8. Enter symbol-editing mode for your movie clip, and choose one of the buttons from the expanded pull-down menu.
9. Add to the `on(release)` event handler by choosing Actions >Browser/Network > getURL.
10. In the URL field, enter `_root`, followed by a dot and then the variable name you initialized in the root Timeline (**Figure 9.12**).
11. Check the Expression checkbox.
12. Test your movie.

    When you click your pull-down menu to expand it and then choose the button to which you assigned the `getURL` action, Flash retrieves the information stored in the variable on the root Timeline. If you had not specified the root Timeline in the URL field of the `getURL` action, Flash would look within the movie clip for that variable and would not be able to find it.

Global variables

If you want to have access to a variable no matter where you are, you can initialize a global variable. A global variable does not have a specific scope but is scoped to all Timelines. A global variable is like the Key or the Mouse object in that you can access it from any Timeline simply by referencing its name.

You can initialize a global variable by preceding it with the identifier `_global`. After the variable is initialized, you can read its contents from anywhere in your Flash movie with just the variable name. If you want to modify the contents of your global variable, use the `_global` identifier with the variable name, and assign new values.

To initialize a variable with a global scope:

1. Select the first frame of the main Timeline, and open the Actions panel.
2. Choose Actions > Variables > set variable.
3. Put your pointer in the Variable field, and choose Objects > Core > _global.
4. Enter a dot following the `_global` identifier; then enter a name for your variable.
5. In the Value field, enter a value for your variable (**Figure 9.13**).

   Your global variable is established. Although the variable is initialized in the root Timeline, you can access its contents of this variable from anywhere in your Flash movie without having to specify a target path (**Figure 9.14**).

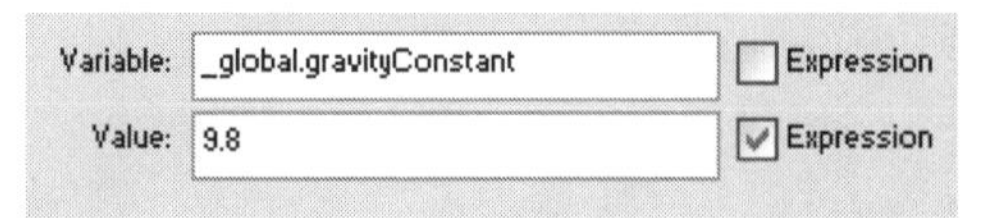

Figure 9.13 The global variable called `gravityConstant` contains the value 9.8. You can use this variable from any Timeline in the movie just by using its name, `gravityConstant`.

```
_global.gravityConstant = 9.8;

VFinal = _root.rocket.VInital +
          (gravityConstant * _root.myTime)
```

Figure 9.14 After a global variable is initialized (top), you can use it anywhere. Notice that in the example statement (bottom), which calculates the final velocity (`VFinal`) based on `gravityConstant` and two more variables (called `VInitial` and `myTime`), target paths are unnecessary for `gravityConstant`.

```
myRotation=45&mySize=150
```

Figure 9.15 Two variables and their values written in MIME format. In this example, the variables are saved in a text document called data.txt.

Loading External Variables

You don't actually have to initialize variables inside your movie. Flash lets you keep variables outside your Flash movie in a text document that you can load whenever you need the variables. This way, you can change the variables in the text document easily and thereby change the Flash movie without even having to edit the movie. Build a quiz, for example, with variables holding the questions and answers. Keep the variables in a text document, and when you want to change the quiz, simply edit the text document. You can also set up the variables in the text document to be generated automatically with server-side scripts based on other external data. Then your Flash movie can read the variables in the text document with only the most recent or user-customized values.

The external text document can contain as many variables as you want, but it needs to be in MIME format, which is a standard format that CGI scripts use. The variables are written in the following form:

```
variable1=value1&variable2=value2&variab
le3=value3
```

The variable/value pairs are separated by a single ampersand (&) symbol.

Variables can be loaded into either a specified level or a specified movie clip. In both cases, you must remember the variables' scope when you want to retrieve their values.

To load external variables:

1. Launch a simple text editor, and open a new document.

   On the Mac, SimpleText is a good application; in Windows, Notepad works well.

2. Write your variable names and their values in the standard MIME format (**Figure 9.15**).

continues on next page

3. Save your text document in the same directory where your Flash movie will be saved.

   It doesn't matter what you name your file, but it helps to keep the name simple and to stick to a standard three-letter extension.

4. In Flash, open a new document.

5. Select the first keyframe of the root Timeline, and open the Actions panel.

6. Choose Actions > Browser/Network > loadVariables (Esc + lv).

7. In the URL field, enter the path to your text file, and leave the Expression checkbox unchecked.

   Because your SWF file and the text file will be in the same directory, you can simply enter the text file's name.

8. From the Location pull-down menu, choose Level, and keep the 0 in the field (**Figure 9.16**).

   Flash loads the variables from your text file into level 0, or the root Timeline. Now your variables are available and scoped to `_root`.

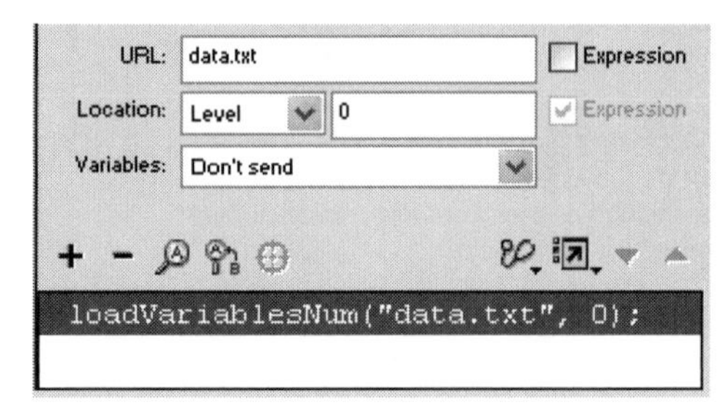

Figure 9.16 The `LoadVariablesNum` statement loads the variables from the data.txt file into level 0.

To test your loaded variables:

1. Continuing the preceding task, create a movie-clip symbol, drag an instance of it to the Stage, and give it a name in the Property Inspector.

2. Select the first frame of the main Timeline, and open the Actions panel.

3. Assign an `onRelease` event handler to your movie-clip instance.

4. Choose Actions > Movie Clip Control > setProperty.

5. Choose Rotation from the Property pull-down menu.

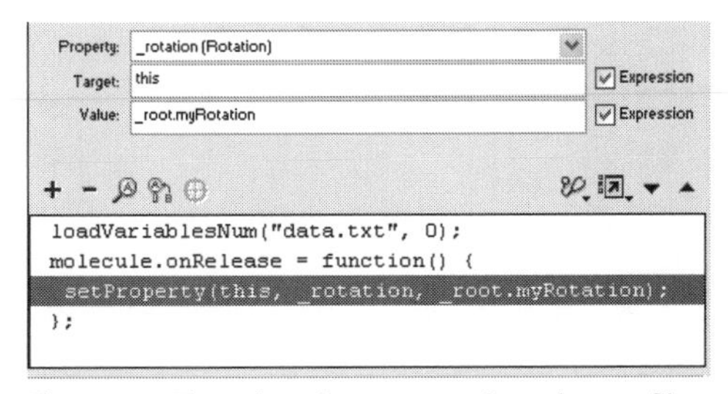

Figure 9.17 The value of `myRotation` from the text file is used to set the rotation property of the movie clip called molecule.

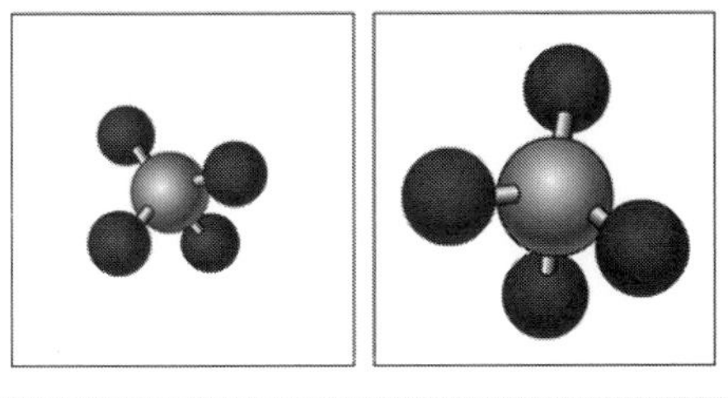

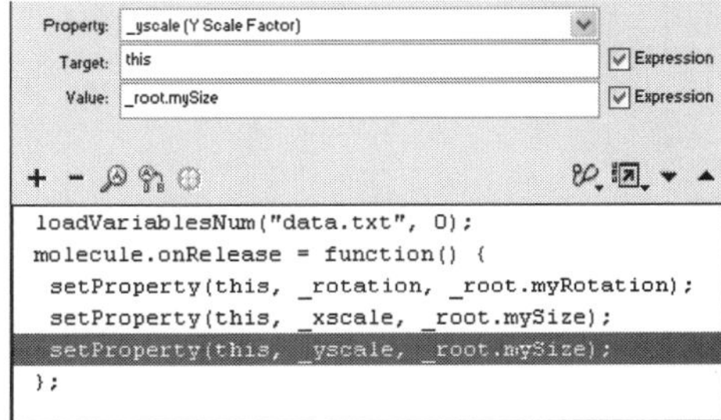

Figure 9.18 Two additional `setProperty` actions change the scale of the movie clip, using the `mySize` variable from the text file. The pictures at the top show the movie clip called molecule before the user clicks it (left) and after the user clicks it (right).

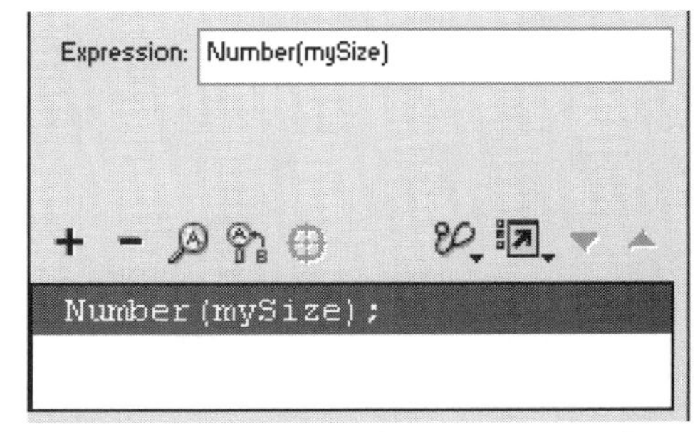

Figure 9.19 Use the Number function to convert the contents of a variable to a number data type. If the value of the variable called `mySize` is `"150"`, the Number function converts it to 150.

6. In the Target field of the Parameters pane, enter `this`.
7. In the Value field, enter the target path to the loaded variable.

   Because the variables are loaded into level 0, you need to enter `_root` or `_level0` before the variable name.
8. Check both Expression checkboxes (**Figure 9.17**).

   When you click your movie clip, Flash uses the externally loaded variable as the value of this movie clip's rotation.
9. Add another `setProperty` action to use the second loaded variable (**Figure 9.18**).
10. Export your movie as a SWF, and save it in the same directory as your text file.

✔ Tips

- The variables you specify in an external text file are loaded into Flash as strings, making quotation marks around string values unnecessary. Flash automatically converts strings to numbers for certain operations and actions. In the preceding example, Flash knows to use a number for the `_rotation`, `_xscale`, and `_yscale` properties. So the string values `"45"` and `"150"` are used as number values 45 and 150. If you want to tell Flash explicitly to use a number, you can apply the `Number` function. Choose Functions > Conversion Functions > Number, and enter your variable name for its parameter (**Figure 9.19**).
- Write your variable and value pairs in an external text file without any line breaks, spaces, or other punctuation except the ampersand. Although you may have a harder time reading the file, Flash will have an easier time understanding it.

The LoadVars object

When you want to have more control over the loading of external variables and other data, you can use the LoadVars object instead of the `loadVariables` action. The LoadVars object provides its own properties, methods, and events to handle and manage incoming (and outgoing) data. You can test how much of the external data has loaded with the method `getBytesLoaded()`, for example, or you can test the success or failure of a load with the event `onLoad`.

Using the LoadVars object requires that you first create an instance with a constructor function. After the instance is instantiated, use the `load()` method to bring external variables from a text file into the object. As is the case with the `loadVariables` action, the variables must be in MIME format.

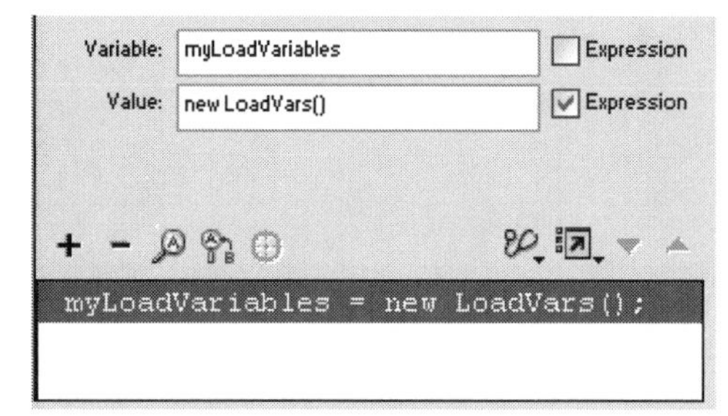

Figure 9.20 The new instance called `myLoadVariables` is created from the LoadVars object.

To load external variables with the LoadVars object:

1. Create a text document containing the names of variables and their values in MIME format, just as you did in the preceding section.
2. In a new Flash document, select the first frame of the main Timeline, and open the Actions panel.
3. Choose Actions > Variables > set variable.
4. In the Variable field, enter a name for your LoadVars object.
5. With the mouse pointer in the Value field, choose Objects > Client/Server > LoadVars > new LoadVars. Check the Expression box (**Figure 9.20**).

   An instance of the LoadVars object is created.
6. Choose Objects > Client/Server > LoadVars > Methods > load.

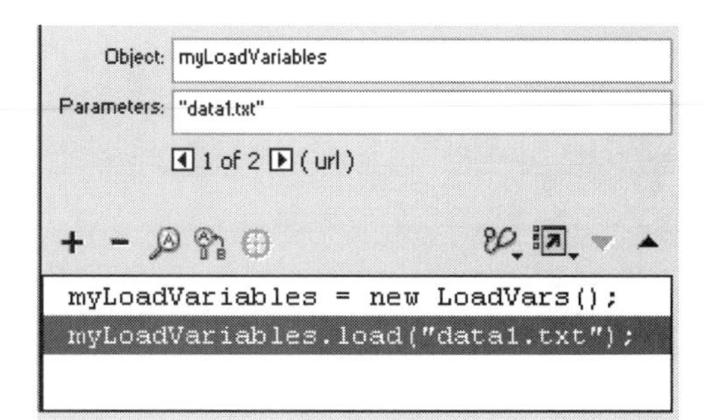

Figure 9.21 The `load()` method loads the data.txt file from the same directory as the Flash movie and puts the variables in the `myLoadVariables` object.

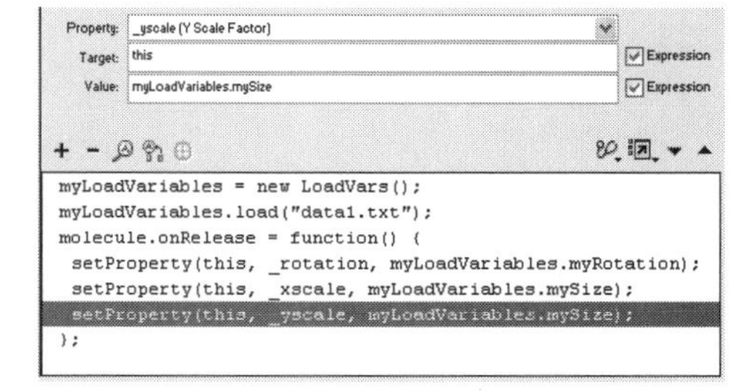

Figure 9.22 The variables in the `myLoadVariables` object change the rotation and scale of the movie clip called molecule.

7. In the Object field, enter the name of your LoadVars object.
8. In the Parameters field, enter the path to the text file that contains your variables.

   If your SWF file and the text file will reside in the same directory, you can enter just the text file's name. Enclose the path or file name in quotation marks (**Figure 9.21**).

   Flash calls the `load()` method, which loads the variable and value pairs from the external text file into the LoadVars object.
9. Use the loaded external variables within your Flash movie.

   The variables are scoped to the LoadVars object, so you must remember to include that object in your target path (**Figure 9.22**).

After you call the `load()` method for your LoadVars object, you can check and respond to the success or failure of the load. Use the `onLoad` event handler for this purpose. In this handler, you specify a parameter—the word `success` or `fail`—that determines whether the handler responds to a successful load or a failed load. One example:

```
myLoadVars.onLoad = function(success) {
   trace("data loaded okay!");
};
```

Another example:

```
myLoadVars.onLoad = function(fail) {
   trace("data failed to load!");
};
```

To detect the completion of loaded data:

1. Continuing with the file you used in the preceding task, select the first frame of the main Timeline, and open the Actions panel.
2. Select the `load()` method.
3. Choose Objects > Client/Server > LoadVars > Events > onLoad.

   Your `onLoad` event handler appears after the `load()` call.
4. In the Object field, enter the name of your LoadVars object.
5. Keep the Parameters field as it is, with the word `success` in it (**Figure 9.23**).

   This event handler is triggered when an attempt to load data occurs and is successful. If you want to detect a failed load, enter `fail` in the Parameters field.
6. Choose actions to be performed when the `load()` call is successful.

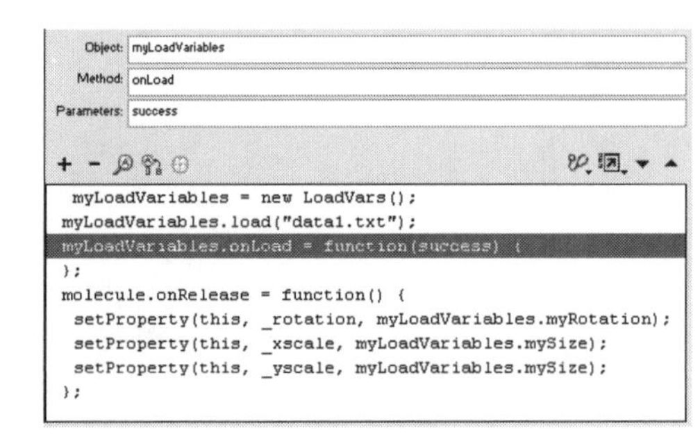

Figure 9.23 The `onLoad` event handler for the myLoadVariables object will be triggered when the `load()` method succeeds. Nothing is written inside the event handler yet.

Loading variables from HTML tags

Via the `loadVariables` action and the LoadVars object, you can load variables from external text files in MIME format into your movie. But you can also access variables that are placed in the HTML page accompanying your SWF file. Those variables are integrated with the `<OBJECT>` and `<EMBED>` tags and are loaded into the SWF automatically. By putting variables in the HTML, you eliminate the need to use a `loadVariables` action or the LoadVars object.

To load variables from the HTML <OBJECT> and <EMBED> tags:

1. Open the HTML document that gets created with your SWF file when you publish your movie.
2. Find the <OBJECT> tag, which should be followed by a series of <PARAM NAME VALUE> tags that tell the browser how to display the movie.
3. Insert your variables as follows:

   `<PARAM NAME=FlashVars VALUE= "myRotation=45&mySize=150">`

   `FlashVars` is the name of the parameter, and the value is a string of variable names/value pairs in MIME format.
4. Find the <EMBED> tag, which should be followed by a series of parameters that tell the browser how to display the movie.
5. Insert your variables as follows:

   `FlashVars="myRotation=45&mySize=150"`

   Inserting the `FlashVars` parameter into both the <OBJECT> and <EMBED> tags is required for cross-browser compatibility (**Figure 9.24**).
6. Save the modified HTML document, and open it in a browser.

   The HTML page provides the variables to its SWF file; no action within the SWF file is necessary to load them. The variables are scoped to the `_root` Timeline.

```
<OBJECT classid="clsid:D27CDB6E-AE6D-11cf-96B8-444553540000"
 codebase="http://download.macromedia.com/pub/shockwave/cabs/flash/swflas
 WIDTH="550" HEIGHT="400" id="myMovie" ALIGN="">
      <PARAM NAME=movie VALUE="myMovie.swf">
      <PARAM NAME=FlashVars VALUE="myRotationVariable=45">
      <PARAM NAME=quality VALUE=high>
      <PARAM NAME=bgcolor VALUE=#FFFFFF>
<EMBED src="myMovie.swf"
      quality=high bgcolor=#FFFFFF
      FlashVars="myRotationProperty=45"
      WIDTH="550"
      HEIGHT="400"
      NAME="myMovie"
      ALIGN=""
      TYPE="application/x-shockwave-flash"
      PLUGINSPAGE="http://www.macromedia.com/go/getflashplayer">
</EMBED>
</OBJECT>
```

Figure 9.24 A portion of the HTML page shows where the `FlashVars` parameters are inserted.

Storing and Sharing Information

Although variables enable you to keep track of information, they do so only within a single playing of a Flash movie. When your viewer quits the movie, all the information in variables is lost. When the viewer returns to the movie, the variables are again initialized to their starting values with `set variable` commands or are loaded from external sources.

You can have Flash remember the current values of your variables even after a viewer quits the movie, however. The solution is to use SharedObjects. SharedObjects save information on a viewer's computer, much as browsers save information in cookies. When a viewer returns to a movie that has saved a SharedObject, that object can be loaded back in, and the variables from the previous visit can be used.

You can use SharedObjects in a variety of ways to make your Flash site much more convenient for repeat visitors. You can store visitors' high scores in a game, or you can store their login names so that they don't have to type them again. Perhaps you have created a complex puzzle game, so you could store the positions of the pieces; for a long animated story, you could store the user's current location.

Using SharedObjects requires you to put information that you want to keep in the `data` property of a named SharedObject. The statement `mySharedObject.data.highscore=200` would store the high-score information in the mySharedObject object. The method `getLocal()` creates or retrieves a SharedObject, and the method `flush()` stores the `data` properties. In the following example, the *x* and *y* positions of a draggable movie clip are saved and can be retrieved when the viewer returns to the movie later.

```
myMC.onPress = function() {
  startDrag(this);
};
myMC.onRelease = function() {
  stopDrag();
};
```

Figure 9.25 This code in the main Timeline makes the movie clip called myMC a draggable one.

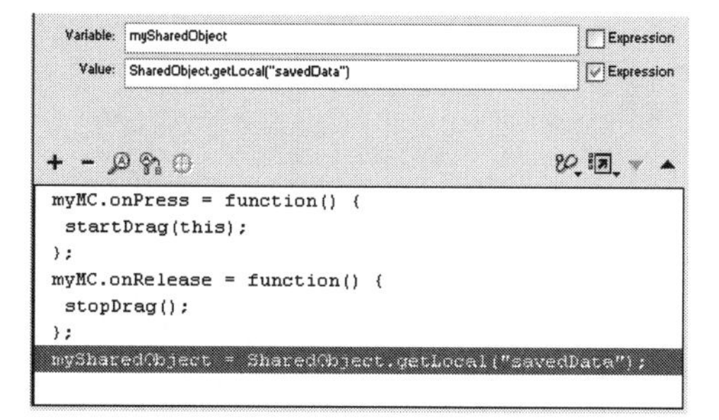

Figure 9.26 The `getLocal()` method creates the SharedObject called savedData.

To store information on a user's computer:

1. Create a movie clip, place an instance of it on the Stage, and give it a name in the Property Inspector.
2. Select the first frame of the main Timeline, and open the Actions panel.
3. Assign a `startDrag()` action to the movie clip's `onPress` handler and a `stopDrag()` action to its `onRelease` handler to create a draggable movie clip (**Figure 9.25**).

   Review Chapter 7 for more information about draggable movie clips.
4. Select the ending curly brace of the `onRelease` event handler.

   Your next ActionScript statement will appear after the event handlers.
5. Choose Actions > Variables > set variable.
6. In the Variable field, enter `mySharedObject` as the name of your SharedObject.
7. In the Value field, enter `SharedObject.getLocal("savedData")`, and check the Expression checkbox (**Figure 9.26**).

   Flash creates a SharedObject called savedData. You can reference this object with the name you entered in the Variable field (mySharedObject). If the SharedObject already exists from a previous visit, Flash retrieves the object instead of creating one.
8. Create a button, place an instance of it on the Stage, and give it a name in the Property Inspector.

   You will assign actions to this button to save the position of your draggable movie clip in your SharedObject.
9. Select the main Timeline, and in the Actions panel, assign an `onRelease` handler to your button.

continues on next page

10. Choose Actions > Variables > set variable.

11. In the Variable field, enter `mySharedObject.data.myMCX`.

12. In the Value field, enter the name of your draggable movie clip, followed by a dot and then the _x property. Check the Expression box (**Figure 9.27**).

    The *x* position of your draggable movie clip is assigned to the `myMCX` property of the data property of your SharedObject. The name `myMCX` is a property name that you make up.

13. Repeat steps 10 through 12 to assign the *y* position of your draggable movie clip to `mySharedObject.data.myMCY`.

14. Choose Actions > Miscellaneous Actions > evaluate.

15. In the Expression field, enter `mySharedObject.flush()`(**Figure 9.28**).

    Calling the `flush()` method saves all the information in the data property of your SharedObject on the viewer's computer.

✔ Tips

- If the `flush()` method is not called explicitly, the information in the data property of your SharedObject will be saved automatically when the viewer quits the movie. The `flush()` method enables you to choose when to save information.

- Many kinds of information can be stored in the data property of a SharedObject, such as numbers, strings, and even objects such as an array. Just remember to assign the information to a property of the data property of a SharedObject, as in `mySharedObject.data.name="Russell"` rather than `mySharedObject.data="Russell"`.

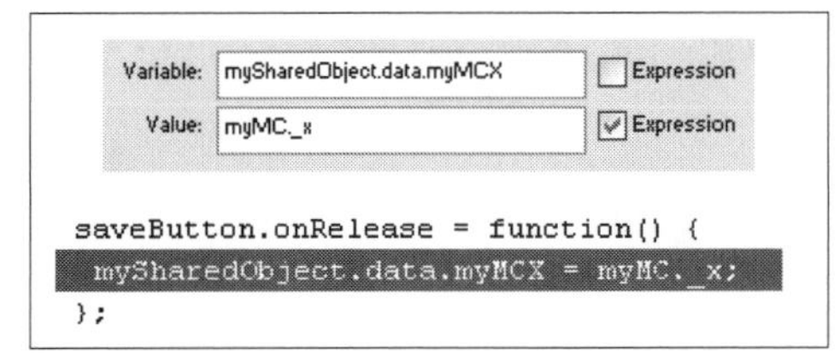


```
saveButton.onRelease = function() {
  mySharedObject.data.myMCX = myMC._x;
};
```

Figure 9.27 To save information, assign it to a property of the `data` property of your SharedObject. Here, the draggable movie clip's x position is saved in `mySharedObject.data.myMCX`.

```
saveButton.onRelease = function() {
  mySharedObject.data.myMCX = myMC._x;
  mySharedObject.data.myMCY = myMC._y;
  mySharedObject.flush();
};
```

Figure 9.28 This portion of the code in the main Timeline shows the `onRelease` handler for the button called saveButton. When a viewer clicks this button, the current *x* and *y* positions of the draggable movie clip are put into the SharedObject and saved on the user's computer.

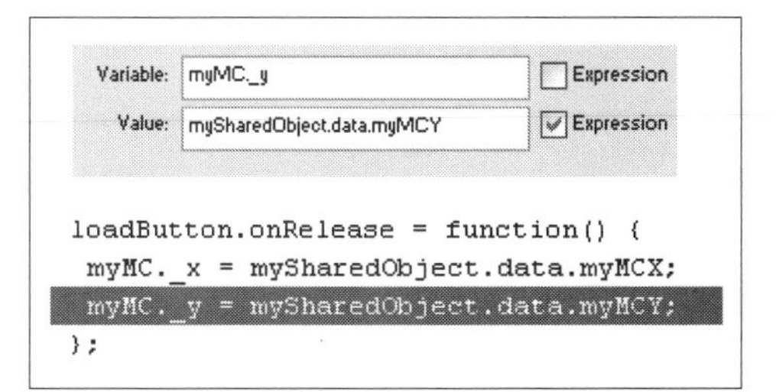

Figure 9.29 This portion of the code in the main Timeline shows the `onRelease` handler for the button called loadButton. When a viewer clicks this button, the draggable movie clip's *x* and *y* positions are set to the values in the SharedObject.

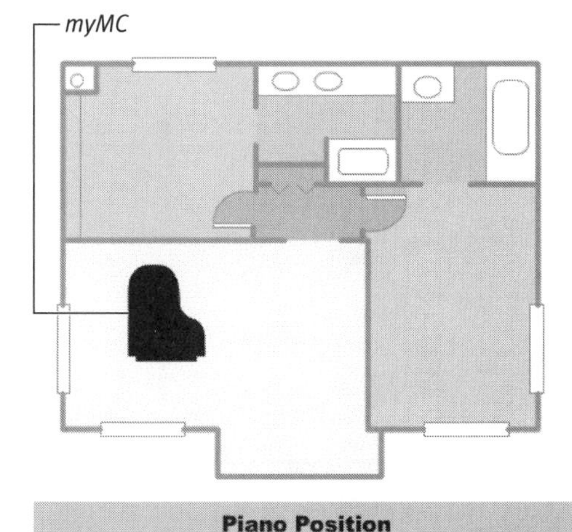

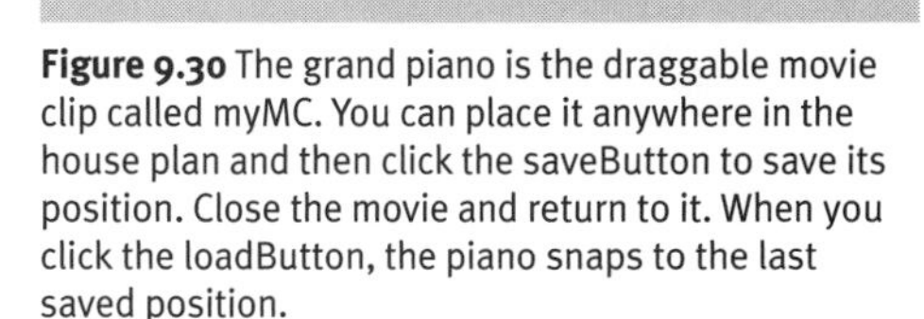

Figure 9.30 The grand piano is the draggable movie clip called myMC. You can place it anywhere in the house plan and then click the saveButton to save its position. Close the movie and return to it. When you click the loadButton, the piano snaps to the last saved position.

To retrieve information from a user's computer:

1. Continuing with the file you used in the preceding task, create a second button, place an instance of it on the Stage, and give it a name in the Property Inspector.

   You will assign actions to this second button, which will retrieve `mySharedObject.data` and move your draggable movie clip to the position where you last saved it.

2. Select the main Timeline, and in the Actions panel, assign an `onRelease` handler to this second button.

3. Choosing two `set variable` actions, assign the `myMCX` and `myMCY` properties of `mySharedObject.data` to the movie clip (**Figure 9.29**).

   The two statements are:

   ```
   myMC._x = mySharedObject.data.myMCX;
   myMC._y = mySharedObject.data.myMCY;
   ```

   These statements retrieve the `myMCX` and `myMCY` values from the viewer's computer and move the draggable movie clip called myMC.

4. Test your movie.

   Drag the movie clip to any position on the Stage, click the first button to save its position, quit the test movie, and test it again. When you click the second button to retrieve the saved information, your movie clip moves to the position where you saved it (**Figure 9.30**).

To clear information on a user's computer:

- Use the keyword `Null` or `Undefined` to clear information that you've saved in a SharedObject.

  Consider the following statements:

  ```
  mySharedObject.data.myMCX=Null
  mySharedObject.data.myMCY=Null
  ```

  These statements remove the `myMCX` and `myMCY` properties.

SharedObjects, Permission, and Local Disk Space

The default amount of information that Flash Player allows you to store on a viewer's computer is set at 100 KB. If you create a SharedObject that exceeds this amount, a dialog box appears over the Stage, asking permission from the viewer (**Figure 9.31**). Viewers can allow the request or deny it. If they deny the request, the SharedObject is not saved, and the method `flush()` returns a value of `false`. If users allow the request, the SharedObject is saved, and the method `flush()` returns `true`. When the dialog box is open, the method `flush()` returns the string `"pending"`.

Figure 9.31 Flash asks to store more information than the viewer currently allows. This request comes from `local`, which is your own computer.

Viewers can change their local storage settings at any time by right-clicking (Windows) or Ctrl-clicking (Mac) the movie and then choosing Settings from the contextual menu (**Figure 9.32**). They can choose never to accept information from a particular domain or to accept varying amounts (10 KB, 100 KB, 1 MB, 10 MB, or unlimited). Local storage permission is specific to the domain (which appears in the dialog box), so future movies from the same domain can save SharedObjects according to the same settings.

Figure 9.32 From the Flash Player menu (top), access the Settings dialog box. You can decide how much information a particular domain can save on your computer. This setting is for local, which is your own computer.

If you know that the information you save to a viewer's computer will grow, you can allow more space initially by defining a minimum disk space for the `flush()` method. Calling the method `mySharedObject.flush(1000000)` saves the SharedObject and reserves 1,000,000 bytes (1 MB) for the information. If Flash asks the viewer to allow disk space for the SharedObject, it will ask for 1 MB. After the permission is given, Flash won't ask for more space until the SharedObject exceeds 1 MB or the viewer changes his or her local storage settings.

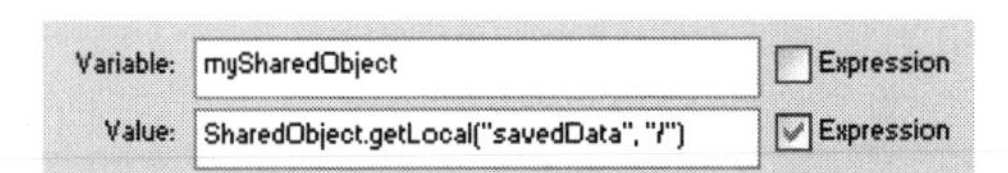

Figure 9.33 The second parameter of the `getLocal()` method determines the local path of the SharedObject and its location on the viewer's computer. The single slash indicates the top-level directory of the domain where the Flash movie resides.

Flash keeps track of a SharedObject that is saved on the viewer's computer by remembering the name of the object as well as the location of the movie that created it. The location of the movie is known as its *local path*. By default, the local path is the relative path from the domain name to the file name. So if your movie is at www.myDomain.com/flash/myMovie.swf, its local path is `"/flash/myMovie.swf"`. Flash lets you specify a different local path when you use the `getLocal()` method so that you can store a SharedObject in a different place. If you have multiple movies, you can define a SharedObject with the same name and a common local path, allowing all the movies to access the same SharedObject and share its information.

Valid local paths for a SharedObject include all the directories in which your movie sits. Do not include the domain name, and do not specify any other directories in the domain. Remember, you are not telling Flash to store information on the server; you are telling Flash to store information locally on the viewer's computer (the host), and the local path helps Flash keep track of the SharedObject. Because local paths are relative to a single domain, a SharedObject can be shared only with multiple movies in the same domain.

To store information that multiple movies can share:

1. Continuing with the file that you created in the preceding task, in the Actions panel, select the `getLocal()` method.
2. Within the parentheses of the `getLocal()` method, add a second parameter.
3. After the SharedObject name, enter a comma; then enter `"/"` for the local path (**Figure 9.33**).

continues on next page

Flash will save the SharedObject called mySharedObject with the local path "/". This entry represents the top-level directory.

4. In a new Flash document, create a movie clip, put an instance on the Stage, and give it a name in the Property Inspector.

   This movie clip will move to a new position determined by the SharedObject you created in your first movie.

5. Select the first frame of the main Timeline, and open the Actions panel.

6. Choose Actions > Variables > set variable.

7. In the Variable field, enter `mySharedObject`.

8. In the Value field, enter `SharedObject.getLocal("savedData", "/")`.

   Flash retrieves the SharedObject called "`savedData`" with the local path "`/`" from the viewer's computer.

9. Choose two more `set variable` actions, and assign the properties in the data property of the SharedObject to the movie clip (**Figure 9.34**).

   The two statements are:

```
anotherMC._x =mySharedObject.data.myMCX;
anotherMC._y =mySharedObject.data.myMCY;
```

   These statements retrieve the `myMCX` and `myMCY` values from the SharedObject and reposition the movie clip called anotherMC.

10. Test your movies.

    Play the first movie, drag your movie clip around the Stage, click the first button to save its position in a SharedObject, and close the movie. Now open your second movie. Flash reads the information in the SharedObject created by the first movie and positions its movie clip in the same place as the first (**Figure 9.35**).

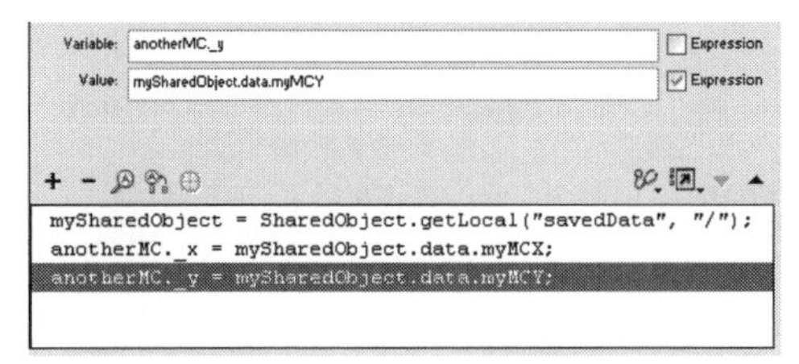

Figure 9.34 In this second Flash movie, the `getLocal()` method retrieves the same SharedObject that was saved in the first Flash movie. (The `getLocal()` method uses the same name and local path in its parameters.) The *x* and *y* positions of the movie clip called anotherMC are set to the values in the SharedObject.

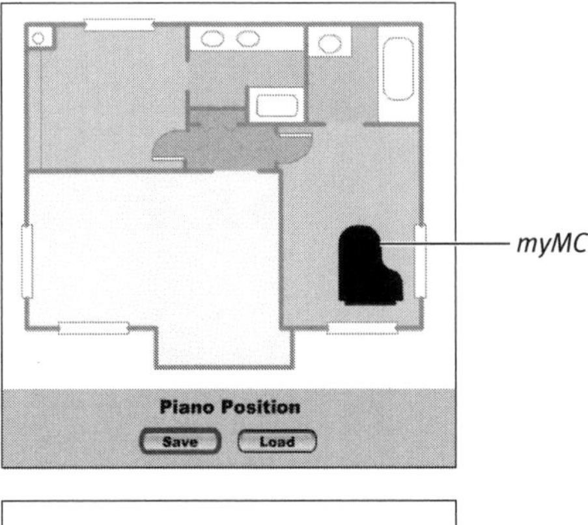

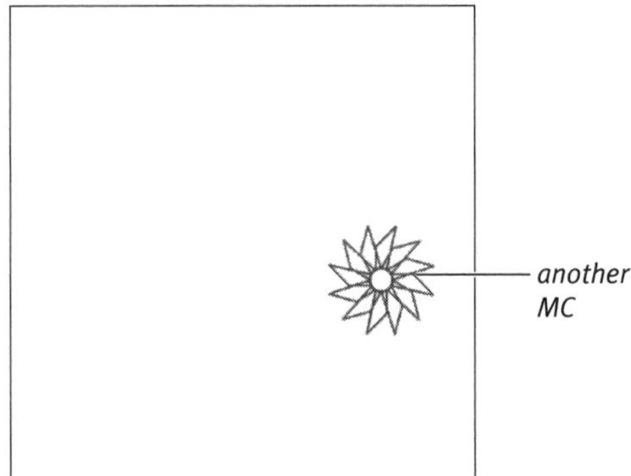

Figure 9.35 When the position of the piano in the first Flash movie (top) is saved, you can open the second Flash movie (bottom), and its movie clip snaps to the position of the piano. Both movies use the same SharedObject.

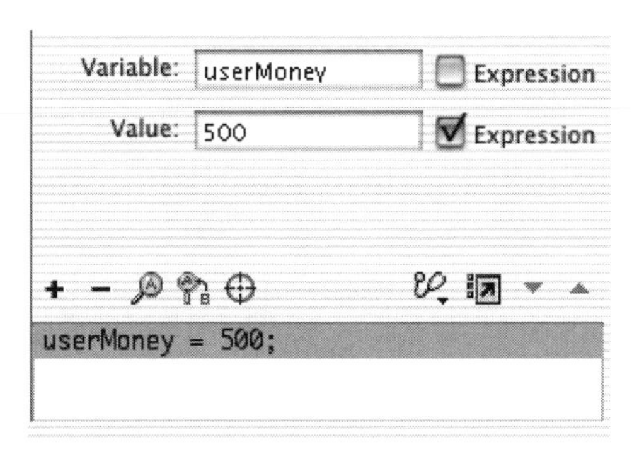

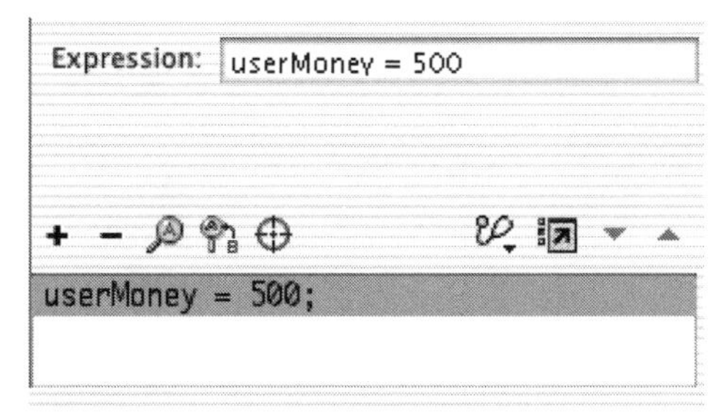

Figure 9.36 The `set variable` action (top) and the `evaluate` action (bottom) create equivalent scripts. In the `evaluate` action, you must enter your own assignment operator.

Table 9.3

Common Operators

Symbol	Description
+	Addition
-	Subtraction
*	Multiplication
/	Division
%	Modulo; calculates the remainder of the first number divided by the second number. 7%2 results in 1.
++	Increases the value by one increment. x ++ is equivalent to x = x + 1.
--	Decreases the value by one increment. x -- is equivalent to x = x - 1.
+=	Adds a value and assigns it to the variable. x += 5 is equivalent to x = x + 5.
-=	Subtracts a value and assigns it to the variable. x -= 5 is equivalent to x = x - 5.
*=	Multiplies by a value and assigns it to the variable. x *= 5 is equivalent to x = x * 5.
/=	Divides by a value and assigns it to the variable. x /= 5 is equivalent to x = x / 5.

Modifying Variables

Variables are useful because you can always change their contents with updated information about the status of the movie or your viewer. Sometimes, this change involves assigning a new value to the variable. At other times, the change means adding, subtracting, multiplying, or dividing the variable's numeric values, or modifying a string by adding characters. The variable `myScore`, for example, could be initialized at 0. Then, for every goal a player makes, the `myScore` variable changes in increments of 1. The job of modifying information contained in variables falls upon *operators*—symbols that "operate" on data.

Assignment and arithmetic operators

The assignment operator (=) is a single equal sign that assigns a value to a variable. You've already used this operator in the action `set variable`, which automatically puts the assignment operator between the entries of the Variable field and the Value field. You can also use the `evaluate` action, which gives you an empty Expression field in the Parameters pane. In that field, you enter your variable name and a value, with the assignment operator between the two entries (**Figure 9.36**). **Table 9.3** lists the other common operators.

Operators are the workhorses of Flash interactivity. You will use them often to perform calculations behind the scenes—adding the value of one variable to another, or changing the property of one object by adding or subtracting the value of a variable, for example. The following task is a simple example of how you can use operators to modify a variable that affects the graphics in a movie. You will create a button that increases the value of a variable each time the button is clicked. That variable is used to set the rotation of a movie clip.

To change incrementally a variable that affects a movie-clip property:

1. Create a movie clip, place an instance of it on the Stage, and give it a name in the Property Inspector.
2. In the first keyframe of the root Timeline, initialize a variable called `myRotation` to 0.
3. Create a button symbol, and place an instance of it on the Stage.
4. Select the button, and in the Actions panel, choose Actions > Movie Control > on. Next, choose Actions > Miscellaneous Actions > evaluate.
5. In the Expression field, enter `myRotation += 10` (**Figure 9.37**).

   The statement adds 10 to the current value and reassigns the sum to the variable called `myRotation`.
6. Select the movie clip, and in the Actions panel, choose Actions > Movie Clip Control > onClipEvent.
7. Select the `EnterFrame` event in the Parameters pane.
8. Choose Actions > Movie Clip Control > setProperty.
9. From the Property pull-down menu, choose Rotation.
10. In the Target field, enter `this`.
11. In the Value field, enter `_root.myRotation`.
12. Check both Expression checkboxes (**Figure 9.38**).

    The `enterFrame` event handler makes the `setProperty` action run continuously. This code assigns the rotation of the movie clip to the value of the `myRotation` variable, which the user can increase by clicking the button.

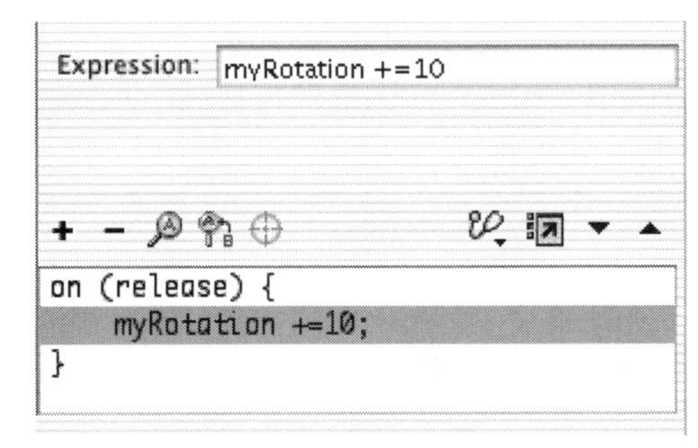

Figure 9.37 Each time the button is clicked, its actions increase the `myRotation` variable by 10.

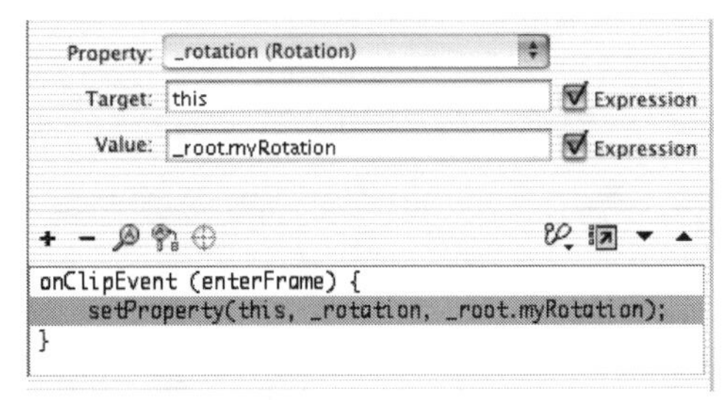

Figure 9.38 The rotation of the current movie clip is updated continually to the value of the `myRotation` variable in the root Timeline.

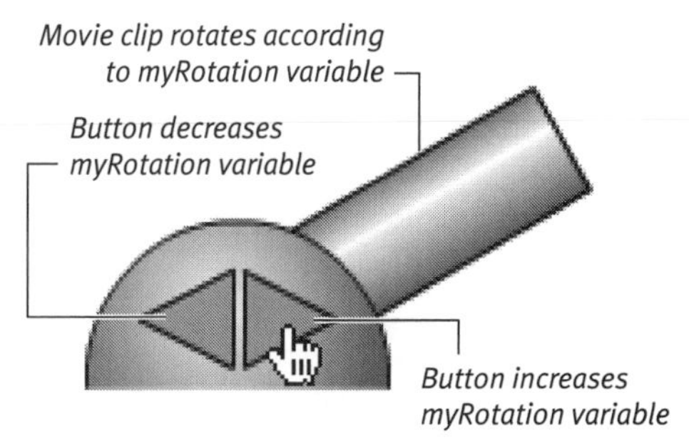

Figure 9.39 The turret of this cannon is the movie clip whose rotation property changes according to the `myRotation` variable.

13. Place another instance of the button on the Stage.

14. Assign a decrement assignment `operator` (-=) to the rotation variable to have it decrease its value each time the button is clicked.

    This code will control the rotation of the movie clip in the opposite direction (**Figure 9.39**).

✔ Tips

- To perform more-complicated mathematical calculations (such as square root, sine, and cosine) or string manipulations on your variables and values, you must use the Math object or the String object. You'll learn about these objects in Chapters 10 and 11.
- The same arithmetic rules of associativity (remember them from math class?) apply when Flash evaluates expressions, which means that certain operators take precedence over others. The most important rule is that multiplication and division will be performed before addition and subtraction. 3 + 4 * 2, for example, gives a very different result from 3 * 4 + 2.
- Use parentheses to group variables and operators so that they are calculated before other parts of the expression are evaluated. (3+2)*4 will return a value of 20, but without the parentheses, 3+2*4 will return a value of 11.
- Use the modulo operator (%) to check whether a variable is an even or an odd number. The statement `myNumber%2` returns 0 if `myNumber` is even or 1 if `myNumber` is odd. Use this logic to create toggling functionality. You can count the number of times a viewer clicks a light switch, for example. If the count is even, you could turn the light on; if the count is odd, you could turn the light off.

Concatenating Variables and Dynamic Referencing

The addition operator (+) adds the values of numeric data types. But it can also put together string data types. The expression "Hello" + "world", for example, results in the string "Hello world". This kind of operation is called *concatenation*. You can even mix strings, numbers, and variables to create expressions that create new objects or variables dynamically. For example, a common practice for naming duplicate movie-clip instances is to concatenate a variable with the name of the original movie clip. The variable is simply a counter that increases by 1 each time a duplicate is made. If the movie-clip name is mushroom, and the variable name is counter, you can concatenate a new name with the following expression:

```
"mushroom" + counter
```

The result will be something like mushroom1 or mushroom2, depending on the value of counter. The new names of the duplicated movie clips are assigned dynamically with a concatenated expression (**Figure 9.40**).

This kind of concatenation to reference an object dynamically works because it happens within a parameter field with its Expression checkbox checked. Flash knows to treat the contents of that field as an expression. What happens if you don't have the option of checking an Expression checkbox? Consider this statement in the Script pane of the Actions panel:

```
"myVariable" + counter = 5
```

This statement doesn't make sense to Flash and causes an error. You must instruct Flash to resolve the left side first and then treat it as a variable before you can assign a value to it. The way to do that is to use the array access operators.

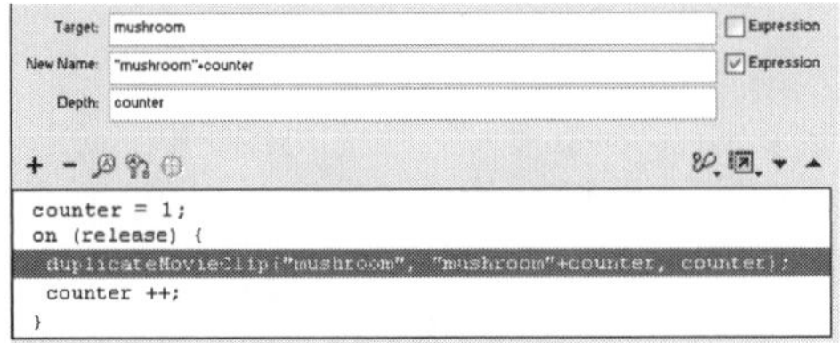

Figure 9.40 The duplicateMovieClip action makes a copy of the movie clip called mushroom. The name of the copy is assigned dynamically, based on the concatenation of "mushroom" and the value of the variable called counter. The first click creates a movie clip called mushroom1, the second click creates mushroom2, and so on. This dynamic assignment is possible because of the checked Expression checkbox next to the New Name field in the Parameters pane.

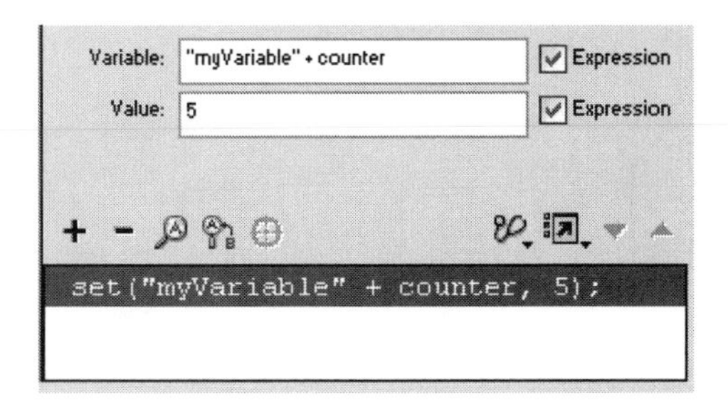

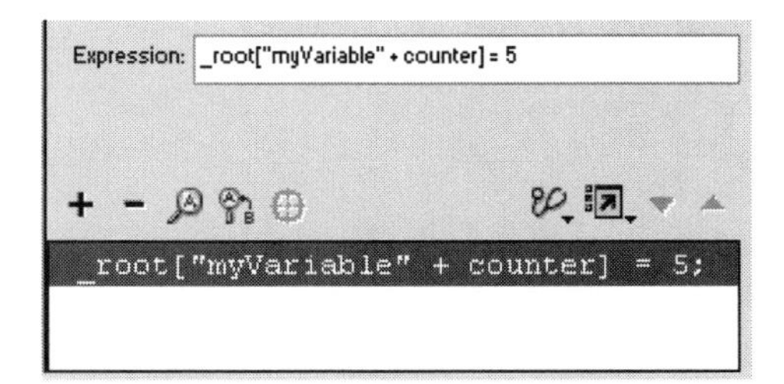

Figure 9.41 Dynamic referencing of variables with the Expression checkboxes checked in `set variable` (top) and with the array access operators (bottom). If `counter` = 1, the result of both assignments will be to initialize a variable called `myVariable1` to the value 5.

Array access operators

When you want to reference a variable or an object dynamically, and you are not given an option to check an Expression checkbox, use the array access operators. The array access operators are the square brackets (located on the same keys as the curly braces). They get their name because they usually are used to access the contents of an Array object, but they are just as useful for accessing the contents of other objects.

What does this capability mean? Think of the main Timeline as being a `_root` or a `_level0` movie-clip object; variables and objects sitting in the main Timeline are its contents. So a variable called `myVariable` initialized in the main Timeline can be targeted with the array access operators as follows:

```
_root[myVariable]
```

Notice that there is no dot between the object (`_root`) and the square brackets. The array access operators automatically resolve concatenated expressions within the square brackets. So, the statement

```
_root["myVariable" + counter] = 5
```

is equivalent to a statement you can create with `set variable`, and checking the Expression checkbox next to the Variable field (**Figure 9.41**).

Using the array access operators also enables you to call methods and change the properties of dynamically referenced objects with dot syntax. If you want to modify an object's transparency, for example, you can do so this way:

```
_root["mushroom" + counter]._alpha = 50
```

Depending on the value of `counter`, a particular movie clip in the root Timeline will become 50 percent transparent. If you want to make a movie clip play, you can call its method like this:

```
_root["myClip" + counter].play()
```

To reference a variable dynamically and assign a value:

1. Choose Actions > Variables > set variable.
2. In the Variable field, enter an expression, and check the Expression checkbox.
3. In the Value field, enter a value for your variable, and leave the Expression checkbox unchecked if the value is a string.

   Flash resolves the expression in the Variable field and assigns the value to it (refer to Figure 9.41, top).

or

1. Choose Actions > Miscellaneous Actions > evaluate.
2. In the Expression field, enter the parent of the variable, followed by an opening square bracket, an expression, a closing square bracket, an equal sign, and a value.

   Flash resolves the expression within the square brackets and assigns the value to it (refer to Figure 9.41, bottom).

To reference an object dynamically and call its method:

1. Choose a method for your object.
2. In the Object field, enter its parent object, followed by an opening square bracket, an expression, and a closing square bracket (**Figure 9.42**).

   Flash resolves the expression between the square brackets and calls the method for that object.

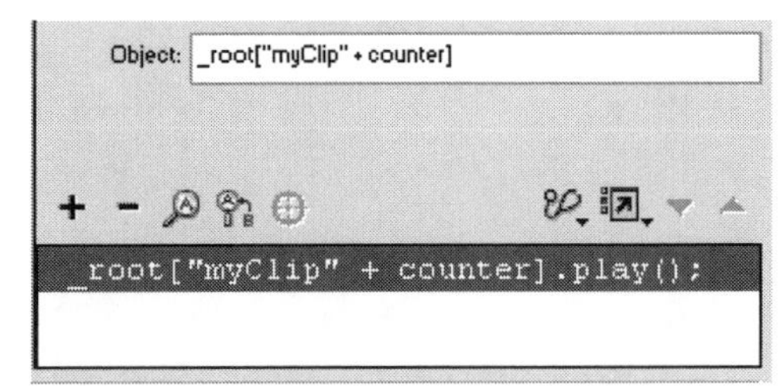

Figure 9.42 Use the array access operators to dynamically reference an object and then call one of its methods. If `counter` = 1, this statement targets the movie clip called myClip1 in the main Timeline and then makes it play.

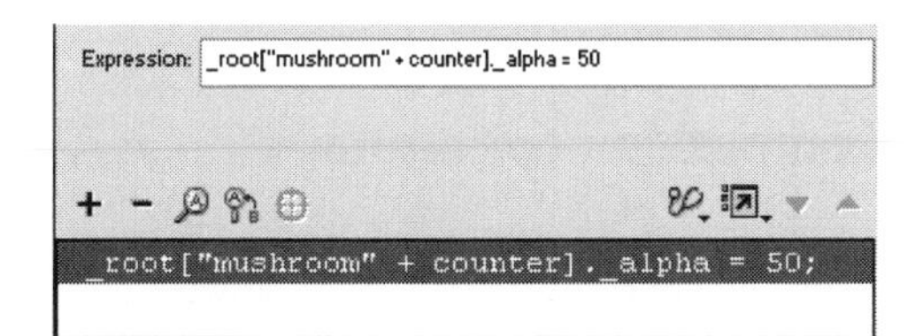

Figure 9.43 Use the array access operators to dynamically reference an object and then evaluate or modify one of its properties. If `counter` = 1, this statement targets the movie clip called mushroom1 in the main Timeline and changes its transparency to 50 percent.

To reference an object dynamically and change its property:

1. Choose Actions > Miscellaneous Actions > evaluate.
2. In the empty Expression field in the Parameters pane, enter the parent object, followed by an opening square bracket, an expression, a closing square bracket, a dot, a property, an equal sign, and finally a value (**Figure 9.43**).

   Flash resolves the expression between the square brackets and assigns the value on the right of the equal sign to the object.

Dynamic Referencing with the eval Function

You can also resolve an expression for dynamic referencing by using the `eval` function, which reads an expression and returns the value as a single string. You can modify an object's transparency with the following statement:

```
eval ("mushroom" + counter)._alpha = 50
```

Or you can call a method of an object like this:

```
eval ("mushroom" + counter).play()
```

Notice that the `eval` function accomplishes the same task as the array access operators. Which technique should you use? You should learn and use the array access operators for dynamic referencing. The `eval` function is an older function that was useful before recent ActionScript objects and syntax made it redundant. The array access operators are preferable because they are less taxing on the processor and result in more compact code that's easier to read.

In addition, in some cases the `eval` function fails to give predictable results. You cannot use `eval` to assign values directly to variables, for example. The statement `eval("myVariable" + counter) = 5` will fail.

Testing Information with Conditional Statements

Variables and expressions go hand in hand with conditional statements. The information you retrieve, store in variables, and modify in expressions will be useful to you only when you can compare it with other pieces of information. Conditional statements let you do this kind of comparison and carry out instructions based on the results. The logic of conditional statements is like the sentence "If abc is true, then do xyz," and in Flash, you define abc (the condition) and xyz (the consequence).

Conditional statements begin with the statement `if()`. The parameter that goes between the parentheses is the *condition*—a statement that compares one thing with another. Is the variable `myScore` greater than the variable `alltimeHighScore`? Is the `_droptarget` property for my draggable movie clip unequal to the target path for the garbageCan movie clip? Does the `_currentFrame` property of the root Timeline equal 10? These are typical examples of conditions.

How do you construct conditions? You use comparison operators.

Comparison operators

A *comparison operator* evaluates the expressions on both sides of itself and returns a value of `true` or `false`. **Table 9.4** summarizes the comparison operators.

When the condition is evaluated and the condition holds true, Flash performs the consequences within the `if` statement's curly braces. If the condition turns out to be false, all the actions within the curly braces are ignored (**Figure 9.44**).

Table 9.4

Comparison Operators

Symbol	Description
==	Equality
===	Strict equality (value and data type must be equal)
<	Less than
>	Greater than
<=	Less than or equal to
>=	Greater than or equal to
!=	Not equal to
!==	Strict inequality

```
if (condition) {
 consequence1;
 consequence2;
 consequence3;
}
```

Figure 9.44 If, and only if, the condition within the parentheses is true, consequence1, consequence2, and consequence3 are all performed. If the condition is false, all three consequences are ignored.

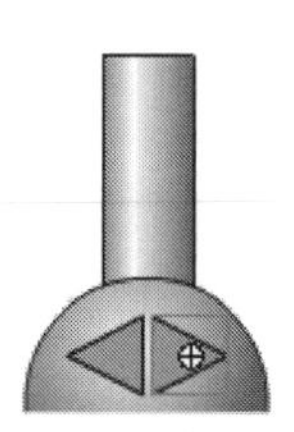

Condition: myRotation > 90

```
on (release) {
 myRotation += 10;
 if (myRotation > 90) {
 }
}
```

Figure 9.45 Add a condition that tests the `myRotation` variable.

Movie-clip rotation at 90

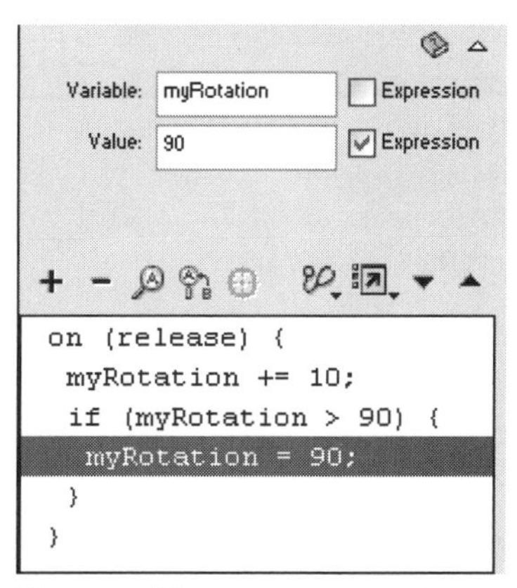

Figure 9.46 The cannon turret can't rotate past 90 degrees, because the `if` statement won't allow the variable `myRotation` to increase beyond 90.

In the following task, you will use the same file that you created to rotate a cannon turret in the "Modifying Variables" section earlier in this chapter. You want to constrain the rotation of the turret to a maximum of 90 degrees, so you will construct a conditional statement to have Flash test whether the value of its rotation is greater than 90. If it is, you will keep its rotation at 90, preventing the turret from rotating past the horizontal plane.

To create a conditional statement:

1. Continuing with the task that demonstrates the rotation of a movie clip (see "Modifying Variables" earlier in this chapter), select the button, and open the Actions panel.
2. After the variable incrementally increases by 10, add a conditional statement by choosing Actions > Conditions/Loops > if (Esc + if).
3. In the Condition field, enter the variable name, followed by the > symbol and then 90 (**Figure 9.45**).

   Flash tests to see whether the variable is greater than 90.
4. Choose Actions > Variables > set variable.
5. In the Variable field, enter your variable name.
6. In the Value field, enter 90, and check the Expression checkbox (**Figure 9.46**).

   If the variable exceeds 90, Flash resets the variable to 90. This setting prevents the cannon turret from rotating past the horizontal plane.

continues on next page

7. Choose the other button that decreases the rotation variable, and create a similar conditional statement to test whether the variable is less than –90.
8. If the condition is true, set the variable to –90.

✔ Tips

- Any action residing outside the `if` statement will be performed regardless of whether the condition in the `if` statement is `true` or `false`. Consider the following script:

```
if (myVariable == 10) {
      myVariable = 20;
   }
myVariable = 30;
```

  After Flash runs this block of code, `myVariable` will always be set to 30, even if the condition `myVariable == 10` is `true`. The last statement is executed no matter what.

- A common mistake is to mix up the assignment operator (=) and the comparison operator for equality (==). The single equal sign assigns whatever is on the right side of it to whatever is on the left side. Use the single equal sign when you are setting and modifying properties and variables. The double equal signs compare the equality of two things; use them in conditional statements.

A simple but powerful and widely applicable use of the `if` statement is to monitor the state of a button click and to provide continuous actions as long as the button is held down. This kind of functionality is sometimes called a *continuous-feedback button.* A continuous-feedback button causes change even when it's held down at a constant state. When you click and hold down a button, for example, you can increase the sound volume (like a television remote control) until you let go. A simple button event cannot accomplish this functionality.

The solution requires you to toggle the value of a variable based on the state of the button. When you click the button, you can set a variable called `pressing` to `true`. When you release the button or move your pointer away from the button, the variable `pressing` is set to `false`. Within an `onEnterFrame` handler, you can monitor the status of the variable continuously with an `if` statement. If `pressing` is `true`, you can perform an action. As long as `pressing` remains `true`, those actions will continue to be executed.

When you build your continuous-feedback button, you will actually use a movie clip. This procedure allows you to assign both button events (`onPress` and `onRelease`) as well as clip events (`onEnterFrame`) to the instance.

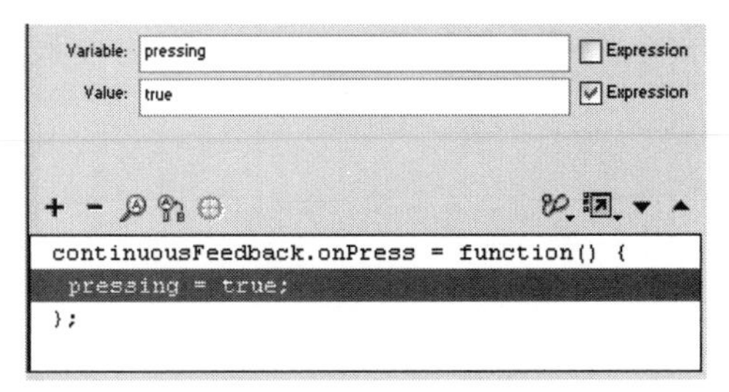

Figure 9.47 The variable called `pressing` keeps track of whether the movie clip called continuousFeedback is being pressed or released. When the movie clip is pressed, `pressing` is set to `true`.

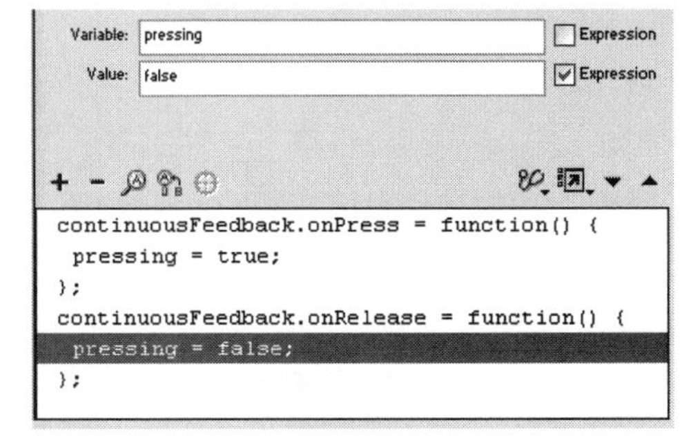

Figure 9.48 The variable called `pressing` keeps track of whether the movie clip called continuousFeedback is being pressed or released. When the movie clip is released, `pressing` is set to `false`.

To create a continuous-feedback button:

1. Create a movie-clip symbol, place an instance of it on the Stage, and give it a name in the Property Inspector.
2. Select the first frame of the main Timeline, and open the Actions panel.
3. Choose Objects > Movie > Movie Clip > Events > onPress.
4. In the Object field, enter the name of your movie-clip instance.
5. Choose Actions > Variables > set variable.
6. In the Variable field, enter a name.
7. In the Value field, enter `true`, and check the Expression checkbox (**Figure 9.47**).

   The variable is set to `true` whenever the button is pressed. Note that the Value field is an expression, so `true` is treated correctly as a Boolean data type, not a string data type.
8. Select the closing brace of the `onPress` handler, and choose Objects > Movie > Movie Clip > Events > onRelease.
9. In the Object field, enter the name of your movie-clip instance.
10. Choose Actions > Variables > set variable.
11. In the Variable field, enter the same variable name you entered for the `onPress` handler.
12. In the Value field, enter `false`, and check the Expression checkbox (**Figure 9.48**).

    The variable is set to `false` whenever the button is released.

continues on next page

13. Select the closing brace of the onRelease handler, and choose Objects > Movie > Movie Clip > Events > onEnterFrame.
14. In the Object field, enter the name of your movie-clip instance.
15. Choose Actions > Conditions/Loops > if
16. In the Condition field, enter the variable name, followed by two equal signs and then true (**Figure 9.49**).

    The condition tests whether the button is being pressed.
17. Choose an action as a consequence that you want to be performed as long as the button is held down (**Figure 9.50**).

✔ Tip

- To refine the continuous-feedback interaction, you can add an onDragOut event to your onRelease handler in Expert mode, as follows:

```
continuousFeedback.onRelease =
continuousFeedback.onDragOut =
function(){
}
```

  Now if your viewer releases the movie clip *or* if the pointer wanders off the movie clip, the continuous actions will stop.

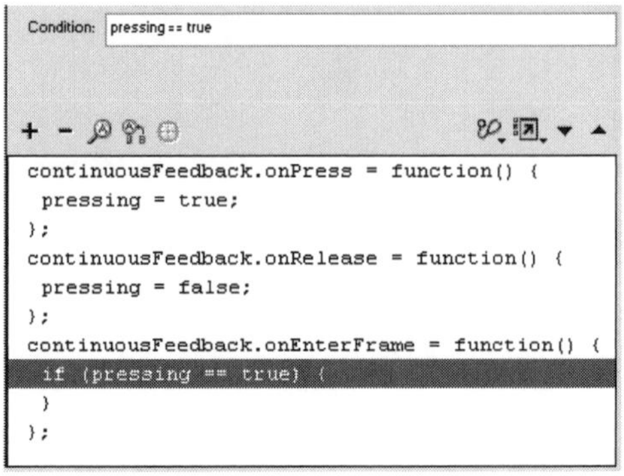

```
Condition: pressing == true

continuousFeedback.onPress = function() {
  pressing = true;
};
continuousFeedback.onRelease = function() {
  pressing = false;
};
continuousFeedback.onEnterFrame = function() {
  if (pressing == true) {
  }
};
```

Figure 9.49 The status of the pressing variable can be monitored continuously by an if statement inside an onEnterFrame handler.

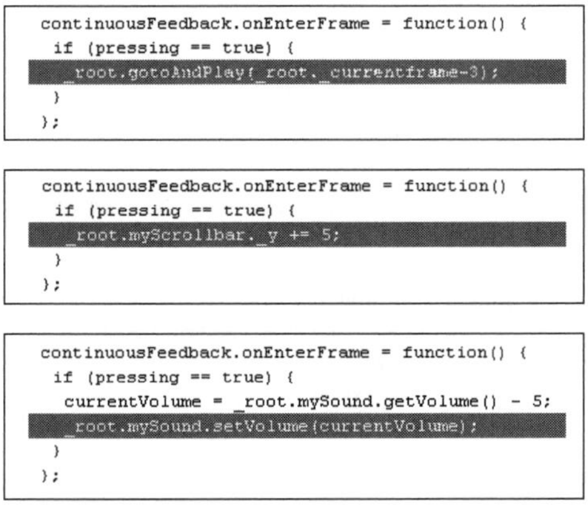

```
continuousFeedback.onEnterFrame = function() {
  if (pressing == true) {
    _root.gotoAndPlay(_root._currentframe-3);
  }
};
```

```
continuousFeedback.onEnterFrame = function() {
  if (pressing == true) {
    _root.myScrollbar._y += 5;
  }
};
```

```
continuousFeedback.onEnterFrame = function() {
  if (pressing == true) {
    currentVolume = _root.mySound.getVolume() - 5;
    _root.mySound.setVolume(currentVolume);
  }
};
```

Figure 9.50 Three examples of how a continuous-feedback button can affect a movie. At top, when the button is held down, Flash moves the playhead three frames behind the current frame, creating a rewind button. In the middle, when the button is held down, a movie clip called myScrollbar moves down the Stage, like a regular scroll bar. At the bottom, when the button is held down, the volume of the Sound object called mySound decreases.

Providing Alternatives to Conditions

In many cases, you'll need to provide an alternative response to the conditional statement. The `else` statement lets you create consequences when the condition in the `if` statement is `false`. The `else` statement was introduced in Chapter 7 as the way to detect dropped movie clips. In that example, the `if` statement tested whether a movie clip was dropped on another movie clip. When the statement was `true`, the dropped movie clip disappeared, and when the statement was `false`, the `else` statement made the dropped movie clip bounce back to its original position. The `else` statement takes care of any condition that the `if` statement doesn't cover.

The `else` statement has to be used in conjunction with the `if` statement and follows the syntax and logic of this hypothetical example:

```
if (daytime) {
   goToWork;
} else {
   goToSleep;
}
```

Use `else` for either-or conditions—something that can be just one of two options. In the preceding example, there are only two possibilities: It is either daytime or nighttime. Situations in which the `else` statement can be useful include collision detection, true/false or right/wrong answer checking, and password verification.

To use else for the false condition:

1. Create a radio-button movie clip as demonstrated in Chapter 5.

   The movie clip should have buttons that toggle between an on and an off state.

2. Place an instance of the movie clip on the Stage, and give it a name in the Property Inspector.
3. Select the movie-clip instance, and open the Actions panel.
4. Choose Actions > Movie Clip Control > onClipEvent.
5. Keep the `Load` event selected.
6. Choose Actions > Variables > set variable.
7. In the Variable field, enter a variable name.

continues on next page

8. In the Value field, enter `false`, and check the Expression checkbox (**Figure 9.51**).

   When this movie clip loads into memory, the variable is initialized to `false`.

9. Enter symbol-editing mode for the radio-button movie clip.

10. Select the button in the off state that sends the playhead to the on state.

11. Add another statement below the `gotoAndStop` action by choosing Actions > Variables > set variable.

12. In the Variable field, enter the name of the variable you initialized in the clip event handler.

13. In the Value field, enter `true`, and check the Expression checkbox (**Figure 9.52**).

    When you click the radio button, your variable is set to `true`.

14. Select the button in the on state that sends the playhead to the off state.

15. Add another statement below the `gotoAndStop` action by choosing Actions > Variables > set variable.

16. In the Variable field, enter the name of the variable you initialized in the clip event handler.

17. In the Value field, enter `false`, and check the Expression checkbox (**Figure 9.53**).

    Pressing the radio button again to turn it off sets your variable to `false`.

18. Create a button symbol, and place an instance of it on the Stage.

19. Select the button instance, and in the Actions panel, choose Actions > Movie Control > on. Next, choose Actions > Conditions/Loops > if.

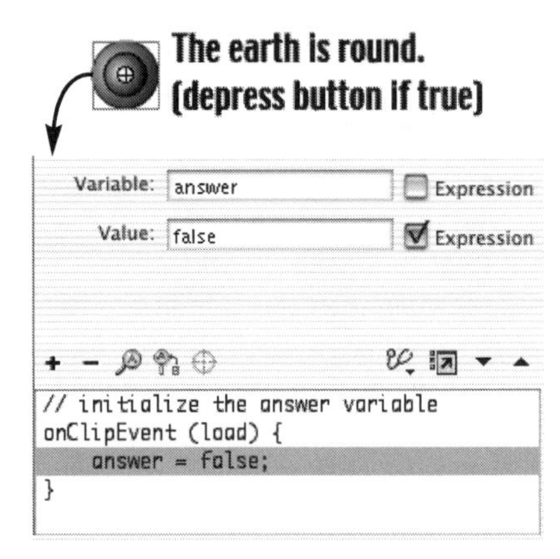

Figure 9.51 The radio-button movie clip initializes the `answer` variable to the Boolean value `false`.

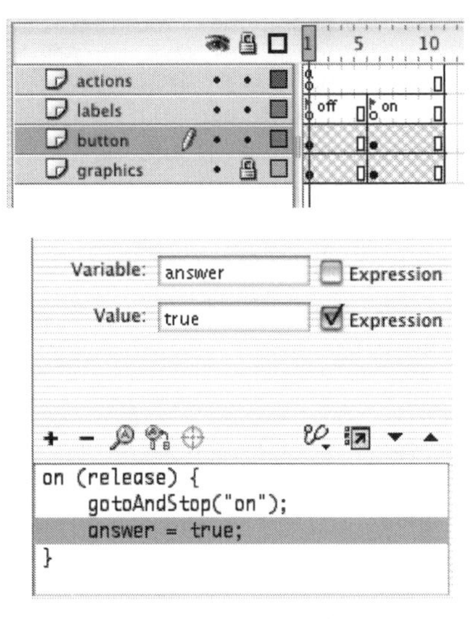

Figure 9.52 The button in the off state changes the `answer` variable to `true` and moves the playhead to the on state.

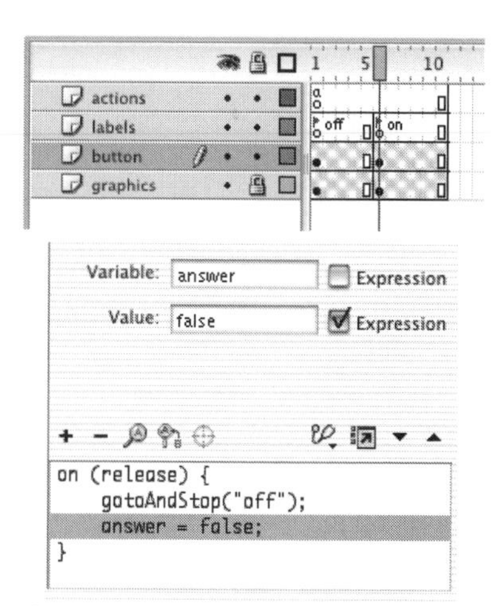

Figure 9.53 The button in the on state changes the answer variable to `false` and moves the playhead to the off state.

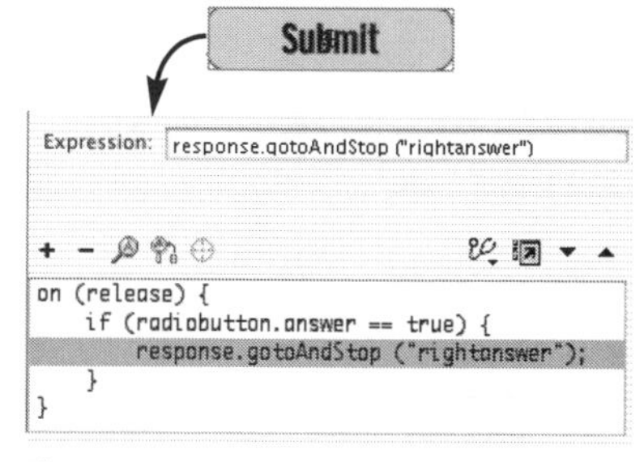

Figure 9.54 The button tests the answer variable, which is scoped to the radio-button movie clip. If the condition is `true`, another movie clip, called response, goes to another frame to display a message.

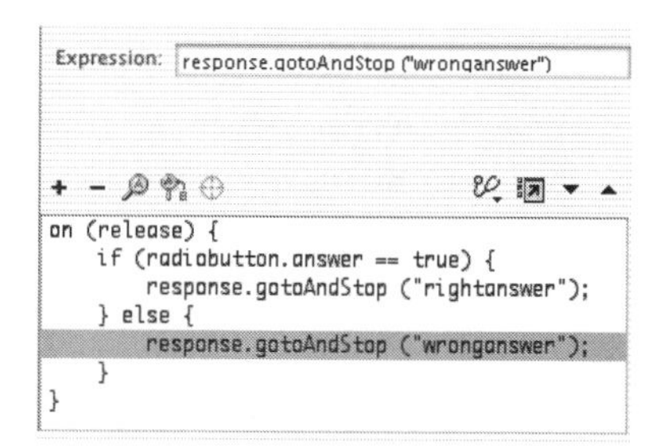

Figure 9.55 The `else` statement makes the response movie clip go to a different frame when the answer variable is `false`.

20. In the Condition field, enter the target path and variable name, and test whether the variable is `true`.

    Remember that your variable is scoped to the movie clip, not to the root Timeline.

21. Choose an action as a response to the `true` condition (**Figure 9.54**).

22. Choose Actions > Conditions/Loops > else (Esc + el).

23. Choose another action as a response to the `false` condition (**Figure 9.55**).

✔ Tips

- To add an `else` statement to an `if` statement with multiple consequences, you must select the last line within the `if` statement's curly braces.
- By default, the `else` statement "cuddles" the closing brace of the `if` statement to show that they belong together. In the Auto Format options, however, you can change the Script pane's formatting to put the `else` statement on its own line.

Branching Conditional Statements

If you have multiple possible conditions and just as many consequences, you need to use more complicated branching conditional statements that a single `else` statement can't provide. If you create an interface to a Web site or a game that requires keyboard input, for example, you would want to test which keys are pressed and respond appropriately to each key press. Flash gives you the `else if` statement, which lets you construct multiple responses, as in the following hypothetical example:

```
if (sunny) {
   bringSunglasses;
} else if (raining) {
   bringUmbrella;
} else if (snowing) {
   bringSkis;
}
```

Each `else if` statement has its own condition that it evaluates and its own set of consequences to perform if that condition returns `true`. Only one condition in the entire `if-else if` code block can be true. If more than one condition is `true`, Flash performs the consequences for the first `true` condition it encounters and ignores the rest. In the preceding example, even if it is both sunny *and* snowing, Flash can perform the consequence only for the sunny condition (`bringSunglasses`), because it appears before the snowing condition. If you want the possibility of multiple conditions to be `true`, you must construct separate `if` statements that are independent, like the following:

```
if (sunny) {
   bringSunglasses;
}
if (raining) {
   bringUmbrella;
}
if (snowing) {
   bringSkis;
}
```

The following example uses the Key object and branching conditional statements to move and rotate a movie clip according to different key presses.

To use else if for branching alternatives:

1. Create a movie-clip symbol, place an instance of it on the Stage, and give it a name in the Property Inspector.
2. Select the first frame of the main Timeline, and open the Actions panel.
3. Choose Objects > Movie > Movie Clip > Events > onEnterFrame.
4. In the Object field, enter the name of the movie-clip instance.
5. Choose Actions > Conditions/Loops > if.
6. In the Condition field, enter `Key.isDown(Key.UP)`.

   The first condition uses the `isDown()` method of the Key object to test whether the up-arrow key is pressed.
7. Choose Actions > Miscellaneous Actions > evaluate.

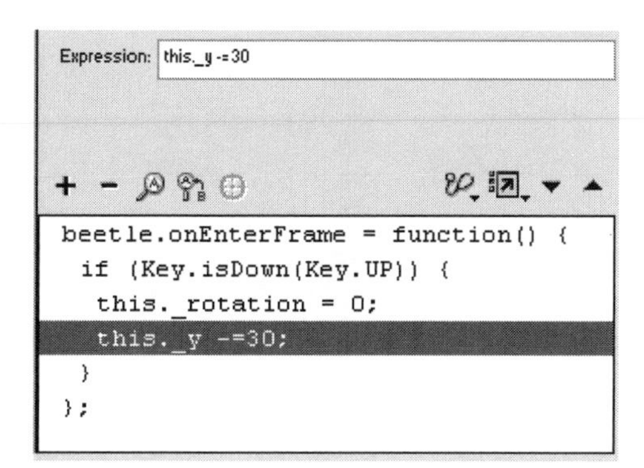

Figure 9.56 If the up-arrow key is pressed, this movie clip is rotated to 0 degrees and is repositioned 30 pixels up the Stage.

8. In the Expression field, enter `this`, followed by a dot, the property `_rotation`, an equal sign, and 0.

9. Again, choose Actions > Miscellaneous Actions > evaluate.

10. In the Expression field, enter `this`, followed by a dot, the property `_y`, a minus sign and equal sign (`-=`), and `30`.

    The two statements rotate the movie clip so that the head faces the top and subtract 30 pixels from its current *y* position, making it move up the Stage. Recall that the operator -= means "subtract this amount and assign the result to myself" (**Figure 9.56**).

11. Choose Actions > Conditions/Loops > else if (Esc + ei).

12. In the Condition field, enter `Key.isDown(Key.RIGHT)`.

13. Create two more expressions with the `evaluate` action to set the rotation of the movie clip to 90 and add 30 pixels to its *x* position.

14. Choose Actions > Conditions/Loops > else if.

15. In the Condition field, enter `Key.isDown(Key.DOWN)`.

16. Create two more expressions with the `evaluate` action to set the rotation of the movie clip to 180 and add 30 pixels to its *y* position.

17. Choose Actions > Conditions/Loops > else if.

18. In the Condition field, enter `Key.isDown(Key.LEFT)`.

continues on next page

19. Create two more expressions with the `evaluate` action to set the rotation of the movie clip to 270 and subtract 30 pixels from its *x* position.

20. Test your movie.

    Your series of `if` and `else if` statements tests whether the user presses the arrow keys and moves the movie clip accordingly (**Figure 9.57**). Now you have the beginnings of a game of Frogger!

✔ Tip

- The conditions for this task did not include the comparison operator for equality (==). For Boolean data types and methods that return Boolean values, you don't need to compare them explicitly to the value `true`. So the following two conditions are identical:

```
if (Key.isDown(Key.LEFT))
if (Key.isDown(Key.LEFT)==true)
```

The switch, case, and default actions

Another way to create alternatives to conditions is to use the `switch`, `case`, and `default` actions instead of the `if` statement. These actions provide a different way to test the equality of an expression. The syntax and logic follow this hypothetical example:

```
switch (weather) {
   case sun :
      bringSunglasses
      break;
   case rain :
      bringUmbrella
      break;
   case snow :
      bringSkis
      break;
   default:
      stayHome
}
```

```
beetle.onEnterFrame = function() {
  if (Key.isDown(Key.UP)) {
    this._rotation = 0;
    this._y -=30;
  } else if (Key.isDown(Key.LEFT)) {
    this._rotation = -90;
    this._x -=30;
  } else if (Key.isDown(Key.RIGHT)) {
    this._rotation = 90;
    this._x += 30;
  } else if (Key.isDown(Key.DOWN)) {
    this._rotation = 180;
    this._y += 30;
  }
};
```

Figure 9.57 The complete script (bottom) has four conditions that use `if` and `else if` to test whether the up-, left-, right-, or down-arrow key is pressed. The rotation and position of the movie clip (this beetle, top) change depending on which condition holds true.

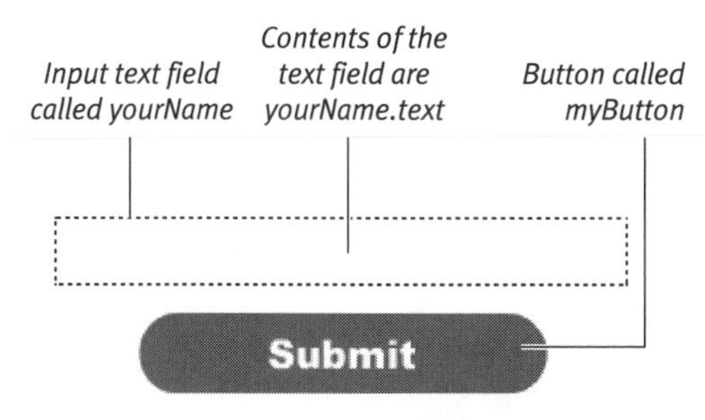

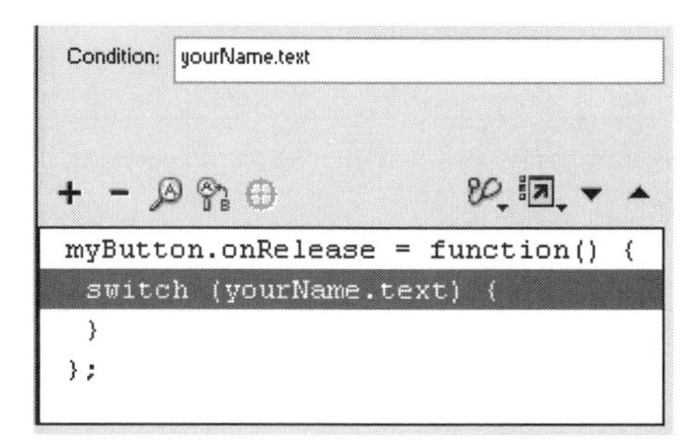

Figure 9.58 Enter `yourName.text` in the Condition field of the `switch` statement.

Flash compares the expression in the `switch` parentheses to each of the expressions in the `case` statements. If the two expressions are equal, the actions after the colon are performed. (If `weather` is equal to `sun`, `bringSunglasses` will happen.) The `break` action is necessary to break out of the `switch` code block after a case has matched. Without it, Flash will run through all the actions following it. The `default` action, which is optional, provides the case if no other cases match the `switch` expression.

A subtlety to keep in mind is that the `switch` and `case` statements test for a strict equality. A strict equality is represented by three equal signs (===); it compares both the value and the data type of two expressions.

In the following example, you'll create an input text field for your viewers to enter their names. When viewers click the Submit button, you can use the `switch` and `case` statements to compare what they typed in the text field with some known users.

To use switch and case for branching alternatives:

1. Select the text tool, and drag out a text field on the Stage.
2. In the Property Inspector, select Input Text, and give the text field a name.
3. Create a button, place an instance below the text field, and give your button instance a name in the Property Inspector.
4. Select the first frame of the main Timeline, and open the Actions panel.
5. Assign an `onRelease` event handler to your button.
6. Choose Actions > Conditions/Loops > switch.
7. In the Condition field, enter the name of your input text field, followed by a dot and then `text` (**Figure 9.58**).

continues on next page

The `switch` statement will check the equality of the contents of the input text field with the expressions in the case statements.

8. Choose Actions > Conditions/Loops > case.
9. In the Condition field, enter "Adam" (**Figure 9.59**).
10. Choose an action to be performed when the contents of the text field match "Adam" (**Figure 9.60**).
11. Choose Actions > Conditions/Loops > break.

    The `break` action discontinues the current code block and makes Flash go on to any ActionScript after the `switch` statement.
12. Repeat steps 8 through 11, but replace "Adam" with a different user's name (**Figure 9.61**).

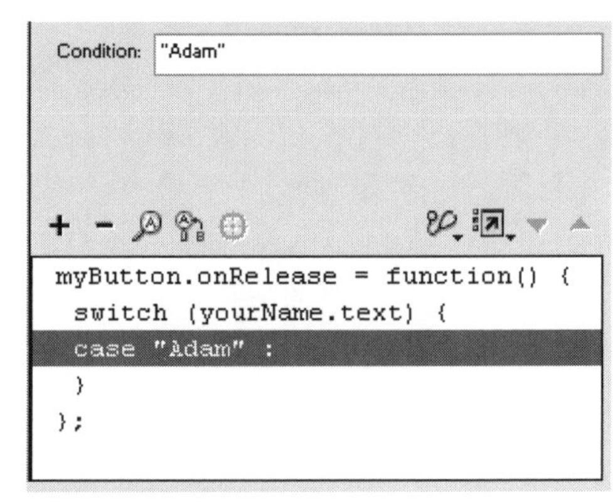

Figure 9.59 Flash will test whether `yourName.text` is equal to the string "Adam".

Figure 9.60 If `yourName.text==="Adam"`, the function called AdamFunction is triggered.

```
myButton.onRelease = function() {
 switch (yourName.text) {
 case "Adam" :
  AdamFunction();
  break;
 case "Betty" :
  BettyFunction();
  break;
 }
};
```

Figure 9.61 Create additional cases to test their equality against the `switch` expression.

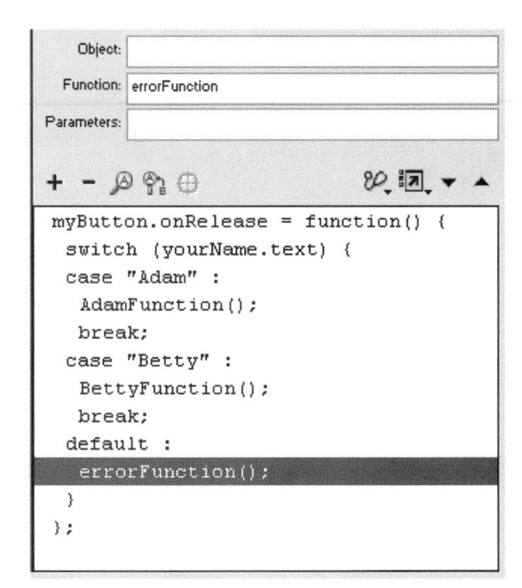

Figure 9.62 If the expression in the switch statement doesn't match either "Adam" or "Betty", the default action will be performed. It's helpful if you think of the default action as being like the else action. Both actions define the consequences when the condition fails.

```
beetle.onEnterFrame = function() {
  switch (true) {
  case Key.isDown(Key.UP) :
   this._y -= 30;
   this._rotation = 0;
   break;
  case Key.isDown(Key.LEFT) :
   this._x -= 30;
   this._rotation = -90;
   break;
  case Key.isDown(Key.RIGHT) :
   this._x += 30;
   this._rotation = 90;
   break;
  case Key.isDown(Key.DOWN) :
   this._y += 30;
   this._rotation = 180;
  }
};
```

Figure 9.63 The full script to move a beetle movie clip with the arrow keys, using switch and case instead of the if statement.

13. Choose Actions > Conditions/Loops > default.

14. Choose an action to be performed when the contents of the text field don't match any of the cases (**Figure 9.62**).

15. Test your movie.

✔ Tip

- What would the switch and case statements look like for the keyboard-controlled beetle in the preceding example? To create identical interactivity, you can enter the value true for the switch parameter and test it against each key press in separate case statements (**Figure 9.63**). It may look backward, but it works!

Combining Conditions with Logical Operators

You can create compound conditions with the logical operators && (AND), || (OR), and ! (NOT). The operators combine two or more conditions in one `if` statement to test for more-complicated scenarios. You could test whether the up-arrow key and the right-arrow key are pressed together to make a movie clip move diagonally, for example. Or you could test whether a draggable movie clip is dropped on one valid target or another. You could use the NOT operator to test whether a variable contains a valid email address whose domain is not restricted.

The following task uses the same file that you created to move a movie clip from the keyboard. You will combine conditions to have Flash test for combination key presses to move the movie clip diagonally.

To combine conditions:

1. Continuing with the file that moves a movie clip with the keyboard arrow keys, select the first frame of the main Timeline, and open the Actions panel.
2. Select the first `if` statement.
3. In the Condition field, place your pointer at the end of the existing condition.
4. Choose Operators > Logical Operators > &&.
5. Enter your second condition after the two ampersands (**Figure 9.64**).

   Both conditions appear in the Condition field, separated by the && operator.
6. Change the actions within the `if` statement to rotate and move the movie clip diagonally (**Figure 9.65**).

```
Condition: Key.isDown(Key.UP) && Key.isDown(Key.RIGHT)
```

Figure 9.64 The logical && operator joins these two expressions so that both the up- and right-arrow keys must be pressed for the whole condition to be `true`.

```
if (Key.isDown(Key.UP) && Key.isDown(Key.RIGHT)) {
  this._rotation = 45;
  this._y -=15;
  this._x +=15;
}
```

Figure 9.65 The first portion of the script shows that when both up- and right-arrow keys are pressed, the beetle rotates 45 degrees and moves diagonally top and right.

7. Continue to add `else if` statements with combined conditions for the other three diagonal key presses while keeping the four conditions for the cardinal directions (**Figure 9.66**).

   Using the && logical operator to combine two conditions, Flash checks whether the user presses two key combinations.

✔ Tip

- You can nest `if` statements within other `if` statements, which is equivalent to using the logical && operator in a single `if` statement. These two scripts test whether both conditions are `true` before setting a new variable:

```
if (yourAge >= 12) {
   if (yourAge <=20) {
      status = "teenager";
   }
}
```

or

```
if (yourAge >= 12 && yourAge <=20) {
   status = "teenager";
}
```

```
beetle.onEnterFrame = function() {
    if (Key.isDown(Key.UP) && Key.isDown(Key.RIGHT)) {
        this._rotation = 45;
        this._y -=15;
        this._x +=15;
    } else if (Key.isDown(Key.DOWN) && Key.isDown(Key.RIGHT)) {
        this._rotation = 135;
        this._y +=15;
        this._x +=15;
    } else if (Key.isDown(Key.UP) && Key.isDown(Key.LEFT)) {
        this._rotation = -45;
        this._y -=15;
        this._x -=15;
    } else if (Key.isDown(Key.DOWN) && Key.isDown(Key.LEFT)) {
        this._rotation = -135;
        this._y +=15;
        this._x -=15;
    } else if (Key.isDown(Key.UP)) {
        this._rotation = 0;
        this._y -= 30;
    } else if (Key.isDown(Key.LEFT)) {
        this._rotation = -90;
        this._x -=30;
    } else if (Key.isDown(Key.RIGHT)) {
        this._rotation = 90;
        this._x += 30;
    } else if (Key.isDown(Key.DOWN)) {
        this._rotation = 180;
        this._y += 30;
    }
};
```

Figure 9.66 The complete script contains combined conditions for two key presses as well as conditions for a single key press.

Looping Statements

With looping statements, you can create an action or set of actions that repeat a certain number of times or while a certain condition holds true. Repeating actions are often used to build *arrays*, which are special kinds of variables that hold data in a structured, easily accessible way. The looping action makes sure that each piece of data is put in a particular order or retrieved in a particular order. You'll learn more about arrays in Chapter 11.

In general, use looping statements to execute actions automatically a specific number of times by using an incremental variable. That incremental variable modifies the parameters of each successive method in the loop or modifies certain properties of objects that are created. You can generate intricate patterns by duplicating movie clips or dynamically drawing lines and shapes with looping statements. Use looping statements to change the properties of a whole series of movie clips, modify multiple sound settings, or alter the values of a set of variables.

There are three kinds of looping statements—the `while`, `do while`, and `for` actions—but they all accomplish the same task. The first two statements perform loops while a certain condition holds true. The third statement performs loops by using a built-in counter and condition.

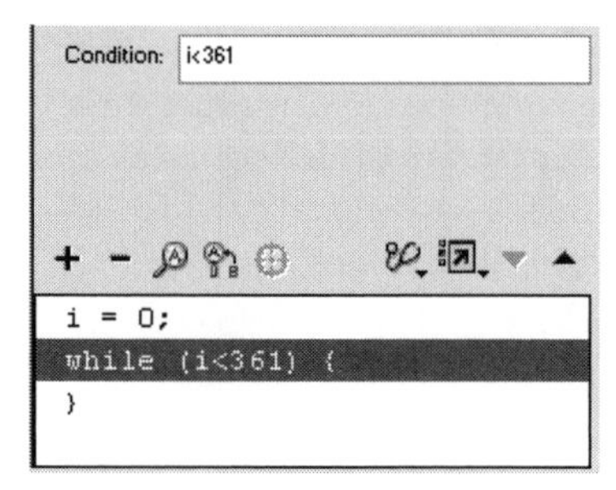

Figure 9.67 Initialize the variable `i`, and create the condition that must be `true` for the loop to continue. As long as the variable `i` is less than 361, this loop will run.

To use the while statement to duplicate movie clips:

1. Create a movie-clip symbol, place an instance of it on the Stage, and give it a name in the Property Inspector.
2. Select the first frame of the main Timeline, and open the Actions panel.

```
Expression: _root["oval" + i]._alpha = (i/360)*100

i = 0;
while (i<361) {
 duplicateMovieClip(oval, "oval"+i, i);
 _root["oval" + i]._rotation = i;
 _root["oval" + i]._alpha = (i/360)*100;
}
```

Figure 9.68 The oval movie clip is duplicated, and its duplicate is rotated and changed in transparency.

```
Expression: i += 10

i = 0;
while (i<361) {
 duplicateMovieClip(oval, "oval"+i, i);
 _root["oval" + i]._rotation = i;
 _root["oval" + i]._alpha = (i/360)*100;
 i += 10;
}
```

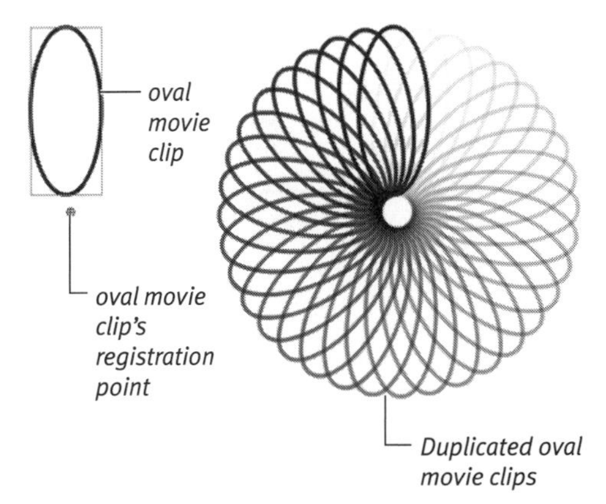

Figure 9.69 At the end of each loop, the variable `i` increases by 10. This loop will run 37 times. The oval movie clip (left) is the basis for the pattern (right) made with the looping statement.

3. Choose Actions > Variables > set variable.
4. In the Variable field, enter `i`.
5. In the Value field, enter 0, and check the Expression checkbox.

   The variable `i`, `j`, or `k` is often used as a loop counter.
6. Choose Actions > Conditions/Loops > while (Esc + wh).
7. In the Condition field, enter `i < 361` (**Figure 9.67**).
8. Assign any actions that you want to run while the condition remains `true` (`i` is less than 361).

   For this example, add a `duplicateMovieClip` action and two statements that rotate and modify the transparency of the duplicates (**Figure 9.68**).
9. Choose Actions > Miscellaneous Actions > evaluate.
10. In the Expression field, enter `i += 10`, or use the equivalent statement `i = i + 10`.

    Each time the loop runs, the variable `i` increases by an increment of 10. When it exceeds 361, the condition that the `while` statement checks at each pass becomes `false`. Flash ends the loop (**Figure 9.69**).

The do while statement

The do while (Esc + do) statement is similar to the while statement, except that the condition is checked at the end of the loop rather than the beginning. This means that the actions in the loop are executed at least once. The same script in the preceding task could be written with the do while statement, as shown in **Figure 9.70**.

```
i = 0;
do {
 duplicateMovieClip(oval, "oval"+i, i);
 _root["oval" + i]._rotation = i;
 _root["oval" + i]._alpha = (i/360)*100;
 i += 10;
} while (i < 361);
```

Figure 9.70 The equivalent do while statement.

The for statement

The for (Esc + fr) statement provides a built-in counter and parameters for increments or decrements to the counter, so you don't have to write separate statements. The parameter fields for the for statement are Init, which initializes the counter variable; Condition, which is the expression that is tested; and Next, which determines the amount of increment or decrement of the counter variable. The preceding task could be written with a for statement, as shown in **Figure 9.71**.

```
for (i = 0; i < 361; i += 10) {
 duplicateMovieClip(oval, "oval"+i, i);
 _root["oval" + i]._rotation = i;
 _root["oval" + i]._alpha = (i/360)*100;
}
```

Figure 9.71 The equivalent for statement. You can read the parameters this way: Start my counter at 0. As long as it is smaller than 361, perform the following actions. Then add 10 to my counter and repeat.

✔ Tips

- Do not use looping statements to build continuous routines to check a certain condition. Real-time testing should be done with the if statement in an enterFrame event handler or from a setInterval function call. When Flash executes looping statements, the display remains frozen, and no mouse or keyboard events can be detected.
- Make sure that the increments to your variables are inside the curly braces of the while or do while statements. If they aren't, the condition will never be met, and Flash will be stuck executing the loop infinitely. Fortunately, Flash warns you about this problem when it detects an infinite loop (**Figure 9.72**).

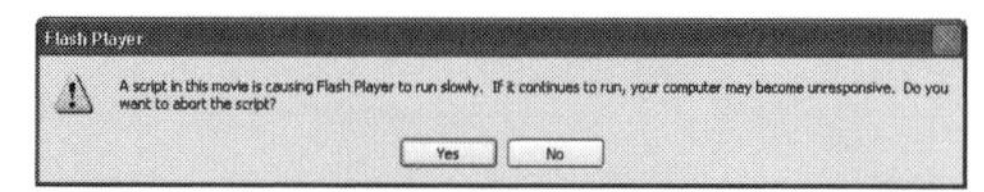

Figure 9.72 This warning dialog box appears when you inadvertently run an infinite loop.

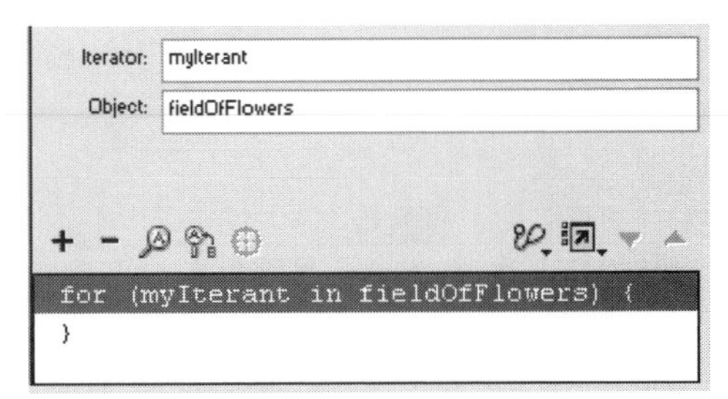

Figure 9.73 The variable called `myIterant` will loop through the objects inside the movie clip called fieldOfFlowers.

The for..in loop

Another kind of loop, called the `for..in` loop, is used specifically to look through the properties or elements of an object. You don't use a `counter` variable, as you do for the other kinds of loops. Instead, you use a variable called an iterant (or iterator), which references each property or element in an object. You can use the iterant in expressions within the `for..in` loop to modify each of the object's properties. If you had a movie clip called parentMovieClip that contained many child movie clips, you could use the `for..in` loop to reference each child this way:

```
for (myIterant in parentMovieClip) {
parentMovieClip[myIterant]._rotation = 90;
}
```

This `for..in` statement would look inside the parentMovieClip, using the variable `myIterant` to reference each child movie clip. The expression within the curly braces rotates every child movie clip inside the parent movie clip.

To use the for..in loop to reference elements inside a movie clip:

1. Create a movie-clip symbol that contains many child movie clips.
2. Drag an instance of the parent movie clip to the main Stage, and give it a name in the Property Inspector.
3. Select the first frame of the main Timeline, and open the Actions panel.
4. Choose Actions > Conditions/Loops > for..in.
5. In the Iterator field, enter a name.
6. In the Object field, enter the name of your parent movie-clip instance (**Figure 9.73**).

continues on next page

7. Choose Actions > Miscellaneous Actions > evaluate.

8. In the Expression field, enter an expression that references each child movie clip with the iterant and modifies its property (**Figure 9.74**).

   In this example, all the child movie clips rotate the same amount.

✔ Tip

- Enter `_root` in the Object field of the `for..in` statement, and you can reference all the objects (buttons, text fields, and movie clips) that sit on the main Stage.

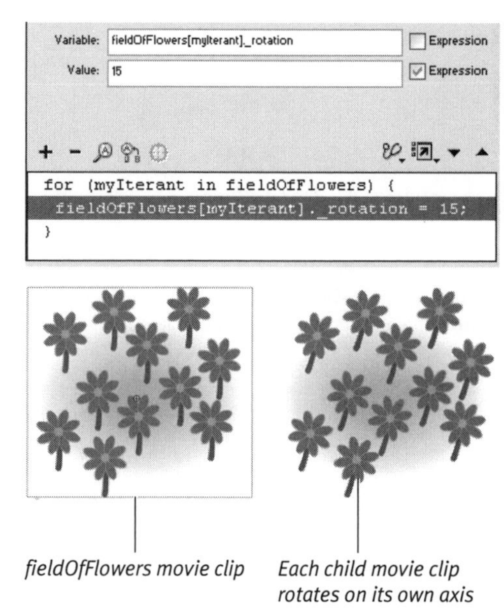

Figure 9.74 Using the array access operators, dynamically reference each child movie clip within fieldOfFlowers and modify the rotation of those clips.

CONTROLLING TEXT

You know that Flash lets you create visually engaging text elements—such as titles, labels, and descriptions—to accompany your graphics, animation, and sound. But did you know that you can do more with text than just set the style, color, and size? Flash text can be *live*, meaning that your viewers can enter text in the Flash movie as it plays, as well as select and edit the text. And Flash text can be dynamic, so it can update during playback. The text that viewers can enter is called *input text*, and the text that you can update during playback is called *dynamic text*. Both input and dynamic text are part of the class called the TextField object. Input and dynamic text provide a way to receive complex information from the viewer and tailor your Flash movie by using that information. You can use input text, for example, to let your viewers enter their names and then use that information to personalize the messages that appear throughout the movie. Or you can develop online tutorials that use input text for short-answer responses and dynamic text for customized feedback.

During author time, you use the text tool and the Property Inspector to create your text fields. But you can also create text fields at run time, dynamically defining their properties (such as background color) or formatting (such as setting font size and style with the TextFormat object). This control of text fields' content and appearance lets you animate text purely through ActionScript, making it responsive to the viewer and to different events.

Two additional objects—the Selection object and the String object—help control the information within text fields. You will use these objects to analyze and manipulate the text or the placement of the insertion point within the text. You can catch a viewer's misspellings or incorrectly entered information, for example, before using the text in your Flash movie or passing it on to an outside application for processing.

This chapter explores some of the many possibilities of the TextField, TextFormat, Selection, and String objects and introduces the tools you can use to integrate text and control the information exchange between your Flash movie and your audience.

Input Text

You can build your Flash project to gather information directly from the viewer—information such as a login name and password, personal information for a survey, answers to quiz questions, requests for an online purchase, or responses in an Internet chat room. You assign these user inputs, which Flash calls *input text*, to a variable so that they can be passed along to other parts of the Flash movie for further processing or sent to a server-side application through the CGI `GET` or `POST` method.

The following task demonstrates how you can use input text to let your user control the parameters of an action. In this case, you will accept information from the viewer in an input text field and use that information to load a URL.

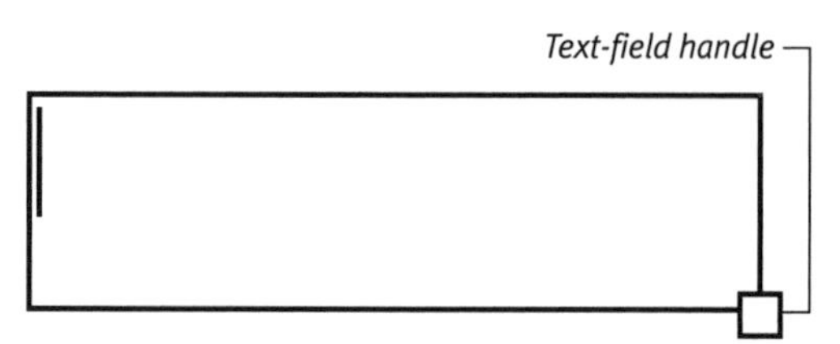

Figure 10.1 A text field is created with the text tool. You can resize the text field with the handle in the bottom-right corner.

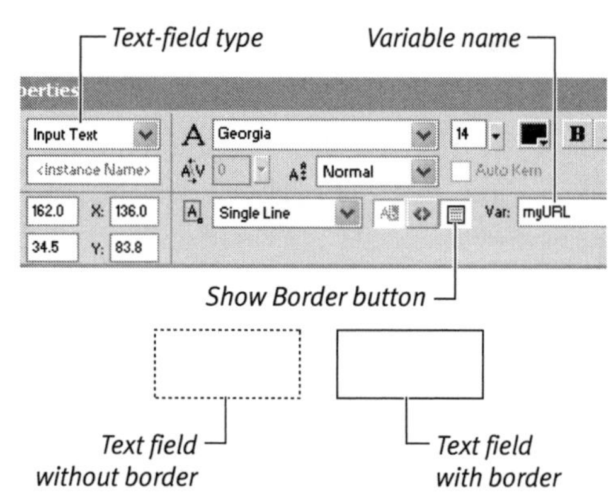

Figure 10.2 The Property Inspector defines the text field as input text. The variable name is `myURL`, and the Show Border button is selected. A text field without a border (bottom left) appears on your Stage in authoring mode with a dotted border. A text field with a border (bottom right) has a solid black border and a white background.

To use input text to request a URL:

1. Choose the text tool in the Tools palette, and drag out a text field on the Stage (**Figure 10.1**).
2. In the Property Inspector, choose Input Text from the pull-down menu.

   Your selected text field becomes input text, allowing text entry during playback.
3. In the Variable field of the Property Inspector, enter the name of your variable.

   Any text entered as the input text during playback is assigned to and stored in this variable.
4. Click the Show Border button in the Property Inspector.

   Your text box is drawn with a black border and a white background (**Figure 10.2**).

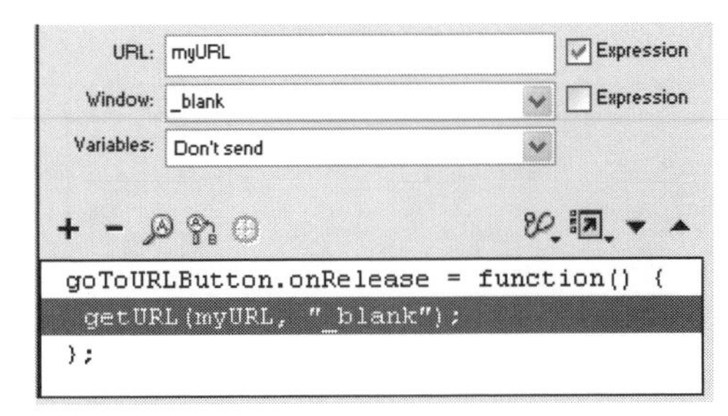

Figure 10.3 The actions assigned to the button called goToURLButton load the URL with the variable `myURL` in a new browser window.

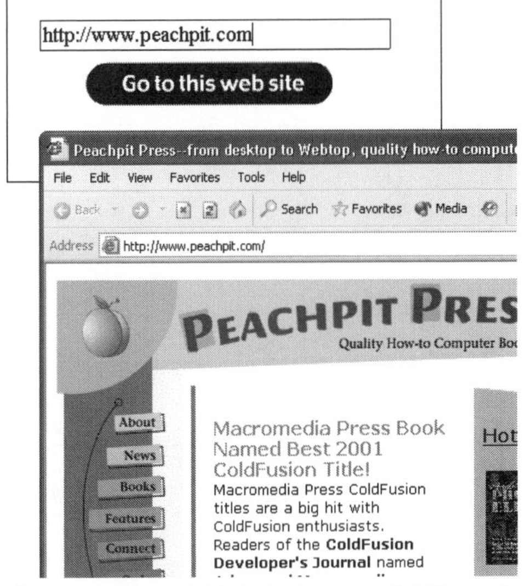

Figure 10.4 The variable in the input text field is used as the URL for the `getURL` action. Note that the viewer must include the protocol http:// in the input text field.

5. Create a button symbol, place an instance of the button on the Stage below the text field, and name the button instance in the Property Inspector.
6. Select the first frame of the main Timeline, and open the Actions panel.
7. Assign an `onRelease` handler to the button.
8. Choose Actions > Browser/Network > getURL.
9. In the URL field of the Parameters pane, enter your input text-field variable name, and check the Expression checkbox.
10. Choose _blank from the Window pop-up menu (**Figure 10.3**).
11. Test your movie.

    When your viewer enters a URL in the text field, the address is stored in the variable. Then, when the viewer clicks the button, Flash opens a new browser window and loads the specified Web site (**Figure 10.4**).

✔ Tip

- You can put initial text in an input text field to instruct viewers on what to enter. Put *Enter Web site address here* in your text field, for example, so that viewers know to replace that phrase with their Web site address. Or you could start them off by putting *http://* in the text field so that it's there already.

Dynamic Text

For text that you control—such as scores in an arcade game, the display of a calculator, or the percentage-of-download progress of your Flash movie—take advantage of Flash's dynamic-text option. Whereas input text fields accept information from the viewer, dynamic text fields output information to the viewer. As is the case with input text, you can assign a variable to dynamic text, and the contents of this variable are displayed in the text field.

In the following task, you will create an input text field and a dynamic text field. When viewers enter the temperature, in Celsius, in the input text field, Flash will convert the value to Fahrenheit and display it in the dynamic text field.

To use dynamic text to output expressions:

1. Choose the text tool in the Tools palette, and drag out a text field onto the Stage.
2. In the Property Inspector, choose Input Text from the pull-down menu.
3. In the Variable field, enter the name of the input-text variable (**Figure 10.5**).

   Your selected text field becomes input text, allowing text entry during playback.
4. Again, choose the text tool, and drag out another text field on the Stage.
5. In the Property Inspector, this time choose Dynamic Text from the pull-down menu.

   Your selected text field becomes dynamic text, allowing you to display and update text in that field.
6. In the Variable field of the Property Inspector, enter the name of the variable for the dynamic text (**Figure 10.6**).

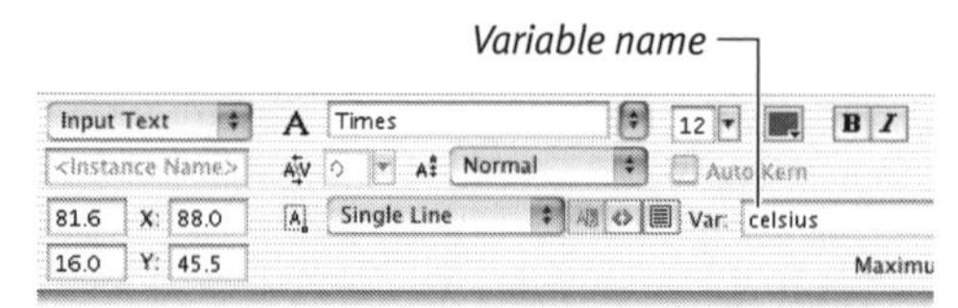

Figure 10.5 Enter `celsius` as the variable name for your input text field.

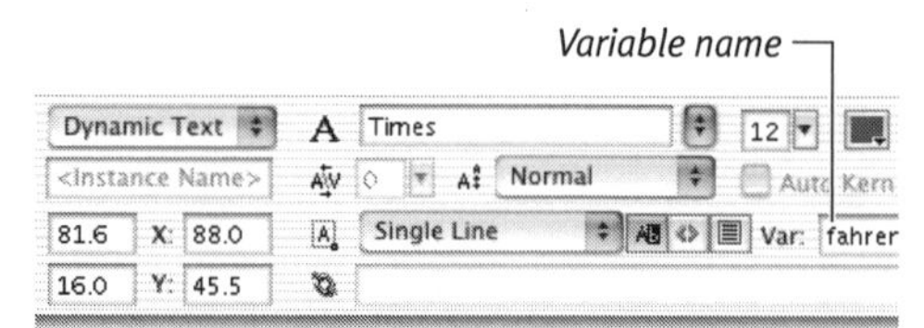

Figure 10.6 Enter `fahrenheit` as the variable name for your dynamic text field.

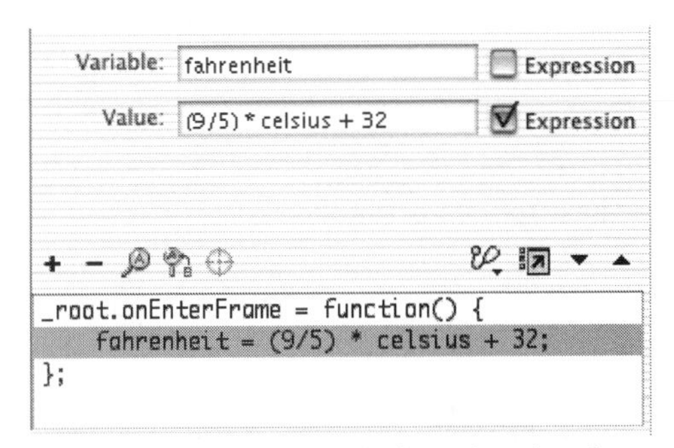

Figure 10.7 This statement calculates the value of `fahrenheit` from the expression in the Value field.

fahrenheit dynamic text
celsius input text

Enter temperature in celsius
Celsius 22
Fahrenheit 71.6

Figure 10.8 The dynamic text-field variable (`fahrenheit`) updates its contents when new input text (`celsius`) is entered.

7. Select the first frame of the main Timeline, and open the Actions panel.
8. Choose Objects > Movie > Movie Clip > Events > onEnterFrame.
9. In the Object field, enter `_root`.

   The `onEnterFrame` event is triggered continuously, providing a way to do the conversion of Celsius to Fahrenheit in real time.
10. Choose Actions > Variables > set variable.
11. In the Variable field, enter the name of your dynamic text variable.
12. In the Value field, enter a formula that incorporates the input-text variable, and check the Expression checkbox (**Figure 10.7**).
13. Test your movie.

    Flash displays the value of the dynamic text variable based on the information that the viewer enters in the input text field (**Figure 10.8**). The calculation is done in real time, and the display is updated any time the input text changes.

✔ Tip

- Use dynamic text to show the contents of variables as a debugging tool. If you are developing a complicated Flash movie involving multiple variables, you can create a dynamic text field to display the variables' current values so that you know how Flash is processing the information. In Chapter 12, you'll learn other ways to track variables, but this way, you can integrate the display of variables into your movie.

Selecting Text-Field Options

The Property Inspector offers many options for an input or dynamic text field (**Figure 10.9**). The two most important fields to fill are Name and Variable . The Name field contains the instance name of your text field, letting you target it to modify its properties and call its methods. The Variable field, as you have learned, contains the variable name that holds any information currently in the text field. The other options let you modify the way text appears:

- The Line Type pull-down menu defines how text will fit into the text field. Single Line forces entered text to stay on one row in the text field. If text goes beyond the limits of the text field, the text begins to scroll horizontally. Multiline No Wrap allows entered text to appear on more than one row in the text field if the viewer presses the Return key for a carriage return. Multiline automatically puts line breaks in text that goes beyond the text field. Password disguises the letters entered in the text box with asterisks; use this option to hide sensitive information such as a password from people looking over your viewer's shoulder.
- The Selectable button allows your viewers to select the text inside the text field. (This button is not available for input text, because input text is—by nature—always selectable.)
- The Render As HTML button allows text formatted with HTML 1.0 tags to be displayed correctly.
- The Show Border button draws a black border and white background around your text field. Deselect this option to leave the text field invisible, but be sure to draw your own background or border so that viewers can find your text field on the Stage.
- The Maximum Characters field puts a limit on the amount of text your viewer can enter. If you want the viewer to enter his or her home state by using only the two-digit abbreviation, for example, enter 2 in this field. (This option is available only for input text.)
- The Character button brings up the Character Options dialog box, where you can choose to embed font outlines with your exported SWF so that your text field displays antialiased type in the font of your choice. Keep in mind that this option increases your file size.
- The Format button brings up the Format Options dialog box, where you can choose paragraph spacing and alignment options.

✔ Tip

- Unfortunately, dynamic and input text fields do not support vertical text. Vertical text is allowed only for static text.

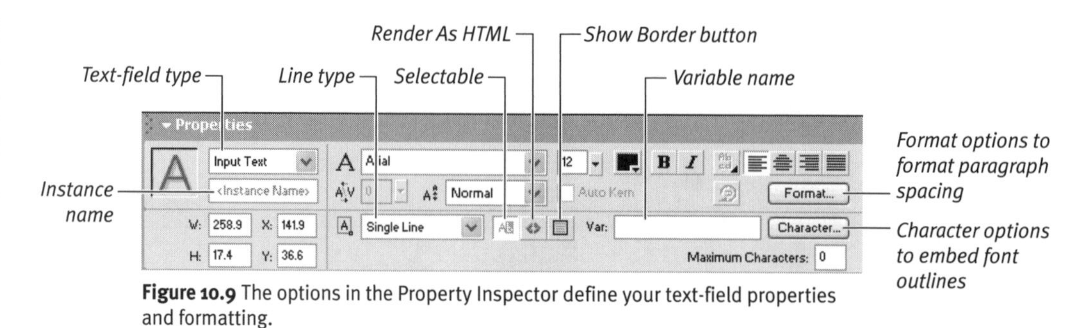

Figure 10.9 The options in the Property Inspector define your text-field properties and formatting.

Embedding Fonts and Device Fonts

Embedding font outlines via the Character Options dialog box ensures that the font you use in the authoring environment is the same one that your audience sees during playback. This operation is done by default for static text, but you must choose the option when you create input text or dynamic text. When you don't embed fonts in your movie, Flash uses the closest font available on your viewer's computer and displays it as aliased text (**Figure 10.10**).

Why wouldn't you choose to embed font outlines all the time? Embedding fonts dramatically increases the size of your exported SWF file, because the information needed to render that font is included. You can keep the file size down by embedding only the characters that your viewers will use in the text field. If you ask viewers to enter numeric information in an input text field, for example, you can embed just the numbers of the font outline. All the numbers would be available during movie playback; the other characters would be disabled and would not display at all.

Another way to maintain small file sizes and eliminate the problem caused by viewers' not having the matching font is to use device fonts. Device fonts appear at the beginning (Windows) or end (Mac) of your Font Style pull-down menu. The three device fonts are _sans, _serif, and _typewriter. This option finds the fonts on a viewer's system that most closely resemble the specified device font. Following are the corresponding fonts for the device fonts:

On the Mac

- _sans maps to Helvetica.
- _serif maps to Times.
- _typewriter maps to Courier.

In Windows

- _sans maps to Arial.
- _serif maps to Times New Roman.
- _typewriter maps to Courier New.

When you use device fonts, you can be assured that your viewer sees text that is very similar to the text in the authoring environment. Be aware of two warnings about device fonts, however: They do not display antialiased, and they cannot be tweened or masked.

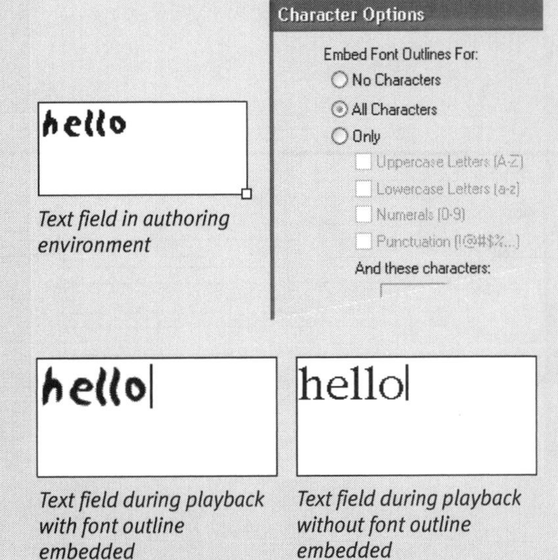

Figure 10.10 A text field using a font in authoring mode (top) displays differently during playback on a computer that doesn't have the font, depending on whether the font outlines are embedded (bottom).

Concatenating Text

Using dynamic text to *concatenate*, or connect, input text with other variables and strings lets you work with expressions in more flexible ways and also allows you to create more-personalized Flash interactions with your viewers. You can have viewers first enter their names in an input text field called yourName, and in a dynamic text field, you can set its variable to:

```
"Hello, "+yourName+", welcome to Flash!"
```

Your viewers will see their own names concatenated with your message.

In an earlier task in this chapter, you created a Flash movie that loaded a URL based on input text. By concatenating the input-text variable called `myURL` in the expression `"http://"+myURL`, you eliminate the requirement that your viewer type the Internet protocol scheme before the actual Website address.

Use this strategy in combination with other Flash actions to develop flexible, customizable functions and interfaces. In the following example, you concatenate input text from a customer to compile the information in the correct layout automatically and then use the `print` action to print a complete receipt or order form.

To concatenate text fields for custom printing:

1. Choose the text tool in the Tools palette, create several input text fields, and give each of them a unique variable name in the Property Inspector (**Figure 10.11**).
2. Create a movie-clip symbol, and enter symbol-editing mode for that movie clip.
3. In the first keyframe of the movie clip, assign a `stop` action, and leave this first keyframe empty of any graphics.

   The `stop` action prevents this movie clip from playing and cycling endlessly.

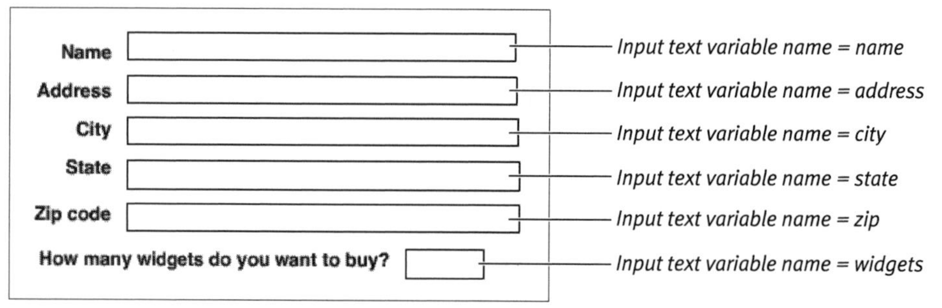

Figure 10.11 Define six input text fields with unique variable names.

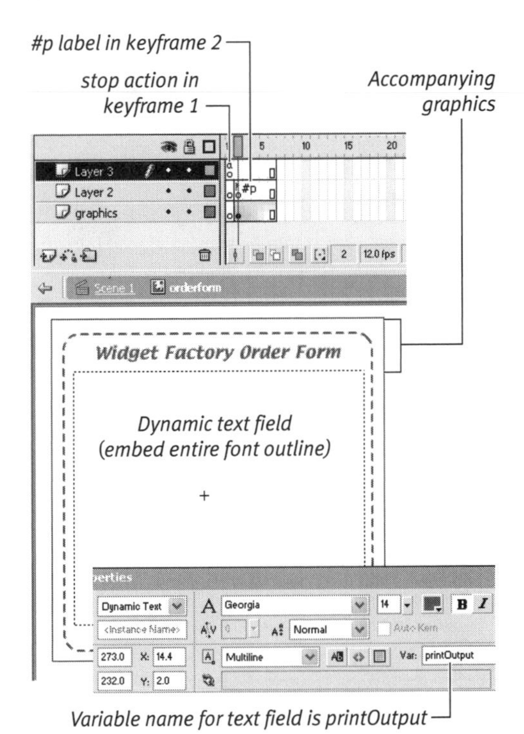

Figure 10.12 The dynamic text field is laid out in keyframe 2 with graphics ready to print.

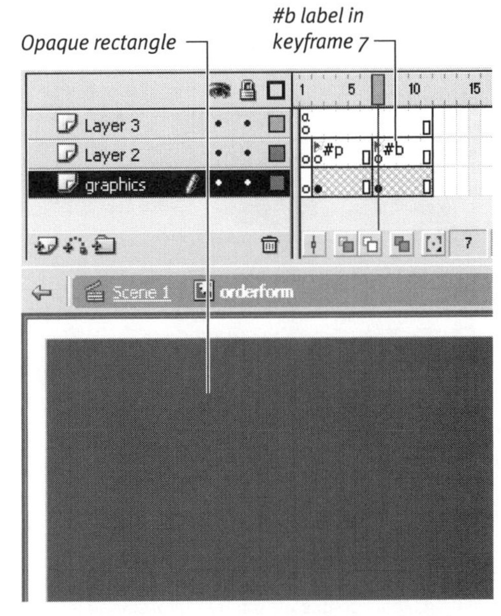

Figure 10.13 The opaque rectangle defines the print area for all the keyframes marked with the #p label.

4. Insert a new keyframe at frame 2, label the new keyframe #p, and create a large dynamic text field in it.

5. In the Property Inspector, choose Multiline from the Line Type pull-down menu, enter a variable name, embed the entire font outline through the Character Options dialog box, and add graphics you want to include in the printed piece (**Figure 10.12**).

   The dynamic text field will display concatenated information, and the #p label identifies this keyframe to print.

6. Insert another keyframe later in the Timeline, label this keyframe #b, and draw a large opaque rectangle that covers the same area covered by the dynamic text field in the preceding keyframe (**Figure 10.13**).

   The #b label identifies this keyframe as the print area.

7. Return to the root Timeline, drag an instance of the three-keyframe movie clip you just created to the Stage, and give the instance a name in the Property Inspector.

8. Create a button symbol, and drag an instance of it to the Stage.

9. Select the instance, and open the Actions panel.

10. Choose Actions > Movie Control > on.

11. Choose Actions > Variables > set variable.

12. In the Variable field, enter the target path to the dynamic text variable.

continues on next page

13. In the Value field, enter a combination of strings and the input text variables to concatenate the user-entered information into a compact, printable form; also, check the Expression checkbox (**Figure 10.14**).

    Use escape sequences such as \r for carriage returns.

14. Choose Actions > Printing > print (**Figure 10.15**).

15. From the Print pull-down menu, choose As Vectors.

16. Choose Target from the location pull-down menu, enter the name of your movie-clip instance, and check the Expression checkbox.

17. Choose Movie from the Bounding pull-down menu as the bounding box.

18. Test your movie.

    When your viewer enters information into the input text fields and then clicks the button, the dynamic text in the movie clip concatenates the input text variables and displays the information in the keyframe labeled #p. Then the `print` action prints this keyframe (**Figure 10.16**).

✔ Tips

- You can also hide a movie clip that's on the Stage from the viewer but still have it available for printing by setting the `_visible` property to `false`. Changing the visibility property of a movie clip doesn't affect how it prints.

- It's important that you embed fonts for dynamic text fields sent to the printer. Embedding fonts for a text field results in a much better-quality print.

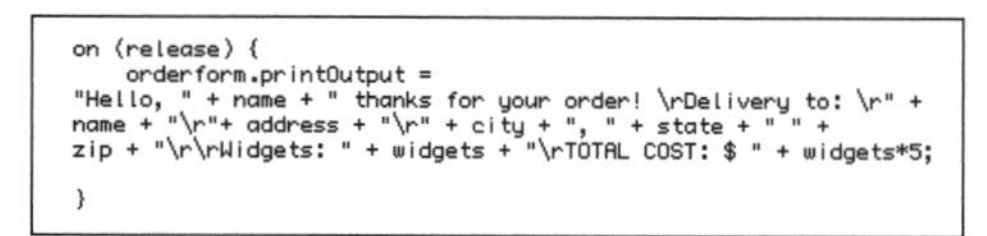

```
on (release) {
    orderform.printOutput =
"Hello, " + name + " thanks for your order! \rDelivery to: \r" +
name + "\r"+ address + "\r" + city + ", " + state + " " +
zip + "\r\rWidgets: " + widgets + "\rTOTAL COST: $ " + widgets*5;

}
```

Figure 10.14 The target path to the dynamic text field called printOutput includes the movie clip called orderform. The dynamic text field displays a string that concatenates the input text variables and totals the cost of ordered widgets by multiplying the variable by 5.

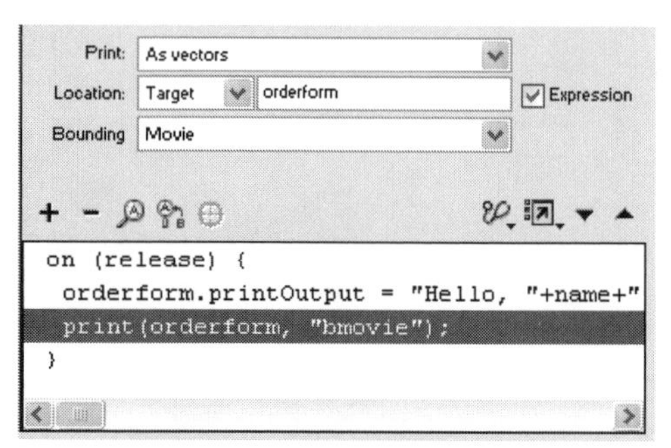

Figure 10.15 The `print` statement sends the information in the #p frame to the printer.

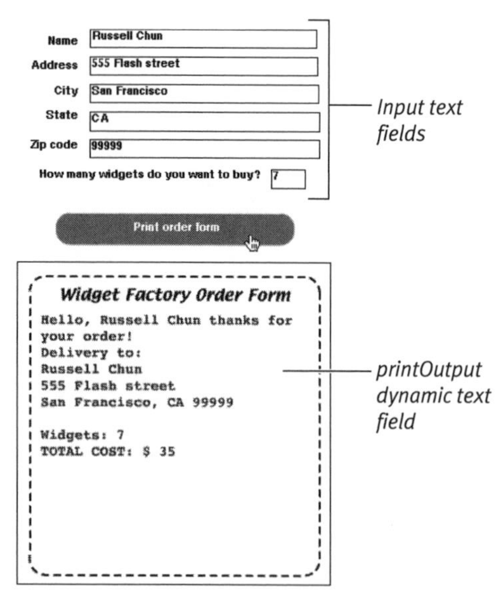

Figure 10.16 The Flash movie (top) provides input text fields that compile the entered information in a dynamic text field and print it (bottom).

Displaying HTML

Flash can display HTML 1.0–formatted text in dynamic text fields. When you mark up text with HTML tags and assign the text to a dynamic text variable, Flash will interpret the tags and preserve the formatting. This means that you can integrate HTML pages inside your Flash movie, maintaining the styles and functional HREF anchors.

Common HTML Tags Supported by Text Fields

- <A HREF> Anchor tag to create hot links
- <B> Bold style
- <FONT COLOR> Font-color style
- <FONT FACE> Font-face style
- <FONT SIZE> Font-size style
- <I> Italics style
- <P> Paragraph
- <U> Underline style

A useful combination is to load HTML-formatted text into dynamic text fields with the action `loadVariables`. Simply by changing the HTML that resides outside the Flash file, you can update the information that displays during playback of your movie. This feature can be very convenient, because you don't have to open the Flash file to make periodic edits, and a server-side script or even a user who's unfamiliar with Flash can make the necessary updates.

To load and display HTML in a dynamic text field:

1. Open a text-editing application or a WYSIWYG HTML editor, and create your HTML document.
2. At the very beginning of the HTML text, add a variable name and the assignment operator (the equal sign [=]).
3. Save the text file (**Figure 10.17**).

continues on next page

```
HTMLpage=<HTML><BODY>
<B>This is an HTML page</B></P>
This contains <I>simple</I> HTML 1.0 tags that <FONT FACE="ARIAL">Flash</FONT> can
understand. Flash will display HTML formatted text when the HTML option is checked in
Dynamic Text in the Text Options panel.</P>
</P>
A HREF will also work to create links to Web sites! For example, if you <FONT
COLOR="#0000FF"><u><A HREF="http://www.macromedia.com">click here</A></u></FONT>, you
will be sent to Macromedia's Web site.</BODY></HTML>
```

Figure 10.17 The HTML text is assigned to the variable called `HTMLpage` and saved as a separate document.

4. In Flash, select the first keyframe in the root Timeline, and open the Actions panel.
5. Choose Actions > Browser/Network > loadVariables.
6. In the URL field, enter the name of the text file you just created.
7. Keep the Location options set to Level and 0 (**Figure 10.18**).

   Flash loads the text file that contains the variable into level 0.
8. Choose the text tool, and drag out a large text field that nearly covers the Stage.
9. In the Property Inspector, choose Dynamic Text and Multiline, and check the Render As HTML button.
10. Give the text field a variable name (**Figure 10.19**).
11. Create a button symbol, and place an instance of it on the Stage.
12. Select the instance, and open the Actions panel.
13. Choose Actions > Movie Control > on.
14. Choose Actions > Variables > set variable.
15. In the Variable field, enter the name of your dynamic text variable.
16. In the Value field, enter the variable you assigned to the text file. Check the Expression box (**Figure 10.20**).
17. Export a SWF file to the same directory that contains your text file.

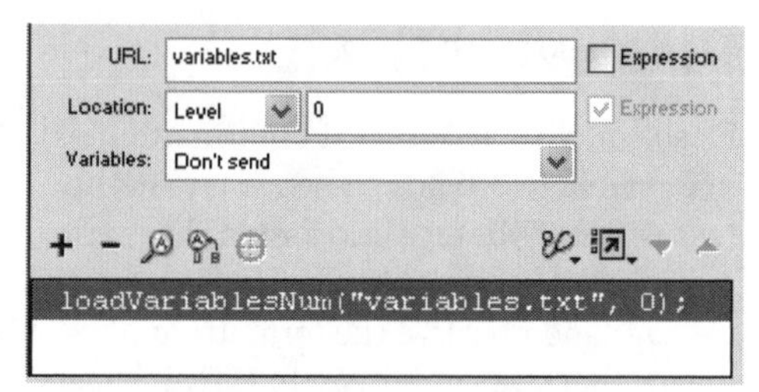

Figure 10.18 This frame action loads the file variables.txt, which contains the variable holding HTML text.

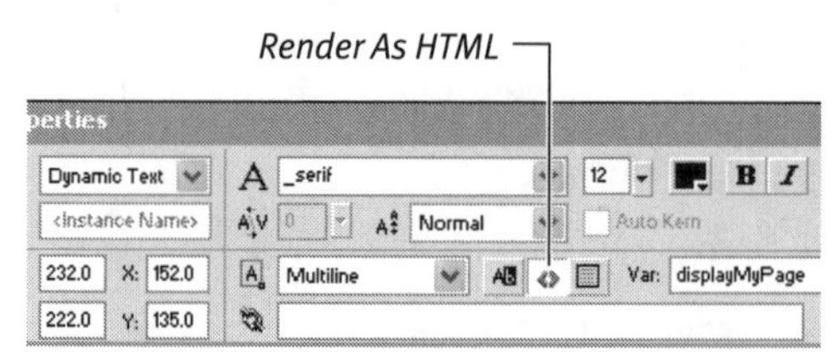

Figure 10.19 Enter `displayMyPage` as the variable name for your dynamic text field, and click the Render As HTML button.

Figure 10.20 The dynamic text-field variable called `displayMyPage` shows the contents of the variable `HTMLpage`.

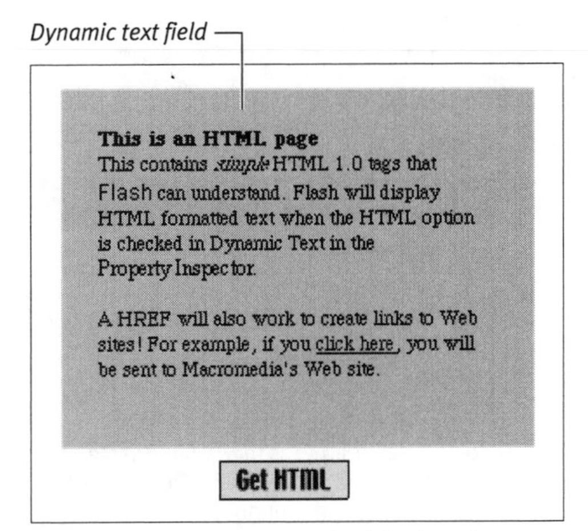

Figure 10.21 The dynamic text field displays the HTML-formatted text.

18. Play the SWF in either Flash Player or a browser.

When your viewer clicks the button, Flash sets the dynamic text variable to the external variable in the text file, which holds HTML-formatted text. The dynamic text field displays the information, preserving all the style and format tags (**Figure 10.21**).

✔ Tips

- Because only a limited number of HTML tags are supported by dynamic text, you should do a fair amount of testing to see how the information displays. When Flash doesn't understand a tag, it simply ignores it.
- The anchor tag (`<A>`) normally appears underlined and in a different color in browser environments. In Flash, however, the hot link is indicated only by the pointer's changing to a finger. To create the underline and color style for hot links manually, apply the underline tag (`<U>`) and the font-color tag (`<FONT COLOR="#0000FF">`).
- The HTML tags override any style settings you assign in the Property Inspector for your dynamic text. If you choose red for your dynamic text, when you display HTML text in the field, the `<FONT COLOR>` tag would modify the text to a different color.

Tweening Text Fields

If you place text fields in movie-clip symbols, you can apply motion tweens to them just as you can with other symbol instances. This technique lets you create titles and banners that not only can be updated dynamically, but also can move across the screen, rotate, and shrink or grow. Imagine a blimp traveling across the Stage with a giant scoreboard attached to its side. By using a dynamic text field as the scoreboard on the blimp graphic, you can update scores or have messages appear as the blimp floats. You could use the same method to create a stock ticker-tape monitor, with the stock prices moving across the screen. Or you could create a game that displays the current status of an individual player right next to the player's icon as it moves around the Stage.

Eventually, you'll learn to animate text fields just with ActionScript. Even so, keep in mind that you will still rely on tweens, or a combination of tweens and ActionScript, for many kinds of motions. Making text follow a path, for example, is a challenge better solved with tweens than with ActionScript alone.

To create a moving dynamic text field:

1. Select the text tool, and drag out a text field on the Stage.
2. In the Property Inspector, choose Dynamic Text and Single Line; give the text field a variable name; and embed the entire font outline through the Character Options dialog box (**Figure 10.22**).
3. Select your text field, and choose Insert > Convert to Symbol (F8) from the main toolbar.

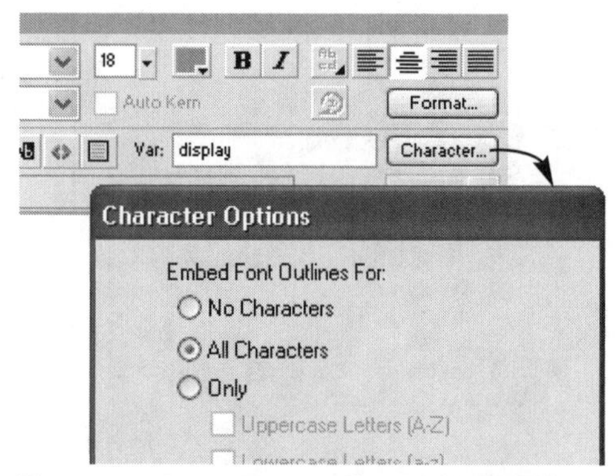

Figure 10.22 Enter `display` as the variable name for your dynamic text field, and embed all font outlines from the Character Options button.

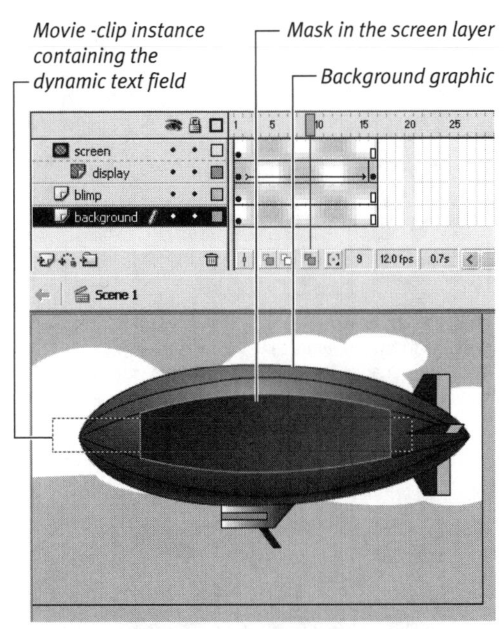

Figure 10.23 On the main Timeline, tween the movie-clip instance that contains the dynamic text field. This movie-clip instance (the dotted rectangle) moves across the Stage behind a mask of the scoreboard on the blimp.

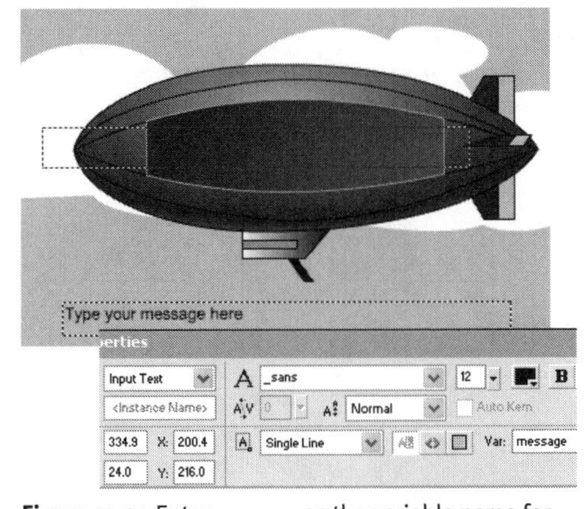

Figure 10.24 Enter `message` as the variable name for the input text field.

4. In the dialog box that appears, name your symbol and choose Movie Clip as the behavior; then click OK.

   Flash puts your dynamic text field inside a movie-clip symbol and places an instance of it on the Stage.
5. In the Property Inspector, name the movie-clip instance.
6. Create a motion tween of the movie-clip instance moving across the Stage (**Figure 10.23**).
7. Select the text tool, and drag out another text field below the tween of the movie-clip instance.
8. In the Property Inspector, choose Input Text and Single Line, and give this text field a variable name (**Figure 10.24**).
9. Select the main Timeline, and open the Actions panel.
10. Choose Objects > Movie > Movie Clip > Events > onEnterFrame.
11. In the Object field, enter `_root`.
12. Choose Actions > Variables > set variable.
13. In the Variable field, enter the target path to the dynamic text variable.

continues on next page

14. In the Value field, enter the input text variable, and check the Expression checkbox (**Figure 10.25**).

    The dynamic text field is updated continuously with the contents of the input text field.

15. Test your movie.

    When your viewer enters information in the input text field, that information is assigned to the dynamic text field inside the movie clip, and the updated text moves across the screen (**Figure 10.26**).

✔ Tip

- It's important to include the entire font outline in a dynamic text field when you tween it (change its rotation and alpha, especially) or when it's part of a masked layer. If the font outline is not included, the text field won't tween properly or show up behind the mask.

Figure 10.25 Assign the input text-field variable called `message` to the dynamic text-field variable called `display`. Because the dynamic text field is inside a movie clip, the target path is `displayInMC.display`.

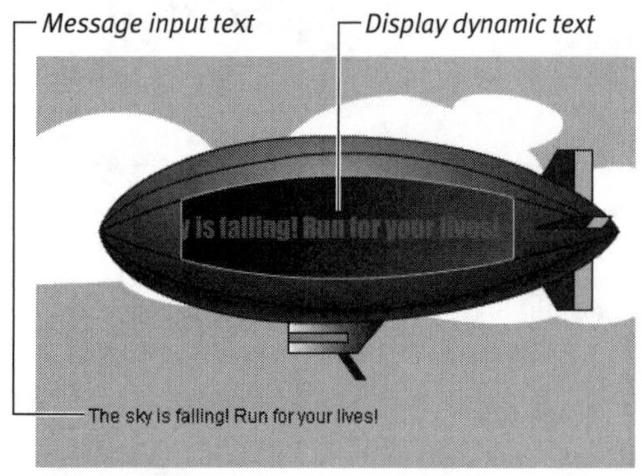

Figure 10.26 Flash tweens the dynamic text field (top) containing any message your viewer enters in the input text field (bottom).

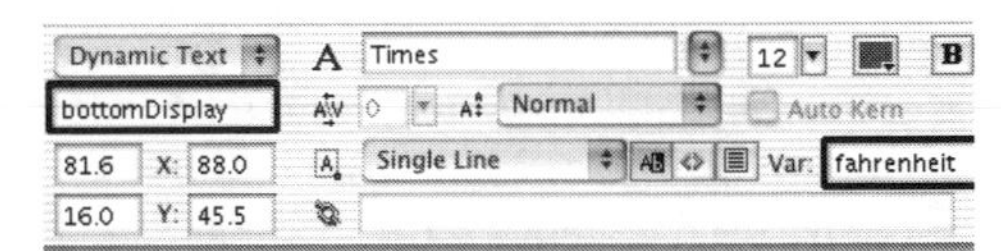

Figure 10.27 The Instance name and Variable name (highlighted with bold rectangles) of a text field are different identifiers and must be unique.

TextField Properties

When you drag an input or dynamic text field on the Stage with the text tool, you are creating an instance of the TextField object. Before you can have access to its methods and properties, however, you must name your text field in the Property Inspector so that you can identify it with ActionScript.

The instance name of a text field is very different from the variable name that you've been using so far in the chapter (**Figure 10.27**). The variable name simply holds the contents of the text field. The instance name, on the other hand, identifies the text field for targeting purposes. When you can target the text field, you can evaluate or modify its many properties. These properties determine the kind and display of the text field. The property `type`, for example, defines an input or dynamic text field; `border` determines whether the text field has one; and `_rotation` controls the angle of the text field.

Table 10.1 summarizes the properties of the TextField object. Many of these properties are identical to the ones you can set in authoring mode in the Property Inspector. In addition, you can use the properties common to the Movie Clip and the Button object, such as `_rotation`, `_alpha`, `_x`, `_y`, `_width`, `_height`, `_xscale`, `_yscale`, `_name`, `_visible`, `tabEnabled`, and `tabIndex`.

continues on next page

By far the most important TextField property is `text`. The `text` property holds the current contents of a text field. So the statement `myTextField.text = "Congratulations!"` would display the string `Congratulations!` in the text field called myTextField. Isn't that the same as a text field's variable name? Yes, it is, and you can use either the `text` property or the variable name to evaluate and modify the contents of a text field. But you'll find that more methods reference the instance name of a text field than its variable name, which makes the variable name somewhat limited.

Table 10.1

TextField Properties

Property	Value	Description
text	A string	The contents of the text field.
type	"dynamic" or "input"	Specifies a dynamic or input text field.
autosize	"none", "left", "center", or "right"	Controls automatic alignment and sizing so that a text field shrinks or grows to accommodate text.
background	true or false	Specifies whether the text field has a background fill.
backgroundColor	A hex code	Specifies the color of the background (visible only when border = true).
border	true or false	Specifies whether the text field has a border
borderColor	A hex code	Specifies the color of the border.
textColor	A hex code	Specifies the color of the text.
textWidth	A number, in pixels	Specifies the width of the text (read-only).
textHeight	A number, in pixels	Specifies the height of the text (read-only).
length	A number	Specifies the number of characters in a text field (read-only).
scroll	A number	Specifies the top line visible in the text field.
bottomscroll	A number	Specifies the bottom line visible in the text field (read-only).
hscroll	A number	Specifies the horizontal scrolling position of a text field. 0 defines the position where there is no scrolling. Values are in 1/20-pixel units
maxscroll	A number	Specifies the maximum value for the scroll property (read-only).
maxhscroll	A number	Specifies the maximum value for the hscroll property (read-only).
restrict	A string	Specifies the allowable characters in the text field,
maxChars	A number	Specifies the maximum number of characters allowable.
variable	A string	Specifies the name of the text-field variable
embedFonts	true or false	Specifies whether fonts are embedded. You must create a font symbol and export it for ActionScript in its Linkage properties.
html	true or false	Specifies whether the text field renders HTML tags.
htmlText	A string	Specifies the contents of a text field when html = true.
multiline	true or false	Specifies whether the text field can display more than one line.
wordWrap	true or false	Specifies whether the text field breaks lines automatically.
selectable	true or false	Specifies whether the contents of the text field are selectable.
password	true or false	Specifies whether input text is disguised.
tabEnabled	true or false	Specifies whether the text field can receive focus when using the Tab key.
tabIndex	A number	Specifies the order of focus when using the Tab key.

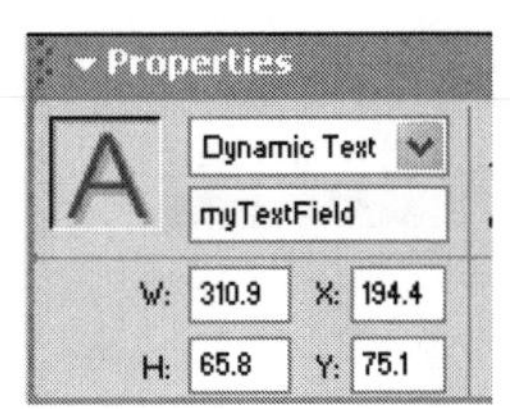

Figure 10.28 The dynamic text field is called myTextField.

Variable: myTextField.textColor Expression
Value: 0xff0000 Expression

```
myTextField.textColor = 0xff0000;
```

Figure 10.29 The `textColor` property of the text field called myTextField is set to red.

Black border *Light-green background*

(x = 200, y = 50) *Embedded font*

```
myTextField.textColor = 0xff0000;
myTextField.text = "Welcome to Flash MX";
myTextField.embedFonts = true;
myTextField.background = true;
myTextField.backgroundColor = 0xDFFCB8;
myTextField.border = true;
myTextField._x = 200;
myTextField._y = 50;
```

Welcome to Flash MX

```
with (myTextField) {
 textColor = 0xff0000;
 text = "Welcome to Flash MX";
 embedFonts = true;
 background = true;
 backgroundColor = 0xDFFCB8;
 border = true;
 _x = 200;
 _y = 50;
}
```

Figure 10.30 The script (above) modifies many properties of the text field called myTextField, resulting in the text in the middle. If you have many properties to change, use the `with` action to alter the scope temporarily, as shown in the bottom script.

To modify the properties of the text field:

1. Select the text tool in the Tools palette, and drag out a text field on the Stage.
2. In the Property Inspector, select Dynamic Text, give the text field a name in the Instance Name field, and leave all other options at their default settings (**Figure 10.28**).
3. Select the first frame of the main Timeline, and open the Actions panel.
4. Select Actions > Variables > set variable.
5. In the Variable field, enter the name of your text field.
6. With your pointer still in the Variable field, choose Objects > Movie > TextField > Properties > textColor.
7. In the Value field, enter `0xff0000`, and check the Expression checkbox.

   The completed statement changes the color of the text to red (**Figure 10.29**).
8. Repeat steps 5 through 7, choosing different properties and values to modify your text field (**Figure 10.30**).

continues on next page

✔ Tips

- To modify the font, font size, and other characteristics of the text, you must use the TextFormat object, which we discuss later in this chapter.
- If you modify the properties `_alpha` and `_rotation`, you must embed the font outlines for your text field. If you don't, the text won't be modified correctly.
- The properties `_x` and `_y` refer to the top-left corner of the text field.
- The properties `_width` and `_height` change the pixel dimensions of the text field but do not change the size of the text inside the text field. The properties `_xscale` and `_yscale`, on the other hand, will scale the text.

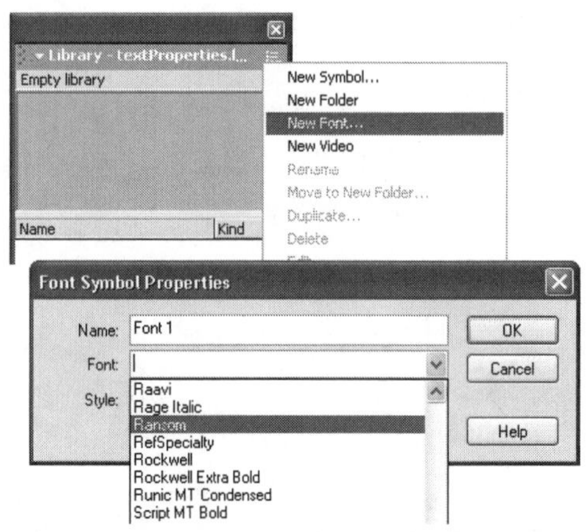

Figure 10.31 Choose New Font from the Library window's Options pull-down menu (top) to create a font symbol. Choose your font in the Font Symbol Properties dialog box (below). The Name field contains the name of the symbol that will appear in the library.

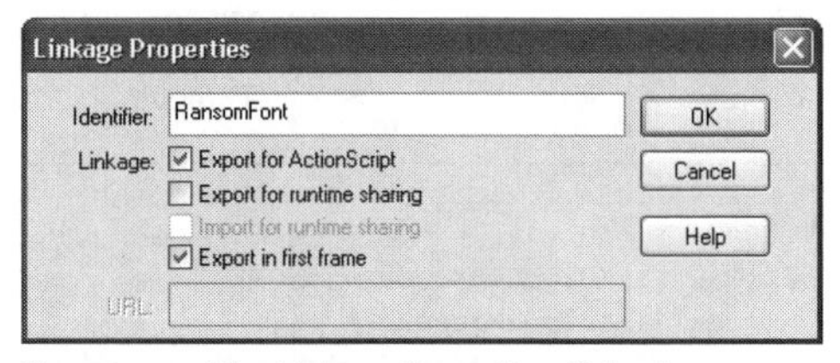

Figure 10.32 The Linkage Properties dialog box enables you to export your font symbol for use in ActionScript. The Identifier field contains the name that you will use in ActionScript to refer to this font.

Embedding Fonts: Creating Font Symbols for ActionScript Export

When you set the `embedFonts` property of a TextField to `true`, you must provide the font outline in the exported SWF. This process involves creating a font symbol in the library and marking it for ActionScript export. If you don't, Flash won't know to make the font available when it publishes your movie. In the library, choose New Font from the Options pull-down menu. In the Font Symbol Properties dialog box that appears, select the font in the list (**Figure 10.31**). Click OK, and you'll have a new font symbol in your library. Select the symbol, and choose Linkage from the Options pull-down menu. In the Linkage Properties dialog box that appears, select Export for ActionScript, and choose an identifier for your font symbol (**Figure 10.32**). Click OK. Your font symbol will be exported to the SWF. When you set the `embedFonts` property to `true` via ActionScript, the font symbol will be available.

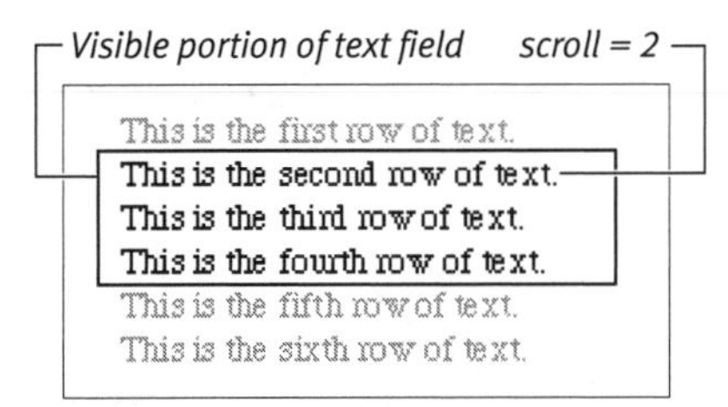

Figure 10.33 The `scroll` property is the first visible row of text within a text field.

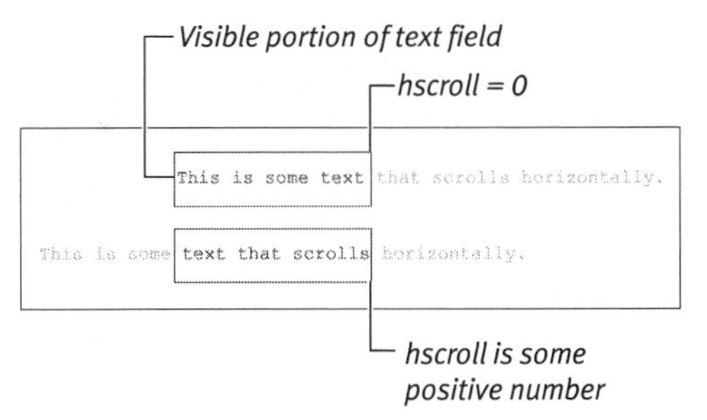

Figure 10.34 The `hscroll` property is relative to the point at which there is no scrolling. The value of `hscroll` increases as horizontal scrolling occurs.

Controlling text-field scrolling

The TextField properties `scroll`, `maxscroll`, `hscroll`, `maxhscroll`, and `bottomscroll` all give information about the position of text within a text field that may be too small to fit in its borders.

When the information in a multiline text field exceeds its defined boundaries, Flash displays only the current text (unless you set the `autosize` property to fit the information). Text that can't fit within the text field is hidden from view but still accessible if the viewer clicks inside the text field and drags up or down. You can display different portions of the hidden text dynamically by defining the properties `scroll` and `hscroll`.

Think of the text field as being a window that shows only a portion of a larger piece of text. Each row of text has an index value. The top row is 1, the second row is 2, and so on. The `scroll` property refers to the topmost visible row. The `bottomScroll` property refers to the bottommost visible row. So the visible portion of a text field is the rows from `scroll` to `bottomscroll`, and as new lines of text scroll up or down, those properties change (**Figure 10.33**).

If a line of text exceeds the width of its text field, you can use `hscroll` to display different portions of its horizontal scrolling. The point on the right edge of the text field where the initial text is visible has an `hscroll` value of 0. The value of `hscroll` is measured in 1/20-pixel units, and as `hscroll` increases, the text scrolls to reveal more of itself (**Figure 10.34**).

continues on next page

You can retrieve the value of `scroll` and `hscroll` so that you know exactly which portion of the text your viewer is currently looking at, or you can modify their values to force your viewer to look at a particular portion. It is common to provide interface controls so that viewers themselves can control the scrolling of text, just as they control the scroll bars in a Web browser or any window on the computer screen. In the following task, you'll create interface controls of this kind.

To create a vertical scrolling text field:

1. Select the text tool in the Tools palette, and drag out a text field onto the Stage.
2. In the Property Inspector, choose Input Text, enter an instance name; choose Multiline from the pull-down menu; and click the Show Border button (**Figure 10.35**).
3. Create a button symbol of an arrow pointing up, place an instance of the button on the Stage, and give it a name in the Property Inspector.
4. Place a second instance of the button on the Stage, choose Modify > Transform > Flip Vertical to make the second button point down, and give the down-arrow button a name in the Property Inspector.
5. Align both buttons vertically next to the input text field (**Figure 10.36**).
6. Select the first frame of the main Timeline, and open the Actions panel.
7. Assign an `onPress` handler to the up-arrow button.
8. Choose Actions > Variables > set variable.
9. In the Variable field, enter the variable name `pressing`.

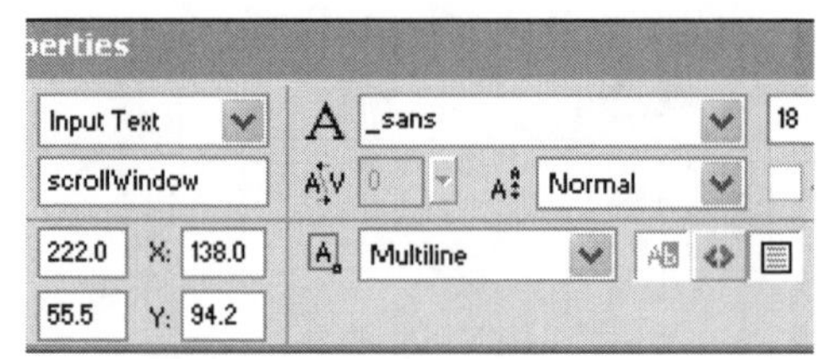

Figure 10.35 Enter scrollwindow as the instance name of your text field.

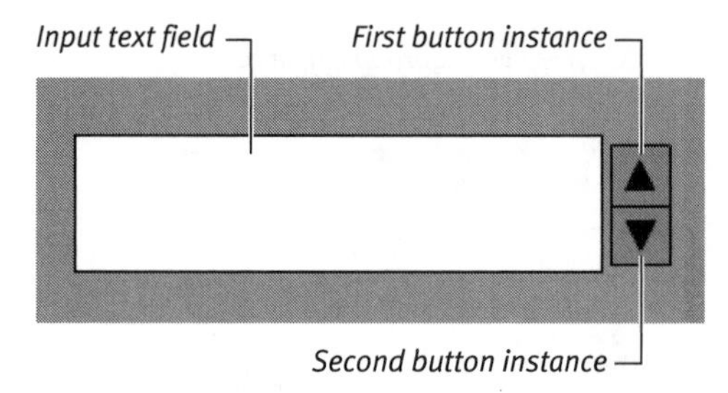

Figure 10.36 Place two buttons next to the input text field.

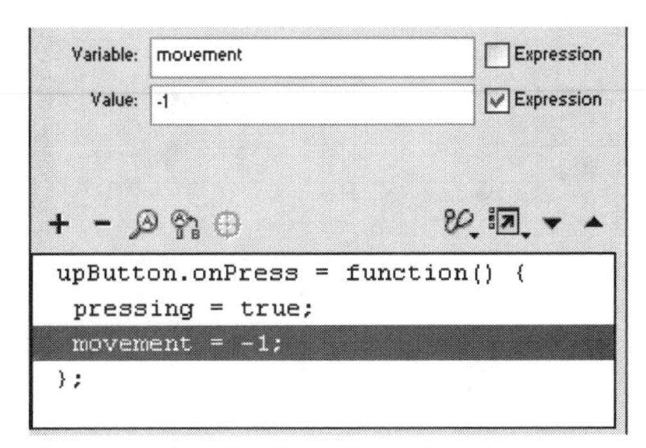

Figure 10.37 Pressing the upButton button sets the variable `pressing` to `true` and the variable `movement` to –1.

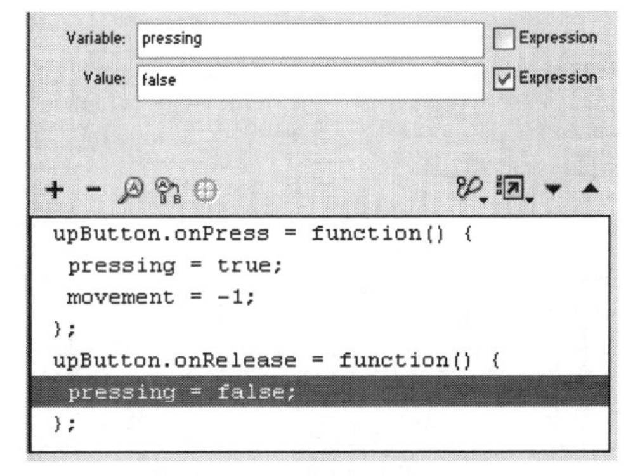

Figure 10.38 Releasing the upButton button sets the variable `pressing` to `false`.

```
upButton.onPress = function() {
 pressing = true;
 movement = -1;
};
upButton.onRelease = function() {
 pressing = false;
};
downButton.onPress = function() {
 pressing = true;
 movement = 1;
};
downButton.onRelease = function() {
 pressing = false;
};
```

Figure 10.39 The script so far, as shown in the Script pane of the Actions panel.

10. In the Value field, enter the Boolean value `true`, and check the Expression checkbox.
11. Again, choose Actions > Variables > set variable.
12. In the Variable field, enter the variable name `movement`.
13. In the Value field, enter –1, and check the Expression checkbox (**Figure 10.37**).

    When the mouse button is pressed, the variable `pressing` is set to `true`, and the variable movement is set to –1.
14. Assign an `onRelease` handler to the up-arrow button.
15. Choose Actions > Variables > set variable.
16. In the Variable field, enter the variable name `pressing`.
17. In the Value field, enter the Boolean value `false` and check the Expression checkbox.

    When the mouse button is released, the variable `pressing` is set to `false` (**Figure 10.38**).
18. Select the down-arrow button, and enter the same statements in the Actions List of the Actions panel, except assign the variable `movement` to 1 when the mouse button is pressed (**Figure 10.39**).

continues on next page

19. Assign an onEnterFrame handler to the root Timeline.

20. Choose Actions > Conditions/Loops > if.

21. In the Condition field, enter pressing == true.

22. Choose Actions > Variables > set variable.

23. In the Variable field, enter the name of the input text field, followed by a dot and then the property scroll.

24. In the Value field, enter the name of the input text field, followed by a dot and then the property scroll; add the value of the variable movement, and check the Expression checkbox (**Figure 10.40**).

    Flash continuously checks to see whether one of the buttons is pressed. If so, Flash adds the value of movement to the current scroll property. If the up-arrow button is pressed, the scroll value is decreased by 1. If the down-arrow button is pressed, the scroll value is increased by 1 (**Figure 10.41**).

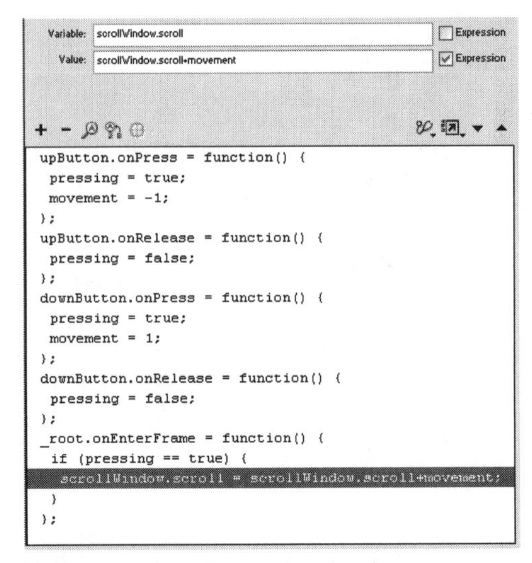

Figure 10.40 The actions assigned to the onEnterFrame handler continuously add the value of the variable movement to the scroll property of scrollwindow when pressing is true.

Enter text in this input text
box. Use the up and down
buttons on the right to

Figure 10.41 The buttons on the right increase or decrease the value of the scroll property of the input text field.

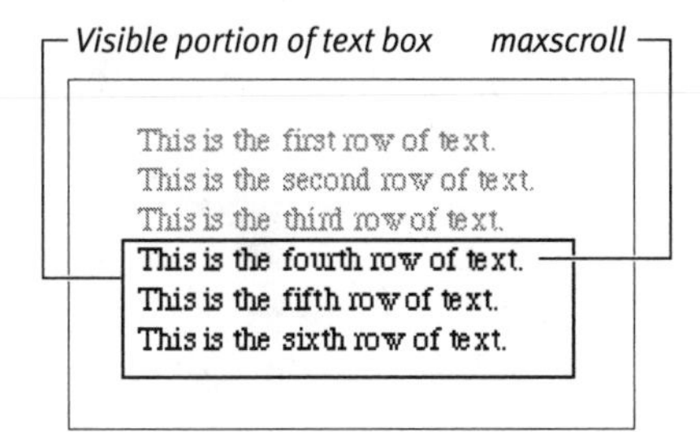

Figure 10.42 The `maxscroll` property refers to the maximum value of the `scroll` property. This value is the value of `scroll` when the last line of text is visible. In this example, `maxscroll` = 4.

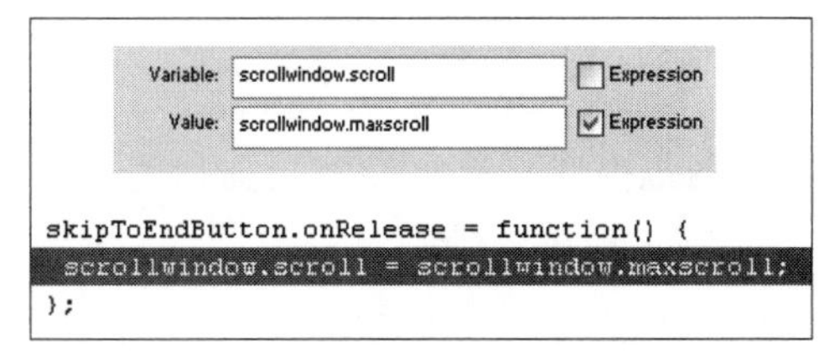

Figure 10.43 A portion of the Script pane shows the `onRelease` handler for a button called skipToEndButton. `maxscroll` is assigned to the `scroll` property of scrollwindow.

Whereas the `scroll` property defines the first visible text row in a text field, the `maxscroll` property defines the maximum allowable value for `scroll` in that text field. This row appears at the top of the text field when the last line of text is visible (**Figure 10.42**). You can't change the value of `maxscroll`, because it's defined by the amount of text and the size of the text field itself, but you can read its value. Assign the value of `maxscroll` to `scroll`, and you can scroll the text to the bottom of the text field automatically. Or you can calculate the value of `scroll` proportional to `maxscroll` and build a draggable scroll bar that reflects and controls the text's position within the text field.

To scroll to the end of a text field:

1. Continuing with the preceding task, create a new button symbol, drag an instance of it to the Stage, and give it a name in the Property Inspector.
2. Select the first frame of the main Timeline, and open the Actions panel.
3. Assign an `onRelease` handler to your latest button.
4. Choose Actions > Variables > set variable.
5. In the Variable field, enter the name of the text field, followed by a dot and then the property `scroll`.
6. In the Value field, enter the name of the text field, followed by a dot and then the property `maxscroll`, and check the Expression checkbox (**Figure 10.43**).

   When the viewer clicks this button, the current value of `maxscroll` for the text field is assigned to `scroll`. The text automatically moves so that the last line is visible.

To create a horizontal scrolling text field:

1. Select the text tool in the Tools palette, and drag out a text box onto the Stage.
2. In the Property Inspector, choose Input Text; enter an instance name, choose Single Line from the pull-down menu; and check the Show Border button (**Figure 10.44**).
3. Create a button symbol of a right-pointing arrow, place an instance of the button on the Stage, and give it a name in the Property Inspector.
4. Place a second instance of the button on the Stage, choose Modify > Transform > Flip Horizontal to make the second button point left, and give the left-arrow button a name in the Property Inspector.
5. Align both buttons horizontally above the input text field (**Figure 10.45**).
6. Select the first frame of the main Timeline, and open the Actions panel.
7. Assign code to the right- and left-arrow buttons as you did to the down- and up-arrow buttons in the preceding task.

   Your code should look similar to this:

```
rightButton.onPress = function() {
    pressing = true;
    movement = 20;
}
rightButton.onRelease = function() {
    pressing = false;
}
leftButton.onPress = function() {
    pressing = true;
    movement = -20;
}
leftButton.onRelease = function() {
    pressing = false;
```

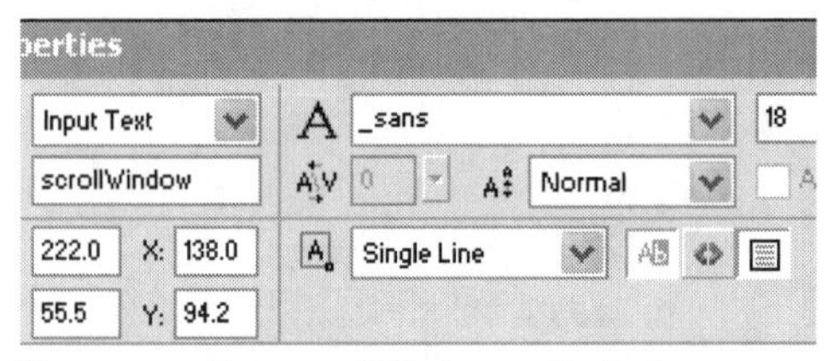

Figure 10.44 Enter scrollWindow as the instance name of your input text field.

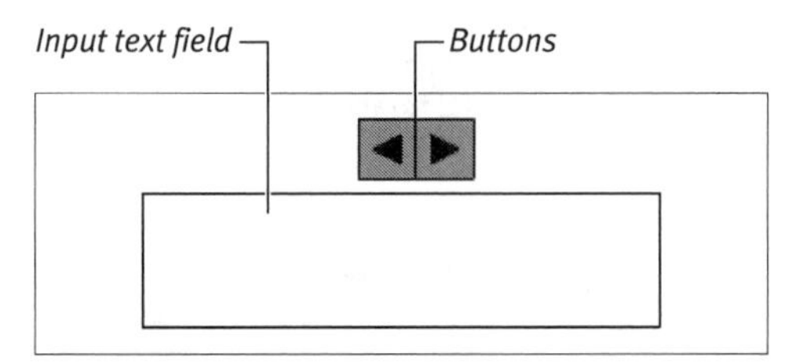

Figure 10.45 Align two buttons above your input text field.

```
Variable: scrollWindow.hscroll                    [ ] Expression
Value: scrollWindow.hscroll+movement              [✓] Expression

rightButton.onPress = function() {
 pressing = true;
 movement = 20;
};
rightButton.onRelease = function() {
 pressing = false;
};
leftButton.onPress = function() {
 pressing = true;
 movement = -20;
};
leftButton.onRelease = function() {
 pressing = false;
};
_root.onEnterFrame = function() {
 if (pressing == true) {
  scrollWindow.hscroll = scrollWindow.hscroll+movement;
 }
};
```

Figure 10.46 The actions assigned to the `onEnterFrame` handler continuously add the value of the variable `movement` to the `hscroll` property of scrollwindow when `pressing` is `true`.

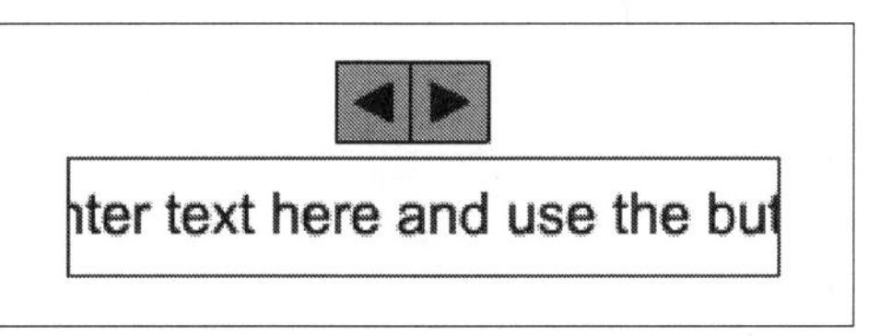

Figure 10.47 The buttons above the input text field increase or decrease the value of the `hscroll` property of the input text field.

8. Assign an `onEnterFrame` handler to the root Timeline.
9. Choose Actions > Conditions/Loops > if.
10. In the Condition field, enter `pressing == true`.
11. Choose Actions > Variables > set variable.
12. In the Variable field, enter the name of the input text field, followed by a dot and then the property `hscroll`.
13. In the Value field, enter the name of the input text field, followed by a dot and then the property `hscroll`; add the value of the variable `movement`; and check the Expression checkbox (**Figure 10.46**).

    Flash continuously checks to see whether one of the buttons is pressed. If so, Flash adds the value of `movement` to the current `hscroll` property. If the right-arrow button is pressed, the `hscroll` value increases by 20, moving the text to the left by 1 pixel. If the down-arrow button is pressed, the `hscroll` value decreases by 20, moving the text to the right by 1 pixel (**Figure 10.47**).

Sometimes in authoring mode, you'll want to restrict the size of your text field so that its contents are scrollable. You can create a text field that already contains text so that much of it is hidden from view by defining your text field as scrollable.

To define a scrollable text field in authoring mode:

1. Select the text tool in the Tools palette, and drag out a text field on the Stage.
2. Choose Text > Scrollable from the main menu's toolbar.

   The resizing handle at the bottom-right corner of your text field fills in with black, indicating that the text field is scrollable. Although your text field remains resizable, any text that does not fit in the text field will begin to scroll (**Figure 10.48**).

   or

   Shift-double-click the resizing handle of the text field.

   The handle turns black, and the text field becomes scrollable.

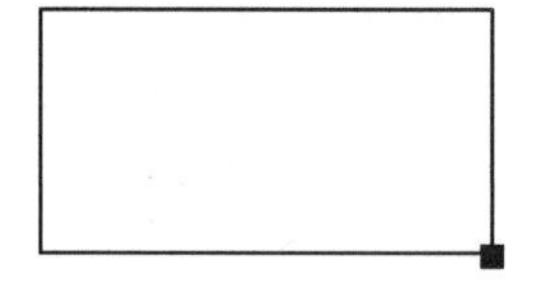

Figure 10.48 When you define a text field as scrollable in authoring mode, the resizing handle turns black (top). You can enter text in authoring mode, but the size of the text field will remain constant, hiding text that can't fit and allowing scrolling (bottom).

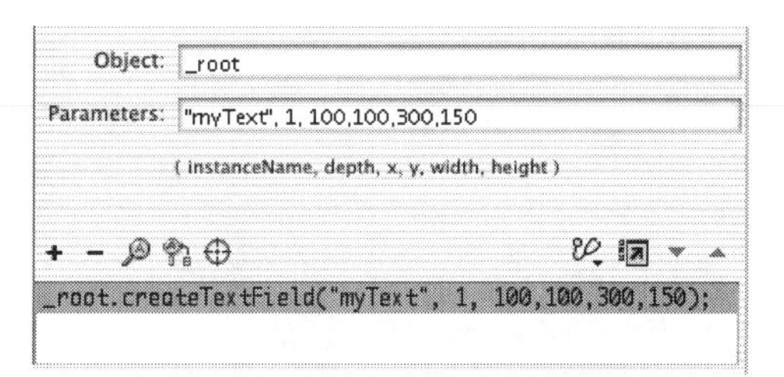

Figure 10.49 A text field called myText that is 300 pixels wide by 150 pixels tall will be created on the root Timeline at x = 100, y = 100, in depth level 1.

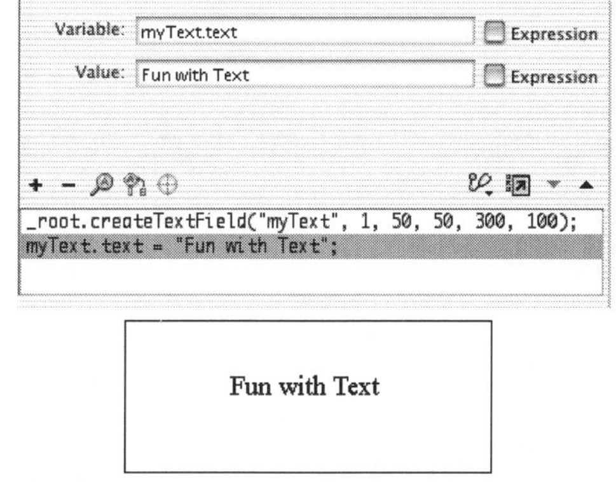

Figure 10.50 The contents of the `text` property of myText appear on the Stage. The default format for a dynamically created text field is black 12-point Times New Roman (Windows) or Times (Mac).

Generating Text Fields Dynamically

If you need to have text appear in your movie based on a viewer's interaction, you have to be able to create a text field during run time. You can generate text fields dynamically with the movie-clip method `createTextField()`. The method creates a new text field, which you must attach to a movie clip. You can choose the root Timeline as the movie clip to which it is attached, and your text field will be placed on the main Stage. You also must specify the text field's depth level, its *x* and *y* positions, and its width and height in pixels. For example:

```
_root.createTextField("newTF", 1,
100,100,200,50)
```

This statement creates a new text field called newTF on the main Stage in depth level 1. Its top-left corner is positioned at x = 100, y = 100, and it is 200 pixels wide by 50 pixels tall.

To create a text field on the main Stage:

1. Select the first frame of the main Timeline, and open the Actions panel.
2. Choose Objects > Movie > Movie Clip > Methods > createTextField.
3. In the Object field, enter `_root`.
   The new text field will be created in the root Timeline (the main Stage).
4. In the Parameters field, enter a name (in quotation marks), a depth level, *x* position, *y* position, width, and height, separating the parameters with commas (**Figure 10.49**).
   A text field is created on the main Stage. To see it, assign text to it with the `text` property (**Figure 10.50**).

To remove a text field that was created dynamically:

1. Choose Objects > Movie > TextField > Methods > removeTextField.
2. In the Object field, enter the name of the text field you want to remove (**Figure 10.51**).

   The text field deletes itself when this method is performed. You can use this method to remove only text fields created by the movie-clip method `createTextField()`.

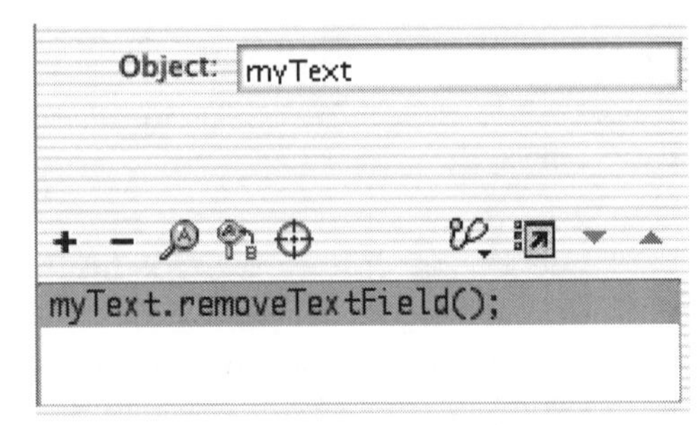

Figure 10.51 The dynamically generated text field called myText is removed.

The Default TextField Appearance

When you create a text field dynamically with the `createTextField()` method, it has the following default properties:

```
type = dynamic
selectable = true
multiline = false
password = false
wordWrap = false
background = false
border = false
html = false
embedFonts = false
restrict = null
maxChars = null
variable = null
autoSize = none
```

The text field also has the following default format properties (which you can change with the TextFormat object):

```
font = Times New Roman (Windows)
font = Times (Mac)
size = 12
textColor = 0x000000
bold = false
italic = false
underline = false
align = "left"
leftMargin = 0
rightMargin = 0
indent = 0
leading = 0
URL = ""
Target = ""
bullet = false
```

Options controlled by TextFormat properties

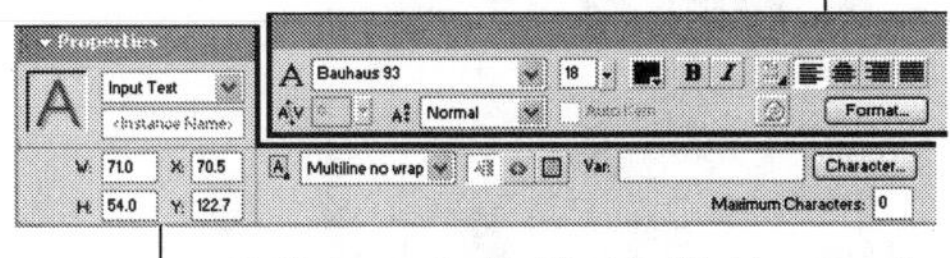

Options controlled by TextField properties

Figure 10.52 The Property Inspector can be divided into sections of options controlled by TextFormat properties and options controlled by TextField properties.

Modifying Text in Text Fields

Although the properties of a text field can define the way text behaves and the way the text field itself appears, the properties don't control the formatting of the text that it contains. For that task, you need to use the TextFormat object. The TextFormat object controls character and paragraph formatting, which are also options available in authoring mode in the Property Inspector. Notice that the Property Inspector is divided into sections of options that are controlled by the TextField object and those that are controlled by the TextFormat object (**Figure 10.52**). **Table 10.2** summarizes the properties of the TextFormat object.

continues on next page

Table 10.2

TextFormat Properties

Property	Value	Description
size	A number	Specifies the point size of the text.
font	A string	Specifies the font of the text. You must create a font symbol and export it for ActionScript in its Linkage properties. Use the Linkage Identifier for the font value. Works only when embedFonts = true.
color	A hex number	Specifies the color of the text.
underline	true or false	Specifies whether the text is underlined.
italic	true or false	Specifies whether the text is italicized.
bold	true or false	Specifies whether the text is bold.
bullet	true or false	Specifies whether text is in a bulleted list.
leading	A positive number	Specifies the space between lines, in points.
align	"left", "center", or "right"	Specifies the alignment of text within the text field.
indent	A number	Specifies the point indentation of new paragraphs.
blockIndent	A number	Specifies the point indentation of the entire text.
rightMargin	A number	Specifies the space between the text and the right edge, in points,
leftMargin	A number	Specifies the space between the text and the left edge, in points.
tabStops	An array of numbers	Specifies the point distances of custom tab stops.
URL	A string	Specifies the URL that the text links to.
target	A string	Specifies the target window where a hyperlink is displayed.

To change the formatting of text in a text field, first create a new instance of the TextFormat object, like so:

```
myFormat = new TextFormat()
```

Then assign new values to the property of your TextFormat object:

```
myFormat.size = 48
```

Finally, call the `setTextFormat()` method for your text field. This method is a method of the TextField object, not of the TextFormat object.

```
myTextField.setTextFormat(myFormat)
```

This statement will change the text size in the text field called myTextField to 48 points.

To modify the text formatting of a text field:

1. Create a new font symbol in the library, and export it for ActionScript in the Linkage Properties dialog box (**Figure 10.53**).
2. Select the text tool, and drag out a text field on the Stage.
3. In the Property Inspector, choose Input or Dynamic Text; enter an instance name; choose a different font from the one you marked for export in step 1; and embed its font outline.
4. Enter some text in the text field (**Figure 10.54**).

   You will use the TextFormat object to modify this text field.
5. Select the first frame of the main Timeline, and open the Actions panel.
6. Choose Actions > Variables > set variable.
7. In the Variable field, enter a name for your new TextFormat object.

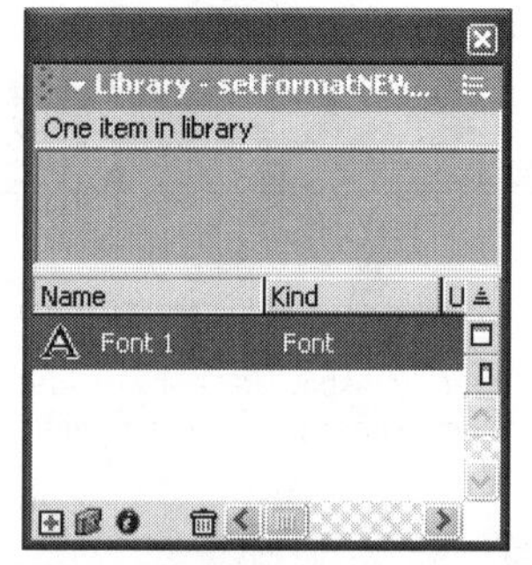

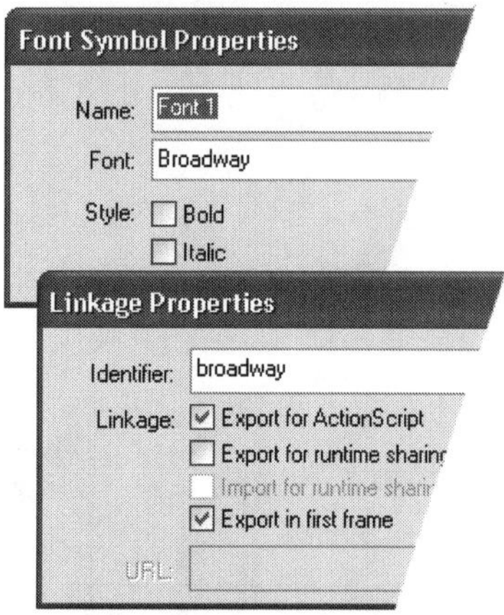

Figure 10.53 Create a font symbol, and export it for ActionScript. This font is identified as Broadway.

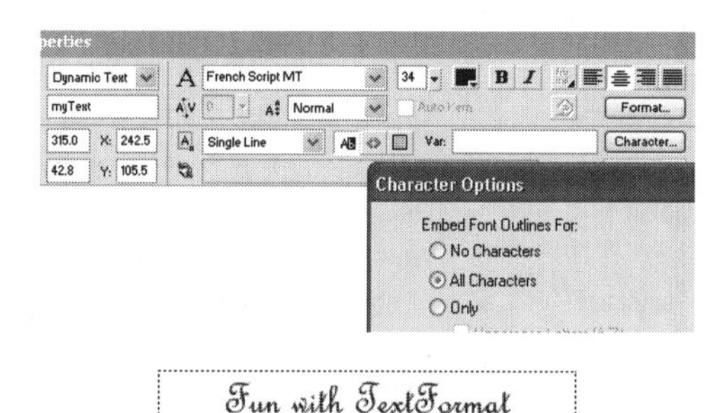

Figure 10.54 Create a text field called myText. The outline for this text field's font (French Script MT) is embedded.

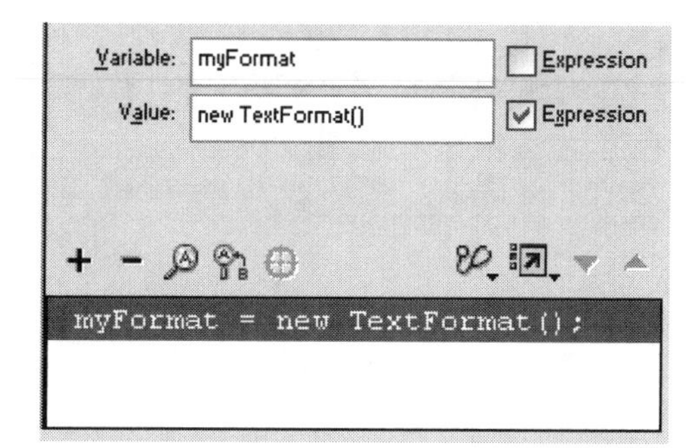

Figure 10.55 Instantiate a TextFormat object called myFormat.

Figure 10.56 Assign the Broadway font that you have marked for export.

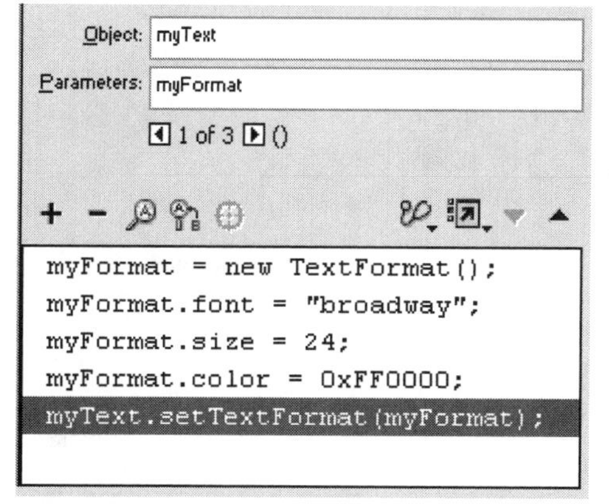

Figure 10.57 Assign the new format to your text field called myText.

8. Put your pointer in the Value field, and choose Objects > Movie > TextFormat > new TextFormat. Check the Expression box (**Figure 10.55**).

   A new TextFormat object is instantiated.

9. Choose Actions > Variables > set variable.

10. In the Variable field, enter the name of your TextFormat object.

11. Choose Objects > Movie > TextFormat > Properties > font.

12. In the Value field, enter the identifier of the exported font symbol (**Figure 10.56**).

13. Continue creating `set variable` statements to assign values to the properties of your TextFormat object.

14. Choose Object > Movie > TextField > Methods > setTextFormat.

15. In the Object field, enter the name of the text field you created in step 2.

16. In the Parameters field, enter the name of your TextFormat object (**Figure 10.57**).

    The TextFormat object is used as the parameter for the `setTextFormat()` method.

continues on next page

17. Test your movie.

    Flash creates a TextFormat object. The properties of the object are passed through the `setTextFormat()` method and modify the existing contents of the text field (**Figure 10.58**).

Fun with TextFormat

Figure 10.58 The original text (in Figure 10.54) changes to red 24-point Broadway.

✔ Tips

- The `setTextFormat()` modifies only existing text in the text field. If you add more text after the `setTextFormat()` method is called, that text will have its original formatting.
- You can also use a variant: the `setNewTextFormat()` method. This method modifies any new text that appears in the text field. Existing text is unaffected. Use `setNewTextFormat()` when you want to distinguish existing text from new text with different formatting.

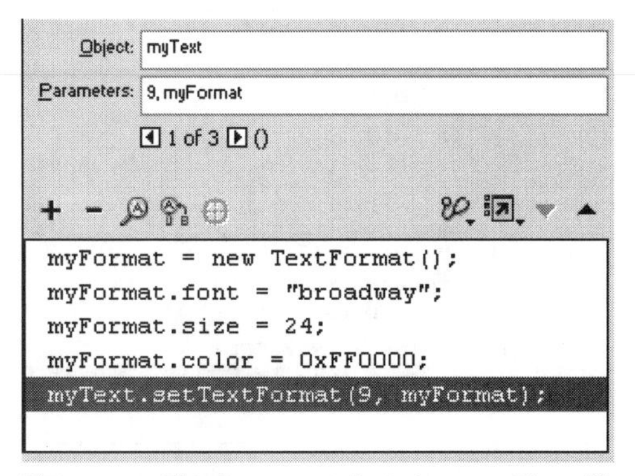

Figure 10.59 The character at the index 9 position will change formats.

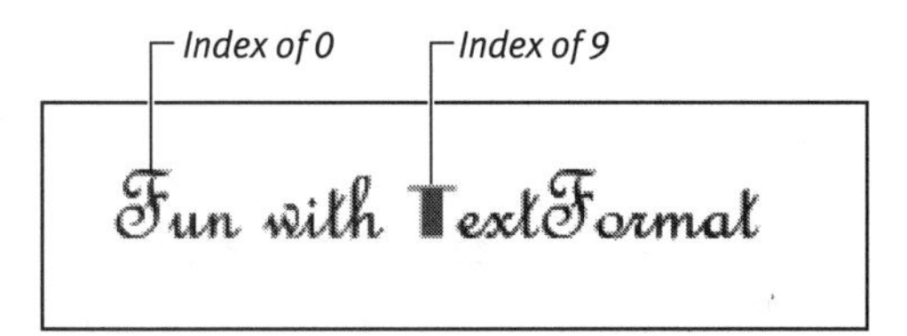

Figure 10.60 While the rest of the text stays the same, the *T* character at index 9 changes to red 24-point Broadway.

The `setTextFormat()` method enables you to format the entire text field, a single character, or a span of characters. You must specify the position in the string that's in your text field. The position is known as the *index*. The index of the first character is 0, the index of the second character is 1, and so on. If you use an index as the first parameter of the `setTextFormat()` method, that single character will be affected. If you use a beginning index and an ending index as the first and second parameters, the span of characters between the two indexes, including the beginning index, will be affected.

To modify the text formatting of a single character:

1. Continuing with the file you created in the preceding example, select the first frame of the main Timeline, and open the Actions panel.
2. Select the statement in the Script pane that contains the `setTextFormat()` method.
3. In the Parameters field, enter an index before the TextFormat object's name, separating the two parameters with a comma (**Figure 10.59**).
4. Test your movie.

   Flash modifies the format of a single character (**Figure 10.60**).

To modify the text formatting of a span of characters:

1. Continuing with the file you used in the preceding example, select the first frame of the main Timeline, and open the Actions panel.
2. Select the statement in the Script pane that contains the `setTextFormat()` method.
3. In the Parameters field, enter a beginning index and an ending index before the TextFormat object's name, separating the three parameters with commas (**Figure 10.61**).
4. Test your movie.

   Flash modifies the format of the span of characters (**Figure 10.62**).

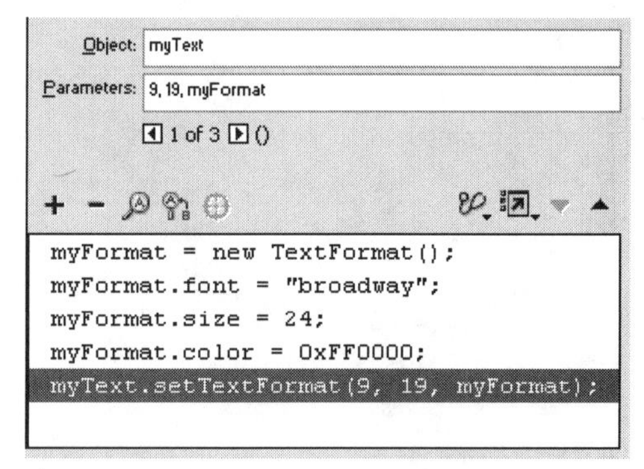

Figure 10.61 The characters beginning at index 9 and up to, but not including, index 19 will change formats.

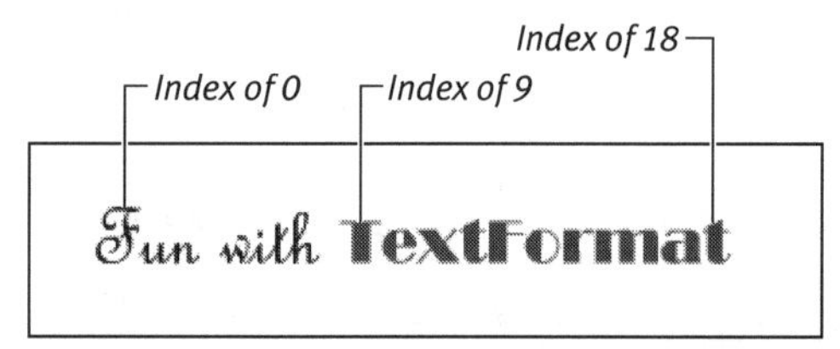

Figure 10.62 While the rest of the text stays the same, the word *TextFormat* from index 9 to index 18 changes to red 24-point Broadway. Although the method specifies the indexes 9 and 19, the last index is not included in the selection.

Creating dynamic text animations

Using a combination of TextFormat properties and TextField properties, you can animate text entirely with ActionScript to make its motion respond dynamically to run-time events or to viewer interaction. You can also use ActionScript to do things to text that are difficult, if not impossible, with normal tweens, such as swapping characters' styles or animating the color of the text independently of the color of its background.

```
_root.createTextField("blinkingSign", 1, 200, 100, 10, 10);
blinkingSign.text = "Open 24 hours! Visit us!";
blinkingSign.autosize = "center";
blinkingSign.embedFonts = true;
```

Figure 10.63 Create the text field called blinkingSign, and set its `text`, `autosize`, and `embedFonts` properties.

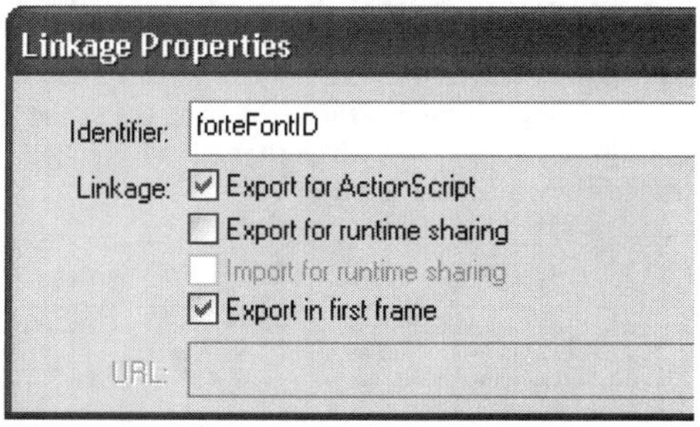

Linkage Properties
Identifier: forteFontID
Linkage: Export for ActionScript
Export for runtime sharing
Import for runtime sharing
Export in first frame
URL:

Figure 10.64 This font symbol is marked for export and identified as forteFontID.

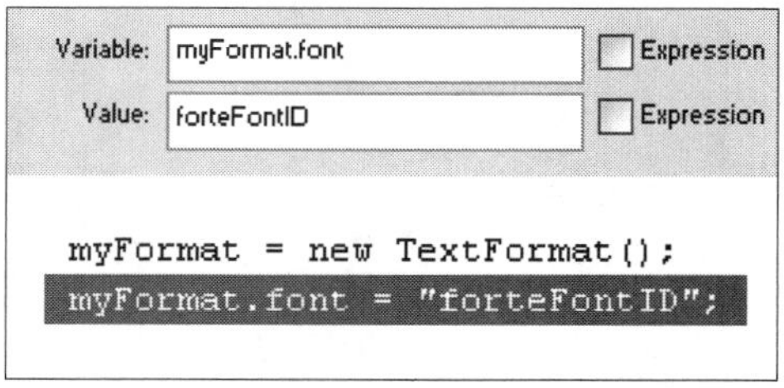

Variable: myFormat.font Expression
Value: forteFontID Expression

```
myFormat = new TextFormat();
myFormat.font = "forteFontID";
```

Figure 10.65 A portion of the Script pane shows a new TextFormat object is created, and the fontForteID is used as the new font.

In the following demonstration, a text field is generated and animated dynamically by being modified with `setInterval` statements and an `onEnterFrame` event handler.

To animate text:

1. Create a text field on the root Timeline with the method `createTextField()`, and place it in depth level 1 on the center of the Stage.

   The size of the text field doesn't matter.

2. Assign text to the text field's `text` property, set `autosize` to "`center`", and set `embedFonts` to `true`.

   The code should look like **Figure 10.63**.

3. Because you are embedding the font, make sure that you create a font symbol in the library.

4. In Linkage Property dialog box, mark the font symbol for export for ActionScript, and give it a name in the Identifier field (**Figure 10.64**).

5. Now create your TextFormat object with the constructor function, and set the `font` property of the object to the font that you marked for export (**Figure 10.65**).

6. Choose Actions > Miscellaneous Actions > setInterval.

7. In the Parameters field, enter `makeRed`, followed by a comma and then 100.

   The function called `makeRed` will be invoked every 100 milliseconds.

8. Again, choose Actions > Miscellaneous Actions > setInterval.

9. In the Parameters field, enter `makeBlue`, followed by a comma and then 200.

   The function called `makeBlue` will be invoked every 200 milliseconds.

continues on next page

10. Choose Actions > User-Defined Functions > function.

11. In the Name field, enter makeRed.

    Your makeRed function is created.

12. Assign the value 0xff0000 to the color property of your TextFormat object.

13. Choose Objects > Movie > TextField > Methods > setTextFormat.

14. In the Object field, enter the name of your text field.

15. In the Parameters field, enter the name of your TextFormat object.

    When the makeRed function is invoked, your text field turns red (**Figure 10.66**).

16. Repeat steps 10 through 15 to create a function called makeBlue. For the color property of the TextFormat object, use the hex code 0x0000ff.

    When the makeBlue function is invoked, your text field turns blue.

17. Choose Objects > Movie > Movie Clip > Events > onEnterFrame.

18. In the Object field, enter _root.

19. Increase the size property of the TextFormat object by 1 and then call the setTextFormat() method again (**Figure 10.67**).

    The onEnterFrame handler continuously increases the font size of your text field.

20. Test your movie (**Figure 10.68**).

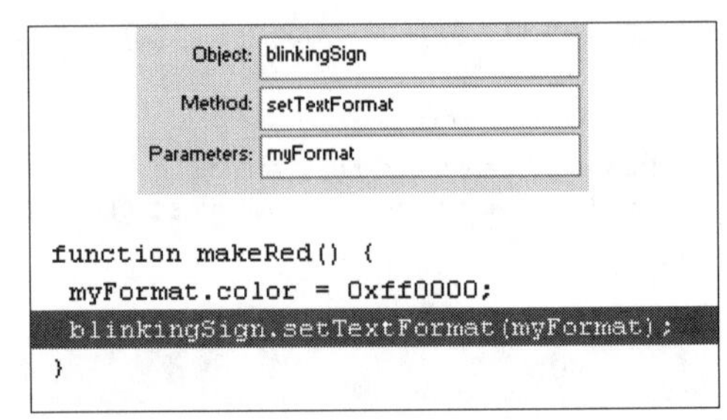

Figure 10.66 A portion of the Script pane shows the function called makeRed, which changes the text field called blinkingSign to a red Forte font.

```
_root.createTextField("blinkingSign", 1, 200, 100, 10, 10);
blinkingSign.text = "Open 24 hours! Visit us!";
blinkingSign.autosize = "center";
blinkingSign.embedFonts = true;
myFormat = new TextFormat();
myFormat.font = "forteFontID";
setInterval(makeRed, 100);
setInterval(makeBlue, 200);
function makeRed() {
 myFormat.color = 0xff0000;
 blinkingSign.setTextFormat(myFormat);
}
function makeBlue() {
 myFormat.color = 0x0000ff;
 blinkingSign.setTextFormat(myFormat);
}
_root.onEnterFrame = function() {
 myFormat.size++;
 blinkingSign.setTextFormat(myFormat);
};
```

Figure 10.67 The full script. The functions makeRed and makeBlue are invoked alternately by the setInterval actions, which change their formatting to make the text blink. At the same time, the onEnterFrame handler continuously increases the size of the text.

Open 24 hours! Visit us!

Figure 10.68 The text field animates by growing and blinking red and blue.

Manipulating Text-Field Contents

When you define a text field as input text, you give your viewers the freedom to enter and edit information. You've seen how this information can be used in expressions with other actions or concatenated and displayed in dynamic text fields. Often, however, you need to analyze the text entered by the viewer before using it. You may want to tease out certain words or identify the location of a particular character or sequence of characters. If you require viewers to enter an email address in an input field, for example, you can check to see whether that address is in the correct format by looking for the @ symbol. Or you could check a customer's telephone number, find out the area code based on the first three digits, and personalize a directory or news listing with local interests.

This kind of parsing, manipulation, and control of the information within text fields is done with a combination of the Selection object and the String object. The Selection object lets you control the focus of multiple text fields and the position of the insertion point within a focused text field. The String object lets you retrieve and change the characters inside a text field.

The Selection Object

The Selection object controls the selection of characters in text fields. Unlike most objects, the Selection object doesn't need a constructor function to be instantiated before you can use it, because there can be only one insertion-point position or selection in a Flash movie at a time. So the Selection object will always refer to that one position or selection.

The methods of the Selection object affect a text field in two ways: It can control which text field is currently active, or *focused*, and it can control where the insertion point is positioned within that text field. **Table 10.3** summarizes the methods of the Selection object.

Table 10.3

Methods of the Selection Object

Method	Description
getBeginIndex()	Retrieves the index at the beginning of the selection
getEndIndex()	Retrieves the index at the end of the selection
getCaretIndex()	Retrieves the index of the insertion-point position
setSelection (beginIndex, endIndex)	Positions the selection at a specified beginIndex and endIndex
getFocus()	Retrieves the instance name of the active text field
setFocus (instanceName)	Sets the focus of the text field specified by the instance name

Controlling the Focus of Text Fields

You can have only one focused object on the Stage at any time. If you have multiple text fields on the Stage, you need to be able to control which one is focused before you can retrieve or assign the insertion-point location or selection. The `getFocus()` and `setFocus()` methods of the Selection object let you do this.

The method `getFocus()` returns a string of the absolute path to the text field by using the `_level0` term. If the selected text field called yourName is on the root Timeline, for example, and you call the `getFocus()` method, the returned value is: "`_level0.yourName`".

It's important to remember that the returned value is a string and that the `_level0` term is used. If you compare the `getFocus()` method with a path name using `_root` or `this`, or forget the quotation marks, then Flash won't recognize the path. The `getFocus()` method returns a value of `null` if there is no focused text field on the Stage.

The `setFocus()` method takes one parameter, which is the text field you want to give focus. You must use a string for the path to specify the text field, although you can use either an absolute or relative path. `setFocus("scoreboard")`, for example, will make the text field called scoreboard active.

To set the focus of a text field:

1. Select the text tool in the Tools palette, and drag out two separate text fields on the Stage.
2. In the Property Inspector, choose Input Text, give each field an instance name, and click the Show Border button for both text fields.
3. Select the first frame of the main Timeline, and open the Actions panel.
4. Create a new listener object from the generic Object class (**Figure 10.69**).
5. Assign the onKeyDown event to your listener.
6. Choose Actions > Variables > if.
7. In the Condition field, enter `Key.isDown(Key.LEFT)`.

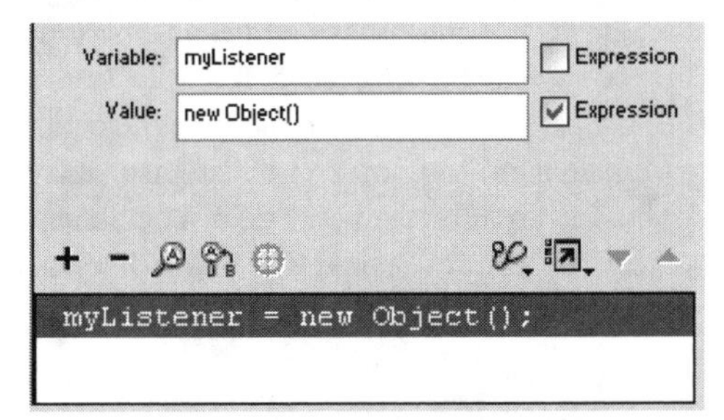

Figure 10.69 Create the listener called `myListener`.

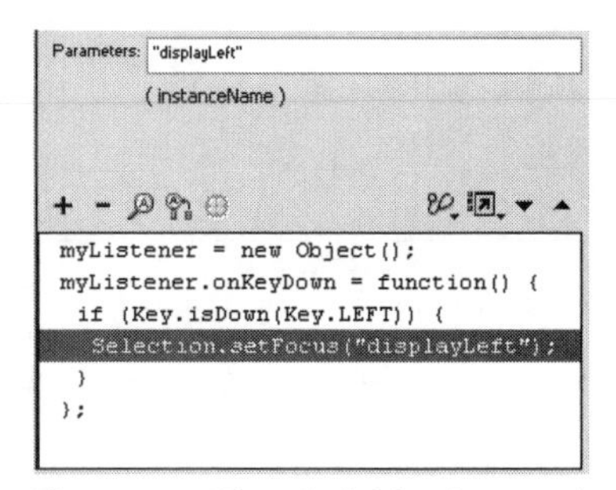

Figure 10.70 When the left key is pressed, Flash focuses the first input text field, called displayLeft.

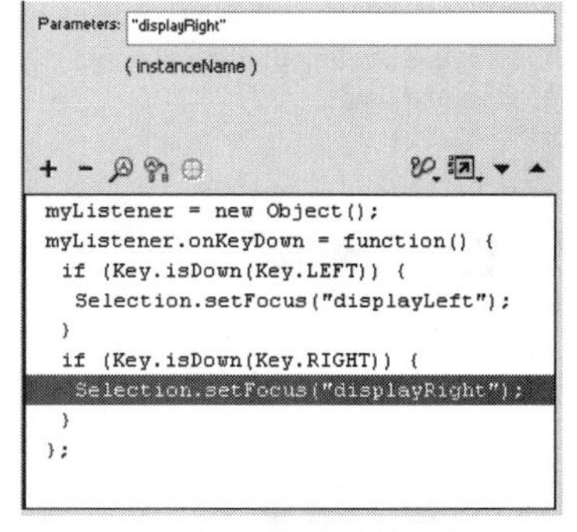

Figure 10.71 When the right key is pressed, Flash focuses the second input text field, called displayRIght.

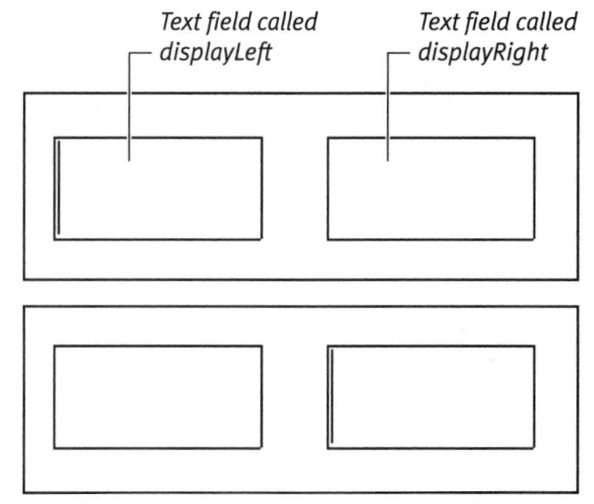

Figure 10.72 The focus of text fields is controlled by the left and right keys. At top, the left text field is focused (the blinking insertion point is visible inside the text field). At bottom, the right text field is focused.

8. Choose Objects > Movie > Selection > Methods > setFocus.
9. In the Parameters field, enter the name of the first input text field, in quotation marks (**Figure 10.70**).

   When the left key is pressed, Flash focuses the first input text field.
10. Select the closing brace of your `if` statement, and choose Actions > Conditions/Loops > if.
11. In the Condition field of your second `if` statement, enter `Key.isDown(Key.RIGHT)`.
12. Choose Objects > Movie > Selection > Methods > setFocus.
13. In the Parameters field, enter the name of the second input text field, in quotation marks (**Figure 10.71**).

    When the right key is pressed, Flash focuses the second input text field.
14. Register your listener to the Key object with the method `addListener()`.
15. Test your movie.

    Flash detects when the right or the left key is pressed on the keyboard and changes the selected text field (**Figure 10.72**). If you disable the automatic focusing with the Tab key, you can build your own way to navigate and select multiple text fields.

In the next task, you will display the name of the focused text field in the Output window by using the method `getFocus()`. (The Output window appears only in authoring mode; it is used for testing and verification purposes.)

To get the focus of a text field:

1. Continuing with the file you created in the preceding task, select the closing brace of the last `if` statement.
2. Choose Actions > Miscellaneous Actions > trace.
3. Put your pointer in the Message field, and choose Objects > Movie > Selection > Methods > getFocus.
4. Check the Expression checkbox (**Figure 10.73**).
5. Test your movie.

   When you use the right and left keys to change the focus of the text fields, Flash displays their target paths in the Output window (**Figure 10.74**).

```
Message: Selection.getFocus()    [✓] Expression

myListener = new Object();
myListener.onKeyDown = function() {
  if (Key.isDown(Key.LEFT)) {
    Selection.setFocus("displayLeft");
  }
  if (Key.isDown(Key.RIGHT)) {
    Selection.setFocus("displayRight");
  }
  trace(Selection.getFocus());
};
Key.addListener(myListener);
```

Figure 10.73 Add a `trace` statement to display the name of the focused text field.

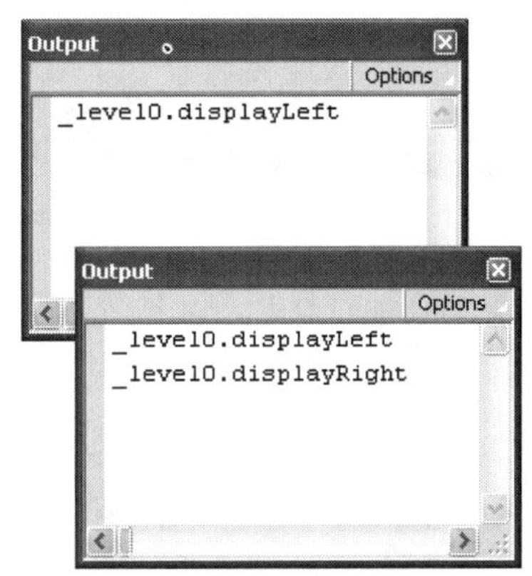

Figure 10.74 The Output window when the left key is pressed (top) and when the right key is pressed immediately afterward (bottom).

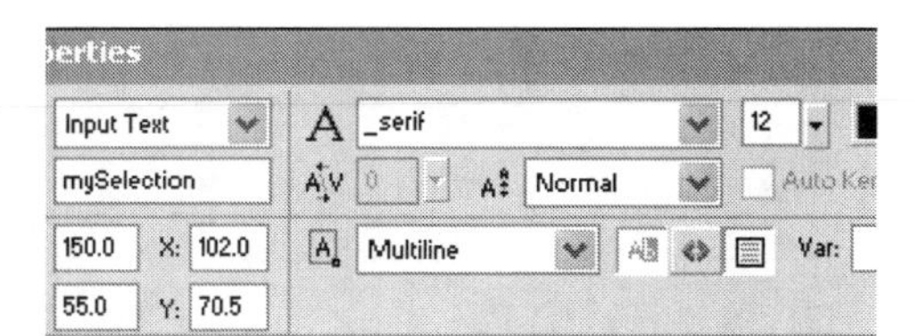

Figure 10.75 Enter mySelection as the instance name for your input text field.

Controlling the Selection Within Text Fields

When you have a focused text field, either by using ActionScript or by a viewer's clicking it with the pointer, you can control the selection or insertion-point position inside it. This technique lets you direct your viewers' attention to particular characters or words they've entered, perhaps to point out errors or misspellings. It also lets you keep track of the insertion-point position, much the way that the `_xmouse` and `_ymouse` properties let you keep track of the location of the viewer's mouse pointer. You can also select certain parts of the text field and replace just those portions with different text.

The position of each character in a string is numbered and used as the index for the methods of the Selection object, just like the index for the `setTextFormat()` method. The first character is assigned the index of 0, the second character is 1, and so on. If an insertion point isn't positioned within a text field when Flash retrieves the selection index, it returns a value of –1.

To identify the position of the insertion point in a text field:

1. Select the text tool, and drag out a text field on the Stage.
2. In the Property Inspector, choose Input Text and Multiline from the pull-down menus; give the input text field an instance name; and click the Show Border button (**Figure 10.75**).
3. Select the text tool, and drag out a second text field on the Stage.

continues on next page

4. In the Property Inspector, choose Dynamic Text and Multiline from the pull-down menus; give the dynamic text field an instance name; and click the Show Border button (**Figure 10.76**).

5. Select the first frame of the main Timeline, and open the Actions panel.

6. Choose Objects > Movie > Movie Clip > Events > onEnterFrame.

7. In the Object field, enter `_root`.

8. Choose Actions > Variables > set variable.

9. In the Variable field, enter the name of the dynamic text field, followed by a dot and then the `text` property.

10. Put your insertion point in the Value field, and choose Objects > Movie > Selection > Methods > getCaretIndex. Check the Expression box (**Figure 10.77**).

11. Test your movie.

    Initially, the dynamic text field displays –1 because the input text field is not focused. When your viewer begins to type in the input text field, Flash updates the dynamic text field to display the insertion point's position (**Figure 10.78**).

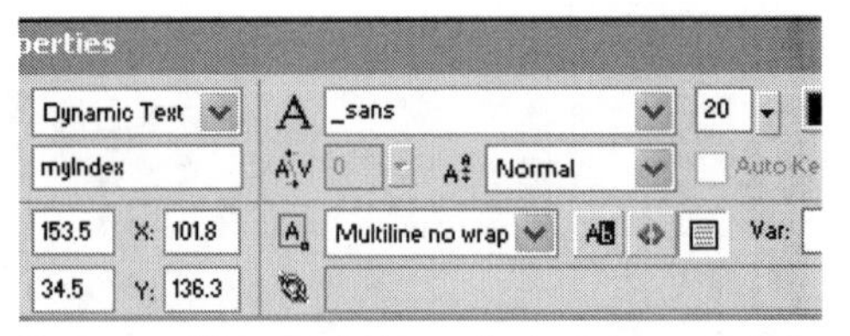

Figure 10.76 Enter myIndex as the instance name for your dynamic text field.

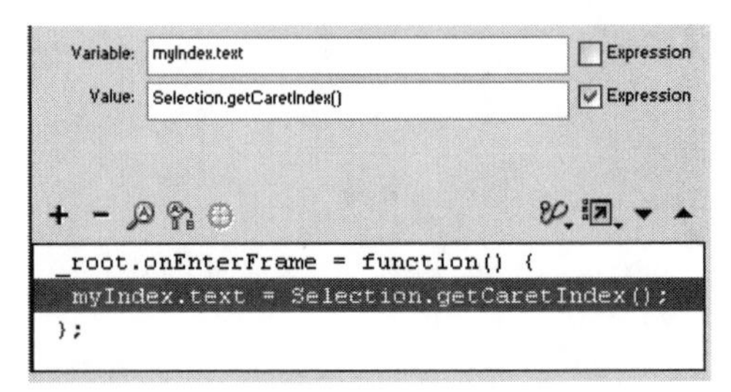

Figure 10.77 Flash assigns the position of the insertion point, or caret, to the contents of the text field called myIndex.

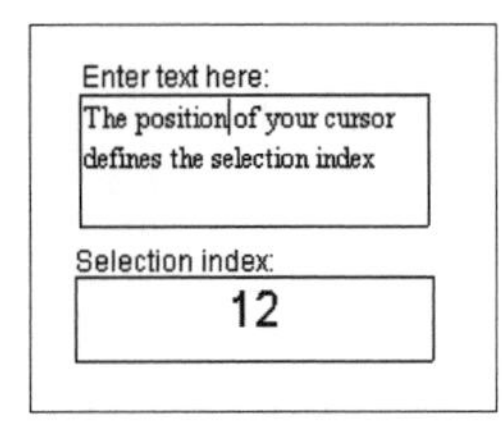

Figure 10.78 The current index of the insertion point is 12. The first letter *T* is 0. The space between *position* and *of* is 12.

Carrots are good to eat.

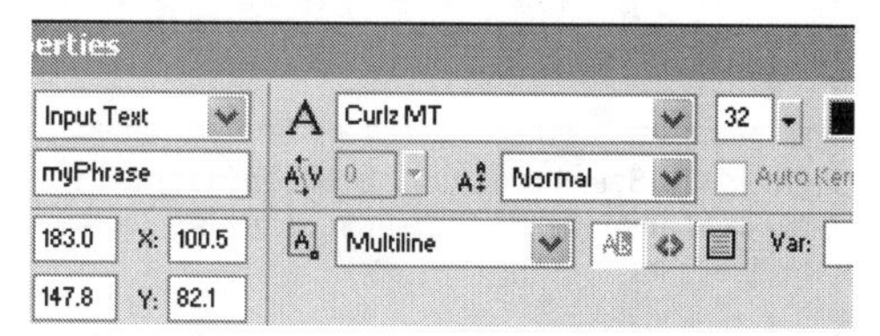

Figure 10.79 Create the text field called myPhrase.

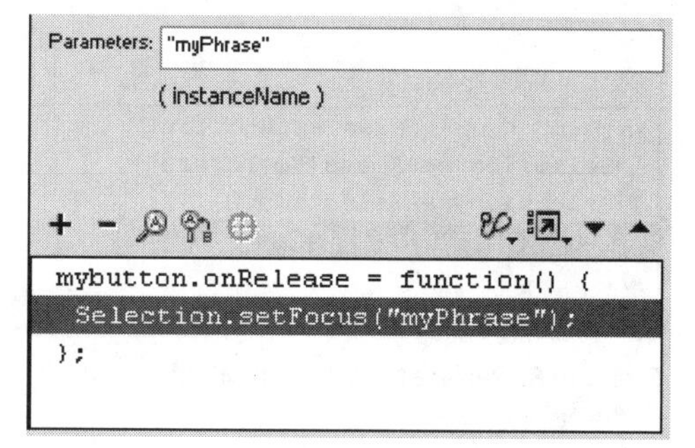

Figure 10.80 Set the focus to the text field called myPhrase.

You can choose a portion of the text field's contents with `Selection.setSelection()` and then replace it with the TextField method `replaceSel()`. In the next example, you will replace a portion of the text field with different text when you click a button.

To change the selection in a text field:

1. Select the text tool in the Tools palette, and drag out a text field on the Stage.
2. Enter the phrase *Carrots are good to eat.*
3. In the Property Inspector, choose Input Text and Multiline; enter an instance name; and embed the font that you want to use (**Figure 10.79**).
4. Create a button symbol, place an instance on the Stage, and give it a name in the Property Inspector.
5. Select the first frame of the main Timeline, and open the Actions panel.
6. Assign an `onRelease` handler to your button.
7. Choose Objects > Movie > Selection > Methods > setFocus.
8. In the Parameters field, enter the name of your text field, in quotation marks (**Figure 10.80**).

   When you click this button, Flash focuses the text field. (The focus moves from your button to the text field.)
9. Choose Objects > Movie > Selection > Methods > setSelection.

continues on next page

10. In the Parameters field, enter 0, followed by a comma and then 7 (**Figure 10.81**).

    The `setSelection()` method selects all the characters between its first parameter and its second parameter, inclusive of the first parameter. So this `setSelection()`selects the first seven characters (index 0 to index 6) of the text field.

11. Choose Objects > Movie > TextField > Methods > replaceSel.

12. In the Object field, enter the name of your text field.

13. In the Parameters pane, enter a replacement for the selection (**Figure 10.82**).

    Make sure that the replacement word is in quotes.

14. Test your movie.

    When you click the button, the `setSelection()` method selects the word *Carrots*, and the `replaceSel()` method replaces it with the word *Burritos* (**Figure 10.83**).

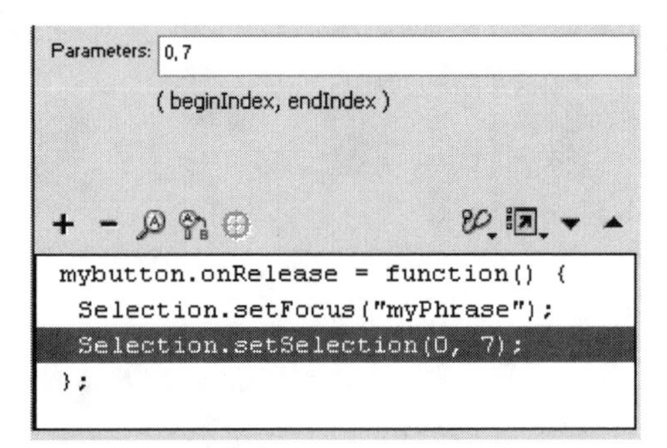

Figure 10.81 Select everything between index 0 (inclusive) and index 7. The word *Carrots* is selected.

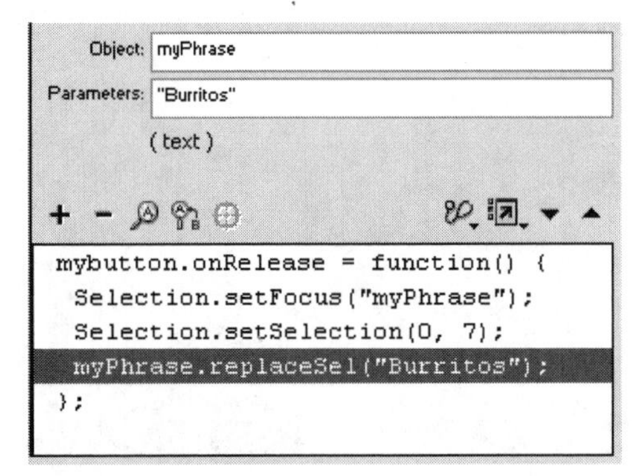

Figure 10.82 Replace the selection with the word *Burritos*.

Figure 10.83 The original text field (top) and the text field after the selection is replaced (bottom). Notice that the insertion point is positioned just after the new selection.

Table 10.4

Selection and TextField Events

Event	Description
onSetFocus	Happens when a new text field receives focus. When used as a TextField event, the handler can take one parameter: oldFocus. When used as a Selection event, the handler can take two parameters—oldFocus and newFocus—and requires a listener.
onChanged	Happens when the contents of a text field change. This TextField event can also be assigned to a listener.
onScroller	Happens when one of the text-field properties—scroll or hscroll—changes. This TextField event can also be assigned to a listener.
onKillFocus	Happens when a text field loses focus. The handler for this TextField event can take one parameter: newFocus.

Detecting Changes in the Text Field

Often, you'll want to capture information from a text field only when the viewer has entered something new. Or you'll want to respond when a viewer has selected a particular text field. You can detect these changes in text fields with event handlers and listeners. Flash provides a variety of them through the Selection object and the TextField object (**Table 10.4**).

In this section, you'll look at two important TextField events:onSetFocus and onChanged.

The onSetFocus event happens when a text field receives focus, because a viewer clicked inside the text field or pressed the Tab key in a browser, or because you used the setFocus() ActionScript command. Each text field has its own onSetFocus event. You can use an optional parameter in an onSetFocus event handler that can tell you what the previously focused text field was. For example:

```
myTF.onSetFocus = function(oldFocus){
trace ("you came from" + oldFocus)
}
```

In this handler, when you focus the text field called myTF, the Output window displays a message telling you where the previous focus was. If the previous focus was not a text field, oldFocus = null.

The onChanged event happens when the viewer changes the contents of a text field. A viewer can click inside a text field and select portions of the text, but the onChanged event is triggered only when the viewer adds to, deletes, or changes its contents.

In the following task, you will create multiple input text fields. You will detect which text field your viewer selects and display a customized message in a dynamic text field.

To detect the focus of a text field:

1. Select the text tool, and drag out a text field on the Stage.
2. In the Property Inspector, choose Input Text and Single Line from the pull-down menus, and enter an instance name for this input text field.
3. Select the text tool again, and create two more input text fields.
4. In the Property Inspector, enter unique instance names for the new input text fields.
5. Select the text tool, and drag out a fourth text field on the Stage.
6. In the Property Inspector, choose Dynamic Text and Multiline from the pull-down menus, and enter an instance name for this dynamic text field (**Figure 10.84**).
7. Select the first frame of the main Timeline, and open the Actions panel.
8. Choose Objects > Movie > TextField > Events > onSetFocus.
9. In the Object field, enter the name of your first input text field. Delete the term `oldFocus` that appears in the Parameters field (**Figure 10.85**).
10. Choose Actions > Variables > set variable.
11. In the Variable field, enter the name of your dynamic text field, followed by a dot and then the `text` property.
12. In the Value field, enter a message that gives instructions to the viewer for the text field that he or she selected (**Figure 10.86**).

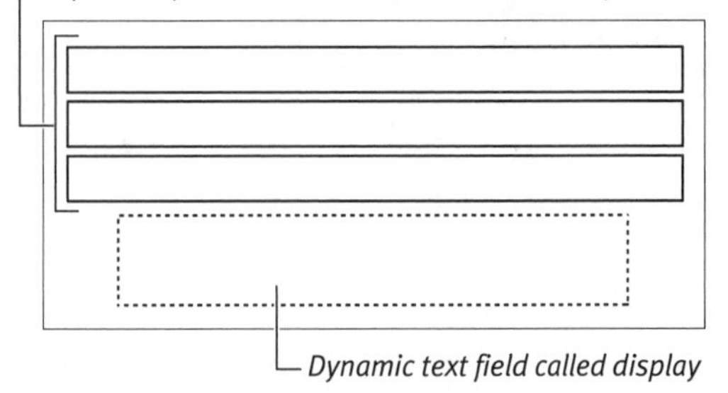

Figure 10.84 Create three input text fields (top) and one dynamic text field (bottom).

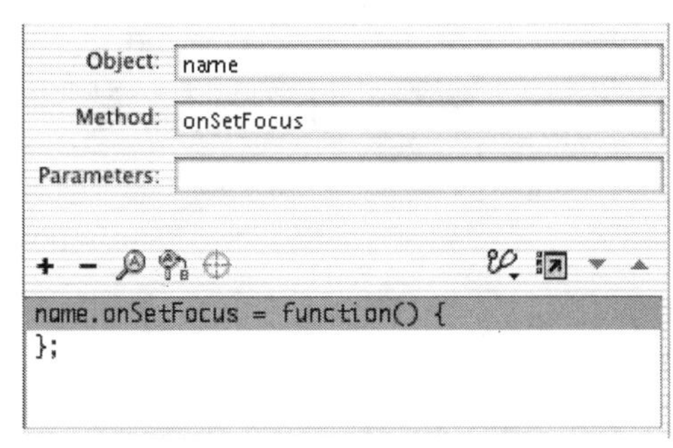

Figure 10.85 The onSetFocus event handler is assigned to the first input text field, called name.

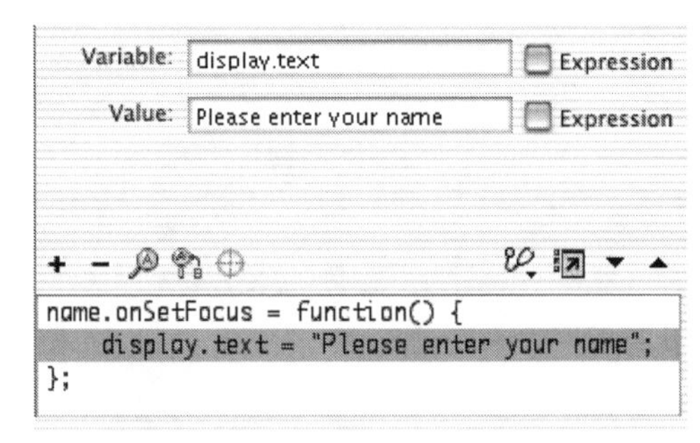

Figure 10.86 When the input text field called name is focused, the bottom dynamic text field tells the viewer to enter his or her name.

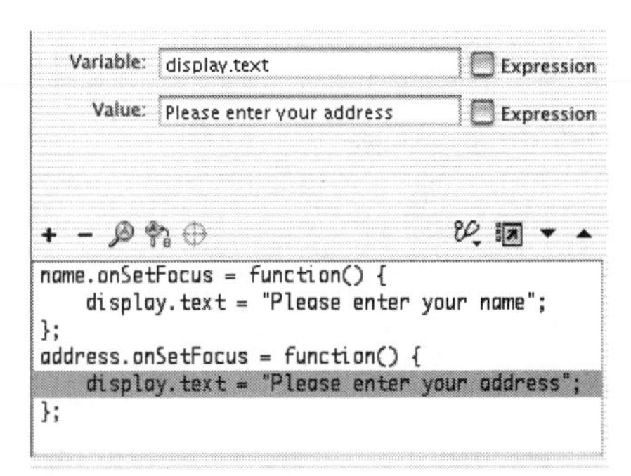

Figure 10.87 When the input text field called address is focused, the bottom dynamic text field tells the viewer to enter his or her address.

Variable: display.text — Expression
Value: Please select a text field — Expression

```
name.onSetFocus = function() {
    display.text = "Please enter your name";
};
address.onSetFocus = function() {
    display.text = "Please enter your address";
};
city.onSetFocus = function() {
    display.text = "Please enter your city";
};
display.text = "Please select a text field";
```

Figure 10.88 The last statement displays a message when the viewer initially encounters this movie.

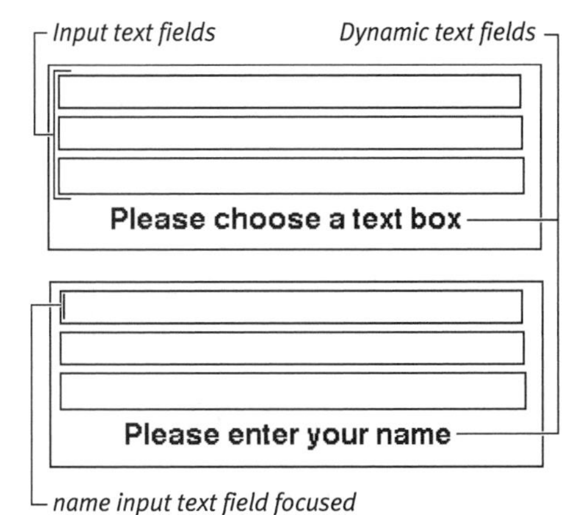

Figure 10.89 A different message appears for each focused input text field. This example shows the start of this movie (top) and the top field focused (bottom).

13. Select the closing brace of the `onSetFocus` handler, and choose Objects > Movie > TextField > Events > onSetFocus.

14. In the Object field, enter the name of your second input text field.

    Another `onSetFocus` handler appears below the first.

15. Choose Actions > Variables > set variable.

16. Assign a message to the `text` property of the dynamic text field, giving instructions to the viewer (**Figure 10.87**).

17. Add another `onSetFocus` handler to detect when the third input text field has received focus, and have the dynamic text field change in response.

18. Add a statement outside all the `onSetFocus` handlers that gives initial instructions to the viewer before any of the text fields receive focus.

    The final script should look like **Figure 10.88**.

19. Test your movie.

    When your viewer first sees your Flash movie, none of the text fields is focused, so the message in the dynamic text field tells the viewer what to do. When the viewer selects a text field, Flash detects which one it is (**Figure 10.89**).

To detect a change in the contents of a text field:

1. Select the text tool, and drag out a text field on the Stage.
2. In the Property Inspector, choose Input Text and Single Line from the pull-down menus, and enter an instance name for this input text field.
3. Select the first frame of the main Timeline, and open the Actions panel.
4. Choose Objects > Movie > TextField > Events > onChanged.
5. In the Object field, enter the name of your text field (**Figure 10.90**).
   Your onChanged handler is created.
6. Assign actions within the curly braces of the onChanged handler.
   Any additions, deletions, or changes in the contents of this text field will trigger the actions within this handler.

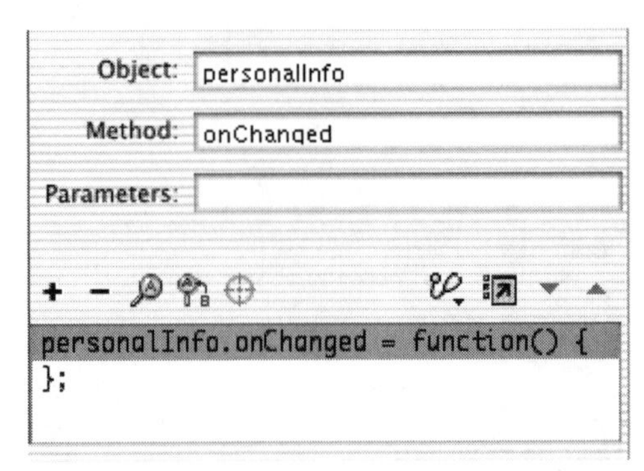

Figure 10.90 When the contents of the text field called personalInfo change, this event handler will be triggered.

✔ Tip

- The onChanged event does not detect changes in a text field via ActionScript. Only user-entered changes trigger the event.

The String Object

You can apply the methods and properties of the String object to analyze and manipulate string data types. The String object can tell you the position of a certain character, for example, or what character occupies a certain position. You can also dissect just a portion of the string and put that part, called a *substring*, into a new string, or you can concatenate substrings and strings. You can even change the lowercase and uppercase styles of different parts of the string. **Table 10.5** summarizes several methods and properties of the String objects.

You can perform all this parsing and shuffling of strings without first having to create an instance of the String object. Flash does this automatically by creating a temporary String object that it discards after the work of the method is completed.

Like those of the Selection and TextField objects, the indices of the String object are based on the positions of the characters in the string; the first character is assigned an index of 0.

✔ Tip

- You can use the `String` function to convert the value of any variable, expression, or object to a string before applying the methods of the String object. If your variable `radioButton` is a Boolean data type, the statement `String (radioButton)` returns the string `"true"` or `"false"`. Now you can manipulate the actual characters with the methods of the String object.

Table 10.5

Methods and Properties of the String Object

Method or Property	Description
indexOf(searchString, fromIndex)	Searches the string and returns the index of the first occurrence of a substring specified in the parameter searchString. The optional fromIndex parameter sets the starting position of the search.
lastIndexOf(searchString, fromIndex)	Searches the string and returns the index of the last occurrence of a substring specified in the parameter searchString. The optional fromIndex parameter sets the starting position of the search.
charAt(index)	Returns the character at the specified index position.
substring(indexA, indexB)	Returns the string between the indexA and indexB parameters.
substr(start, length)	Returns the string from the start index with the specified length.
concat(string1,...,stringN)	Concatenates the specified strings.
toLowerCase()	Returns a string that contains all lowercase characters.
toUpperCase()	Returns a string that contains all uppercase characters.
length	A property that returns the length of the string.

Analyzing Strings

Use the methods of the String object to identify a character or characters in a string. The following tasks analyze input text fields to verify that the viewer has entered the required information.

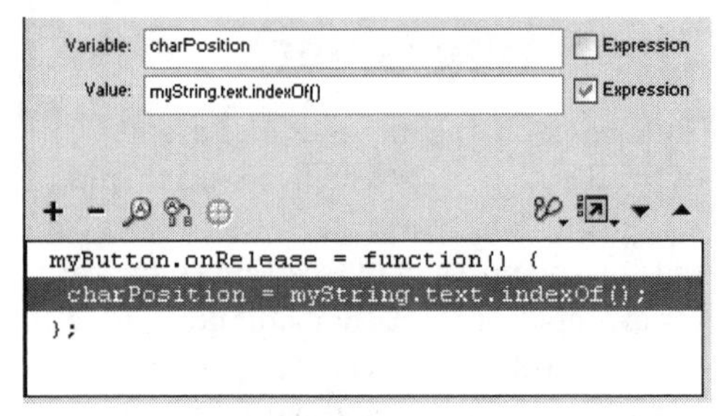

Figure 10.91 Assign the `indexOf()` method to `myString.text` to search its contents for a specific character. The parameters for the `indexOf()` method have not yet been defined.

To identify the position of a character:

1. Select the text tool in the Tools palette, and drag out a text field on the Stage.
2. In the Property Inspector, choose Input Text and Single Line from the pull-down menus, and enter an instance name for this input text field.
3. Create a button symbol, place an instance of it on the Stage, and give it a name in the Property Inspector.
4. Select the first frame of the main Timeline, and open the Actions panel.
5. Assign an `onRelease` handler to your button.
6. Choose Actions > Variables > set variable.
7. In the Variable field, enter a variable name.
8. In the Value field, enter the name of your input text field, followed by a dot and then the `text` property.
9. With the insertion point still in the Value field, choose Objects > Core > String > Methods > indexOf.

   The `indexOf()` method appears after the `text` property. This method takes two parameters: `searchString` and `fromIndex`. The parameter `searchString` is the specific character you want to identify in the string. The parameter `fromIndex`, which is optional, is the starting position in the string (**Figure 10.91**).

10. Between the parentheses of the indexOf() method, enter the character you want to find.

    Make sure that you include quotation marks around the character.

11. Check the Expression checkbox next to the Value field (**Figure 10.92**).

    When your viewer enters information in the input text field and clicks the button you created, Flash searches the contents of the input text field for the specified character and assigns its position to your variable. Use this variable in the methods of the Selection, TextField, and String objects to modify the information further.

✔ Tips

- The flip side of the method indexOf() is charAt(). This method returns the character that occupies the index position you specify for a string. You could use this method to verify that the first, second, and third character correspond to numbers for a certain area code of a telephone number, for example.

- If the character you search for with indexOf() occurs more than once in the string, Flash returns the index of only the first occurrence. Use the method lastIndexOf() to retrieve the last occurrence of the character.

- If you want to retrieve all the occurrences of a certain character, you must use several iterations of the method indexOf(). Use its optional second parameter, fromIndex, which begins the search at a specific index. Imagine that the text field called input contains the string "home/images/vacation". Then assign this script:

```
slash1 = input.text.indexOf ("/")
slash2 = input.text.indexOf
("/", slash1+1)
```

  The first statement assigns the variable slash1 to the first occurrence of the slash symbol in the string input (slash1 = 4). The second statement searches for the slash symbol again but starts the search at the next character after the first slash (at index 5, or the *i* in *images*). By constructing a while or a do while loop, you can make Flash march down the string, starting new searches as it finds occurrences of the character. Do this until the returned value of the indexOf() method equals the value of the lastIndexOf() method.

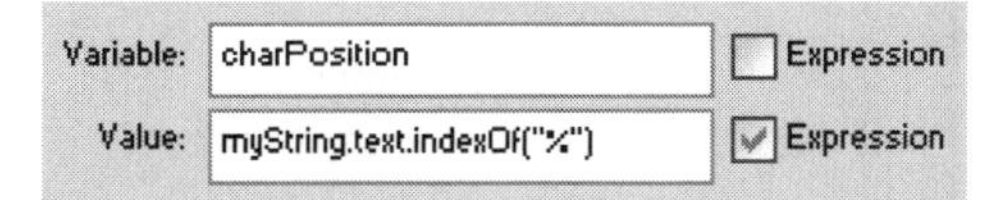

Figure 10.92 This indexOf method searches myString.text for the % sign and puts the index in the variable characterPosition.

If Flash searches a string with the `indexOf()` or `lastIndexOf()` method and doesn't find the specified character, it returns a value of –1. You can use this fact to check for missing characters within a string. If `indexOf("%") == -1`, for example, you know that the percentage symbol is missing from the string. In the next task, you search an input text field for the @ symbol and the period to check whether an email address has been entered correctly.

To check for a missing character:

1. Select the text tool, and drag out a text field on the Stage.
2. In the Property Inspector, choose Input Text and Single Line from the pull-down menus, and enter an instance name for this input text field.
3. Select the text tool again, and drag out another text field on the Stage.
4. In the Property Inspector, choose Dynamic Text and Multiline from the pull-down menus, and enter an instance name for this dynamic text field (**Figure 10.93**).
5. Create a button symbol, place an instance of the button on the Stage between the input text field and the dynamic text field, and give the button a name in the Property Inspector (**Figure 10.94**).
6. Select the first frame of the main Timeline, and open the Actions panel.
7. Assign an `onRelease` handler to the button.
8. Choose Actions > Conditions/Loops > if.
9. In the Condition field, enter the name of the input text field, followed by a dot and then the property `text`.

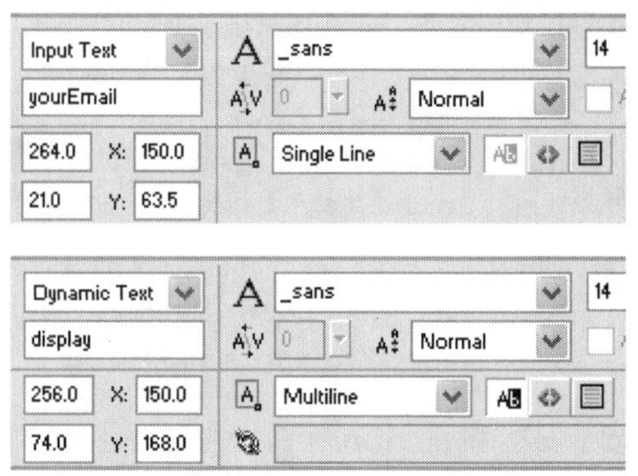

Figure 10.93 Enter yourEmail as the instance name for your input text field, and enter display as the instance name for your dynamic text field.

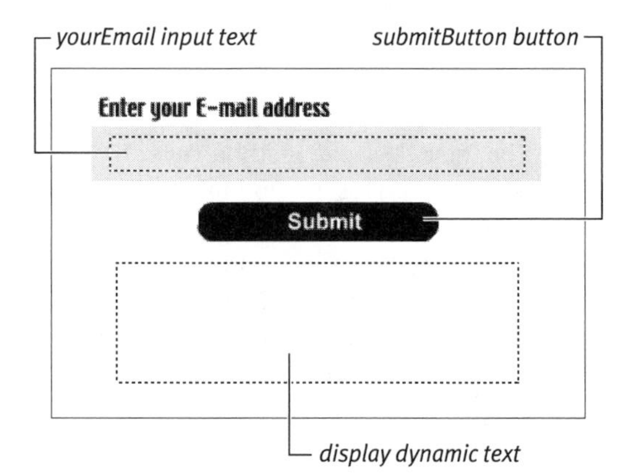

Figure 10.94 Place the input text field at the top, the button in the middle, and the dynamic text field at the bottom.

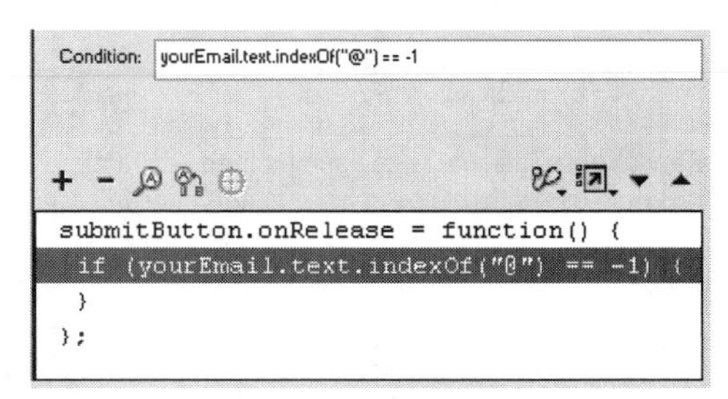

Figure 10.95 If the @ symbol is missing from the string inside `yourEmail.text`, this condition will hold true.

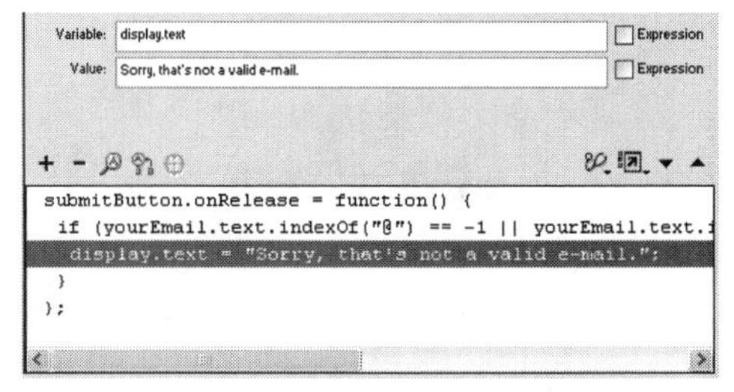

Figure 10.96 The message in the Value field appears in the dynamic text field called display.

10. With your insertion point still in the Condition field, choose Objects > Core > String > Methods > indexOf.

    The `indexOf()` method appears after the `text` property of your text field.

11. Between the parentheses of the `indexOf()` method, enter `"@"`.

    Make sure that you include the quotation marks.

    Flash searches the input text field for the @ symbol.

12. Complete the rest of the condition so that the whole statement looks like the following:

    `yourEmail.text.indexOf ("@") == -1`

    This condition checks to see whether the @ symbol in the string within `yourEmail.text` is not present (**Figure 10.95**).

13. In the same Condition field, enter the logical `OR` operator, `||`.

14. Add a second condition that checks whether a period (.) is not present in this string:

    `yourEmail.text.indexOf (".") == -1`

15. Choose Actions > Variables > set variable.

16. In the Variable field, enter the name of your dynamic text field, followed by a dot and then the `text` property.

17. In the Value field, enter a message that notifies your viewer of a problem with the input (**Figure 10.96**).

continues on next page

18. Choose Actions > Conditions/Loops > else.
19. Choose Actions > Variables > set variable.
20. Send an alternative message to the contents of the dynamic text field that thanks your viewer for submitting an email address (**Figure 10.97**).
21. Test your movie.

    When the viewer clicks the button after entering an email address in the input text field, Flash checks the string for both the @ symbol and a period, and returns the indexes of those symbols. If either index is –1, the viewer receives a message that the input is incorrect. Otherwise, the viewer receives a thank-you message (**Figure 10.98**).

✔ Tip

- Use the `indexOf()` or `lastIndexOf()` method to check for a character or sequence of characters. If you specify a string as the parameter, such as `indexOf(".org")`, Flash returns the index of the first occurrence of the sequence `.org` that appears in the string.

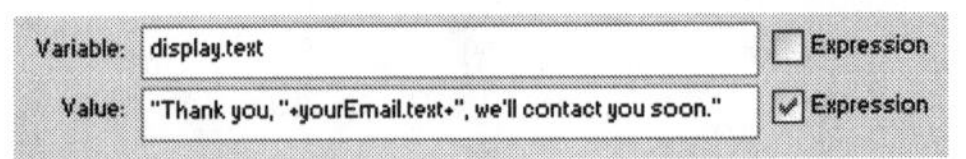

Figure 10.97 This message appears in the dynamic text field called display when the condition is false.

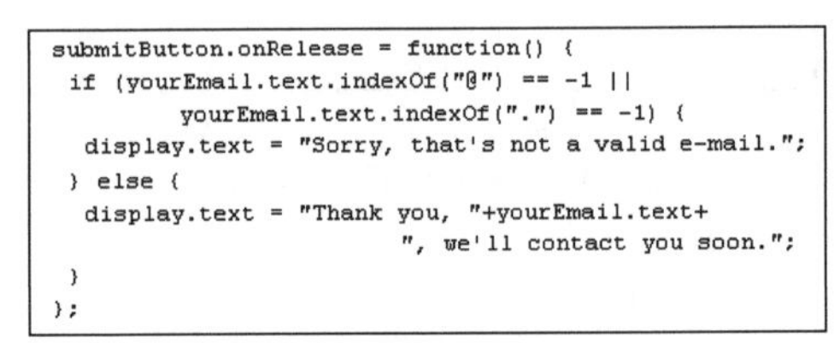

```
submitButton.onRelease = function() {
  if (yourEmail.text.indexOf("@") == -1 ||
          yourEmail.text.indexOf(".") == -1) {
    display.text = "Sorry, that's not a valid e-mail.";
  } else {
    display.text = "Thank you, "+yourEmail.text+
                        ", we'll contact you soon.";
  }
};
```

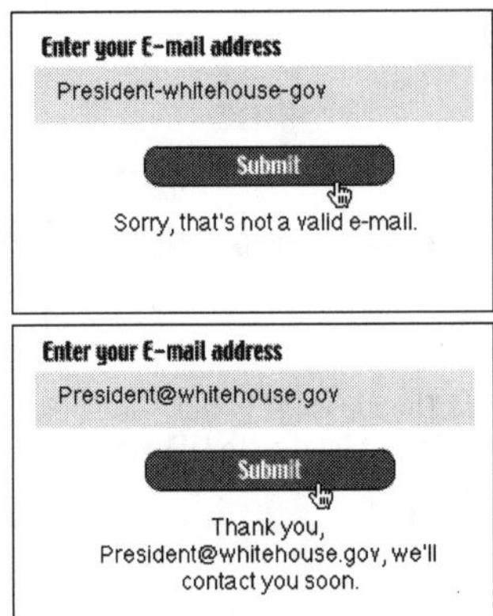

Figure 10.98 The full script (top). Entering an incorrect email address in the input text field results in a warning displayed in the dynamic text field (middle). Entering an email address with an @ sign and a period results in a thank-you message displayed in the dynamic text field (bottom).

```
if (yourEmail.text.length == 0) {
  display.text = "Please enter something";
}
```

Figure 10.99 Flash checks whether the string inside yourEmail.text is empty and displays an appropriate message.

The String object has one property, `length`, that contains the value of the number of characters in a string. This property is a read-only property that is useful for checking the relative positions of characters. If you are building an online purchasing interface with input text fields for prices, you can check the input text to see whether a period character is three positions before the length of the input string in the following expression:

```
input.text.indexOf(".") ==
input.text.length - 3
```

If this condition is true, you could treat the last two digits as a decimal.

The following task refines the preceding example of verifying an email address. You will have Flash make sure that the length of the input isn't 0 (meaning that the viewer hasn't entered anything).

To check the length of a string:

1. Continuing with the file you used in the preceding task, select the main Timeline, and open the Actions panel.
2. Select the ending brace of the `else` statement.
3. Add another `if` statement.
4. In the Condition field, check the length of the string.

   The expression should look like the following:

   `yourEmail.text.length == 0`
5. Assign text to the dynamic text field to notify the viewer that the input text field is empty.

   When your viewer clicks the button, Flash also checks the length of the input text field to see whether anything has been entered (**Figure 10.99**).

Rearranging Strings

When you have information about the position of certain characters and the length of a string, you can select a portion of the string and put it in a new variable. Flash provides tools to get specific selections from a string and put them together with other strings via methods such as `concat()`, `fromCharCode()`, `slice()`, `split()`, `substr()`, and `substring()`. Many of these methods are similar. In this section, we will discuss only `substring()`, to get a specific portion of a string, and `concat()`, to put several strings together. You can use a combination of these two methods to control the information that flows from input text fields into the rest of your Flash movie and back out into dynamic text fields.

The following task copies the current selection that the viewer has made and pastes it into a dynamic text field.

To get selected portions of strings:

1. Select the text tool, and drag out a text field on the Stage.
2. In the Property Inspector, choose Input Text and Multiline from the pull-down menus, and enter an instance name for this input text field (**Figure 10.100**).
3. Drag out another text field on the Stage.
4. In the Property Inspector, choose Dynamic Text and Multiline from the pull-down menus, and enter an instance name for this dynamic text field (**Figure 10.101**).
5. Create a button symbol, and place an instance of it on the Stage between the input text field and the dynamic text field (**Figure 10.102**).

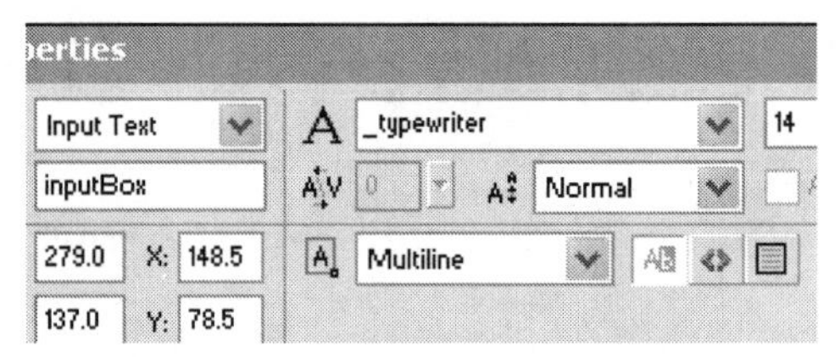

Figure 10.100 Enter inputBox as the instance name for your input text field.

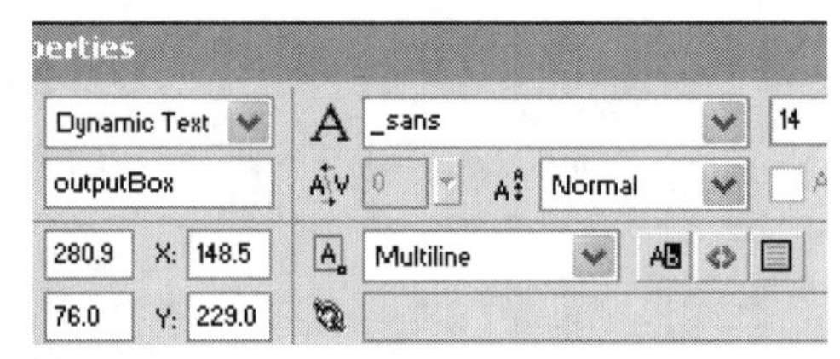

Figure 10.101 Enter outputBox as the instance name for your dynamic text field.

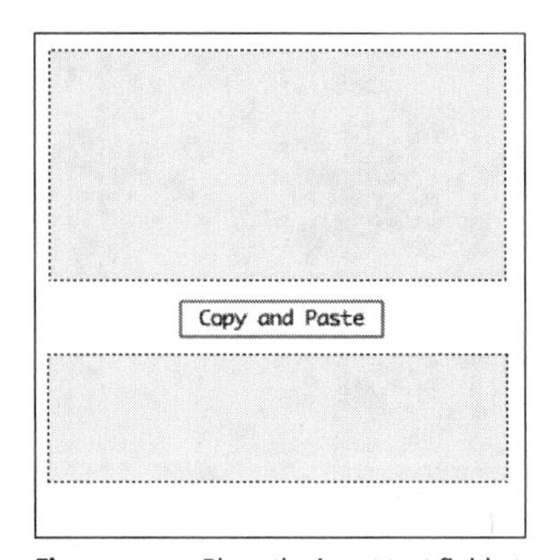

Figure 10.102 Place the input text field at the top, the button in the middle, and the dynamic text field at the bottom.

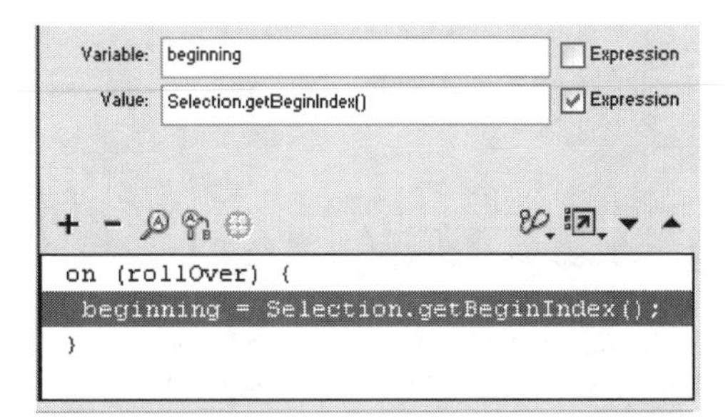

Figure 10.103 The variable called `beginning` contains the position of the start of the selection.

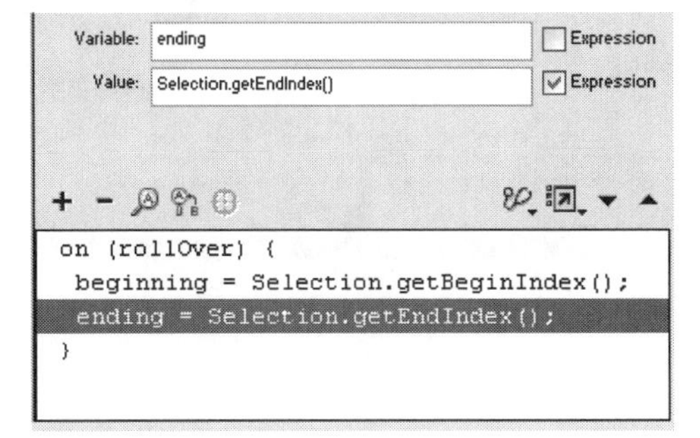

Figure 10.104 The variable called `ending` contains the position of the end of the selection.

6. Select the button, and open the Actions panel.
7. Choose Actions > Movie Control > on. Select the Roll Over event.
8. Choose Actions > Variables > set variable.
9. In the Variable field, enter a variable name.
10. In the Value field, choose Objects > Movie > Selection > Methods > getBeginIndex, and check the Expression checkbox (**Figure 10.103**).

    The position of the start of the selection is assigned to this variable.
11. Choose Actions > Variables > set variable.
12. In the Variable field, enter another variable name.
13. Place your insertion point in the Value field, and choose Objects > Movie > Selection > Methods > getEndIndex.
14. Check the Expression checkbox next to the Value field (**Figure 10.104**).

    The position of the end of the selection is assigned to this variable.
15. Choose Actions > Variables > set variable.
16. In the Variable field, enter another variable name.
17. In the Value field, enter the name of the input text field, followed by a dot and then the `text` property.
18. Choose Objects > Core > String > Methods > substring.

    The `substring()` method appears after your `text` property. This method takes two parameters: `indexA` and `indexB`. `indexA` defines the start of the sequence of characters you want to grab, and `indexB` defines the end of the sequence.

continues on next page

19. Between the parentheses of the `substring()` method, enter your variable for the beginning of the selection and then your variable for the end of the selection, separating them with commas.

20. Check the Expression checkbox next to the Value field (**Figure 10.105**).

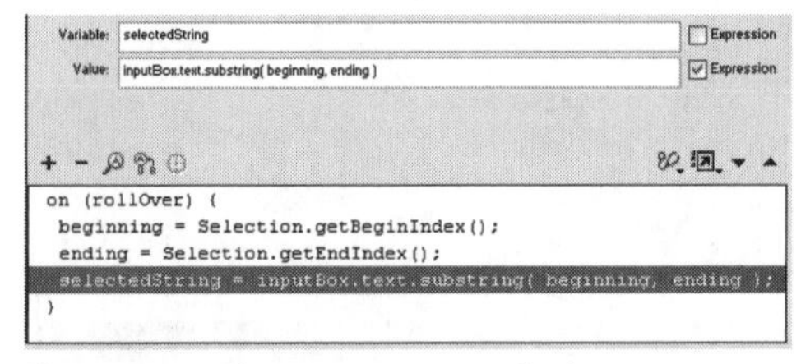

Figure 10.105 The `substring()` method creates a substring out of the string inside `inputBox.text` between indexes `beginning` and `ending`.

21. Create a new event handler by choosing Actions > Movie Control > on.

22. Select the `Release` event.

23. Choose Actions > Variables > set variable.

24. Assign the variable holding the selected substring to the `text` property of the dynamic text field (**Figure 10.106**).

    Your viewer can enter information in the input text field and select portions of the text. When the viewer's mouse rolls over the button that you created, Flash captures the position of the selection and puts the substring into another variable. When your viewer clicks the button, the substring appears in the dynamic text field (**Figure 10.107**).

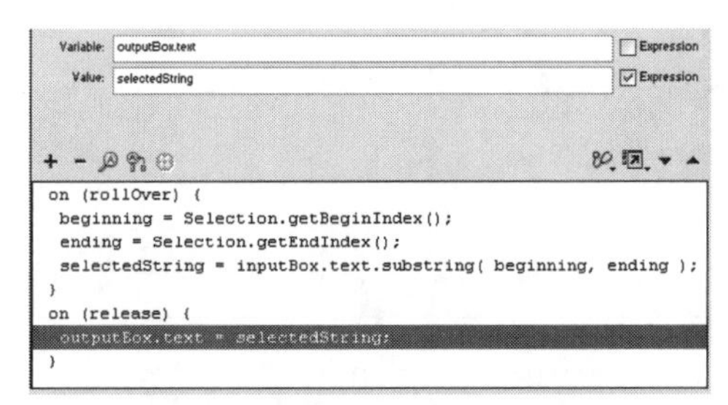

Figure 10.106 The contents of outputBox display the contents of the variable called `selectedString`.

✔ Tip

- You might wonder why the Selection methods are assigned to the `Roll Over` event rather than the `Release` event. That's because Flash must maintain the focus of a text field to capture information about the position of the insertion point or the selection. When the viewer clicks a button, the text field loses focus, and the selection disappears. Assigning the information about the selections to the `Roll Over` event ensures that you have it before it is lost.

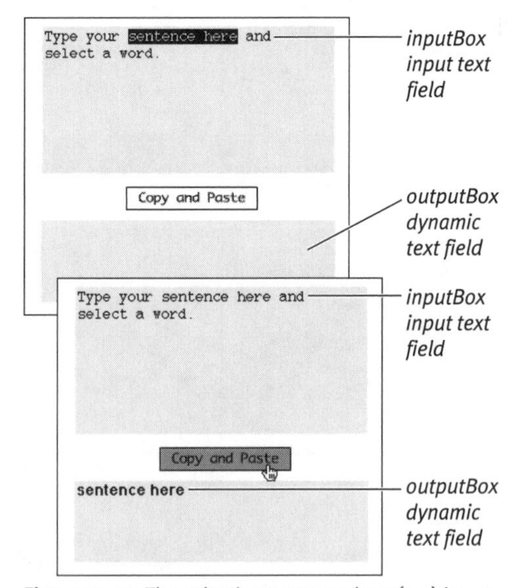

Figure 10.107 The selection *sentence here* (top) is put in a substring and displayed in the dynamic text field below the button (bottom).

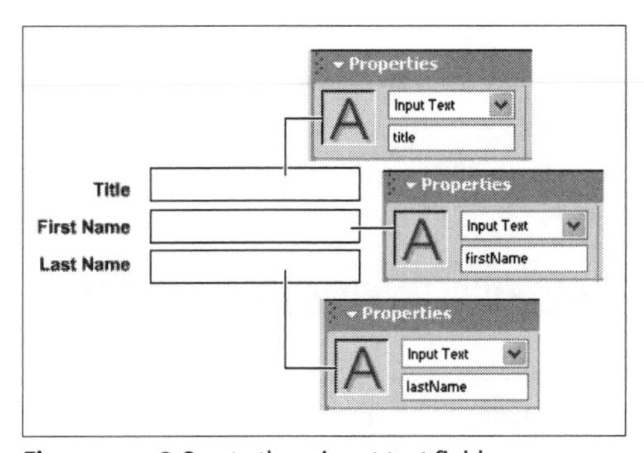

Figure 10.108 Create three input text fields.

Refining Email Verification with the substring() Method

You can apply the `substring()` method to the example for email verification to refine the feedback message. Instead of displaying a thank-you message directed at the full email address, for example, you can personalize it somewhat by stripping out everything that comes after the @ symbol. That way, your thank-you message is directed just at the user name, which is often the user's actual name (or close to it). Set the dynamic text field `text` property to:

```
"Thank you, " + yourEmail.text.substring
(0, (yourEmail.text.indexOf("@"))) + ",
we'll contact you soon."
```

The substring returns the selection from the first character (index 0) to the @ character.

With the method `concat()`, you can put together strings you've dissected in an order that's more useful. The parameters of the `concat()` method are individual expressions, separated by commas, that you want to combine. The `concat()` method accomplishes the same thing as the addition operator (+), which is discussed earlier in this chapter and in Chapter 9. The following two statements are equivalent:

```
"Hello, ".concat (firstName, " ", lastName);
"Hello, " + firstName + " " + lastName;
```

To combine two separate strings:

1. Select the text tool, and drag out a text field on the Stage.
2. In the Property Inspector, choose Input Text and Multiline from the pull-down menus, and enter an instance name for this input text field.
3. Select the text tool again, and drag out two more input text fields with the same settings as the first.
4. In the Property Inspector, give these input text fields different instance names (**Figure 10.108**).
5. Select the text tool, and drag out a fourth text box on the Stage.
6. In the Property Inspector, choose Dynamic Text and Multiline from the pull-down menus, and enter an instance name for this dynamic text field.
7. Create a button symbol, and place an instance of it on the Stage.
8. Select the button symbol, and open the Actions panel.

continues on next page

9. Choose Actions > Movie Control > on.
10. Leave the `Release` event checked.
11. Choose Actions > Variables > set variable.
12. In the Variable field, enter the name of your dynamic text field, followed by a dot and then the `text` property.
13. In the Value field, enter the name of the first input text field, followed by a dot and then the `text` property.
14. Choose Objects > Core > String > Methods > concat.

    The `concat()` method appears in the Value field following the `text` property for the first text field. You still need to supply the parameters of the `concat()` method, which are values that will be concatenated (**Figure 10.109**).
15. For the parameters of the `concat()` method, enter the `text` properties of the second and third input text fields and spaces, separating all your parameters with commas.
16. Check the Expression checkbox (**Figure 10.110**).
17. Test your movie.

    When the viewer enters information in the input text fields and then clicks the button, Flash concatenates the contents of the three input text fields and displays them in the dynamic text field (**Figure 10.111**).

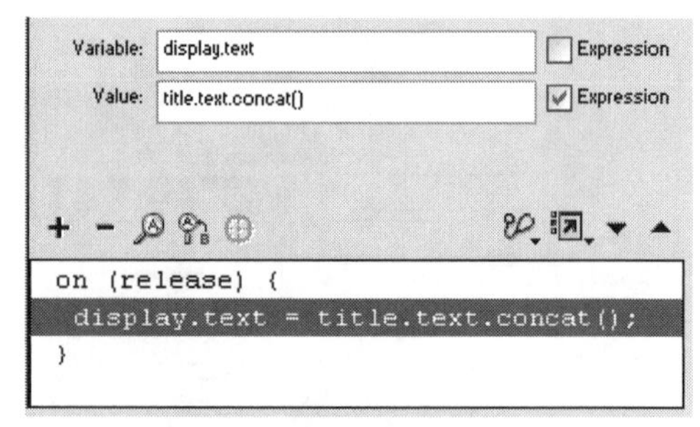

Figure 10.109 The `concat()` method combines the values specified in its parameters, which have not yet been defined here, with the string inside `title.text`.

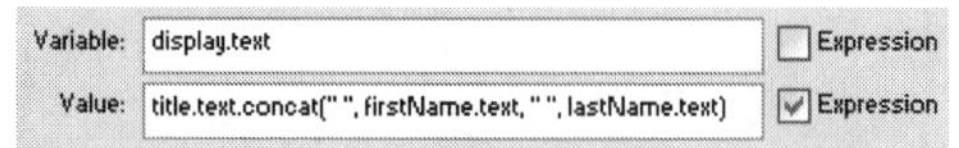

Figure 10.110 This `concat()` method is equivalent to `title.text + " " + firstName.text + " " + lastName.text`.

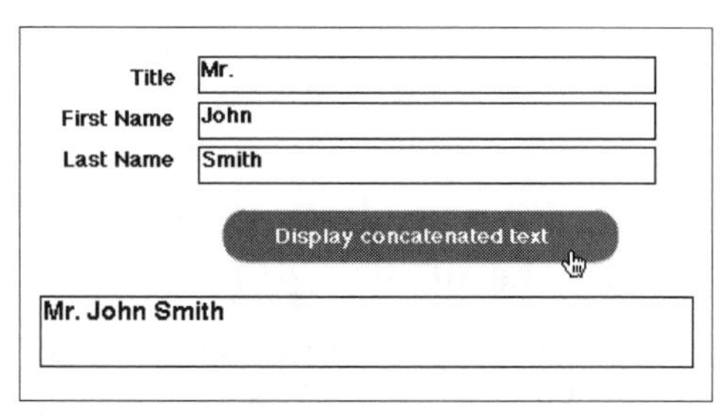

Figure 10.111 Flash concatenates the top three input text fields into one string in the bottom dynamic text field.

Modifying Strings

You can perform two simple methods on a string to modify its characters: `toUpperCase()` and `toLowerCase()`. Both methods return a string with all uppercase letters or all lowercase letters. If you want to modify only certain letters to uppercase or lowercase, first you'll need to create substrings of those specific characters, as discussed in the preceding section. Modify the substrings to uppercase or lowercase; then put the string back together with `concat()`.

To change the case of characters in strings:

1. Select the text tool, and drag out a text field on the Stage.
2. In the Property Inspector, choose Input Text and Single Line from the pull-down menus, and enter an instance name for this input text field.
3. Select the text tool, and drag out another text field on the Stage.
4. In the Property Inspector, choose Dynamic Text and Single line from the pull-down menus, and enter an instance name for this dynamic text field.
5. Create a button symbol, and place an instance of it on the Stage.
6. Select the button symbol, and open the Actions panel.
7. Choose Actions > Movie Control > on.
8. Leave the `Release` event checked.
9. Choose Actions > Variables > set variable.

continues on next page

10. In the Variable field, enter the `text` property of your dynamic text field.

11. In the Value field enter the `text` property of your input text field.

12. Choose Objects > Core > String > Methods > toUpperCase.

13. Check the Expression checkbox.

    The `toUpperCase()` method appears in the Value field after the `text` property of your input text field. No parameters are required (**Figure 10.112**).

14. Test your movie.

    When your viewer enters text in the input text field and clicks the button you created, Flash converts the entire string to uppercase and displays the results in the dynamic text field (**Figure 10.113**). Note that the method does not change the original string that calls it. In this example, the contents of myInput remain as they were originally.

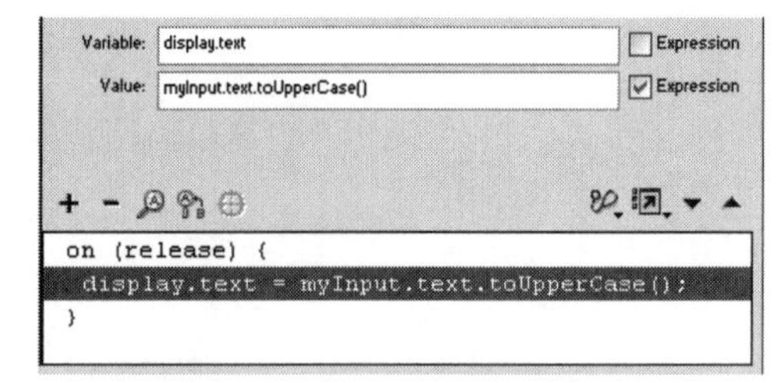

Figure 10.112 The `toUpperCase()` method creates a string from `myInput.text` and converts that string to uppercase characters.

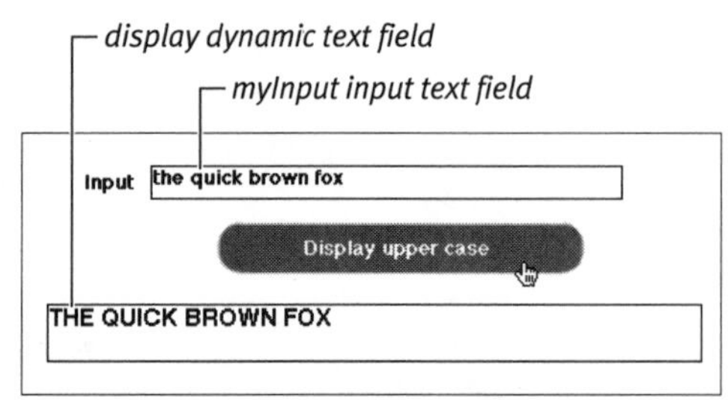

Figure 10.113 The results of the `toUpperCase()` method shown in the dynamic text field called display.

MANIPULATING INFORMATION

11

The information that you store in variables, modify in expressions, and test with conditional statements often needs to be processed and manipulated by mathematical functions such as square roots, sines, cosines, and exponents. Flash can perform these calculations with the Math object, which lets you create formulas for complicated interactions between the objects in your movie and your viewer or for sophisticated geometry in your graphics. The Math object, for example, allows you to model the correct trajectory of colliding objects or the effects of gravity for a physics tutorial, calculate probabilities for a card game, or generate random numbers to add unpredictable elements to your movie. Much of the information you manipulate sometimes needs to be stored in arrays to give you better control of your data and a more efficient way to retrieve it. You can use the Array object to keep track of ordered data such as shopping lists, color tables, and scorecards.

When the information you need depends on the time or the date, you can use the Date object to retrieve the current year, month, or even millisecond. Build clocks and timers to use inside your Flash movie, or send the time information (along with a viewer's profile) to a server-side script.

All this information handling and processing is easier when you use functions. Build functions that string together separate actions and methods to accomplish many tasks at the same time. Build a single function, for example, that automatically attaches a sound, plays it, and adjusts the volume level and pan settings based on the parameters you provide. You can even build functions to customize your own classes. Extend the capabilities of predefined Flash objects by creating your own methods and properties for your customized objects. This chapter explores the variety of ways you can manipulate information with added complexity and flexibility and shows you how to integrate the objects you've learned about in previous chapters.

Calculating with the Math Object

The Math object lets you access trigonometric functions such as sine, cosine, and tangent; logarithmic functions; rounding functions; and mathematical constants such as pi and e. **Table 11.1** summarizes the methods and properties of the Math object. As with the Key, Mouse, Selection, and Stage objects, you don't need to instantiate the Math object to call on its methods or properties, and all the Math object's properties are read-only values that are written in all capital letters. You precede the method with the object name, `Math`.

To calculate the square root of 10, for example, you write:

```
myAnswer = Math.sqrt (10)
```

The calculated value is put in the variable `myAnswer`. To use a constant, use similar syntax:

```
myCircum = Math.PI * 2 * myRadius
```

The mathematical constant pi is multiplied by 2 and the variable `myRadius`, and the result is put into the variable `myCircum`.

Table 11.1

Methods and Properties of the Math Object

Method or Property	Description
abs(number)	Calculates the absolute value. Math.abs(-4) returns 4.
acos(number)	Calculates the arc cosine.
asin(number)	Calculates the arc sine.
atan(number)	Calculates the arc tangent.
atan2(y, x)	Calculates the angle (in radians) from the x axis to a point on the y axis.
ceil(number)	Rounds the number up to the nearest integer. Math.ceil (2.34) returns 3.
cos(number)	Calculates the cosine of an angle, in radians.
exp(number)	Calculates the exponent of the constant e.
floor(number)	Rounds the number down to the nearest integer. Math.floor (2.34) returns 2.
log(number)	Calculates the natural logarithm.
max(x, y)	Returns the larger of two values. Math.max (2, 7) returns 7.
min(x, y)	Returns the smaller of two values. Math.min (2, 7) returns 2.
pow(base, exponent)	Calculates the exponent of a number.
random()	Returns a random number between 0 and 1 (not including 1).
round(number)	Rounds the number to the nearest integer. Math.round (2.34) returns 2.
sin(number)	Calculates the sine of an angle, in radians.
sqrt(number)	Calculates the square root.
tan(number)	Calculates the tangent of an angle, in radians.
E	Euler's constant; the base of natural logarithms.
LN2	The natural logarithm of 2.
LOG2E	The base-2 logarithm of e.
LN10	The natural logarithm of 10.
LOG10E	The base-10 logarithm of e.
PI	The circumference of a circle divided by its diameter.
SQRT1_2	The square root of 1/2.
SQRT2	The square root of 2.

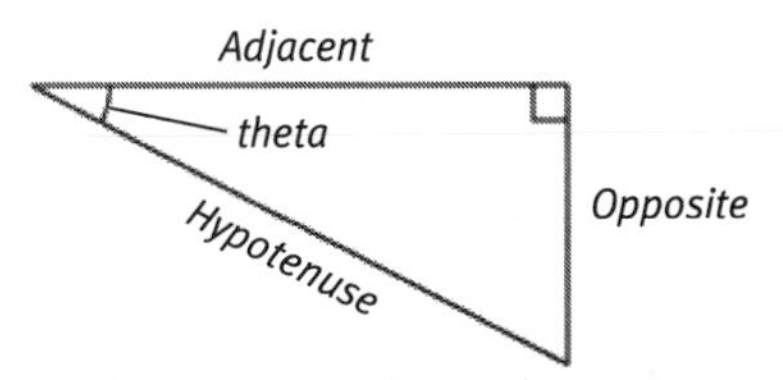

Sin theta = opposite/hypotenuse
Cos theta = adjacent/hypotenuse
Tan theta = opposite/adjacent

Figure 11.1 The angle, theta, of a right triangle is defined by sin, cos, and tan and by the length of the three sides.

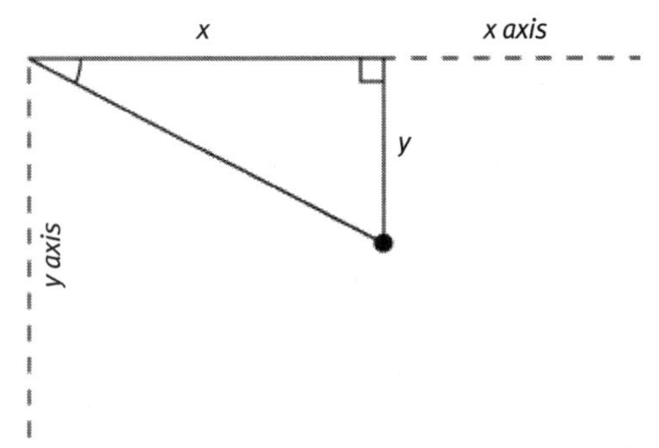

Figure 11.2 A point on the Stage makes a right triangle with x (adjacent side) and y (opposite side).

Calculating Angles with the Math Object

The angle that an object makes relative to the Stage or to another object is useful information for creating many game interactions, as well as for creating dynamic animations and interfaces based purely in ActionScript. To create a dial that controls the sound volume, for example, you need to compute the angle at which your viewer drags the dial relative to the horizontal or vertical axis and then change the dial's rotation and sound's volume accordingly. Calculating the angle also requires that you brush up on some of your high-school trigonometry, so a review of some basic principles related to sine, cosine, and tangent is in order.

The mnemonic device SOH CAH TOA can help you keep the trigonometric functions straight. This acronym stands for Sine = Opposite over Hypotenuse, Cosine = Adjacent over Hypotenuse, and Tangent = Opposite over Adjacent (**Figure 11.1**). Knowing the length of any two sides of a right triangle is enough information for you to calculate the other two angles. You will most likely know the lengths of the opposite and adjacent sides of the triangle because they represent the y and x coordinates of a point (**Figure 11.2**). When you have the x and y coordinates, you can calculate the angle (theta) by using the following mathematical formulas:

```
Tan theta = opposite/adjacent
```

or

```
Tan theta = y/x
```

or

```
theta = ArcTan (y/x)
```

In Flash, you can write this expression by using the Math object this way:

```
myTheta = Math.atan(this._y/this._x)
```

continues on next page

Alternatively, Flash provides an even easier method that lets you define the y and x positions without having to do the division. The `atan2()` method accepts the y and x positions as two parameters, so you can write the equivalent statement:

```
myTheta = Math.atan2(this._y, this._x)
```

Unfortunately, the trigonometric methods of the Math object require and return values in radians, which describe angles in terms of the constant pi—easier mathematically, but not so convenient if you want to use the values to modify the `_rotation` property of an object. You can convert an angle from radians to degrees, and vice versa, by using the following formulas:

```
Radian = Math.PI/180 * degrees
Degrees = radian * 180/Math.PI
```

The following tasks calculate the angles of a draggable movie clip and display the angles (in degrees) in a dynamic text field.

To calculate the angle relative to the Stage:

1. Create a movie-clip symbol, place an instance of it on the Stage, and give the movie-clip instance a name in the Property Inspector.

   In this example, the movie-clip instance is called circle.

2. Create a dynamic text field on the Stage, choose Single Line in the Property Inspector, and give the dynamic text field an instance name.

   In this example, the text field is called myDegrees.

3. Select the first frame of the main Timeline, and open the Actions panel.
4. Choose Actions > Movie Clip Control > startDrag.
5. In the Target field, enter `circle`, and check the Expression checkbox.
6. Check the Constrain to Rectangle and Lock Mouse to Center checkboxes.
7. Enter `0` in the L field, `0` in the T field, `Stage.width` in the R field, and `Stage.height` in the B field (**Figure 11.3**).

   The center of the movie clip follows your viewer's pointer and is constrained to the boundaries of the Stage.

8. Choose Objects > Movie > Movie Clip > Events > onEnterFrame.
9. In the Object field, enter `_root`.
10. Choose Actions > Variables > set variable.
11. In the Variable field, enter a name for a variable that will hold the angle in radians.
12. Place your insertion point in the Value field, and choose Objects > Core > Math > Methods > atan2.

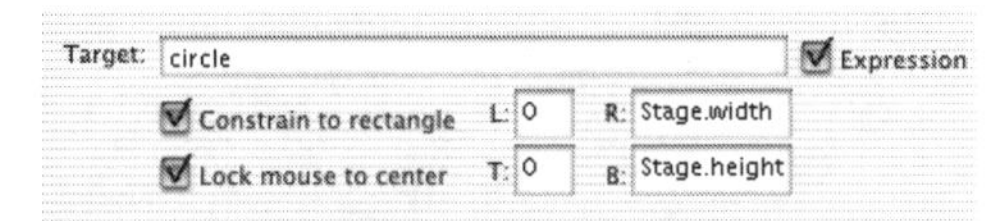

Figure 11.3 This `startDrag` action makes the movie clip follow the pointer and constrains it within the boundaries of the Stage's width and height.

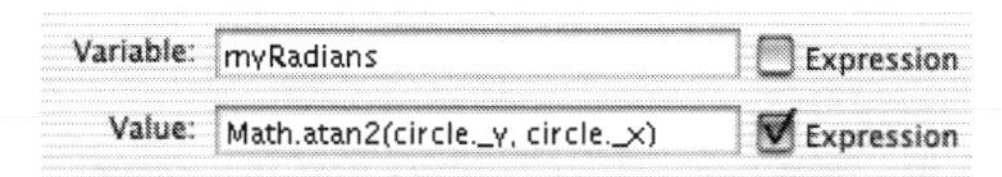

Figure 11.4 The `Math.atan2()` method calculates the angle that the movie clip called circle makes with the origin (top-left corner of the Stage).

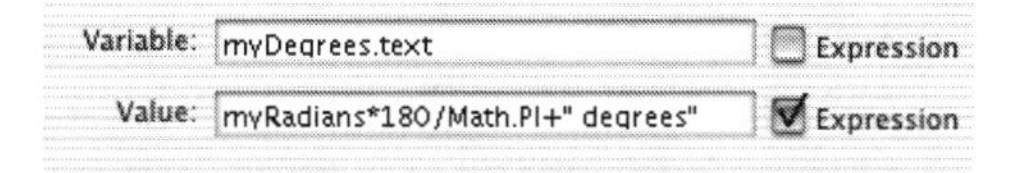

Figure 11.5 The dynamic text field called myDegrees displays the angle in degrees.

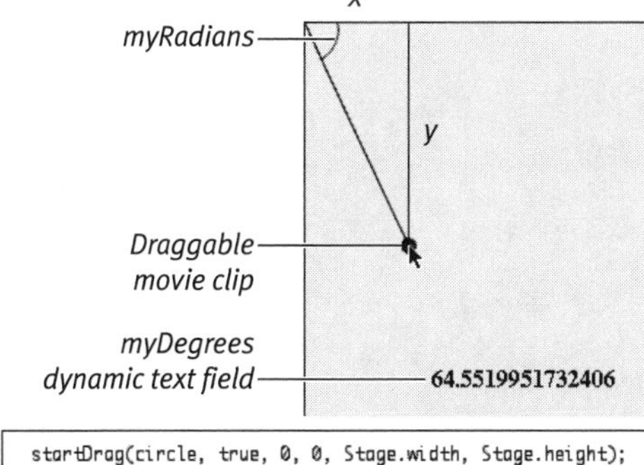


```
startDrag(circle, true, 0, 0, Stage.width, Stage.height);
_root.onEnterFrame = function() {
    myRadians = Math.atan2(circle._y, circle._x);
    myDegrees.text = myRadians*180/Math.PI+" degrees";
};
```

Figure 11.6 The full script as it appears in the Script pane (below). The movie clip makes an angle of approximately 65 degrees below the x axis. The lines have been drawn in to show the right triangle.

13. Between the parentheses of the `atan2()` method, enter `circle._y`, followed by a comma and then `circle._x`, and check the Expression checkbox (**Figure 11.4**).

    Flash calculates the arc tangent of the y position of the movie clip divided by the x position of the movie clip and returns the value in radians.

14. Choose Actions > Variables > set variable.

15. In the Variable field, enter `myDegrees.text`.

16. In the Value field, enter an expression that multiplies your variable that holds the radian angle by 180 and divides it by the constant pi:

    `myRadians * 180/Math.PI`

17. Check the Expression checkbox, and concatenate the string `"degrees"` to the end of the expression.

    The angle is converted from radians to degrees and assigned to the contents of the dynamic text field (**Figure 11.5**).

18. Test your movie.

    As the viewer moves the pointer around the Stage, the movie clip follows the pointer. Flash calculates the angle that the movie clip makes with the x axis of the root Timeline and displays the angle (in degrees) in the dynamic text field (**Figure 11.6**).

To calculate the angle relative to another point:

1. Continuing with the file you used in the preceding task, create another movie-clip symbol, place an instance of it on the Stage, and give it a name in the Property Inspector.

   In this example, the name is myReferencePoint.

2. Select first frame of the main Timeline, and open the Actions panel.

3. Select the statement that calculates the angle from the `atan2()` method, and change the expression to read:

   ```
   Math.atan2
   ((circle._y -myReferencePoint._y),
   (circle._x -myReferencePoint._x))
   ```

   By subtracting the y and x positions of the reference point from the draggable movie clip's position, Flash calculates the y and x distances between the two points (**Figure 11.7**).

4. Test your movie.

   As the viewer moves the pointer around the Stage, the movie clip follows the pointer. Flash calculates the angle that the draggable movie clip makes with the stationary movie clip and displays the angle (in degrees) in the dynamic text field.

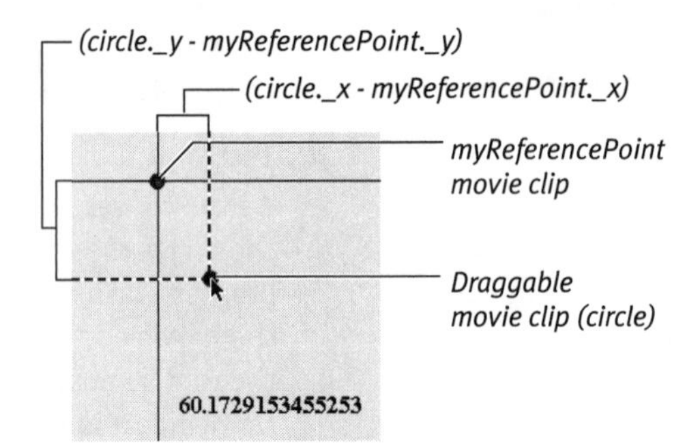

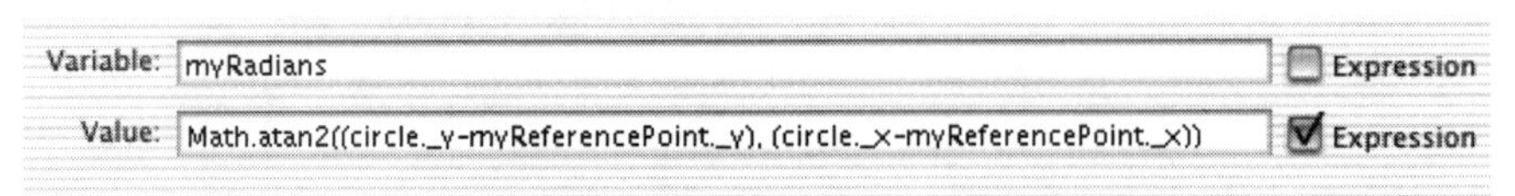

Figure 11.7 The difference between the y positions of the circle movie clip and the myReferencePoint movie clip is the y parameter for `Math.atan2()`. The difference between the x positions of the circle movie clip and the myReferencePoint movie clip is the x parameter for `Math.atan2()`.

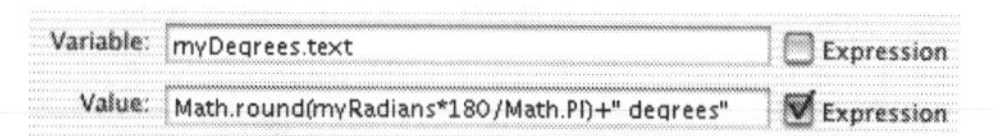

Figure 11.8 The expression within the parentheses is rounded to the nearest integer and displayed in the dynamic text field called myDegrees.

So far, the returned values for your angles have had many decimal places. Often, you will need to round those values to the nearest whole number (or integer) so that you can use those values as parameters in methods and properties. Use `Math.round()` to round values to the nearest integer, `Math.ceil()` to round to the closest integer greater than or equal to the value, and `Math.floor()` to round to the closest integer less than or equal to the value.

To round a number to an integer:

1. Continuing with the file you used in the preceding task, select the first frame of the main Timeline, and open the Actions panel.
2. Select the statement that converts the angle from radians to degrees.
3. Place your insertion point in the Value field in front of the expression, and enter the method `Math.round`.

   Use parentheses to group the expression that converts radians to degrees (**Figure 11.8**).

   Flash converts the angle from radians to degrees and then applies the `Math.round()` method to that value, returning an integer.

You can apply the methods that calculate angles and round values to create a draggable rotating dial. The approach is to calculate the angle of the mouse's position to the center point of the dial and then set the `_rotation` property of the dial to the angle.

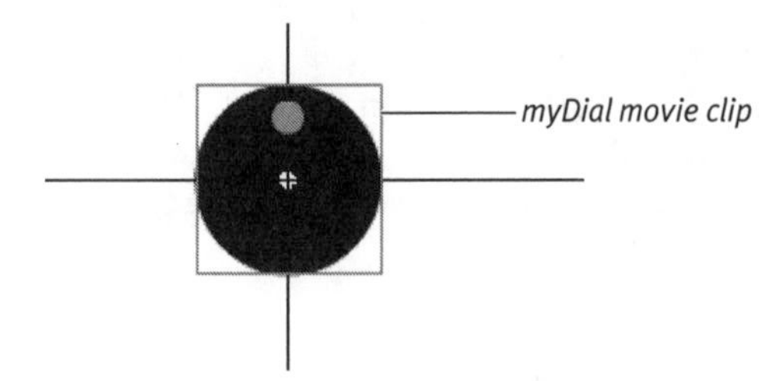

Figure 11.9 Place a circular movie clip called myDial on the Stage.

To create a draggable rotating dial:

1. Create a movie-clip symbol of a dial, place an instance of it on the Stage, and give it a name in the Property Inspector.

   In this example, the name is myDial (**Figure 11.9**).

2. Select the first frame of the main Timeline, and open the Actions panel.
3. Assign an `onPress` handler for your movie clip.
4. Choose Actions > Variables > set variable.
5. In the Variable field, enter the variable name `pressing`.
6. In the Value field, enter `true`, and check the Expression checkbox (**Figure 11.10**).
7. Switch to Expert mode (Ctrl-Shift-E for Windows, Cmd-Shift-E for Mac), and assign a handler for both the `onRelease` event and the `onReleaseOutside` event for your movie clip.
8. Switch back to Normal mode (Ctrl-Shift-N for Windows, Cmd-Shift-N for Mac), and choose Actions > Variables > set variable.
9. In the Variable field, enter the variable name `pressing`.

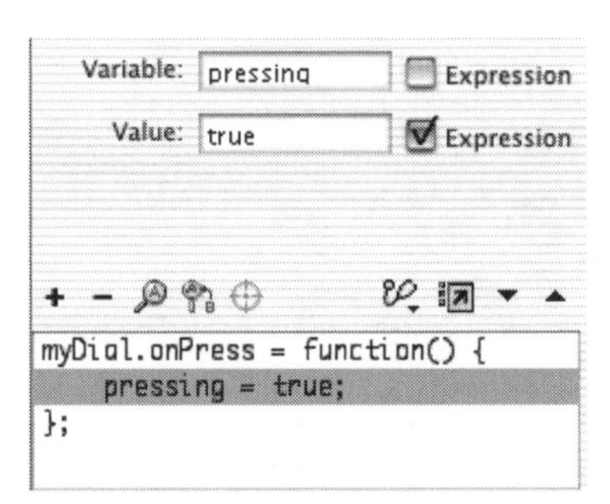

Figure 11.10 Set `pressing` to `true` when the button is pressed.

```
myDial.onPress = function() {
    pressing = true;
};
myDial.onRelease = myDial.onReleaseOutside=function () {
    pressing = false;
};
```

Figure 11.11 Set `pressing` to `false` when the button is either released or released outside the button's hit area. The compound handler that combines the `onRelease` and `onReleaseOutside` events is created in Expert mode.

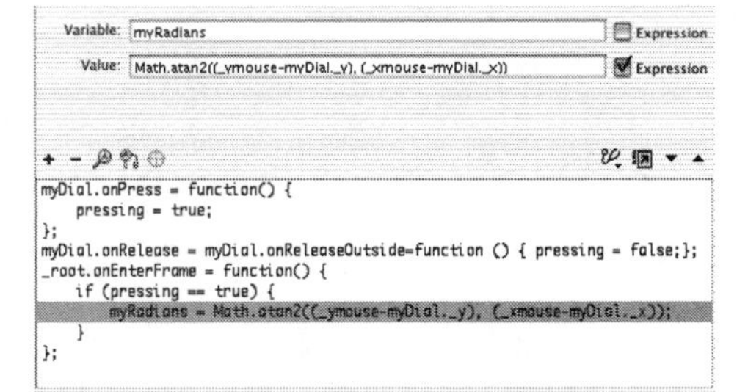

Figure 11.12 The variable `myRadians` contains the calculated angle between the pointer and the movie clip.

10. In the Value field, enter `false`, and check the Expression checkbox (**Figure 11.11**).

    The variable called `pressing` keeps track of whether your viewer is pressing or not pressing this movie clip.

11. Select the closing brace of your last event handler, and choose Objects > Movie > Movie Clip > Events > onEnterFrame.

12. In the Object field, enter `_root`.

13. Choose Actions > Conditions/Loops > if.

14. In the Condition field, enter `pressing == true`.

15. Choose Actions > Variables > set variable.

16. In the Variable field, enter a variable name.

17. In the Value field, enter the following, and check the Expression checkbox:

    `Math.atan2((_ymouse-myDial._y), (_xmouse-myDial._x))`

    Flash calculates the angle between the viewer's pointer and the center of the movie clip (**Figure 11.12**).

18. Choose Actions > Variables > set variable.

19. In the Variable field, enter a variable name.

continues on next page

20. In the Value field, enter an expression to convert radians to degrees and round the result to an integer, and check the Expression checkbox (**Figure 11.13**).

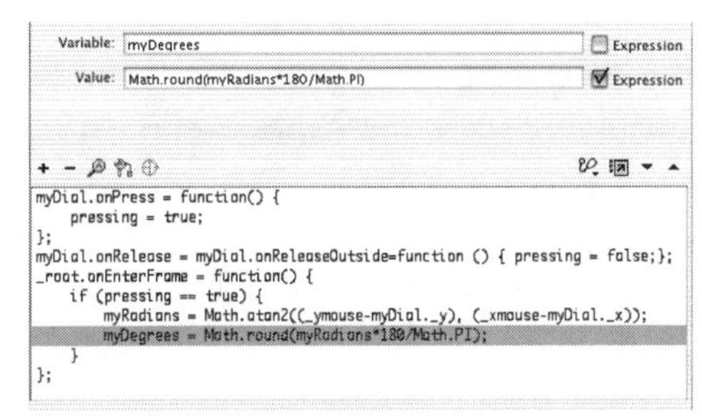

Figure 11.13 The angle is converted from radians to degrees, rounded to the nearest integer, and assigned to the variable called `myDegrees`.

21. Choose Actions > Variables > set variable.

22. In the Variable field, enter `myDial._rotation`.

23. In the Value field, enter your variable that holds the angle in degrees, and add 90; then check the Expression checkbox.

    The rotation of the movie clip is assigned to the calculated angle. The 90 is added to compensate for the difference between the calculated angle and the movie-clip rotation property. A value of 0 for `_rotation` corresponds to the 12 o'clock position of a movie clip, but a value of 0 corresponds to the 3 o'clock position of the calculated arcTangent angle, so adding 90 equalizes them (**Figure 11.14**).

24. Test your movie.

    When viewers press the button in the dial, they can rotate it by dragging it around its center point. When they release the button, the dial stops rotating.

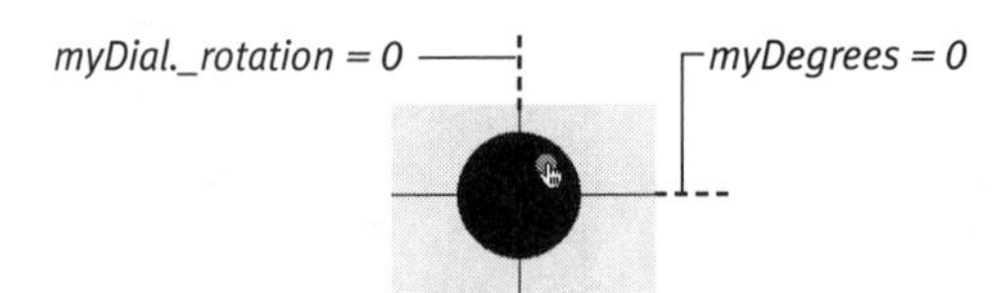


```
myDial.onPress = function() {
    pressing = true;
};
myDial.onRelease = myDial.onReleaseOutside=function () { pressing = false;};
_root.onEnterFrame = function() {
    if (pressing == true) {
        myRadians = Math.atan2((_ymouse-myDial._y), (_xmouse-myDial._x));
        myDegrees = Math.round(myRadians*180/Math.PI);
        myDial._rotation = myDegrees+90;
    }
};
```

Figure 11.14 The final statement within the `if` statement modifies the rotation of the myDial movie clip. The rotation of myDial is set at `myDegrees + 90` to account for the difference between the reference point of the trigonometric functions and Flash's `_rotation` property.

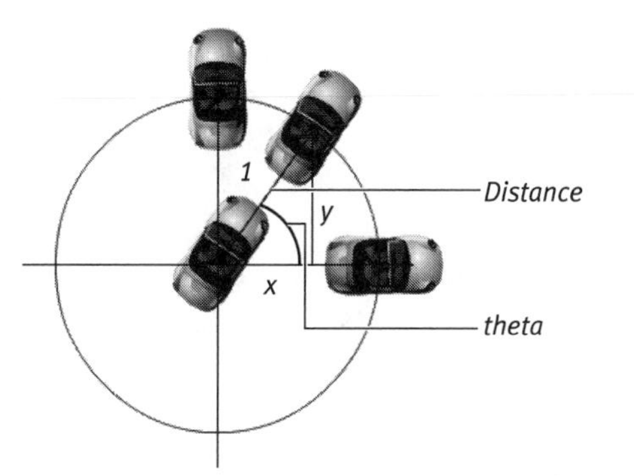

Figure 11.15 The x and y components of this car, which moves a certain distance, is determined by the cosine and sine of its angle, theta.

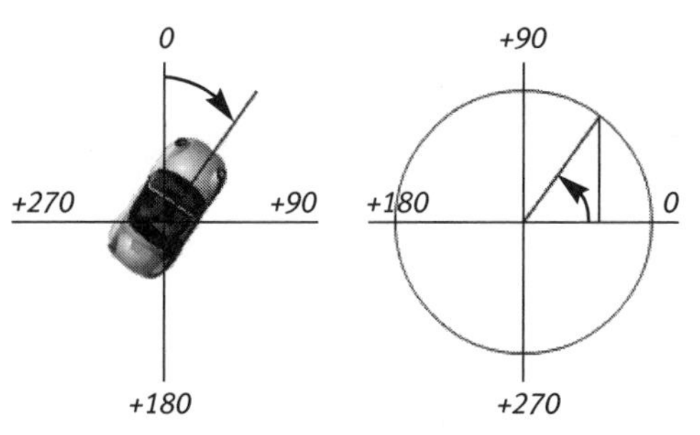

Figure 11.16 The rotation property of a movie clip begins from the vertical axis and increases in the clockwise direction (left). Values for sine and cosine angles begin from the horizontal axis and increase in the counterclockwise direction (right).

Using Sine and Cosine for Directional Movement

When you want to control how far an object on the Stage travels based on its angle, you can use the sine and cosine trigonometric functions. Suppose that you want to create a racing game featuring a car that your viewer moves around a track. The car travels at a certain speed, and it moves according to where the front of the car is pointed.

Calculating just how far the car moves in any direction requires the `Math.sin()` and `Math.cos()` methods of the Math object. The new location of the car is determined by the x and y components of the triangle that is formed by the angle of the car. When the car is angled up, the y component is 1, and the x component is 0. When the car is angled to the right, the y component is 0, and the x component is 1. When the car is angled somewhere between up and right, the sine and cosine of the angle give you the x and y contributions (**Figure 11.15**). The sine of the angle determines the magnitude of the y component, and the cosine of the angle determines the magnitude of the x component. Sine and cosine, however, are based on angles that begin at 0 degrees from the horizontal axis. The rotation property, on the other hand, is based on angles that begin at 0 degrees from the vertical axis (**Figure 11.16**). Moreover, the y component for the sine function is positive above the origin of the circle and negative below it. When you deal with a movie clip's coordinate space, you must do two transformations: Subtract the rotation property from 90 to get the angle for sine and cosine, and then use the negative value of sine for the change in the y direction:

```
myCar._x += Math.cos(90-rotation);
myCar._y += -Math.sin(90-rotation);
```

continues on next page

In the following task, you will create a movie clip whose rotation can be controlled by the viewer. The movie clip has a constant velocity, so it will travel in the direction in which it is pointed, just as a car moves according to where it is steered.

To create a controllable object with directional movement:

1. Create a movie-clip symbol, place an instance of it on the Stage, and name it in the Property Inspector.
   In this example, the name is car.
2. Select the first frame of the main Timeline, and open the Actions panel.
3. Choose Objects > Movie > Movie Clip > Events > onEnterFrame.
4. In the Object field, enter `_root`.
5. Choose Actions > Conditions/Loops > if.
6. In the Condition field, enter the following:
   `Key.isDown (Key.LEFT)`
   Flash checks to see whether the left-arrow key is pressed.
7. Choose Actions > Miscellaneous Actions > evaluate.
8. In the Expression field, enter `car._rotation -= 10`.
   Flash subtracts 10 from the current rotation property of the movie clip car when the left-arrow key is pressed (**Figure 11.17**).
9. Choose Actions > Conditions/Loops > else if.
10. In the Condition field, enter the following:
    `Key.isDown (Key.RIGHT)`
    Flash checks to see whether the right-arrow key is pressed.
11. Choose Actions > Miscellaneous Actions > evaluate.

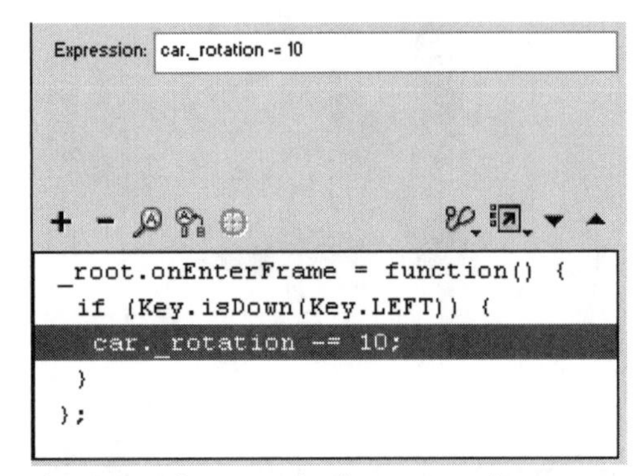

Figure 11.17 The car movie clip rotates 10 degrees counterclockwise when the left-arrow key is pressed.

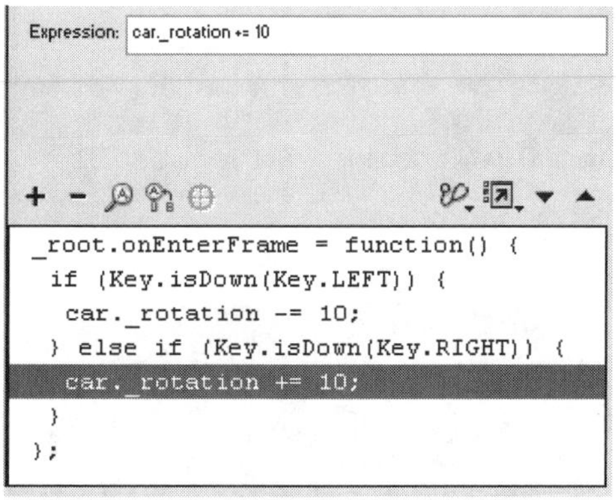

Expression: car._rotation += 10

```
_root.onEnterFrame = function() {
  if (Key.isDown(Key.LEFT)) {
    car._rotation -= 10;
  } else if (Key.isDown(Key.RIGHT)) {
    car._rotation += 10;
  }
};
```

Figure 11.18 The car movie clip rotates 10 degrees clockwise when the right-arrow key is pressed.

Variable: myAngle ☐ Expression
Value: 90 - car._rotation ☑ Expression

```
_root.onEnterFrame = function() {
  if (Key.isDown(Key.LEFT)) {
    car._rotation -= 10;
  } else if (Key.isDown(Key.RIGHT)) {
    car._rotation += 10;
  }
  myAngle = 90 - car._rotation;
};
```

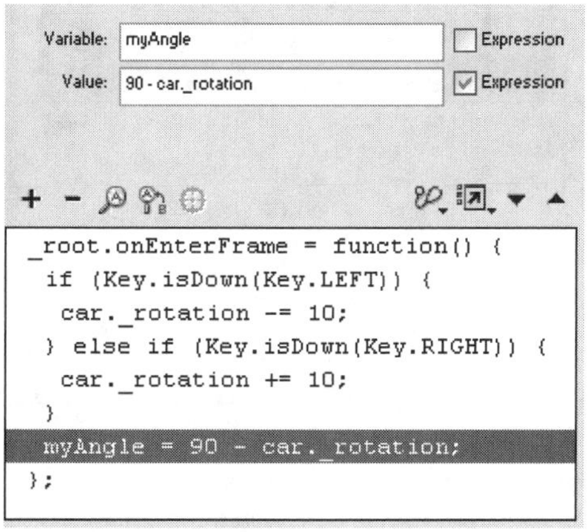

Figure 11.19 The variable `myAngle` will be used as the angle for sine and cosine.

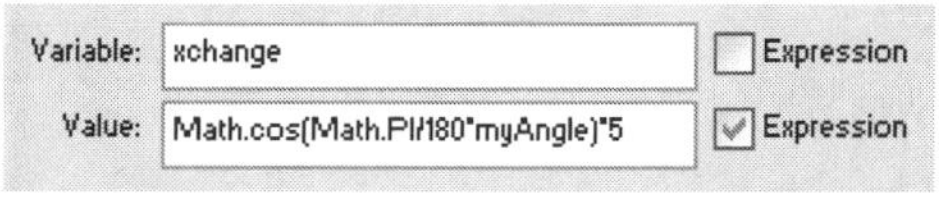

Variable: xchange ☐ Expression
Value: Math.cos(Math.PI/180*myAngle)*5 ☑ Expression

Figure 11.20 The cosine of the movie clip's angle is calculated and assigned to `xchange`.

12. In the Expression field, enter `car._rotation += 10`.

    Flash adds 10 to the current rotation property of the movie clip car when the right-arrow key is pressed (**Figure 11.18**).

13. Select the closing brace of the `else if` action, and choose Actions > Variables > set variable.

14. In the Variable field, enter `myAngle`.

15. In the Value field enter the expression `90 - car._rotation`. Check the Expression box (**Figure 11.19**).

    When you subtract the rotation property of the movie clip from 90 to get the equivalent angle for use in the sine and cosine functions.

16. Choose Actions > Variables > set variable.

17. In the Variable field, enter the variable name `xchange`.

18. Put your insertion point in the Value field, and choose Objects > Core > Math > Methods > cos.

    The `Math.cos()` method appears in the Value field.

19. Between the parentheses of the `Math.cos()` method, enter an expression to convert `myAngle` from degrees to radians; multiply the entire expression by 5; and check the Expression checkbox next to the Value field (**Figure 11.20**).

    The variable `xchange` represents the magnitude of the x component. Multiplying by 5 increases the magnitude of the change so that the movie clip moves a little faster in the x direction.

20. Choose Actions > Variables > set variable.

21. In the Variable field, enter the variable name `ychange`.

continues on next page

22. Put your insertion point in the Value field, and choose Objects > Core > Math > Methods > sin.

    The `Math.sin()` method appears in the Value field.

23. Between the parentheses of the `Math.sin()` method, enter an expression to convert `myAngle` from degrees to radians; multiply the entire expression by 5 and make it negative by placing a minus sign in front of the expression; and check the Expression checkbox next to the Value field (**Figure 11.21**).

    The variable `ychange` represents the magnitude of the y component. Multiplying by 5 increases the magnitude of the change so that the movie clip moves a little faster in the y direction. You must use the negative value for the change in the y direction to compensate for the discrepancy between the coordinate space for sine and the coordinate space for the movie clip.

24. Choose Actions > Miscellaneous Actions > evaluate.

25. In the Expression field, enter `car._x += xchange`.

    Flash adds the value of `xchange` to the current x position of the movie clip.

26. Choose Actions > Miscellaneous Actions > evaluate.

27. In the Expression field, enter `car._y += ychange`.

    Flash adds the value of `ychange` to the current y position of the movie clip.

28. Test your movie.

    When your viewer presses the left- or right-arrow key, the rotation of the movie clip changes. The x and y positions change as well, calculated from the angle of the movie clip. The movie clip moves according to where its nose is pointed (**Figure 11.22**).

Figure 11.21 The negative sine of the movie clip's angle is calculated and assigned to `ychange`.

```
_root.onEnterFrame = function() {
  if (Key.isDown(Key.LEFT)) {
    car._rotation -= 10;
  } else if (Key.isDown(Key.RIGHT)) {
    car._rotation += 10;
  }
  myAngle = 90 - car._rotation;
  xchange = Math.cos(Math.PI/180*myAngle)*5;
  ychange = -Math.sin(Math.PI/180*myAngle)*5;
  car._x += xchange;
  car._y += ychange;
};
```

Figure 11.22 The final script is shown at the bottom. As the movie clip of the car rotates, the x and y components are calculated from cosine and sine, and the car's new position is defined.

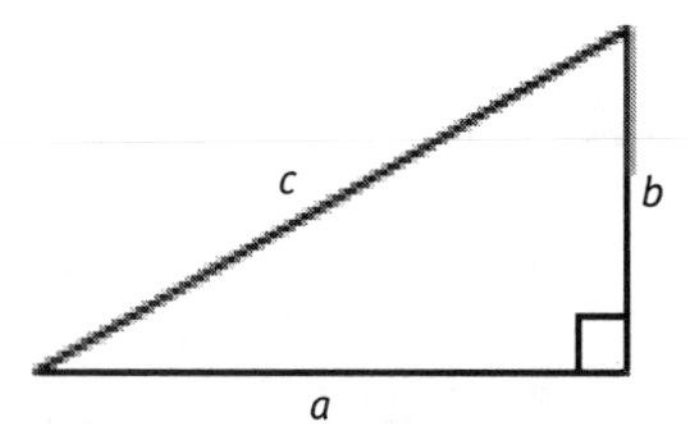

Figure 11.23 This right triangle has sides a, b, and c.

Calculating Distances with the Math Object

Using the Pythagorean theorem, Flash makes it possible for you to calculate the distance between two objects. This technique can be useful for creating novel interactions among interface elements—graphics, buttons, or sounds that react in proportion to their distance from the viewer's pointer, for example. You can also create games that have interaction based on the distance between objects and the player. A game in which the player uses a net to catch goldfish in an aquarium, for example, can use the distance between the goldfish and the net to model the behavior of the goldfish. Perhaps the closer the net comes to a goldfish, the quicker it swims away.

The distance between any two points is defined by the equation

$a^2 + b^2 = c^2$

or

c = square root $(a^2 + b^2)$

The variables `a` and `b` are the lengths of the sides of a right triangle, and `c` is the length of the hypotenuse (**Figure 11.23**). Using Flash's `Math.sqrt()` and `Math.pow()` methods, you can calculate the distance between the points on the hypotenuse with the following expression:

```
c = Math.sqrt ((Math.pow (a, 2)) +
(Math.pow (b, 2)))
```

To calculate the distance between the pointer and another point:

1. Create a movie clip, place an instance of it on the Stage, and give it a name in the Property Inspector.

   In this example, the name is myReference.

2. Select the first frame of the main Timeline, and open the Actions panel.

3. Choose Objects > Movie > Mouse > Listeners > onMouseMove.

4. In the Object field, enter `_root`.

5. Choose Actions > Variables > set variable.

6. In the Variable field, enter `xDistance`.

7. In the Value field, enter `_xmouse - myReference._x`, and check the Expression checkbox.

   The distance between the x position of the pointer and the x position of the movie clip is assigned to the variable `xDistance` (**Figure 11.24**).

8. Choose Actions > Variables > set variable.

9. In the Variable field, enter `yDistance`.

10. In the Value field, enter:

    `_ymouse - myReference._y`

    Check the Expression box next to the Value field.

    The distance between the y position of the pointer and the y position of the movie clip is assigned to the variable `yDistance` (**Figure 11.25**).

11. Choose Actions > Variables > set variable.

12. In the Variable field, enter the name `myDistance`.

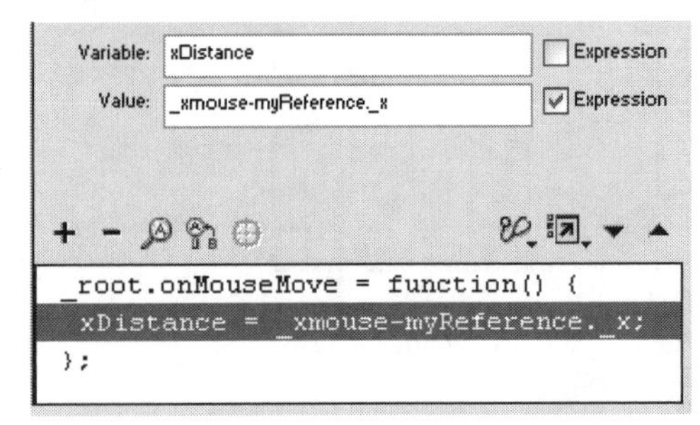

Figure 11.24 The difference between the x position of the pointer and the x position of the movie clip called myReference is the distance between them on the x axis.

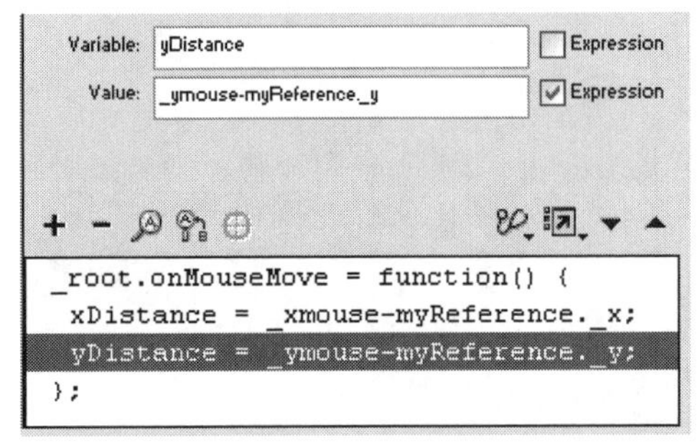

Figure 11.25 The difference between the y position of the pointer and the y position of the movie clip called myReference is the distance between them on the y axis.

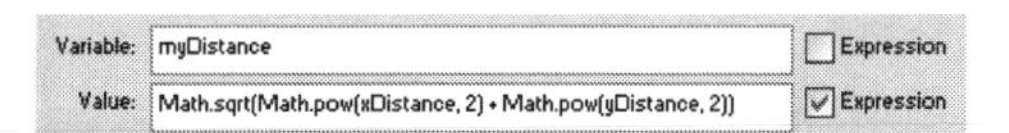

Figure 11.26 The distance between the two points is calculated from the variables `xDistance` and `yDistance`.

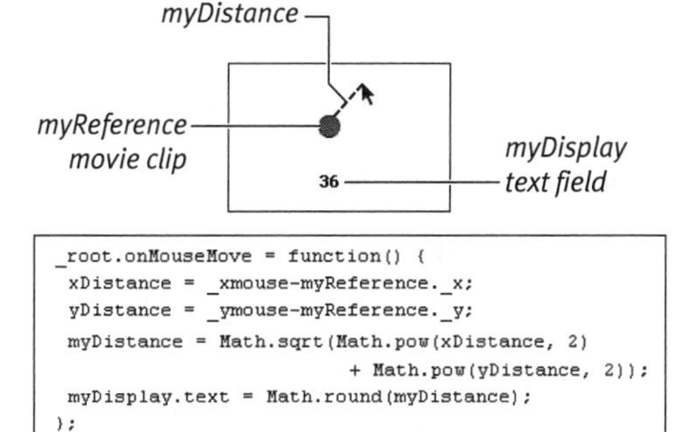

Figure 11.27 The full script is shown at the bottom. The dynamic text field called myDisplay displays an integer of `myDistance`.

13. Put your insertion point in the Value field, and choose Objects > Core > Math > Methods > sqrt.

    The `Math.sqrt()` method appears in the Value field.

14. While your insertion point is between the parentheses of the `Math.sqrt()` method, choose Objects > Core > Math > Methods > pow.

15. Enter `xDistance` and `2` as the parameters of the `Math.pow()` method.

16. Add another `Math.pow()` method with the parameters `yDistance` and `2` (**Figure 11.26**).

    Flash calculates the square of `xDistance` and adds it to the square of `yDistance`; then it calculates the square root of that sum.

17. Create a dynamic text field on the Stage, and give it an instance name.

18. Choose Actions > Variables > set variable.

19. Assign the value of `myDistance` to the `text` property of the dynamic text field on the Stage (**Figure 11.27**).

20. Test your movie.

    As the pointer moves around the movie clip, Flash calculates the distance between points in pixels.

Generating Random Numbers

When you need to incorporate random elements into your Flash movie, either for a design effect or for game play, you can use the Math object's `Math.random()` method. The `Math.random()` method generates random numbers between 0 and 1 (including 0 but not including 1) with up to 15 decimal places in between. Typical return values are:

```
0.242343544598273
0.043628738493829
0.7567833408654
```

You can modify the random number by multiplying it or adding to it to get the span of numbers you need. If you need random numbers between 1 and 10, for example, multiply the return value of `Math.random()` by 9 and then add 1, as in the following statement:

```
Math.random() * 9 + 1
```

You will always multiply `Math.random()` by a number to get your desired range and then add or subtract a number to change the minimum and maximum values of that range. If you need an integer, apply the `Math.round()` method to round the number to the nearest integer.

To generate a random number:

1. Create a button symbol, and place an instance of it on the Stage.
2. Create a dynamic text field, and give it an instance name in the Property Inspector.
3. Select the button instance, and open the Actions panel.
4. Choose Actions > Movie Control > on.
5. Choose Actions > Variables > set variable.
6. In the Variable field, enter the name of your text field, followed by a dot and then the `text` property.
7. Place your insertion point in the Value field, choose Objects > Core > Math > Methods > random, and check the Expression checkbox.

   The `Math.random()` method appears in the Variable field (**Figure 11.28**).

   When you click the button, a new random number between 0 and 1 is generated and displayed in the dynamic text field.

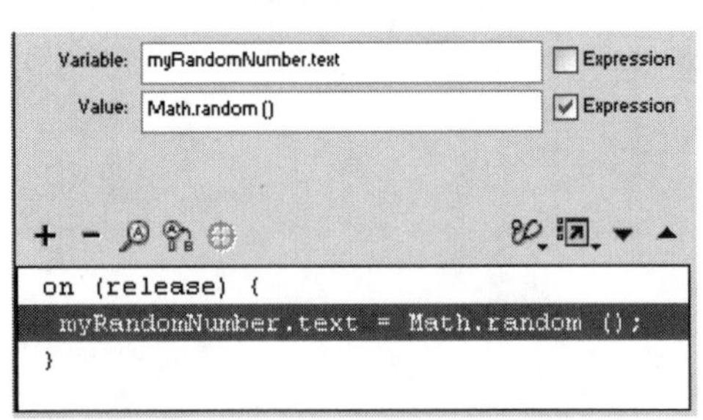

Figure 11.28 A random number between 0 and 1 is displayed in the text field called myRandomNumber when the button is clicked.

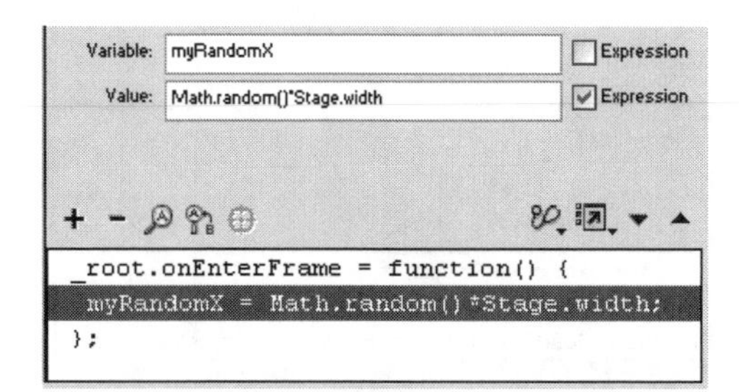

Figure 11.29 A random number between 0 and the width of the Stage is assigned to the variable myRandomX.

Use randomly generated numbers to add unpredictable animated elements to your movie. Enemy ships in an arcade game could appear anywhere to attack the player. You can make Flash deal random cards from a deck of cards so that every hand is different. Or for a test, you can shuffle the order in which the questions appear. The following task demonstrates how random numbers can modify property values by setting the x and y properties of a movie clip.

To use random numbers as property values:

1. Create a movie-clip symbol, place an instance of it on the Stage, and give it a name in the Property Inspector.
2. Select the first frame of the main Timeline, and open the Actions panel.
3. Choose Objects > Movie > Movie Clip > Events > onEnterFrame.
4. In the Object field, enter `_root`.
5. Choose Actions > Variables > set variable.
6. In the Variable field, enter a variable name.
7. In the Value field, enter `Math.random () * Stage.width`, and check the Expression checkbox.

   Flash generates a random number between 0 and the width of the current Stage (**Figure 11.29**).
8. Again, choose Actions > Variables > set variable.
9. Assign a second variable to a random number between 0 and the height of the Stage.
10. Choose Actions > Variables > set variable.

continues on next page

11. In the Variable field, enter the x position of your movie clip.
12. In the Value field, enter the variable name for the first randomly generated number, and check the Expression checkbox (**Figure 11.30**).

    The movie clip's x position is set to the first random number.
13. Choose Actions > Variables > set variable.
14. In the Variable field, enter the y position of your movie clip.
15. In the Value field, enter the variable name for the second randomly generated number, and check the Expression checkbox.

    The movie clip's y position is set to the second random number (**Figure 11.31**).
16. Test your movie.

    The x and y positions of your movie clip are set randomly, making your movie clip jump around the Stage.

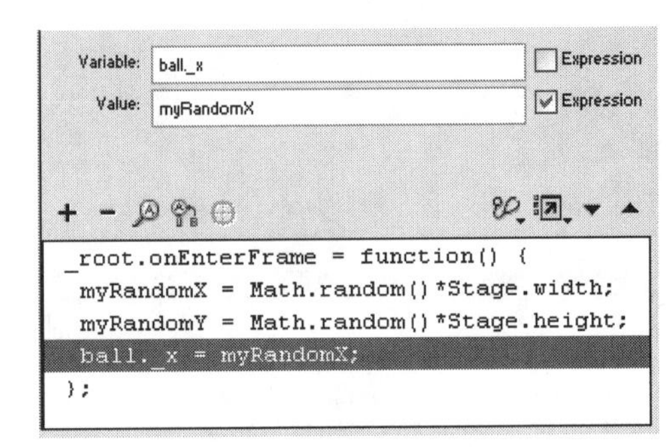

Figure 11.30 The x position of the movie clip is set to myRandomX.

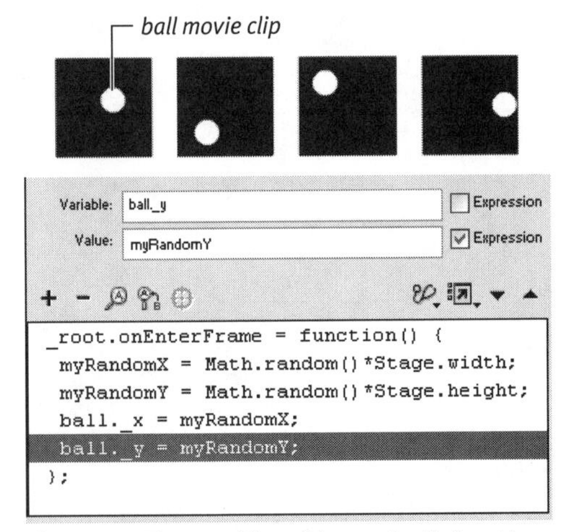

Figure 11.31 The y position of the movie clip is set to myRandomY. The movie clip changes its position on the Stage randomly (top).

✔ Tips

- The `Math.random()` method replaces the `random` action used in earlier versions of Flash. Although the `random` action still works, it is deprecated, so you should stick to using the Math object to generate your random numbers.
- Although most properties, such as _x and _y, can accept noninteger values that are generated from the `Math.random()` method (as in the preceding example), some properties require integers. The `_currentFrame` property, which determines the current frame number of a Timeline, must be given as an integer. Use the `Math.round()` method to convert a fraction to an integer and then apply it to the `_currentFrame` property.

Index	Value
0	"monitor"
1	"mouse"
2	"keyboard"
3	"CPU"
4	"modem"
5	"speakers"

Figure 11.32 An array is like a two-column table with an Index column and a corresponding Value column.

Ordering Information with Arrays

When you have many pieces of related information that you want to store, you may need to use the Array object to help arrange that information. *Arrays* are containers that hold data, just as variables do, except that arrays hold data in a specific sequence, called an *index*. The index begins at 0 and is numbered sequentially so that each piece of data corresponds to an index, as in a two-column table (**Figure 11.32**). Because each piece of data is ordered numerically, you can retrieve and modify the information easily—and, most important, automatically—just by referencing its index. Suppose that you're building a foreign-language tutorial and want to search the content of a viewer's text input for important vocabulary words. You can store those words in an array, so that index 0 holds the first vocabulary word, index 1 holds the second word, and so on. By using a looping statement, you can check the input text against each entry in the array automatically.

The indexes of an array are referenced with the square bracket, as in the following:

```
myArray[4]
```

The square brackets are known as array access operators. This statement accesses the data in index 4 of the array called `myArray`. The number of entries defines the length of an array, so the length of the array in Figure 11.32 is 6. You can think of an array as being a sequence of ordered variables. You could convert the variables `myScores0`, `myScores1`, `myScores2`, and `myScores3` to a single array called `myScores` of length 4 with indices between 0 and 3. Because you have to handle only one array object instead of four separate variables, using arrays makes information easier to manage.

continues on next page

The data that arrays hold can be mixed. So you could have a number in index 0, a string in index 1, and a Boolean value in index 2. You can change the data in any index in an array at any time, just as you can with variables. The length of arrays is not fixed, either, so arrays can grow or shrink to accommodate new information as needed.

Creating an array involves two steps. The first is to use a constructor function to instantiate a new array from the Array object, as in this example:

```
myArray = new Array()
```

The second step is to fill, or *populate*, your array with data. One way to populate your array is to assign the data to each index in separate statements, like this:

```
myArray [0] = "Russell";
myArray [1] = "Rebecca";
myArray [2] = "Clint";
myArray [3] = "Kathy";
```

Another way to assign the data is to put the information as parameters within the constructor function:

```
myArray = new Array ("Russell", "Rebecca",
"Clint", "Kathy")
```

The second way is a more-compact way of populating your array, but you are restricted to entering data in sequence.

To create an array:

1. Select the first keyframe of the Timeline, and open the Actions panel.
2. Choose Actions > Variables > set variable.
3. In the Variable field, enter a name for your array.
4. Put your insertion point in the Value field, and choose Objects > Core > Array > new Array.
5. Check the Expression checkbox next to the Value field.

   The `new Array()` constructor function appears in the Value field. Flash instantiates a new array (**Figure 11.33**).
6. Choose Actions > Variables > set variable.
7. In the Variable field, enter the name of your new array, followed by an index within square brackets.
8. In the Value field, enter the data you want to store in the array at that index position (**Figure 11.34**).
9. Continue choosing `set variable` actions, or use `evaluate` actions (Actions > Miscellaneous Actions > evaluate) to assign more data to the array.

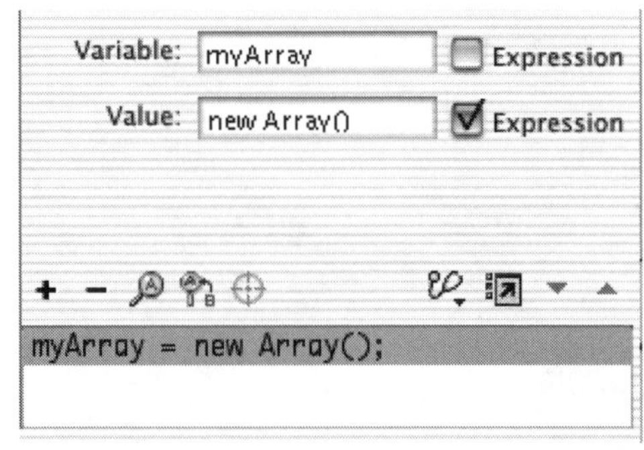

Figure 11.33 A new array called `myArray` is instantiated.

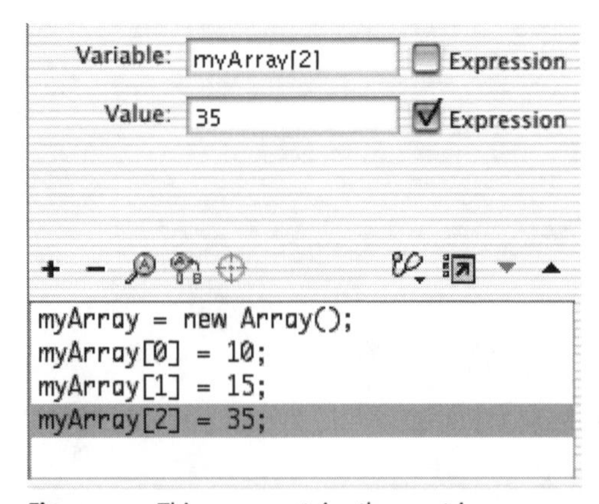

Figure 11.34 This array contains three entries.

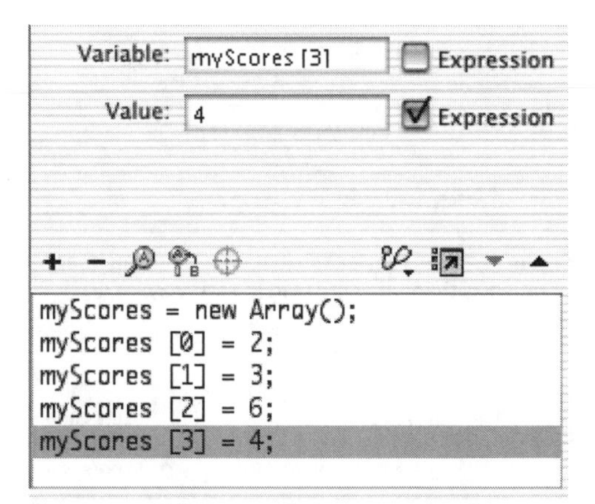

Figure 11.35 This array, called myScores, has four entries.

Because the entries contained in arrays are indexed numerically, they lend themselves nicely to looping actions. By using looping actions such as `while`, `do while`, and `for`, you can have Flash go through each index and retrieve or assign new data quickly and automatically. To average the scores of many players in an array without a looping action, for example, you would have to total all their scores and divide by the number of players, like this:

```
mySum = myScores[0] + myScores[1] +
myScores[2] + ...
myAverage = mySum/myScores.length;
```

The property `length` defines the number of entries in the array.

Using a looping action, however, you can calculate the `mySum` value this way:

```
for (i=0; i<myScores.length; i++) {
  mySum = mySum + myScores[i];
}
myAverage = mySum/myScores.length;
```

Flash starts at index 0 and adds each indexed entry in the array to the variable `mySum` until it reaches the end of the array.

To loop through an array:

1. Select the first keyframe of the Timeline, and open the Actions panel.
2. Choose Actions > Variables > set variable, and instantiate a new array called `myScores`.
3. Choose Actions > Variables > set variable, and populate your `myScores` array with numbers representing scores (**Figure 11.35**).
4. Create a button symbol, and place an instance of the button on the Stage.
5. Select the button instance, and open the Actions panel.
6. Choose Actions > Movie Control > on.
7. Choose Actions > Conditions/Loops > for.

continues on next page

8. In the Init field, enter `i=0`.
9. In the Condition field, enter `i<myScores.length`.
10. In the Next field, enter `i++`.

    Flash begins with the counter variable `i` set at the value 0. It increases the variable by increments of 1 until the variable reaches the length of the array called `myScores` (**Figure 11.36**).
11. Choose Actions > Variables > set variable.
12. In the Variable field, enter `mySum`.
13. In the Value field, enter `mySum + myScores[i]`, and check the Expression checkbox.

    For each index of the `myScore` array, Flash adds the value in that index to `mySum`. When the value of `i` reaches the value of `myScores.length`, Flash jumps out of the `for` loop and stops adding any more index values. Therefore, the last addition is `myScores [myScores.length-1]`, which corresponds to the last index of the array (**Figure 11.37**).
14. Select the ending curly brace of the `for` statement, and choose Actions > Variables > set variable.

    The next statement appears after the curly brace outside the `for` statement.
15. In the Variable field, enter `myAverage.text`.
16. In the Value field, enter the expression `mySum/myScores.length`, and check the Expression checkbox (**Figure 11.38**).
17. Create a dynamic text field on the Stage with the instance name `myAverage`.
18. Test your movie.

    When you click the button on the Stage, Flash loops through the `myScores` array to add all the data entries and divides the total by the number of entries. The average is displayed in the dynamic text field on the Stage.

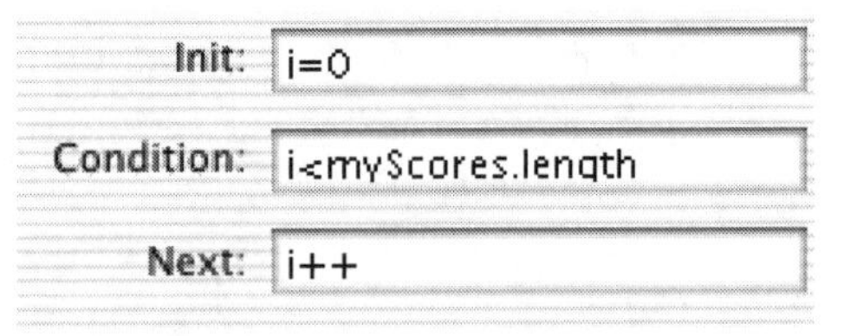

Figure 11.36 This `for` action loops the same number of times as there are entries in the array `myScore`.

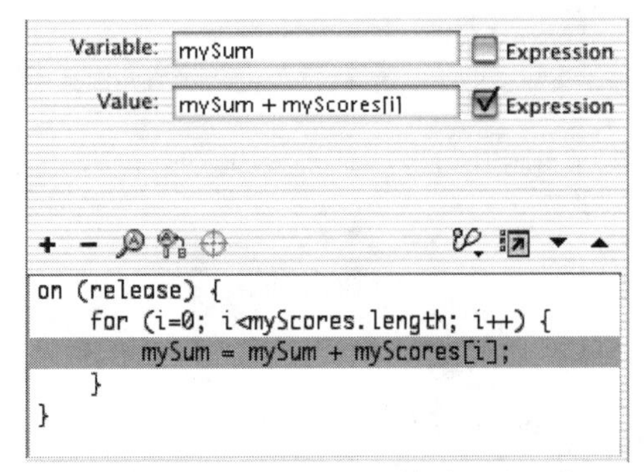

Figure 11.37 The variable `mySum` adds the value of every entry in the array.

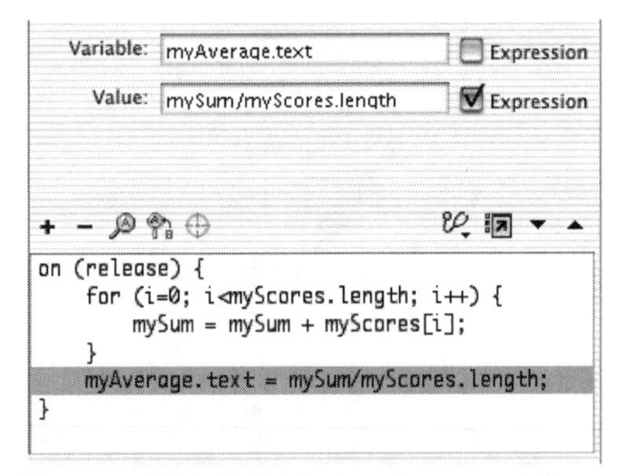

Figure 11.38 Outside the `for` loop, the average value of the entries in the array is calculated and displayed in the text field called myAverage.

The methods of the Array object let you sort, delete, add, and manipulate the data in an array. **Table 11.2** summarizes the methods of the Array object. It's convenient to think of the methods in pairs. `shift()` and `unshift()`, for example, both modify the beginning of an array; `push()` and `pop()` both modify the end of an array; and `slice()` and `splice()` both modify the middle of an array.

continues on next page

Table 11.2

Methods of the Array Object

Method	Description
concat(array1,...,arrayN)	Concatenates the specified values and returns a new array.
join(separator)	Concatenates the elements of the array, inserts the separator between the elements, and returns a string. The default separator is a comma.
pop()	Removes the last element in the array and returns the value of that element.
push(value)	Adds elements to the end of the array and returns the new length.
shift()	Removes the first element in the array and returns the value of that element.
unshift(value)	Adds elements to the beginning of the array and returns the new length.
slice(indexA,indexB)	Returns a new array beginning with indexA and ending with (indexB-1).
splice(index,count,elem1,...,elemN)	Inserts or deletes elements. Set count to 0 to insert specified values starting at index. Set count > 0 to delete the number of elements starting at and including index.
reverse()	Reverses the order of elements in the array.
sort()	Sorts an array by using the < operator. Numbers are sorted in ascending order, and strings are sorted alphabetically.
sortOn(fieldName)	Sorts an array based on the fieldName parameter.
toString()	Returns a string with every element concatenated and separated by a comma.

Following is an example of how some of these methods operate:

Statement	Value of myArray
myArray = new Array(2,4,6,8)	2, 4, 6, 8
myArray.pop()	2, 4, 6
myArray.push(1,3)	2, 4, 6, 1, 3
myArray.shift()	4, 6, 1, 3
myArray.unshift(5,7)	5, 7, 4, 6, 1, 3
myArray.splice(2,0,8,9)	5, 7, 8, 9, 4, 6, 1, 3
myArray.splice(3,2)	5, 7, 8, 6, 1, 3
myArray.reverse()	3, 1, 6, 8, 7, 5
myArray.sort()	1, 3, 5, 6, 7, 8

✔ Tips

- It's important to note which methods of the Array object modify the original array and which ones return a new array. `concat()`, `join()`, `slice()`, and `toString()` return a new array or string and do not alter the original array. `myNewArray = myArray.concat(8)`, for example, puts `8` at the end of `myArray` and assigns the resulting array to `myNewArray`. The original `myArray` is not affected. Also note that some methods modify the array as well as return a specific value. These two things are not the same. The statement `myArray.pop()` for example, modifies myArray by removing the last element and also returns the value of that last element. So in the following example:

  ```
  myArray = new Array (2, 4, 6, 8);
  myPop = myArray.pop();
  ```

  The value of `myPop` is `8`, and the value of `myArray` is now `2, 4, 6`.

- An easy way to remember the duties of some of these methods is to think of the elements of your array as being a stack. (In fact, *stack* is the programmer's term,) An array is often thought of as being like a stack of books or a stack of cafeteria trays on a spring-loaded holder. The bottom of the stack is the first element in an array. When you `push` an array, imagine that you literally push a new tray on top of the stack to add a new element. When you `pop` an array, you "pop," or remove, the top tray from the stack (the last element). When you `shift` an array, you take out the bottom tray (the first element) so that all the other trays shift down into new positions.

Two-Dimensional Arrays

We've compared an array with a two-column table, in which the index is in one column and its contents are in a second column. What if you want to keep track of information that requires rows as well as columns, like a traditional spreadsheet? The solution is to nest an array inside another one to create what's known as a two-dimensional array. This type of array creates two indexes for every piece of information. To keep track of a checker piece on a checkerboard, for example, you can use a two-dimensional array to reference its row and its column (**Figure 11.39**).

For the three rows, create three separate arrays and populate them with numbers:

```
Row0 = new Array(1,2,3)
Row1 = new Array(4,5,6)
Row2 = new Array(7,8,9)
```

Now you can put those three arrays inside another array, like so:

```
gameBoard = new Array()
gameBoard[0] = Row0
gameBoard[1] = Row1
gameBoard[2] = Row2
```

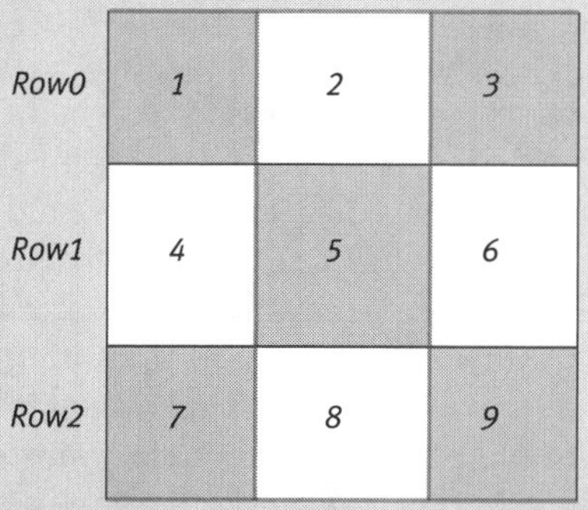

Row0	1	2	3
Row1	4	5	6
Row2	7	8	9

Figure 11.39 You can use a two-dimensional array to map a simple checkerboard and keep track of what's inside individual squares. Each row is an array. The rows are put inside another array.

To access or modify the information of a checkerboard square, first use one set of square brackets that references the row. The statement, `gameBoard[2]`, references the array called `Row2`. Then, by using another set of square brackets, you can reference the column within that row. So the statement `gameBoard[2][0]` accesses the number 7.

Keeping Track of Movie Clips with Arrays

Sometimes, you'll have to deal with many movie clips on the Stage at the same time. Keeping track of them all and performing actions to modify, test, or evaluate each one can be a nightmare unless you use arrays to help manage them all. Imagine that you are creating a game in which your viewer has to avoid falling rocks from the sky. You can use the hitTest() method to see whether each falling-rock movie clip intersects with the viewer. But if there are 10 rocks on the Stage, that potentially means 10 separate hitTest() statements. You can better manage the multiple falling rocks by putting them in an array. Doing so allows you to perform the hitTest() on one array instead of on many separate movie clips.

Put a movie clip into an array by referencing its name with array access operators, like so:

```
rockArray[0]=_root["fallingRock0"]
rockArray[1]=_root["fallingRock1"]
rockArray[2]=_root["fallingRock2"]
```

These statements put the movie clip called fallingRock0 in index 0 of the array called rockArray, the movie clip called fallingRock1 in index 1, and the movie clip called fallingRock2 in index2. Now you can reference the movie clips through the array. This statement changes the transparency of the movie clip fallingRock2:

```
rockArray[2]._alpha = 40
```

You can even call methods this way:

```
rockArray[2].hitTest(_xmouse, _ymouse, true)
```

This statement checks to see whether the fallingRock2 movie clip intersects with the mouse pointer.

The following examples combine looping statements to populate an array with movie clips automatically. When the array is full of movie clips, you can perform the same action, such as modifying a property or calling the hitTest(), on all the movie clips by referencing the array.

To populate an array with duplicate movie clips:

1. Create a movie-clip symbol, place an instance of it on the Stage, and give it a name in the Property Inspector.

   In this example, the name is block.

2. Select the first frame of the main Timeline, and open the Actions panel.
3. Choose Actions > Variables > set variable.
4. In the Variable field, enter a name for your array.
5. In the Value field, choose Objects > Core > Array > new Array, and check the Expression checkbox.

   Your array object is instantiated (**Figure 11.40**).

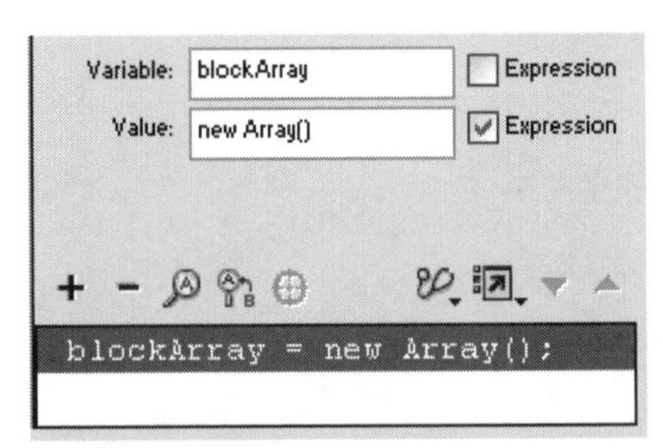

Figure 11.40 A new array called blockArray is instantiated.

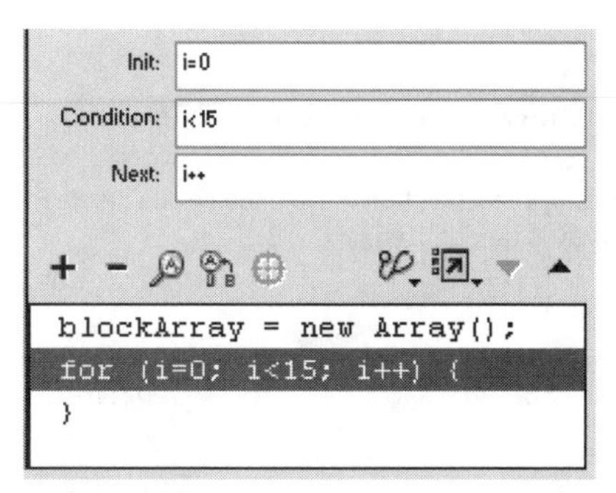

Figure 11.41 Create a `for` statement that uses a counter that begins at 0 and ends at 14, increasing by 1 with each loop.

```
Target: block
New Name: "block" + i
Depth: i
blockArray = new Array();
for (i=0; i<15; i++) {
  duplicateMovieClip(block, "block" + i, i);
}
```

Figure 11.42 The movie clip called block on the Stage is duplicated and automatically given a new name based on the loop variable `i`.

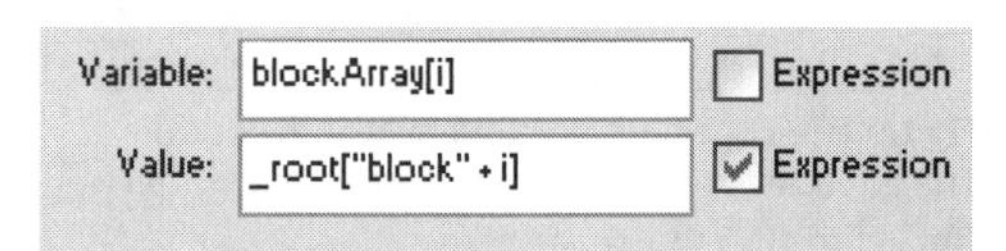

Figure 11.43 Each duplicate is referenced dynamically with the square brackets (in the Value field) and put in `blockArray`. The movie clip block0 is in `blockArray[0]`, the movie clip block1 is in `blockArray[1]`, and so on.

6. Choose Actions > Conditions/Loops > for.
7. In the Init field, enter `i=0`; in the Condition field, enter `i<15`; and in the Next field, enter `i++` (**Figure 11.41**).

   This loop will occur 15 times, starting when `i=0` and ending when `i=14`.
8. Choose Actions > Movie Clip Control > duplicateMovieClip.
9. In the Target field, enter `block` (the name of your movie clip).
10. In the New Name field, enter `"block" + i`; and in the Depth field, enter `i`.
11. Check the Expression checkboxes for both the Target field and the New Name field (**Figure 11.42**).

    Flash duplicates the block movie clip and gives each duplicate a unique name based on the variable `i`. The first duplicate is called block0, the second is called block1, and so on.
12. Choose Actions > Variables > set variable.
13. In the Variable field, enter `blockArray[i]`. In the Value field, enter `_root.["block"+i]`, and check the Expression box.

    Each new duplicate is put inside a different index of your array (**Figure 11.43**).

Now that your array is populated with movie clips, you can reference them easily with just the array's index value to change their property.

To reference movie clips inside an array (part 1, modify properties):

1. Continuing with the file you created in the preceding task, select the main Timeline, and open the Actions panel.
2. Select the last statement within the `for` statement.

   Your next statement will still appear within the `for` statement, but after the duplicates are made and placed inside your array.
3. Choose Actions > Variables > set variable.
4. In the Variable field, enter `blockArray[i]._x`.
5. In the Value field, enter `Math.random()*Stage.width`, and check the Expression checkbox (**Figure 11.44**).

   A random number between 0 and the width of the current Stage is generated and assigned to the x position of every movie clip inside `blockArray`.
6. Choose Actions > Variables > set variable.
7. In the Variable field, enter `blockArray[i]._y`.
8. In the Value field, enter `Math.random()*Stage.height`, and check the Expression checkbox (**Figure 11.45**).

   A random number between 0 and the height of the current Stage is generated and assigned to the y position of every movie clip inside `blockArray`.
9. Test your movie.

   The `for` loop generates duplicate movie clips automatically and puts them inside your array. At the same time, it references the movie clips inside the array and changes their x and y positions based on a random number (**Figure 11.46**).

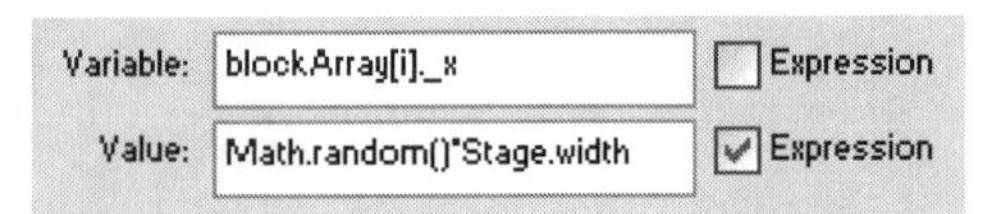

Figure 11.44 The x position of each movie clip inside `blockArray` is randomized.

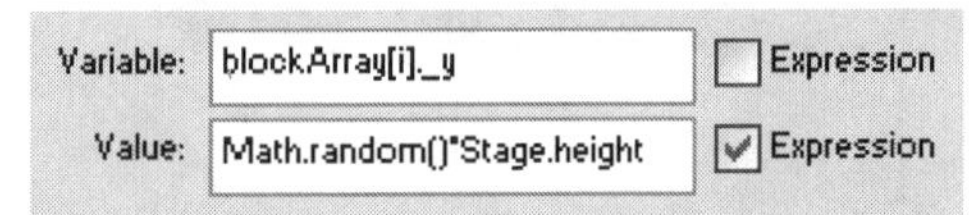

Figure 11.45 The y position of each movie clip inside `blockArray` is randomized.

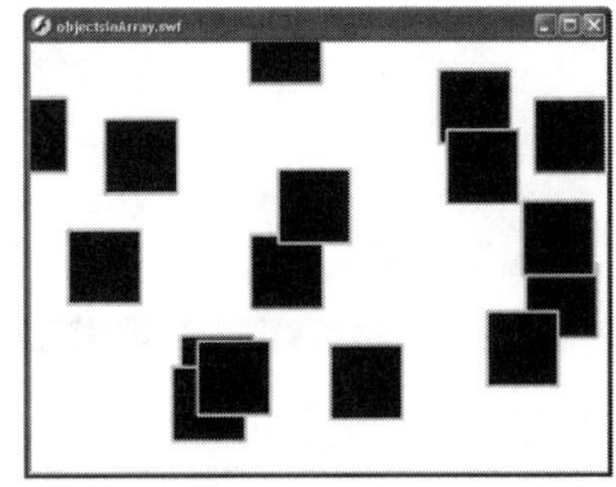

```
blockArray = new Array();
for (i=0; i<15; i++) {
 duplicateMovieClip(block, "block"+i, i);
 blockArray[i] = _root["block"+i];
 blockArray[i]._x = Math.random()*Stage.width;
 blockArray[i]._y = Math.random()*Stage.height;
}
```

Figure 11.46 The full script is shown at the bottom. The duplicate movie clips scatter randomly within the boundaries of your Stage.

```
Init: i=0
Condition: i<15
Next: i++

blockArray = new Array();
for (i=0; i<15; i++) {
 duplicateMovieClip(block, "block"+i, i);
 blockArray[i] = _root["block"+i];
 blockArray[i]._x = Math.random()*Stage.width;
 blockArray[i]._y = Math.random()*Stage.height;
}
_root.onEnterFrame = function() {
 for (i=0; i<15; i++) {
 }
};
```

Figure 11.47 Enter the same loop parameters for the for loop as you did for the first loop that generated your duplicates.

```
Condition: blockArray[i].hitTest(_xmouse,_ymouse, true)

blockArray = new Array();
for (i=0; i<15; i++) {
 duplicateMovieClip(block, "block"+i, i);
 blockArray[i] = _root["block"+i];
 blockArray[i]._x = Math.random()*Stage.width;
 blockArray[i]._y = Math.random()*Stage.height;
}
_root.onEnterFrame = function() {
 for (i=0; i<15; i++) {
  if (blockArray[i].hitTest(_xmouse, _ymouse, true)) {
  }
 }
};
```

Figure 11.48 Flash checks every movie clip inside blockArray to see whether the clips intersect with the mouse pointer.

Now you'll check to see whether the viewer's pointer touches any of the movie-clip duplicates. Instead of checking each duplicate separately, you loop through the array again and check all the duplicates at the same time.

To reference movie clips inside an array (part 2, call a method):

1. Continuing with the file you used in the preceding task select the main Timeline, and open the Actions panel.
2. Create an onEnterFrame handler after the for statement. In the Object field of the onEnterFrame handler, enter _root.
3. Choose Actions > Conditions/Loops > for.
4. In the Init field, enter i=0; in the Condition field, enter i<15; and in the Next field, enter i++ (**Figure 11.47**).
5. Choose Actions > Conditions/Loops > if.
6. In the Condition field, enter blockArray[i] to reference each movie clip inside the array.
7. With the pointer still in the Condition field, choose Objects > Movie > Movie Clip > Methods > hitTest.
8. Between the parentheses of the hitTest() method, enter the parameters _xmouse, _ymouse, and true (**Figure 11.48**).

continues on next page

9. Choose a consequence for the `if` statement.

   For this example, choose Actions > Miscellaneous Actions > evaluate.

10. In the Expression field, enter `blockArray[i]._alpha = 30` (**Figure 11.49**).

11. Test your movie.

    When the `for` loop is performed, all the movie clips inside `blockArray` are tested to see whether they intersect with the pointer. Because the `for` loop is within an `onEnterFrame` handler, this checking is done continuously. If a positive intersection occurs, that particular movie clip turns 30 percent transparent (**Figure 11.50**).

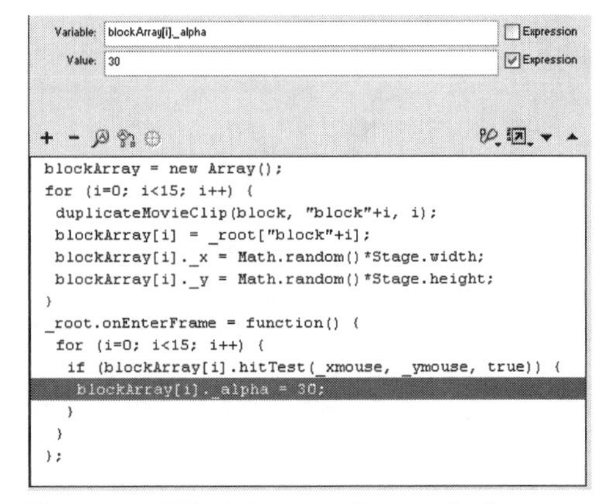

Figure 11.49 If Flash detects an intersection between a movie clip and your pointer, that particular movie clip changes transparency.

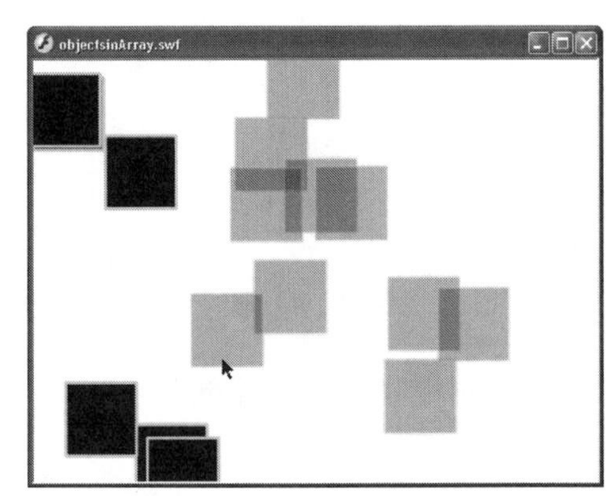

Figure 11.50 The pointer has passed over many of the movie clips on the right side of this movie. Use this technique to manage multiple movie clips for game interactivity.

Table 11.3

Methods of the Date Object	
METHOD	DESCRIPTION
getDate()	Returns the day of the month as a number between 1 and 31.
getDay()	Returns the day of the week as a number between 0 (Sunday) and 6 (Saturday).
getFullYear()	Returns the year as a four-digit number.
getHours()	Returns the hour of the day as a number between 0 and 23.
getMilliseconds()	Returns the milliseconds.
getMinutes()	Returns the minutes as a number between 0 and 59.
getMonth()	Returns the month as a number between 0 (January) and 11 (December).
getSeconds()	Returns the seconds as a number between 0 and 59.

Using the Date and Time

The Date object lets you retrieve the local or universal (GMT) date and time information from the clock in your viewer's computer system. Using the Date object, you can retrieve the year, month, date, day of the week, hour, minute, second, and millisecond. Use the Date object and its methods to create accurate clocks in your movie or to find information about certain days and dates in the past. You can create a Date object for your birthday, for example, by specifying the month, date, and year. Using methods of the Date object, you can retrieve the day of the week for your Date object that tells you what day you were born.

First, you need to instantiate the Date object with the constructor function `new Date()`. Then you can call on its methods to retrieve specific time information. **Table 11.3** summarizes the common methods for retrieving the dates and times.

To create a clock:

1. Create a dynamic text field on the Stage, and give it an instance name in the Property Inspector.
2. Select the first frame of the main Timeline, and open the Actions panel.
3. Choose Objects > Movie > Movie Clip > Events > onEnterFrame.
4. In the Object field, enter `_root`.
5. Choose Actions > Variables > set variable.
6. In the Variable field, enter the name of a new Date object.

continues on next page

7. Place your insertion point in the Value field, choose Objects > Core > Date > new Date, and check the Expression checkbox.

   The `new Date()` constructor function appears in the Value field. Your Date object is instantiated (**Figure 11.51**). If you don't specify any parameters of the Date object, you create a generic date object that you can use to retrieve current date and time information. If you specify the parameters of the Date object, you create an object that references a specific date or time.

8. Choose Actions > Variables > set variable.
9. In the Variable field, enter `currentHour`.
10. In the Value field, enter the name of your Date object.
11. With your insertion point still in the Value field, choose Objects > Core > Date > Methods > getHours, and check the Expression checkbox.

    The `getHours()` method appears after the name of your Date object. Flash retrieves the current hour and puts the returned value in your variable called `currentHour` (**Figure 11.52**).

12. Repeat step 11 to retrieve the current minute with the `getMinutes()` method and the current second with the `getSeconds()` method, and assign the returned values to variables (**Figure 11.53**).
13. Choose Actions > Conditions/Loops > if.
14. In the Condition field, enter `currentHour > 12`.
15. Choose Actions > Variables > set variable.

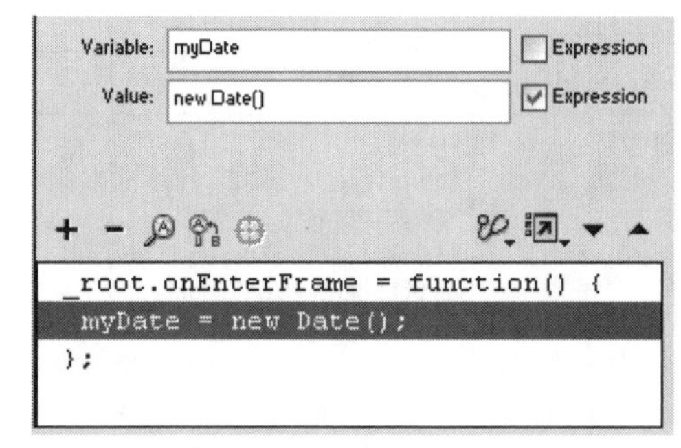

Figure 11.51 The myDate Date object is instantiated inside an `onEnterFrame` handler.

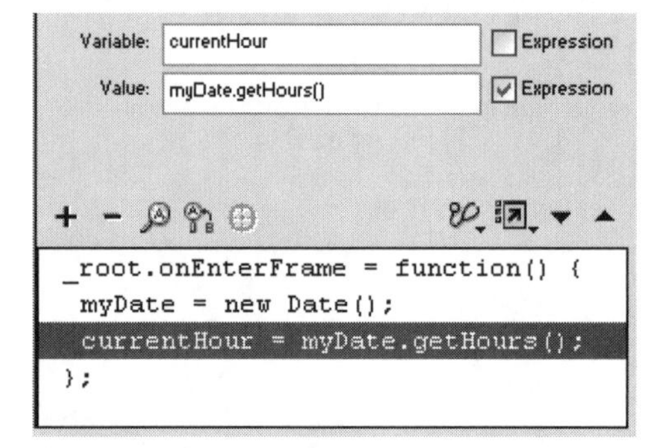

Figure 11.52 The current hour is assigned to the variable `currentHour`.

```
_root.onEnterFrame = function() {
 myDate = new Date();
 currentHour = myDate.getHours();
 currentMinute = myDate.getMinutes();
 currentSecond = myDate.getSeconds();
};
```

Figure 11.53 The current hour, minute, and second are retrieved from the computer's clock and assigned to different variables.

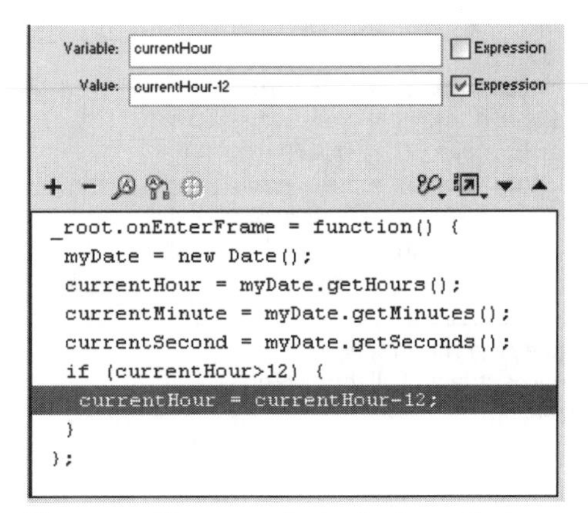

Figure 11.54 The returned value for the method getHours() is a number from 0 to 23. To convert the hour to the standard 12-hour cycle, subtract 12 from values greater than 12.

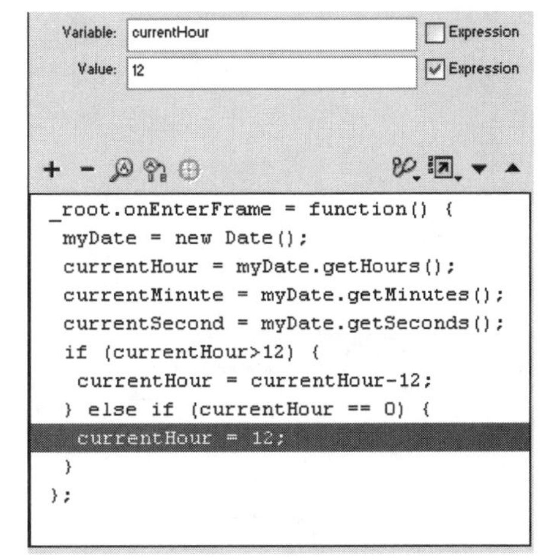

Figure 11.55 Because there is no 0 on our clocks, have Flash assign 12 to any hour that has the value 0.

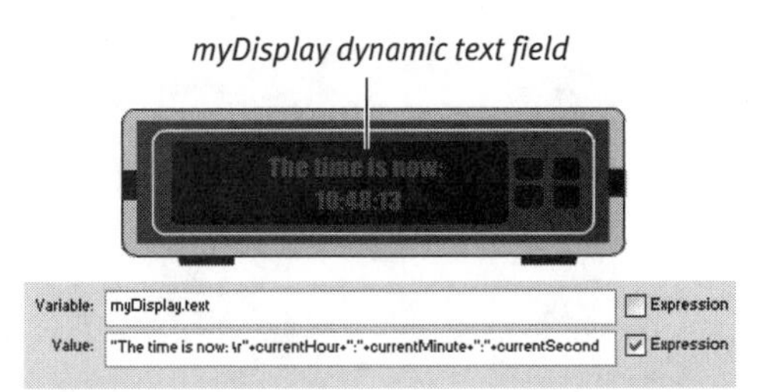

Figure 11.56 The dynamic text field (top) displays the concatenated values for the hour, minutes, and seconds.

16. In the Variable field, enter `currentHour`, and in the Value field, enter `currentHour-12`. Check the Expression box (**Figure 11.54**).
17. Choose Actions > Conditions/Loops > else if.
18. In the Condition field, enter `currentHour == 0`.
19. Choose Actions > Variables > set variable.
20. In the Variable field, enter `currentHour`.
21. In the Value field enter 12, and check the Expression checkbox (**Figure 11.55**).
22. Select the closing brace of the `else if` statement, and choose Actions > Variables > set variable.
23. In the Variable field, enter the name of your text field, followed by a dot and then the `text` property.
24. In the Value field, concatenate the variable names for the hour, the minute, and the second with appropriate spacers between them, and check the Expression checkbox (**Figure 11.56**).
25. Test your movie.

    The dynamic text field displays the current hour, minute, and second in the 12-hour format.

✔ Tip

- Note that minutes and seconds that are less than 10 display as single digits, such as 1 and 2, rather than as 01 and 02. Refine your clock by adding conditional statements to check the value of the current minutes and seconds, and add the appropriate 0 digit.

The returned values for the getMonth() and getDays() methods of the Date object are numbers instead of string data types. The getMonth() method returns values from 0 to 11 (0 = January), and the getDays() method returns values from 0 to 6 (0 = Sunday). To correlate these numeric values with the names of the months or days of the week, you can create arrays that contain this information. You can create an array that contains the days of the week with the following statements:

```
daysofWeek = new Array ();
daysofWeek[0] = "Sunday";
daysofWeek[1] = "Monday";
daysofWeek[2] = "Tuesday";
daysofWeek[3] = "Wednesday";
daysofWeek[4] = "Thursday";
daysofWeek[5] = "Friday";
daysofWeek[6] = "Saturday";
```

To create a calendar:

1. Create a dynamic text field on the Stage, and give it an instance name in the Property Inspector.
2. Select the first keyframe of the Timeline, and open the Actions panel.
3. Choose Actions > Variables > set variable.
4. In the Variable field, enter a name for a new array that will hold the days of the week.
5. In the Value field, enter the constructor function new Array(), and check the Expression checkbox.
6. In a series of statements, assign to each index of your new array a string representing the names of the days of the week (**Figure 11.57**).
7. Choose Actions > Variables > set variable.
8. In the Variable field, enter a name for a second new array, which will hold the months of the year.

```
daysofWeek = new Array( );
daysofWeek[0] = "Sunday";
daysofWeek[1] = "Monday";
daysofWeek[2] = "Tuesday";
daysofWeek[3] = "Wednesday";
daysofWeek[4] = "Thursday";
daysofWeek[5] = "Friday";
daysofWeek[6] = "Saturday";
```

Figure 11.57 The array daysofWeek contains strings of all the days of the week.

```
daysofMonth = new Array ();
daysofMonth[0] = "January";
daysofMonth[1] = "February";
daysofMonth[2] = "March";
daysofMonth[3] = "April";
daysofMonth[4] = "May";
daysofMonth[5] = "June";
daysofMonth[6] = "July";
daysofMonth[7] = "August";
daysofMonth[8] = "September";
daysofMonth[9] = "October";
daysofMonth[10] = "November";
daysofMonth[11] = "December";
```

Figure 11.58 The array daysofMonth contains strings of all the months.

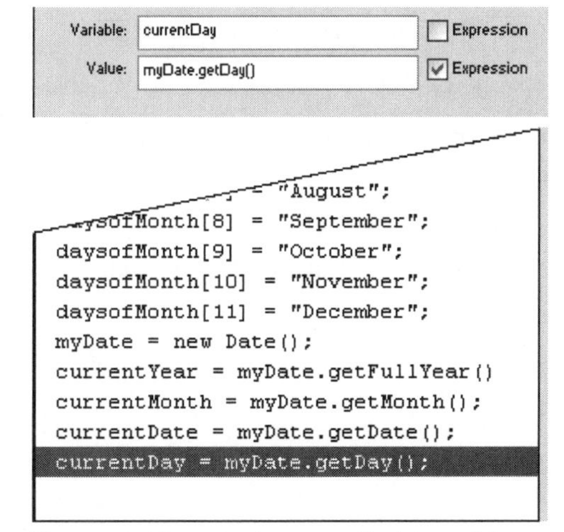

Figure 11.59 The current year, month, date, and day are retrieved from the computer's clock and assigned to new variables.

Variable: myDisplay.text ☐ Expression
Value: daysofWeek[currentDay] ☑ Expression

Figure 11.60 The value of the variable currentDay is a number between 0 and 6. The expression in the Value field retrieves the correct string in the array corresponding to the current day.

9. In the Value field, enter the constructor function `new Array()`, and check the Expression checkbox.

10. In a series of statements, assign to each index of your second new array a string representing the names of the months of the year (**Figure 11.58**).

11. Choose Actions > Variables > set variable.

12. In the Variable field, enter the name of your new date object.

13. In the Value field, enter the constructor function `new Date()` without any parameters, and check the Expression checkbox.

14. In a series of statements, call the `getFullYear()`, `getMonth()`, `getDate()`, and `getDay()` methods, and assign their values to new variables (**Figure 11.59**).

15. Choose Actions > Variables > set variable.

16. In the Variable field, enter the name of your dynamic text field, followed by a dot and then the `text` property.

17. In the Value field, enter the name of your array that contains the days of the week, and put in the variable containing the `getDay()` returned value as its index (**Figure 11.60**).

18. Concatenate the array that contains the days of the month, and put the variable containing the `getMonth()` returned value as its index.

continues on next page

19. Concatenate the other variables that hold the current date and year (**Figure 11.61**).

20. Test your movie.

    Flash gets the day, month, date, and year from the system clock. The names of the specific day and month are retrieved from the array objects you initialize in the first keyframe, and the information is displayed in the dynamic text field.

Another way to provide time information to your viewer is to use the Flash function `getTimer`. This function returns the number of milliseconds that have elapsed since the Flash movie started playing. You can compare the returned value of `getTimer` at one instant with the returned value of it at another instant, and the difference gives you the elapsed time between those two instances. Use the elapsed time to create timers for games and activities in your Flash movie. You can time how long it takes for your viewer to answer questions correctly in a test or give your viewer only a certain amount of time to complete the test. Or you can award more points in a game if the player successfully completes a mission within an allotted time.

Because `getTimer` is a function and not an object, you don't need to use a constructor function to instantiate it, which makes it a very simple and convenient way to get elapsed times.

To create a timer:

1. Create a dynamic text field on the Stage, and give it an instance name in the Property Inspector.
2. Select the first frame of the main Timeline, and open the Actions panel.
3. Choose Objects > Movie > Movie Clip > Events > onMouseDown.
4. In the Object field, enter `_root`.
5. Choose Actions > Variables > set variable.
6. In the Variable field, enter `startTime`.
7. Put your insertion point in the Value field, and choose Functions > getTimer.

   The `getTimer` function appears in the Value field.

continues on next page

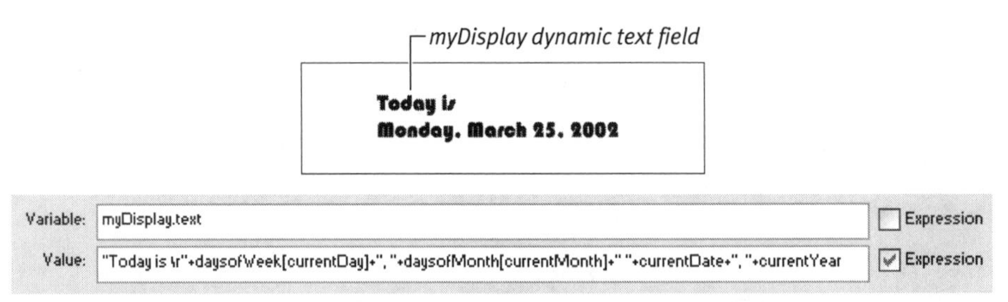

Figure 11.61 The day, month, date, and year information is concatenated and displayed in the myDisplay text field (top).

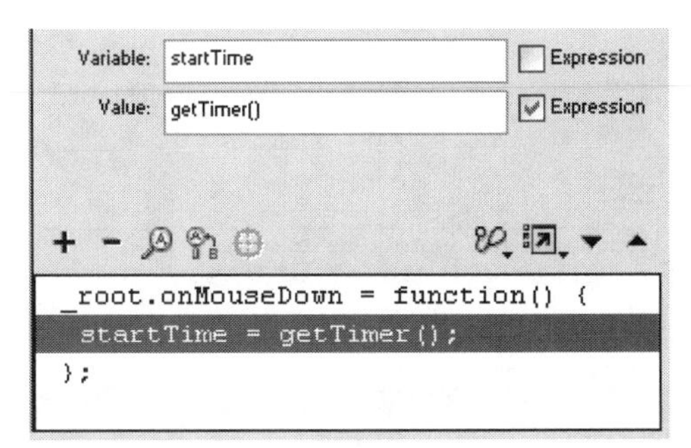

Figure 11.62 When the viewer presses the mouse button, the `getTimer` function retrieves the time elapsed since the start of the Flash movie. That time is put in the variable `startTime`. (If the mouse button is not pressed, the value of `startTime` defaults to 0.)

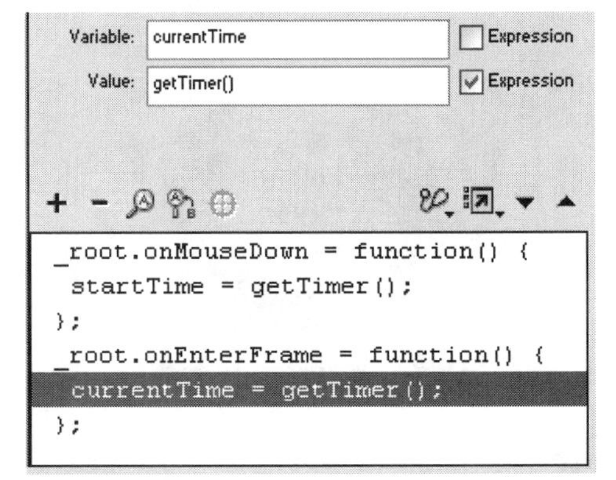

Figure 11.63 On an ongoing basis, the `getTimer` function retrieves the time elapsed since the start of the Flash movie. That time is put in the variable `currentTime`.

8. Check the Expression checkbox (**Figure 11.62**).

   Whenever the mouse button is pressed, the time that has passed since the movie started playing is assigned to the variable called `startTime`.

9. Choose Objects > Movie > Movie Clip > Events > onEnterFrame.

10. In the Objects field, enter `_root`.

11. Choose Actions > Variables > set variable.

12. In the Variable field, enter `currentTime`.

13. Put your insertion point in the Value field, and choose Functions > getTimer.

    The `getTimer` function appears in the Value field.

14. Check the Expression checkbox. (**Figure 11.63**).

15. Choose Actions > Variables > set variable.

16. In the Variable field, enter `elapsedTime`.

continues on next page

17. In the Value field, enter `(currentTime-startTime)/1000`, and check the Expression checkbox.

    Flash calculates the difference between the current timer and the timer at the instant a mouse button is clicked. The result is divided by 1,000 to give seconds (**Figure 11.64**).

18. Choose Actions > Variables > set variable.

19. Assign the variable `elapsedTime` to the `text` property of your dynamic text field (**Figure 11.65**).

20. Test your movie.

    Flash displays the time elapsed since the last instant the viewer pressed the mouse button. Experiment with different event handlers to build a stopwatch with Start, Stop, and Lap buttons.

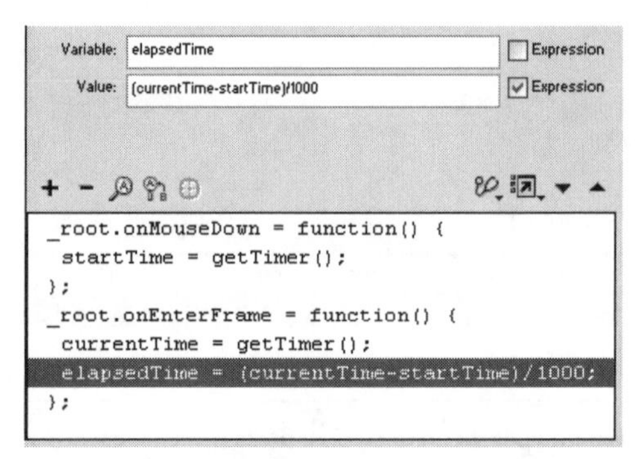

Figure 11.64 The variable `elapsedTime` is the time between the two instances of time recorded in the variables `startTime` and `currentTime`.

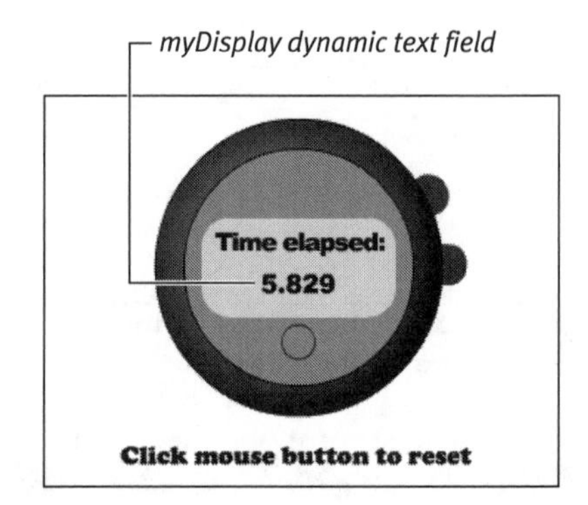

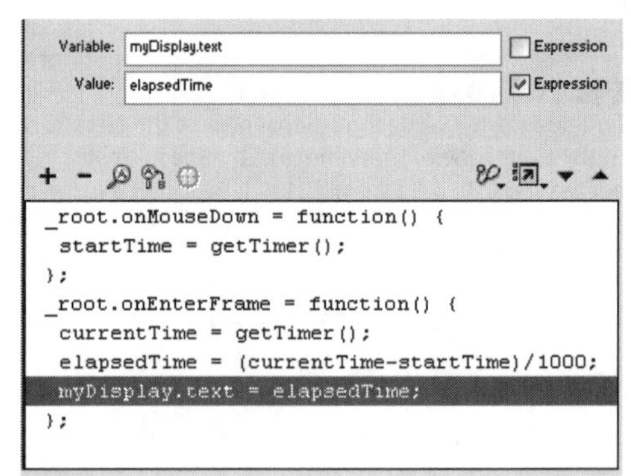

Figure 11.65 The value of `elapsedTime` is displayed in the text field called myDisplay (top).

Building Reusable Scripts

When you need to perform the same kind of manipulation of information multiple times, you can save time and reduce code clutter by building your own functions. You used functions in previous chapters, mostly as event handlers. When you assign an anonymous function to an event, for example, that function is triggered whenever the event happens. But whether they are anonymous or named, functions have the same job: They group related statements to perform a task that you can invoke from anywhere, at any time. You decide how to mix and match ActionScript statements as needed.

To create a function, use the function command in the Actions toolbox (Actions > User-Defined Functions > function), and give your function a name. Your statement could look something like this:

```
function doExplosion () {
}
```

Any actions within the curly braces of the function are performed when the function is called. You call this function by name, just like this: `doExplosion()`.

The following task builds a function that creates a Sound object, attaches a sound, starts it, and sets the volume. By consolidating all these methods, you can play the sound with just one call to a single function—and do so multiple times from different places in your movie.

To build and call a function:

1. Select the first keyframe of the main Timeline, and open the Actions panel.
2. Choose Actions > User-Defined Functions > function (Esc + fn).
3. In the Name field, enter a name for your function.
4. Leave the Parameters field empty.

   The function statement appears in the Script pane with a set of curly braces. All statements included within the curly braces become part of the function; they will be performed when the function is called (**Figure 11.66**).
5. Choose Actions > Variables > set variable.
6. In the Variable field, enter the name of a new Sound object.

continues on next page

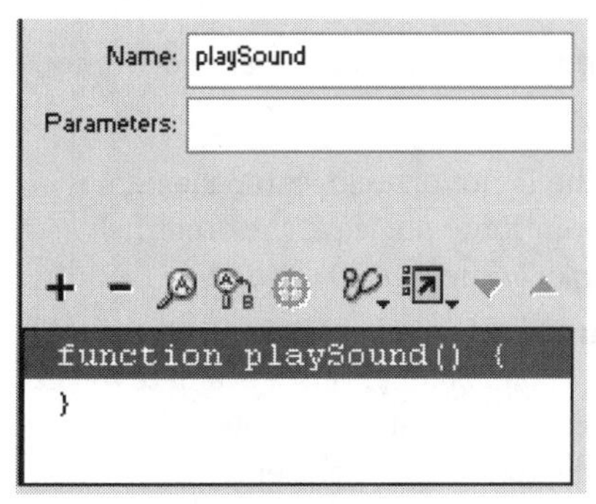

Figure 11.66 This function is called `playSound` and contains no parameters.

7. In the Value field, enter the constructor function `new Sound()`, and check the Expression checkbox (**Figure 11.67**).

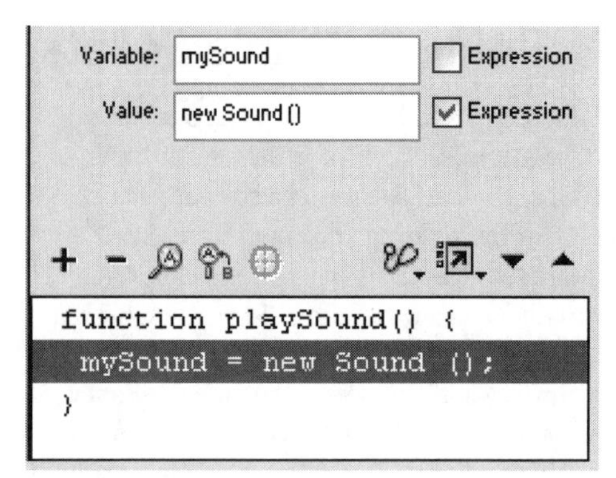

Figure 11.67 The new Sound object called mySound is instantiated.

8. Assign the three following methods that attach the sound, start playing it, and set its volume (**Figure 11.68**):

```
mySound.attachSound ("musicID")
mySound.start (0,2)
mySound.setVolume (50)
```

   Alternatively, you can switch to Expert mode and place the three statements within a `with` action:

```
with (mySound) {
    attachSound ("musicID");
    start (0, 2);
    setVolume (50);
}
```

```
function playSound() {
 mySound = new Sound ();
 mySound.attachSound("musicID");
 mySound.start(0, 2);
 mySound.setVolume(50);
}
```

Figure 11.68 When the function `playSound` is called, the three methods of the Sound object are performed.

9. Create a button symbol, and place an instance of the button on the Stage.
10. Select the button, and open the Actions panel.
11. Choose Actions > Movie Control > on.
12. Choose Actions > User-Defined Functions > call function.
13. In the Function field, enter the name of your function; leave the other fields blank (**Figure 11.69**).

   You can also simply choose Actions > Miscellaneous Actions > evaluate to get a new statement line in the Script pane. In the Expression field, enter the name of your function with parentheses (**Figure 11.70**).

   The function that you created on the main Timeline is called when this button is clicked.

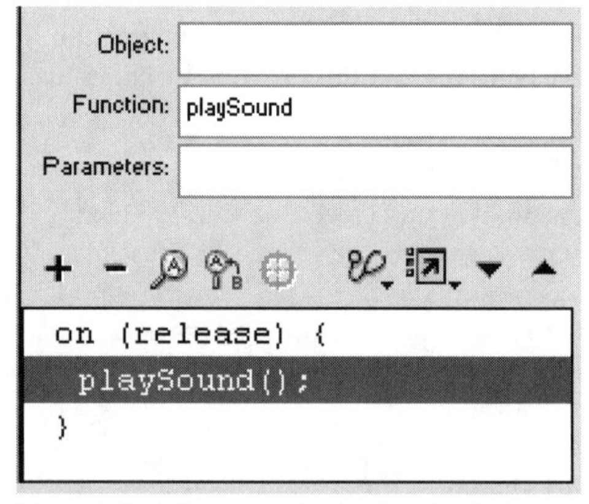

Figure 11.69 Call your function by choosing Actions > User-Defined Functions > call function.

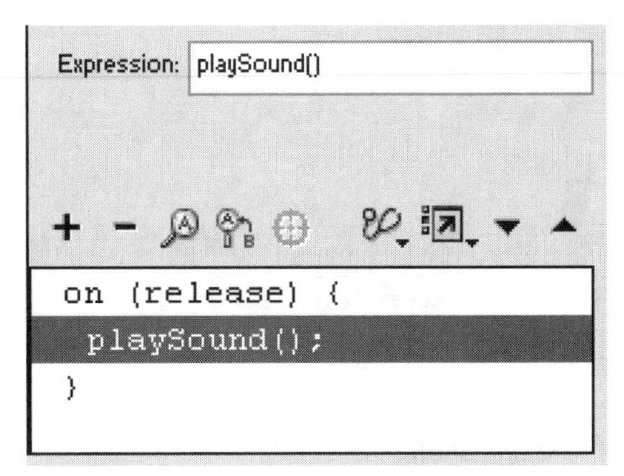

Figure 11.70 You can also call your function by choosing Actions > Miscellaneous Actions > evaluate and entering your function name with parentheses in the Expression field.

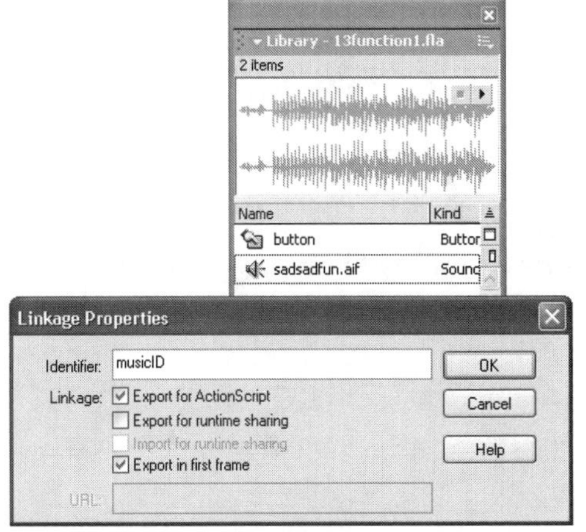

Figure 11.71 The Linkage Properties dialog box for an imported sound. Select Export for ActionScript, and enter a name in the Identifier field.

14. Import a sound clip.

15. In the Linkage Properties dialog box (accessed from the Library options pulldown menu), check the Export for ActionScript checkbox, and enter a name in the Identifier field (**Figure 11.71**).

16. Test your movie.

Your function is defined in the first keyframe of the main Timeline. When your viewer clicks the button on the Stage, Flash calls the function, which creates a new Sound object, attaches the sound, and starts playing it at a specified volume level.

✔ Tips

- You can initialize variables that are called *local variables*, which are scoped only within the function. Local variables expire at the end of the function and won't conflict with variables you've initialized elsewhere. You initialize local variables in the Actions panel by choosing Actions > Variables > var (Esc + vr). Use local variables to keep your functions independent and self-contained. That way, you can copy and paste functions from one project to another easily, without having to worry about conflicts with duplicate variable names.

- Remember that the scope of a function is defined in the Timeline on which it is created. If you call a function that was created on the main Timeline from within a movie clip, the actions from the function still pertain to the main Timeline.

Parameters and returned values

When you define a function, you can tell it to perform a certain task based on parameters that you provide, or *pass*, to the function at the time you call on it. This arrangement makes functions more flexible, because the work they do is tailored to particular contexts. In the preceding task, for example, you can define the function to accept a parameter for the sound volume. When you call the function, you also provide a value for the sound volume and the function incorporates that value in the `setVolume()` method.

To build a function that accepts parameters:

1. Continuing with file you used in the preceding task, select the first keyframe, and open the Actions panel.
2. Select the function statement.
3. In the Parameters field, enter `sndLoop` and `sndVolume`, separated by a comma.

   These names are the parameters for your function. You can name your parameters whatever you like (as long as they conform to the standard naming rules for variables and objects), and you can have as many parameters as you like (**Figure 11.72**).
4. Select the `start()` method within your function, and replace the loop parameter with `sndLoop`.
5. Select the `setVolume()` method, and replace the volume parameter with `sndVolume`.

   The parameters `sndLoop` and `sndVolume` will be used to play the sound for a certain number of loops and at a certain volume (**Figure 11.73**).

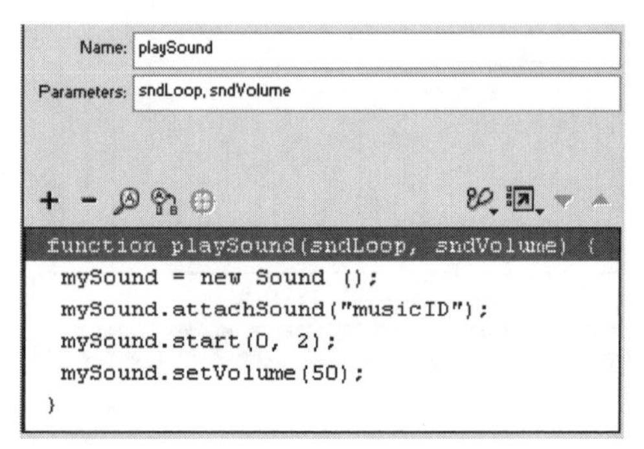

Figure 11.72 The function `playSound` accepts the parameters `sndLoop` and `sndVolume` and then passes them to the statements within its curly braces (which are not yet defined).

```
function playSound(sndLoop, sndVolume) {
 mySound = new Sound ();
 mySound.attachSound("musicID");
 mySound.start(0, sndLoop);
 mySound.setVolume(sndVolume);
}
```

Figure 11.73 The final script for a function that accepts and passes parameters. The parameters of the function `playSound` modify the `start()` method and the `setVolume()` method.

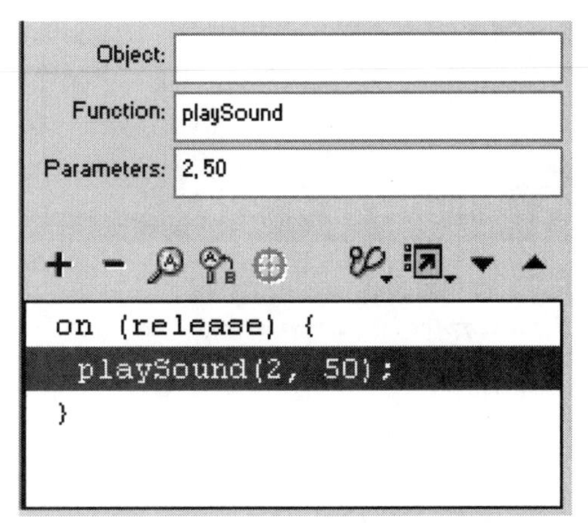

Figure 11.74 The function `playSound` is called, passing the parameters 2 and 50. The sound "musicID" starts playing and loops twice at a volume of 50.

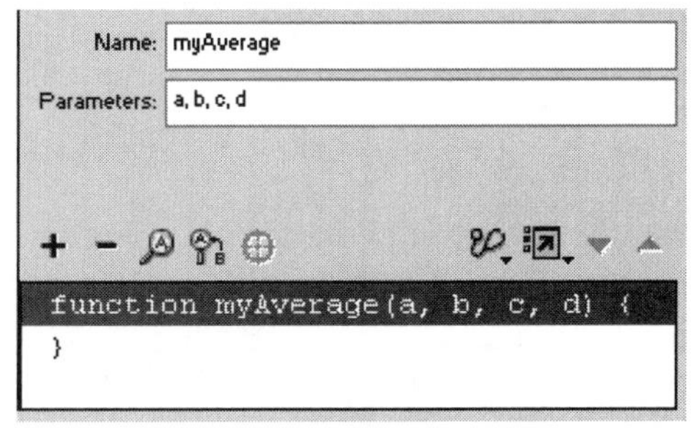

Figure 11.75 The function `myAverage` accepts the parameters `a`, `b`, `c`, and `d`.

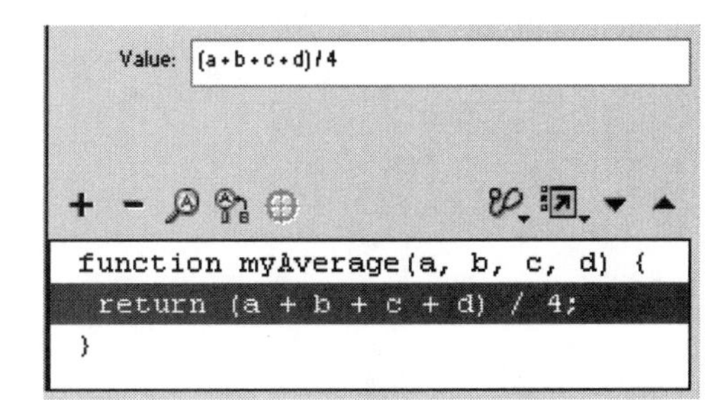

Figure 11.76 The `return` action evaluates the expression and makes the result available to the statement that called the function.

6. Select the button instance on the Stage.
7. In the Actions panel, select your function call.
8. In the Parameters field, enter a value for the `sndLoop` parameter and a value for the `sndVolume` parameter, separate the two values with a comma (**Figure 11.74**).
9. Test your movie.

   The actual values of the parameters that pass to the function are defined when you call the function. Another button may call the same function with different values for the parameters.

When you pass parameters to a function, you often want to know the results of a particular calculation. To make your function report a resulting calculation, use the `return` action. The `return` action, defined in your function statement, returns the value of any expression that you want to know when you call a function.

To build a function that returns values:

1. Select the first keyframe of the main Timeline, and open the Actions panel.
2. Choose Actions > User-Defined Functions > function.
3. In the Name field, enter a name for your function.
4. In the Parameters field, enter `a, b, c, d` (**Figure 11.75**).
5. Choose Actions > User-Defined Functions > return (Esc + rt).
6. In the Value field, enter an expression to average the four parameters.

   This function returns the value of the expression (**Figure 11.76**).

continues on next page

7. Select the text tool in the Tools palette, create a dynamic text field on the Stage, and give the text field an instance name in the Property Inspector.
8. Create a button symbol, and place an instance of it on the Stage.
9. Select the instance, and in the Actions panel, choose Actions > Movie Control > on.
10. Choose Actions > Variables > set variable.
11. In the Variable field, enter the name of your text field, followed by a dot and then the `text` property.
12. In the Value field, enter the name of your function and four values for its parameters, separating the values with commas; then check the Expression checkbox (**Figure 11.77**).

    These four values pass to the function, where it is processed. The function returns a value back to where it was called. The returned value is assigned to the dynamic text field, where it is displayed.
13. Test your movie.

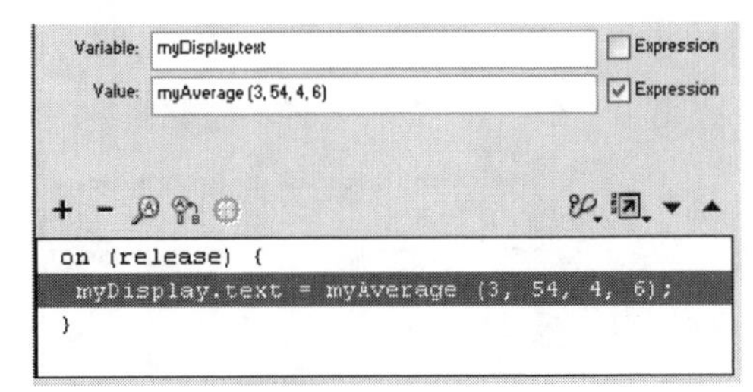

Figure 11.77 The function `myAverage` is called, and the returned value appears in the myDisplay dynamic text field.

✔ Tip

- The `function` action replaces the `call` action used in previous versions of Flash. Although the `call` action still works, it can't pass parameters or receive returned values as easily as the `function` action does.

The Arguments object

Sometimes, you want to build a function that can accept a variable number of parameters. Building a function that calculates a mathematical average, for example, is much more useful when you can input as many or as few numbers as you want. The Arguments object can help solve this problem. The Arguments object is an array that contains the number of parameters that are passed to a function, as well as their values. Every function has an Arguments object, which you can use without instantiation.

In the preceding task, you defined a function with the following script:

```
function myAverage(a, b, c, d) {
   return (a + b + c + d)/4;
}
```

You called the function like so:

```
myAverage (3, 54, 4, 6);
```

The Arguments object for this function would be an array with four elements:

```
Arguments[0]=3
Arguments[1]=54
Arguments[2]=4
Arguments[3]=6
```

The `length` property of the Arguments object returns the number of entries in the array. So for this function, `Arguments.length = 4`.

The following task builds a function that can accept any number of parameters and calculates their average with the Arguments object.

To use the Arguments object to handle a variable number of parameters passed to a function:

1. Select the first frame of the main Timeline, and open the Actions panel.
2. Choose Actions > User-Defined Functions > function.
3. In the Name field, enter a name for your function; leave the Parameters field blank (**Figure 11.78**).
4. Choose Actions > Variables > set variable.
5. In the Variable field, enter `total`.

continues on next page

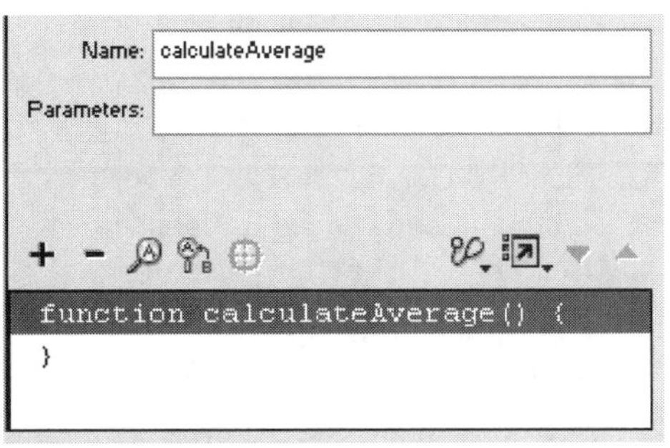

Figure 11.78 Create the function called `calculateAverage`, and do not define any parameters.

6. In the Value field, enter `0`. Check the Expression box.

   The variable called `total` will hold the sum of the numbers you will pass to this function. Each time this function is called, `total` will be reset to 0.

7. Choose Actions > Conditions/Loops > for.

8. In the Init field, enter `i=0`; in the Conditions field, enter `i<Arguments.length`; and in the Next field, enter `i++`.

   This loop statement will be performed as many times as there are elements in the Arguments array.

9. Choose Actions > Miscellaneous Actions > evaluate.

10. In the Expression field, enter `total += Arguments[i]`.

    The variable `total` adds the value of each element in the `Arguments` array to itself. This adds up all the parameters that are passed to the function (**Figure 11.79**).

11. Select the closing brace of the `for` statement, and choose Actions > User-Defined Functions > return.

12. In the Value Field, enter `total/(Arguments.length)`.

    The function returns the average of all the parameters that are passed to it (**Figure 11.80**).

```
Expression: total += Arguments[i]

function calculateAverage() {
  total = 0;
  for (i=0; i<Arguments.length; i++) {
    total += Arguments[i];
  }
}
```

Figure 11.79 All the parameters that are passed to this function are stored in the `Arguments` array, and the variable called `total` adds them up.

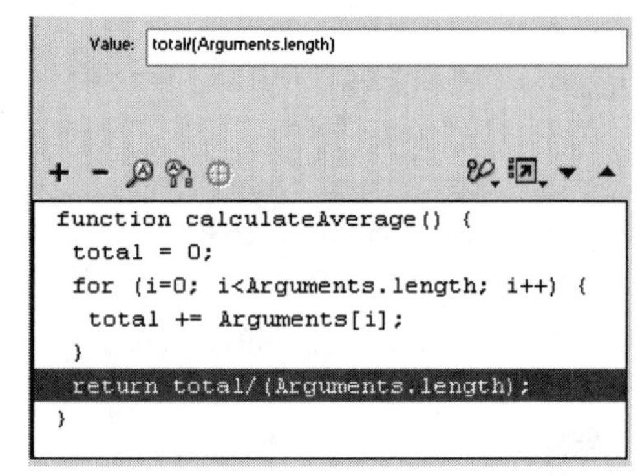

Figure 11.80 The sum of all the parameters is divided by the number of parameters. The result is returned to the statement that called the function.

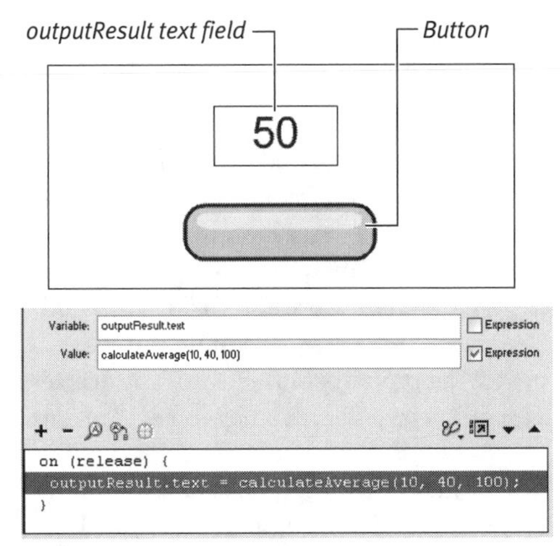

Figure 11.81 Three parameters are passed to the `calculateAverage` function, and the average is displayed in the outputResult text field.

13. Create a dynamic text field on the Stage, and give it an instance name in the Property Inspector.

In this example, the instance name is outputResult.

14. Create a button symbol, and place an instance on the Stage.

15. Select the button instance, and open the Actions panel.

16. Choose Actions > Movie Control > on.

17. Choose Actions > Miscellaneous Actions > evaluate.

18. In the Expression field, enter the following:

```
outputResult.text =
calculateAverage(10, 40, 100);
```

When this button is clicked, the numbers `10`, `40`, and `100` are passed to the function. The average is calculated and returned, where it is displayed in the dynamic text field called outputResult (**Figure 11.81**). You can pass any number of parameters to the `calculateAverage` function and still get a mathematical average.

Building Custom Classes with Functions

You can use functions not only to combine multiple actions in a single task or a single event handler, but also to define the properties and methods of new classes, so you can organize and customize information in your scripts for easier access and storage and to create functionality that Flash doesn't provide. After you create a custom class, use a constructor function to instantiate an object of your class. Consider this simple function:

```
function Circle (whatRadius){
  this.radius = whatRadius;
}
```

This function defines a class called Circle that has the property called radius. You instantiate an object from this class by using the constructor function, as in the following:

```
myCircle = new Circle (100);
```

This statement creates a new object called myCircle out of the Circle class. The parameter 100 is passed to the function and used to set the radius property. The new object has the property radius with a value of 100 (in dot syntax, myCircle.radius = 100).

Now that you've created a custom Circle class, you'll want to create a custom method for it. You define what you want your method to do within a function statement and then assign it to your class. You make a method "belong" to a class by assigning it to the prototype property of the class. The prototype property affects all new objects made from its class, so that all new objects are said to inherit the method. The method startDrag(), for example, is shared with all movie-clip instances of the MovieClip class. Assign a new method to your class like so:

```
Circle.prototype.getArea=function(){
    return (Math.PI *
    this.radius*this.radius)
}
```

The method getArea() calculates the area of a Circle object based on its radius property and returns that value. This method is assigned to the prototype property of the Circle class. Assign a second method to your class like so:

```
Circle.prototype.setArea=function(whatArea)
{
this.radius=Math.sqrt(whatArea/Math.PI)
}
```

The method setArea() changes the radius property of a Circle object based on the area you want it to be.

To call either method from your object, you would write the statement myCircle.getArea() to retrieve the area or myCircle.setArea(300) to change myCircle so that its area is 300.

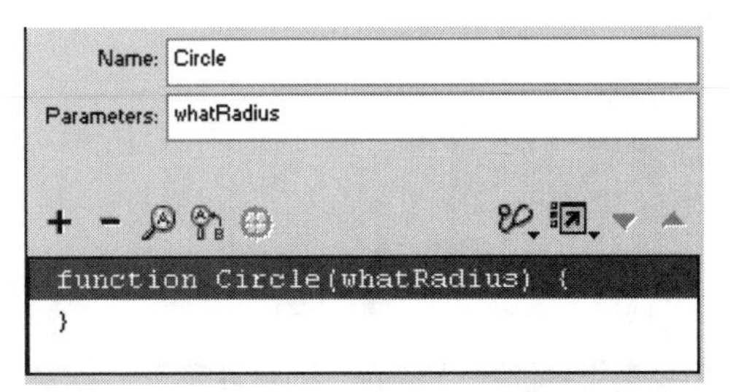

Figure 11.82 The function called `Circle` requires the parameter `whatRadius`.

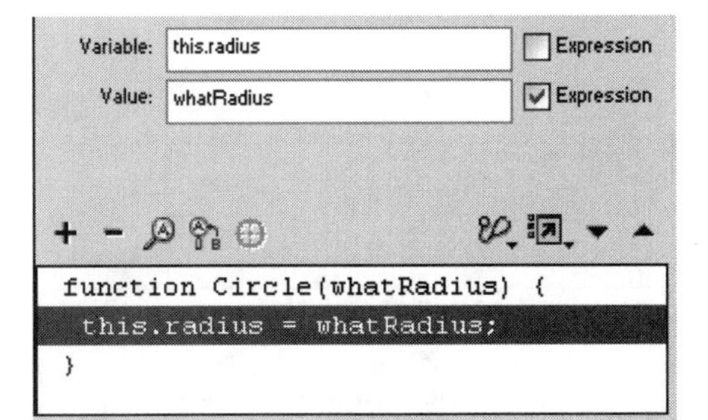

Figure 11.83 The `Circle` class contains one property, called `radius`. It will be defined when you instantiate an object and pass the parameter `whatRadius` through the constructor function.

By using functions to create your own classes, properties, and methods, you have a powerful and flexible way to go beyond the classes that Flash provides.

To create a custom class:

1. Select the first keyframe of the main Timeline, and open the Actions panel.
2. Choose Actions > User-Defined Functions > function.
3. In the Name field, enter `Circle`.
4. In the Parameters field, enter the parameter name `whatRadius` (**Figure 11.82**).
5. Choose Actions > Variables > set variable.
6. In the Variable field, enter `this`, followed by a dot and then a property name.
7. In the Value field, enter the name of the parameter `whatRadius` that you defined in the function statement.

   This function defines the class called `Circle` with one property. The keyword `this` refers to the instances that will be made from the `Circle` class. Check the Expression box (**Figure 11.83**).

✔ Tip

- This `Circle` class isn't literally a graphic circle on the Stage. When you create a `Circle` class, it's simply an abstract container of data that is useful for holding methods and properties together.

To define a method of a custom class:

1. Continuing with the file you used in the preceding task, select the first keyframe of the main Timeline, and open the Actions panel.
2. Select the closing curly brace of the function.

   The next action you add will appear outside the function.
3. Choose Actions > User-Defined Functions > method.
4. In the Object field, enter `Circle.prototype`.
5. In the Method field, enter the name of your method, `getArea`.

   The method `getArea()` is assigned to the `Circle` class and will be available to all the objects you create from it (**Figure 11.84**).
6. Choose Actions > User-Defined Functions > return.
7. In the Value field, enter an expression that calculates the area of the Circle object based on its `radius` property:

   `Math.PI*this.radius*this.radius`

   The method `getArea()` calculates the area and returns the result (**Figure 11.85**).
8. Select the closing curly brace of the method.

   The next action you add will appear outside the method.
9. Choose Actions > User-Defined Functions > method.

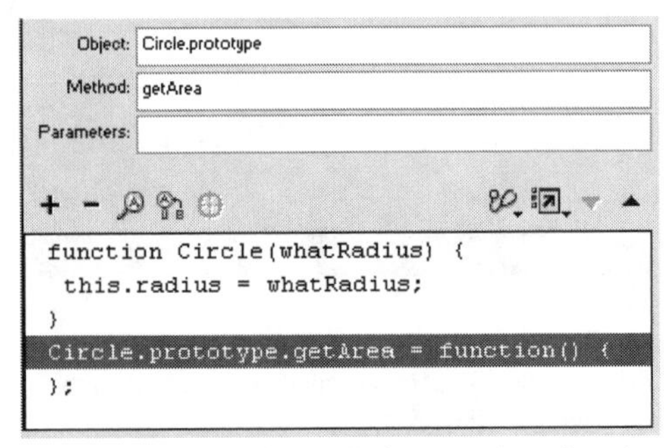

Figure 11.84 The method called `getArea` is assigned to the `prototype` property of the `Circle` class, making `getArea` available to all Circle objects.

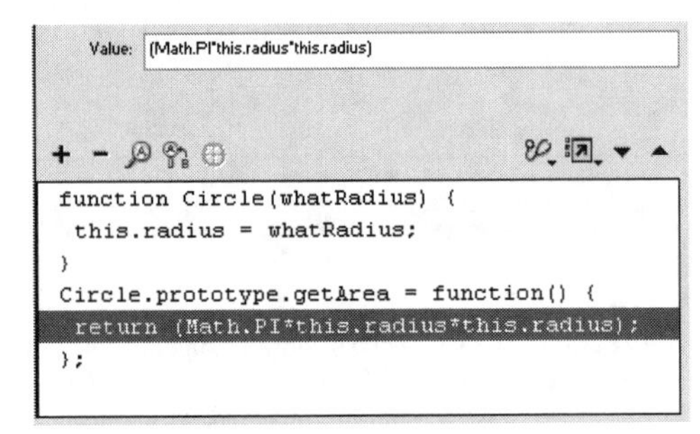

Figure 11.85 The method called `getArea` returns the area of a Circle object based on its `radius` property.

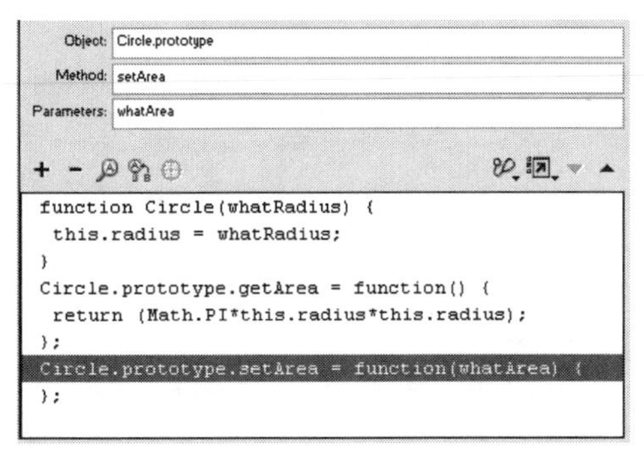

Figure 11.86 The method called `setArea` is assigned to the `prototype` property of the Circle class, making `setArea` available to all circle objects. This method requires one parameter, called `whatArea`.

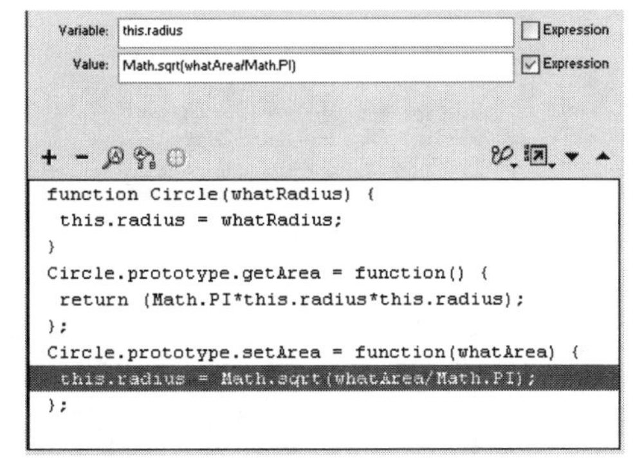

Figure 11.87 The method called `setArea` sets a new area of a Circle object. As a result, the `radius` property changes.

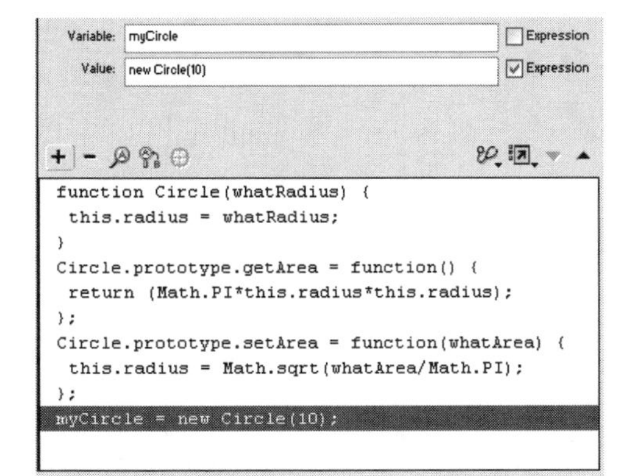

Figure 11.88 Instantiate a new object from the `Circle` class with a constructor function. The new object called `myCircle` has a radius of 10.

10. In the Object field, enter `Circle.prototype`.
11. In the Method field, enter the name of a second method, `setArea`.
12. In the Parameters area, enter `whatArea` (**Figure 11.86**).

    When you call this function, you must provide a parameter (`whatArea`).
13. Choose Actions > Variables > set variable.
14. In the Variable field, enter `this.radius`.
15. In the Value field, enter an expression that calculates the radius of the Circle object based on the `whatArea` parameter: `Math.sqrt(whatArea/Math.PI)`. Check the Expression box.

    The method `setArea()` modifies the `radius` property based on a new area of the Circle object (**Figure 11.87**).

To instantiate an object from a custom class:

1. Continuing with the file you used in the preceding task, select the first keyframe of the Timeline, and open the Actions panel.
2. Select the closing brace of the last statement in the Script pane.
3. Choose Actions > Variables > set variable.
4. In the Variable field, enter the name for your new object.
5. In the Value field, enter `new Circle(10)`, and check the Expression checkbox (**Figure 11.88**).

   A new object is instantiated from your `Circle` class, with its property defined by the value passed to the function. This new object inherits the methods `setArea()` and `getArea()`.

To call a method of a custom class:

1. Continuing with the file you used in the preceding task, create a button symbol, and drag an instance to the Stage.
2. Select the button, and open the Actions panel.
3. Choose Actions > Movie Control > on.
4. Choose Actions > User-Defined Functions > call function.
5. In the Object field, enter your object name.
6. In the Method field, enter the name of one of your methods, `setArea`.
7. In the Parameters field, enter `300` as the parameter of the method (**Figure 11.89**).

   When this button is clicked, the `setArea()` method is called, and the radius of your object changes so that its area is 300.

Figure 11.90 shows the complete script that creates the custom class and methods.

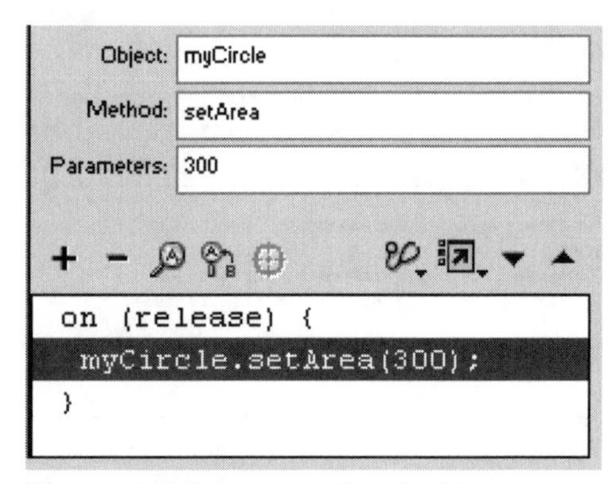

Figure 11.89 Call the `setArea()` method for `myCircle`. The area of `myCircle` is now `300`.

```
function Circle(whatRadius) {
 this.radius = whatRadius;
}
Circle.prototype.getArea = function() {
 return (Math.PI*this.radius*this.radius);
};
Circle.prototype.setArea = function(whatArea) {
 this.radius = Math.sqrt(whatArea/Math.PI);
};
myCircle = new Circle(10);
```

```
on (release) {
 myCircle.setArea(300);
}
```

Figure 11.90 The top script defines the `Circle` class with a `radius` property and two methods, `getArea()` and `setArea()`. The last statement instantiates a new object called `myCircle` of `radius 10`. The bottom script calls the `setArea()` method for `myCircle`.

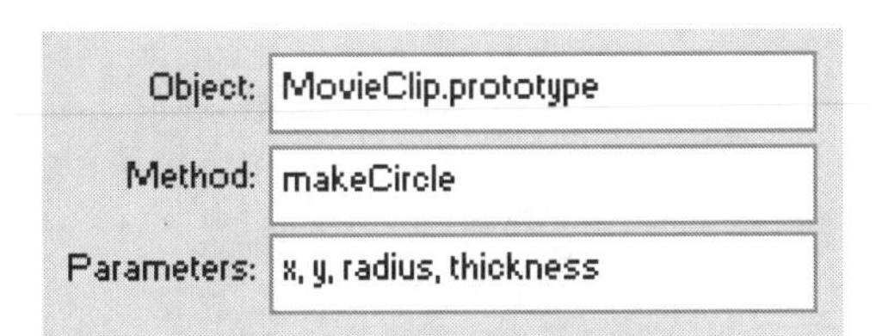

Figure 11.91 The `makeCircle()` method is assigned to the `MovieClip` class. This method passes four parameters: `x`, `y`, `radius`, and `thickness`.

Using prototype to extend predefined classes

The `prototype` property is important to ensure that your methods are shared with all the instances of your custom class. This means that you have to define the method for the class only once, saving you time and saving computer memory. But you can also define new methods and properties and assign them to the `prototype` property of *existing* classes. If the `Button` class doesn't have a method that you really need, for example, you can create your own method and assign it to `Button.prototype`:

```
Button.prototype.myMethod=function(){
}
```

All new buttons that you create and put on the Stage can use the method called `myMethod()`.

As another example, you could create your own method to draw circles with the movie clip, combining the existing methods `moveTo()`, `curveTo()`, and `lineStyle()`. Assign your method to `MovieClip.prototype`, and all movie-clip instances can use your method to draw circles.

To assign a new method to an existing class:

1. Select the first frame of the main Timeline, and open the Actions panel.
2. Choose Actions > User-Defined Functions > method.
3. In the Object field, enter the name of an existing class, followed by a dot and then `prototype`.
4. In the Methods field, enter a name for your new method.
5. In the Parameters field, enter any parameters that you want to pass to your method (**Figure 11.91**).

continues on next page

Your method is assigned to the existing class. The names of existing classes can be found below the Objects category of the Actions Toolbox. MovieClip, for example, is the class name for movie clips.

6. Define the actions for your new method between the function parentheses (**Figure 11.92**).

7. In this example, all movie-clip instances inherit the makeCircle() method, so call this method, and pass parameters for its x location, y location, radius, and line thickness (**Figure 11.93**).


```
MovieClip.prototype.makeCircle = function(x, y, radius, thickness) {
 function radians(degrees) {
  return (Math.PI/180)*degrees;
 }
 theta = 45;
 d = radius/Math.cos(radians(.5*theta));
 this.lineStyle(thickness, 0x000000, 100);
 this.moveTo(x+radius, y);
 for (k=(theta/2); k<361; k=k+theta) {
  xControl = d*Math.cos(radians(k));
  yControl = d*Math.sin(radians(k));
  xAnchor = radius*Math.cos(radians(k+(theta/2)));
  yAnchor = radius*Math.sin(radians(k+(theta/2)));
  this.curveTo(x+xControl, y+yControl, x+xAnchor, y+yAnchor);
 }
};
```

Figure 11.92 All the statements within the makeCircle function's curly braces are performed when the method is called. The x and y parameters specify the center of a circle drawn with eight curveTo() segments. radius specifies its size, and thickness specifies the thickness of the line.

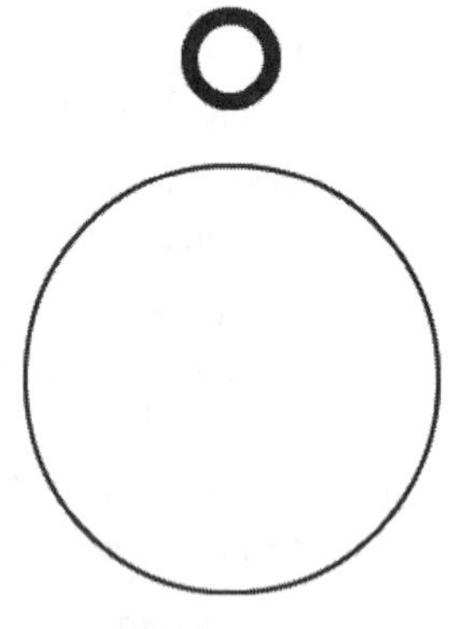

```
_root.makeCircle(200, 300, 100, 2);
_root.makeCircle(200, 150, 20, 8);
```

Figure 11.93 You can use makeCircle() as you do any other method of a movie clip. The top statement creates a circle at x=200, y=300, with a radius of 100 and an outline 2 points thick. The bottom statement creates a circle at x=200, y=150, with a radius of 20 and an outline 8 points thick.

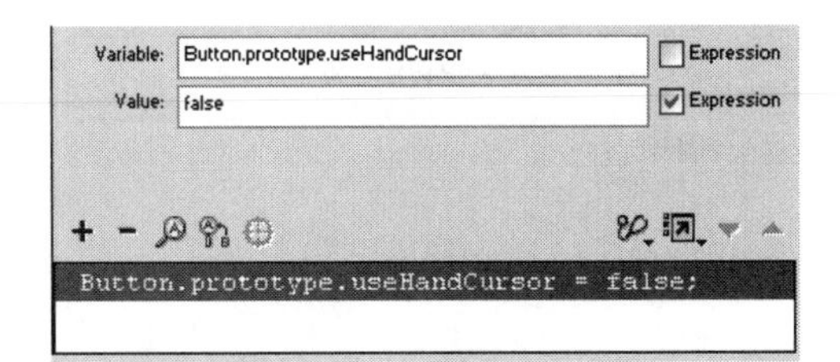

Figure 11.94 All button instances will inherit the property `useHandCursor = false`, so the hand icon will not appear.

Assigning properties to the `prototype` property of a class can also be useful. Consider the following statement:

```
Button.prototype.useHandCursor=false
```

This statement makes all button instances inherit the property and its value, `useHandCursor=false`, so that the hand icon does not appear over any buttons.

To assign a property value to an entire class:

1. Select the first frame of the main Timeline, and open the Actions panel.
2. Choose Actions > Variables > set variable.
3. In the Variable field, enter the name of an existing class, followed by a dot, `prototype`, another dot, and then the name of a property.
4. In the Value field, enter a value of the property (**Figure 11.94**).

   All instances of the class you specify in the Variable field will inherit the property value you specify in the Value field.

Building custom properties

If you want to build your own property, you can do so with the Object method, addProperty(). The addProperty() method enables you to define a new property with a function that gets the property value and another function that sets the property value. This situation allows for the read-write nature of properties.

Wouldn't it be convenient to have a MovieClip property called _color that controls its RGB color? Currently, there are properties like _alpha and _rotation, but nothing that controls the color. So you'll create one. You can add this custom property by using addProperty() on the prototype property of the MovieClip class. The addProperty() method takes three parameters: the name of the new property, the name of the function that gets its value, and the name of the function that sets its value:

```
MovieClip.prototype.addProperty
("_color", getColor, setColor)
```

After you've added the _color property to the MovieClip class, you must define the getColor and setColor functions.

To create a custom property:

1. Select the first frame of the main Timeline, and open the Actions panel.
2. Choose Objects > Core > Object > Methods > addProperty.
3. In the Object field, enter the name of your class (whether it's a custom one that you created or an existing one), followed by a dot and then prototype (**Figure 11.95**).
4. In the Parameters field, enter a name for your new property within quotation marks, followed by the name of a function that gets the property value and then the name of a function that sets the property value, separating your three parameters with commas (**Figure 11.96**).

Figure 11.95 The prototype property determines inheritance for the entire class.

Figure 11.96 The Parameters field for the addProperty() method. The property called _color is added to the MovieClip class. Flash gets the _color property by using the function getColor and sets the _color property by using the function setColor. You must define these two functions.

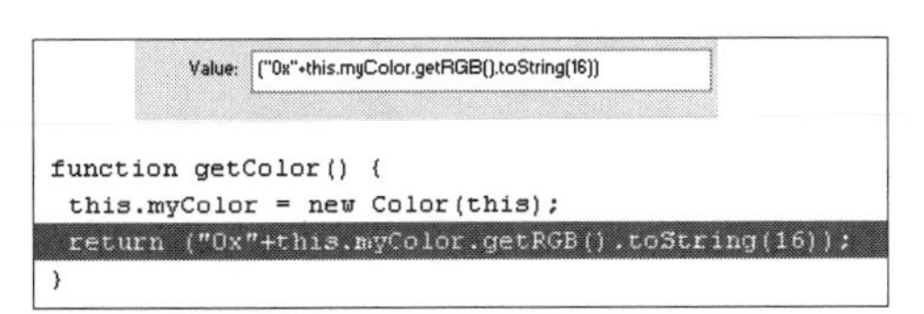

Figure 11.97 The `getColor` function instantiates a new Color object and uses the `getRGB()` method to retrieve the value of the movie clip's color. The `toString()` method converts the value to a hexadecimal representation as a string. The string `"0x"` is added to the front, and the result is returned as the `_color` property.

Object: this.myColor
Method: setRGB
Parameters: hexCode

```
function setColor(hexCode) {
  this.myColor = new Color(this);
  this.myColor.setRGB(hexCode);
}
```

Figure 11.98 The `setColor` function instantiates a new Color object and uses the `setRGB()` method to change the movie clip's color. The parameter that is passed through this function is the value that is assigned to the `_color` property.

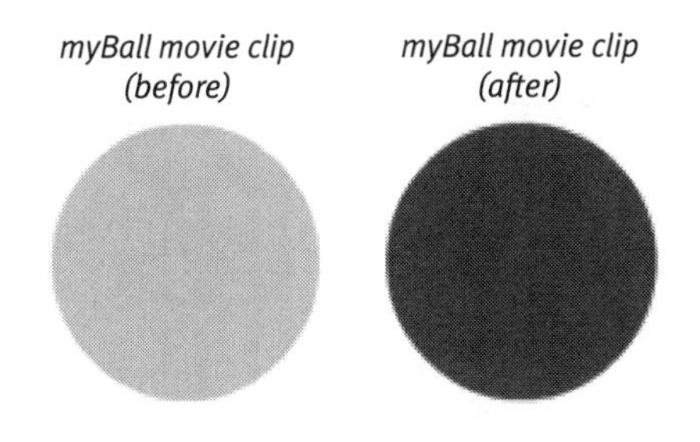


```
myBall._color = 0xFF0000;
```

Figure 11.99 When you assign a hex-code value to the `_color` property of the myBall movie clip, the `setColor` function is invoked, and the movie clip changes color.

In this example, a new property called `_color` is created for the `MovieClip` class. When you get a movie clip's `_color` property, Flash will invoke the function called `getColor`. When you set a movie clip's `_color` property, Flash will invoke the function called `setColor`.

5. Choose Actions > User-Defined Functions > function.
6. In the Name field, enter `getColor`, and within the curly braces of this function, assign actions that get the value of your property (**Figure 11.97**).
7. Select the closing brace of your function, and choose Actions > User-Defined Functions > function.
8. In the Name field, enter `setColor`.
9. In the Parameters field, enter a parameter name, and within the curly braces of this function, assign actions that use the parameter to set the value of your property (**Figure 11.98**).
10. Use your new `_color` property to retrieve or change the RGB color of any movie-clip instance (**Figure 11.99**).

✔ Tip

- If you want your property to be read-only, you don't really need the third parameter in the `addProperty()` method, which specifies the function to set the property's value. In its place, use the keyword `null` and you can read your property but not modify it.

MANAGING CONTENT AND TROUBLESHOOTING

12

As the complexity of your Flash movie increases with the addition of bitmaps, videos, sounds, and animations, as well as the ActionScript that integrate them, you'll need to keep close track of these elements so you can make necessary revisions and bug fixes. After all, the most elaborate Flash movie is useless if you can't pinpoint the one variable that's keeping the whole thing from working. Fortunately, Flash provides several tools for troubleshooting and managing library symbols and code.

This chapter shows you how to create shared library symbols and external ActionScripts that supply common elements—symbols and code—to a team of Flash developers working on a project. You'll learn about components, which are specialized movie clips that contain pre-scripted code that makes common interactivity easy to apply. For example, using components that Flash provides, you can quickly build a scroll bar or a check box, and specify parameters to customize it for your own project without having to build your own from scratch. This chapter also delves into the Movie Explorer, Output window, and Debugger panel, which offer information about the organization and status of your movie. These three windows let you review your ActionScript in context with the other components in your movie, receive error and warning messages, and monitor the changing values of variables and properties as your movie plays.

Finally, you'll learn some strategies for making your Flash movie leaner and faster—optimizing graphics and code, organizing your work environment, and avoiding some common mistakes—guidelines to help you become a better Flash animator and developer.

Sharing Library Symbols

Flash makes it possible for teams of animators and developers to share common symbols of a complex project. Each animator might be working on a separate movie that uses the same symbol—the main character in an animated comic book, for example. An identical symbol of this main character needs to reside in the library of each movie, and if the art director decides to change this character's face, a new symbol has to be copied to all the libraries—that is, unless you create a shared library symbol. There are two kinds of shared symbols: runtime shared symbols and author-time shared symbols.

Runtime Sharing of Symbols

In runtime sharing, one movie provides a symbol for multiple movies to use during runtime. This simplifies the editing process and ensures consistency throughout a Flash project (**Figure 12.1**).

Your viewers also benefit from the shared symbols, since they only have to download them once. For example, a main character would be downloaded just once for the first movie and all subsequent movies using that character.

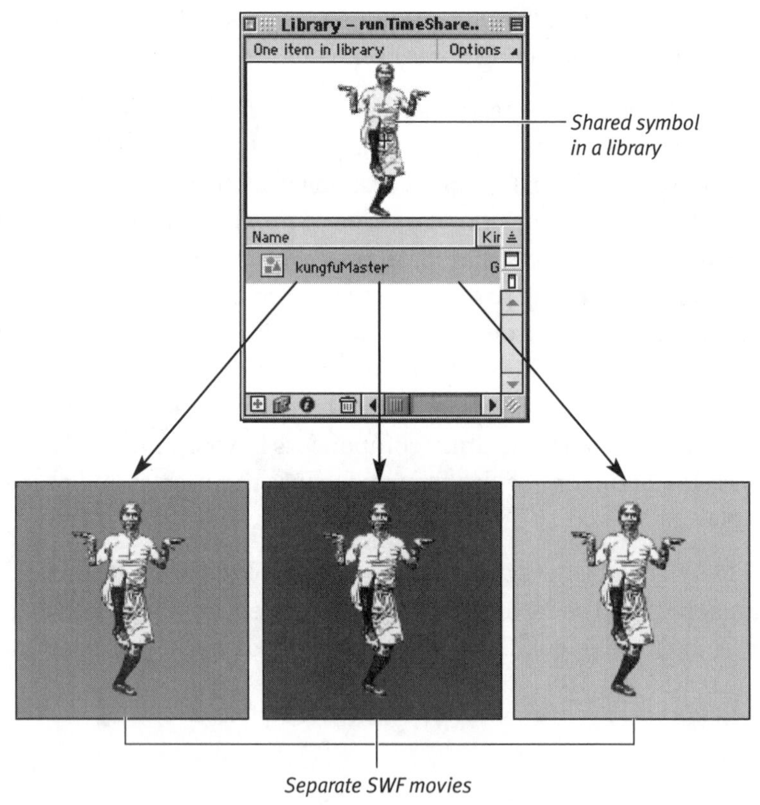

Figure 12.1 A runtime shared symbol (top) lets multiple SWF files use the same symbol.

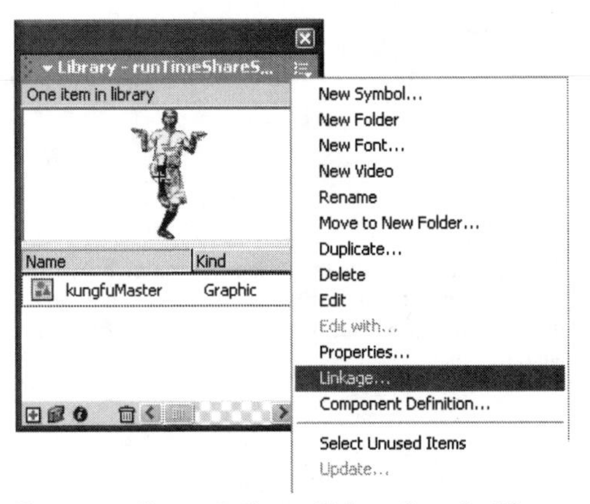

Figure 12.2 Choose Options > Linkage from the Library window's pull-down menu.

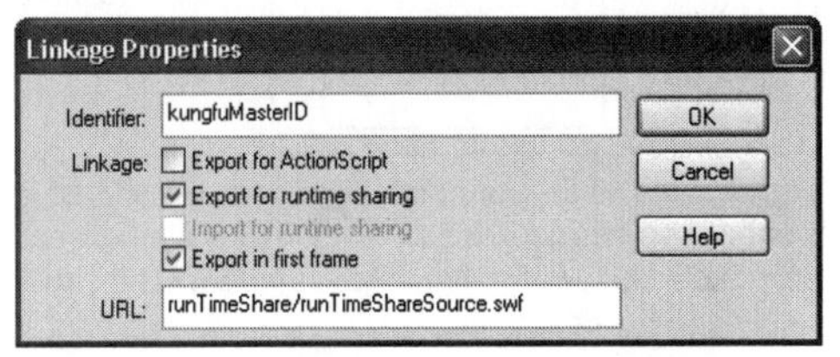

Figure 12.3 To mark a symbol as a shared symbol, it is given an identifier in the Linkage Properties dialog box, selected for export, and given a URL where it can be found. This shared symbol is located in the directory called runTimeShare in the file called runTimeShareSource.swf.

To create a runtime shared library symbol, you mark the symbol for Export for runtime sharing in the Linkage Properties dialog box. When you export the SWF file, the symbol you identified will be available to other SWF movies.

To create a runtime shared symbol:

1. In a new Flash document, create a symbol you want to share. The symbol can be a graphic, button, movie clip, font symbol, sound, or bitmap.
2. In the Library window, select your symbol. From the Options pull-down menu, choose Linkage (**Figure 12.2**).

   The Linkage Properties dialog box appears.
3. From the Linkage choices, select Export for runtime sharing. In the Identifier field, enter a unique name for your symbol. In the URL field, enter the relative or absolute path to the source movie that will share this symbol. Keep the Export in first frame box checked. Click OK (**Figure 12.3**).

   Your selected symbol is now marked for export and available to be shared by other movies.
4. Export your Flash movie as a SWF file and place it in the location you specified in the URL field of the Linkage Properties dialog box.

   This is your source movie that shares its symbol.

Once you create a movie that shares a library symbol, you can create other movies that use it. You do this by opening a new Flash document and creating a symbol. In its Linkage Properties dialog box, mark the symbol to Import for runtime sharing, and enter the name and location of the source symbol. At runtime, your new movie finds, imports, and uses the source symbol.

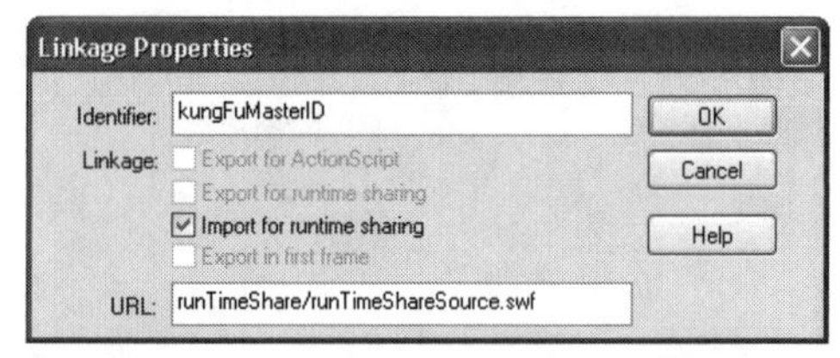

Figure 12.4 In the Linkage Properties dialog box, check the Import for runtime sharing box and enter the Identifier and location of the shared symbol you wish to use.

To use a runtime shared symbol:

1. Open a new Flash document and create a new symbol.

   It doesn't matter what kind of symbol you create (movie clip, graphic, or button) or what content is inside it, because it will be replaced by the shared symbol from the source movie at runtime. This symbol is simply a placeholder.

2. In the Library window, select your symbol. From the Options pull-down menu, choose Linkage.

   The Linkage Properties dialog box appears.

3. From the Linkage choices, select Import for runtime sharing. In the Identifier field, enter the name for the shared symbol in the source movie. In the URL field, enter the path to the source movie. Click OK (**Figure 12.4**).

   Your selected symbol is now marked to find the shared symbol in the source movie and import it.

4. Drag an instance of the symbol onto the Stage and use it in your movie.

5. Export your Flash movie as a SWF file and place it in a location where it can find the source movie (**Figure12.5**).

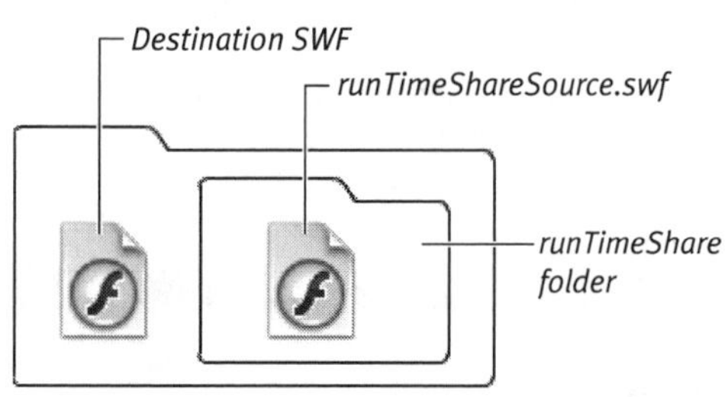

Figure 12.5 The destination SWF imports the shared symbol from the source SWF. The URL field in Figures 12.3 and 12.4 specify where the source SWF is located relative to the destination SWF.

When you play the SWF, it imports the shared symbol from the source movie. The shared symbol takes over the current symbol (**Figure 12.6**).

✔ Tips

- When you make changes and revisions to the shared symbol in the source movie, all the destination movies that use the shared symbol will be automatically updated to reflect the change.
- You can also drag the shared symbol from the source movie's library into the destination movie. The shared symbol will be automatically imported into your destination movie with the correct Linkage Properties options checked and field values entered.
- Unfortunately, you can't assign ActionScript that affects runtime shared symbols. For example, you can't use the methods `attachMovieClip()` or `attachSound()` to dynamically place a shared symbol from the library into your movie. The reason is that a symbol can't be marked for both Import for runtime sharing and Export for ActionScript at the same time.

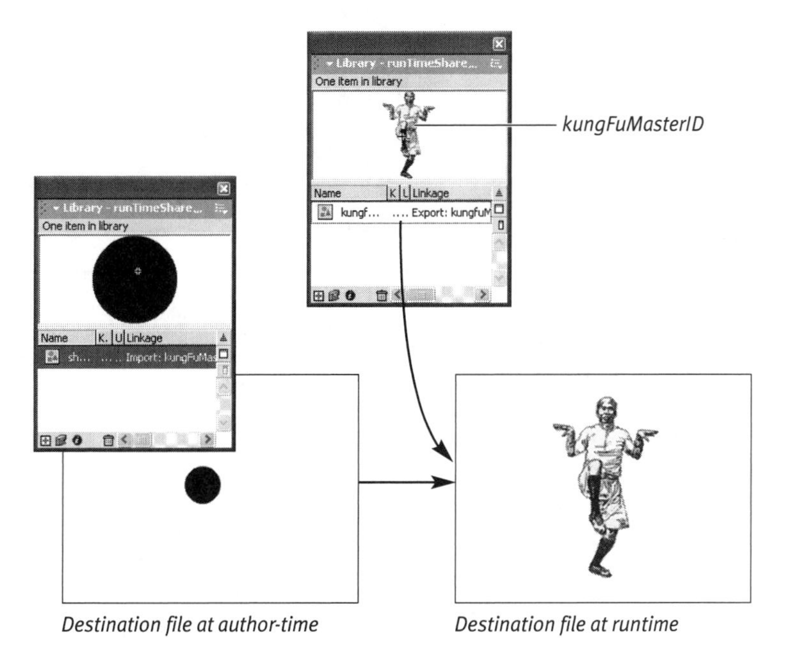

Figure 12.6 The black circle symbol in the destination movie (left) imports the kungFuMasterID shared symbol from the runTimeShareSource.swf at runtime. As a result, the shared symbol appears in the destination SWF (right).

Author-time sharing of symbols

When you want to share symbols among FLA files instead of SWF files, turn to author-time sharing. Author-time sharing lets you choose a source symbol in a particular FLA file so that another FLA file can reference it and keep its symbol up to date. You only have to worry about modifying one FLA file containing the source symbol instead of multiple FLA files that contain the same symbol. Each movie stores its own copy of the common symbol. You can update the symbol to the source symbol whenever you want, or even make automatic updates before you publish a SWF file.

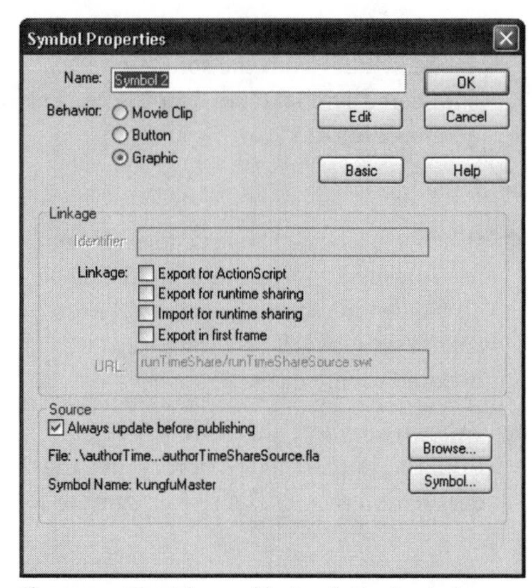

Figure 12.7 The Advanced button in the Symbol Properties dialog box displays more options for Linkage and Source.

To update a symbol with another from a different Flash file:

1. Select the symbol you wish to update in the Library window. From the Options pull-down menu, choose Properties.

   The Symbol Properties dialog box appears.

2. Click Advanced.

   The Symbol Properties dialog box expands to display more options (**Figure 12.7**).

3. In the Source section of the dialog box, click Browse. Select the Flash file that contains the symbol you wish to use to update your currently selected symbol. Click OK (Windows) or Open (Mac).

   The Select Source Symbol dialog box appears, showing a list of all the symbols in the selected Flash file's library.

4. Select a symbol and click OK (**Figure12.8**).

   The Select Source Symbol dialog box closes.

5. In the Symbol Properties dialog box that is still open, note the new source for your symbol (**Figure 12.9**). Click OK.

   The Symbol Properties dialog box closes and your symbol is updated with the symbol you just chose for its new source. Your symbol retains its name, but its content is updated to the source symbol.

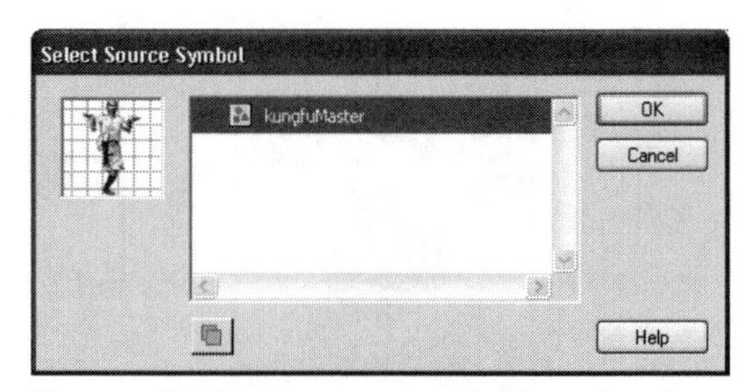

Figure 12.8 Select the source symbol for author-time sharing.

Figure 12.9 The Source area of the Symbol Properties dialog box displays the path to the author-time source symbol and the name of the source symbol.

To make automatic updates to a symbol:

- In the Symbol Properties dialog box, check the Always update before publishing box.

  Whenever you export a SWF from your Flash file, whether by publishing it or by using the Control > Test Movie command, Flash will locate the source symbol and update your symbol.

Runtime Sharing or Author-time Sharing?

Although they may seem similar, runtime and author-time sharing are two very different ways to work with symbols. Each approach is better suited for different types of projects. Runtime sharing is useful when multiple SWF movies can share common assets, decreasing symbol redundancy, file size, and download times. Publish a single SWF file holding all the common symbols that multiple SWF files can access. Author-time sharing, on the other hand, is useful for organizing your workflow before you publish your SWF movie. You can use author-time sharing to keep different symbols in separate FLA files. A "master" FLA file can reference all of the symbols in the separate files and compile them into a single SWF. Working this way, you can have different members of a Flash development team work on different symbols, and rely on author-time sharing to ensure that the final published movie will contain the updated symbols. Compare these two ways of sharing library symbols in **Figure 12.10**.

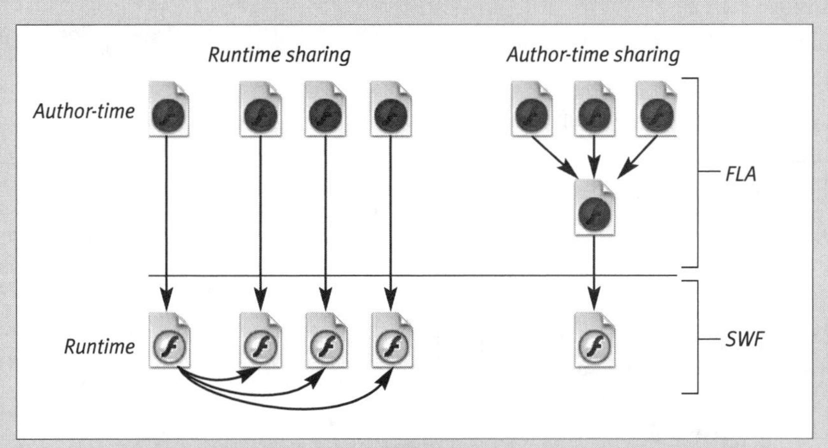

Figure 12.10 During runtime sharing (left), multiple SWF files can share symbols from a single common SWF file. During author-time sharing (right), multiple FLA files can provide updated symbols to a single FLA file that publishes a SWF file to play during runtime.

Sharing Fonts

Just as you can create symbols to share between movies, you can create symbol fonts and share them. After creating a font symbol, you identify it to be exported using the Linkage identifier, in a process identical to the one used to create runtime shared symbols. Use shared fonts to reduce the need to embed the same font outline for multiple movies. When multiple movies share a common font, the font only has to be downloaded once for the first movie, reducing file size and download times for the subsequent movies.

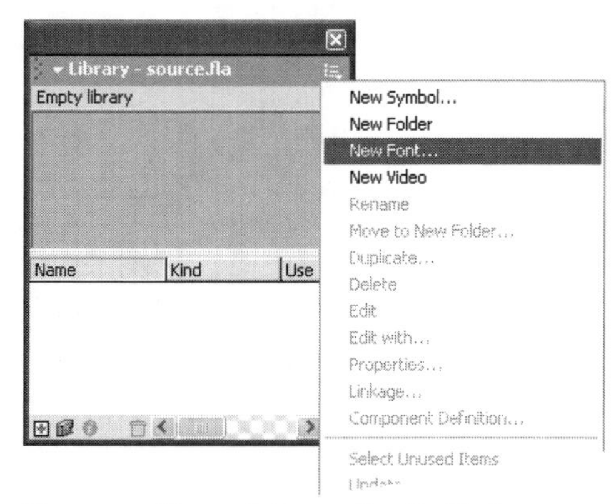

Figure 12.11 Choose Options > New Font in the Library window.

To create a font symbol to share:

1. Open the Library window. From the Options pull-down menu, choose New Font (**Figure 12.11**).

   The Font Symbol Properties dialog box appears.

2. Enter a name for your new font symbol in the Name field. From the Font pull-down menu, select the font you wish to include in your library as a font symbol. Check the optional boxes for Style. Click OK (**Figure 12.12**).

   The font symbol appears in your library.

3. Select your font symbol in the Library window. From the Options pull-down menu, choose Linkage.

   The Linkage Properties dialog box appears.

4. From the Linkage choices, select Export for runtime sharing. In the Identifier field, enter a unique name for your symbol. In the URL field, enter the path for the source movie that will share this font. Click OK (**Figure 12.13**).

   Your selected font symbol is now marked for export and available to be shared by other movies.

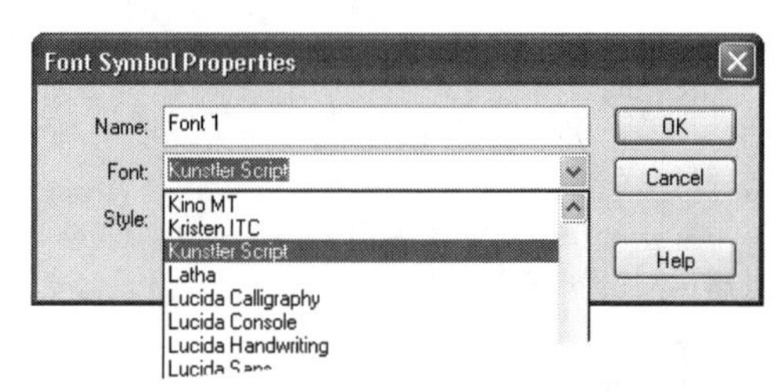

Figure 12.12 Create a font symbol by choosing a font and giving it a name in the Font Symbol Properties dialog box. Here the symbol called Font 1 is created for Kunstler Script.

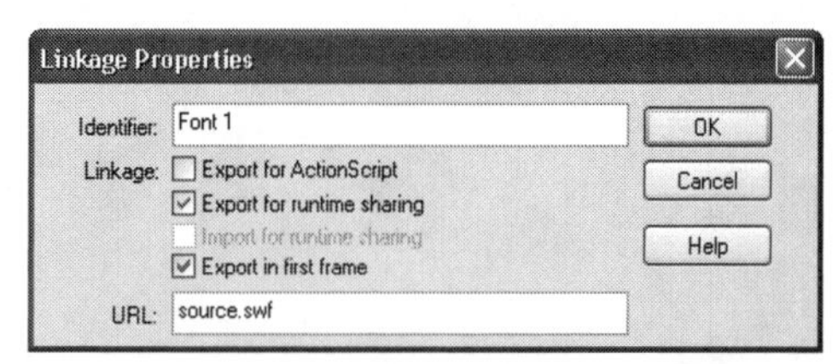

Figure 12.13 In the Linkage Properties dialog box, mark your symbol font for runtime sharing, give it an identifier, and specify its location relative to the destination file that will use the shared font. If the destination and source file will reside in the same directory, you can simply enter the name of the source file in the URL field, as is shown here.

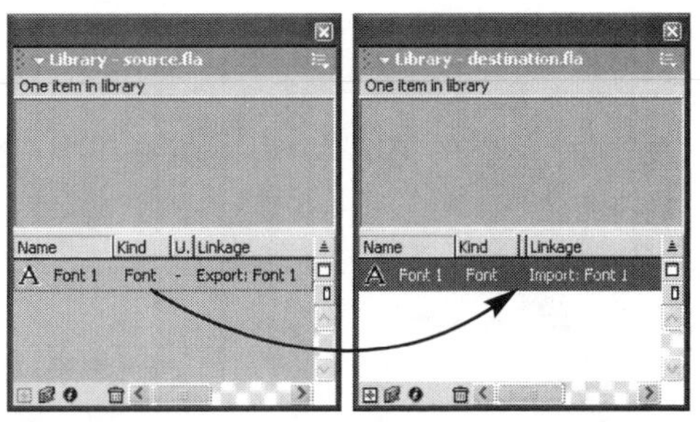

Figure 12.14 Drag the shared font symbol from the source library (left) to the destination library (right).

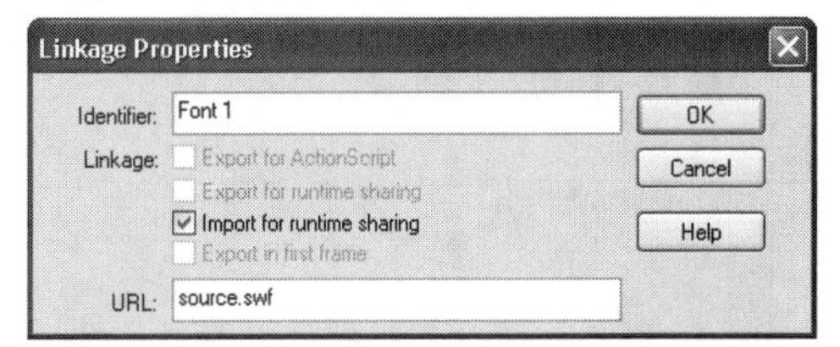

Figure 12.15 The Linkage Properties dialog box for the font symbol in the destination file. This font symbol will import the font called Font 1 from the file called source.swf.

5. Export your Flash movie as a SWF file.

   Your selected font symbol resides in the SWF file. This SWF file provides the shared font to other movies.

To use a shared font symbol:

1. Open a new Flash file (the destination file) where you want to use a shared font symbol.
2. Open the Flash file (the source file) that contains your shared font symbol. Drag the shared font symbol from its library to the library of the destination Flash file.

   The font symbol appears in the library of the destination Flash file. The font symbol is automatically marked as Import for runtime sharing (**Figure 12.14**).
3. In the destination Flash file, select the font symbol in the Library window. From the Options pull-down menu, choose Linkage.

   The Linkage Properties dialog box appears.
4. Confirm that the Import for runtime sharing is checked, the Identifier field contains the name of the shared font symbol in the source movie, and the URL field contains the path to the source movie (**Figure 12.15**). Click OK.

   Your font symbol in the destination movie is now set to share the font symbol in the source movie.

continues on next page

5. Select the text tool in the Tools window. In the Property Inspector, choose the shared font symbol from the pull-down list of available fonts (**Figure 12.16**). Create input text or dynamic text, and be sure to embed all the font outlines in the Character Options.

6. Publish the destination SWF file and the source SWF file.

   The source SWF shares its font with the destination SWF. The destination SWF displays the shared font correctly and with anti-aliasing, but its file size remains small (**Figure12.17**).

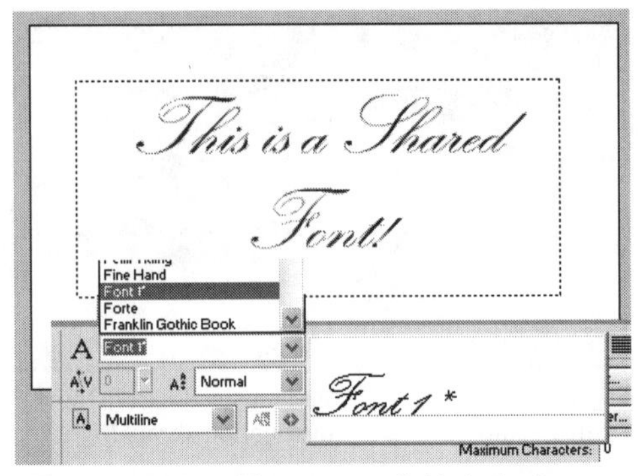

Figure 12.16 Shared fonts are available in the Property Inspector and are distinguished by an asterisk after their names.

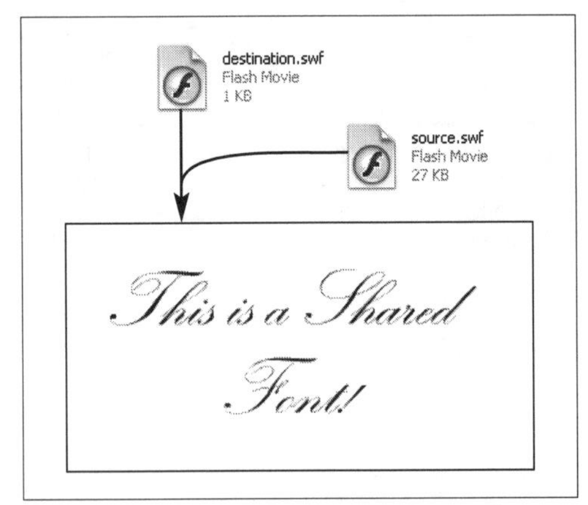

Figure 12.17 The destination.swf file displays the shared font correctly because the font is supplied by the source.swf file. Notice the difference in file size between destination.swf (1 KB) and source.swf (27 KB).

Using Components

There are times when you'll create an interface element, like a scroll bar or a check box, which you'll want to use in multiple projects, but in slightly varying ways. For one movie, you may want your scroll bar to move text vertically, but for another movie, you may want it to move text horizontally. Or you may want to hand off your scroll bar to a designer or animator for their own use, but you want to provide them with easy guidelines so they can customize the scroll bar without recoding any of your ActionScript. How do you develop this modular piece of interactivity that can be easily customized, even by non-ActionScript coders? The solution is to use components. Components are specialized movie clips that have been programmed by one developer to be used by other developers who can easily modify some of the movie clip's functionality. Components are sometimes described as "parameterized" movie clips because you pass parameters to customize the way they look and do their job.

If this sounds very general, it's because components are meant to tackle any sort of task—not just scroll bars, check boxes, and other user-interface elements, but data handling, graphics behaviors, sound manipulation, and many other kinds of interactivity as well. Components are like templates. They provide the general functionality as well as the parameters to help you make them fit your particular needs.

Flash UI Components

Flash provides a set of components of common user interface elements, located in the Components panel (Window > Components). They are the CheckBox, ListBox, RadioButton, ScrollPane, ComboBox, PushButton, and ScrollBar (**Figure 12.18**). Each of these components comes with its own parameters that you define in the Property Inspector. For example, the ComboBox, which works like a pull-down menu, lets you define the number of menu items, their labels, the data to pass when one of the choices is selected, and even an event handler.

continues on next page

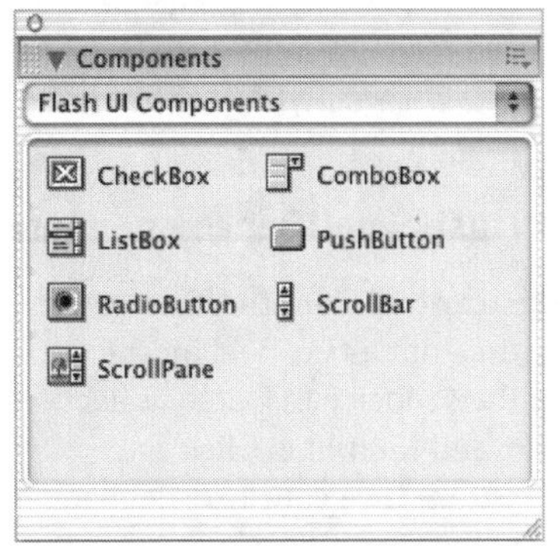

Figure 12.18 The Components panel shows the user-interface components Flash provides to quickly and easily add interactivity to your movie.

You can use the Flash UI components to varying degrees, depending on how much you want to modify them and how willing you are to dig into the custom methods and properties that each component provides. For example, you can change their appearance by editing the graphics within the component movie clips, or by calling the custom method `setStyleProperty()`. Consult the ActionScript dictionary (Help > ActionScript Dictionary) to learn more about each component's unique methods and properties. (They are listed as FCheckBox, FListBox, FRadioButton, FScrollPane, FComboBox, FPushButton, and FScrollBar).

If you don't need anything more than the standard functionality and basic design that the Flash UI components give, they are a great resource to use. Look for more exciting components from Macromedia and from third-party developers. In the following example, you'll use the ScrollBar component to quickly create a scroll bar for an input text field.

To use the Flash ScrollBar component:

1. Select the text tool from the Tools window and drag out a text field on the Stage. In the Property Inspector, select Input Text and Multiline. Click the Borders button. Give your text field an instance name.
2. Choose Window > Components (Ctrl-F7 for Windows, Command-F7 for Mac).

   The Components panel opens and displays the user-interface components that Flash provides.

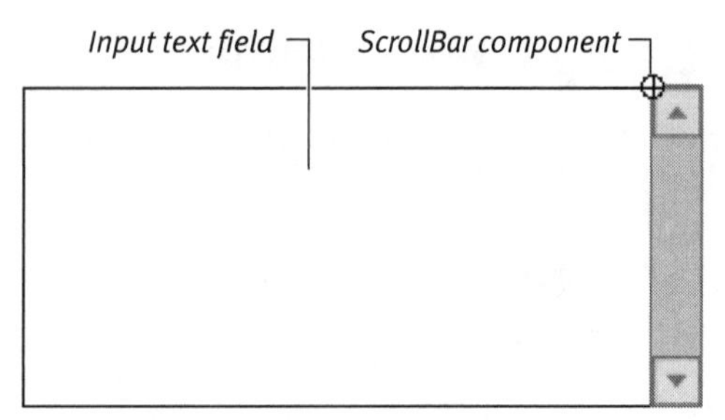

Figure 12.19 The ScrollBar component automatically snaps to the input text field.

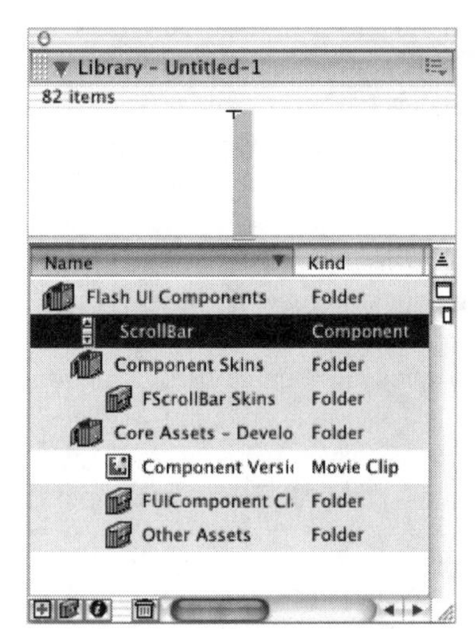

Figure 12.20 When you add a component to your Flash movie, all the necessary symbols are added to the library. The Component Skins folder contains the graphics that define the appearance of your component. The Core Assets folder contains the code that defines its functionality.

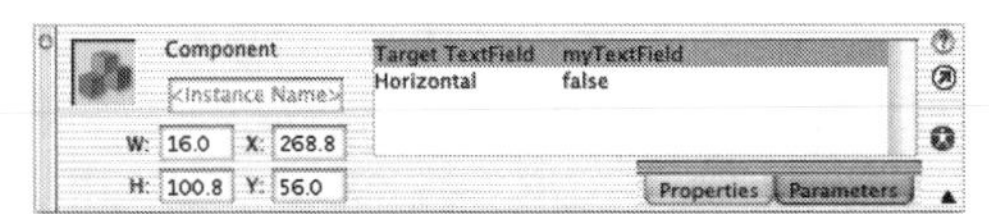

Figure 12.21 The Property Inspector displays the parameters for the ScrollBar component. You can change the parameters to modify its functionality. This ScrollBar will affect the vertical scrolling of the text field called myTextField.

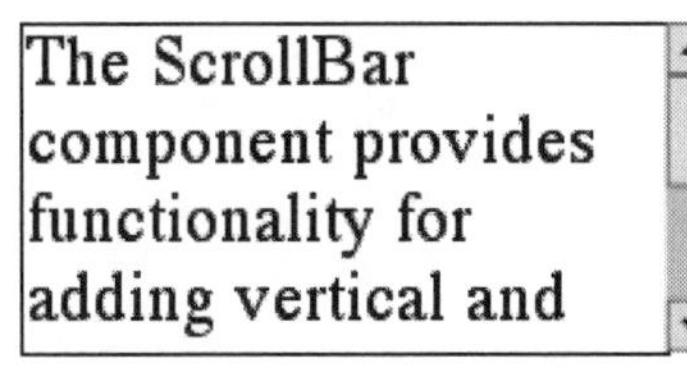

Figure 12.22 The ScrollBar component controls the scrolling of a text field.

3. Select the ScrollBar component, drag it to the Stage, and release it inside the input text field near the right-hand edge.

   The scroll bar component is automatically resized to fit the text field and snaps to its edge (**Figure 12.19**). All the necessary symbols for the component, including the graphics and ActionScript code, are imported into the library (**Figure 12.20**).

4. Select the scroll bar component. Click the Parameters tab of the Property Inspector to see the parameters for the scroll bar.

   The parameters for the scroll bar have been automatically set. The Target TextField parameter is set to the name of your text field and the Horizontal parameter is set to false (**Figure 12.21**). You can click the parameter values to change either the text field target or the scroll bar alignment.

5. Test your movie.

   Enter text into your input text field. As the text exceeds the boundaries of the text field, the contents begin to scroll. The scroll bar automatically updates to reflect the amount of text and its position within the text field. Use the scroll bar to scroll vertically through the text field contents (**Figure 12.22**).

Editing ActionScript

When the code in the Script pane of the Actions panel becomes long and complex, you can check, edit, and manage it using the Options pull-down menu of the Actions panel. In addition to the choices for Normal and Expert mode, the menu options include searching and replacing words, importing and exporting scripts, and printing your scripts, as well as different ways to display your script (**Figure 12.23**).

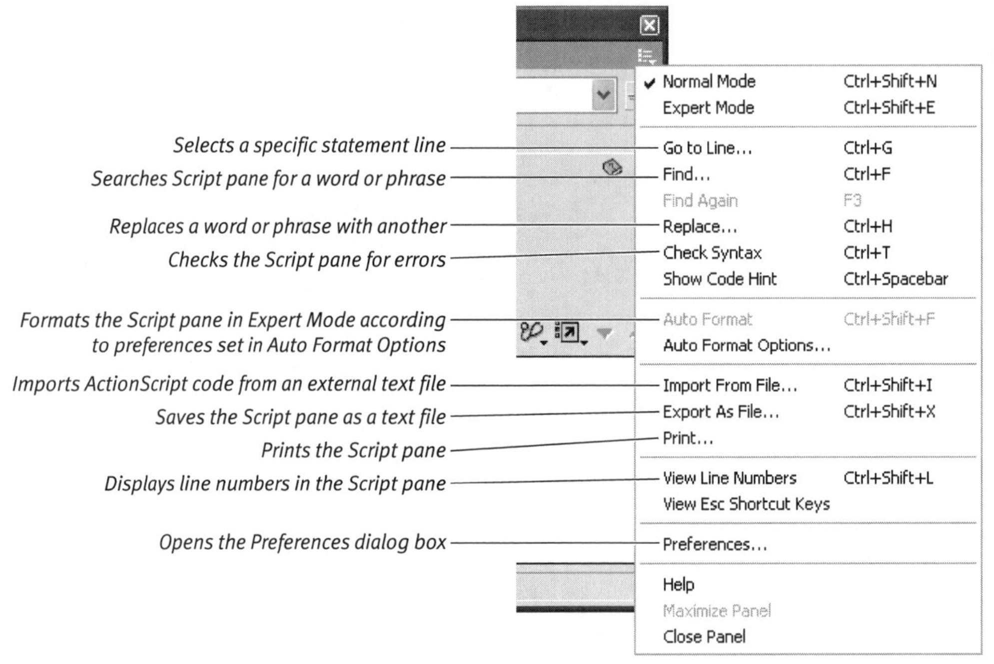

Figure 12.23 The Options pull-down menu of the Actions panel contains editing functions for the Script pane.

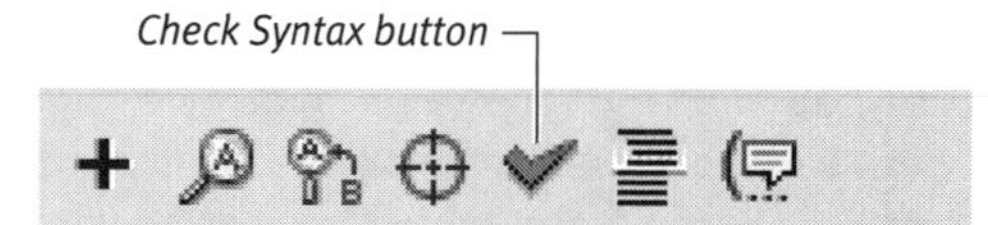

Figure 12.24 The Check Syntax button is the checkmark icon above the Script pane (available in Expert mode).

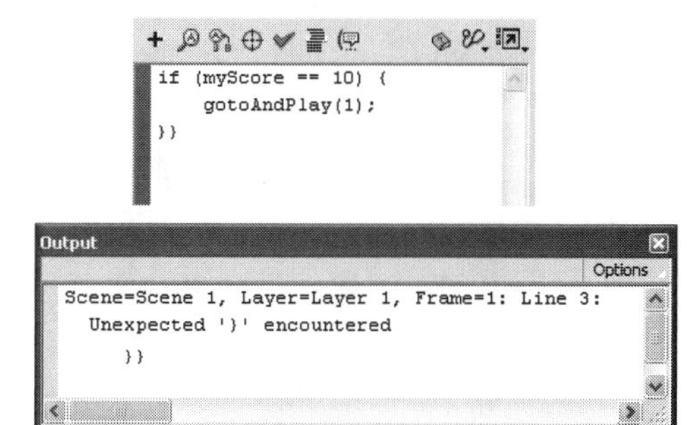

Figure 12.25 The Script pane (above) contains an extra closing curly brace. Flash notifies you of the nature and location of the error in the Output window (below).

To check the syntax in the Script pane:

- In the Actions panel, choose Check Syntax from the Options pull-down menu (Command-T for Mac, Ctrl-T for Windows). In Expert mode, you can also click on the Check Syntax button above the Script pane (**Figure 12.24**).

  Flash checks the script in the Actions List for errors in syntax. If it finds an error, it displays a warning dialog box and reports any errors in an Output window (**Figure 12.25**). Use the information provided in the Output window to locate the error and correct the syntax.

✔ Tip

- Check Syntax reports just the errors in the current Script pane, not for the entire movie.

Use the Find and Replace functions in the Actions panel to quickly change variable names, properties, or even actions. For example, if you created a lengthy script involving the variable redTeamStatus, but change your mind and want to change the variable name, you can replace all instances of redTeamStatus with blueTeamStatus. You could find all the occurrences of the property _x and replace them with _y, or you could find all the occurrences of the action `gotoAndStop` and replace them with `gotoAndPlay`.

To find and replace ActionScript terms in the Script pane:

1. In the Actions panel, choose Replace from the Options pull-down menu (Command-H for Mac, Ctrl-H for Windows).

   The Replace dialog box appears.

2. In the Find what field, enter a word or words that you want Flash to find. In the Replace field, enter a word or words that you want the found words to be replaced with. Check the Match case box to make Flash recognize upper- and lowercase letters (**Figure 12.26**).

3. Click Replace to replace the first instance of the found word, or click Replace All to replace all instances of the found word.

✓ Tips

- The Replace dialog box replaces all the occurrences of a particular word or phrase only in the current Script pane of the Actions panel. In order to replace every occurrence of a certain word in the whole movie, you need to go to each script and repeat this process.
- The Actions panel must be in Expert mode to search for and replace actions.

The Import From File, Export As File, and Print functions of the Actions panel let you work with external text editors or print the contents of the Script pane.

To import an ActionScript:

- Select Import From File from the Options pull-down menu (Command-Shift-I for Mac, Ctrl-Shift-I for Windows). From the dialog box that appears, choose the text file that contains the ActionScript you wish to import. Click Open.

  Flash replaces the contents of the current Script pane with the ActionScript contained in the text file.

To export an ActionScript:

- Select Export As File from the Options pull-down menu (Command-Shift-X for Mac, Ctrl-Shift-X for Windows). Enter a destination filename. Click Save.

  Flash saves a text file that contains the entire contents of the current Script pane. The recommended extension for external ActionScript files is *.as*, as in myCode.as.

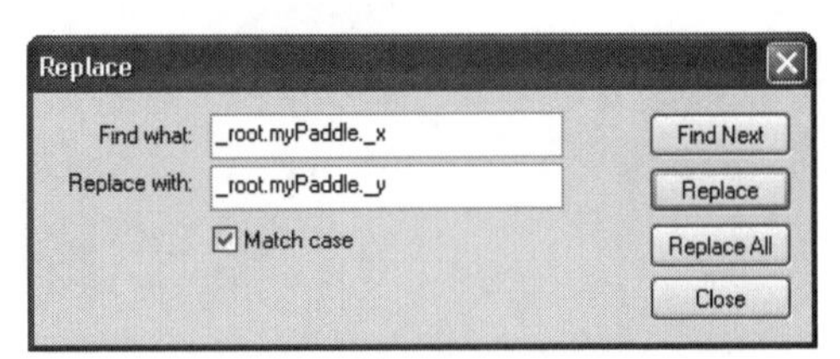

Figure 12.26 Every occurrence of `_root.myPaddle._x` will be replaced with `_root.myPaddle._y`.

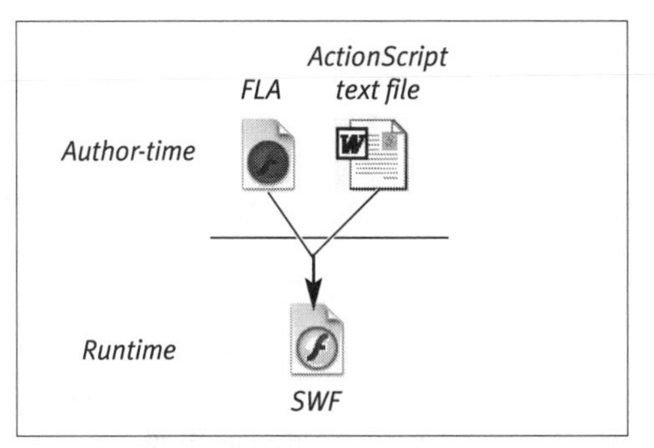

Figure 12.27 The `#include` action integrates ActionScript from an external text file when the FLA exports a SWF. The `#include` action does *not* work at runtime.

```
startDrag(ball, true);
```

Figure 12.28 This is the ActionScript in a text file saved as myCode.as.

Including External ActionScript

You can create external ActionScript files to share common code among multiple movies. Create the ActionScript code that appears many times in different movies, and keep that code in a text file outside the Flash movies. If you need to change the code, you only need to change it in one place.

External code can be incorporated into a Flash movie with the action `#include`. This action pulls in an external text file containing ActionScript and includes it in the existing script in the Script pane.

It's important to point out that the `#include` action to share external ActionScript code is performed when the SWF is published, and not dynamically during runtime. You must re-export your Flash movie in order for Flash to include the most current ActionScript. This means that the `#include` action, although useful, is limited to authoring mode like author-time shared symbols (**Figure 12.27**).

In the following task, the `#include` action is assigned to the first frame of the main Timeline. A text document contains ActionScript. When you export the SWF file, the code in the external text document is incorporated into the script.

To include external ActionScript with the #include action:

1. Open a text-editing application, such as SimpleText for Mac or Notepad for Windows.
2. Write your ActionScript code, and save it as a text document. Do not include any quotation marks around your script. Use the extension *.as* to identify it as an ActionScript file (**Figure 12.28**).

continues on next page

3. Open a new document in Flash. Create a movie-clip symbol, and place an instance of it on the Stage. In the Property Inspector, give it a name. In this example, call it *ball*.
4. Select the first frame of the main Timeline and open the Actions panel.
5. Choose Actions > Miscellaneous Actions > #include (Esc + in).
6. In the Path field, enter the name of your text file that contains ActionScript. Do not include quotation marks, as they are included automatically in the Script pane (**Figure 12.29**).
7. Save your FLA file in the same directory as your ActionScript text file.
8. Export a SWF from your FLA file.

   Flash integrates the code from the text document. If you change the code in the text file, you must re-export the SWF so that Flash can include the latest changes.

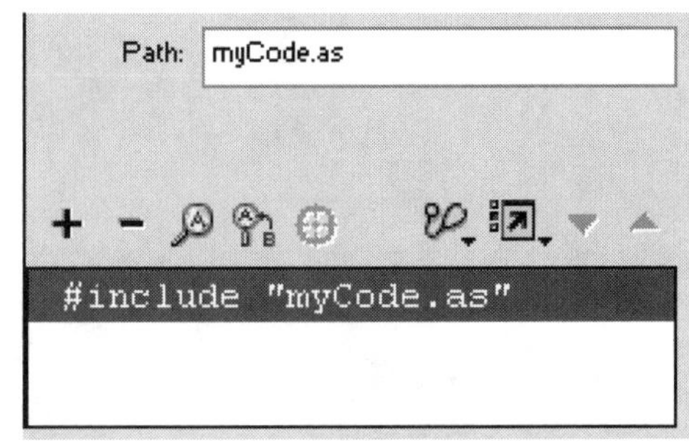

Figure 12.29 When this movie is published, the external text file called myCode.as is included in this Script pane.

✔ Tip

- If you are using the Actions panel in Expert mode to write out your ActionScript manually, do not include a semicolon at the end of a `#include` statement. Although semicolons usually separate ActionScript statements, the `#include` statement is an exception.

Using the Movie Explorer

In order to get a bird's-eye view of your whole Flash movie, you can use the Movie Explorer panel (Option-F3 for Mac, Alt-F3 for Windows). The Movie Explorer is a powerful tool for tracking all the elements of your movie, and it will take you directly to a particular ActionScript, graphic, or frame you want to modify. The Movie Explorer panel can selectively represent the graphical components of a movie and provide information about frames and layers, as well as show ActionScripts assigned to buttons, movie clips, and keyframes. The display list is organized hierarchically, letting you see the relationships between various elements (**Figure 12.30**).

The Movie Explorer even updates itself in real time, so as you're authoring a Flash movie, the panel displays the latest modifications. Use the Movie Explorer to find particular elements in your movie. For example, if you want to find all the instances of a movie clip, you can search for them and have Flash display the exact scene, layer, and frame where each instance resides. You can then quickly go to those spots on the Timeline to edit the instances. You can also edit various elements within the Movie Explorer panel itself, such as the names of symbols or the contents of a text selection. The customized display and quick navigation capabilities of the Movie Explorer make it much easier to find your way around a complex movie.

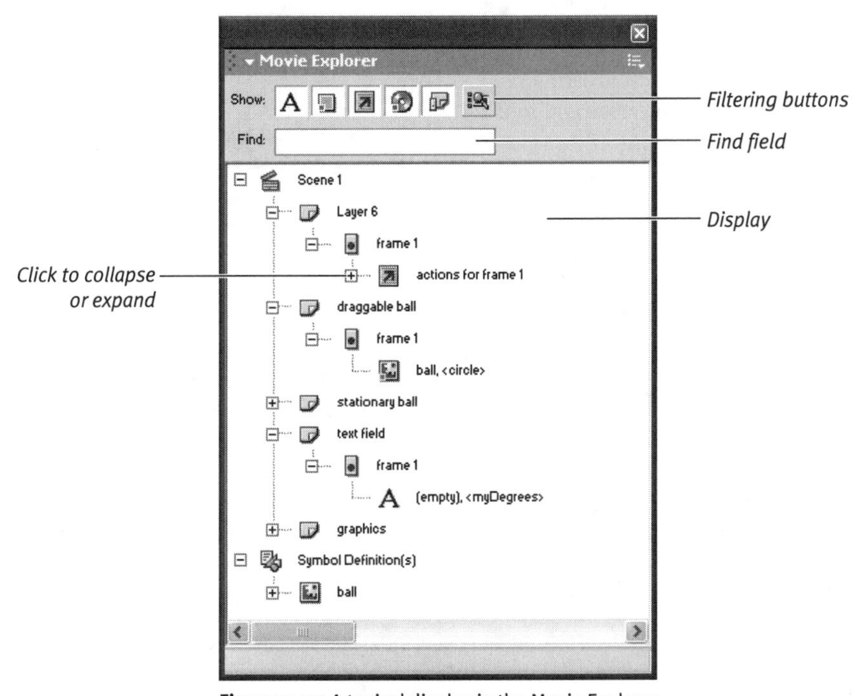

Figure 12.30 A typical display in the Movie Explorer shows various elements of the movie in an expandable hierarchy.

To display different categories of elements:

From the Options pull-down menu at the right of the Movie Explorer panel, select one or more of the following (**Figure 12.31**):

- Show Movie Elements displays all the elements in your movie and organizes them by scene. Only the current scene is displayed.
- Show Symbol Definitions displays all the elements associated with symbol instances that are on the Stage.
- Show All Scenes displays all the elements in your movie in all scenes.

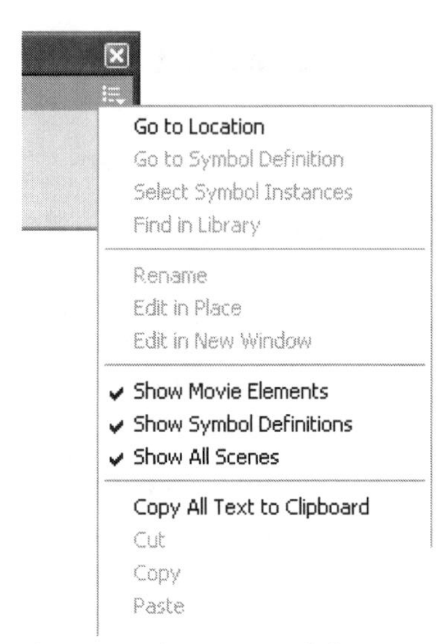

Figure 12.31 The Options pull-down menu of the Movie Explorer panel.

To filter the categories of elements that are displayed:

From the row of filtering buttons at the top of the panel, select one or more to add categories of elements to display (**Figure 12.32**).

- Show Text displays the actual string in a text selection, the font name and font size, and the instance name and variable name for input and dynamic text.
- Show Buttons, Movie Clips, and Graphics displays the symbol names of buttons, movie clips, and graphics on the Stage, as well as the instance names of movie clips and buttons.
- Show ActionScripts displays the actions assigned to buttons, movie clips, and frames.
- Show Video, Sounds, and Bitmaps displays the symbol names of imported video, sounds, and bitmaps on the Stage.
- Show Frames and Layers displays the names of layers, keyframes, and frame labels in the movie.
- Customize which Items to Show displays a dialog box from which you can choose individual elements to display.

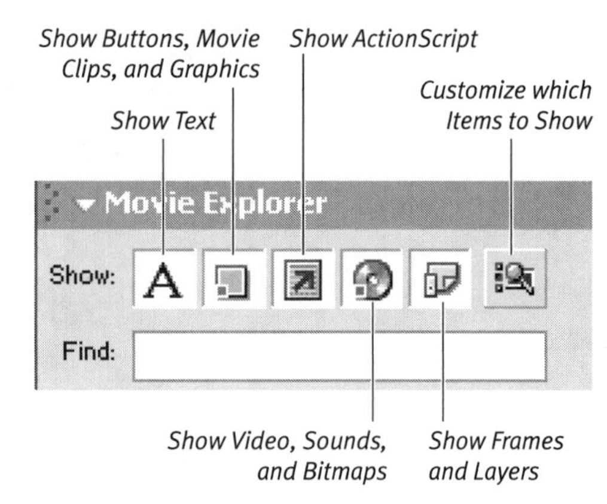

Figure 12.32 The filtering buttons let you selectively display elements.

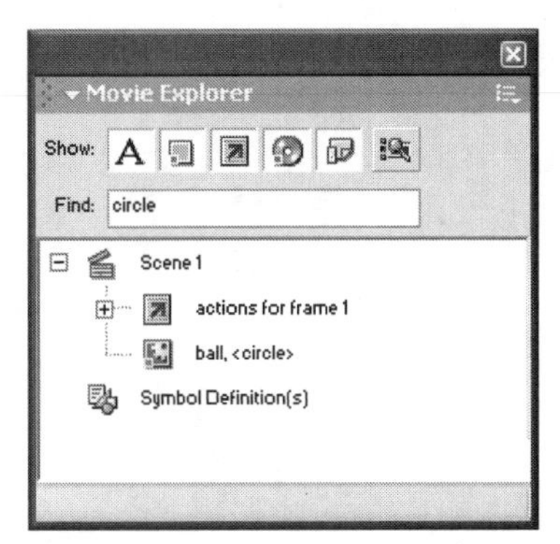

Figure 12.33 Entering a phrase in the Find field displays all occurrences of that phrase in the Display window. Here, the instance named *circle* of the movie-clip symbol called *ball* has been found.

To find and edit elements in the display:

1. Enter the name of the element you wish to find in the Find field at the top of the Movie Explorer panel (**Figure 12.33**).

   All the elements of the movie that contain that name appear in the display list automatically as you type in the field.

2. Click the desired element to select it.

   The element will also be selected on the Timeline and on the Stage. If a scene or keyframe is selected, Flash takes you to that scene or keyframe.

3. From the Options pull-down menu of the Movie Explorer panel, choose Edit in Place or Edit in New Window to go to symbol-editing mode for a selected symbol.

   or

   Choose Rename from the Options pull-down menu.

   The name of the element becomes selectable so that you can edit it.

   or

   Double-click the desired element to modify it. Flash makes the element editable or opens an appropriate window, depending on what type of element it is.

   Double-clicking a symbol (except for sound, video, and bitmaps) opens symbol-editing mode.

   Double-clicking ActionScript opens the Actions panel.

   Double-clicking a scene or layer lets you rename it.

   Double-clicking a text selection lets you edit its contents.

To replace all occurrences of a particular font:

1. In the Find field of the Movie Explorer panel, enter the name of the font you wish to replace.

   All occurrences of that font appear in the display (**Figure 12.34**).

2. Select all the text elements, using Shift-click to make multiple selections.

3. In the Property Inspector, choose a different font and style for all text elements.

   All the selected text elements change according to your choices in the Property Inspector (**Figure 12.35**).

To find all instances of a movie-clip symbol:

- In the Find field of the Movie Explorer panel, enter the name of the movie-clip symbol whose instances you want to find.

  All instances of that movie-clip symbol appear in the display (**Figure 12.36**).

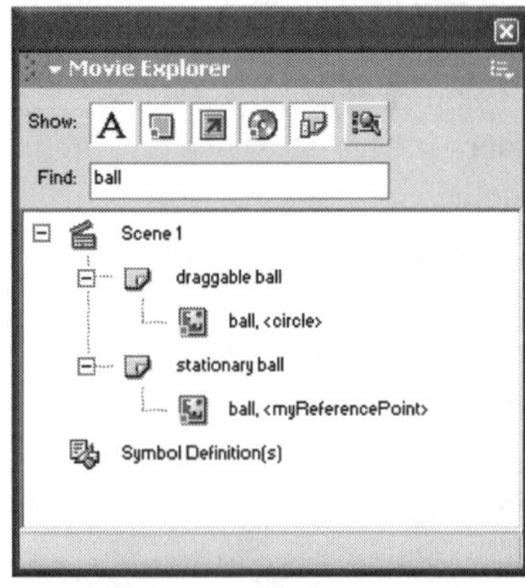

Figure 12.36 Entering the symbol name *ball* in the Find field displays all the instances of the ball symbol. There are two instances listed: one called *circle* in the layer called draggable ball, and another called *myReferencePoint* in the layer called stationary ball.

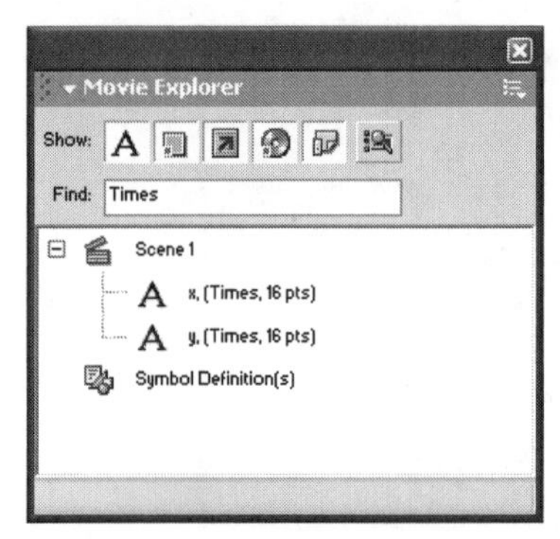

Figure 12.34 All the occurrences of the Times font appear in the Display window.

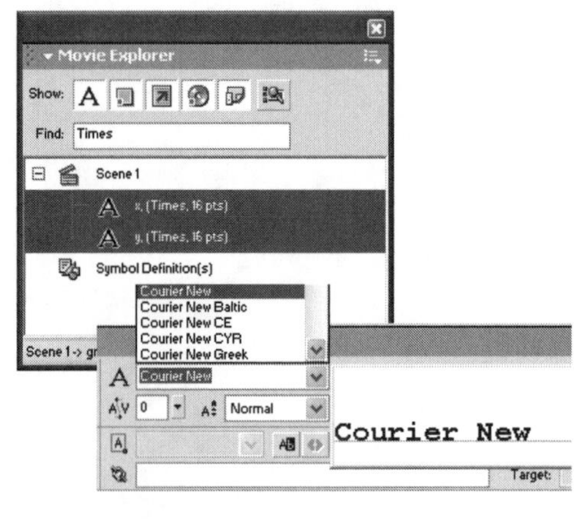

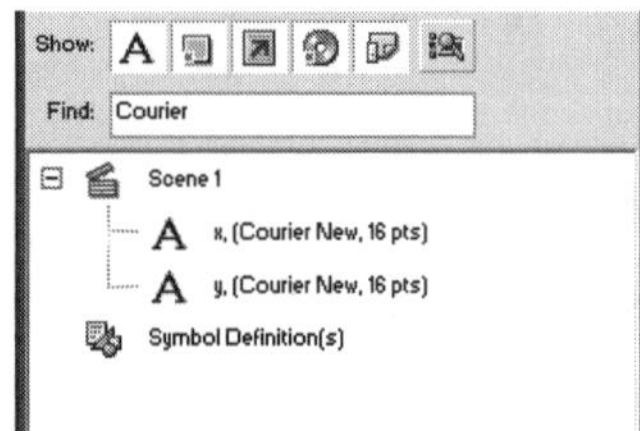

Figure 12.35 With the Times text elements selected, choose a different font, such as Courier New (top) from the Property Inspector. Flash changes those text elements from Times to Courier New (bottom).

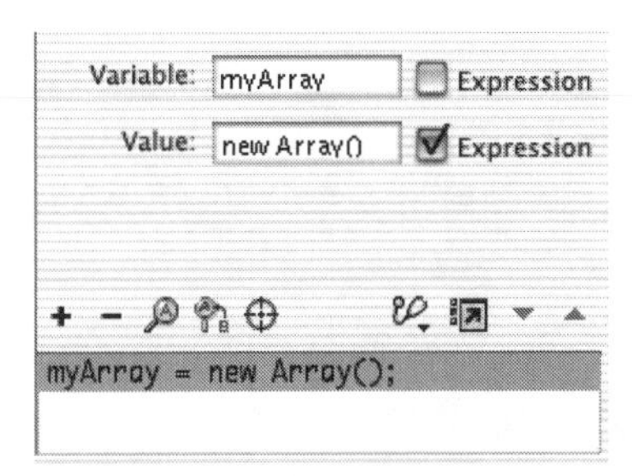

Figure 12.37 The object myArray is created from the new Array constructor function.

Listing Variables and Objects in the Output Window

While the Movie Explorer represents many of a movie's graphic elements and ActionScript, it doesn't display variables or object target paths. For this you use the Output window. Often, while your movie is playing, you will want to know the values of your variables and the target paths of movie clips to determine whether Flash is handling the information correctly. This is especially important when your movie is very complicated, perhaps involving many parameters passing between functions or having dynamically allocated variables. For example, say you want to initialize and populate an array object in the first frame of the Timeline. After assigning the ActionScript to the frame that does the job, you can test your movie, but you won't really know if Flash has correctly populated the array because there's nothing visual on the Stage. In order to see if the array is indeed filled up with the correct values, you can list the variables in the Output window in testing mode. The List Variables command displays all the variables in a movie with their scopes and values.

In the following task, you first create a simple array object, and then assign values to it using a looping statement. In testing mode, you list the movie's variables in the Output window to see the array's final values.

To list variables in the Output window:

1. Select the first frame of the main Timeline, and open the Actions panel.
2. Instantiate a new array object called myArray, as described in Chapter 11 (**Figure 12.37**).

continues on next page

3. Choose Actions > Conditions/Loops > for. In the Init field, enter `i=0`. In the Condition field, enter `i<5`. In the Next field, enter `i++` (**Figure 12.38**).
4. Choose Actions > Variables > set variable. In the Variable field, enter `myArray[i]`. In the Value field, enter `i*5`. Check the Expression box next to the Value field.

   Each time the `for` statement loops, the value of i increases by 1. Flash assigns each entry in the myArray array the value of its index multiplied by 5. This loop populates the myArray array (**Figure 12.39**).
5. Test your movie (Control > Test Movie). In testing mode, from the top menu, choose Debug > List Variables (Command-Option-V for Mac, Ctrl-Alt-V for Windows).

   The Output window opens, displaying all the variables in the movie. The first variable listed is `$version`, which contains information about the version of the Flash player and the system platform. The second variable is the myArray object. Flash lists its location (_level0.myArray), its data type (object of the Array class), and all of its values in each index (0, 5, 10, 15, 20). The third variable is the counter variable, called `i`, that was used in the `for` looping statement (**Figure 12.40**).

✔ Tip

- The List Variables command displays all the variables in a movie at the instant you choose the command from the menu. If the variables change as the movie plays, you need to choose List Variables again in order to see the latest values. For real-time display of variables, use the Debugger panel, described later in this chapter.

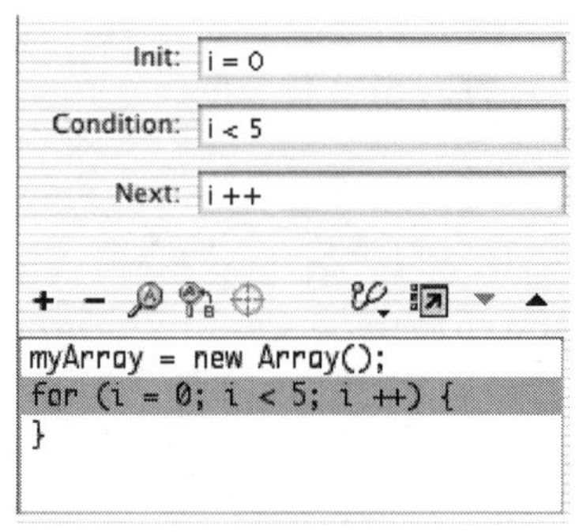

Figure 12.38 Create a loop that begins with i=0 and increases by 1 until it reaches 4.

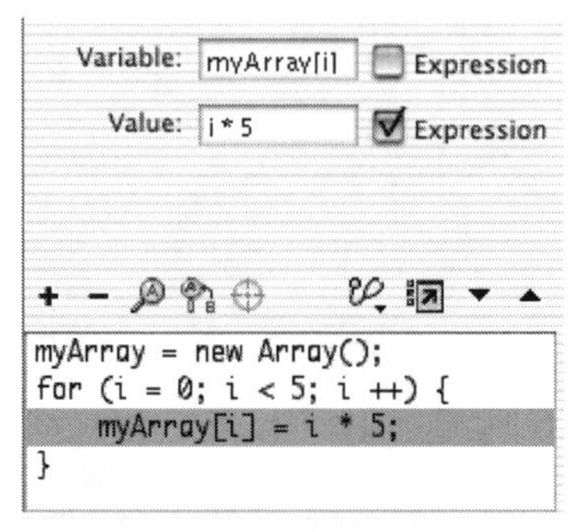

Figure 12.39 The object myArray is automatically filled with the values determined by the looping statement.

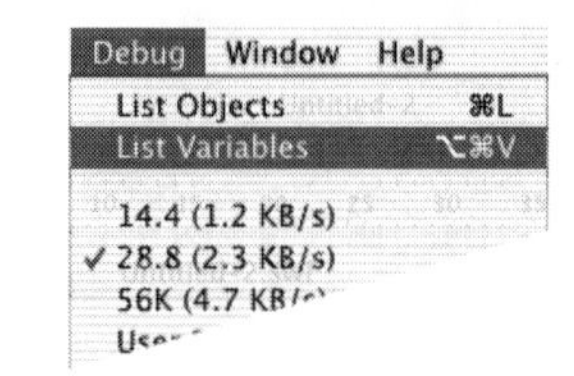

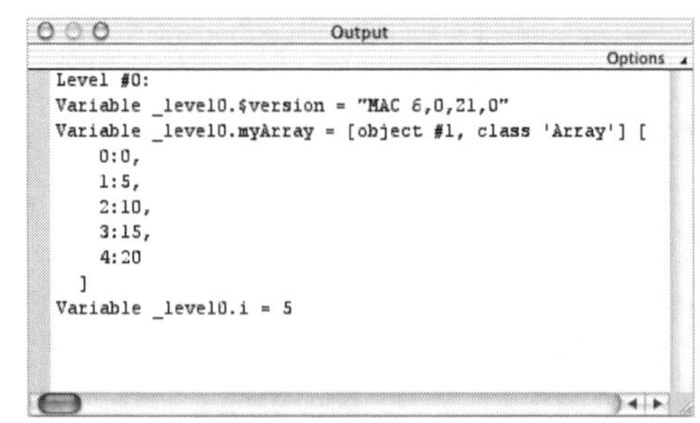

Figure 12.40 Choose Debug > List Variables in testing mode to see all the current variables. The myArray object and its values are listed, verifying the results of the looping statement.

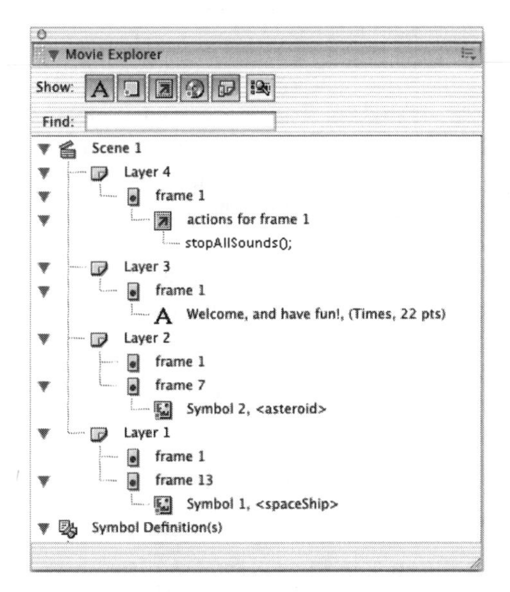

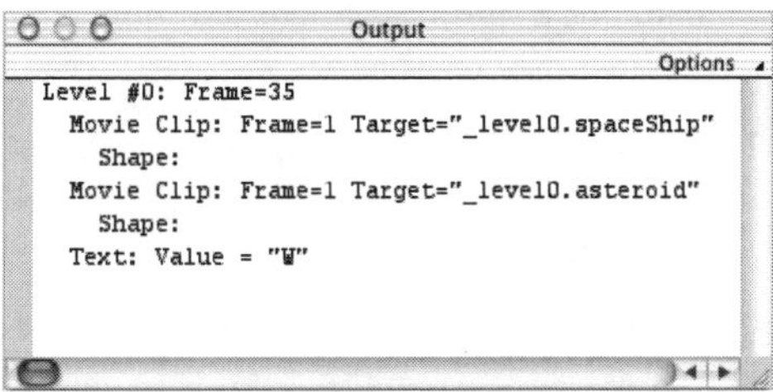

Figure 12.41 The same movie is displayed in the Movie Explorer (top) and the Output window (bottom). The Movie Explorer visually displays the hierarchy of objects. The Output window lists the target path of objects and other graphic elements. Note that the Output window only shows the first letter of a static text field.

Figure 12.42 Choose Debug > List Objects in testing mode.

You can also use the Output window to display a list of the objects in the movie. While the Output window's display is not as graphically appealing as the display in the Movie Explorer, it gives you information about objects that you can't get from the Movie Explorer. The object information listed in the Output window includes the object's level, type of symbol (Movie Clip, Button, Edit Text), or type of graphic (Text, Shape), and the absolute target path of the objects. The target path of objects is the most important bit of information the Output window can tell you directly, although the Movie Explorer can give that to you indirectly. A comparison of the typical information display for the same movie in the Movie Explorer and in the Output window is in **Figure 12.41**.

To list objects in the Output window:

- In testing mode, choose Debug > List Objects (Command-L for Mac, Ctrl-L for Windows) (**Figure 12.42**).

  All the objects in the current state of the movie are displayed in the Output window.

✔ Tip

- As in the command List Variables, the command List Objects only displays the movie's current status. If a movie clip disappears from the Timeline as the movie plays, you need to select List Objects again to update the display of objects in the Output window.

Tracing Variables in the Output Window

Sometimes you'll want to know the status of a variable or expression at a particular point during the playback of your movie. For example, imagine that you've created a game of Pong in which a movie clip of a ball bounces between two other movie clips of paddles. You want to find out, for testing purposes, the position of the paddle at the instant of a collision with the ball. The command List Variables would be very little help because of the rapidly changing variables for the paddle positions. The solution is to use the action `trace`. You can place the action `trace` at any point in the movie to have Flash send a custom message to the Output window during testing mode. The custom message is an expression you create that gives you tailored information at just the right moment. In the Pong example, you could write a trace statement that would look something like:

```
trace ("paddle X-position is " +
myPaddle._x);
trace ("paddle Y-position is " +
myPaddle._y);
```

Place these two trace statements in the `if` statement that detects the collision. At the moment of collision, Flash will send a message to the Output window, and it would look something like:

```
paddle X-position is 25
paddle Y-position is 89
```

You can also use `trace` to monitor the condition of an expression so you can understand the circumstances that change its value. For example, in the following task, you'll create a simple draggable movie clip and another movie clip that remains stationary. You'll assign a `trace` action to display the value of the draggable movie clip's `hitTest()` method, letting you see when and where the value becomes true or false.

To display an expression in the Output window:

1. Create a movie-clip symbol, place an instance of it on the Stage, and name the instance *myMovieClip*.
2. Create another movie-clip symbol, place an instance of it on the Stage, and name the instance *rock*.
3. Select the first frame of the main Timeline and open the Actions panel.
4. Choose Objects > Movie > Movie Clip > Events > onEnterFrame. In the Object field, enter `_root`.
5. Choose Actions > Movie Clip Control > startDrag. Enter `myMovieClip` in the Target field, and check the Expression box. Check the Lock mouse to center box (**Figure 12.43**).
6. Choose Actions > Miscellaneous Actions > trace (Esc + tr).

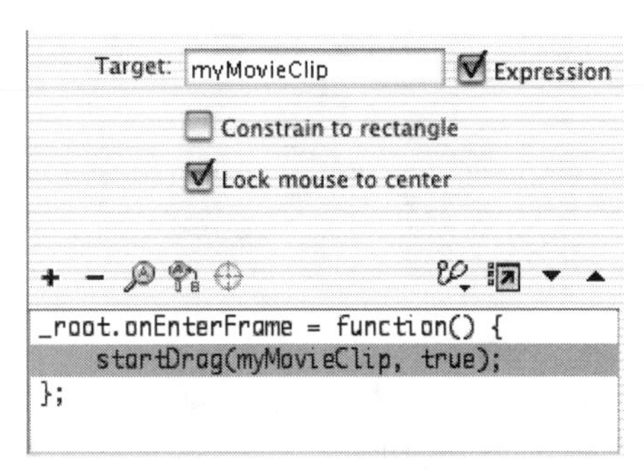

Figure 12.43 The `startDrag` action will make the movie clip called myMovieClip follow the pointer.

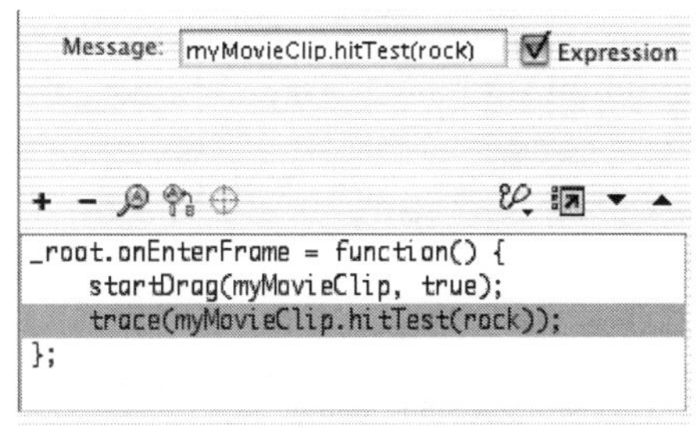

Figure 12.44 The `trace` action evaluates the expression in the Message field and displays the value in the Output window.

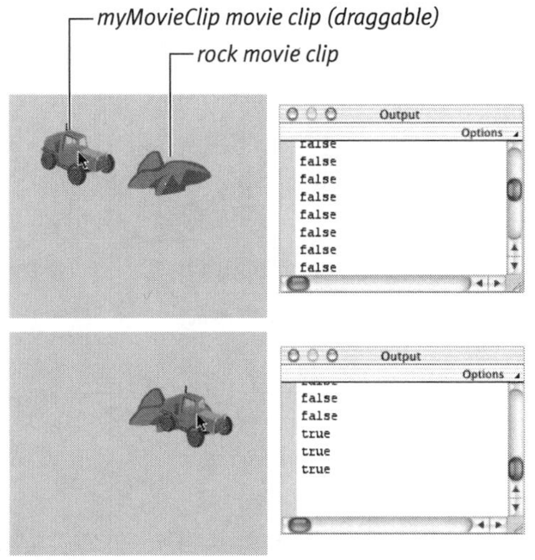

Figure 12.45 The Output window displays false when myMovieClip is clear of the rock movie clip (top). The Output window displays true when there is a collision (bottom).

7. In the Message field, enter the expression:

   `myMovieClip.hitTest(rock)`

   Check the Expression box (**Figure 12.44**).

   Flash evaluates the `hitTest()` method to see if the draggable movie clip collides with the movie clip called rock. The returned value is displayed in the Output window in testing mode.

8. Test your movie.

   The Output window opens, displaying the result of the `trace` action (**Figure 12.45**).

The typeof operator can be used in conjunction with the trace action in order to display the data type of a certain variable. This information is very useful when you begin to encounter problems with unexpected values in your variables. If you suspect that the problem stems from using a variable in ways that are incompatible with its data type, placing a trace action to display the data type will confirm or disprove your suspicions.

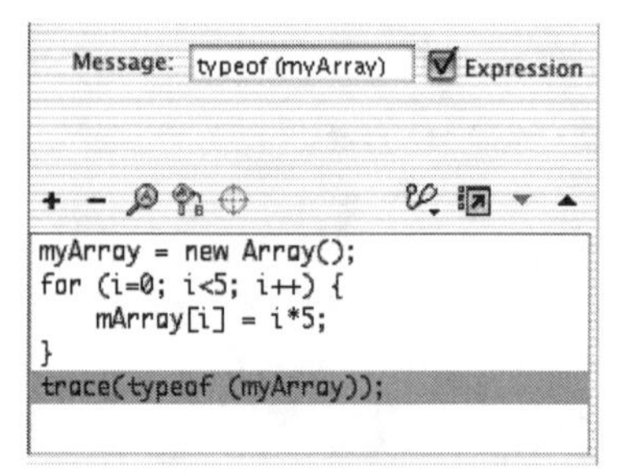

Figure 12.46 The data type of myArray will be evaluated and displayed in the Output window.

To determine the data type of a variable:

1. Continue with the file you created in the previous section, "Listing Variables and Objects in the Output Window." This is the file in which you created an array and populated the array with a looping statement. Select the first frame, and open the Actions panel.
2. Select the ending curly brace of the last statement in the Script pane.
3. Choose Actions > Miscellaneous Actions > trace.
4. In the Message field, choose Operators > Miscellaneous Operators > typeof.
   The typeof operator appears in the Message field.
5. Between the parentheses of the typeof operator, enter the word myArray. Check the Expression box (**Figure 12.46**).
   Flash evaluates myArray and displays its data type in the Output window in testing mode.
6. Add two more trace actions with the typeof operator (**Figure 12.47**).
7. Test your movie. Flash displays the results of the three trace statements in the Output window in testing mode. The first trace displays the data type of myArray as an object. The second trace displays myArray[3] as a number, and the third trace displays myArray.toString() as a string (**Figure 12.48**).

```
myArray = new Array();
for (i=0; i<5; i++) {
 myArray[i] = i*5;
}
trace (typeof (myArray));
trace (typeof (myArray[3]));
trace (typeof (myArray.toString()));
```

Figure 12.47 Add trace actions to evaluate and display the data type of index 3 of myArray and the method toString() of myArray.

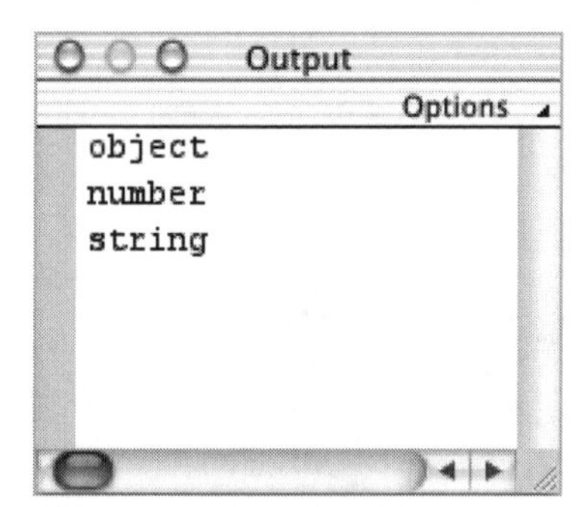

Figure 12.48 The results of the trace action in the Output window.

Debugging

The Debugger panel lets you monitor and modify the values of all the variables and properties in your movie as it plays. You can also examine the values of objects that hold data, such as instances of the Date or Sound objects. Use the Debugger to verify that Flash is manipulating the information in variables the way you want it to, and to test certain conditions or the effects of certain variables quickly. For example, imagine that you created an animation with the variable myVelocity controlling the speed of a spaceship. In the Debugger panel, you can modify the variable myVelocity as the movie plays, to see how it affects the motion of your spaceship. Increase or decrease the value of myVelocity until you are satisfied with the results.

The Debugger panel opens and is active in testing mode when you select Control > Debug Movie. Once open and active, the Debugger displays information in several separate parts: a Display list at the top left, Properties, Variables, and Watch lists below it, a Call stack window at the bottom left, and a Code view on the right (**Figure 12.49**). The Display list shows the root Timeline and the hierarchy of movie clips in that Timeline. You can select the root Timeline or the other movie clips to see the properties belonging to that particular Timeline or to see all the variables within that particular scope. The Code view lets you define breakpoints in your ActionScript so that you can step through the movie line by line to determine where and when some piece of interactivity in your movie is going awry. The call stack at the bottom left displays the names of your function calls as you step through the code.

continues on next page

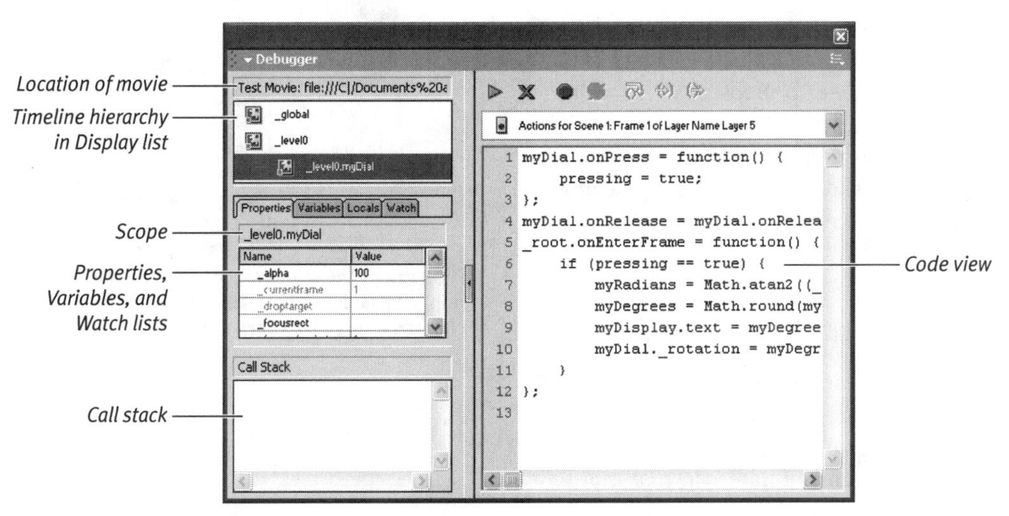

Figure 12.49 The Debugger panel displays a hierarchy of Timelines and their properties and variables on the left side. ActionScript can be displayed on the right side for you to step through the code line by line.

Use the Control menu to rewind, play, and step forward or backward through your movie, frame by frame, as necessary, to scrutinize the movie's properties and variables (**Figure 12.50**).

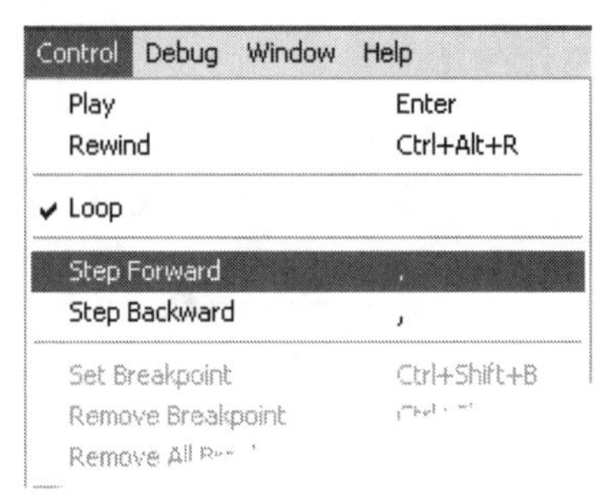

Figure 12.50 Use the Control menu to control the playback of your movie in testing mode.

To access the debugger:

- From the Flash authoring environment, choose Control > Debug Movie (Command-Shift-Return for Mac, Ctrl-Shift-Enter for Windows).

  Flash exports a SWF and enters testing mode. The Debugger panel opens and is activated.

To modify a property or a variable in the Debugger panel:

1. In the Display list of the Debugger panel, select the movie clip whose properties or variables you wish to modify.
2. Click the Properties or the Variables tab.
3. Double-click the field in the Value column next to the property or variable you wish to modify.
4. Enter a new value.

   The new value must be a constant (a string, number, or Boolean value) rather than an expression that refers to another variable or property. For example, it must be 35 instead of `35 + myAlpha`. The movie reflects the new value immediately (**Figure 12.51**).

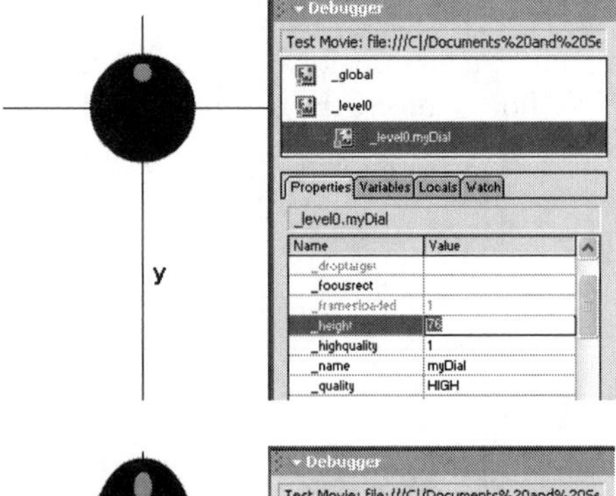

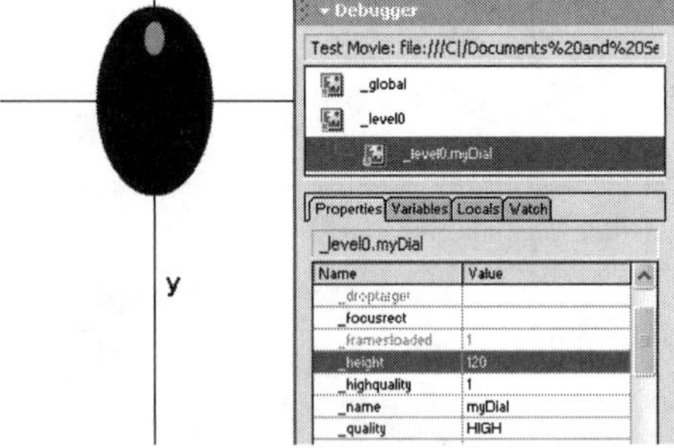

Figure 12.51 The values of properties can be selected (top) and modified (bottom); your movie will reflect changes even while it plays.

✔ Tip

- Certain properties are read-only and are grayed out, indicating that they cannot be modified. For example, the property `_totalframes` is a fixed value determined by the number of frames in your movie.

Figure 12.52 The selected variable (myRadians) is added to the Watch list using the pull-down menu.

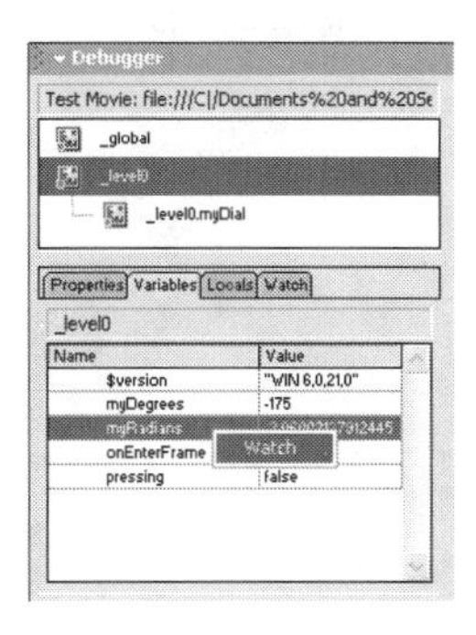

Figure 12.53 The selected variable (myRadians) is added to the Watch list using the display menu.

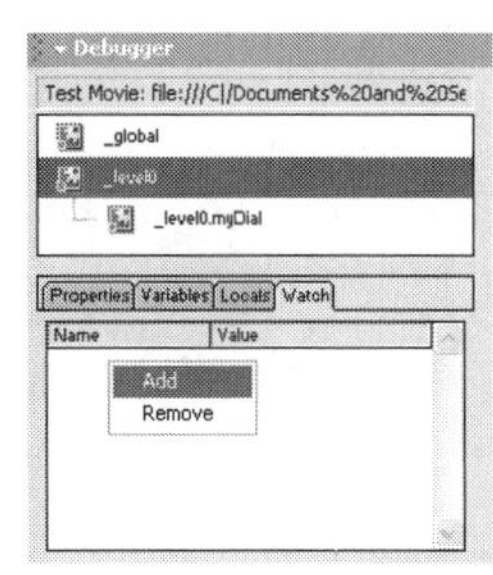

Figure 12.54 Choose Add from the display menu on the Watch list to enter a variable by hand.

The Variables tab in the Debugger panel lets you watch only the variables within the same scope. If you want to watch variables belonging to different scopes, you can use the Watch tab to choose the variables you would like to observe. This lets you create a set of critical variables that are culled in one place for you to watch and modify. The variables in your Watch list are displayed with their absolute target paths in slash syntax.

To add variables to the Watch list:

1. In the Debugger panel, select the root Timeline or a movie clip from the Display list.
2. Select the variable from the Variables tab. From the Options pull-down menu at the top-right corner of the Debugger panel, choose Add Watch (**Figure 12.52**).

   A blue dot appears next to the variable, marking it to be displayed on the Watch list.

   or

   Select the variable from the Variables tab. Control-click (Mac) or right-click (Windows) the variable. Choose Watch from the display menu that appears (**Figure 12.53**).

   A blue dot appears next to the variable, marking it to be displayed on the Watch list.

   or

   From the Watch tab, Control-click (Mac) or right-click (Windows) in the empty list. Choose Add from the display menu that appears (**Figure 12.54**). Enter the absolute target path of the variable in slash syntax.

To remove variables from the Watch list:

- In the Watch list, Control-click (Mac) or right-click (Windows) the variable, and choose Remove from the display menu that appears.
- In the Variables list, Control-click (Mac) or right-click (Windows) the variable, and choose the check-marked Watch.
- In the Variables or Watch list, select the variable and then choose Remove Watch from the Options pull-down menu at the top-right corner of the Debugger panel.

Breakpoints and Stepping through Code

Breakpoints are places in a particular script where you tell Flash to pause so you can more easily inspect the condition of variables and properties and the status of your movie. You can have multiple breakpoints, and you can set them either in the Debugger panel or in the Actions panel.

Once set, you can step through the code, line by line if you need to. Various options let you play through the code or skip function statements as desired.

To set breakpoints in your code:

1. In the active Debugger panel, choose a script from the script pull-down menu.

   ActionScript appears in the Code view on the right-hand side of the Debugger panel.
2. Select a line of code where you want to set a breakpoint. Click the Toggle Breakpoint button or Control-click (Mac) or right-click (Windows) the line of code and select Set Breakpoint.

   Flash adds a red stop sign next to the line number (**Figure 12.55**). When the movie plays in the Debugger, it will stop when it reaches the breakpoint so you can inspect the state of the movie and its variables and properties.

   or

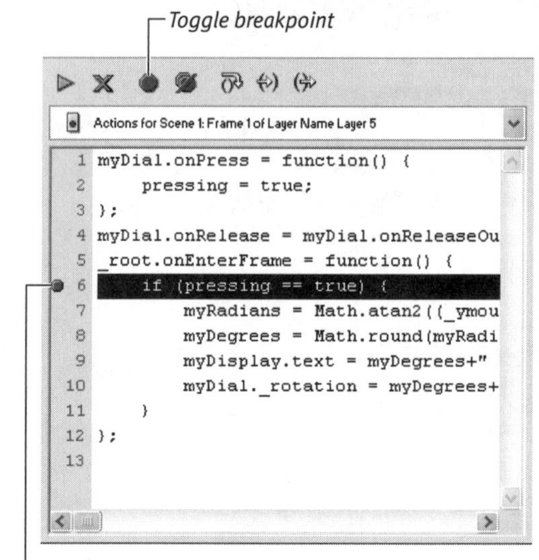

Figure 12.55 A breakpoint is set at line 6 of this ActionScript.

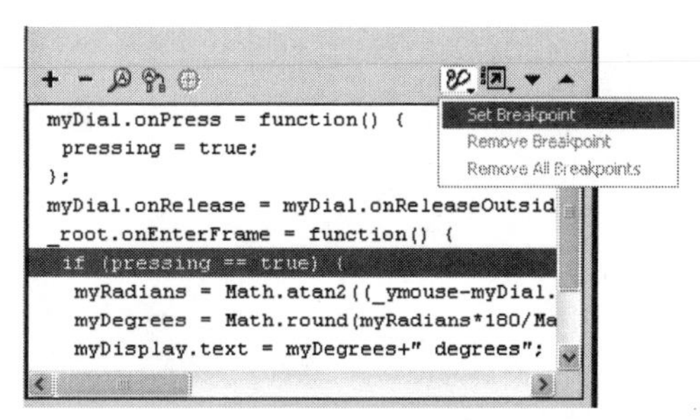

Figure 12.56 In the Actions panel, add a breakpoint from the Debug Options pull-down menu. The breakpoints you set in the Actions panel will be saved in the FLA file.

1. While not in Debug mode, open the Actions panel.
2. Select a line of code where you want to set a breakpoint. Click the Debug Options button above the Script pane and select Set Breakpoint from the pull-down menu (**Figure 12.56**).

   Flash adds a red stop sign next to the line number. When you debug the movie (Control > Debug Movie), the breakpoints will appear in the Debugger panel.

To remove a breakpoint:

- In the Debugger panel, select the breakpoint. Click the Toggle Breakpoint button, or Control-click (Mac) or right-click (Windows) the line of code and select Remove Breakpoint.

  The breakpoint is removed.

  or

- In the Actions panel, select the breakpoint. Click the Debug Options button above the Script pane and select Remove Breakpoint from the pull-down menu, or Control-click (Mac) or right-click (Windows) the line of code and select Remove Breakpoint.

  The breakpoint is removed.

To remove all breakpoints:

- In the Debugger panel, click the Remove All Breakpoints button, or Control-click (Mac) or right-click (Windows) and select Remove All Breakpoints.

  All breakpoint are removed.

  or

- In the Actions panel, click the Debug Options button above the Script pane and select Remove All Breakpoints from the pull-down menu, or Control-click (Mac) or right-click (Windows) and select Remove All Breakpoints.

  All breakpoints are removed.

To step through code:

- Click the Continue button to advance the Debugger through ActionScript code until the next breakpoint is encountered (**Figure 12.57**).

  A yellow arrow marks the line of code where the Debugger is paused.

- Click the Step Over button to skip over a function that you have defined. The debugger continues to the next line after the function call (**Figure 12.58**).

  Although the Debugger steps over a function, the statements inside the function are still performed.

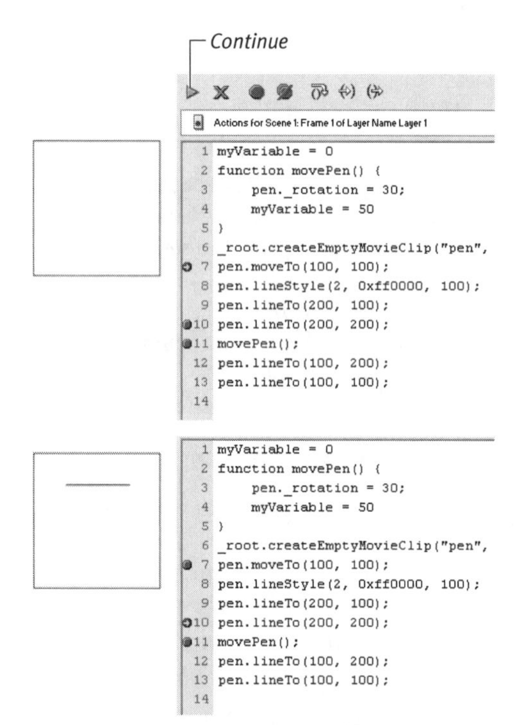

Figure 12.57 The yellow arrow marks the current line where the Debugger is paused. At top, the Debugger is paused at line 7 and the Stage is empty. When you click the Continue button, the Debugger proceeds to the next breakpoint and pauses at line 10 (bottom). The horizontal line segment from (100,100) to (200,100) is drawn. The code at line 10 is not yet performed.

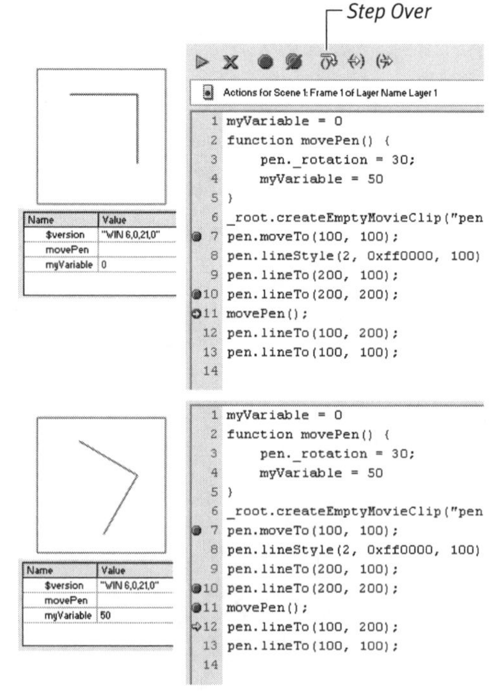

Figure 12.58 At top, the Debugger is paused at line 11 and the Stage shows two line segments. When you click the Step Over button, the Debugger steps over the function called movePen and stops at the first statement after the function call at line 12 (bottom). The statements inside the function are still performed, as you can see by the rotation and the new value for myVariable.

- Click the Step In button to perform the statements inside a function (**Figure 12.59**).
- Click the Step Out button to break out of a function. The debugger continues to the next line after the function call (**Figure 12.60**).

  Although the Debugger steps out of a function, the rest of the statements inside the function are still performed.

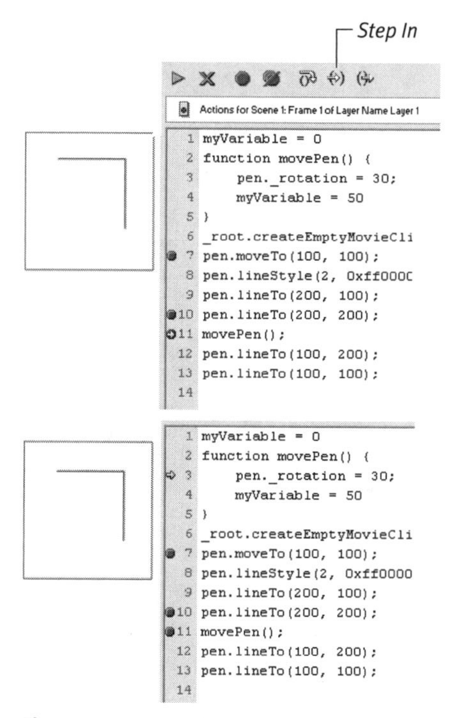

Figure 12.59 At top, the Debugger is paused at line 11 and the Stage shows two line segments. When you click the Step In button, the Debugger proceeds to the next line inside the function called movePen (bottom).

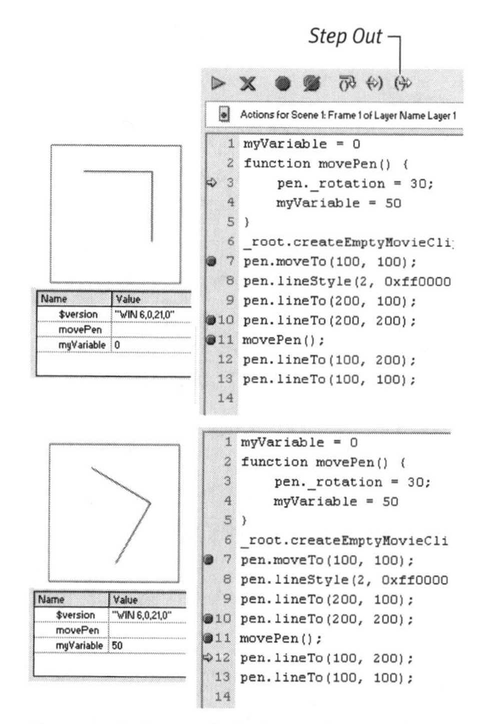

Figure 12.60 At top, the Debugger is paused at line 3 and the Stage shows two line segments. When you click the Step Out button, the Debugger steps out of the function called movePen and stops at the first statement after the function call at line 12 (bottom). The statements inside the function are still performed, as you can see by the rotation and the new value for myVariable.

Remote Debugging

You can also access the Debugger panel of a SWF movie remotely (outside Testing mode). This lets you watch variables and properties and check interactivity when your movie is in a "real-life" setting, such as when it's uploaded to a Web site.

To enable remote debugging, you must select the Debugging Permitted option in the Flash tab of the Publish Settings dialog box. When you publish your movie, a SWD file is also exported. This file contains debugging information that allows you to set breakpoints and step through your code. Keep both the SWF and SWD files together in the same directory and upload them to your Web site. You'll now be able to debug your movie remotely.

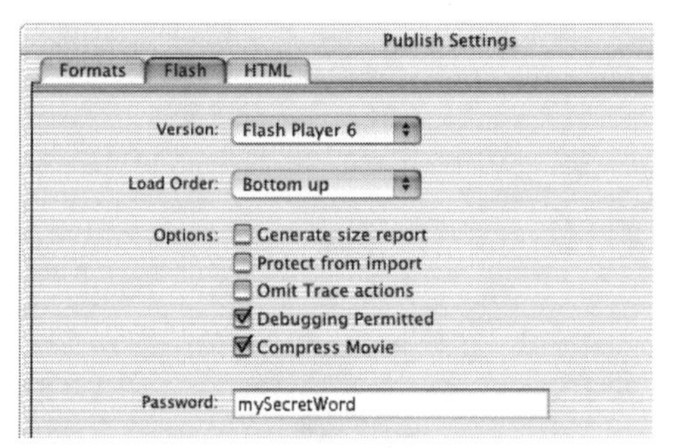

Figure 12.61 To enable remote debugging, check the Debugging Permitted option in the Flash tab of the Publish Settings dialog box. The password mySecretWord will give you access to the debugger.

To debug remotely:

1. Open the Flash file you want to debug. Choose File > Publish Settings.
2. Click the Flash tab. In the list of options, check the Debugging Permitted box. If you wish to protect your movie by limiting debugging access, enter a password in the Password field (**Figure12.61**).
3. Publish your Flash movie.

   Flash exports an HTML, SWF, and a SWD file. Although the SWD file is not required for remote debugging, it is required to set breakpoints and step through code.
4. Keep all three files together and upload them to your Web site, or place them in a desired directory locally on your hard drive.
5. In Flash, choose Window > Debugger.

   The Debugger panel opens.
6. In the Options pull-down menu, choose Enable Remote Debugging (**Figure12.62**).

Figure 12.62 Choose Options > Enable Remote Debugging in the Debugger panel.

Figure 12.63 When remote debugging has been enabled and the SWD file is in the same directory as the SWF file, the Remote Debug dialog box appears, letting you access the Debugger for the remote movie. If you selected a password in the Publish Settings dialog box when you published your movie, enter it in the second dialog box that appears (bottom).

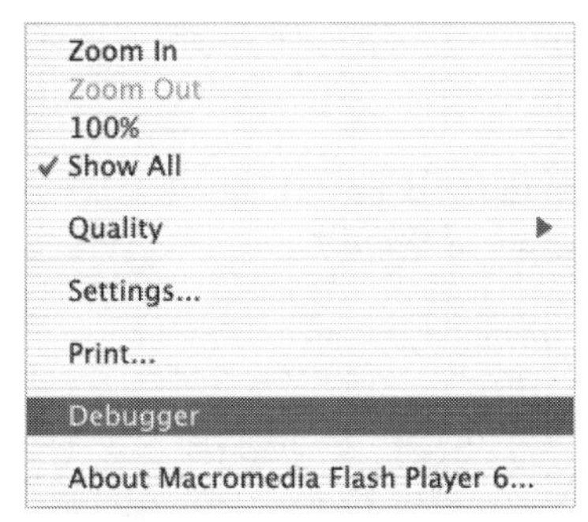

Figure 12.64 You can access the Debugger from the contextual display menu.

7. From your browser or from the Flash stand-alone player, open the SWF file that you've kept either on your computer or uploaded on the Internet.

   The Remote Debug dialog box appears requesting information on where the Flash application is running.

8. Select Local Host, since Flash and the Debugger are on the same (local) computer. Click OK. Enter your password if you had entered one in the Publish Settings (**Figure 12.63**).

   The movie opens in Flash with the Debugger panel active where you can debug the movie.

✔ Tip

- If you don't get the Remote Debug dialog box, or if you've closed the Debugger panel, you can open it by right-clicking (Windows) or Control-clicking (Mac) inside the movie. In the menu that appears, choose Debugger (**Figure 12.64**).

Optimizing Your Movie

Understanding the tools you use to create graphics, animation, sound, and ActionScript is important, but it's equally important to know how best to use them to create streamlined Flash movies. After all, the best-laid designs and animations won't be appreciated if poor construction and clunky code make them too large to download or too inefficient to play easily. To streamline a Flash movie, you use optimizations that keep the file size small, the animations smooth, and the revisions simple. Many different factors affect the file size and performance of the final exported SWF. Bitmaps, sounds, complicated shapes, color gradients, alpha transparencies, and embedded fonts all increase the Flash file size and slow down the movie's performance. Only you can weigh the tradeoffs between the quality and quantity of Flash content, and the size and performance of the movie. Keep in mind the audience to whom you're delivering your Flash movies. Does your audience have Internet connections with T1 lines, or does your audience rely on 28.8 modems? Knowing the answer to this question helps you make more informed choices about what to include in your movie and how to build it.

The following strategies can help you work more efficiently and help you create smaller, more manageable, better performing Flash movies.

To optimize your authoring environment:

- Use layers to separate and organize your content. For example, place all your actions on one layer, all your frame labels on another layer, and all your sounds in still another layer. By using layers, you'll be able to understand and change different elements of your movie quickly (**Figure 12.65**). Having many layers does not increase the size of the final exported SWF file. Use comments in keyframes as well, to explain the different parts of the Timeline.
- Use dynamic text fields in addition to the Output window and Debugger panel to observe variables in your movie. Dynamic text fields let you display expressions and variables in the context of your movie.
- Avoid using scenes in your movie. Although scenes are a good organizational feature for simple movies, Timelines that contain scenes are more difficult to navigate from movie clips. Also, movie-clip instances are not continuous between scenes. Use labels to mark different areas of the Timeline instead.

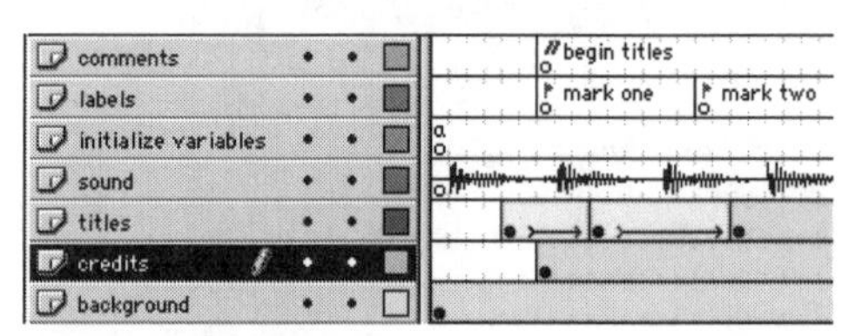

Figure 12.65 Well-organized layers like these are easy to understand and change.

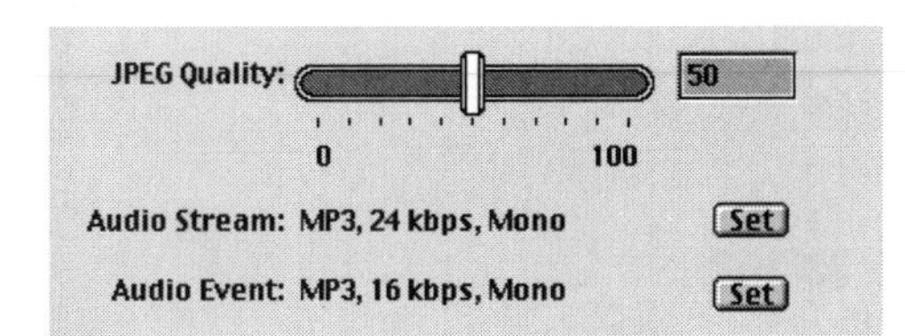

Figure 12.66 The JPEG quality and audio-compression options in the Publish Settings dialog box.

To optimize bitmaps and sounds for playback performance:

- Avoid animating large bitmaps. Keep bitmaps as static background elements if they are large, or make them small for tweening.
- Place streaming sounds on the root Timeline instead of within a movie clip. A movie clip needs to be downloaded in its entirety before playing. A streaming sound on the root Timeline, however, will begin playing as the frames download.
- Use the maximum amount of compression tolerable for bitmaps and sounds. You can adjust the JPEG quality level for your exported SWF file in Publish Settings. You can also adjust the compression settings for the stream sync and event sync sounds separately, so you can keep a higher-quality streaming sound for music and narration, and a lower-quality event sound for button clicks (**Figure 12.66**).
- Avoid using the Trace Bitmap command to create an overly complex vector image of an imported bitmap. The complexity of a traced bitmap can make the file size larger and the performance significantly slower than if you use the bitmap itself.
- Import bitmaps and sounds at the exact size or length that you want to use them in Flash. Although editing within Flash is possible, you want to import just the information you need, to keep the file size small. For example, do not import a bitmap and then reduce it 50 percent to use in your movie. Instead, reduce the bitmap 50 percent first and then import it into Flash.

To optimize graphics, text, and tweening for playback performance:

- Use tweening wherever you can instead of frame-by-frame animation. In an animation, Flash only has to remember the keyframes, making tweening a far less memory-intensive task.
- Tween symbols instead of groups. Each group in the keyframes of a tween must be downloaded, whereas only the single symbol in a tween must be downloaded. Moreover, groups don't allow you to apply instance effects like Tint, Brightness, or Alpha. Using groups in tweens makes editing difficult because you have to apply the same edit on every single group in the keyframes of the tween.
- Avoid creating animations that have multiple objects moving at the same time, or that have large areas of change. Both of these kinds of animations will tax a computer's CPU and slow the movie's performance.
- Break apart groups within symbols to simplify them. Once you're satisfied with an illustration in a symbol, break apart the groups into shapes to "flatten" the illustration out. Flash will have fewer curves to remember and thus have an easier time tweening the symbol instance. Alpha effects on the instance will also affect the symbol as a whole instead of the individual groups within the symbol (**Figure 12.67**).
- Use color gradients and alpha transparencies sparingly.
- Use the Properties Inspector to change the color, tint, and brightness of instances instead of creating separate symbols of different colors.

Figure 12.67 A symbol defined as separate groups (top left) contains more information (top middle) and can produce undesirable transparency effects (top right). A symbol defined as a shape (bottom left) contains less information (bottom middle) and will become transparent as one unit (bottom right).

Figure 12.68 Complex curves and shapes can be simplified without losing their detail.

- Optimize curves by avoiding special line styles (such as dotted lines) and using the pencil tool rather than the brush tool, and by reducing the complexity of curves with Modify > Optimize or Command-Shift-Option-C for Mac, Ctrl-Alt-Shift-C for Windows (**Figure 12.68**).
- Use fewer font styles, and embed only the essential font outlines.

To optimize ActionScript code:

- Try to keep all your code in one place, preferably on the main Timeline, and keep code in just one Layer.
- Use a consistent naming practice for variables, movie clips, objects, and other elements that need to be identified. Consistent and simple names make the job that the variable performs more apparent.
- Use comments within your ActionScript to explain the code to yourself and to other developers who may look at your Flash file for future revisions.
- Think about modularity. This means use smaller, separate components to build your interactivity. For example, use functions to define frequently accessed tasks, use the `#include` action to maintain external scripts, and keep large or common assets outside your movie but available through shared symbols, `loadMovie()`, and `loadSound()`. You'll reduce redundancy, save memory, and make revisions easier.

Avoiding Common Mistakes

When troubleshooting your Flash movie, there are a few obvious places where you should look first to locate what might be common mistakes. These usually involve some simple but critical element, such as overlooking quotation marks or a relative path term, or forgetting to name an instance. Pay close attention to the following warning list to ensure that all your Flash movies are free of bugs.

To avoid common mistakes:

- Double-check the data type of your values. Review the Script pane to make sure that quotation marks are only around string data types. The keyword `this` should not be within quotation marks. Movie-clip target paths can be within quotation marks, but it's good practice to keep them as expressions.
- Double-check the target paths for your movie clips, variables, and objects.
- Remember to name your movie-clip, button, and text field instances.
- Check to see if ActionScript statements are within the correct parentheses or curly braces in the Script pane. For example, verify that statements belonging to an `if` statement or to a function statement are contained within their curly braces.
- Place a `stop` action in the first keyframe of a movie clip to prevent it from playing automatically and looping.
- To test simple actions and simple buttons, remember to choose Enable Simple Frame Actions and Enable Simple Buttons from the Control menu. For more complex button events, you must choose Test Movie from the Control menu.
- Remember that the default setting for your Flash movie in the testing mode is to loop.

✔ Tip

- For additional help and advice on debugging your movie, check out the vast Flash resources on the Web. Begin your search from the Answers panel, a window that links to Flash resources, including Macromedia's Web site, where there is a searchable archive of tech notes and online versions of the user's manual and ActionScript dictionary (**Figure 12.69**). You'll also find links to Web sites with Flash tutorials, articles, FLA source files, bulletin boards, and mailing lists. Check out the CD that accompanies this book for more Flash links and resources.

Figure 12.69 Open the Macromedia Answers panel (Window > Answers) for the latest news, tips, and tutorials.

Object Methods and Properties

A

The following tables summarize the major Flash objects discussed in this book, along with their complete methods and properties. Parameter names are italicized.

Array Object

Method	Description	Parameters
new Array(*length*)	Creates a new Array object.	*length*, optional argument for array length
concat(*array1,…, arrayN*)	Concatenates the specified values and returns a new array.	*array1,…,arrayN*, the elements to be concatenated in a new array
join(*separator*)	Concatenates the elements of the array, inserts the *separator* between the elements, and returns a string.	*separator*, a character or string
pop()	Removes the last element in the array and returns the value of that element.	
push(*value*)	Adds elements to the end of the array and returns the new length.	*value*, the elements to be added to the array
reverse()	Reverses the order of elements in the array.	
shift()	Removes the first element in the array and returns the value of that element.	
slice(*indexA*, *indexB*)	Returns a substring beginning with and including *indexA* and all the elements up to but not including *indexB*.	*indexA*, the starting element (included) *indexB*, the ending element (not included)
sort()	Sorts an array using the less-than (<) operator. Numbers are sorted in ascending order, and strings are sorted alphabetically.	
sortOn(*fieldName*)	Sorts the elements in the array based on a field in the array.	*fieldName*, the field to be used for sorting
splice(*index*, *count*, *elem1,…,elemN*)	Inserts or deletes elements from the array.	*index*, the beginning of the insertion or deletion *count*, the number of elements to be deleted *elem1,…,elemN*, the elements to be inserted
toString()	Returns a string with every element concatenated and separated by a comma.	
unshift(*value*)	Adds elements to the beginning of an array and returns the new length.	*value*, the elements to be added to the array

Property	Description
length	Number of entries in the array.

Button Object

Method	Description
getDepth()	Returns the depth level of a button instance

Property	Description
enabled	Button can receive events, either true or false
tabEnabled	Button can receive keyboard focus with the Tab key; either true or false.
tabIndex	Order of focus when using the Tab key.
trackAsMenu	Track as menu (true) or track as button (false).
useHandCursor	Visibility of the hand icon, either true or false.
_alpha	Transparency from 0 (transparent) to 100 (opaque)
_focusrect	Visibility of the yellow rectangle around a focused button, either true or false
_height	Vertical dimension in pixels
_name	Name of the button instance
_rotation	Rotation in degrees, clockwise from 12 o'clock
_target	Target path of the button instance (read-only)
_visible	Visibility, either true or false
_width	Horizontal dimension, in pixels
_x	x position
_xscale	Percentage of the horizontal dimension
_y	y position
_yscale	Percentage of the vertical dimension

Color Object

Method	Description	Parameters
new Color(*target*)	Creates a new Color object.	*target*, the target path of a movie clip
getRGB()	Returns the numeric value of the color of a movie clip assigned by getRGB().	
getTransform()	Returns the color-transform information of a movie clip assigned by setTransform().	
setRGB(*0xRRGGBB*)	Sets the color of the Color object.	*0xRRGGBB*, the red, green, and blue values for the color
setTransform(*cxform*)	Transforms the color and alpha of the Color object.	*cxform*, an object holding the color-transformation parameters ra, rb, ga, gb, ba, bb, aa, and ab

Date Object *Note: Universal Coordinated Time (UTC) is the same as Greenwich Mean Time.*

Method	Description	Parameters
new Date(*year*, *month*, *date*, *hour*, *min*, *sec*, *ms*)	Creates a new Date object.	*year*, *month*, *date*, *hour*, *min*, *sec*, *ms*, optional arguments for a specific date
getDate()	Returns the date of the month (1-31).	
getDay()	Returns the day of the week (0-6).	
getFullYear()	Returns the four-digit year.	
getHours()	Returns the hour of the day (0-23).	
getMilliseconds()	Returns the millisecond (0-999).	
getMinutes()	Returns the minute (0-59).	

Date Object *Note: Universal Coordinated Time (UTC) is the same as Greenwich Mean Time.*

Method	Description	Parameters
getMonth()	Returns the month (0-11).	
getSeconds()	Returns the second (0-59).	
getTime()	Returns the number of milliseconds elapsed since midnight, January 1, 1970 UTC.	
getTimezoneOffset()	Returns the difference between the local time and UTC, in minutes.	
getUTCdate()	Returns the date of the month (1-31), UTC.	
getUTCday()	Returns the day of the week (0-6), UTC.	
getUTCFullYear()	Returns the four-digit year, UTC.	
getUTCHours()	Returns the hour of the day (0-23), UTC.	
getUTCMilliseconds()	Returns the millisecond (0-999), UTC.	
getUTCMinutes()	Returns the minute (0-59), UTC.	
getUTCMonth()	Returns the month (0-11), UTC.	
getUTCSeconds()	Returns the second (0-59), UTC.	
getYear()	Returns the year calculated from the current year minus 1900.	
setDate(*date*)	Sets the day of the month.	*date*, an integer from 1 to 31
setFullYear (*year*, *month*, *date*)	Sets the year, month, and date.	*year*, a four-digit integer *month*, an optional integer from 0 to 11 *date*, an optional integer from 1 to 31
setHours(*hours*, *minutes*, *seconds*, *ms*)	Sets the hour, minute, second, and millisecond.	*hours*, an integer from 0 to 59 *minutes*, an optional integer from 0 to 59 *seconds*, an optional integer from 0 to 59 *ms*, an optional integer from 0 to 999
setMilliseconds(*ms*)	Sets the millisecond.	*ms*, an integer from 0 to 999
setMinutes(*minutes*, *seconds*, *ms*)	Sets the minute, second, and millisecond.	*minutes*, an integer from 0 to 59 *seconds*, an optional integer from 0 to 59 *ms*, an optional integer from 0 to 999
setMonth(*month*, *date*)	Sets the month and date.	*month*, an integer from 0 to 11 *date*, an optional integer from 1 to 31
setSeconds(*seconds*, *ms*)	Sets the seconds and millisecond.	*seconds*, an integer from 0 to 59 *ms*, an optional integer from 0 to 999
setTime(*value*)	Sets the number of milliseconds elapsed since midnight, January 1, 1970.	*value*, an integer representing the elapsed time
setUTCDate(*date*)	Sets the day of the month, UTC.	*date*, an integer from 1 to 31
setUTCFullYear (*year*, *month*, *date*)	Sets the year, month, and date, UTC.	*year*, a four-digit integer *month*, an optional integer from 0 to 11 *date*, an optional integer from 1 to 31
setUTCHours(*hours*, *minutes*, *seconds*, *ms*)	Sets the hour, minute, second, and millisecond, UTC.	*hours*, an integer from 0 to 59 *minutes*, an optional integer from 0 to 59 *seconds*, an optional integer from 0 to 59 *ms*, an optional integer from 0 to 999
setUTCMilliseconds(*ms*)	Sets the millisecond, UTC.	*ms*, an integer from 0 to 999
setUTCMinutes (*minutes*, *seconds*, *ms*)	Sets the minute, second, and millisecond, UTC.	*minutes*, an integer from 0 to 59 *seconds*, an optional integer from 0 to 59 *ms*, an optional integer from 0 to 999

Date Object *Note: Universal Coordinated Time (UTC) is the same as Greenwich Mean Time.*

Method	Description	Parameters
setUTCMonth (*month*, *date*)	Sets the month and date, UTC.	*month*, an integer from 0 to 11 *date*, an optional integer from 1 to 31
setUTCSeconds (*seconds*, *ms*)	Sets the seconds and millisecond, UTC.	*seconds*, an integer from 0 to 59 *ms*, an optional integer from 0 to 999
setYear (*year*, *month*, *date*)	Sets the four-digit year.	*year*, a four-digit integer *month*, an optional integer from 0 to 11 *date*, an optional integer from 1 to 31
toString()	Returns a string of the values of a Date object.	

Key Object

Method	Description	Parameters
addListener (*whatListener*)	Registers a Listener object to the Key object	*whatListener*, an object assigned with an event handler
getAscii()	Returns the ASCII value of the last key pressed.	
getCode()	Returns the key code of the last key pressed.	
isDown(*keycode*)	Returns true if the specified key is depressed.	*keycode*, the numerical code assigned to each key
isToggled(*keycode*)	Returns true if either the Caps Lock or Num Lock key is depressed.	*keycode*, the numerical code for Caps Lock (20) or Num Lock (144)
removeListener (*whatListener*)	Removes a Listener object	*whatListener*, an object assigned with an event handler

Property (Constant)	Description
BACKSPACE	Key code of the Backspace key
CAPSLOCK	Key code of the Caps Lock key
CONTROL	Key code of the Control key
DELETEKEY	Key code of the Delete key
DOWN	Key code of the down-arrow key
END	Key code of the End key
ENTER	Key code of the Enter key
ESCAPE	Key code of the Escape key
HOME	Key code of the Home key
INSERT	Key code of the Insert key
LEFT	Key code of the left-arrow key
PGDN	Key code of the Page Down key
PGUP	Key code of the Page Up key
RIGHT	Key code of the right-arrow key
SHIFT	Key code of the Shift key
SPACE	Key code of the spacebar
TAB	Key code of the Tab key
UP	Key code of the up-arrow key

Math Object

Method	Description	Parameters
abs(*number*)	Calculates the absolute value.	*number*, any number or expression
acos(*number*)	Calculates the arc cosine.	*number*, a number from –1 to 1
asin(*number*)	Calculates the arc sine.	*number*, a number from –1 to 1
atan(*number*)	Calculates the arc tangent.	*number*, a number
atan2(*y*, *x*)	Calculates the arc tangent.	*y*, the *y* coordinate of a point *x*, the *x* coordinate of a point
ceil(*number*)	Returns the closest integer that is greater than or equal to the *number*.	*number*, a number or expression
cos(*number*)	Calculates the cosine.	*number*, an angle in radians
exp(*number*)	Calculates the constant e to the power of the specified *number*.	*number*, the exponent
floor(*number*)	Returns the closest integer that is less than or equal to the *number*.	*number*, a number or expression
log(*number*)	Calculates the natural logarithm.	*number*, a number or expression
max(*x*, *y*)	Returns the larger value of the two specified parameters.	*x*, a number or expression *y*, a number or expression
min(*x*, *y*)	Returns the smaller value of the two specified parameters.	*x*, a number or expression *y*, a number or expression
pow(*base*, *exponent*)	Calculates the value of *base* raised to the power of *exponent*.	*base*, a number or expression *exponent*, a number or expression
random()	Returns a random number between 0 and 1.	
round(*number*)	Rounds a number to the nearest integer.	*number*, a number or expression
sin(*number*)	Calculates the sine.	*number*, an angle in radians
sqrt(*number*)	Calculates the square root.	*number*, a number or expression
tan(*number*)	Calculates the tangent.	*number*, an angle in radians

Property (Constant)	Description
E	Euler's constant; the base of natural logarithms
LN2	Natural logarithm of 2
LN10	Natural logarithm of 10
LOG2E	Base 2 of logarithm of e
LOG10E	Base 10 of logarithm of e
PI	Ratio of the circle circumference to its diameter
SQRT1_2	Reciprocal of the square root of 1/2
SQRT2	Square root of 2

Mouse Object

Method	Description	Parameters
addListener (*whatListener*)	Registers a Listener object to the Mouse object	*whatListener*, an object assigned with an event handler
hide()	Hides the pointer.	
removeListener (*whatListener*)	Removes a Listener object	*whatListener*, an object assigned with an event handler
show()	Shows the pointer.	

Movie Clip Object

METHOD	DESCRIPTION	PARAMETERS
attachMovie(*idName*, *newName*, *depth*)	Attaches a movie clip from the Library to a movie-clip instance on the Stage.	*idName*, the identifier of the movie- clip symbol in the Library's Linkage property *newName*, the instance name of the attached movie-clip symbol *depth*, the depth level
createEmptyMovieClip (*name*, *depth*)	Creates an instance of a movie clip containing no content on the Stage.	*name*, the instance name depth, the depth level
createTextField (*name*, *depth*, *x*, *y*, *width*, *height*)	Creates a new text field.	*name*, the instance name *depth*, the depth level *x*, the x position *y*, the y position *width*, the horizontal dimension in pixels *height*, the vertical dimension in pixels
duplicateMovieClip (*newName*, *depth*)	Creates another instance of a movie-clip instance on the Stage.	*newName*, the instance name of the duplicate *depth*, the depth level
getBounds (*targetCoordinateSpace*)	Returns the minimum and maximum *x* and *y* positions of the movie clip in the coordinate space of the specified target. The returned object contains the properties xMin, xMax, yMin, and yMax.	*targetCoordinateSpace*, the Timeline whose coordinate space is the reference
getBytesLoaded()	Returns the amount of a movie clip downloaded, in bytes.	
getBytesTotal()	Returns the total size of a movie clip, in bytes.	
getDepth()	Returns the depth level of a movie-clip instance.	
getURL (*URL*, *window*, *variables*)	Loads a URL into a browser window.	*URL*, an Internet address of relative path *window*, optional parameter for browser window or frame *variables*, optional parameter specifying the CGI GET or POST method
globaltoLocal(*point*)	Converts the global coordinates of the point object to coordinates relative to the movie clip.	*point*, an object that contains *x* and *y* coordinates.
gotoAndPlay(*frame*)	Sends the playhead to the specified frame or label and begins playing.	*frame*, the number of the frame or name of the label
gotoAndStop(*frame*)	Sends the playhead to the specified frame or label and stops.	*frame*, the number of the frame or name of the label
hitTest(*x*, *y*, *shapeFlag*)	Returns true if the *x* and *y* coordinates intersect the movie clip.	*x*, the *x* coordinate *y*, the *y* coordinate
hitTest(*target*)	Returns true if the specified target movie clip intersects the movie clip.	*shapeFlag*, true or false parameter that determines if the coordinates intersect the shape of the movie clip (true) or its bounding box (false) *target*, the intersecting movie- clip instance
loadMovie(*URL*, *method*)	Loads an external SWF or JPEG into the movie clip.	*URL*, the path to the external SWF file or JPEG file *method*, optional argument specifying the CGI GET or POST method
loadVariables (*URL*, *method*)	Loads external variables kept in a text file into the movie clip.	*URL*, the path to the external text file *method*, optional argument specifying the CGI GET or POST method
localtoGlobal (*point*)	Converts the coordinates of the point object from a movie clip to coordinates relative to the Stage.	*point*, an object that contains *x* and *y* coordinates.
nextFrame()	Sends the playhead to the next frame and stops.	
play()	Begins playing the movie-clip Timeline at the current position of the playhead.	

Movie Clip Object

METHOD	DESCRIPTION	PARAMETERS
`prevFrame()`	Sends the playhead to the previous frame and stops.	
`removeMovieClip()`	Removes a movie-clip instance created with `createEmptyMovieClip()`, `duplicateMovieClip()`, or `attachMovie()`.	
`setMask(`*maskMC*`)`	Makes the movie clip specified in the parameter into a mask that affects the movie clip that calls this method	*maskMC*, a movie clip
`startDrag(`*lockCenter, left, top, right, bottom*`)`	Makes the movie clip follow the pointer.	*lockCenter*, true or false parameter that determines if the center point of the movie clip is locked to the pointer *left, top, right, bottom*, values to constrain the movie clip's position
`stop()`	Stops the playhead.	
`stopDrag()`	Stops the movie clip from following the pointer.	
`swapDepths(`*depth*`)`	Switches the stacking order of movie clips.	*depth*, the depth level that contains a movie clip to swap
`swapDepths(`*target*`)`		*target*, the movie clip that swaps
`unloadMovie()`	Removes the loaded SWF file in a movie movie-clip instance or a movie clip created at run time or author time.	
DRAWING METHOD	**DESCRIPTION**	**PARAMETERS**
`beginFill` `(`*0xRRGGBB, alpha*`)`	Indicates the fill for the start of a drawing path.	*0xRRGGBB*, the red, green, and blue values for the color *alpha*, an optional value for the transparency
`beginGradientFill` `(`*fillType, colors, alphas, ratios, matrix*`)`	Indicates the gradient fill for the start of a drawing path.	*fillType*, either "radial" or "linear" *colors*, an array containing the hex code colors *alphas*, an array containing the transparency values *ratios*, an array containing the color-distribution values (0-255) *matrix*, an object with the properties *matrixType*, x, y, w, h, and r which determines the gradient orientation
`clear()`	Removes shapes created with the drawing methods	
`curveTo(`*controlX, controlY, anchorX, anchorY*`)`	Creates a curve from the previous point to the anchor point using the control point to determine curvature.	*controlY*, y position of control point *anchorX*, x position of end point *anchorY*, y position of end point *controlX*, x position of control point
`endFill()`	Applies a fill to the paths since the last `beginFill()` or `beginGradientFill()` method.	
`lineStyle(`*thickness, 0xRRGGBB, alpha*`)`	Defines the line style	*thickness*, thickness of the line (0-255) *0xRRGGBB*, optional hex code value for the line color *alpha*, optional value for the transparency of the line
`lineTo(`*x, y*`)`	Draws a line from the previous position to the x and y positions	*x*, the x position of the end point *y*, the y position of the end point
`moveTo(`*x, y*`)`	Moves the current drawing position.	*X*, the new x position *y*, the new y position

Movie Clip Object

PROPERTY	DESCRIPTION
`_alpha`	Alpha transparency from 0 (transparent) to 100 (opaque)
`_currentframe`	Current frame position of the playhead (read-only)
`_droptarget`	Target path of a movie clip that the draggable movie clip is dropped on (in slash notation, read-only)
`_focusrect`	Visibility of the yellow rectangle around a focused movie clip, either true or false
`_framesloaded`	Number of frames that have been downloaded to the viewer's computer (read -only)
`_height`	Vertical dimension in pixels
`_name`	Name of the movie- clip instance
`_rotation`	Rotation in degrees, clockwise from the 12 o'clock position
`_target`	Target path of the movie- clip instance (read -only)
`_totalframes`	Total number of frames in the movie- clip symbol (read -only)
`_url`	The URL of the SWF file loaded into the movie clip (read -only)
`_visible`	Visibility, either true or false
`_width`	Horizontal dimension in pixels
`_x`	*x* position
`_xmouse`	x position of the pointer
`_xscale`	Percentage of the horizontal dimension of the movie- clip symbol
`_y`	*y* position
`_ymouse`	y position of the pointer
`_yscale`	Percentage of the vertical dimension of the movie- clip symbol
`enabled`	Movie clip can receive events, either true or false
`focusEnabled`	Movie clip can receive focus even when it is not acting as a button, true or false.
`hitArea`	Another movie clip that serves as the active area
`tabChildren`	Movie clips inside movie clips can receive focus when using the Tab key, true or false.
`tabEnabled`	Movie clip can receive keyboard focus with the Tab key, either true or false.
`tabIndex`	Order of focus when using the Tab key.
`trackAsMenu`	Track as menu (true) or track as button (false).
`useHandCursor`	Visibility of the hand icon, either true or false.

Selection Object

METHOD	DESCRIPTION	PARAMETERS
`addListener (whatListener)`	Registers a Listener object to the Selection object	*whatListener*, an object assigned with an event handler
`getBeginIndex()`	Returns the index of the start of the selection.	
`getCaretIndex()`	Returns the index of the insertion point.	
`getEndIndex()`	Returns the index of the end of the selection.	
`getFocus()`	Returns the name of the currently focused text field.	
`removeListener (whatListener)`	Removes a Listener object	*whatListener*, an object assigned with an event handler
`setFocus(variableName)`	Sets the focus of a text field.	*variableName*, the name of the text field
`setSelection (beginIndex,endIndex)`	Sets the selection in an editable text field.	*beginIndex*, the start index of the selection *endIndex*, the end index of the selection

Sound Object

Method	Description	Parameters
new Sound (*target*)	Creates a new Sound object.	*target*, the target path for a movie clip
attachSound(*idName*)	Attaches a sound file from the Library to a Sound object.	*idName*, the identifier of your sound in the Library's Linkage property
getBytesLoaded()	Returns the number of bytes (data) loaded for the Sound object.	
getBytesTotal()	Returns the total number of bytes (data) for the Sound object.	
getPan()	Returns the pan level assigned by setPan().	
getTransform()	Returns the sound- transformation information assigned by setTransform().	
getVolume()	Returns the volume level assigned by setVolume().	
loadSound (*url*, *isStreaming*)	Loads an MP3 file	*url*, the path to the MP3 file *isStreaming*, determines if the sound is streaming or not, true or false
setPan(*pan*)	Sets the left–right balance of the sound.	*pan*, a number from –100 (left) to 100 (right)
setTransform(*sxform*)	Sets how the left and right sounds are distributed through the left and right speakers.	*sxform*, an object holding the sound-transformation parameters ll, lr, rr, and rl
setVolume(*volume*)	Sets the percentage of the volume level.	*volume*, a number from 0 (silent) to 100 (normal)
start(*secondsOffset*, *loops*)	Plays the attached sound.	*secondsOffset*, the starting point of the sound (in seconds) *loops*, the number of times the sound loops
stop()	Stops the attached sound.	

Property	Description
duration	Duration of sound in milliseconds
position	Number of milliseconds sound has been playing

Stage Object

Method	Description	Parameters
addListener (*whatListener*)	Registers a Listener object to the Stage object	*whatListener*, an object assigned with an event handler
removeListener (*whatListener*)	Removes a Listener object	*whatListener*, an object assigned with an event handler

Property	Description
align	Alignment of the Flash content ("T", "B, "R", "L", "TR, "TL", "BR", "BL", or "C")
height	Vertical dimension of the Stage in pixels (read-only)
scaleMode	Type of scaling display ("showAll", "noBorder", "exactFit", or "noScale")
showMenu	Contextual control menu accessible with a right-click (Windows) or Ctrl-click (Mac), either true or false
width	Horizontal dimension of the Stage in pixels (read-only)

String Object

METHOD	DESCRIPTION	PARAMETERS
new String (*value*)	Creates a new String object.	*value*, the value of the String object
charAt (*index*)	Returns the character at a specific index.	*index*, the position of the character
charCodeAt (*index*)	Returns the character code at a specific index.	*index*, the position of the character
concat (*string1*,...,*stringN*)	Combines the contents of the specified strings.	*string1*, ...,*stringN*, the strings to be concatenated
fromCharCode (*num1*,...,*numN*)	Returns a string made up of the specified elements.	*num1*,...,*numN*, the characters to be made into a string
indexOf (*searchString*, *fromIndex*)	Returns the index of the first occurrence of a specified character or substring.	*searchString*, the character or characters *fromIndex*, the starting index
lastIndexOf (*searchstring*, *fromIndex*)	Returns the index of the last occurrence of a specified character or substring.	*searchstring*, the character or characters *fromIndex*, the starting index
slice (*indexA*, *indexB*)	Returns a substring between the specified indices including *indexA* but not including *indexB*.	*indexA*, the start of the substring *indexB*, the end of the substring
split (*separator*, *limit*)	Returns an array of two or more substrings based on the *separator*.	*separator*, the character that separates the substrings *limit*, the maximum number of substrings to be put in the array
substr (*start*, *length*)	Returns a substring of a certain length starting at the specified index.	*start*, the starting index *length*, the length of the substring
substring (*indexA*, *indexB*)	Returns a substring between the specified indices.	*indexA*, the start of the substring *indexB*, the end of the substring
toLowerCase()	Returns a string with all lowercase characters.	
toUpperCase()	Returns a string with all uppercase characters.	

PROPERTY	DESCRIPTION
length	The number of characters in a string (read-only)

TextField Object

METHOD	DESCRIPTION	PARAMETERS
addListener (*whatListener*)	Registers a Listener object to the TextField object.	*whatListener*, an object assigned with an event handler
getDepth()	Returns the depth level of a text field	
getFontList()	Returns an array whose elements are the names of all the fonts on the viewer's computer. Use TextField.getFontList() to call the method.	
getNewTextFormat()	Returns a copy of the TextFormat object of newly inserted text in a text field.	
getTextFormat() or getTextFormat(*index*) or getTextFormat (*beginIndex*, *endIndex*)	Returns a TextFormat object of an entire text field, a single character, or a span of characters.	*index*, the position of a character in a text field. *beginIndex*, the starting position of a span of characters *endIndex*, the end position of a span of characters

TextField Object

Method	Description	Parameters
removeListener (*whatListener*)	Removes a Listener object	*whatListener*, an object assigned with an event handler
removeTextField()	Removes a text field created with the createTextField() method	
replaceSel(*text*)	Replaces the current selection in a text field with new text	*text*, the new replacement text
setNewTextFormat (*textFormat*)	Formats newly inserted text according to a text format object.	*textFormat*, a text format object.
setTextFormat (*textFormat*) or setTextFormat (*index*, *textFormat*) or setTextFormat (*beginIndex*, *endIndex*, *textFormat*)	Formats an entire text field, a single character, or a span of characters according to a text format object.	*textFormat*, a text format object. *index*, the position of a character in a text field. *beginIndex*, the starting position of a span of characters *endIndex*, the end position of a span of characters

Property	Description
autosize	Automatic alignment and sizing so a text field shrinks or grows to accommodate text ("none", "left", "center", or "right").
background	Background fill, either true or false.
backgroundColor	Color of the background as a hex code.
border	Border, either true or false.
borderColor	Color of the border as a hex code.
bottomscroll	Bottom line visible in the text field (read-only)
embedFonts	Font symbol embedded, true or false.
hscroll	Horizontal scrolling position of a text field.
html	Render as HTML, either true or false.
htmlText	Contents of an HTML-rendered text field.
length	Number of characters in a text field (read-only)
maxChars	Maximum number of characters allowable.
maxhscroll	Maximum value for the hscroll property (read-only)
maxscroll	Maximum value for the scroll property (read-only)
multiline	Text allowable on more than one line, either true or false.
password	Input text is disguised, either true or false.
restrict	Allowable characters in the text field
scroll	Top line visible in the text field
selectable	Contents selectable by the viewer, either true or false.
tabEnabled	Text field can receive focus from the Tab key, true or false.
tabIndex	Order of focus when receiving focus from the Tab key.
text	Contents of the text field
textColor	Color of the text as a hex code.
textHeight	Height of the text (read-only)
textWidth	Width of the text (read-only)
type	Type of text field ("dynamic" or "input")
variable	Name of the text field variable
wordWrap	Text automatically breaks on multiple lines, either true or false.
_alpha	Transparency from 0 (transparent) to 100 (opaque)

TextField Object

Method	Description
`_focusrect`	Visibility of the yellow rectangle around a focused text field, either true or false
`_height`	Vertical dimension in pixels
`_name`	Name of the text field instance
`_rotation`	Rotation in degrees, clockwise from 12 o'clock
`_target`	Target path of the text field instance (read-only)
`_visible`	Visibility, either true or false
`_width`	Horizontal dimension, in pixels
`_x`	x position
`_xscale`	Percentage of the horizontal dimension
`_y`	y position
`_yscale`	Percentage of the vertical dimension

TextFormat Object

Method	Description	Parameters
`new TextFormat()`	Creates a new text format object.	
`getTextExtent(`*text*`)`	Returns an object with properties width and height specifying the pixel dimensions of a single line of text in the formatting of the text format object.	*text*, a single line of text.

Property	Description
`align`	Alignment of text ("left", "center", or "right").
`blockIndent`	Indentation of the entire text, in points
`bold`	Bold style, either true or false
`bullet`	Bulleted list, either true or false
`color`	Color of text as a hex code.
`font`	Font of the text
`indent`	Indentation of new paragraphs, in points.
`italic`	Italic style, either true or false
`leading`	Space between lines, in points
`leftMargin`	Space of left margin, in points.
`rightMargin`	Space of right margin, in points.
`size`	Size of text, in points.
`tabStops`	Point distances of tab stops as an array of numbers.
`target`	Target window where a hyperlink is displayed.
`underline`	Underline style, either true or false.
`URL`	URL that the text links to.

Keyboard Keys and Matching Key Codes

B

Letters

Letter Key	Key Code
A	65
B	66
C	67
D	68
E	69
F	70
G	71
H	72
I	73
J	74
K	75
L	76
M	77
N	78
O	79
P	80
Q	81
R	82
S	83
T	84
U	85
V	86
W	87
X	88
Y	89
Z	90

Numbers and Symbols

<table>
<tr><th>Key</th><th>Key Code</th><th>Key Object Property</th></tr>
<tr><td>0</td><td>48</td><td></td></tr>
<tr><td>1</td><td>49</td><td></td></tr>
<tr><td>2</td><td>50</td><td></td></tr>
<tr><td>3</td><td>51</td><td></td></tr>
<tr><td>4</td><td>52</td><td></td></tr>
<tr><td>5</td><td>53</td><td></td></tr>
<tr><td>6</td><td>54</td><td></td></tr>
<tr><td>7</td><td>55</td><td></td></tr>
<tr><td>8</td><td>56</td><td></td></tr>
<tr><td>9</td><td>57</td><td></td></tr>
<tr><td>Numbpad 0</td><td>96</td><td></td></tr>
<tr><td>Numbpad 1</td><td>97</td><td></td></tr>
<tr><td>Numbpad 2</td><td>98</td><td></td></tr>
<tr><td>Numbpad 3</td><td>99</td><td></td></tr>
<tr><td>Numbpad 4</td><td>100</td><td></td></tr>
<tr><td>Numbpad 5</td><td>101</td><td></td></tr>
<tr><td>Numbpad 6</td><td>102</td><td></td></tr>
<tr><td>Numbpad 7</td><td>103</td><td></td></tr>
<tr><td>Numbpad 8</td><td>104</td><td></td></tr>
<tr><td>Numbpad 9</td><td>105</td><td></td></tr>
<tr><td>Numbpad *</td><td>106</td><td></td></tr>
<tr><td>Numbpad +</td><td>107</td><td></td></tr>
<tr><td>Numbpad Enter</td><td>108</td><td></td></tr>
<tr><td>Numbpad -</td><td>109</td><td></td></tr>
<tr><td>Numbpad .</td><td>110</td><td></td></tr>
<tr><td>Numbpad /</td><td>111</td><td></td></tr>
<tr><td>Backspace</td><td>8</td><td>BACKSPACE</td></tr>
<tr><td>Tab</td><td>9</td><td>TAB</td></tr>
<tr><td>Clear</td><td>12</td><td></td></tr>
<tr><td>Enter</td><td>13</td><td>ENTER</td></tr>
<tr><td>Shift</td><td>16</td><td>SHIFT</td></tr>
<tr><td>Control</td><td>17</td><td>CONTROL</td></tr>
<tr><td>Alt</td><td>18</td><td></td></tr>
<tr><td>Caps Lock</td><td>20</td><td>CAPSLOCK</td></tr>
<tr><td>Esc</td><td>27</td><td>ESCAPE</td></tr>
<tr><td>Spacebar</td><td>32</td><td>SPACE</td></tr>
<tr><td>Page Up</td><td>33</td><td>PGUP</td></tr>
<tr><td>Page Down</td><td>34</td><td>PGDN</td></tr>
<tr><td>End</td><td>35</td><td>END</td></tr>
<tr><td>Home</td><td>36</td><td>HOME</td></tr>
<tr><td>Left arrow</td><td>37</td><td>LEFT</td></tr>
<tr><td>Up arrow</td><td>38</td><td>UP</td></tr>
</table>

Numbers and Symbols

<table>
<tr><td>Right arrow</td><td>39</td><td>RIGHT</td></tr>
<tr><td>Down arrow</td><td>40</td><td>DOWN</td></tr>
<tr><td>Insert</td><td>45</td><td>INSERT</td></tr>
<tr><td>Delete</td><td>46</td><td>DELETEKEY</td></tr>
<tr><td>Help</td><td>47</td><td></td></tr>
<tr><td>Num Lock</td><td>144</td><td></td></tr>
<tr><td>;:</td><td>186</td><td></td></tr>
<tr><td>=+</td><td>187</td><td></td></tr>
<tr><td>-_</td><td>189</td><td></td></tr>
<tr><td>/?</td><td>191</td><td></td></tr>
<tr><td>`~</td><td>192</td><td></td></tr>
<tr><td>[{</td><td>219</td><td></td></tr>
<tr><td>\|</td><td>220</td><td></td></tr>
<tr><td>]}</td><td>221</td><td></td></tr>
<tr><td>'"</td><td>222</td><td></td></tr>
</table>

Function Keys

Function Key	Key Code
F1	112
F2	113
F3	114
F4	115
F5	116
F6	117
F7	118
F8	119
F9	120
F10	121
F11	122
F12	123

Summary of the Actions Category

C

Descriptions of Actions

Action	Syntax	Key Sequence	Description
break	break;	Esc + br	Breaks out of a looping statement (for, for in, do while, or while) or a switch statement.
call	call (*frame*);	Esc + ca	Performs the script attached to a specified frame label. This action is deprecated, so the action function should be used.
call function	*object*.function (*parameters*);	Esc + cf	Calls the function and passes the specified parameters.
case	case expression: statement;	Esc + ce	Specifies the statements to be performed when the expression matches the switch statement.
clearInterval	clearInterval(*intervalID*);		Stops a setInterval action from executing.
comment	*// comment*	Esc + //	Allows text to be included within the Script pane for commentary only.
continue	continue;	Esc + co	Makes Flash skip the rest of the actions within a looping statement and jump to where the condition is tested.
default	default:*statement*;	Esc + dt	Specifies the statements to be performed when none of the case expressions match the switch statement.
delete	delete *variable*;	Esc + de	Removes a variable.
do while	do { *statement*; } while (*condition*);	Esc + do	Creates a loop that performs statements as long as the specified condition is true.
duplicateMovieClip	duplicateMovieClip (*target*, *newname*, *depth*);	Esc + dm	Creates a copy of a movie-clip instance.
else	else { *statement*; }	Esc + el	Specifies the statements to be performed when the condition in an if statement is false.
else if	else if (*condition*) { *statement*; }	Esc + ei	Specifies the statements to be performed for an alternative condition.
#endinitclip	#endinitclip	Esc + ec	Indicates the end of a code block for initialization. Used to develop new components.

Descriptions of Actions

Action	Syntax	Key Sequence	Description
evaluate	*expression*;	Esc + ev	Adds a new statement line in the Script pane to evaluate an expression.

for	for (*init*; *condition*; *next*) {
	  statement;
	}
		Esc + fr	Creates a loop that performs statements as long as the specified condition is true. The condition usually tests a counter that increases or decreases with each loop.

for..in	for (*iterator* in *object*) {
	  statement;
	}
		Esc + fi	Creates a loop that performs statements on the properties of an object or elements in an array.

fsCommand	fscommand (*command*, *arguments*);	Esc + fs	Sends commands to JavaScript in the browser environment, or to the Flash Player or Projector to control playback.

function	function *name* (*parameters*) {
	  statement;
	}
		Esc + fn	Defines statements that perform a certain task given a set of parameters.

getURL	getURL (*URL*, *window*, *variables*);	Esc + gu	Loads the file at a specified URL (absolute Internet address or relative path) in a browser window. Provides optional arguments specifying the CGI GET or POST method.

goto	gotoAndPlay (*scene*, *frame*);
	gotoAndStop (*scene*, *frame*);
	nextFrame();
	prevFrame();
	nextScene();
	prevScene();
		Esc + go	Sends the playhead to the specified scene, frame number or frame label, and plays or stops there.

if	if (*condition*) {
	  statement;
	}
		Esc + if	Specifies the statements to be performed when a certain condition is true.

#include	#include (*path*)	Esc + in	Incorporates ActionScript from an external text document.
#initclip	#initclip	Esc + ic	Indicates the start of a code block for initialization. Used to develop new components.
loadMovie	loadMovieNum or loadMovie (*URL*, *levelortarget*, *variables*);	Esc + lm	Loads an external SWF file or JPEG file into a level or into a movie clip. Provides optional arguments specifying the CGI GET or POST method.
loadVariables	loadVariablesNum or loadVariables (*URL*, *levelortarget*, *variables*);	Esc + lv	Loads variables from an external text document into a level or a movie clip. Provides optional arguments specifying the CGI GET or POST method.
method	*object*.*method* = function(*parameters*) { }	Esc + md	Creates a method for an object and passes the specified parameters.

on	on (*buttonEvent*) {
	  statement;
	}
		Esc + on	Specifies the statements to be performed when a certain button event occurs. The on handler is always assigned to a button or a movie clip instance.

Descriptions of Actions

Action	Syntax	Key Sequence	Description
`onClipEvent`	`onClipEvent (clipEvent) { statement; }`	Esc + oc	Specifies the statements to be performed when a certain clip event occurs. The `onClipEvent` handler is always assigned to a movie-clip instance.
`play`	`play();`	Esc + pl	Begins playing the movie from the current position of the playhead.
`print`	`print (location, boundingbox);`	Esc + pr	Prints the contents of frames.
`removeMovieClip`	`removeMovieClip (target);`	Esc + rm	Removes a dynamically created movie-clip instance.
`return`	`return value;`	Esc + rt	Returns a value calculated from a function.
`setInterval`	`setInterval(function, interval,parameters);` or `setInterval(object, method, interval, parameters);`		Calls a function or a method at regular intervals.
`set variable`	`variable = value;`	Esc + sv	Assigns a value to a variable.
`setProperty`	`setProperty (target, property, value);`	Esc + sp	Assigns a value to a property of an object.
`startDrag`	`startDrag (target, centered, L, T, R, B);`	Esc + dr	Makes the specified movie clip follow the pointer.
`stop`	`stop();`	Esc + st	Stops the playhead.
`stopAllSounds`	`stopAllSounds ();`	Esc + ss	Stops all sounds from playing.
`stopDrag`	`stopDrag();`	Esc + sd	Stops the movie clip from following the pointer caused by the `startDrag` action.
`switch`	`switch (expression) { }`	Esc + sw	Creates a branching conditional statement by testing whether the expression matches a `case` statement.
`trace`	`trace (message);`	Esc + tr	Displays an expression in the Output window in testing mode.
`unloadMovie`	`unloadMovieNum` or `unloadMovie (levelortarget);`	Esc + um	Removes a loaded movie from a level or a movie clip. Also removes movie clips created at runtime or author-time.
`updateAfterEvent`	`updateAfterEvent();`		Updates the display independently of the frame rate when called within a clipEvent handler or within a function called from the `setInterval` action.
`var`	`var variable = value`	Esc + vr	Defines local variables that are contained within a function.
`while`	`while (condition) { statement; }`	Esc + wh	Creates a loop that performs statements as long as the specified condition is true.
`with`	`with (object) { statement; }`	Esc + wt	Specifies the statements to be performed on an object or movie clip of a certain target path.

Summary of Events and Object Associations

D

Summary of Events and Object Associations

Event		Object Association
onPress	on(press)	Button, Movie Clip
onRelease	on(release)	Button, Movie Clip
onReleaseOutside	on(releaseOutside)	Button, Movie Clip
onRollOver	on(rollOver)	Button, Movie Clip
onRollOut	on(rollOut)	Button, Movie Clip
onDragOut	on(dragOut)	Button, Movie Clip
onDragOver	on(dragOver)	Button, Movie Clip
	on(keyPress "whatKey")	Button
onKeyDown	onClipEvent(keyDown)	Key, Movie Clip
onKeyUp	onClipEvent(KeyUp)	Key, Movie Clip
onMouseDown	onClipEvent(mouseDown)	Mouse, Movie Clip
onMouseUp	onClipEvent(mouseUp)	Mouse, Movie Clip
onMouseMove	onClipEvent(mouseMove)	Mouse, Movie Clip
onEnterFrame	onClipEvent(enterFrame)	Movie Clip
onData	onClipEvent(data)	Movie Clip
onLoad	onClipEvent(load)	Movie Clip, Sound, LoadVars
onUnload	onClipEvent(unload)	Movie Clip
onSetFocus		Button, Movie Clip, Selection, TextField
onKillFocus		Button, Movie Clip, TextField
onChanged		TextField
onScroller		TextField
onSoundComplete		Sound
onResize		Stage

INDEX

B

INDEX

C

F

M

N

INDEX

INDEX

Q

R

S

T

U

V

W

X

Y

Z

D - C d-harrell@nlla.com

sheeraz_uddin99@yah